Women, Science, and Technology

Am. Bio. Teach 2004

Kate - 413-244-7326

Women, Science, and Technology

A Reader in Feminist Science Studies

Edited by

Mary Wyer

Mary Barbercheck

Donna Geisman

Hatice Örün Öztürk

Marta Wayne

Routledge
New York London

Published in 2001 by

Routledge
29 West 35th Street
New York, NY 10001

Published in Great Britain by

Routledge
11 New Fetter Lane
London BC4P 4EE

Routledge is an imprint of the Taylor & Francis Group

Printed in the United States of America on acid-free paper.

Library of Congress Cataloging-in-Publication Data

Women, science, and technology : a reader in feminist science studies / edited by Mary Wyer ... [et al.].

p. cm.

ISBN 0-415-92607-6 (pbk.)

1. Women in science. 2. Women in technology. 3. Feminism and science. I. Wyer, Mary.

Q130.W672 2001
500′.82--dc21

00-046452

We dedicate this book to all those women in science and engineering who have been denied the good friendship and encouragement that have sustained us. Know that we are cheering for you all.

Acknowledgments

We thank the generous goodwill of the North Carolina State University Women's and Gender Studies Program and its director, Laura Severin, for providing us with a nest from which to work on our project. Many other individuals at the university have lent material and intellectual support to the project, including but not limited to Sarah Rajala, James Anderson, Margaret Zahn, Dan Solomon, James Oblinger, Becky Leonard, and Denis Gray. We could not have finished the book without assistance from a patient crew of wonderful women affiliated with the Women's and Gender Studies Program, including especially the intrepid Michelle Feijo, Daphne Holden, Chelsea Earles, and Hope Ziglar. The project was financially supported, in part, by a grant from the National Science Foundation (NSF grant no. HRD-9810454).

Contents

WARNING:

You are about to enter the multidisciplinary world of feminist science studies.

Preface

This book may be unlike anything you have previously encountered, because we cannot fit the material easily into conventional academic categories.[1] Our topics blend research in the humanities, social sciences, sciences, and engineering. We have drawn on elements of the opposing perspectives of empirical positivism and social constructivism in order to ask readers to consider how scientific research contributes both to reproducing inequalities and to documenting and challenging inequalities between women and men in the United States. The five of us—an entomologist, a molecular biologist, a geneticist, an engineer, and a social scientist—became aware of feminist analyses of science for a variety of reasons, some shared, some distinct, as part of a reading group. Our paths would never have crossed but for this shared interest. As we look back on the experience now, it appears to us remarkable that we were able to work together at all. Yet despite our differences, we met regularly over the course of four years. As our interest and commitment to understanding the material grew, so did our common goal of sharing our insights and discoveries. It was a logical extension of our meetings to develop a multidisciplinary course for university students to introduce them to the new scholarship on women in science and engineering. The contents of this book reflect our collaborative work in creating a course on women and gender in science and technology. That we found tireless support from the head of the women's and gender studies program, and that our university had a renewed interest in improving the circumstances for women and minorities in science and engineering, was both fortunate and perfectly timed.

We were pursuing our own interests, but we were also doing something new, working across entrenched boundaries between the so-called hard and soft sciences. Specifically, we wanted to communicate to scientists and to students of science the need to examine critically the political, social, and economic forces behind their research. Likewise, we were trying to communicate to women's studies students and scholars the need to participate in the dialogues that shape scientific research and technological development. Because of the novelty and import of this work, we were awarded a grant to develop courses for the university. We had the intellectual and financial support of several deans within our university. We were provided with travel grants to attend a national meeting to present information about our class. Perhaps most important, we had a chance to work together in an environment of mutual respect, where each of our voices was heard, where our unpolished thoughts had value, where each of our unique sets of talents and shortcomings blended with and complemented the others, producing a resource that no one person could have matched. Not that we worked without conflict—quite the contrary.

Because we came from very different backgrounds, we had different philosophies about the scientific material that we planned on discussing. It would have been difficult, for example, for those of us trained in genetics to accept without reservation a social-constructivist view of human biology and behavior. Likewise, the social scientist questioned precisely the positivist perspective of knowledge and "truth" that most scientists hold dear. However, instead of having our philosophical positions dictate the nature of our work and working environment, we found that over time we were much more committed to working through all of our differences than we were to maintaining disciplinary allegiances. What began as an assumption of goodwill toward one another and a deep regard and respect for one another became the foundation on which our intellectual community was built.

We stopped trying to convince each other of our individual positions and created a safe space in which we could express our differences without hesitation. We all learned from listening to one another and having the opportunity to explore our own biases. So, unintentionally, in trying to imagine the kind of social, political, and economic environment in which an inclusive and perhaps more objective science could be conducted, we had created exactly the kind of working environment we had previously only imagined: a place where we could both speak about and practice our beliefs without being censored or having to censor ourselves. The value and joy of working under such circumstances only strengthened our resolve to continue our collaboration.

Given all of the interpersonal and intellectual rewards for working together, we were surprised to learn that many of our colleagues did not approve of our initiative or appreciate its value. Some of the obstacles we encountered were explicit examples of resistance to change. There were institutional challenges to the course, stemming from the difficulty of trying to work with more than one college within the university at a time. We had to sort out which college in the university would get what kind of credit for the actual teaching, and whether the course could be taken for whatever kind of credit needed by students from the different colleges at the university. In order to get the course approved, someone from the credit-giving college had to be the professor listed in the course guide (what was an entomologist doing teaching a humanities course?), and so on. Within our own departments there were persistent challenges to the value of teaching such a course in the first place. In one of the more devastating incidents that we faced, one of us had to leave her department and find support in a completely different college at the university in order to continue pursuing research in this area. Even the students in our first class were skeptical. The interactive discussion format of the class and the content of the course were completely unfamiliar to students trained in the sciences, and in their final evaluations they were critical of both.

In retrospect it was probably naïve of us not to expect our colleagues to say: "Why are you wasting your time teaching that?" or "I hope you are going to teach a real science class next time." We should have expected our students to think we were teaching them biased material, showing them only one side of the story. We should have expected someone in the class to believe that affirmative action is nothing more than a "quota system" for hiring women and minorities. And we should have recognized the choices that we were making all along: that we were expanding the jobs for which we were paid, as scientists, as students of science, into new responsibilities because of our commitment to this work; that in deciding we had work to do together in community, we were undertaking a fundamental paradigm shift in how we lived our individual lives. In the very act of working together we have given significance and vitality to our interest in feminist scholarship and its diffusion into the sciences and engineering. We will be continuing this work together as long as we are able, and we will work on our own, too, if that time comes.

Negotiating a middle ground between positivism and social constructivism was not simply a matter of philosophical debate for us; it went to the heart of how we would use scientific materials in the course. It was one thing to read and discuss Anne Fausto-Sterling's explicitly feminist critique of research on sex differences in the human brain, but it is quite another to expose students to emerging and controversial research in evolutionary biology on the genetic bases of animal behavior. Some arenas of scientific research, including sociobiology and evolutionary psychology, have jumped into the behavioral genetics juggernaut. These arenas are suspect within feminist frameworks because the research that emerges is so often and so easily (though seldom thoughtfully) defended in terms of a potential contribution to understanding social inequalities between the sexes, even while it legitimates those very inequalities. Though Ruth Bleier's classic critique of sociobiology (included herein) points out the flawed logic and inadequate experimentation behind such claims, the popular press is nonetheless rife with them. How would we teach students to appreciate the importance of women's contributions to genetics research (of which there are many) when at the same time we were asking them to consider how this research is subject to social influences? If women are interpreting their research results the same way men are, then doesn't that mean that scientific knowledge is truly "objective," that no matter who does the research the findings will be the same? When women in science publish research supporting the notion that the social inequalities of human culture are genetic, does that mean we should accept those inequalities as unchangeable and inevitable? Does it mean that women in science are politically shortsighted when they contribute to such work, that they are trained in a male-centered science and so unable to see the flaws therein? Or does it mean that there is something more subtle going on?

The search for material for our course, and for an organizing premise for the material, led us to the conclusion that there was a need for a book to make the work in feminist analyses of science more accessible to undergraduates and readers new to this topic. For the purposes of this book, we define a feminist perspective on science and technology as one that recognizes that our personal experiences, perspectives, and context are necessarily a part of creating scientific knowledge, and that a lack of awareness of this inescapable aspect of human activity has led to a body of scientific work that uncritically reinscribes inequalities between women and men in our society. All researchers come to the questions they study with their particular personal and social backgrounds and with professional interests to protect and foster. A feminist perspective acknowledges this and makes it a visible part of critical inquiry about our own and others' research. What a feminist perspective offers, then, is a recognition that scientists locate themselves by fields—for instance, molecular genetics—which in turn locate them historically and culturally in science. Scientists work within the culture of science. The culture consists of particular groups of scientists, in particular laboratories, who share beliefs, habits, knowledge, achievements, experimental practices, techniques or skills, and a history of conflicting ideas, interests, priorities, and personalities. In this sense, a feminist perspective shares common ground with social studies of science in general. In addition, in feminist analyses, women's interests, contributions, and activities are at the center. Improving the lives of women and increasing our participation and visibility throughout the social, political, economic, and scientific fabric of our culture are constant and unwavering goals. We hope that students in science, women and men alike, will learn to see a feminist perspective as an important resource in their research and teaching.

Notes

1. In this book we often use the terms *women* and *feminist.* This is for convenience only and does not stem from a belief that either of these categories is monolithic or invariable. There are innumerable differences among women and their situations, and we acknowledge that their outlooks, concerns, and needs are equally innumerable. There are also many schools of feminism, each with its own grounding theories and projects. For a discussion of the many feminist schools of thought relative to science, see Sandra Harding, *The Science Question in Feminism* (Ithaca, N.Y.:

Cornell University Press, 1986), and Sue Rosser, "Applying Feminist Theories to Women in Science Programs," *Signs: Journal of Women in Culture and Society* 24, 1 (1999): 171–200. For a treatment of the interactions of race, ethnicity, gender, and science, see Sandra Harding, ed., *The "Racial" Economy of Science* (Bloomington: Indiana University Press, 1993).

Introduction: Science and Feminism

Since the emergence of women's studies initiatives in academia in the 1980s and 1990s, there has been a steady stream of challenges to the received wisdom of the humanities and social sciences. By placing women at the center of analysis, by asking the simple question: "What about women?" researchers revealed the ways in which the grounding assumptions in a variety of disciplines excluded women. In the fields of literary studies, history, psychology, philosophy, sociology, and anthropology, the exclusion of women as subjects of study mattered. It mattered because the interesting questions, grounding assumptions, and accepted answers all changed once women were brought into the picture. The fields grew, in short, as a result of including women as subjects of study.[1]

Many science and engineering fields have been untouched by these developments. There are several reasons for this: (1) Where the subject matter does not include any people, the absence of women as subjects of study may seem irrelevant. (2) In disciplines where there are few or no women in a position to promote change, there are few who have a vested interest in challenging the status quo. (3) Scientists and engineers do not usually have the training to consider the social dynamics that have shaped their fields, and so most assume that scientific perspectives are necessarily "objective" and outside the influence of these dynamics. (4) Most women's studies scholars come from the humanities and social sciences, so their work does not address or challenge issues in the physical, biological, or engineering sciences. (5) Whatever their discipline, faculty evaluations of their peers tend to reinforce disciplinary boundaries by demanding that research and teaching address discipline-specific questions. Those who focus on women's lives must cross these institutionally determined boundaries, leaving themselves vulnerable to criticism from colleagues and the institution.

This book is our attempt to begin breaching those boundaries to help ensure that readers have the knowledge and perspectives they need to participate fully in the research, teaching, and public-policy decision-making of the twenty-first century. To the extent that women continue to be second-class citizens socially, economically, and politically, the issue of our access to training and expertise in scientific and technological fields has renewed urgency in the face of the growing centrality of these fields in a global economy. The belief that scientific and feminist perspectives are incompatible contributes to a persistent ignorance about the importance of scientific and technological innovations in shaping the conditions of women's lives, the limitations of research and teaching that exclude women, and the talents and abilities of women in science and engineering. It is our goal to confront this ignorance.

The Scientific Method

We generally think of scientific perspectives as true, as factual. They are assumed to be perspectives untainted by political considerations. They produce reliable and complete knowledge that we can use with predictable results. In a world full of uncertainties, facts and truth lead us to clarity and understanding. In contrast, we often think of feminist perspectives in quite different terms. Feminist perspectives create knowledge that challenges what we take for granted to be true and factual. Feminist knowledge provokes change. It encourages us to ask new questions about how to understand the world around us. Feminists are often accused of being politically biased, of creating knowledge that is not purely "objective." What could these two perspectives—feminist and scientific—possibly have in common? We argue that they share many commitments, including an emphasis on understanding the social and physical worlds in which we live, and on striving toward more complete descriptions of those worlds.

What is science, exactly? What sets science apart from any other way to gather information or explain how something works? How do we differentiate between scientific knowledge and nonscientific knowledge? Everyone has some notion of what science is and what scientists do. If we were to watch a group of people working in a laboratory while they were dissecting animals and arguing about their data, and if we knew nothing of science, we might describe them naïvely like this:

> Perhaps these animals are being processed for eating. Maybe we are witnessing oracular prophecy through the inspection of rat entrails. Perhaps the individuals spending hours discussing scribbled notes and figures are lawyers. Are the heated debates in front of the blackboard part of a gambling contest? Perhaps the occupants of the laboratory are hunters of some kind, who, after patiently lying in wait by a spectrograph for several hours, suddenly freeze like a gun dog fixed on a scent.[2]

However, most of us have had some exposure to images of real or imagined scientists in television, movies, and advertising. Yet most scientists do not spend their days in the jungle searching for plants that cure cancer or jungle fever (as in the movie *Medicine Man*), genetically engineering dinosaurs (as in the movie *Jurassic Park*), or trying to communicate with extraterrestrial allies (as in the movie *Contact*). So what do ordinary scientists do that defines their activity as science? Most scientists would define science as an approach called the scientific method. The scientific method encompasses the procedures and principles regarded as necessary for scientific investigation and the production of scientific knowledge. The scientific method is actually quite simple in concept and is made up of the following steps:

1. Observations are made of objects or events, either natural or produced by experimentation. From these observations a falsifiable hypothesis is developed.
2. The hypothesis is tested by conducting repeatable experiments.
3. If the experiments refute the hypothesis, it is rejected, and new hypotheses are formulated.
4. Hypotheses that survive are condensed into generalized empirical relationships, or laws.[3]
5. Laws are synthesized into larger theories that explain the nature of the empirical relationships and provide a conceptual framework for understanding how the natural world operates.

Ideally, then, the facts of nature are uncovered by a stepwise winnowing-out of inadequate hypotheses and refinement of the remaining hypotheses. The explanations or facts that remain are considered true until someone is able to falsify them using the scientific method. Therefore, ideally, scientists must be prepared to abandon or alter hypotheses, laws, and theories when new knowledge contradicts them. However, as readers will learn, science does not always proceed in this idealized way. The major questions in feminist analyses of science concern the degree to which the scientific method ensures that the knowledge produced is unbiased and untouched by the social or political commitments of the researchers.

Scientific Behavior and the Scientific Method

In using the scientific method, it is assumed that scientists will adhere to a number of behavioral norms.[4] These are truisms or prescriptions for the behavior needed in order to arrive at scientific knowledge. They contain the essence, or spirit, of scientific inquiry. The scientific norms describe the ethics to which the community of science subscribes, and form an informal code by which the behavior of most scientists is judged by their peers. The scientific norms include (1) originality (scientific results should be original); (2) detachment (the motive of scientists should be the advancement of science, and the scientist should have no psychological commitment to a particular point of view); (3) universality (results of experiments formulated within the scientific method transcend person, time, and place); (4) skepticism (all claims should be scrutinized for error); and (5) public accessibility (all scientific knowledge should be freely available to anyone).[5]

The characteristics listed above are ideals, and many working scientists would admit that in doing science it can be difficult to live up to them. We can get a better understanding of why these qualities are accepted as norms by examining the philosophical and historical roots of Western science.

A Brief History of the Scientific Method: The Standard Story

Science as a method of knowing has a long history associated with and informed by European-Greek philosophy. Science as a practice has been promoted for at least four hundred years as a unique form of knowledge production whose power transcends the peculiarities of time and place. This strong association with Western philosophy has influenced how scientists and society think about science. Some influential philosophers who are credited with formalizing our ideas about science as a way of knowing and as a practice are Aristotle, Galileo, Sir Isaac Newton, René Descartes, Sir Francis Bacon, Sir Karl Popper, and Thomas Kuhn.

From Aristotle we inherited the approach of formal logical deduction. In this method one uncovers the truth by postulating premises, then using deduction to derive the conclusions that follow from the premises. A common example used to illustrate deductive logic is:

Premise 1: All men are mortal.

Premise 2: Socrates is a man.

Conclusion: Socrates is mortal.

However, the following example uses the same logic:

Premise 1: All men are mortal.

Premise 2: Marie Curie is not a man.

Conclusion: Marie Curie is not a mortal.

As developed by Aristotle in his *Physics,* the method of logical deduction can be used whether or not the premises are true. The method merely requires that the conclusion follow from the premises. The conclusion is considered valid as long as the correct method for deducing the conclusion is used. As you will learn, there are many examples from throughout history of this type of error. Presumably true premises, or assumptions, have been (and are still) made about women or people of color that have resulted in false "scientific" conclusions about these groups. Aristotle never advocated experiments or even observations to serve as a check on the validity of his underlying premises or conclusions. In the received history of science, that did not happen until Galileo developed the practice of experimentation and Bacon formalized his ideas on inference to general instances from specific observations.[6]

Galileo is credited with the notion of conducting experiments under controlled conditions. If the scientist has a hypothesis about how something works, she or he must construct an experiment in which all the variables except the one of interest are held constant. The scientist can then measure the variable of interest. Until Galileo, most important discussions about the natural world were conducted as theoretical debates rather than through practice. Newton is credited with the formalization of the idea of the description of nature in mathematical terms and invented the idea and means of using mathematics to analyze experimental data. From Descartes we inherited the dominant mode of analysis in science, which is Cartesian reductionism. Some assumptions of this mode are that the whole is equal to the sum of the parts, that the parts can exist in isolation, and that causes are unambiguously separate from effects.

Sir Francis Bacon developed the idea of a laboratory and codified the procedure for research now called the scientific method. He is considered by many scientists to be the originator of the scientific method. According to Bacon, scientific inquiry begins with the careful recording of observations in a disinterested, impartial, and totally objective way. The observations should not be influenced by any prior prejudice or theoretical preconception. When enough observations are accumulated, the investigator generalizes from these, via the process of induction, to some hypothesis describing a general pattern present in the observations.

Karl Popper was probably one of the most influential philosophers of science in modern times. Popper recognized that there was a problem with Baconian induction for producing scientific knowledge. The difficulty with induction is that you cannot be certain that what you observed in the past will be true in the future. Also, it is not possible to be totally objective, because the decisions about what is a relevant observation will inevitably be influenced heavily by background assumptions, which are often highly theoretical in character. For example, in his book *Paradigms Lost* mathematician John Casti offers the following illustration of the problem of induction:

> You may remember on IQ or college board tests where a sequence of numbers is given and you are supposed to pick the right continuation of the sequence as a demonstration of your intelligence. Suppose the initial sequence is {1, 2, 4, 8} and you are asked to choose the natural continuation of the sequence. Some possible answers would be {16, 32, 64, 128} (doubling) or {9, 11, 15} (differences in original sequence) or {who do we appreciate} (high school football stadium). In the absence of context, that is, additional information, there is no such thing as a "natural" continuation of the sequence. The "right" answer is dictated by sociological considerations rather than any kind of objective reality for number sequences.[7]

Because of the problem of induction, most scientists consider that the only way to produce legitimate scientific knowledge is through the scientific method based on testing of falsifiable hypotheses, rather than by amassing observations. The hypotheses must be falsifiable, because one can show conclusively that a hypothesis is false but not that it is true. To refute or falsify a hypothesis, only one piece of evidence is needed. For example, consider the hypothesis that all ravens are black. We can make observations of ravens in many locations. Even if all the ravens that we see are black, we cannot verify the hypothesis, because we cannot observe every raven in the world. If we observe even one white raven, then the hypothesis is falsified, and this leads to more-refined hypotheses, perhaps about factors that influence the distribution or occurrence of black ravens as opposed to white ones. In Popper's use of the scientific method, learning about nature is carried out by a process of eliminating false hypotheses. In the pursuit of scientific knowledge scientists come closer and closer to the truth through a series of falsified observations or experiments, but they can never know if they have reached their goal of scientific fact.[8]

Thomas Kuhn, a physicist who published *The Structure of Scientific Revolutions* in 1962, challenged Popper's philosophy of science. Many would argue that Kuhn's book launched a field of research into the practices of science, sometimes called science studies, whose project has been to show how social phenomena deflect science practice from the presumed ideal. Kuhn challenged the fundamental assumptions that scientists are objective about and receptive to new ideas. Kuhn argued that every scientist works within a distinctive paradigm, which is an intellectual framework that influences the way nature is perceived. Scientists, just like the rest of humanity, carry out their day-to-day business within a framework of presuppositions about what constitutes a problem, a solution, and a method. This background of shared assumptions makes up a paradigm, and at any given time a particular scientific community will have a prevailing paradigm that shapes and directs research in a field of science. Paradigms have great utility and practical value, because without them no one would know how to set up an experiment and collect data.

A paradigm is like a filter through which scientists see and construct research problems, and a paradigm shift (or in Kuhn's terms, a scientific revolution) takes place when a new filter transforms the scientist's perspective. Once this shift takes place, the next generation of scientists is trained according to the new vision of truth. According to Kuhn, there is no such thing as an empirical observation or fact; we always see by interpretation, and the interpretation we use is filtered through the prevailing paradigm. Because paradigms are influenced by the social and economic contexts in which scientists live and work, science is not independent of the broader culture, but is itself an integral part of culture.[9]

Kuhn described two phases of science, normal and revolutionary. During a normal phase in science, the level of consensus is high, and most scientists working in a field accept the validity of the current paradigm. During a revolutionary phase consensus breaks down, but in time it will again consolidate, this time around the new paradigm. During periods of normal science, observations are influenced by theory, as opposed to theory being influenced by observations, and therefore the data that scientists collect are theory-laden. Rather than experimental and observational data being the determinant of the course of science, theories determine what evidence is looked for and what evidence is taken seriously. During normal science, scientists accept almost without question the dominant scientific theories in their research areas even if there are observations that the theory is unable to explain or which suggest that the theory is wrong. Failure of an experiment to confirm a theory or achieve results expected by a widely accepted theory casts doubts not on the theory, but upon the ability of the experimenter.[10] Kuhn contends that the observer, the theory, and the equipment are all an expression of that point of view as well. If Kuhn's ideas about science are accurate, then several of the scientific norms and an essential foundation of the scientific method, objectivity (that the observer can be essentially separate from the experimental apparatus used to test the theory and the subject being studied), are open to challenge.

Women and the Development of Western Science

You may have noticed that the "story" of the development and philosophies of science outlined above lacks any mention of the contributions that women made to the development of science. Very little is known of women's involvement in science in the ancient world. In ancient Egypt women were able to attend medical school, mainly to specialize in midwifery.[11] Western science is largely a European-Greek invention, and we have inherited the tradition of Western philosophy and the ideals of reason and objectivity from white males, many of whom have been demonstrably sexist or misogynist.[12] For example, Aristotle, who rejected his teacher Plato's moderate views on women, promoted the traditional Greek view that women were inferior to men and incapable of rational thought. During the Middle Ages in Europe, education centered on the cathedral schools for boys and men, which later developed into universities. Women could join convents, which provided education for upper-class girls and women. In this way medieval women could participate in science-related activities. Two such women were the Abbess of Hohenburg, Harrad, who wrote the encyclopedia *Hortus deliciarum* to teach convent students, and Hildegard of Bingen, who wrote the book *On Nature and Man, the Moral World and the Material Universe, the Spheres, the Winds and the Humours, Birth and Death, on the Soul, the Resurrection of the Dead, and the Nature of God.* In Italy opportunities for women were much broader, and upper-class women were able to participate in university life both as students and as teachers, especially in medical schools.

The period from the fifteenth century through the eighteenth century is considered an especially important era in the development of modern science. Women's involvement in science at this time seems to have been restricted by the persistence of women's subordinate social and presumed inferior biological status. Francis Bacon saw women as an impediment to the achievements of men and believed that women should be avoided altogether. His dismissal of women is somewhat ironic given that Bacon's writings on the philosophy of science are threaded with sexual imagery and metaphor. Bacon's vision of science was articulated as mastery of man over nature, with nature characterized as a bride and science as the means to bind her to the will of men.[13]

It has been argued that the underlying metaphors of the identification of nature, subjectivity, and emotion with women and the identification of culture, objectivity, and reason with men have provided a rationale for the exploitation and control of both women and nature. Ideologies of gender, nature, and science that arose in the seventeenth century supported the increasing split between men's and women's worlds and between the public and private spheres, and supported the exclusion of women from intellectual pursuits such as science.[14]

Although formal educational opportunities for women existed mainly in the highest socioeconomic classes, we know that women during this time were interested in science, and corresponded and studied with their contemporary male scientists.[15] For example, Descartes corresponded on scientific topics with several women, including Princess Elizabeth of Bohemia and Queen Christina of Sweden, among others. Margaret Cavendish (1617–1673), the duchess of Newcastle, produced fourteen books on subjects from natural history to atomic physics. Emilie du Châtelet (1706–1749) exchanged ideas with the foremost mathematicians and scientists of Paris and earned a reputation as a physicist and interpreter of the theories of Leibniz and Newton. She duplicated Newton's experiments in the great hall of her château.

During the seventeenth and eighteenth centuries, upper-class women in England and France participated in scientific discussion in salons. The grand salons of Paris were run almost exclusively by women. Influential women, effectively acting as intellectual power brokers, were patrons of young men hoping to make careers in science.[16] Unfortunately, the great majority of men who were aided by these unconventional women produced writings that either ignored women entirely or upheld the most traditional views of them. The salons and the women who ran them were ridiculed even by the influential men who benefited from the interactions there. For example, Rousseau, in his novel *Emile*, wrote: "I would a thousand times rather have a homely girl . . . than a learned lady and a wit who would make a literary circle of my house. . . . A female wit is a scourge to her husband, her children, her friends, her servants, to everybody. From the lofty height of her genius, she scorns every womanly duty, and she is always trying to make a man of herself." The German philosopher Immanuel Kant wrote that women such as the marquise du Châtelet, who "carries on fundamental conversations about mechanis[,] . . . might just as well have a beard."[17]

And yet women developed at least three science-related fields: midwifery, nursing, and home economics.[18] These fields have generally been ignored by historians of science, perhaps because most historians of science have been men who focused on the achievements of men. Nonaristocratic European women participated in scientific activities through the craft tradition as daughters, wives, and apprentices; independent artisans; or widows who inherited the family business. The participation of these women in fields such as astronomy, physics, and the natural sciences in the seventeenth and eighteenth centuries has been largely unacknowledged, presaging the "invisible assistants"—the many women who worked in laboratories but seldom received credit for their contributions—of the nineteenth and twentieth centuries.

During the eighteenth century treatises on physics, chemistry, and natural history became popular, and lectures in these areas were attended by women. Popular scientific newspapers and journals arose to satisfy women's interest in these topics. This accepted interest prepared society to at least acknowledge the possibility of a woman scientist. By the nineteenth century women participated in some aspects of almost all science, mainly in data gathering but also in idea creation. Educational reforms, the Industrial Revolution, and political changes increased the ability of women to be active in science, which has resulted in increasing the contributions of women to science practice and theory up to the present day's participation levels.[19]

Becoming a Scientist

It is one thing to talk about the scientific method and how it developed historically, but it is quite another to consider how research actually is done. In Western society rarely can someone who is not formally trained produce information that will be accepted as scientific fact. As with many professions, in science there is a long accreditation/training period in which the aspirant not only gains technical knowledge, but is also introduced to the paradigms, culture, and norms of the field. In the United States the training period usually starts in high school with coursework focused on mathematics and science, continues through undergraduate education, and includes more specialized training at the graduate level. Today, research scientists most often work in academic settings, government research organizations, or industry.[20] Usually scientists are aided in their work by support staff who have varying levels of academic and scientific training, and who may or may not be given credit by the scientific community for their work. The acceptance of the scientific information they produce depends upon consensus by other scientists in the field, and therefore scientists act as gatekeepers on the production of scientific facts.

Building Consensus in Science

Information collected through the scientific method is not automatically accepted as scientific fact by the scientific community. The scientific community accepts scientific knowledge through a process of consensus building. Theoretically, consensus is based on the unbiased evaluation of the empirical evidence.

There are many necessary steps after experimentation in order to convince other scientists that a new piece of information is a "fact." For instance, Dr. Susan A. Scientist at Prestigious University has conducted experiments to test the hypothesis that the moon actually consists of blue, rather than green, cheese. After her brilliant discovery, she writes up her experiments in manuscripts that detail the methods used, the results, and the significance of her results relative to other knowledge in her field, and submits them to a scientific journal. The editor of the journal sends her manuscript to two or more of her peers for anonymous review. If the reviewers and the editor of the journal agree that Dr. Scientist's research is repeatable and the results are valid and significant, her manuscript will be published. At the same time Dr. Scientist will attend scientific conferences and present her results formally as lectures and informally in discussion with other scientists to make them aware of her results and to convince them of its validity.

When the manuscript is published it becomes available for the scrutiny of other scientists, who may or may not challenge any aspect of Dr. Scientist's research: her methods, the results, or her interpretation of the results. Sometimes, in the case of especially significant research, results will be announced in the popular media at the same time as they are published in the scientific literature.

Unfortunately, sometimes a scientist's research is challenged not only on the merits of the research, but on the personal characteristics of the scientist herself. For example, James Watson, a recipient of the Nobel prize for his development of the model of the helical structure of DNA, describes Rosalind Franklin, another scientist investigating the structure of DNA in this way:

> I suspect that in the beginning Maurice hoped that Rosy would calm down. By choice she did not emphasize her feminine qualities. Though her features were strong, she was not unattractive and might have been quite stunning had she taken even a mild interest in clothes. This she did not. There was never lipstick to contrast with her straight black hair. Clearly, Rosy had to go or be put in her place. The real problem, then was Rosy. The thought could not be avoided that the best home for a feminist was in another person's lab.[21]

Rosalind Franklin died of cancer at the age of thirty-seven in 1958, just four years before the Nobel prize was awarded to Watson, Francis Crick, and Maurice Wilkins. Until recently the critical importance of Franklin's research for the description of the structure of DNA was not generally acknowledged. The unauthorized use of Franklin's crystallographic data allowed Watson and Crick to develop the structural model for DNA.[22]

Sometimes the results of scientific research take many years to be accepted, especially if they challenge the validity of currently held beliefs of what has been previously accepted as a scientific fact. The research of Barbara McClintock, who received the Nobel prize in 1988 for her research in corn genetics, is a good example of this. Her results, which challenged then-current beliefs about the static behavior of genes on chromosomes, were not fully appreciated until forty years after she had completed her experiments.

A Multidisciplinary Perspective

Understanding that scientists are people who do research within particular social and historical contexts requires looking at science as a social activity. As we have pointed out, the scientific method is an approach that philosophers and scientists developed and formalized over time. This method allows scientists to collect and evaluate data systematically and then develop generalizations that provide a shared conceptual framework for information exchange and interpretations of natural phenomena. From a social constructivist perspective, the method and the knowledge that results from it are socially constructed. This means that human activity has produced the knowledge. Scientists (or anyone who does research) can only represent their understandings of the natural world according to the conventions of their disciplinary theories, vocabulary, and professional practices. These conventions constrain how and what they can credibly claim about the natural world. Within the social constructivist view, language mediates our understanding of nature because it is through language that all humans learn about and represent the world. In contrast, the positivist perspective sees knowledge as facts that humans uncover rather than produce. Knowledge about the natural world is something that is revealed to the scientist by careful hypothesis development and testing. Language is a transparent medium through which humans relay their insights. Within the positivist view, nothing of importance rests on language.[23]

In this book we borrow from each of these perspectives. We argue that social processes leading to scientific knowledge can produce adequate and useful explanations of the natural world. At the same time, they can also produce inadequate and regressive explanations and theories. Feminist science studies seek to sort out which is which in relation to women. *Women, Science and Technology* is meant to give readers tools for doing the same. Though many classic texts in feminist scholarship on science are difficult reading in their original form for most newcomers to the field, the analyses detailed in the texts nonetheless provide valid and useful insights about even the most current scientific research. To make these readings more available, we have excerpted from them and included section introductions that provide background information on the salient points of key arguments.

When deciding how to organize this book, given our diverse interests and expertise, we agreed on a list of five major questions: Who does science? How does culture shape science? How does science shape culture? Can we redefine and reform science to include feminist perspectives? How can feminist perspectives on science and technology improve the day-to-day lives of women (and men)? These questions are a distillation of the issues raised in the five sections. There is interplay between the sections, in itself an example of the complexity of feminist analyses of science. For example, the answer to the question "Who does science?" is inseparable from the question of how culture shapes science. The five questions we ask are thus an organizing device that focuses readers' attention around core issues in order to survey the material. The overlaps among sections are meant to open debate and foster discussions about their inseparability.

In our first section, titled "High Hopes, Broken Promises, and Persistence: Educating Women for Scientific Careers," we include as a backdrop a brief overview of the history of women's exclusion from—and struggles to obtain training in—the sciences. The book's sequence of readings begins with accounts of women's experiences in science as outsiders in their training programs. Other essays in section 1 review the qualitative and quantitative data on why women decide to avoid or pursue scientific careers and on how they fare in those professions relative to men.

We take the theme of exclusion into "Science, Sex, and Stereotypes: Cultural Images of Science and Scientists," our second section, exploring how our cultural images of men and women shape our beliefs about who can and cannot be scientists. We examine images of scientists drawn from the culture of science as well as images drawn from the culture at large, including in particular advertising images from scientific publications. We have also included readings on the culture and language of science and how they affect the climate for women and relationships between men and women in science.

The continuity between, and intertwining of, science and culture is the theme organizing the third section, "Constructing Gender, Constructing Science: How Ideas about Women and Men Shape Science and Technology." We explore why it matters to science that women generally have been excluded from scientific culture, and why it matters that where women have been able to make contributions, these have been lost, ignored, or appropriated. Some of the most persuasive examples of the effects of culture on science come from work used expressly to reinscribe dominant social paradigms, such as studies from the nineteenth century "proving" that women are inherently inferior to men or that Africans and Asians are inferior to Europeans. In these cases, it is clear (at least in hindsight) that investigators were predisposed to finding results that were consistent with their beliefs.[24] However, predispositions in scientists' interpretations are not limited to the nineteenth century—they also occur in contemporary theoretical assumptions, interpretation of data, experimental design, or language use. So, for instance, the exclusive use of male subjects in health research until the early 1990s was assumed to be "scientific" even though it leads to a nonrepresentative sample (excluding 51 percent of the population), because the male body was accepted as the norm.[25] It is acceptable to use terms such as *sexy, penetrating,* and *seminal* to describe exciting research, because male sexuality is considered the norm.[26] It is possible for researchers to refer to sperm as "active" and eggs as "passive" because male dominance in relation to women is considered the norm.[27]

In the fourth section, "New Science, New Knowledge: Bringing Feminist Perspectives into Science and Technology Studies," we consider the question "Can we redefine and reform science to include feminist perspectives?" Feminist science is not simply or necessarily science by women. It is science that investigates topics considered irrelevant or obvious by men but which are nonetheless important to improving women's lives. It is science that recognizes the place of scientists in a social system. Striving for objectivity, for complete detachment of observer from observed, may seem irreconcilable with many feminist philosophies. However, the critical issue is not whether objectivity can be accomplished, but rather whether it is a useful tool. If it is useful, and we think it is, then there clearly is a place for feminist science—science done outside of and analyzing the traditional male-centered viewpoint—because it enhances scientific knowledge by enlarging the circle of legitimate questions and topics, and because feminist perspectives can help in the detection and analysis of distorting biases. Paradoxically, acknowledging bias is often a crucial step toward more complete, meaning more objective, descriptions of the world. In the absence of social and cultural diversity in science, however, it is hard to imagine a vigorous discussion of such biases taking place.

The closing section of the book, "Reproducible Insights: Women Creating Knowledge, Social Policy, and Change," explores how feminist perspectives on science and technology can improve the day-to-day lives of women (and men). This involves looking at what happens when scientific knowledge is translated into use in public policy, corporate decision making, or technological innovation. The topics included in section 5 range from an analysis of environmental policy to a critique of welfare policy. Current economic and social trends mean that the more scientifically literate we all are, the better able we will be to make informed decisions about everything, from our personal medical care to emerging local, state, and federal legislation about new technologies. In addition, the United States is becoming a country in which an increasingly diverse majority of the educated will need to have training in scientific or engineering fields in order to reach their career potential.[28] Feminist perspectives on science and technology provide an intellectual map that can help readers find their way through the morass of available information. Understanding how social dynamics shape our educational experiences and options, workplace experiences and job opportunities, and the directions and content of scientific knowledge and technological innovation reduces the distance between the "experts" and the "citizens." Similarly, scientific and technological knowledge can ground feminist teaching and learning in contemporary issues, inviting feminist scholars to consider if (or how) our theories and research are adequately informed by those disciplines in which women are just beginning to make their presence felt.

Notes

1. For a compendium reviewing the development of women's studies across the disciplines, including in particular the emergence of research on women of color and on masculinity, see Cheris Kramarae and Dale Spender, *The Knowledge Explosion: Generations of Feminist Scholarship,* (New York: Teachers College Press, 1992).
2. Bruno Latour and Steven Woolgar, *Laboratory Life: The Social Construction of Scientific Facts* (Princeton, N.J.: Princeton University Press, 1986).
3. Empiricism is the practice of the search for knowledge by observation and experiment, so if information is empirical, it was determined from experiment, observation, or experience, rather than derived from theory.
4. Robert Merton, *The Sociology of Science: Theoretical and Empirical Investigations* (Chicago: University of Chicago Press, 1973).
5. For the classic description of these norms, see Merton, *The Sociology of Science.* See also J. Woodward and D. Goodstine, "Conduct, Misconduct, and the Structure of Science," *American Scientist* 84 (1996): 479–90.
6. M. Peltonen, ed., *The Cambridge Companion to Bacon* (New York: Cambridge University Press, 1996).
7. John Casti, *Paradigms Lost: Images of Man in the Mirror of Science* (New York: Morrow, 1989), 30.
8. Karl Popper, *The Logic of Scientific Discovery* (London: Hutchinson, 1959).
9. Thomas Kuhn, *The Structure of Scientific Revolutions* (Chicago: University of Chicago Press, 1970).
10. Barbara McClintock is one such scientist. Her scientific insights in genetics were so advanced in comparison to her colleagues' that they were not readily accepted as she was publishing them, though now her work is recognized as important and valid by the scientific community. See E. F. Keller, *A Feeling for the Organism: The Life and Work of Barbara McClintock,* (New York: Freeman, 1983).
11. M. B. Ogilvie, *Women in Science: Antiquity through the Nineteenth Century* (Cambridge, Mass.: MIT Press, 1983).
12. L. M. Antony and C. Witt, eds., *A Mind of One's Own: Feminist Essays on Reason and Objectivity* (Boulder, Colo.: Westview Press, 1993); R. Agonito, *History of Ideas on Women* (New York: Perigee, 1977).
13. E. F. Keller, *Reflections on Gender and Science* (New Haven, Conn.: Yale University Press, 1985).
14. C. Merchant, *The Death of Nature* (London: Wildwood House, 1980); V. Plumwood, *Feminism and the Mastery of Nature* (New York: Routledge, 1993).
15. B. S. Anderson and J. P. Zinsser, *A History of Their Own: Women in Europe from Prehistory to the Present,* vol. 2 (New York: Harper and Row, 1988).
16. L. Schiebinger, *The Mind Has No Sex? Women in the Origins of Modern Science* (Cambridge, Mass.: Harvard University Press, 1989).
17. Anderson and Zinsser, *A History of Their Own;* Schiebnger, *The Mind Has No Sex?* 146. Schiebinger explains that the beard is a symbol of virility. Kant believed that the education of women ran counter to natural law and that science is masculine in character. The cite is to *Kants Werke,* ed. Wilhelm Dilthey (Berlin, 1909–1919), 2:229–30.
18. Ogilvie, *Women in Science.*
19. For the most current national information about the percentage of women among science and engineering degree earners, see National Science Foundation data at their website, www.nsf.gov.

20. For a discussion on women doing science in nontraditional places, see M. A. Eisenhart and E. Finkel, *Women's Science: Learning and Succeeding from the Margins* (Chicago: University of Chicago Press, 1998).
21. J. Watson, *The Double Helix: A Personal Account of the Discovery of the Structure of DNA* (New York: Atheneum, 1968), 20–21.
22. For a view of Rosalind Franklin that differs greatly from that of Watson's, see Anne Sayre, *Rosalind Franklin and DNA* (New York: Norton, 1975).
23. Popper, *The Logic of Scientific Discovery.*
24. S. J. Gould, *The Mismeasure of Man* (New York: Norton, 1981).
25. S. V. Rosser, *Women's Health—Missing from U.S. Medicine,* (Bloomington: Indiana University Press, 1994).
26. C. Cohn, "Wars, Wimps, and Women: Talking Gender and Thinking War," in M. Cooke and A. Woollacott, eds., *Gendering War Talk* (Princeton, N.J.: Princeton University Press, 1993).
27. E. Martin, *The Woman in the Body* (Boston: Beacon Press, 1987).
28. Sigma Xi, *Entry-level Undergraduate Courses in Science, Mathematics and Engineering: An Investment in Human Resources* (Research Triangle Park, N.C.: Sigma Xi, 1990); William Greider, *One World, Ready or Not: The Manic Logic of Global Capitalism* (New York: Simon and Schuster, 1997).

SECTION 1

HIGH HOPES, BROKEN PROMISES, AND PERSISTENCE

EDUCATING WOMEN FOR SCIENTIFIC CAREERS

In the United States, the history of women's participation in science is entangled with debates about women's intellectual capacities and their roles and responsibilities in relation to men and children. Until the mid-1800s, most women were expressly and specifically excluded from all but basic literacy education, since it was thought that educated women would engage in deviant social and political behavior. It was said that women would refuse to do housework and would disobey their husbands if their education was too advanced. They would become masculinized and expect to be included in men's activities. They would try to take over men's jobs. If women knew too much, their intellects would undermine their health and that of their children. The education of women was against the natural order; God would not approve. By the mid-1800s advocates for women's education argued that women could not fulfill their God-given duties to their husbands without a complete education, but the depth and range of subjects deemed appropriate for women's minds was a matter of controversy.[1]

By the late 1800s scientists had published a number of studies that purported to document a decrease in the health of upper-middle-class white women due to the strain education was putting on women's limited intellectual capacities. (The physiological impact of education on working-class white women and African Americans was dismissed as an issue, since it was assumed that they would not seek higher education.) These studies argued that the strain of learning Latin, Greek, or advanced mathematics drew blood to the brain and away from women's reproductive organs. Education threatened white female fertility and racial superiority, and it upset the progress of human evolution. Indeed, the uterus was considered to be the "controlling organ" in the female body, "as if the Almighty, in creating the female sex, *had taken the uterus and build up a woman around it*" (emphasis in original).[2]

Though elementary education was available to women, these attitudes were prevalent enough in the eighteenth century that the general literacy rate for women (defined as the ability to write one's own name) was half that of men—estimated at 40 percent for women and 80 percent for men. By the middle of the nineteenth century, historians estimate, literacy rates for white women and men became about equal, but for the African-American women literacy rates remained at about 50 percent. Even with these restricted educational opportunities, there were some early American white women who contributed to scientific knowledge through research and writing. In the 1750s, for instance, Jane Colden, taught by her botanist father, identified and classified over three hundred species of plants in the Hudson River Valley. She is best known for her work with the gardenia, which she identified and described.[3]

A contributing factor to white women's increased literacy was the emergence of female academies, which were private schools for upper-class white women. These schools created audiences for general texts on science topics. So, for instance, in 1785 Rousseau's posthumously published *Letters on the Elements of Botany Addressed to a Lady* appeared. In addition, women wrote popular science texts, participating in the process of educating the reading public about basic science. In 1796 Priscilla Bell Wakefield published her *Introduction to Botany in a Series of Familiar Letters,* which was in print in England and America for fifty years. A few years later Jane Marcet published her *Conversations on Chemistry,* of which there were fifteen editions before 1860.[4]

The belief that it was unnatural for women to be educated began to give way to the idea that education improved the ability of women to do what was most natural to them: be mothers and wives. The popularity of science texts directed at women legitimated the idea that women were interested in and could understand scientific information, leading the way to the introduction of science topics into the curriculum for women and girls who were less privileged. Emma Hart Willard argued that it was the responsibility of the state to fund the advanced education of all women, because women were responsible for the character of future American citizens. In 1819 Willard founded the Troy Female Seminary in New York and secured public funding of secondary education for women. She offered the first classes available to women in mathematics, physics, physiology, and natural history. Her sister, Almira Hart Lincoln, published *Familiar Lectures on Botany* in 1829, which sold 275,000 copies in the next forty years, appearing in seventeen editions. Lincoln became wealthy writing and publishing popular texts in botany, chemistry, and natural philosophy. Ironically, she did not believe that women should become scientists, only that science would make women better wives and mothers, enriching their domestic lives.[5]

Changes in attitudes toward women, in particular the idea that women were entitled to a publicly funded education, just as were men, provoked dramatic changes in the educational opportunities available to women. New colleges sprang up that were dedicated to the education of women. Public, land-grant institutions opened across the country as new states entered the Union, and some of these opened their doors to women. In the meantime, some women were being educated in science by their fathers or husbands, as they had been for centuries. These two processes contributed to a slow but steady growth in the number of women who gained access to scientific knowledge. In 1833 Oberlin College opened its doors, announcing that it would be coeducational and that it would accept African-American students. Private women's colleges opened later in the century, including Vassar College (1865), Smith College (1871), Wellesley College (1875), and Barnard College (1889).

Maria Mitchell is perhaps the earliest woman who was a professional scientist in the United States. She was educated by her father and worked part time as a librarian on Nantucket while she did research in her father's laboratory. In 1847, at the age of twenty-eight, she discovered a new comet and became something of a celebrity as the first woman elected to the American Academy of Arts and Sciences (1848) as well as one of the first women in the American Philosophical Society of Philadelphia (1869). She was hired at the newly opened Vassar College (1865) as a professor of science, one of the first women in the United States to be so. Mitchell was always aware of her unique presence in the field and was an advocate for including women in science. She was the founding president of the Association for the Advancement of Women and reported routinely to members on women's advances and setbacks in science. In her 1875 presidential address she said: "In my younger days, when I was pained by the half-educated, loose, and inaccurate ways which we [women] all had, I used to say, 'how much women need exact science,' but since I have known some workers in science who were not always true to the teachings of nature, who have loved self more than science, I have now said, 'how much science needs women.'"[6]

All women in the United States confronted resistance to their participation in science, no matter how talented, but those who had money or whose fathers were scientists could secure some training despite the obstacles. African-American women in general did not have these advantages, but there were important exceptions. Josephine Silone Yates, for instance, became the first African-American woman professor of science when she was appointed head of the Natural Sciences Department at Lincoln University in Missouri. She was born in 1859 to a well-respected, established, and educated family in Mattituck, New York. She was taught reading, writing, and arithmetic at home before entering school. Her parents saw that she had the best available educational opportunities, sending her to black private schools as well as Newport, Rhode Island, public schools (in which she was the only black student). She finished a four-year high-school course of study in just three years and went on to receive the highest score ever recorded on the Rhode Island state teachers' examination. In 1879 she became head of the department of natural sciences at Lincoln University. Because state law prohibited married women from holding teaching positions, she resigned her position in 1889 in order to marry. At this point she, like Maria Mitchell, became an activist on behalf of women, and from 1901 to 1906 she was president of the National Association of Colored Women. Despite Yates's considerable talents and interests in science, prevailing beliefs about women and African Americans severely restricted her access to the career opportunities and research environments necessary for scientific achievement.[7]

In general, the first generation of women scientists who were employed as faculty at women's colleges and historically black colleges and universities published little because they carried heavy teaching responsibilities and they had uneven research backgrounds given their exclusion from most graduate programs in the United States. Because of laws prohibiting married women from teaching, many women literally dedicated their lives to the education of a new generation of women scientists. They never married and stayed on faculties for thirty to forty years, often retiring to a cottage near campus with a sister or retired colleague. When they died, the colleges frequently honored them with an endowed chair or a building named after them. Students would write obituaries defending their lack of publications and celebrating their commitment to educating students. Many bequeathed their estates to the colleges that had been the center of their adult lives.[8]

Their efforts and dedication were having an effect, however slow and dispersed it must have seemed at the time. By 1889 a total of twenty-five doctorates had been awarded to women in the United States, six of them in science. By 1900 another 204 doctorates had been awarded to women, with thirty-six of them in science. These increases, as small as they seem, mark the end of men's exclusive claim to scientific expertise and the beginning of women's entry into scientific professions.[9]

This change has not been an even and easy one, however. The increasing numbers of women who had advanced training led to discussions about the need for expanded job opportunities for women. Science was no longer considered, at least among women who had doctorates in science, simply as a way to improve their domestic skills as mothers and wives. Still, the old attitudes did not completely give way. Expansions in scientific research directions and practices led to larger research staffs, and the expansion of land-grant institutions led to more research staffs in science, all of which opened opportunities for women. Limited by stereotypes about women, however, employers defined these new jobs as "women's work." So, for instance, in astronomy the use of new technologies, including spectroscopes and cameras, meant that there was a need for fewer "observers" (i.e., men) and more "assistants" (i.e., women). Women were thought to be especially good at detailed and methodical work, and they would work for less money. So they were hired to pore over mountains of astronomical photographs, and though many made important contributions to astrophysics, their work did not lead to wages that matched men's or to advancement and recognition on the job.[10]

For this next generation, there is story after story of highly qualified and talented women, dedicated to their research, who were employed in low-paying, sometimes nonpaying, jobs. They were exploited for their skills and abilities, but they were nonetheless willing to do difficult and tedious work because it was the only work available to them in science. One researcher, psychologist Leta Stetter Hollingworth, used her scientific expertise to question the assumptions that grounded these employment practices. Hollingworth decided to challenge the notion that women and men had different physical, motor, and intellectual abilities, since women's workplace opportunities were severely constrained by beliefs about sex differences in these abilities. A student at Barnard, she was a self-proclaimed feminist who was provoked to undertake this research when she had to resign her teaching position upon marrying. Between 1913 and 1916 she published a series of academic studies on sex differences in work performance that concluded such differences did not exist.[11]

There were others, particularly in the suffrage movement, who, like Hollingworth, argued that women were not different from or inferior to men in any way. But their voices were overwhelmed by public acceptance of the idea that fundamental and biological differences between the sexes were a natural fact informing social arrangements. The two world wars opened doors for women's participation in science as part of the war effort, though after the wars ended, women were required to leave their positions. Still, optimism ran high. In 1921 the president of Bryn Mawr declared that "the doors of science have been thrown wildly open to women," and in that decade an annual average of 50 doctorates in the sciences were awarded to women. By the end of the 1930s, 165 doctorates in the sciences were awarded annually to women. Barriers to African-American women's participation also began to fall. In 1933 Ruth Moore became the first African American to be awarded a doctorate in bacteriology (Ohio State University); in 1935 Jessie Mark became the first African American to be awarded a doctorate in botany (Iowa State University); and in 1940 Roger Arliner Young became the first African American to be awarded a doctorate in zoology (University of Pennsylvania).[12]

The second world war, in particular, had a dramatic impact on employment opportunities for women who had scientific training as the federal government's investment in science grew exponentially. Women scientists were in demand as the scientific labor force expanded. Women were allowed entry into a variety of settings from which they had previously been excluded, particularly in academia. Women were appointed temporary department chairs, were hired as faculty, and enrolled as graduate students. They were recruited into careers in science and engineering with a barrage of books and articles that painted a cheery picture of the prosperous and fulfilling futures that awaited them. Unfortunately, conservative social attitudes prevailed in the postwar period, as women were displaced by returning veterans taking advantage of the generous terms of the GI Bill and the Serviceman's Readjustment Act of 1944, which provided veterans with up to five years of full tuition plus living expenses.[13] As campus enrollments bulged, quotas were set on the number of women students admitted, so that male students could be housed in women's dorms. Despite admission caps for graduate women, the number of science doctorates awarded to women continued to increase steadily, from 120 in 1940 to 290 in 1954. But because the number of men in science programs was skyrocketing, the percentage of doctorates awarded to women shrank to only 6 percent of the total.[14]

A few extraordinary women continued to work productively in science, however, and international recognition for women as scientists in the United States became a reality when in 1947 Gerta Cori, a biochemist (and a wife and mother), became the first American women to win a Nobel prize for medicine. Resistance to women in science continued, however. One California housewife and educator, Olive Lewis, in 1948 published an article in the American Medical Association journal *Hygeia* arguing that scientists who were mothers were always so preoccupied with their own domestic problems that they did not do much good work of their own and even often disrupted the experiments of their colleagues. Still, such attitudes did not discourage increases in the number of women from becoming scientists. Between 1947 and 1963 a total of 782 doctorates were awarded to women in chemistry, 1,107 in the biosciences, 236 in mathematics, and 40 in engineering.[15]

By the second half of the twentieth century women had established their interest in scientific careers and their ability to compete with men for the privileges of practicing science. However, new barriers in hiring and promotion emerged, particularly for careers in academia, where the most prestigious positions were to be filled. In 1958 there were 138 doctorates awarded to women in the biosciences, but only twenty-six women in this pool were hired into jobs in colleges and universities. In the physical sciences, seventy-four women earned doctorates that year, but only twenty-six were hired into colleges and universities.[16]

Women in science organized to confront this trend. A series of national initiatives to eliminate discrimination in U.S. higher education sprang up as a response to concerns raised by the modern women's movement in the 1960s. Academic women in sociology, anthropology, and psychology published a series of articles and books that documented gender inequalities in the employment status of women in their fields. These efforts prompted changes in discriminatory policies on the enrollment, funding, and housing of women on college campuses. As increasing numbers of women were accepted into majors in the sciences, and as increasing numbers of women were accepted and graduated from doctoral programs, the number of women scientists on college campuses, in industry, and in government grew.

Despite these increases in the overall numbers of women doctorates, an individual was often the only woman in a graduate program. Sarah Blaffer Hrdy, an anthropologist, offers this account in the acknowledgments for one of her essays to describe her experiences in the 1970s:

> In the preface to her recent book "Mother Care," my colleague in behavioral biology Sandra Scarr (1984, p. ix) notes, "I wish I could thank all the wonderful graduate school professors who helped me to realize the joys of combining profession and motherhood;

> unfortunately there weren't any at Harvard in the early 1960s." A decade later, things at Harvard—at least in the biologically oriented part of Harvard that I encountered—had changed remarkably little. As I think back on those postgraduate years (my undergraduate experience at Harvard was a wonderful and very different story), I cannot recall a single moment's fear of success, but what I do distinctly recall was the painful perception that there were professors and fellow students (no women in those years) who acted as if they feared that I might succeed. Intellectually, it was a tremendously exciting environment, filled with stimulation and occasionally inspirational teachers and coworkers. It was also an environment that was socially and psychologically hostile to the professional aspirations of women. But there were exceptions, exceptions made all the more significant because they were rare.[17]

Promoting access to education and careers as scientists and engineers is only part of the story, however.[18] A handful of women scientists began to examine how sexism and male-centered perspectives could influence scientific theories and empirical research. Among the earliest was primatologist Donna Haraway, who in 1978 published a groundbreaking feminist theoretical critique of primate behavior studies.[19] Another pioneer was Harvard biologist Ruth Hubbard, who published, along with colleagues, one of earliest collections of essays examining the ways in which scientific understandings of women's biology were gender-biased, in *Women Look at Biology Looking at Women* (1979). Hrdy, a sociobiologist, was one of the first feminists to challenge sociobiological arguments about male superiority, in *The Woman that Never Evolved* (1981). Perhaps influenced by the early work of the pioneering Ruth Herschberger in *Adam's Rib* (1948), neurobiologist Ruth Bleier began publishing articles on social influences on biology in the 1970s and produced a major study, *Science and Gender,* in 1984. At the same time, physicist Evelyn Fox Keller began publishing articles exploring objectivity, gender, and feminism, followed by a major theoretical essay that appeared in *Signs: Journal of Women in Culture and Society* in 1982. Similarly, biologist Anne Fausto-Sterling's *Myths of Gender: Biological Theories about Women and Men* appeared in 1985. Sue Rosser, also a biologist, took this work in new directions when in the mid-1980s she began to write on integrating feminist perspectives into science education, publishing *Female-Friendly Science: Applying Women's Studies Methods and Theories to Attract Students to Science* in 1990. Since then, a wide variety of articles and books has elaborated the theoretical groundwork laid by these scientists, enriching our understanding of feminist perspectives in/on the sciences with philosophy, literature, sociology, anthropology, psychology, history, and cultural and technology studies.

The growth of work by and about women in science is testimony to the intellectual richness that feminist perspectives can bring to science and science studies. Yet despite two decades of research, and despite a wealth of new information and perspectives on the causes of women's underrepresentation in science, women remain outsiders in scientific culture. The essays in this section focus on the experiences of women in a variety of fields, the processes that exclude them, the ways in which they have responded to these exclusionary practices, and analyses of the connections between women's exclusion and key ideologies in the scientific community. We have divided the section into two parts, "Education: Out of the Frying Pan . . ." and "Careers: . . . And into the Fire," in order to emphasize that women face persistent and distinct challenges throughout both their education and their careers.

The first two readings in this section are autobiographical. Aimee Sands's interview with Evelynn Hammonds, "Never Meant To Survive: A Black Woman's Journey," and Evelyn Fox Keller's "The Anomaly of a Woman in Physics" provide firsthand accounts of the personal and social barriers to women's success in science. Hammonds describes the double jeopardy she felt as an African-American woman in physics. Keller recalls her painful experiences in the physics department at Harvard in the late 1950s and relates how she transformed her feelings of rage about the blatant biases and differential treatment of men and women students into political consciousness. Both articles describe the alienation and self-doubt engendered by being part of an extreme minority. Both Keller and Hammonds doubted their own abilities before questioning the culture of science that worked against their survival. The broader focus helped them to understand that the difficulties they confronted were not of their own making. Their stories are also about strength, self-realization, and eventual success—Fox Keller as a molecular biologist and philosopher of science, and Hammonds as a physicist and historian of science.

Hammonds's and Keller's accounts are compelling examples of how individual women experience discrimination. But what are the social processes within higher education that lead women toward or away from careers in science or engineering? In "Gender Constructs and Career Commitment: The Influence of Peer Culture on Women in College," Margaret Eisenhart and Dorothy Holland present an analysis of the profound influence of peer culture and social processes on young women's academic path toward or away from scientific careers. The article reviews theories of socialization of gender roles, need fulfillment, and reproduction of subordinate status and presents the results of an ethnographic study of black and white women students at two southern universities. In this study the universities' influence on the women's career-related decisions paled in comparison to peer influence and consideration of gender norms. Among the women studied, academic success and interest in science were often given a negative connotation, and science majors were thought of as weird and socially inept. (In section 2 we will continue to examine the popular image of science and scientists and how this image reflects cultural ideas about who can and cannot do science.) Most of the women in Eisenhart's and Holland's study believe that social and peer success were more critical than academic success for women.

The last reading in this group, "Snow Brown and the Seven Detergents," by Banu Subramaniam, is written in the form of a fairy tale that tells the story of a young woman from India who travels to the United States to become a scientist. The hero, Sneha, is troubled by her experiences in graduate school and seeks advice from two authorities: the Senior White Patriarch and the Wise Matriarch. Her dreams about becoming a scientist fade, however, as her confidence erodes in the face of the racism and sexism that she encounters.

The next group of readings explores issues that confront those who have succeeded in becoming professional scientists. Two short essays, one by Dara Horn on the ways in which women's contributions to science have been lost and one by Christine Wennerás and Agnes Wold on the peer review process, point to specific cases in which scientific knowledge generated by women has been devalued. In "Nine Decades, Nine Women, Ten Nobel Prizes: Gender Politics at the Apex of Science," Hilary Rose reviews the obstacles that even the most remarkable women scientists have faced on their way to the highest recognition of achievement in science, a Nobel prize. Rose also tells the stories of women who were overlooked—whose achievement might have been recognized in a more equitable world. Rose points out historical and social factors that played into recognition (or nonrecognition) of the women included in the chapter. She describes how the late timing of the award in the lives of women Nobel prize winners differs from awards made to men, rendering award-winning women less influential on young scientists and less able to broker the power that accompanies the prize.

The last reading in this section, by sociologist Harriet Zuckerman, summarizes research that focuses on identifying the variety of factors that foster gender differences in scientific careers. Researchers have offered four general explanations for gender differences in the levels of success achieved by women and men in science: (1) that women and men differ in their abilities; (2) that discrimination reduces the opportunities for success available to women; (3) that women and men differ in their commitments to a career and family; and (4) that there are gender differences in the small advantages and disadvantages that accumulate over the course of scientists' education and careers. Zuckerman concludes on a less than hopeful note, saying that the slow pace of changes in opportunities for women in science and engineering in the twentieth century suggests that full equality is a distant hope.

NOTES

[1] See Janice Law Trecker, "Sex, Science, and Education," in this volume. See also Glenda Riley, "Origins of the Argument for Improved Female Education," *History of Education Quarterly* 9, 4 (winter 1969): 455–70.

[2] Margaret Rossiter, *Women Scientists in America: Struggles and Strategies to 1940* (Baltimore: Johns Hopkins University Press. 1982), 2–3; Janice Law Trecker, "Sex, Science and Education," *American Quarterly* 26, 4 (1974): 352–66. Quote is from Barbara Ehrenreich and Deirdre English, *For Her Own Good: 150 Years of the Experts' Advice to Women* (New York: Doubleday, 1978), 108.

[3] Sally Schwager, "Educating Women in America", *Signs: Journal of Women in Culture and Society* 12, 2 (1987): 333–72, esp. 339–40; Rossiter, *Women Scientists to 1940,* 2–3.

[4] Schwager, "Educating Women in America"; Rossiter, *Women Scientists to 1940.* See also H.J. Mozans, *Woman in Science* (Notre Dame, Ind.: University of Notre Dame Press, 1991 [1913]).

[5] Rossiter, *Women Scientists to 1940,* 4–7; Schwager, "Educating Women in America," 340–46.

[6] Pamela Mack, "Straying from Their Orbits: Women in Astronomy in America," in G. Kass-Simon and P. Farnes, eds., *Women of Science: Righting the Record* (Bloomington: Indiana University Press, 1990); quote from Rossiter, *Women Scientists to 1940,* 14–15.

[7] Darlene Clark Hine et al., eds., *Black Women in America* (New York: Carlson Publishing, 1993).

[8] Rossiter, *Women Scientists to 1940,* 19–21.

[9] Ibid., 35.

[10] Mack, "Straying from Their Orbits," 81–91; Rossiter, *Women Scientists to 1940,* 55–57.

[11] Stephanie Shields, "Ms. Pilgrim's Progress: The Contributions of Leta Stetter Hollingworth to the Psychology of Women," *American Psychologist* 30 (1975): 852–57.

[12] Rossiter, *Women Scientists to 1940,* 127; Hine et al., *Black Women in America.*

[13] Women veterans were technically also eligible (there were some 400,000), but this was not widely known or applied. Margaret Rossiter, *Women Scientists in America: Before Affirmative Action, 1940–1972* (Baltimore: Johns Hopkins University Press, 1995), 30–31.

[14] Ibid., 30–33.

[15] Ibid., 41; National Science Foundation, *Women, Minorities, and Persons with Disabilities in Science and Engineering* (Washington, D.C.: NSF, 1994).

[16] Rossiter, *Women Scientists 1940–1972,* 195–96.

[17] Sarah Blaffer Hrdy, "Empathy, Polyandry, and the Myth of the Coy Female," in Ruth Bleier, ed., *Feminist Approaches to Science* (New York: Teachers College Press, 1991), 141.

[18] The full integration of women into science and engineering education challenges assumptions about the professionalization process itself. Even when male scientists are supportive of women students, gender dynamics can shape the mentor-student relationship in unproductive ways. See Banu Subramaniam and Mary Wyer, "Assimilating the 'Culture of No Culture' in Science: Feminist Interventions in (De)Mentoring Graduate Women," *Feminist Teacher* 12, 1 (June 1998): 12–28.

[19] Donna Haraway. "Animal Sociology and a Natural Economy of the Body Politic, Part I. A Political Physiology of Dominance," and "Part II. The Past Is the Contested Zone: Human Nature and Theories of Production and Reproduction in Primate Behavior Studies," *Signs: Journal of Women in Culture and Society* 4, 1 (1978): 21–36, 37–60.

EDUCATION:
Out of the Frying Pan . . .

THE ANOMALY OF A WOMAN IN PHYSICS

Evelyn Fox Keller

A couple of months ago I was invited to give a series of lectures at a major university as one of a "series of distinguished guest lecturers" on mathematical aspects of biology. Having just finished teaching a course on women at my own college, I somehow felt obliged to violate the implicit protocol and address the anomalous fact of my being an apparently successful woman scientist. Though I had experienced similar vague impulses before, for a variety of reasons arising from a mix of anger, confusion, and timidity, it had never seemed to me either appropriate or possible to yield to such an impulse. Now, however, it seemed decidedly inappropriate, somewhat dishonest, and perhaps even politically unconscionable to deliver five lectures on my work without once making reference to the multitude of contradictions and conflicts I had experienced in arriving at the professional position presumed on this occasion. Therefore, in a gesture that felt wonderfully bold and unprofessional, I devoted the last lecture to a discussion of the various reasons for the relative absence of women in science, particularly in the higher ranks. The talk formed itself—with an ease, clarity, and lack of rancor that amazed me. I felt an enormous sense of personal triumph. Somehow, in the transformation of what had always appeared to me an essentially personal problem into a political problem, my anger had become depersonalized, even defused, and a remarkable sense of clarity emerged. It suggested to me that I might, now, be able to write about my own rather painful and chaotic history as a woman in science.

Origins are difficult to determine and obscure in their relation to final consequences. Suffice it to say that in my senior year of college I decided I would be a scientist. After several years of essentially undirected intellectual ambition, I majored in physics partly for the sake of discipline and partly out of the absence of any clear sense of vocation; and in my last year I fell in love with theoretical physics.

I invoke the romantic image not as a metaphor, but as an authentic, literal description of my experience. I fell in love, simultaneously and inextricably, with my professors, with a discipline of pure, precise, definitive thought, and with what I conceived of as its ambitions. I fell in love with the life of the mind. I also fell in love, I might add, with the image of myself striving and succeeding in an area where women had rarely ventured. It was a heady experience. In my adviser's fantasies, I was to rise, unhampered, right to the top. In my private fantasies, I was to be heralded all the way.

It was 1957. Politics conspired with our fantasies. Graduate schools, newly wealthy with National Science Foundation money, competed vigorously for promising students, and a promising female student was a phenomenon sufficiently unique to engage the interest and curiosity of recruiters from Stanford to Harvard. Only Cal Tech and Princeton were closed to me—they were not yet admitting women—and I felt buoyant enough to challenge them. I particularly wanted to go to Cal Tech to study with Richard Feynman—a guru of theoretical physics—on whose work I had done my senior thesis. In lieu of my being accepted at Cal Tech, an influential friend of mine volunteered to offer Feynman a university chair at MIT, where I would be admitted. Heady indeed.

Even then I was aware that the extreme intoxication of that time was transitory—that it had primarily to do with feeling "on the brink." Everything that excited me lay ahead. I had fantasies of graduate school and becoming a physicist; what awaited me, I thought, was the fulfillment of those fantasies. Even the idea of "doing physics" was fantasylike. I could form no clear picture of myself in that role, had no clear idea of what it involved. My conception of a community of scholars had the airiness of a dream. I was intoxicated by a vision that existed primarily in my head.

Well, Feynman was not interested in leaving Cal Tech, and so I went to Harvard. More accurately, I was pressured, and eventually persuaded, by both a would-be mentor at Harvard and my adviser, to go to Harvard. At Harvard I was promised the moon and the sun—I could do anything I wanted. Why I was given this extraordinary sales pitch seems, in retrospect, all but inexplicable. At the time, it seemed quite natural. I dwell on the headiness of this period in order to convey the severity of the blow that graduate school at Harvard actually was.

The story of my graduate school experience is a difficult one to tell. It is difficult in part because it is a story of behavior so crude and so extreme as to seem implausible.

Moreover, it is difficult to tell because it is painful. In the past, the telling of this story always left me so badly shaken, feeling so exposed, that I became reluctant to tell it. Many years have passed, and I might well bury those painful recollections. I do not because they represent a piece of reality—an ongoing reality that affects others, particularly women. Even though my experiences may have been unique—no one else will share exactly these experiences—the motives underlying the behavior I am going to describe are, I believe, much more prevalent than one might think, and detectable in fact in behavior much less extreme.

I tell the story now, therefore, because it may somehow be useful to others. I *can* tell the story now because it no longer leaves me feeling quite so exposed. Let me try to explain this sense of exposure.

Once, several months into my first year in graduate school, a post-doctoral student in an unusual gesture of friendliness offered me a ride home from a seminar and asked how I was doing. Moved by his gesture, I started to tell him. As I verged on tears, I noticed the look of acute discomfort on his face. Somehow, I had committed a serious indiscretion. It was as if I had publicly disrobed. Whatever I said, then and always after, it somehow seemed I had said too much. Some of this feeling remains with me even now as I write this article. It is a consequence of the assumption in the minds of others that what I am describing must have been a very personal, private experience—that is, that it was produced somehow by forces within myself. It was not. Although I clearly participated in and necessarily contributed to these events, they were *essentially* external in origin. That vital recognition has taken a long time. With it, my shame began to dissolve, to be replaced by a sense of personal rage and, finally, a transformation of that rage into something less personal—something akin to a political conscience.

That transformation, crucial in permitting me to write this, has not, however, entirely removed the pain from the process of recollecting a story that retains for me considerable horror. If I falter at this point, it is because I realize that in order for this story to be meaningful, even credible, to others, I must tell it objectively—I must somehow remove myself from the pain of which I write. The actual events were complex. Many strands weave in and out. I will describe them, one by one, as simply and as fairly as I can.

My first day at Harvard I was informed, by the very man who had urged me to come, that my expectations were unrealistic. For example, I could not take the course with Schwinger (Harvard's answer to Feynman) that had lured me to Harvard, and I ought not concern myself with the foundations of quantum mechanics (the only thing that did concern me) because, very simply, I was not, could not be, good enough. Surely my ambition was based on delusion—it referred to a pinnacle only the very few, and certainly not I, could achieve. Brandeis, I was told bluntly, was not Harvard, and although my training there might have earned me a place at Harvard, distinction at Brandeis had no meaning here. Both I and they had better assume I knew nothing. Hence I ought to start at the beginning. The students they really worried about, I was informed, were those who were so ignorant and naive that they could not apprehend the supreme difficulty of success at Harvard.

These remarks were notable for their blatant class bias and arrogance, as well as for their insistent definition of me on the basis of that bias—a gratuitous dismissal of my own account that I experienced recurrently throughout graduate school. The professor's remarks were all the more remarkable in that I had expressed exactly the same intentions in our conversation the previous spring and had then been encouraged. What could account for this extraordinary reversal? There had been no intervening assessment of my qualifications. Perhaps it can be explained simply by the fact that the earlier response was one of someone in the position of selling Harvard, while now it seemed there was an obligation to defend her. (It is ironic that universities should be associated with the feminine gender.) Nor was it coincidental, I suspect, that this man was shortly to assign to one of the senior graduate students (male, of course) the task of teaching me how to dress.[1]

Thus began two years of almost unmitigated provocation, insult, and denial. Lacking any adequate framework—political or psychological—for comprehending what was happening to me, I could only respond with personal rage: I felt increasingly provoked, insulted, and denied. Where political rage would have been constructive, personal rage served only to increase my vulnerability. Having come to Harvard expecting to be petted and fussed over (as I had been before) and expecting, most of all, validation and approval, I was entirely unprepared for the treatment I received. I could neither account for nor respond appropriately to the enormous discrepancy between what I expected and what I found. I had so successfully internalized the cultural identification between male and intellect that I was totally dependent on my (male) teachers for affirmation—a dependency made treacherous by the chronic confusion of sexuality and intellect in relationships between male teachers and female students. In seeking intellectual affirmation, I sought male affirmation, and thereby became exquisitely vulnerable to the male aggression surrounding me.

I had in fact been warned about the extreme alienation of the first year as a graduate student at Harvard, but both my vanity and my naiveté permitted me to ignore these warnings. I was confident that things would be different for me. That confidence did not last long. Coming from everywhere, from students and faculty alike, were three messages. First, physics at Harvard was the most difficult enterprise in the world; second, I could not possibly understand the things I thought I understood; and third, my lack of fear was proof of my ignorance. At first, I adopted a wait-and-see attitude and agreed to take the conventional curriculum, though I privately resolved to audit Schwinger's course. Doing so, as it turned out, seemed such an act of bravado that, daily, all eyes turned on me as I entered the class and, daily, I was asked by half a dozen people with amusement if I still thought I understood. Mysteriously, my regular courses seemed manageable, even easy, and as I became increasingly nervous about my failure to fear properly, I spent more and more evenings at the movies. In time, the frequent and widespread iteration of the message that I could not understand what I thought I understood began to take its toll. As part of a general retreat, I stopped attending Schwinger's course.

[1] My attire, I should perhaps say, was respectable. It consisted mainly of skirts and sweaters, selected casually, with what might have been called a bohemian edge. I wore little or no makeup.

I had begun to lose all sense of what I did or did not understand, there and elsewhere. That I did well in my exams at the end of the semester seemed to make no difference whatever.

Meanwhile, it was clear that I was becoming the subject—or object—of a good deal of attention in the Physics Department. My seriousness, intensity, and ambition seemed to cause my elders considerable amusement, and a certain amount of curiosity as well. I was watched constantly, and occasionally addressed. Sometimes I was queried about my peculiar ambition to be a theoretical physicist—didn't I know that no woman at Harvard had ever so succeeded (at least not in becoming a *pure* theoretical physicist)? When would I too despair, fail, or go elsewhere (the equivalent of failing)? The possibility that I might succeed seemed to be a source of titillation; I was leered at by some, invited now and then to a faculty party by others. The open and unbelievably rude laughter with which I was often received at such events was only one of many indications that I was on display—for purposes I could either not perceive or not believe. My fantasy was turning into nightmare. . . .

It is sometimes hard to separate affront to oneself as a person from affront to one's sensibilities. Not only do they tend to generate the same response—one feels simply affronted—but it is also possible (as I believe was true here) that the motives for both affronts are not unrelated. I went to graduate school with a vision of theoretical physics as a vehicle for the deepest inquiry into nature—a vision perhaps best personified, in recent times, by Einstein. The use of mathematics to further one's understanding of the nature of space, time, and matter represented a pinnacle of human endeavor. I went to graduate school to learn about foundations. I was taught, instead, how to do physics. In place of wisdom, I was offered skills. Furthermore, this substitution was made with moralistic fervor. It was wrong, foolhardy, indeed foolish, to squander precious time asking why. Proper humility was to bend to the grindstone and learn techniques. Contemporary physics, under the sway of operationalism, had, it seemed, dispensed with the tradition of Einstein—almost, indeed, with Einstein himself. General relativity, the most intellectually ambitious venture of the century, seemed then (wrongly) a dead subject. Philosophical considerations of any sort in the physical sciences were at an all-time low. Instead, techniques designed to calculate nth-order corrections to a theory grievously flawed at its base were the order of the day. . . .

My naiveté and idealism were perfect targets. Not only did I not know my place in the scheme of things as a woman, but by a curious coincidence, I was apparently equally ingenuous concerning my place as a thinker. I needed to be humbled. Though I writhed over the banality of the assignments I was given, I did them, acknowledging that I needed in any case to learn the skills. I made frequent arithmetic errors—reflecting a tension that endures within me even today between the expansiveness of conception and the precision of execution, my personal variation perhaps of the more general polar tension in physics as a whole. When my papers were returned with the accuracy of the conception ignored and the arithmetic errors streaked with red—as if with a vengeance—I wondered whether I was studying physics or plumbing. Who has not experienced such a wrenching conflict between idealism and reality? Yet my fellow students seemed oddly untroubled. From the nature of their responses when I tried to press them for deeper understanding of the subject, I thought perhaps I had come from Mars. Why, they wondered, did I want to know? That they were evidently content with the operational success of the formulas mystified me. Even more mystifying was the absence of any appearance of the humility of demeanor that one would expect to accompany the acceptance of more limited goals. I didn't fully understand then that in addition to the techniques of physics, they were also studying the techniques of arrogance. This peculiar inversion in the meaning of humility was simply part of the process of learning how to be a physicist.

It was intrinsic to the professionalization, and what I might even call the masculinization, of an intellectual discipline.

To some extent the things I describe here are in the nature of the academic subculture. They reflect the perversion of academic style—familiar in universities everywhere—a perversion that has become more extensive as graduate schools have tended to become increasingly preoccupied with professional training. My experiences resemble those of many graduate students—male and female alike. What I experienced as a rather brutal assault on my intellectual interests and abilities was I think no accident, but rather the inevitable result of the pervasive attempt of a profession to make itself more powerful by weeding out those sensibilities, emotional and intellectual, that it considers inappropriate. Not unrelated is a similar attempt to maintain the standards and image of a discipline by discouraging the participation of women—a strategy experienced and recounted by many other women. Viewed in this way, it is perhaps not surprising that the assault would be most blatant in a subject as successful as contemporary physics, and in a school as prestigious as Harvard.

Perhaps the most curious, undoubtedly the most painful, part of my experience was the total isolation in which I found myself. In retrospect, I am certain that there must have been like-minded souls somewhere who shared at least some of my disappointments. But if there were, I did not know them. In part, I attribute this to the general atmosphere of fear that permeated the graduate student body. One did not voice misgivings because they were invariably interpreted to mean that one must not be doing well.[2] The primary goal was to survive, and, better yet, to *appear* to be surviving, even prospering. So few complaints were heard from anyone. Furthermore, determined not to expose the slightest shred of ignorance, few students were willing to discuss their work with any but (possibly) their closest friends. I was, clearly, a serious threat to my fellow students' conception of physics as not only a male stronghold but a male *retreat*, and so I was least likely to be sought out as a colleague. I must admit that my own arrogance and ambition did little to allay their anxieties or temper their resistances. To make matters even worse, I shared with my fellow classmates the idea that a social or sexual relationship could only exist between male and female students if the man was "better" or "smarter" than the woman—or at the very least, comparable. Since both my self-definition and my performance labeled me as a superior student, the field of sociability and companionship was considerably narrowed.

There was one quite small group of students whom I did view as like-minded and longed to be part of. They too were concerned with foundations; they too wanted to know why. One of them (the only one in my class) had in fact become a close friend during my first semester. Though he preached to me about the necessity of humility, the importance of learning through the tips of one's fingers, the virtue of precision—he also listened with some sympathy. Formerly a Harvard undergraduate, he explained to me the workings of Harvard and I explained to him how to do the problems. With his assistance, I acquired the patience to carry out the calculations. We worked together, talked together, frequently ate together. Unfortunately, as the relationship threatened to become more intimate, it also became more difficult—in ways that are all too familiar—until, finally, he decided that he could no longer afford the risk of a close association with me. Out of sympathy for his feelings, I respected his request that I steer clear of him and his friends—with the consequence that I was, thereafter, totally alone. The extent of my isolation was almost as difficult for *me* to believe as for those to whom I've attempted to describe it since. Only once, years later in a conversation with another woman physicist,

---

[2] Indeed, most people then and later assumed I had done badly—particularly after hearing my story. Any claims I made to the contrary met with disbelief.

did I find any recognition. She called it the "sea of seats": you walk into a classroom early, and the classroom fills up, leaving a sea of empty seats around you.

Were there no other women students? There were two, who shared neither my ambition, my conception of physics, nor my interests. For these reasons, I am ashamed to say, I had no interest in them. I am even more ashamed to admit that out of my desire to be taken seriously as a physicist I was eager to avoid identification with other women students who I felt could not be taken seriously. Like most women with so-called male aspirations, I had very little sense of sisterhood.

Why did I stay? The Harvard Physics Department is not the world. Surely my tenacity appears as the least comprehensible component of my situation. At the very least, I had an extraordinary tolerance for pain. Indeed, one of my lifelong failings has been my inability to know when to give up. The very passion of my investment ruled out alternatives.

I had, however, made some effort to leave. At the very beginning, a deep sense of panic led me to ask to be taken back at Brandeis. Partly out of disbelief, partly out of the conviction that success at Harvard was an invaluable career asset, not to be abandoned, I was refused, and persuaded to continue. Although I had the vivid perception that rather than succeed I would be undone by Harvard, I submitted to the convention that others know better; I agreed to suspend judgment and to persevere through this stinging "initiation rite." In part, then, I believed that I was undergoing some sort of trial that would terminate when I had proven myself, certainly by the time I completed my orals. I need be stoic only for one year. Unfortunately, that hope turned out to be futile. The courses were not hard, never became hard in spite of the warnings, and I generally got A's. But so did many other students. Exams in fact were extremely easy.

When I turned in particularly good work, it was suspected, indeed sometimes assumed, that I had plagiarized it. On one such occasion, I had written a paper the thesis of which had provoked much argument and contention in the department. This I learned, by chance, several weeks after the debate was well underway. In an effort to resolve the paradox created by my results, I went to see the professor for whom I had written the paper. After an interesting discussion, which incidentally resolved the difficulty, I was asked, innocently and kindly, from what article(s) I had copied my argument.

The oral exams, which I had viewed as a forbidding milestone, proved to be a debacle. My committee chairman simply failed to appear. The result was that I was examined by an impromptu committee of experimentalists on mathematical physics. Months later, I was offered the following explanation: "Oh, Evelyn, I guess I owe you an apology. You see, I had just taken two sleeping pills and overslept." The exam was at 2:00 P.M. Nevertheless, I passed. Finally, I could begin serious work. I chose as a thesis adviser the sanest and kindliest member of the department. I knocked on his door daily for a month, only to be told to come back another time. Finally I gained admittance, to be advised that I'd better go home and learn to calculate.

My second year was even more harrowing than the first. I had few courses and a great deal of time that I could not use without guidance. I had no community of scholars. Completing the orals had not served in any way to alleviate my isolation. I was more alone than ever. The community outside the physics department, at least that part to which I had access, offered neither solace nor support. The late fifties were the peak of what might be called home-brewed psychoanalysis. I was unhappy, single, and stubbornly pursuing an obviously male discipline. What was wrong with me? In one way or another, this question was put to me at virtually every party I attended. I was becoming quite desperate with loneliness. And as I became increasingly lonely I am sure I became increasingly defensive, making it even more difficult for those who might have been sympathetic to me or my plight to approach me to commiserate. Such support might have made a big difference. As it was, I had neither colleagues nor lovers, and not very many friends. The few friends I did have viewed my situation as totally alien. They gave sympathy out of love, though without belief. And I wept because I had no friend whose ambition I could identify with. Was there no woman who was doing, had done, what I was trying to do? I knew of none. My position was becoming increasingly untenable. . . .

I recognize that this account reads in so many ways like that of a bad marriage—the passionate intensity of the initial commitment, the fantasies on which such a commitment (in part) is based, the exclusivity of the attachment, the apparent disappearance of alternative options, the unwillingness and inability to let go, and finally, the inclination to blame oneself for all difficulties. Although I can now tell this story as a series of concrete, objective events that involved and affected me, at the time I eventually came to accept the prevalent view that what happened to me at Harvard simply manifested my own confusion, failure, neurosis—in short that *I* had somehow "made" it happen. The implications of such internalization were—as they always are—very serious.

Now I had to ask *how* I had "made" it happen—what in me required purging? It seemed that my very ambition and seriousness were at fault, and that these qualities—qualities I had always admired in others—had to be given up. Giving up physics, then, seemed to mean giving up parts of me so central to my sense of myself that a meaningful extrication was next to impossible. I stayed on at Harvard, allowing myself to be convinced once again that I must finish my degree, and sought a dissertation project outside the Physics Department.

After drifting for a year, I took advantage of an opportunity to do a thesis in molecular biology while still nominally remaining in the Physics Department. That this rather unusual course was permitted indicated at least a recognition, on the part of the then chairman, of some of the difficulties I faced in physics. Molecular biology was a field in which I could find respect, and even more important, congeniality. I completed my degree, came to New York to teach (physics!), married, bore children, and ultimately began to work in theoretical biology, where I could make use of my training and talents. This proved to be a rewarding professional area that sustained me for a number of critical years. If my work now begins to take me outside this professional sphere, into more political and philosophical concerns, this reflects the growing confidence and freedom I have felt in recent years.

Inner conflict, however, was not to disappear with a shift in scientific specialization. While it is true that I was never again to suffer the same acute—perhaps bizarre—discomfort that I did as a graduate student in physics, much of the underlying conflict was to surface in other forms as I assumed the more conventional roles of wife, mother, and teacher. The fundamental conflict—between my sense of myself as a woman and my identity as a scientist—could only be resolved by transcending all stereotypical definitions of self and success. This took a long time, a personal analysis, and the women's movement. It meant establishing a personal identity secure enough to allow me to begin to liberate myself from everyone's labels—including my own. The tension between "woman" and "scientist" is not now so much a source of personal struggle as a profound concern.

After many years, I have carved out a professional identity very different from the one I had originally envisioned, but one that I cherish dearly. It is, in many important ways, extraprofessional. It has led me to teach in a small liberal arts college that grants me the leeway to pursue my interests on my own terms and to combine the teaching I have come to love with those interests, and that respects me for doing so. It has meant acquiring the courage to seek both the motives and rewards for my intellectual efforts more within myself. Which is not to say that I no longer need affirmation from others;

but I find that I am now willing to seek and accept support from different sources—from friends rather than from institutions, from a community defined by common interests rather than by status.

As I finished writing this essay, I came across an issue of the annals of the *New York Academy of Sciences* (March 15, 1973) devoted to "Successful Women in the Sciences." The volume included brief autobiographical accounts of a dozen or so women, two of whom were trained in physics and one in mathematics. Because material of this kind is almost nonexistent, these first-person reports are an important contribution "to the literature." I read them avidly. More than avidly, for the remarks of these women, in their directness and honesty, represent virtually the only instance of professional circumstances with which to compare my own experience.

It may be difficult for those removed from the mores of the scientific community to understand the enormous reticence with which anyone, especially a woman, would make public his or her personal impressions and experiences, particularly if they reflect negatively on the community. To do so is not only considered unprofessional, it jeopardizes one's professional image of disinterest and objectivity. Women, who must work so hard to establish that image, are not likely to take such risks. Furthermore, our membership in this community has inculcated in us the strict habit of minimizing any differences due to our sex. I wish therefore to congratulate women in the mainstreams of science who demonstrate such courage.

Their stories, however, are very different from mine. Although a few of these women describe discrete experiences similar to some of mine, they were generally able to transcend their isolation and discomfort, and in their perseverance and success, to vindicate their sex. I am in awe of such fortitude. In their stories I am confirmed in my sense that with more inner strength I would have responded very differently to the experiences I've recorded here. The difficulty, however, with success stories is that they tend to obscure the impact of oppression, while focusing on individual strengths. It used to be said by most of the successful women that women have no complaint precisely because it has been demonstrated that with sufficient determination, anything can be accomplished. If the women's movement has achieved anything, it has taught us the folly of such a view. If I was demolished by my graduate school experiences, it was primarily because I failed to define myself as a rebel against norms in which society has heavily invested. In the late fifties, "rebel" was not a meaningful word. Conflicts and obstacles were seen to be internal. My insistence on maintaining a romantic image of myself in physics, on holding to the view that I would be rewarded and blessed for doing what others had failed to do, presupposed a sense of myself as special, and therefore left me particularly vulnerable. An awareness of the political and social realities might have saved me from persisting in a search for affirmation where it could not and would not be given. Such a political consciousness would have been a source of great strength. I hope that the political awareness generated by the women's movement can and will support young women who today attempt to challenge the dogma, still very much alive, that certain kinds of thought are the prerogative of men.

NEVER MEANT TO SURVIVE*
A Black Woman's Journey:
An Interview with Evelynn Hammonds by Aimee Sands

Aimee. What was it that sparked becoming a scientist in your mind?

Evelynn. I thought I'd like to be a scientist when at nine I had my first chemistry set. I had such a good time with all the experiments. I wanted to know more, and I wanted to get the advanced Gilbert chemistry set so I could do more interesting experiments.

A. Who gave you the chemistry set?

E. My father. And he gave me a microscope a year later. I always had sets like that. I had chemistry sets or microscopes or building sets or race car sets or different kinds of project-kit things to build stuff. My father and I always spent some time together working on them, and he was always interested in what I was finding out . . . figuring out. . . .

A. When did you start doing science in school?

E. We always had science in elementary school. The, you know, "go out and look at the plants," and the general basic (I guess in elementary school) science curriculum that I took along with everything else. I didn't think of taking more science courses than just the requirements until I was in high school. But I really liked science, I always did. But my basic interest was that I wanted to go to a good college. So I wanted to have a good background to do that. And I felt that the more science and math I could take the better off I would be.

So I started seriously . . . I guess in my high school we had to take up through chemistry, but then I went on and took physics. We only had math up through trigonometry, but I begged my math teacher to let us have a pre-calculus class because I wanted to go on. And that pre-calculus class came about because in my junior year in high school I was accepted into a National Science Foundation summer program for high achievers in mathematics for high school students. So I spent the summer in Emory University studying math.

There were three Black students in the program, and we were all just totally baffled by what was going on. We were taking a course in analytical geometry when we didn't know what analytical geometry was. We were taking an introductory course in group theory, and I can't remember the third course, but, some of the concepts it seemed all the other students had studied before and we hadn't studied at all, 'cause all three of us had gone to segregated high schools or recently integrated high schools. And it was a very painful experience because I felt that I was as smart as the other kids, the white kids in the class, but I had this gap in my background. I didn't know what to do about it, how to go and find the information I didn't have, and I didn't know how to prove I was still good, even though I didn't understand what was going on in class.

A. Did you know what the gap was even called? What you were missing?

---

*The phrase "never meant to survive" is from a line in a poem "A Litany for Survival" by Audre Lorde, published in *A Black Unicorn* (New York: Norton, 1978).

E. No, I didn't have any words for it. It was just very painful. The three of us sort of haunted the libraries trying to find the books that would help us understand what was going on. It was supposed to be a summer program, so we were supposed to have fun, but the three of us weren't having fun at all. We were miserable and scared, and wondered if we were going to make it. And I was also completely angry at my parents and at my teachers that I'd had at my high school, who I felt hadn't pushed me and hadn't given me the right preparation. And that was the beginning for me to begin to understand that I'd had a deficient education . . . because I'd gone to predominantly Black schools, that that deficiency showed up most strongly in math and science. So it made me angry and made me start looking over what had happened to me.

A. What did you see?

E. I felt I'd been cheated . . . I felt I'd been denied that opportunity to have a good education because I was a Black person and I lived in the South. So I went back to my high school, and I took another year of science when I didn't have to. And I took another year of math and asked my teacher for the pre-calculus course.

A. Did that turn out to be what you were missing? Pre-calculus?

E. In part.

A. I want to go back a little before the Emory experience, when you were in grade school and high school. Were there teachers that encouraged your interest in science? I mean you said you took what everyone else took, and you implied by that you didn't have any special interest in school and it sounds like your special interest was more outside of school with the chemistry stuff. Is that right?

E. Yeah, uh . . . in elementary school and probably in junior high and the early years of high school I pursued my interest outside. I'd read books, science books and books about science and ideas just on my own, and I would talk to the few friends that I had who were interested in those things.

A. Were there teachers who encouraged or discouraged you or did they just not know anything about that side of your life?

E. Most of my teachers didn't know that I was doing it. It would show up when I'd come back to school that I had read all this interesting stuff, and I'd talk about it in class. They were very encouraging but they didn't push or anything. I always had—particularly math and science—teachers who took an interest in me most of the way—*except,* I have to say, for a couple of the times when I was being bused. I had two teachers, both math, one science, who were just outright racist and . . . one math teacher, who would, if I raised my hand for a question (I was the only Black student in the class) she would stop, call the roll, ask everybody if they had a question, skip my name and *then* ask me what my question was at the end. So I had those kinds of experiences. Or I never quite had enough points to make an A on a test or . . . I always seemed to get an A−. It always seemed there were points to be taken off for something—you know that kind of stuff—and I noticed. Those were the kinds of things I didn't know how to fight, at that time.

A. Why do you think it was that those kinds of experiences didn't discourage you from pursuing science?

E. Because I was angry, and I wasn't going to let that stop me. And . . . because my parents wouldn't have let me stop, to a certain extent. If I had given that kind of reason they wouldn't have—they would have thought I was unacceptable—especially my mother.

A. What would she have said?

E. She would have said that I could stop it if I didn't *like* it, but I couldn't stop because someone was discriminating against me—or making it difficult for me—because I had to understand people were going to make it difficult for me in the world because I was Black. . . .

A. Describe the remainder of your college years and what happened?

E. I entered Spelman College in the Dual Degree Program, which was a program between the five Black colleges and the Atlanta University Center and Georgia Tech where students would spend 2½ years at one of the Black colleges and then 2½ years at Georgia Tech and at the end of that time have bachelors degrees from both schools.

It was important to me to have the experience of being at Spelman. Even though I rebelled at first, I began to like being there. At the end of my junior year at Spelman, I was about to begin my time at Georgia Tech. I had declared at Spelman that I was a physics major, so I was predominantly taking most of my physics classes at Morehouse because Spelman College actually didn't have a Physics Department. So there I was again—there were about four women in my class, at Morehouse.

It was in the spring of that year, that I really came to terms with what it was going to mean to be a female and be a serious scientist, because at that time we had a speaker who was Shirley Jackson, who had just gotten her Ph.D. in physics from MIT and was the first Black woman to do so. She came and spoke, and it created quite a furor in our department and a whole conversation engendered about whether or not women could be women and scientists at the same time.

It was really an ugly way that it all came about. In choosing officers for a society of physics students organization, the men students in the class fought really seriously against any women being officers of the organization. In the midst of that election all the faculty members, who were male, voted for the male students. Afterwards they apologized to me for doing so. It just started coming out more and more that you couldn't be a serious scientist and a woman. That was a prevailing attitude in the department. I was startled, I was completely shocked. I had never had anybody, the Black students I had gone to school with, question whether or not I could do what I wanted to do. I expected opposition from white people, and I expected that to be because I was a Black person, but I never expected opposition because I was a woman. In my usual fashion I went to the library to find out about Black women in science and women scientists . . . and there was *nothing!* Then I started getting worried.

At the end of that school term I went for a summer at Bell Laboratories to the Summer Research Program for Minorities and Women. It was a great program! We would go up to the labs, and we were given scientists to work with. We had a project for the summer, and we could report on it at a big presentation we had at the end of the summer, or lots of us were able to get our names on the work published in scientific journals. So it was a really good program. That also really honed my interest in being a scientist because I really like the projects that I worked on there, and I did well. I got a paper published with my name on it as one of the authors. It was exciting to be around famous people. The labs were well equipped so I got to see I . . . I remember saying to the person who was my advisor for the summer, that I was really interested in lasers, and he pointed to a laser sitting on the table, and I didn't know that was what a laser looked like [laugh]. I had only seen really small ones because we didn't have that kind of equipment at Morehouse. We had minimal equipment. So here I am saying, "I love lasers," and "I'm really interested in them," and I don't know what they look like! I was really embarrassed.

But I didn't encounter any opposition at Bell Labs. All of us were there because we were bright, and we were encouraged to do well and to take the opportunity we were being given there seriously. Though among the students themselves there was still *a lot* of talk about women not being serious scientists, and that was difficult, and I began to see it as more and more of a problem. I was *very* angry about it, and I thought of myself as a feminist for the first time as a result of that experience, both in the spring at school and the summer at Bell Labs.

A. What year was this?

E. This was 1974. . . .

A. What about your family, were they of any help at this point?

E. Let me clarify at this point. I wasn't getting discouraged by teachers or other scientists at Bell Labs at all. I was getting a lot of encouragement, also from my professors at Morehouse. I wasn't getting encouraged by my *peers*, though. That's where it was coming from. . . . All the social pressure. To give up going out with someone because I wanted to stay home and work was seen as weird. *I* was seen as weird and different, and *wrong*!—somehow not being a "right kind of woman." And *that* was what was disturbing me a lot.

And what I got by reading about the women's movement and reading all those books was that I wasn't the only woman in this world that was having this problem. That helped me tremendously, even though I was one of the few . . . I didn't know any other feminists! I was a—you know—bookstore feminist. Certainly there were women around me beginning to call into question men making outrageous sexist remarks. So reading about the women's movement helped me a lot, and the women that I met in the summer program at Bell Labs were also beginning to think of themselves seriously as having careers in science—going to graduate school, getting a Ph.D., and being serious scholars. So we were beginning to talk about it, beginning to see what was happening in terms of our relationships in the social world that we lived in.

So I left Bell Labs at the end of that summer and came back to face Georgia Tech. And that was something. What I faced there was that I was the only woman in my engineering class and one of the three Black students. The racism was unbelievable! . . .

A. So you moved from Spelman and Morehouse which were sister/brother Black colleges over to a predominantly white college?

E. Predominantly male. And the students in the Dual Degree Program were viewed by many people as only there because of affirmative action programs. It was felt if we didn't have good enough grades to come to Georgia Tech from the beginning, then we weren't as strong as other students, and we didn't deserve to be there. We were only there because the government was forcing them to let us in—that was the prevailing view of us.

A. So, on the whole, your experience at Georgia Tech—how would you sum it up insofar as your experience as a Black woman in science?

E. I think it was an extremely *difficult* period for me. If I hadn't had the support to pursue physics, if I hadn't had (after my first year at Georgia Tech) another summer at Bell Labs where I had that same nurturing, encouraging environment, I would not have gone on. At Georgia Tech the people there were *not* interested in Black students' development at all. So just basic things—like going into somebody to ask, "what's going to be on a test"—you could *never* get that information from people. We were being *denied* that kind of information; we were being left out of the environment there in really serious ways. It was as if you—and there were Black students who did *well* and they were *really bright*—they could really get the information on their own and didn't need to have other students to bounce ideas off and help them understand. They really basically did it on their own, and they were real bright—the students who did it. Those who weren't struggled *a lot,* with no encouragement whatsoever, I think. The people in the Dual Degree Program administration basically told us we were going to have a tough time, and nobody was going to help us out. Being a woman—nobody wanted to address that at all.

A. Wasn't that an issue there?

E. For me it was. I was going to lab and having a male lab partner who would set up the experiment. What we would usually do is set the experiment up, run the experiment, and get our data. They'd usually come in and set it up and want me to take notes. If I got in and *I* set it up, usually they would take it apart, and I would have to fight with some guy about "Don't take it apart." They just assumed I couldn't set it up correctly!

A. These were white *and* Black guys?

E. Yes. So I had to deal with that all the time, and it was very hard. But I wasn't the only Black woman in that program who started out; I was the only Black woman in my class, in the Dual Degree Program, who finished. And I was not the brightest woman. I know that. The other three women were stronger in math than me, and two of them were certainly stronger in chemistry. I was definitely the strongest in physics, but they didn't finish because of the lack of encouragement. I feel that very strongly. I don't think it was anything intellectual. I think it was the lack of encouragement. One woman—the other woman who was a physics major—when it was time to transfer to Georgia Tech, she was so terrified of what we heard about how hard it was—about the pressures—that she refused to go. She stayed at Spelman where it was more comfortable for her.

A. It sounds as if the fact that you majored in physics was ultimately what saved you. You also mentioned a professor who helped you along at Georgia Tech, and the other woman, I guess, didn't have that person?

E. No, they didn't and they didn't finish. I think it was the lack of encouragement from professors, what people felt was going to be a hostile atmosphere at Georgia Tech that they didn't want to face. *And* the fact that again, what was happening in our personal lives was that more and more we were experiencing "you can't be a woman and do this." That pull from boyfriends, from male friends, was causing a lot of conflict. And there was nobody to talk to about that who wasn't just saying "you have to be tough," and that was the only solace that we had. So it was very hard . . . and I'd always look around to see who was there and wonder why people weren't with me now that I'd started out with. And I know that for those women, that's why they weren't there.

A. It seems like you got to be tough in terms of racism but not in terms of sexism, how come? I mean it worked as a way to keep going for you when you were facing racism, not when you were facing sexism, is that right?

E. Ah, both. I guess I was prepared to face the fact that I was going to be having difficulties because I was Black. I wasn't *prepared* to face difficulties because I was female. And there were just too few people around to even acknowledge it and help me understand it. I think that there were lots of people around to talk to about how tough it was to be Black and do this. There were just too few people around, I think, until I came to MIT.

A. And it also sounds like, starting with your family, there was a real strong identification of racism as white people's problem, but sexism was *not* strongly identified as men's problem so that you would more easily internalize that.

E. I did internalize a lot of that and see it as my own deficiency. And that created a lot of doubt for me and was just hard for me to deal with. But I was still excited enough about science and physics to keep going. I had *no* intention of being an electrical engineer, at all. So I applied to MIT and was accepted, and I received a fellowship from Xerox. So, I was ready to leave Atlanta and turn my back on that and start. I really saw myself as a serious science student at that time, and I really saw coming to MIT as a big adventure.

And being at MIT was very difficult; again, I faced the racism and the sexism. And even in some ways it was as overt as at Georgia Tech, and in other ways that I felt in the end was more damaging . . . it was very subtle. I think the sexual, the male/female issues were probably stronger then. And my growing, *growing* consciousness as a feminist was almost like—at first I had no words and no one to talk to, and then, when I found them, my whole way of looking at the world changed. I think it's difficult for women students to continue in graduate school, to go onto the Ph.D. without being very single-minded and not let themselves be distracted . . . it's real important to do that. But the nature of the system . . . I have to say sometimes that the feminism distracted me. It made it hard for me to tolerate what I saw around me. It made it hard for me to tolerate the way I saw women treated when they came to speak. And I'd sit there in the back of the room and hear professors and fellow students talk about how the woman was dressed, and not ever talk about the content of her presentation. And there were very few women who came to talk at MIT in the Physics Department. So that was real disheartening. As my feminist consciousness grew, I was in great conflict about this. Did I really want to be involved with these people? The *culture* of physics was beginning to bother me a lot when I saw what was happening. And the work was hard, and I was beginning to have a lot of doubts about whether I could do the work.

A. But you were really a success as a young physicist.

E. I was. My research was successful. As a physics student, I was not successful. I was having a hard time with my courses, for the most part. I was having a hard time with my exams. but I was doing good research.

A. Did your problems in the courses and exams have to do with the atmosphere that you were experiencing there in terms of the sexism you described before?

E. I think a lot of it, again, is not being prepared for MIT in certain kinds of ways . . .

A. In the educational holes again?

E. Yeah, the educational holes. My first week at MIT, the first person I had as a sort of advisor on which courses to take suggested that I start with freshman physics . . . essentially saying I should start all over!

A. This is graduate school?

E. Graduate school. And I was angry. I was very angry. I was insulted. What that meant was that instead of taking . . . you know looking at the educational holes and saying where do I really need to build up . . . I was mad! I was determined that I was going to take what every other graduate student was going to take. And the hell with them! Which was a mistake. Because there were some things I shouldn't have taken. I remember there were times when people said I had a chip on my shoulder. But, I remember that all of us Black students that came in that year, there were four of us, felt the same way; we felt we had been insulted. We felt we were being . . . um . . . we couldn't ask anybody and get a *reasonable* answer. It was an *unreasonable* answer to say to me I had to take freshman physics. We didn't want to be seen as deficient! We didn't want to be seen as, you know, not supposed to be there once again! This whole thing I think, really results from affirmative action; there are a lot of people who are resentful about affirmative action and they tended to label us. We didn't want to be labeled as deficient students. We wanted to be students and pursue our work like everybody else. There was lots of students . . . in fact, there was a student I had gone to Georgia Tech with, who came in and had (you know) educational holes in the same areas because . . .

A. Was he a white student?

E. Yeah, a white student. Because if you go to a . . . anybody who went to say a small college coming to MIT may not have the whole range of courses, or the background that lots of students that have gone to larger research institutions as undergraduates might have had. That's true across the board. And white students are given more reasonable, and in this case, the white student that I knew, was given more reasonable advice—"You should take junior-level this, or the senior undergraduate course in this." *Not* that he should take freshman physics. If someone had said to me, "take junior level quantum mechanics or junior or senior level this," I would have said, "fine." You know, uh, but we didn't get that kind of advice. Because I knew it was racist, it angered me. And I went with the anger—I went with the emotional response. And I didn't have any way to distance myself and say, "wait a minute, what do I really need to do?"

A. And once again, there was nobody to help you distance yourself?

E. Yeah, exactly.

A. You were again on your own?

E. Yeah. We were on our own. We were the other Black students that we had for support. There were very few people around that had just been through the department. Cheryl Jackson was the only Black woman who had ever been through the department and managed to survive, through to the Ph.D., and she had studied under the only *Black* professor in the department. There was nobody who had that step back and was there to say, "take this approach to being successful."

A. Why were the Black students isolated? How did that come about?

E. I don't know how it comes about anywhere, but we were. In certain ways, we banded together. We all knew each other—except for one. Three of us had been at Bell Labs together—the summer program. So we stuck together because we knew each other. And we were isolated because it took us a long time to be willing to reach out of our group to other people and nobody reached towards us. So I don't see on white campuses, it's simply that Black students isolate themselves. The few Black students there who are in a class stick together; the other white students don't feel like they can reach across into that group and make alliances and work with people. So I think it's on both sides, because I think when *I* reached outside of that group there were people willing to be friends with me and study with me and stuff. But they didn't reach out.

A. What do you mean "they didn't reach out?" I missed what you meant.

E. When I was ready to reach outside of my group of Black students, there were people who were receptive to that. But there weren't white students who were coming around who were trying to reach into *our* group.

A. What was the role of your advisor in encouraging you to get through or not encouraging you to get through this time at MIT?

E. My advisor was very encouraging in a sense. He wanted me to get through, but I thought he was real tough on me, and that was hard. And I don't know if I can say that it's a lot more complicated than that. I think in part it was difficult for him to know *how* to advise a student like me.

A. Like *you* meaning what?

E. Black and female. And not just advise, I mean to move to the next step. An *advisor* just imparts information to you. A *mentor* really prepares you in a larger way to become a part of the profession in the same way that they are. I think that was difficult for him.

A. How long did you stay at MIT?

E. 3½ years.

A. And did you in fact get a Ph.D.?

E. No.

A. What happened?

E. I chose to leave.

A. Why?

E. I chose to leave because I finished my Master's degree work, and I had to prepare for my Ph.D. exams, and I really came to a crisis. I didn't know if I really wanted to go on. I questioned whether I really wanted to be a physicist.

A. Is that because you questioned that you wanted to do physics?

E. I didn't question . . . I don't think I really questioned whether or not I wanted to do physics. I questioned whether or not I could really *be* a physicist. I questioned whether or not I had the skills. I questioned whether or not I was going to make it through my exams. I had a lot of doubts, and it was a real crisis for me. So I decided to leave.

A. What about the factor that you mentioned before, the social milieu of doing science? Did that play a role in this decision?

E. Oh yeah. I mean it was clear to me that I was going to be the only Black woman. You know, the social experience of going to an international conference and being the only Black woman there was difficult. That's the kind of isolation that was beginning to bother me tremendously. People were very nice to me, but I didn't have any friends. I didn't have anybody that I was close to that I could share my work with. And I knew that it wasn't going to get any better; it was going to continue, and I was going to continue to be isolated. And that isolation . . . that's what I mean by the culture of it was bothering me. It was the isolation. It was the fact that Black scientists are questioned more severely. Our work is held up to greater scrutiny; we have a difficult time getting research, getting university positions. All of that, and I didn't really want to fight that. One of my friends, the other Black woman who finished MIT, was supposed to come to a particular international conference, so I was feeling ok. "Well, she was going to be there, I'll be fine." And she decided not to come, because a piece of work that she was doing wasn't finished, and she knew that she was going to be given a really difficult time and asked very pointed questions about her work that she was not prepared to face. So she chose not to come. But that meant I was there alone. Ok, so what does that mean? That the three Black women in physics that I knew in the entire country at that time if we weren't all at the same conference we were going to be alone. And as I said before, my consciousness as a feminist was growing and growing. I wanted to become more active. Raising the issues of racism and sexism and trying to get my degree out of that department seemed to be at odds and more and more difficult for me. I would spend more time on those kinds of issues than I would on my science sometimes. So I was in a lot of conflict and that's why I chose to leave.

A. You said that you experienced sexism as an overriding problem at MIT when we first started talking about it. But the way you talked about it since then it really sounds like it was racism that really affected you the most.

E. They are *not* separate. Because they aren't separate in me. I am always Black and female. I can't say "well, that was just a sexist remark" without wondering would he have made the same sexist remark to a white woman. So, does that make it a racist, sexist remark? You know, I don't know. And that takes a lot of energy to be constantly trying to figure out which one it is. I don't do that anymore, I just take it as, you know, somebody has some issues about *me* and who *I am* in the world. *Me* being Black, female and wanting to do science and be taken seriously. That's it.

GENDER CONSTRUCTS AND CAREER COMMITMENT
The Influence of Peer Culture on Women in College

Margaret A. Eisenhart and Dorothy C. Holland

When we first met Paula[1] in 1979, she had come to college with a straight *A* average from high school and planned to major in biology and become a doctor. During her freshman year, she did not find her courses, including calculus and chemistry, particularly difficult, but she did find them "boring" and often could not make herself go to class or study. By the end of her freshman year, she decided to switch her concentration to nursing ("because my grades aren't high enough for med school"). During the first semester of her sophomore year, she missed the deadline for application to the nursing program and decided instead to try for an education degree. In the middle of her sophomore year, Paula had this to say about her career-related decisions during college: "Since I've been here, I've changed my mind about 1,000 times. . . . And, like right now, I feel like . . . just not working would be the greatest thing in the world—just taking care of children and not studying." Paula eventually settled on a social science field as her major and graduated in 1983. After graduation, she enrolled in a management trainee program, worked in a department store, and got married. In 1987, she had this to say about careers: "[My husband and I] want to have successful careers . . . his is a career where I feel like mine is a job. So, my career goals are for his career more so than mine. . . . I'm trying to be there to help [him] when I can."

Paula's case is not atypical of the college women we have been following since 1979. Despite the removal of legal barriers to women's participation in high-status occupations, the implementation of affirmative action programs, and the efforts of the women's movement, we found women—with the opportunity to attend college, with strong high school records, and with expressed commitments to pursue careers—who continued to make "career decisions" like Paula's, decisions that seemed to be leading them into "traditional" roles for women in the work force.[2] This essay is about the social processes that encourage bright young college women in the United States to continue to make career-related choices like Paula's.

Some researchers have suggested that the underrepresentation of women with careers is declining, especially for privileged young women. R. W. Connell, D. J. Ashenden, S. Kessler, and G. W. Dowsett (1982:96–97) in their study of one hundred Australian middle school students report that some of the girls at elite schools were seriously considering professional careers. The authors predict that these girls will grow up to challenge the traditional model of adult femininity as wife, mother, and volunteer and, by becoming career women, they will redefine work and family and instigate changes in gender relations in Australia (175–77; see also Kessler et al. 1985). Several studies of American college freshmen in the late 1970s and early 1980s reveal large increases in the percentage of women enrolled in traditionally male fields of engineering, math, and science (Astin et al. 1983; Boli, Allen, and Payne 1983; Hafner 1985). These authors hope that this trend will continue and presumably set the stage for more women to pursue careers in these high-status, traditionally male-dominated fields.

Although we take these increases to be a sign of change, we are not convinced that this cohort of privileged young women will, in large numbers, continue into careers—

careers in the sense of "job sequences that require a high degree of commitment and that have a continuous developmental character" (Rapoport and Rapoport 1976:9). Our longitudinal study (1979–87) of university women,[3] many of whom started college with interests in math and science majors at two southern universities, revealed that their commitment to careers remained low or diminished during college. Why do such women "decide" not to pursue careers?

Many others have tried to answer this question before, citing such factors as nonsupportive socialization, gender-specific motivation patterns, and subtle forms of institutional discrimination. In this essay we argue that school-based peer groups and their associated cultures play an important—and relatively unrecognized—role in guiding women toward traditional positions in the work force. These peer cultures encourage women to see themselves as (potential) romantic partners with men, and they are virtually silent on the subject of academic work or future careers. In such a context, individual women find that commitment to academic work and a career is difficult to preserve or expand. Ideas about the importance and value of academic work and careers—ideas that the women bring with them to college . . . —are not compelling enough to keep many women from being redirected by the pull of the peer culture. . . .

GENDER CONSTRUCTS AND CAREER PATHS

. . . The women we talked to and observed led us to the realm of their informal peer groups and the powerful mediating role of these groups in creating a context for college women's career-related decisions. The school's contribution seemed pale by comparison.

What we found was that the meaning of gender for these college women was being learned and enacted primarily in peer group interactions and that this process, though surely begun much earlier in the women's lives, was still unfolding and changing while the women were in college. The peer cultures at both schools (although different in some respects) encouraged women to assess themselves in terms of their romantic relationships with and their attractiveness to men. In contrast, women's success at schoolwork or in future careers was not of much consequence in the peer culture. As far as the peer culture was concerned, women could excel or not in schoolwork, and they might or might not have serious career plans. These areas were viewed as matters of individual capability, effort, and preference. What was appraised and rated in the peer culture was how successful women were in their romantic relationships. Thus, to understand the effect of gender constructions on the women's schoolwork models and career plans, it is first necessary to discuss the peer system and the way it construes gender.

The Pull of the Peer System

Ostensibly, women and men go to college for the purposes of furthering their "education" and acquiring the credentials necessary for future careers; yet, there is more to college life than studying, classes, and examinations. Helen Horowitz (1987), in her historical account of college life in the United States, argues that, since the late eighteenth century, the campus peer system has dominated most students' lives at college: "[There is a tradition of] peer consciousness sharply at odds with that of the faculty . . . dating from the late eighteenth century. . . . Classes [were] the price one had to pay for college life . . . 'a little space of time . . . where the young made a world to suit themselves'" (11–12).

When the women in our study went to college, they found themselves in a world of peers. The women spent most of their time around age-mates; were constantly exposed to peer-organized activities; learned age-mates' interpretations and evaluations of all aspects of university life; had most of their close, intimate relationships with age-mates on campus; and learned ways to understand and evaluate themselves from these peers. The women were, of course, familiar with peer cultures when they came to college. Peer groups are an important feature of American students' lives in high school (Coleman 1961; Schwartz 1972) and even in elementary school (Eisenhart and Holland 1983); however, at Bradford and SU [the colleges—the first historically black, the second historically white—in our study] the peer groups were more intense. As at other residential colleges, students lived, worked, and played with their peers, and they had contact with other groups, such as family, much less frequently and perhaps only at long distance.

Especially for women students, the peer culture was organized around male-female relationships. Activities were evaluated according to the opportunities they offered to meet men or to enact romantic relationships. Such activities as being invited to parties, going to mixers and bars, and assisting at male-dominated events were highly appraised in the peer culture. It was considered, for example, more desirable to be a fraternity sweetheart or little sister than a sorority sister and more fun to support men's sports as cheerleaders, majorettes, flag girls, managers, and even spectators than to be involved in women's sports.

In the survey we conducted, respondents were asked how much importance they attributed to fifty-five different kinds of campus activities, which were identified during the ethnographic study. Of these fifty-five activities, thirteen were directly related to schoolwork or a career. Almost twice as many (twenty-three) were peer-dominated, and most of these, including socializing, friendships, and romantic relationships, were rated equal to or more important than work-related activities (Holland and Eisenhart 1981:23–27).

In the ethnographic interviews and observations, the women's talk concerned men, their own and others' physical appearances, and social activities. Paula put it this way: "[When I'm with my girlfriends,] we always talk about our boyfriends, or how we wish we had boyfriends, or how fat we are—we all say that. . . . None of us have to lose weight, but we just want to be thinner. . . . I'm gonna lose weight and clear up my face and [grow] my hair out, so I'll be all beautiful this summer." Aleisha described a long and detailed conversation she had with her "girlfriends": "I came back [to school] and there was actually a list of five [guys]. . . . It just accumulated. . . . All of them are so hard to choose from. . . . Me and my girlfriends were sitting in the room and I am telling them this, and they said, 'All right, who's got the most money? Who's got the most prestige? Who's the nicest? Who's the best looking?' We just debated it back and forth. . . . It was just really even because of all of them, each person had something the other four didn't have. . . . I had the hardest time making up my mind."

Another study at SU suggested that the students had a cultural model of intimate male-female relationships that consisted of a taken-for-granted scenario of how such relationships develop (Holland and Skinner 1987) and that the model informed women's talk, feelings, and thoughts about such relationships (D. C. Holland n.d.). Interviews from Bradford suggest a very similar model.

According to the model, an attractive man and an attractive women are drawn to each other. The man shows his interest by appreciating the woman's special qualities and by treating her well, as demonstrated, for example, in giving her gifts and taking her nice places. The woman, in turn, reveals her affection for him and allows the relationship to become more intimate. By participating in romantic relationships, one gains prestige as well as intimacy. Because men and women tend to match up by attractiveness, men—especially attractive men—validate a woman's prestige and vice versa.

Women, it should be noted, were more dependent on romance for prestige than were men. For women, attractiveness to men was the main source and indicator of prestige in the peer culture. Men had several sources of prestige, such as sports or campus offices (see also Horowitz 1987:208). To gain some measure of prestige in the peer system at Bradford and SU, women had to be involved in romantic relationships. One of the women summed it up this way: "Girls always want to have the guy everybody would talk about. . . . You *have* to have a boyfriend for this and that."

A desire for heterosexual intimacy also was considered "natural." A woman could not singly declare a lack of interest in men that she could for, say, mathematics, history, or any or all of her courses. For various reasons, including the inability to find a good match, limited knowledge or expertise about how to find or keep a romantic partner, and in a few cases other salient interests, the women in our study were not equally successful in this peer system (see D. C. Holland n.d. and Holland and Eisenhart 1988a for more detail about this). They were, however, all liable to evaluation in terms of the system, and they all knew it.

In the peer system with its emphasis on romantic relationships, other aspects of college life were important but secondary. On both campuses, women's relationships with other women were formed in the shadow of relationships with men. Although the women went about their female-female relationships differently at Bradford and SU, the outcome was the same: weaker and secondary relationships among women. The women at Bradford emphasized self-reliance and control over information about their relationships with men to the point that it was difficult for them to achieve trusting relationships with women. The women at SU relied on their female friends to support them in their efforts to find and keep desirable men, but once a romantic partner was found, they tended to spend time with female friends only when their boyfriends were unavailable (Holland and Eisenhart 1989). . . .

Struggles to Manage Schoolwork and Peers

Although schoolwork was de-emphasized in the peer group system, doing schoolwork could not be relegated to a secondary place as easily as some other things, such as female-female relationships. No system existed to propel women into close female-female relationships, but the academic system did exert pressure on women, making it necessary for them to pay some attention to schoolwork if they wanted to stay in school. The dynamic created between the peer and academic systems on the two campuses produced a tension that most women mentioned. During the course of the ethnographic study, all of the women in our study struggled—some more, some less—with what they perceived to be the competing demands of schoolwork and peers.

For most, the two systems were viewed as competing domains: time spent studying was time spent away from peers, and time with peers meant little schoolwork was accomplished. One SU woman described the situation as a choice of identity: one could be a "bookworm" or a person who liked to "have fun." Della at Bradford described the same dichotomy in another way: "The ones that did all the book studying, they had no social life; the ones that didn't do no book work, they had a lot [of social life]."

None of the women wished to be viewed as one or the other of these extreme types. When they arrived at college, they all wanted, and expected, to be successful in both school and in the peer system. Almost from the beginning though, they talked about needing to study more and "party" less. Most were surprised to find schoolwork took more time than they had given it in high school, and they struggled to complete it and do other things as well. One woman at SU had this to say: "I always liked school, ever since I was very young . . . but here I haven't done anything for enjoyment in so long. . . . All I do is work. . . . It always came so easy for me in high school, and now I've got to *compete* with somebody just to get a spot [in medical school], so I almost never have time to do anything with my friends . . . I'm going crazy."

This struggle with the demands of schoolwork was evident in the survey responses too. One of the survey questions asked about people and activities that had taken more time than expected over the semester and thus caused the women to cut back on the other things they normally did. Schoolwork was felt to be extraordinarily demanding by the largest percentage; over 80 percent of the women on both campuses felt that some aspects of schoolwork had taken an unexpectedly large amount of their time. Jobs and peer relationships were much less likely to be seen as taking up an untoward amount of time.

The women said their peers complained if they devoted too much time to schoolwork. One Bradford woman put it this way: "Guys will tell you, 'Come on, let's go out.' And if you tell him you have to study, he'd probably be upset. Some of my friends tell me I'm a party-pooper . . . cause I usually have to study. A lot of times when [my two closest friends] have somewhere to go, they won't ask me. . . . This sort of bothered me 'cause they were having a good time and I wasn't."

Jobs, unlike both schoolwork and peers, could be ignored. One woman described her typical day as follows: "[I] go to class, go to work, go out to dinner with some friends, relax with [friends], and watch TV [with friends]." When she got a couple of Cs on tests, she decided, "Work's [the job's] the bother; there's no time left for studying. . . . I think I'm going to have to quit work. You think I'm gonna let that work bother me? Nah!"

Occasionally, the women spoke admiringly of other women who could keep peer activities from getting out of control. For example, Della described an older "girl" on her hall as follows: "She's a girl that sets a good example as a very studious person. . . . I see her studying all the time. . . . She lets you know that studying is very important . . . that you can't just all the time have a bunch of friends over to go out all the time. There's a time for everything; she lets you know." Della knew that failure to manage both could have long-term implications: "My sister . . . has messed up her life along the way, and she's still messing up . . . having so many men until she don't even have [time] to work."

The women expressed a need to study more, but they often would also remark that they studied a lot already and were not very motivated to do more. Correspondingly, the women often let themselves be drawn into peer activities. One student explained what happened as she and her suitemates were preparing to leave her room for a night of studying for the next day's exams: "We had a spontaneous party . . . everyone was here . . . till two in the morning. We made all kinds of daiquiris. . . . My parents called [during the party] and I never knew it. They couldn't believe we partied the night before exams. I can't believe we did. I've never done anything like that in my life." . . .

It appears the women at Bradford and SU wanted and expected to do well both in schoolwork and with their peers, but schoolwork seemed to interfere with peer activities by demanding too much time. Peer-related activities, on the other hand, were more fun and readily available; hence, they threatened to overwhelm schoolwork.

Schoolwork and Careers

Given this peer culture and the constant invitations to women to develop themselves as romantic and social types, how do college women understand and prepare for careers? What happens to their views of themselves as learners or schoolworkers? How do they further their commitment to career?

We found that although the women shared basic ideas about schoolwork, classes, grades, and professors, they differed in their views of the purpose of college work. We have elsewhere described these alternative views as "cultural models" (Holland and Eisenhart 1988b). The women brought to college a view of both the purpose of schoolwork and themselves in school, in the form of these models or orientations. The peer culture provided a system that competed with schoolwork. It derailed some women but not others, and some sooner than others, depending on the woman's model of schoolwork.

We identified three distinctive models of schoolwork held by the women in our ethnographic study. The models were organized around the motives for doing schoolwork and can be described as (1) work in exchange for "getting over" (i.e., finishing college and thereby obtaining college credentials); (2) work in exchange for "doing well" (i.e., receiving good grades or other academic accolades); and (3) work in exchange for learning from experts. These models of schoolwork affected the women's interpretation of grades, evaluation of teachers, decisions about studying, choices of courses and majors, and feelings about their own performance. During the three-semester period of the main study, each woman seemed to hold one model as a dominant one; however, some were aware of the alternative models and sometimes entertained other models themselves or at least pieces of them (see Holland and Eisenhart 1988b for a detailed presentation of the models).

"Getting Over" and Enjoying Peers

Nine women (eight at Bradford and one at SU) held the first model of schoolwork. All the women in this group seemed to be quite certain what they wanted to major in. They came to college with a major chosen in high school or before, said they fully intended to pursue that major through college, and kept the same major as long as they remained in college. These women did not believe they needed to make outstanding grades or otherwise demonstrate special mastery in academic areas; they were simply trying to make good enough grades to finish school and get the credential they believed necessary to make them eligible for the type of future job they envisioned. They did not find the content of schoolwork compelling. Della's comment was typical: "I just did enough [schoolwork] to get over; hey, that's all." . . .

With two exceptions, the women with the "getting over" model (all of whom had been good students in high school) had no serious trouble doing "well enough" in their schoolwork and having time enough for friends. For them, only minor adjustments were necessary to participate in both worlds. One woman in this group put it this way: "I like biology; it wasn't hard at all. I came out with a *B*. . . . I didn't ever go to class. . . . I was doing a lot of things with my friends. . . . I didn't learn anything, but I passed all my tests." Another said, "I never did bad to where I needed to change my ways." Della provides another example. As mentioned earlier, when she started to have some trouble in her classes, she decided to quit her part-time job, but with no regrets, to have more time to study and to preserve her "free time" with her friends and boyfriends. . . .

"Doing Well" and Succumbing to Peers

The seven women (one at Bradford; six at SU) who held the model of schoolwork for doing well were the most vulnerable to *reducing* career commitment in college as they tried to handle the demands of both peer and academic systems. These women viewed the work they did in college as a way of gaining recognition for their natural abilities and skills. One of them put it this way: "I always wanted to achieve the best, to be the best that I could academically. I always wanted to make *As* . . . if I made a *B*, I felt I was a failure within." From the vantage point of this model, doing well in college should be easy for those who are naturally good at the kinds of tasks or the subject matter of school. That is, good grades should be attainable without a lot of hard work; it should be possible to make high grades *and* have time to be with friends and do other enjoyable things.

All of the women in this group, like most of the others, faced the situation of having to work harder in college to get the same grades they did in high school. In general, those with the "getting over" models chose not to work harder and so made lower grades. For those whose major orientation toward schoolwork was the idea of doing well, there was more of a problem. Not being able to do well was a challenge to their identity as a "good student." Not doing well in a particular subject area was a blow to their notion of why they were in college—to study a subject at which they were naturally good.

. . . Kelly, for example, was faced with reconciling herself to a lower rank after only a few weeks of college. In response, she dropped her goal of becoming a doctor and switched to a social science field before the end of her first semester. About what happened to her, Kelly said, "I came from a background of good grades, tops in the class, never really worrying about it," but in college, "I'm just a face in the crowd . . . just average here. . . . It's a lot harder than I thought . . . I wish I could have done a lot better." Linda, another SU woman who scaled down her commitment to schoolwork and switched her major to a field she perceived as less demanding, also talked about the problem of "being average" at college: "I don't want to be average. . . . But, right now, I guess that's what I'll have to content myself with because I don't know if I can do any better." . . .

As they reduced their commitment to schoolwork, these women began to devote more time and energy to romantic and other peer relationships. They all spent their freshmen and sophomore years worried about finding the right man with whom to share a romantic relationship. . . . In sum, it appeared that as these women divested themselves of strong student or schoolwork-related identities, they invested more of themselves in romantic identities. As schoolwork became less central to their lives, romantic relationships became more important. (For a detailed description of this process, see Holland and Eisenhart 1990). . . .

Learning from Experts and Managing Peers

The women with this model (two at Bradford, two at SU) believed the purpose of doing academic work at college was to master an area of expertise one wished to pursue into the future. Although concerned about grades and obtaining their degrees, these women were more concerned about finding people in the university setting they considered "expert," especially in their subject of interest. For them, low grades were setbacks but were taken as an indication of one's lack of mastery, not of one's unsuitability for major or career. Professors were sought out not because they were easy or entertaining but because they could teach a subject of interest. One woman in this group said, "I love speech and English. I like writing and I like talking about what I write, but it's the proper way of [doing it] that I have trouble comprehending. I want to major in [English] and I want to get it down solid. . . . It's a lot to learn. But since I got to college . . . the instructor . . . he's an expert and I'm an amateur. . . . He's published five or six books and he knows every corner of a good paper. . . . I always wanted an instructor that was real strict on the way I write and he is. . . . He's been critiquing me hard. That's why if I get a good grade, I'll feel like I've accomplished something."

These women also participated in peer activities and romantic relationships; however, they had a sense of wanting to contain these activities so they could pursue their other interests. One of the women in this group, Karla, chose a boyfriend with extraordinary demands on his time and had this to say about dates: "[My boyfriend] is my favorite date. . . . He's very busy; he usually can get free for only one night a week. He's a workaholic. . . . [But] he allows me as much freedom as I want. . . . My main complaint [about another guy who wants to go out with her] is that he is continually calling me. He wants to take up all my time. . . . I feel like a dog trying to take a walk with this slow little human dragging behind." Because her boyfriend could only go out occasionally and she was not very interested in the activities of her other peers, Karla managed to be free, relative to women in the other groups, to pursue her career interests at college. . . .

The women with the "learning from experts" model came to college with a cultural model that made learning important to them, were able to sustain their model throughout our study, and had the ability or luck to keep their romantic and other peer relationships from taking time away from school-related interests. Unlike the women with the "doing well" orientation, these women were not derailed by lower grades. Unlike the women with the "getting over" orientation, these women saw themselves as directly profiting from meaningful activities rather than putting in time doing arbitrary exercises for the purpose of obtaining a degree in the distant future. These women had and were able to maintain a commitment to themselves as students. All of them graduated from college with their original major or with an augmented version of their original major. All of them pursued their college majors into graduate work or a job in their field. In contrast to the few (only three: Linda, Lisa, and Natalie, or 17.6 percent) with other schoolwork orientations who pursued their majors in any way after graduating from college, 100 percent of the women with the "learning from experts" model pursued their college career interests after graduation.

SUMMARY

In sum, the competing demands of schoolwork and the peer system were handled in different ways depending on the woman's schoolwork model. The general outcomes fell into two patterns. The first pattern predominated. Sixteen of the twenty-one women whose cases we analyzed from the ethnographic study held the models of schoolwork in exchange for "getting over" or for "doing well." As discussed, they received little support from the peer culture for developing or maintaining a commitment to career during college. One other woman, Lisa, let her boyfriend control her decisions about her schoolwork and her career. Of these seventeen, only one, Natalie, pursued her college major into her own career, without consideration of a man in her life. Perhaps because of the strong support she received for her chosen career from her family, especially from her father, she, unlike the others, did not become very involved in the peer system at college.

The second type of outcome for the ethnographic sample was quite different. The four women who held the view of schoolwork as "learning from experts" were able to maintain and, in some cases, further develop a commitment to career in college.

The pattern that predominated in the ethnographic study appeared to predominate in the survey responses as well. In general, the survey responses from the women on the two campuses were consistent with the pattern found in the ethnographic study. At Bradford, the survey responses suggested that the model of schoolwork for "getting over" was most common among the women on campus; at SU, the model of schoolwork for "doing well" seemed to be the most prevalent. If this is an accurate summary of the situation on the two campuses, it appears a large proportion of the women, regardless of campus, had orientations to schoolwork that easily derailed them. Their experiences on campus eroded their views of their future careers and they were drawn to committing considerable time and energy to the campus peer system.

Notes

We are indebted to the National Institute of Education, the University of Research Council of the University of North Carolina at Chapel Hill, and the College of Education of Virginia Polytechnic Institute and State University for their funding of this research. We are especially grateful to the women in the study and the interviewers who assisted us.

1. All proper names and place names used in reference to the study are pseudonyms.
2. We use the term *traditional* to refer loosely to the general pattern of female participation in certain college majors, occupations, and other adult activities. Correspondingly, the term *nontraditional* is used to refer to majors, occupations, and other activities conventionally associated with men and usually considered to be higher-status, more lucrative, and more career-oriented than those associated with women.
3. A full account of the study is in Holland and Eisenhart (1990).

References

Anyon, Jean. 1981. "Social Class and School Knowledge." *Curriculum Inquiry* 11(1):3–42.

Astin, Alexander W., K. C. Green, W. S. Korn, and M. Maier. 1983. *The American Freshman: National Norms for Fall 1983.* Los Angeles: UCLA Higher Research Institute.

Astin, Helen S. 1983. "The Meaning of Work in Women's Lives: A Sociopsychological Model of Career Choice and Work Behavior." *The Counseling Psychologist* 12(4):117–26.

Boli, John, Mary Lou Allen, and Adrienne Payne. 1983. "Women and Men in Introductory Undergraduate Mathematics and Chemistry Courses." Paper presented at the Annual Meeting of the American Educational Research Association, Montreal, Canada.

Bowles, Samuel, and Herbert Gintis. 1976. *Schooling in Capitalist America.* New York: Basic Books.

Brophy, Jere, and Thomas Good. 1974. *Teacher-Student Relationships: Causes and Consequences.* New York: Holt, Rinehart and Winston.

Coleman, James S. 1961. *The Adolescent Society.* New York: Free Press.

Connell, R. W., D. J. Ashenden, S. Kessler, and G. W. Dowsett. 1982. *Making the Difference: Schools, Families and Social Division.* Sydney: George Allen and Unwin.

Eccles, Jacquelynne S. 1987. "Gender Roles and Women's Achievement-Related Decisions." *Psychology of Women Quarterly* 11:135–72.

———. 1989. "Girl Friendly Instruction in Math and the Sciences." Paper presented at the University of Colorado, Boulder.

Eccles, Jacquelynne S., and J. Jacobs. 1986. "Social Forces Shape Math Participation." *Signs: Journal of Women in Culture and Society* 11:367–80.

Eder, Donna. 1985. "The Cycle of Popularity: Interpersonal Relations among Female Adolescents." *Sociology of Education* 58:154–65.

Eder, Donna, and Stephen Parker. 1987. "The Cultural Production and Reproduction of Gender: The Effect of Extracurricular Activities on Peer-Group Culture." *Sociology of Education* 60:200–213.

Eisenhart, Margaret A. 1985. "Women Choose Their Careers: A Study of Natural Decision Making." *Review of Higher Education* 8:247–70.

Eisenhart, Margaret A., and Dorothy C. Holland. 1983. "Learning Gender from Peers: The Role of Peer Groups in the Cultural Transmission of Gender." *Human Organization* 42:321–22.

Fordham, Signithia, and John U. Ogbu. 1986. "Black Students' School Success: Coping with the 'Burden of Acting White.'" *Urban Review* 18(3):176–206.

Gaskell, Jane. 1985. "Course Enrollment in the High School: The Perspective of Working-Class Females." *Sociology of Education* 58:48–59.
Goffredson, Linda S. 1981. "Circumscription and Compromise: A Developmental Theory of Occupational Aspirations." *Journal of Counseling Psychology* 28:545–79.
Hafner, Anne L. 1985. "Gender Differences in College Students' Educational and Occupational Aspirations: 1971–1983." Paper presented at the Annual Meeting of the American Educational Research Association, Chicago, Illinois.
Holland, Dorothy C. n.d. "How Cultural Systems Become Desire: A Case Study of American Romance." Unpublished manuscript.
Holland, Dorothy C., and Margaret A. Eisenhart. 1981. *Women's Peer Groups and Choice of Career: Final Report.* Washington, D.C.: National Institute of Education.
———. 1988a. "Moments of Discontent: University Women and the Gender Status Quo." *Anthropology and Education Quarterly* 19(2):115–38.
———. 1988b. "Women's Ways of Going to School: Cultural Reproduction of Women's Identities as Workers." In *Class, Race, and Gender in American Education,* ed. L. Weis. Albany: SUNY Press.
———. 1989. "On the Absence of Women's Gangs in Two Southern Universities." In *Women in the South: An Anthropological Perspective,* ed. H. Mathews. Athens: University of Georgia Press.
———. 1990. *Educated in Romance: Women, Achievement, and College Culture.* Chicago: University of Chicago Press.
Holland, Dorothy C., and Debra Skinner. 1987. "Prestige and Intimacy: The Cultural Model behind American's Talk about Gender Types." In *Cultural Models in Language and Thought,* ed. D. Holland and N. Quinn. New York: Cambridge University Press.
Holland, J. L. 1985. *Making Vocational Choices: A Theory of Vocational Personalities and Work Environments.* Englewood Cliffs, N.J.: Prentice-Hall.
Horowitz, Helen L. 1987. *Campus Life: Undergraduate Cultures from the End of the Eighteenth Century to the Present.* New York: Alfred A. Knopf.
Hunter College Women's Studies Collective. 1983. *Women's Realities, Women's Choices.* New York: Oxford University Press.
Kessler, S., D. J. Ashenden, R. W. Connell, and G. W. Dowsett. 1985. "Gender Relations in Secondary Schooling." *Sociology of Education* 58:34–48.
Lees, Sue. 1986. *Losing Out: Sexuality and Adolescent Girls.* London: Hutchinson.
Nespor, Jan. 1989. "Gender, Ethnicity, and Organizational Structure in the Choice of a College Major." Paper presented at the American Educational Research Association, April, San Francisco, California.
Ogbu, John U. 1974. *The Next Generation: An Ethnography of Education in an Urban Neighborhood.* New York: Academic Press.
———. 1978. *Minority Education and Caste: The American System in Cross-Cultural Perspective.* New York: Academic Press.
———. 1988. "Class Stratification, Racial Stratification, and Schooling." In *Class, Race, and Gender in American Education,* ed. L. Weis. Albany: SUNY Press.
Rapoport, Rhona, and Robert N. Rapoport. 1976. *Dual-Career Families Reexamined: New Integrations of Work and Family.* London: Martin Robertson.
Schwartz, G. 1972. *Youth Culture: An Anthropological Approach.* Addison-Wesley Module in Anthropology, No. 17. Reading, Mass.: Addison-Wesley.
Spradley, James P. 1979. *The Ethnographic Interview.* New York: Holt, Rinehart and Winston.
———. 1980. *Participant Observation.* New York: Holt, Rinehart and Winston.
Tittle, Carol K., and Sharon L. Weinberg. 1984. "Job Choice: A Review of the Literature and a Model of Major Influences." Paper presented at the Annual Meeting of the American Educational Research Association, New Orleans, Louisiana.
Valli, Linda, 1986. *Becoming Clerical Workers.* Boston: Routledge and Kegan Paul.
Willis, Paul. 1977. *Learning to Labor: How Working Class Kids Get Working Class Jobs.* New York: Columbia University Press.

SNOW BROWN AND THE SEVEN DETERGENTS
A Metanarrative on Science and the Scientific Method

Banu Subramaniam

Once upon a time, deep within a city in the Orient, lived a young girl called Snehalatha Bhrijbhushan. She spent her childhood merrily playing in the streets with her friends while her family and the neighbors looked on indulgently. "That girl, Sneha [as they called her], is going to become someone famous someday," they would all say. Sneha soon became fascinated with the world of science. One day she announced, "I am going to sail across the blue oceans to become a scientist!"

There was silence in the room. "You can be a scientist here, you know."

"But I want to explore the world," said Sneha. "There is so much to see and learn."

"Where is this place?" they asked.

"It's called the Land of the Blue Devils."

"But that is dangerous country," they cried. "No one has ever been there and come back alive."

"Yes, I know," said Sneha. "But I have been reading about it. It is in the Land of the Kind and Gentle People. In any case, I can handle it."

Her friends and family watched her animated face and knew that if anyone could do it, it would be brave Sneha, and so they relented. The city watched her set out and wished her a tearful farewell. She promised to return soon and bring back tales from lands afar. For forty-two days and nights Sneha sailed the oceans. Her face was aglow with excitement, and her eyes were filled the stars. "It's going to be wonderful," she told herself.

And so one fine day she arrived in the Land of the Blue Devils. She went in search of the Building of Scientific Truth. When she saw it, she held her breath. There it stood, tall and slender, almost touching the skies. Sneha shivered. "Don't be silly," she told herself. She entered the building. The floors were polished and gleaming white. It all looked so grand and yet so formidable. She was led into the office of the Supreme White Patriarch. The room was full. "Welcome, budding Patriarchs," he said, "from those of us in the Department of the Pursuit of Scientific Truth. But let me be perfectly frank. These are going to be difficult years ahead. This is no place for the weak or the emotional or the fickle. You have to put in long, hard hours. If you think you cannot cut it, you should leave now. Let me introduce you to our evaluation system. Come with me."

He led them across the hall into a huge room. At the end of the room stood a mirror, long and erect and oh so white. "This is the Room of Judgment," he continued. "The mirror will tell you how you're doing. Let me show you." He went to the mirror and said, "Mirror, mirror on the wall, who is the fairest scientist of them all?"

"You are, O Supreme White Patriarch!" said the mirror.

The Patriarch laughed. "That is what all of you should aspire to. And one day when it calls out your name, you will take my place. But until then, you will all seek Truth and aspire to be number one. We want fighters here, Patriarchs with initiative and genius. And as for those who are consistently last in the class for six months . . . well, we believe they just do not have the ability to pursue Scientific Truth, and they will be expelled. Go forth, all ye budding Patriarchs, and find Scientific Truth."

Everyone went their way. Sneha found herself in the middle of the hallway all alone. "Go find Truth?" she said to herself. Was this a treasure hunt? Did Truth fall from the sky? She was very confused. This was not what she had thought it would be like. She went looking for her older colleagues. "Where does one find Scientific Truth?" she asked.

"Well," said he, "first you have to find the patronage of an Associate Patriarch or an Assistant Patriarch. You will have a year to do that. Until then, you take courses they teach you and you learn about Truths already known and how to find new Truths. During this time you have to learn how to be a scientist. That is very important, but don't worry, the mirror will assist you."

"How does the mirror work?" asked Sneha.

"Well, the mirror is the collective consciousness of all the Supreme White Patriarchs across the Land of the Kind and Gentle People. They have decided what it takes to be the ideal scientist, and it is what we all must dream of and aspire and work toward if we want to find Scientific Truth. You must check with the mirror as often as you can to monitor your progress."

Sneha tiptoed to the Room of Judgment, stood in front of the mirror, and said, "Mirror, mirror on the wall, who is the fairest scientist of them all?"

The mirror replied, "Not you, you're losing this game, you with the unprounceable name!"

Sneha was very depressed. Things were not going as she had expected. "Oh, mirror," she cried, "everything has gone wrong. What do I do?"

"More than anything," said the mirror, "you have to learn to act like a scientist. That's your first task. Deep within the forests lives the Wise Matriarch in the House of the Seven Detergents. Go see her, she will help you."

Sneha set out to meet the Wise Matriarch. "Come in, child," she said. "What seems to be the problem?" She appeared to be a very kind woman, and Sneha poured out her misery.

"I know this is a very difficult time for you, but it is also a very important one," the Matriarch said.

"Why do they call you the Wise Matriarch?" Sneha inquired.

"I joined the Department of the Pursuit of Scientific Truth some twenty years ago," the Matriarch replied. "That is why I understand what you're going through. I was expelled. When the department offered me this position, I felt I could begin changing things. Over the years I have advised many budding Patriarchs. You could say I've earned my reputation.

"My child," she went on, "this is where the department sends its scientific misfits. Let me show you what they would like me to have you do." She led Sneha to a room, and in it stood seven jars. "These are the seven detergents," she said. "With them you can wash away any part of yourself you don't want. But the catch is that once you wash it away, you have lost it forever."

Sneha was excited. "First I'd like to get rid of my name and my accent. The mirror told me that."

The Wise Matriarch shook her head, "My child, do not give away your identity, your culture—they are part of you, of who you are," she cried.

"But," said Sneha, "I've always dreamed of being a scientist. I spent all my savings coming here, and I cannot go back a failure. This is truly what I want." Sneha got into the Great Washing Machine with the first detergent. *Rub-a-dub-a-dub, rub-a-dub-a-dub,* went the detergent.

"You may come out now, Snow Brown. Good luck."

Snow Brown went back amazed at how differently her tongue moved. For the next week she met the other budding Patriarchs, decided on her courses, and went out socializing with her colleagues. But everything was new in this land: how people ate and drank, even what people ate and drank. She felt stupid and ignorant. And just as she expected, when she went to the mirror, it told her that such behavior was quite unscientific and that she had to learn the right etiquette. Off she went again to the House of the Seven Detergents and used two other detergents that worked their miracles in the Great Washing Machine.

"Now I act like everyone else," she said, satisfied.

Snow Brown went to her classes. She thought them quite interesting. But the professors never looked her in the eye and never asked for her opinions. "Maybe they think I'm stupid," she said to herself. In class discussions everyone spoke up. Some of the things they said were pretty stupid, she thought. And so she would gather up her courage and contribute. She was met with stony silence. On some occasions others would make the same point, and the professor would acknowledge it and build on it.

She knew the mirror would be unhappy with her, and sure enough, she was right. "You have to be more aggressive," it said. "It doesn't matter so much what you say as how you say it."

"But that's ridiculous," she said. "Most of what is said is just plain dumb. Have you listened to some of them? They like the sound of their voices so much."

"That may be true, but that is the way. You have to make an impression, and sitting and listening like a lump of clay is not the way. And another thing—why did you let the others operate the machine in the lab? You have to take initiative."

"That was a ten-thousand-dollar machine. What if I broke it? I've never used it before."

"Leave your Third World mentality behind. The Patriarchs see it as a lack of initiative. They think you are not interested. You have to shoot for number one, be the very best. You have to act like a scientist, like a winner. Girl, what you need is a good dose of arrogance and ego."

Snow Brown was a little perturbed. She was disturbed by what she saw around her. Did she really want to act like some of the people she had met? What had happened to kindness, a little humility, helping each other? Just how badly did she want this, anyway? Her family was going to hate her when she went back. They would not recognize her. She thought long and hard and finally decided to go ahead.

She went back to the House of the Seven Detergents and used the anti–Third World detergent. When the Great Washing Machine was done, she came striding out, pride oozing out of every pore. The next day the Supreme White Patriarch called for her. "So, what kind of progress are you making in your search for Scientific Truth?" he asked.

"Well," she said, "the mirror has kept me occupied with learning to act like a scientist. Surely you can't expect me to make as much progress as the others, considering."

"We don't like students making excuses, Snow Brown. You had better make some progress, and real soon. There is no place for laziness here."

Snow Brown started developing some of her ideas. She went to the mirror to talk them over.

"I'm thinking of working with mutualisms," she said. "Organisms associate with each others in numerous ways ecologically. They can both compete for the same resources as in competition. Some live off other organisms, and that's called parasitism. When organisms get into ecological relationships with each other that are mutually beneficial, it's called mutualism."

"To be frank, Snow Brown, I would recommend studying competition or parasitism."

"But most of the studies of ecological interactions have focused on them," Snow Brown said. "I am amazed that there has been so little study of mutualisms. We know of some examples, but just how prevalent mutualisms are is still up in the air. For all we know, they may be a fundamental principle that describes demographic patterns of organisms on our planet."

"Whoa! Whoa!" cried the mirror. "You're getting carried away with your emotions. We would all like a and-they-lived-happily-ever-after kind of fairy tale. You are violating one of the fundamentals of doing science—objectivity. You don't pursue a study because you think it would be 'nice.' You base it on concrete facts, data. Then you apply the scientific method and investigate the problem."

"I do agree that the scientific method may have merit," she said. "I will use it to study mutualisms. But tell me, why do you think competition has been so well studied?"

"That's because competition is so important. Just look around you," the mirror replied. "Are the Patriarchs working with each other for their mutual benefit, or are they competing? This is what I do—promote competition. It is nature's way."

"Aha!" cried Snow Brown triumphantly. "You throw emotionalism and subjectivity at me. Listen to yourself. You are reading into nature what you see in yourself. I happen to believe that mutualisms are very important in the world. The Patriarchs have decided to work with a particular model. It doesn't mean that it's the only way."

"Get realistic," said the mirror, laughing. "You need the patronage of an Associate or Assistant Patriarch. You need to get money from the Supreme White Patriarch to do the research. Don't forget you need to please the Patriarch to get ahead. And you are still way behind in the game. This is not the time to get radical, and you are not the person to do it."

Convinced that pragmatism was the best course,the overconfident Snow Brown developed her ideas, talked in classes, and aggressively engaged the Patriarchs in dialogue. She was supremely happy. Things were finally going her way. She went to the mirror and said, "Mirror, mirror on the wall, who is the fairest scientist of them all?"

And the mirror replied, "It sure ain't you, Snow Brown. You're still the last one in town."

Snow Brown could not believe her ears. "I act and think like everyone around me. I am even obnoxious at times. What could I possibly still be doing wrong?"

"You're overdoing it," said the mirror. "You don't know everything. You should be a little more humble and subservient."

"Am I hearing things? I don't see anyone else doing that. This place does not validate that. You told me that yourself. What is really going on here?"

"When I advised you last," answered the mirror, "I advised you the way I would advise anyone, but I've been watching how the other Patriarchs interact with you. Apparently their expectations of you are different. You're brown, remember?"

Snow Brown was furious. She stormed out and went to the House of the Seven Detergents, and the sixth detergent washed her brownness away. She was now Snow White. She marched back to the Department of Scientific Truth. All the Patriarchs stared at her. They suddenly realized that what stood before them was a woman, and a beautiful one at that.

"Well, am I white enough for the lot of you now?" she demanded.

"Oh, but you're too pretty to be a scientist," cried the Supreme Patriarch.

"You can be a technician in my lab," said another.

"No, in mine!" urged yet another.

The Wise Matriarch had been right. Sneha had now lost her whole identity, and for what? Why had she not seen this coming? she asked herself. How could she ever have been the fairest scientist? How could she have been anything but last when judged by a mirror that wanted to produce clones of the Supreme White Patriarch? She went to the House of the Seven Detergents.

"It's too late, my child," said the Wise Matriarch. "You cannot go back now. I warned you about it. I wish I had more resources to support you and others like you. I have seen this happen far too often. It is important for you to communicate this to others. You must write down what has happened to you for future generations."

Two days later they discovered Sneha's cold body on the floor of her room. Her face looked tortured. In her sunken eyes was the resigned look of someone who had nothing more to lose to the world she had come to live in. On the nightstand by her body rested a tale entitled "Snow Brown and the Seven Detergents."

ENDING 1: AND INJUSTICE PREVAILS

The Patriarchs stood around the body. "It is so sad," said one. "But she was too emotional, a very fuzzy thinker. Some people are just not meant to pursue Scientific Truth. I wish they would accept it and leave instead of creating all this melodrama."

The other Patriarchs nodded in agreement at the unfortunate event.

"There is no reason for anyone to see this story, is there?" said the Patriarch who had initially spoken.

The others concurred, and they poured the last detergent on her. When they were done, there was nothing left. No pathetic face, no ugly reminders, no evidence.

ENDING 2: INTO EMPIRICISM

Snow Brown in her subversive wisdom sent copies of her story and insights to all in the department. There were some who kept the tale alive. It soon became apparent that there were dissenters within the Patriarchy. They broke their silence, and the movement slowly grew. Scientists began forming coalitions, talking and supporting each other in forming pockets of resistance. They questioned the power inequities. Why are most Patriarchs white? Why are most of them men? Over many decades the negotiations continued. Women scientists and scientists of color rose in the power structure. The collective consciousness was now male, female, and multicolored. But it was still supreme. It was privileged. The Pursuit for Truth continued, although new Truths emerged—Truths from the perspective of women, from the black, brown, yellow, red and the white. The world had become a better place.

ENDING 3: A POSTMODERN FANTASY

The story of Snow Brown spread like wildfire. The Land of the Blue Devils was ablaze with anger and rage. The Wise Matriarch and a number of budding Patriarchs stormed the Department of the Pursuit of Scientific Truth and took it over. The mirror was brought down. The Room of Judgment was transformed into the Room of Negotiation. In their first meeting after all this occurred, the scientists sat together. "We need a different model," they said. They dismantled the positions of the Supreme White Patriarch, the Emeritus Patriarch, the Associate Patriarch, the Assistant Patriarch, and the Young Patriarch. "We will be self-governing," they decided. They debunked the myth that truth was a monolithic entity. "Truth is a myth," they said. "One person's truth is often privileged over someone else's. This is dangerous. The Patriarchs privileged their worldview over all others. This distorts knowledge and makes an accurate description of the world impossible." Together they decided they could help each other in reconstructing science and rewriting scientific knowledge. The House of the Seven Detergents was dismantled, and the detergents were rendered invisible. The new Department of Scientific Endeavor was very productive. Its faculty and students solved many problems that had eluded the world for years. They became world renowned, and their model was adopted far and wide.

If you are ever in the forests in the Land of the Blue Devils and come across the voice of an old-school scientist arguing vociferously, you know you have stumbled across the ghosts of Snow Brown and the Seven Detergents.

CAREERS:
. . . And into the Fire

THE SHOULDERS OF GIANTS

Dara Horn

I have always been fascinated by scientists, because they appear to be the only people in the world who are immune to personal pettiness. Most people's careers are based on getting ahead, perhaps even at the expense of others. Scientists' goals, on the other hand, are not personal but collective. We imagine that their work is exclusively dedicated to the betterment of humankind.

As a student of literature, I am often asked to consider the life stories, motives, and intentions of the authors whose work I examine. If I were studying politics or history, I would concern myself even more with the personal conduct of the people I studied. But while a juicy biography of Darwin or Einstein would certainly make a good read, there exists a widespread belief among nonscientists that the motivations of researchers are secondary to their discoveries. Scientists are somehow outside of society, freed from its concerns in order to pursue knowledge for us all—or so those of us who are not scientists like to believe.

I imagine that most essays in this section of the book will address the effects of science on society, whether good or bad. But the story I am about to tell demonstrates the effects of society on science—effects that have the potential to be very damaging. In 1925 a twenty-five-year-old graduate student at Harvard discovered what the universe is made of. It was one of the most astonishing discoveries in the history of astronomic research. The problem was that no one believed her.

You have probably never heard of British-born Cecilia H. Payne (later Cecilia Payne-Gaposchkin), who in 1923 came to the United States to study stellar spectra at the Harvard College Observatory. In a remarkably short time Payne managed to quantify and classify the stellar spectra in the plate collection at the observatory, arriving at the startling conclusion that stars are "amazingly uniform" in their composition and that hydrogen is millions of times more abundant than any other element in the universe. Her doctoral dissertation, "Stellar Atmospheres" (1925), demonstrated her theory concerning the chemical composition of stars and earned her the first doctoral degree ever offered to either man or woman by Harvard's astronomy department. A few years later Otto Struve, an eminent astronomer, called it "the most brilliant Ph.D. thesis ever written" (p. 20).[1]

But in 1925 other scholars in the field were less impressed—or perhaps less courageous. Most astronomers at the time believed that stars were made of heavy elements. When her manuscript was presented to Henry Norris Russell, the leading contemporary astronomer dealing with stellar spectra, he wrote that her ideas concerning hydrogen's prevalence were "impossible" (p. 19). The director of Harvard's Observatory, Harlow Shapley, trusted Russell and convinced Payne to dilute her conclusion substantially. By the end of these machinations Payne, despite the data in her thesis, asserted in writing that the abundance of hydrogen that she had detected was "almost certainly not real" (p. 20). Later, the same scholars who had led her to weaken her thesis steered her away from continuing her work on the observatory's spectra, the area where she had demonstrated both promise and brilliance. At the observatory she was pitted against one of Russell's students, thereby impeding the progress of both, and her research was redirected toward photometry and variable stars, which she studied for the rest of her career. Four years later Russell published a paper of his own announcing that the sun is made mostly of hydrogen.

Payne-Gaposchkin eventually became Harvard's first female tenured professor and later the first female department chair, but her "promotion" did not come until 1956, when a new observatory director finally conceded that she deserved the position and a new university president finally permitted it. She had been passed over for positions several times; once, when the observatory sought to fill a professorship, Shapley, unable to acknowledge the fact that an excellent candidate was standing in front of him, said to her, "What this Observatory needs is a spectroscopist" (p. 223). But by then, at Russell's suggestion, she had already been "pushed against my will into photometry" (p. 223).

Since her death, in 1979, the woman who discovered what the universe is made of has not received so much as a memorial plaque. Her newspaper obituaries did not mention her greatest discovery. Even today, when it has become fashionable for historians to highlight the accomplishments of great female scientists, other astronomers are given precedence, or her name is listed as merely one of many. But there is no need to visit an astronomy hall of fame to see how faint the memory of Payne-Gaposchkin has become. A glance at any elementary physical science textbook will do the trick. Every high-school student knows that Isaac Newton discovered gravity, that Charles Darwin discovered evolution, and that Albert Einstein discovered the relativity of time. But when it comes to the composition of our universe, the textbooks simply say that the most abundant atom in the universe is hydrogen. And no one ever wonders how we came to know this.

I believe that Payne-Gaposchkin's work on stellar spectra was stopped in its tracks by three factors that had absolutely nothing to do with astronomy: she was a woman, she was young, and she was outstanding. The first and second of these factors led other people to underestimate her, either by mistaking her genius for foolishness or by assuming (and perhaps even hoping) that she could not possibly be capable of doing what she did. The third, the brilliance that placed her research beyond the understanding of those who were supposedly older and wiser, ultimately made her underestimate herself—a fact that she acknowledged later in life. Long after the 1920s, when Otto Struve began working on a history of astrophysics, he offered to include her prior discovery of a particular effect in stellar spectra. But Payne-Gaposchkin was too angry with herself to accept. "I was to blame for not having pressed my point," she insisted. "I had given into authority when I believed I was right. That is another example of How Not To Do Research" (p. 169). Her marriage to astronomer Sergei Gaposchkin seems to have made her even more vulnerable. His work was in variable stars, and Payne-Gaposchkin soon found herself devoting almost all of her research to that field. This, in addition to the challenge of raising their three children, caused her to abandon spectroscopy altogether. In her autobiography, however, she rarely expresses frustration with anyone other than herself.

But more than underestimation and disbelief were working against her. If Payne had merely been misunderstood, her colleagues would have surely encouraged her to continue working on stellar spectra once they realized that she was right. But they did not. Instead, even after the importance of her work had become obvious, Payne was still cajoled into abandoning her specialty. I believe this stemmed not from scientific concerns about the merit of her research, but from something simpler and more universal, an emotion that every scientist and nonscientist can understand. When dressed in the guise of science, jealousy becomes much more destructive than usual, for it can curtail our knowledge of the world. We will probably never be able to confirm why Russell and Shapely made the decisions that they made. Yet it is clear that discrimination as well as personal bitterness precluded scientific progress at many levels throughout Payne-Gaposchkin's career. In her case, one might argue that the public was lucky. Her revelation is ours, even if we do not know her name. But what of the discoveries that might have been made if she had continued working on stellar spectra for another twenty years? Can we even begin to estimate the magnitude of the loss?

Like most people, I have almost no scientific training. What I know about scientific research comes from newspapers, magazines, television programs, and a few ill-remembered high-school chemistry classes. But like most people, I have been taught to see science as an entirely pure and objective pursuit of knowledge, embarked upon for the benefit of people like me. This assumption may be ridiculous. Yet as knowledge expands beyond my grasp it is an assumption that I have to make in order to avoid living in a state of perpetual and paralyzing doubt.

So if I read in the newspaper that a fat substitute is safe for consumption, I do not question it. If a television program tells me that there is no cure for a particular disease, I believe it. If my college textbook explains to me that the universe is made of hydrogen but does not tell me who discovered it, I trust that this fact was so obvious that it did not even need to be discovered. Along with millions of others, I have placed my faith in scientists—not because I am dull-witted, but because their pursuit is reputed to be noble and disinterested, unmarred by the jealousies and desires that motivate most of us. Perhaps I am naive, but then so are many others. If scientists let us down, we will not know it.

The greatest loss to scientific research comes not from anything inherent in science, but rather from something inherent in society: our love of stars, particularly metaphoric ones. As students, we learn to associate the phenomena of our world with the names of the people who discovered them—never with their personalities, or with their networks of teachers and fellow researchers, or with the bibliographies of works upon which they built their own. On the elementary level, evolution is taught not as evolution, but as Darwinian evolution. We study not relativity, but Einstein's theory of relativity. Our textbooks supply us with Planck's constant, Avogadro's number, and Newton's laws. Scarcely a theorem exists without someone's name attached to it, regardless of how many people may have contributed to it.

After spending so many years listening to the great geniuses' names repeated again and again, a young student entering the sciences might understandably believe that the supreme goal of the scientist is not to reach for the stars, but rather to become one. After all, among the constellations of scientific giants, do we ever see the light of their instructors, their colleagues, or those who were their inspirations? Isaac Newton once said of himself, "If I have seen further than other men, it is because I have stood upon the shoulders of giants." But what happens when no one is content to offer his shoulders?

I am not in a position to judge how typical or unusual Payne-Gaposchkin's experience might be today. Nevertheless, I urge scientists to aspire to that which the rest of us already assume is taking place: the effort to ensure that research is not just a solitary effort geared toward individual reward, but a joint effort to push back the boundaries of knowledge. That should be the highest and most impassioned goal. As the sciences become more specialized, stardom will become more elusive. Scientists will then be faced with a choice: to become more competitive in their quest for glory or to become more sincere in their quest for truth. The most crucial contributions to knowledge come not only from those who make revolutionary revelations, but also from those who know how to appreciate and nurture the talents of others.

Cecilia Payne-Gaposchkin wrote in her autobiography that she hoped to be remembered for what she considers her greatest discovery: "I have come to know that a problem does not belong to me, or to my team, or to my Observatory, or to my country; it belongs to the world" (p. 162). The shoulders of that discovery are the only ones strong enough to support us.

Notes

1. All quotations are from Cecilia Payne-Gaposchkin, *Cecilia Payne-Gaposchkin: An Autobiography and Other Writings,* 2nd ed., ed. K. Haramundanis (Cambridge: Cambridge University Press, 1986).

NEPOTISM AND SEXISM IN PEER-REVIEW

Christine Wennerås and Agnes Wold

Throughout the world, women leave their academic careers to a far greater extent than their male colleagues.[1] In Sweden, for example, women are awarded 44 per cent of biomedical PhDs but hold a mere 25 per cent of the postdoctoral positions and only 7 per cent of professorial positions. It used to be thought that once there were enough entry-level female scientists, the male domination of the upper echelons of academic research would automatically diminish. But this has not happened in the biomedical field, where disproportionate numbers of men still hold higher academic positions, despite the significant numbers of women who have entered this research field since the 1970s.

REASONS FOR LACK OF SUCCESS

Why do women face these difficulties? One view is that women tend to be less motivated and career-oriented than men, and therefore are not as assiduous in applying for positions and grants. Another is that women are less productive than men, and consequently their work has less scientific merit. Yet another is that women suffer discrimination due to gender. We decided to investigate whether the peer-review system of the Swedish Medical Research Council (MRC), one of the main funding agencies for biomedical research in Sweden, evaluates women and men on an equal basis. Our investigation was prompted by the fact that the success rate of female scientists applying for postdoctoral fellowships at the MRC during the 1990s has been less than half that of male applicants.

Our study strongly suggests that peer reviewers cannot judge scientific merit independent of gender. The peer reviewers overestimated male achievements and/or underestimated female performance, as shown by multiple-regression analyses of the relation between defined parameters of scientific productivity and competence scores.

In the peer-review system of the Swedish MRC, each applicant submits a curriculum vitae, a bibliography and a research proposal. The application is reviewed by one of 11 evaluation committees, each covering a specified research field. The individual applicant is rated by the five reviewers of the committee to which he or she has been assigned. Each reviewer gives the applicant a score between 0 and 4 for the following three parameters: scientific competence; relevance of the research proposal; and the quality of the proposed methodology. The three scores given by each reviewer are then multiplied with one another to yield a product score that can vary between 0 and 64. Finally, the average of the five product scores an applicant has received is computed, yielding a final score that is the basis on which the applicants to each committee are ranked.

The MRC board, which includes the chairmen of the 11 committees, ultimately decides to whom the fellowships will be awarded. Usually each committee chooses between one and three of the top-ranked applicants. Of the 114 applicants for the 20 postdoctoral fellowships offered in 1995, there were 62 men and 52 women, with a mean age of 36 years, all of whom had received a PhD degree within the past five years. Most of the female applicants had basic degrees in science (62 per cent), and the rest had medical (27 per cent) or nursing (12 per cent) degrees; the corresponding figures for the male applicants were 38, 59 and 3 per cent.

Traditionally, peer-review scores are not made public, and indeed the MRC officials initially refused us access to the documents dealing with evaluation of the applicants.

In Sweden, however, the Freedom of the Press Act grants individuals access to all documents held by state or municipal authorities. Only documents defined as secret by the Secrecy Act are exempt, for example those that may endanger the security of the state, foreign relations or citizens' personal integrity. Accordingly, we appealed against the refusal of the MRC to release the scores.

In 1995, the Administrative Court of Appeal judged the evaluation scores of the MRC to be official documents. Hence, to our knowledge, this is the first time that genuine peer-reviewer evaluation sheets concerning a large cohort of applicants has become available for scientific study.

We found that the MRC reviewers gave female applicants lower average scores than male applicants on all three evaluation parameters: 0.25 fewer points for scientific competence (2.21 versus 2.46 points); 0.17 fewer points for quality of the proposed methodology (2.37 versus 2.54); and 0.13 fewer points for relevance of the research proposal (2.49 versus 2.62). Because these scores are multiplied with each other, female applicants received substantially lower final scores compared with male applicants (13.8 versus 17.0 points on average). That year, four women and 16 men were awarded postdoctoral fellowships.

As shown by these figures, the peer reviewers deemed women applicants to be particularly deficient in scientific competence. As it is generally regarded that this parameter is related to the number and quality of scientific publications,[2–5] it seemed reasonable to assume that women earned lower scores on this parameter than men because they were less productive. We explored this hypothesis by determining the scientific productivity of all 114 applicants and then comparing the peer-reviewer ratings of groups of male and female applicants with similar scientific productivity.

PRODUCTIVITY VARIABLES

We measured the scientific productivity of each applicant in six different ways. First, we determined the applicant's total number of original scientific publications, and second, the number of publications on which the applicant was first author. Both figures were taken from the applicant's bibliography, which we double-checked in the Medline database. (We call these measures 'total number of publications' and 'total number of first-author publications'.)

To take into account the fact that the prestige of biomedical journals varies widely, we constructed measures based on journals' impact factors. The impact factor of a scientific journal is listed in the independent Institute of Scientific Information's *Journal Citation Reports*, and describes the number of times an average paper published in a particular journal is cited during one year. Our third measure was to add together the impact factors of each of the journals in which the applicant's papers were published, generating the 'total impact measure' of the applicant's total number of publications.

Fourth, we generated the 'first-author impact measure' by adding together the impact factors of the journals in which the applicant's first-author papers appeared. The unit of measure for both total impact and first-author impact is 'impact points', with one impact point equalling one paper published in a journal with an impact factor of 1.

Fifth, using the science citation database, we identified the number of times the applicant's scientific papers were cited during 1994, which yielded the measure 'total citations'. And sixth, we repeated this procedure for papers on which the applicant was first author, giving the measure 'first-author citations.'

FIGURE 1 The mean competence score given to male (red squares) and female (blue squares) applicants by the MRC reviewers as a function of their scientific productivity, measured as total impact. One impact point equals one paper published in a journal with an impact factor of 1. (See text for further explanation.)

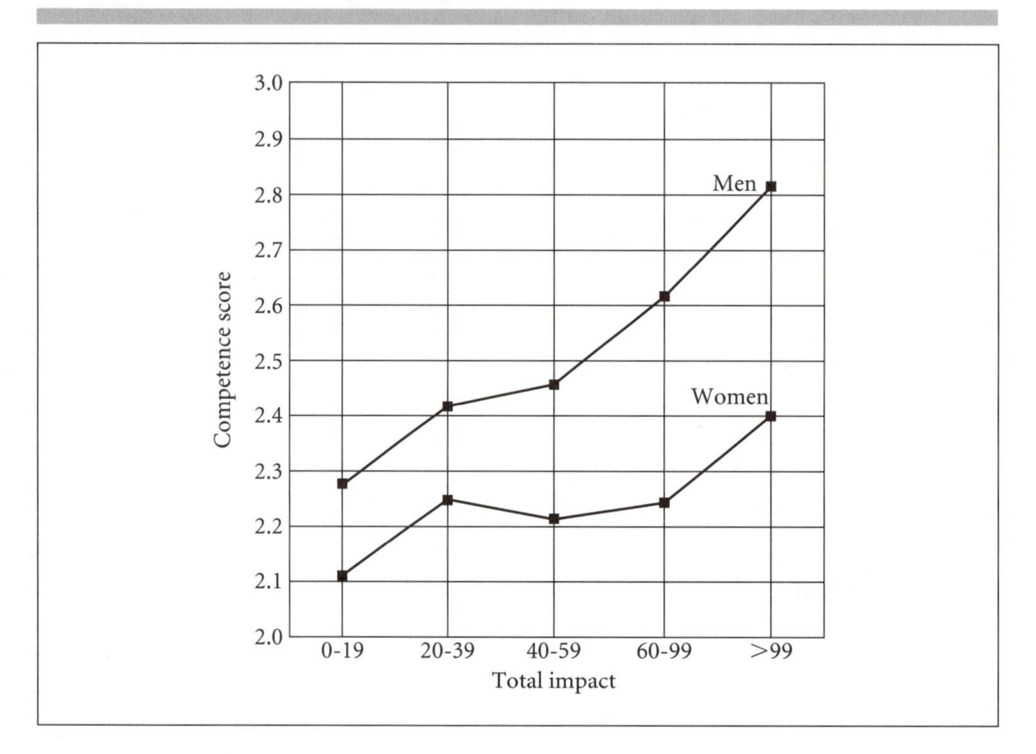

Did men and women with equal scientific productivity receive the same competence rating by the MRC reviewers? No! As shown in Fig. 1 for the productivity variable 'total impact', the peer reviewers gave female applicants lower scores than male applicants who displayed the same level of scientific productivity. In fact, the most productive group of female applicants, containing those with 100 total impact points or more, was the only group of women judged to be as competent as men, although only as competent as the least productive group of male applicants (the one whose members had fewer than 20 total impact points).

WHY WOMEN SCORE LOW

Although the difference in scoring of male and female applicants of equal scientific productivity suggested that there was indeed discrimination against women researchers, factors other than the applicant's gender could, in principle, have been responsible for the low scores awarded to women. If, for example, women were mainly to conduct research in areas given low priority by the MRC, come from less-renowned universities, or have less collaboration with academic decision-makers, their lower scores could depend on such factors, rather than on their gender *per se.*

To determine the cause of women's lower scores, we performed a multiple-regression analysis, which reveals the factors that exert a primary influence on a certain outcome (for example competence scores) and the size of such an influence. Multiple regression permits the elimination of factors whose influence on a certain outcome merely reflects their dependence on other factors.

In the multiple-regression analysis, we assumed that the competence scores given to applicants are linearly related to their scientific productivity. We constructed six different multiple-regression models, one for each of the productivity variables outlined above. In each of these models, we determined the influence of the following factors on the competence scores: the applicant's gender; nationality (Swedish/non-Swedish); basic education (medical, science or nursing school); scientific field; university affiliation; the evaluation committee to which the applicant was assigned; whether the applicant had had postdoctoral experience abroad; whether a letter of recommendation accompanied the application; and whether the applicant was affiliated with any of the members of the evaluation committee. The last piece of information is noted on the MRC evaluation protocols, in which case the reviewer in question is not allowed to participate in the scoring of that applicant. It was as frequent for female (12 per cent) as for male (13 per cent) applicants to be associated with a committee member.

The outcome of the regression analysis is shown in Table 1. Three out of the six productivity variables generated statistically significant models capable of predicting the competence scores the applicants were awarded: total impact, first-author impact and first-author citations. The model that provided the highest explanatory power was the one based on total impact ($r^2 = 0.47$). In all three models, we found two factors as well as scientific productivity that had a significant influence on competence scores: the gender of the applicant and the affiliation of the applicant with a committee member.

According to the multiple-regression model based on total impact, female applicants started from a basic competence level of 2.09 competence points (the intercept of the multiple regression curve) and were given an extra 0.0033 competence points by the reviewers for every impact point they had accumulated. Independent of scientific productivity, however, male applicants received an extra 0.21 points for competence. So, for a female scientist to be awarded the same competence score as a male colleague, she needed to exceed his scientific productivity by 64 impact points (95 per cent confidence interval: 35–93 impact points).

This represents approximately three extra papers in *Nature* or *Science* (impact factors 25 and 22, respectively), or 20 extra papers in a journal with an impact factor of around 3, which would be an excellent specialist journal such as *Atherosclerosis, Gut, Infection and Immunity, Neuroscience* or *Radiology.* Considering that the mean total impact of this cohort of applicants was 40 points, a female applicant had to be 2.5 times more productive than the average male applicant to receive the same competence score as he ($(40 + 64)/40 = 2.6$).

FRIENDSHIP BONUS

According to the same multiple-regression model, applicants who were affiliated with a committee member received competence scores 0.22 points higher than applicants of the same gender and scientific productivity who lacked such ties (Table 1). This 'affiliation bonus' was worth 67 impact points (confidence interval: 29 to 105 impact points). Hence, an applicant lacking personal ties with the reviewers needed to have 67 more impact points than an applicant of the same sex who was associated with one of the reviewers, to be perceived as equally competent. So, although MRC policy does not allow 'biased' reviewers to participate in the scoring of applicants they are associated with, this rule was insufficient, as the 'neutral' committee members compensated by raising their scores when judging applicants affiliated with one of their peers.

Because the affiliation bonus was of the same magnitude as the 'male gender' bonus, a woman applicant could make up for her gender (–0.21 competence points)

TABLE 1 Factors that Significantly Influenced Peer Reviewers' Rating of Scientific Competence, According to Three Multiple Regression Models.

	Scientific Productivity			Additional Points Given by the Reviewers for the Following Factors			Size of the Influence of the Non-Scientific Factors in Productivity Equivalents		
Multiple regression model based on:	r^2	Intercept	Competence points per productivity unit	Male gender	Reviewer affiliation	Recommendation letter	Male gender	Reviewer affiliation	Unit of measure
Total impact	0.47	2.09	0.0033 *<0.00005**	0.21 *<0.00005*	0.22 *0.0008*	0.10 *0.04*	64 (35–93)[†]	67 (29–105)	Impact points
First-author impact	0.44	2.13	0.0094 *<0.0001*	0.24 *<0.00005*	0.20 *0.005*	NS	25 (14–36)	21 (6–36)	Impact points
First-author citations	0.41	2.17	0.0054 *0.001*	0.23 *<0.00005*	0.23 *0.001*	NS	42 (23–61)	42 (17–67)	Citations during 1994

* Italicized numbers indicate *P*-values for the variable in question.
[†] Numbers in parentheses indicate 95% confidence interval.
NS, not statistically significant, *P*-value > 0.05.

by being affiliated with one of the reviewers (+0.22 competence points). On the other hand, a female (−0.21 competence points) lacking personal connections in the committee (−0.22 competence points) had to present an additional 131 impact points to the MRC reviewers to receive the same competence score as a male applicant affiliated with one of the reviewers.

Such a level of productivity was attained by only three of the 114 applicants, one male and two female. Hence, being of the female gender and lacking personal connections was a double handicap of such severity that it could hardly be compensated for by scientific productivity alone.

The two other regression models, based on first-author impact and first-author citations, yielded almost identical results to the first with regard to the effect of gender and affiliation (Table 1). This congruity was not a statistical artefact due to a high degree of interrelation between the three productivity variables, as the total impact and first-author impact of the applicants were only moderately correlated ($r = 0.63$), as were total impact and first-author citations ($r = 0.62$). We therefore believe that male gender and reviewer affiliation were real determinants of scientific competence in the eyes of the MRC reviewers.

The applicant's nationality, education, field of research or postdoctoral experience did not influence competence scores in any of the models. A letter of recommendation had a positive effect on the competence score in the model based on total impact, but not in the two others (Table 1). By contrast, the evaluation committee that rated individual applicants did influence competence scores, as some committees were 'sterner' in their evaluation of competence than the rest (data not shown). However, an applicant who was assigned to a 'tough' committee had the same chance of being awarded a fellowship as other applicants, as fellowships were distributed based on the rank the applicant acquired within his or her committee and not on absolute score values.

CHANGING THE SYSTEM

The peer-review system, characterized as "the centerpiece of the modern scientific review process,"[6] has been criticized on many grounds, including poor inter-reviewer reliability[2] and because reviewers may favour projects confirming their own views.[7] Our study is the first analysis based on actual peer-reviewer scores and provides direct evidence that the peer-review system is subject to nepotism, as has already been suggested anecdotally.[8–10]

One might argue that young researchers affiliated with peer reviewers are part of a scientific élite that has received superior training and are therefore more competent than average applicants. Indeed, applicants with such ties had higher total impact levels on average than applicants without such connections (data not shown). Hence, applicants with personal alliances justly benefited from higher competence scores because of their higher scientific productivity. However, on top of that, they were given extra competence points not warranted by scientific productivity. We see no reason why an applicant who manages to produce research of high quality despite not being affiliated with a prestigious research group should not be similarly rewarded.

Several studies have shown that both women and men rate the quality of men's work higher than that of women when they are aware of the sex of the person to be evaluated, but not when the same person's gender is unknown.[11–13] It is somewhat surprising that the results of these studies have not discouraged the scientific community from relying on evaluation systems that are vulnerable to reviewer prejudice.

An interesting question that we could not address here is whether the harsher evaluation of female researchers was due to the paucity of women among the peer reviewers. The small number of women reviewers (5 out of 55) and their uneven distribution among the MRC's committees made a statistical analysis of their scoring behaviour impossible. However, a few studies have indicated that female evaluators may be more objective in assessing the achievement of women than their male counterparts[14]. Nevertheless, we are not confident that a simple increase in the percentage of women reviewers would solve the problem of gender-based discrimination.

If gender discrimination of the magnitude we have observed is operative in the peer-review systems of other research councils and grant-awarding organizations, and in countries other than Sweden, this could entirely account for the lower success rate of female as compared with male researchers in attaining high academic rank. The United Nations has recently named Sweden as the leading country in the world with respect to equal opportunities for men and women, so it is not too far-fetched to assume that gender-based discrimination may occur elsewhere. It is therefore essential that more studies such as ours are conducted in different countries and in different areas of scientific research.

An in-depth analysis of other peer-review systems can be achieved only if the policy of secrecy is abandoned. We could perform our study only because of the Swedish Freedom of the Press Act. It is often claimed that secrecy in scoring will protect reviewers from improper influences. But our results cast doubt on these claims. It has also been suggested that the recruitment of peer reviewers of high quality would be impeded if reviewers were not granted anonymity. Such fears seem to be exaggerated because, although reviewer evaluation scores have been accessible to everyone in Sweden since the court ruling of 1995, there have been no large-scale defections of peer reviewers from the evaluation committees.

Most important, the credibility of the academic system will be undermined in the eyes of the public if it does not allow a scientific evaluation of its own scientific evaluation system. It is our firm belief that scientists are the most suited to evaluate research performance. One must recognize, however, that scientists are no less immune than other human beings to the effects of prejudice and comradeship. The development of peer-review systems with some built-in resistance to the weaknesses of human nature is therefore of high priority. If this is not done, a large pool of promising talent will be wasted.

Notes

1. Widnall, S. E. *Science* **241,** 1740–1745 (1988).
2. Cole, S., Cole, J. R. & Simon, G. A. *Science* **214,** 881–886 (1981).
3. Long, J. S. *Social Forces* **71,** 159–178 (1992).
4. Sonnert, G. *Social Stud. Sci.* **25,** 35–55 (1995).
5. Sonnert, G. & Holton, G. *Am. Sci.* **84,** 63–71 (1996).
6. Glantz, S. A. & Bero, L. A. *J. Am. Med. Assoc.* **272,** 114–116 (1994).
7. Ernst, E., Resch, K. L. & Uher, E. M. *Ann. Intern. Med.* **116,** 958 (1992).
8. Forsdyke, D. R. *FASEB J.* **7,** 619–621 (1993).
9. Calza, L. & Gerbisa, S. *Nature* **374,** 492 (1995).
10. Perez-Enciso, M. *Nature* **378,** 760 (1995).
11. Goldberg, P. *Trans-Action* **5,** 28–30 (1968).
12. Nieva, V. F. & Gutek, B. A. *Acad. Manag. Rev.* **5,** 267–276 (1980).
13. O'Leary, V. E. & Wallston, B. S. *Rev. Pers. Soc. Psychol.* **2,** 9–43 (1982).
14. Frieze, I. H. in *Women and Achievement: Social and Motivational Analyses* (eds. Mednick, M. T., Tangri, S. S. & Hoffman, L. W.), 158–171 (Hemisphere, Washington DC, 1975).

NINE DECADES, NINE WOMEN, TEN NOBEL PRIZES
Gender Politics at the Apex of Science

Hilary Rose

Gertrude Elion, Rita Levi-Montalcini, Barbara McClintock, Rosalyn Yalow, Dorothy Crowfoot Hodgkin, Maria Goeppert Mayer, Gerty Cori, Irène Joliot Curie and Marie Curie: nine women, ten Nobel Prizes for science (Marie Curie was awarded prizes both in physics—1903—and in chemistry—1911), distributed over the eighty-five years between 1903 and 1988. They range in age, from Curie receiving her first prize at 36, to the three most recent, Elion, Levi-Montalcini and McClintock, being 71, 77 and 81 respectively. Apart from Irène Joliot Curie, who, at 38, emulated her mother in her youthfulness as well as her scientific talent, and was awarded a prize in 1935, the intermediate group of postwar prizewinners were all in their fifties: Gerty Cori, 53 (1947); Maria Goeppert Mayer, 57 (1963); Dorothy Crowfoot Hodgkin, 54 (1964) and Rosalyn Yalow, 56 (1977). These nine women constitute some 2 per cent of the scientific Nobel Laureates.

Since Nobel prizes are not awarded posthumously a number of commentators, including but not only feminists, viewing the three women honoured in the 1980s, have suggested that longevity is increasingly an additional criterion for women scientists to meet. It seems that the Nobel committee, in responding to the new pressure on it to recognize women scientists, feels safer in going back in history, to acknowledge those whose scientific eminence is unquestionable but who have been previously passed over. Perhaps men with the power to give public recognition suffer from an inability to recognize scientific merit in peer-group women, whereas they have no such problem with peer-aged or even younger men. However, in that a central rationale for awarding the cash-rich Nobel Prize was to free creative scientists from concerns about resources, then these most recently honoured women would seem to be ineligible, and certainly other older men scientists have been explicitly excluded on precisely these grounds.[1]

This anomaly, which in its repetition suggests a response to the increasing claims of gender justice and those of scientific merit, while possibly not at the level of conscious intentionality, is demonstrably effective as a means of constraining reform. The overdue recognition of these distinguished but now older women scientists limits the possibility of their exercising the usual powers of a Nobel Laureate. Their age means that, however brilliant, they are manifestly less likely to be in touch with younger up-and-coming scientists in their own field and less likely to be able to campaign for them. The move also diminishes the pressure to recognize those others, in their forties or fifties, who would be in a phase of their life and career cycle where they might best utilize the reward and the status. Even before the most recent awards, the time gap between their work and its formal recognition was already more strongly marked for women than men.[2] Nor is this unrecognized by the women scientists themselves, though perhaps it takes someone of Rita Levi-Montalcini's social and scientific confidence to reveal publicly her anger at the lapse of time and of the different treatment accorded to those she sees as in every way her peers. She notes that 'Two of my university colleagues and close friends, Salvador Luria and Renato Dulbecco, were to receive the Nobel Prize in Physiology and Medicine, respectively seventeen and eleven years before I would receive the same most prestigious award.'[3]

THE PRIZE AS CULTURAL CAPITAL

While scientific excellence has, with very rare exceptions, been successfully acknowledged by the Nobel Science committees (the Literature and Peace prizes have long had a more contentious record), the institutional and social origins of the Laureates have played a significant part. Just ten colleges, for example, produced 55 per cent of the 71 US Laureates studied by Harriet Zuckerman.[4] In a similar way the history of the nine women Laureates is in a number of ways a microcosm of the history of gender politics in science this century. The Nobel Prize sits at the apex of the status system of science. The Laureates are icons of the fusion of scientific knowledge and cultural power, so that where they are not already members of their national elite groupings of scientists, such as the Royal Society of London or the French or US National Academies, then it is customary that they are rather swiftly elected. Membership of institutionalized national and international scientific elites, as well as confirming such cultural and political power, also offers its bearer the prospect of participation in these institutionalized forms, and hence a close and uncritical relationship with the state. Members of this ultra-elite within science are invited to walk the corridors of power. Governments seeking scientific advice of a politically strategic nature frequently turn to their national academies or to specific disciplinary groups within them. The shadowy JASON group of leading Nobelist and near-Nobelist US physicists advising on US military strategy came into notoriety during the Vietnam war, but has continued ever since, today advising the US government on what is euphemistically termed national security and defence. Nor is the desire for scientific advice limited to powers temporal in the late twentieth century; the Pope, wishing to develop his thoughts on the environment, turned to the collective wisdom of Nobel Laureates, via the Vatican Academy, for advice.

This is a paradox at the heart of the Nobel system: scientific eminence is achieved through a small but innovatory piece of knowledge concerning a specific aspect of chemistry, physics, physiology or medicine, but winning the prize gives its bearers the ability to advise on global sociopolitical issues far outside their range of expertise. Feminists, in order to explain the systematic undervaluing of women within the labour market, have described women as 'inferior bearers of labour'; by contrast Nobel Prize-winners become 'superior bearers of thought', acquiring the power to speak and be listened to on topics where their competence is either at the same level as that of their fellow citizens, or even demonstrably less. Because this cultural power is rather concrete, few people are entirely consistent in their attitudes to its manifestation. Individual scientists have used their cultural capital to support their ideological and political commitments. Thus I have to admit that, like many antiracists, I tend to point out that Nobel Laureate William Shockley received his prize for work on transistors and that he had no special competence to support his unquestionably hereditarian views on intelligence/IQ, but that when anxious to see nuclear power controlled I welcome seeing George Wald throw his political and scientific weight onto the socially critical side of the debate, and am less anxious to point out the modest connection between his Nobel Prize-winning work on receptor pigments in the eye and the scientific debate at issue. Many times have I welcomed the signatures of what seems to be a shrinking handful of anti-militarist British Laureates and FRSs, not least Dorothy Hodgkin and Maurice Wilkins, in protests against military aggression, without dwelling on the cultural power that their welcome presence reinforces.

It would also be ungenerous, particularly in periods when nonconformity with the state carries significant penalties, not to acknowledge the personal courage sometimes entailed. For leading non-Jewish German scientists to oppose the Nazis required an act of courage, as it did for leading US scientists to use their cultural capital to protest against witch-hunting during the height of the McCarthy era; it was much easier to deplore the excesses privately and subscribe to the politics of prudential acquiescence. The physicist Sakharov was rightly admired for his courage in using his cultural capital as the father of the Soviet H-bomb to play a leading role in the human rights movement. And although political persecution has not been a significant issue for British scientists, her anti-militarist activities and marriage to a communist meant that Nobel Laureate crystallographer Dorothy Hodgkin was proscribed from admission to the US except by a special CIA waiver until she was in her eighties. (Presumably the combination of her age and the collapse of the former Soviet Union led the CIA to think that she was not imminently about to engage in the violent overthrow of US liberal democracy.)

Thus I want both to salute individual Laureates and other eminent scientists for their sometimes quite concrete personal courage in the use of their cultural capital, in the face of sanctions which have ranged from exclusion and even death to various levels of social opprobrium, yet also to criticize a system which has amplified the cultural power of science, not least because of the extent to which, during the twentieth century, science has become incorporated and plays a predominantly socially conservative role.[5]

CEREMONY AND SECRECY

. . . The archives of the Royal Society, itself one of the oldest scientific institutions, are accessible after forty years; but those of the Nobel Institute, created at the beginning of this century, are accessible only after fifty years; in consequence proportionately more of the Nobel's iceberg of secrecy is hidden. Such intense and prolonged secrecy about the affairs of the scientific elites, considerably longer even than that of the notoriously secretive British governmental tradition and an anachronism in Sweden, where any citizen may have access to letters written by a minister, is in itself a matter of curiosity.[6] When it is remembered that these elites are choosing to honour creators of 'public knowledge' in science, not trade, military or diplomatic secrets, such secrecy speaks of the sense of cultural and political mystery with which Bacon's masculine knowledge has endowed itself.

The archives made it possible to go behind the public face of the Royal Society, with its discourse of the President being above the election of members, and scientific merit being the only criterion for election, and contrast this with the very particular ways, documented by committee minutes and correspondence, through which actual elite men scientists treated the claims of women scientists and finally came to the understanding that they could no longer exclude women. No such possibility, for other than the early years, exists in the case of the Nobel Prize archives. Lacking this account from the perspective of the powerful who manage such events, the story of the election of the women Laureates has for the greater part to be built from more outsider sources, including biographies, the rather rare autobiography, the occasional interview, and, as an important set of resources which have remained constant over time, the Laureate's Stockholm speech of acceptance, together with the biographical note and the photographic portrait which accompanies its publication.[7]

The occasion of the prize-giving is highly formal, and takes place in the presence of the monarch. It is the Swedish king himself, that symbol of a past military system of power, who awards the medals. The men attending the ceremony are required to wear white tie and tails. While for a number of recent men Laureates, perhaps particularly those from the US, who have rarely been known to wear anything except jeans and checked shirts, such dressing up is something of a novelty, it is also—as Virginia Woolf reminded us for the thirties—still very much part of the life of educated men. The academy has a passion not only for secrecy but for distinctive attire, a surrogate uniform on which medals signifying heroic performance on the field of truth may be displayed. The sharing of the military code and its honours is made all the easier in the Nobel ceremony because it is carried out at such a symbolic level; the constitutional monarch of a neutralist country is at once remote from the military and also the descendant of Gustavus Adolphus, the last Swedish king to die leading his troops in battle.[8]

Novelty and innovation are always central within the award of a Nobel Prize, even though the language has shifted over the decades from the 'land ho' quality of scientific 'discovery' in which the newly recognized phenomenon is equated with finding a new land (or at least new to the discoverers) to what the users doubtless see as a rather more nuanced language of a 'seminal contribution'. Women Laureates have to be innovators in an additional sense. Like the women who were first admitted to the Royal Society, they are likely to be entrants to new and therefore initially low-status areas of science where the discipline has not been fully formed, where there is no clear structure of employment and career, and hence where there is room for unpaid or badly paid pioneers whose passion is knowledge of the natural world. . . .

A DANGEROUS COMBINATION OF LOVE AND SCIENCE: MILEVA EINSTEIN MARÍC

The recently recovered biography of Mileva Einstein Marí c[9] documents the dangerous combination of love and science for women, and its power to render women and their science invisible. After a painful beginning where she conceived a child by Albert Einstein out of wedlock and had the baby adopted, the marriage was initially happy and mutually appreciative. Einstein, for example, explained to a group of Zagreb intellectuals that he needed his wife as 'she solves all the mathematical problems for me'. Two key episodes document the process by which her work, if not actively appropriated, was certainly lost by her to him. In one episode Mileva, through the collaboration with a mutual friend, Paul Habicht, constructed an innovatory device for measuring electrical currents. Having built the device the two inventors left it to Einstein to describe and patent, as he was at that time working in the patent office. He alone signed the publication and patented the device under the name Einstein-Habicht. When asked why she had not given her own name of Einstein Maríc she asked, 'What for, we are both only "one stone" [*Ein stein*]?'. Later when the marriage had collapsed she found that the price of her selfless love and affectionate joke was that her work had become his. She also lost her personal health through trying to do the mathematical work to support his theorizing and simultanously take care of their children. One son suffered from schizophrenia and after the divorce Einstein was mean about keeping up with the alimony.

Troemel-Ploetz[10] points to the even more disturbing episode of the articles published in 1905 in the Leipzig *Annalen der Physik*. Of the five key papers, two of the originally submitted manuscripts were signed also by Mileva, but by the time of their publication, her name had been removed. These two articles, written in what was widely understood as Einstein's golden age, included the theory of special relativity which was to change the nature of physics, and for which he alone received the Nobel prize. Thus although the purpose of the biography was to restore Mileva's name as a distinguished and creative scientist, and not to denigrate Einstein, it inevitably raised the issue of his withholding recognition of Mileva's contribution to the achievement. A number of observers have also commented on the puzzle of Einstein's gift of the prize money to Mileva Maríc even though they were by then separated. This gift-giving was later emulated by George Hoyt Whipple, a Nobel Prize-winner in 1934. Although Whipple had the reputation of being very careful financially, he shared his prize money with Frieda Robsheit Robbins, his co-worker for many years, and with two other women colleagues. In Einstein's and Hoyt Whipple's circumstances, was the money meant to compensate for the system's, and perhaps their own, appropriation of their collaborators' work?

While Mileva's biographer is careful to indicate that Einstein was the creative thinker, she suggests that he could not have realized his theoretical insights without Mileva's mathematics. Between men scientists such a collaboration between theory and technique is rather difficult to ignore; between husband and wife scientists it was—and according to the context still is—rather easy. It was especially so at the turn of the century when bourgeois women, as wives, were only permitted to work as unpaid workers and when scientific work like housework and child care could be constructed—as they were by Mileva—as part of the labour of love. While Trbuhovic Gjuric's biography (not least because it was originally published in Serbian in 1969) has not had the impact of Ann Sayre's study of Rosalind Franklin, it has raised doubts in the physics community,[11] meanwhile feminists will recognize the pattern as characteristic, made possible by that early twentieth century scientific labour market in all its unbridled patriarchal power of appropriation. . . .

APPROPRIATION AND ERASURE: ROSALIND FRANKLIN

Between the awards to the biochemist Gerty Cori and the physicist Maria Goeppert Mayer was the triumphalist story of DNA and its soon-to-be revealed subtext of the appalling treatment of the X-ray crystallographer Rosalind Franklin. The account of the erasure of this outstanding woman scientist and the appropriation of her work was told to a wider audience in 1975 in the biography by Anne Sayre, who along with her crystallographer husband was a personal friend of Franklin's. Sayre's book made public the grave disquiet felt among the crystallographic community,[12] and was received within a political climate newly sensitized by an increasingly powerful women's movement. The story is brief, as was the life of this scientist who died at 37 of cancer. Born into a well-off North London Jewish family, Rosalind Franklin was sent to St Paul's, a fee-paying girls' school which prided itself on the educational performance of its pupils. She went to Cambridge to read science, did postgraduate work on the physical chemistry of coal, worked with the crystallographer Marcel Mathieu in Paris and then accepted a postdoctoral fellowship in the department of biophysics in King's College, London. The laboratory was one of a number interested in the structure of the giant molecule of DNA, which was already thought to be associated in some way with the genetic mechanisms of heredity, and both Franklin and another scientist, Maurice Wilkins, were engaged in making X-ray diffraction photographs of the rather intractable DNA crystals.

The relationship between the two was far from cordial; a matter not made easier by the anti-woman atmosphere at King's, which in the 1950s still excluded women from the common rooms as a matter of course; by the failure of John Randall as the head of department to clarify the lines of authority between the two researchers; and by the assumption of Maurice Wilkins that the woman scientist, who had more technical experience, was in some automatic sense his junior.[13] Lastly, Rosalind Franklin was regarded by a number of her contemporaries as a 'difficult' woman.

While feminism has commented with some sophistication on the construction of 'difficult women', not least in the context of independent and creative women such as Franklin, there has been little discussion in this otherwise much examined story concerning the extent of anti-semitism in educational institutions during the immediate postwar period, and what this meant to any Jewish person with a sense of cultural identity. We know that Rosalind Franklin and her family had such a sense. During the war her father worked with the Jewish Board of Deputies to help refugees, and she helped too during school holidays. At Cambridge she had become friends with the metallurgist and French Jewish refugee Adrienne Weill, who was responsible for Franklin working in Paris with Mathieu, who as a communist had egalitarian attitudes to women scientists and was a committed anti-fascist.

Coming to King's must have been something of a shock, not least after Mathieu's laboratory, for not only was King's very much a male bastion, it was also a bastion of the Church of England. The origins of King's were as a Church of England college established in direct opposition to University College, which had been founded by the Utilitarians to provide university education to unitarians, free thinkers and Jews. Androcentricity and Christian ethnocentrity were thus the twin hallmarks of institutions such as King's. But Christian ethnocentricity in the forties and fifties was not simply a matter of exclusionary or even hostile speech practices; there was also institutionalized anti-semitism, not least in education. A number of direct-grant schools, particularly those in areas where there was a considerable Jewish community, had a Jewish quota to prevent the stereotypically clever Jews flooding out the Christians. In the discourse of the time, Christians as the privileged group were unmarked; marking was reserved for the Jewish others. Nor was anti-semitism limited to negative speech and institutionalized exclusion; it also took violent forms, particularly in areas where the poorer sections of the Jewish community lived. Despite the death camps and the war, anti-semitism was still a virulent force on the streets and a taken-for-granted aspect of everyday British life.

Most of these cruder forms of anti-semitism faded as the objects of racist abuse were changed. The advent of the Caribbean and Asian migration into Britain resulted in Jews being replaced for some years as the scapegoats of racist fears. Because replacement rather than resistance weakened it, the phenomenon of anti-semitism within cultural life remains under-explored, but it was there for Jewish men and women who found a number of elite educational institutions difficult places to study and to work at. To be a woman scientist and Jewish during the immediate postwar period in any laboratory where there was no counter-ideology was to carry a double burden, none the less real for not yet being fully named. It is doubtful if it is even healthy not to be 'difficult' in such a situation.

In the context of the DNA project, success required the collaboration between theoreticians, or model builders, and experimentalists, who would take the X-ray diffraction photographs to provide the empirical evidence to sustain the models. The former, Francis Crick and James Watson, were based in Cambridge and the latter, Maurice Wilkins and Rosalind Franklin, in London. The crux of what was increasingly seen within crystallography as a shabby affair was that Franklin had made the key photographs which clearly indicated the helical form, but that these had been taken, without her permission, by Wilkins to show to the two Cambridge men with whom he was collaborating. In addition a Cambridge colleague, Max Perutz,[14] who was on the Medical Research Council committee which had received Franklin's research report, also showed this privately to Crick and Watson. Although the crucial papers published in *Nature* included one by Franklin and her colleagues, she did not know just how important her photograph had been to Crick and Watson.

For this and other reasons the situation at King's became intolerable and was resolved in the usual way; the woman, not the man, moved. Franklin went to work at Birkbeck with the crystallographer Desmond Bernal. Bernal's communism, like that of Mathieu, meant that his laboratory was a more congenial environment in which to work. She stayed there until her death, with Bernal writing her obituary memoir.

Thus Franklin was already dead when the Nobel Prize in Medicine and Physiology for the DNA work was awarded to Crick, Watson and Wilkins in 1962. Despite the centrality of her contribution, none of the Laureates made a reference in his Stockholm address to her published papers, and Wilkins only spoke of her in very general terms. In Jim Watson's best seller *The Double Helix*, written several years after both Franklin's death and the award of the prize, Rosalind Franklin appears as a bad fairy in the Watson fantasy of himself as artless young man stumbling on the double helix. Despite the enthusiasm shown by a number of men scientists for the 'Jack the Giantkiller' quality of Watson's book,[15] Crick considered suing him. Wilkins would have gone along with the action, but the matter was dropped. Similarly the London Science Museum's construction of the DNA story erased Franklin's contribution until her crystallographer friends and colleagues protested and ensured that her work was acknowledged. However, it was not until Sayre questioned Wilkins directly in 1970 as to the probity of taking the photographs to Cambridge that the masculinist appropriation of the work and the erasure of the woman scientist came into full view.

The interesting and unanswerable speculation must be what would have happened if Franklin had not died, given that the prize can by tradition only be shared between three, and that it was her photograph which provided the critical empirical support to the double helix model. For Franklin herself, gender, 'race' and cancer colluded to diminish her contribution, yet the combination of personal and scientific friends speaking out in the context of a rising women's moment, has meant that her name has become a warning beacon for any who contemplate the erasure of women scientists. . . .

OVERDUE RECOGNITION AND ITS SOCIAL AND SCIENTIFIC IMPLICATIONS

The next three women Laureates were awarded prizes for work which they had done between forty and thirty-five years earlier. Zuckerman's general point that women scientists are recognized later for their work is now made almost grotesque. Very few men, other than the ethologists Konrad Lorenz and Niko Tinbergen, have received prizes in their seventies; and their late recognition was intended to flag the new field of ethology, which was seen as of great scientific interest but which the rules had hitherto precluded. In fact little was said about the new field at their prize-giving ceremony. Tinbergen used the occasion to ramble on about the Alexander method while Lorenz chose to explain/explain away his erstwhile support for the Nazis. (Actually he was rather more active than he indicated in his speech, as he was a member of the Nazi Party, a detail which the revisionist history of science omitted in his obituaries.) By contrast the three women prize-winners neither wandered into therapeutic enthusiasms nor used the occasion to explain away unfortunate political associations. They are intensely professional, each speaking technically and elegantly about her science. Only Rita Levi-Montalcini directly confronted the time gap between her science and its recognition, but not even she, on the occasion of the prize or in her subsequent biography, chose to examine the social and scientific meaning of her late recognition.

BARBARA MCCLINTOCK

The first of the three, Barbara McClintock, presents her biography in a highly detached manner, only touching the events which were 'by far the most influential in my scientific life' in an enigmatic text. None of the social or economic sensitivities which scatter both Hodgkin's and Yalow's biographies appear in this intensely impersonal account. McClintock comes into the world as a student, attending the only course in genetics open to undergraduates at Cornell. For a more intimate account of her childhood and young womanhood we have to read Evelyn Fox Keller's widely read and highly sympathetic biography, which was published just before the prize was awarded.[16]

In both her autobiography and Keller's study we are given a picture of an unusually independent and intellectually purposeful young woman; thus by the time she graduates her research direction is set. Whatever problems there were for some in the economic climate of the 1920s, her self-account gives away nothing. Unlike the earlier generation of US Nobel Laureates, McClintock was American-born. Unlike Yalow and Elion she came from a privileged background and despite the harsh times was essentially naive socially and politically, so that her research fellowship to Germany in 1933, where she encountered Nazism and Aryan genetics, was traumatic, and she fled back to Cornell.

Scientifically the biography is a story of a coherent intellectual and academic trajectory, unusual among women and only achievable where women are either without children or have such resources that others take adequate care of them. She reports that she completed her PhD and began a collaborative study locating maize genes to the appropriate one of the ten maize chromosomes. It is as if it is at this point that her history as a scientist begins, and it is the only moment where the dry impersonal prose becomes suffused with the warmth of remembered friendship: 'a sequence of events occurred of great significance to me. It began with the appearance in the fall of 1927 of George W. Beadle (a Nobel laureate) . . . to start studies for his PhD degree with Professor Rollins A. Emerson.' She then goes on to describe the close-knit group which grew up and which drew in any interested graduate students. 'For each of us this was an extraordinary period . . . Over the years members of this group have retained the warm personal relationship that our early association generated. The communal experience profoundly affected each one of us.' We are, from very early on in the autobiography, flagged that this scientist is working as an accepted group member within an elite setting.

Despite a widespread reading of Keller's biographical study as implying that in some way McClintock was not adequately recognized in science, there is little solid evidence of this, except that she did not receive the accolade of a Nobel prize until she was 81 (perhaps not insignificantly, shortly after the publication of the acclaimed Keller biography). Yet McClintock had long been an acknowledged member of the scientific elite, and she was, as Keller points out, early spoken of as a 'genius'—a compliment which is more rarely made by one scientist about another than by the media. She was the third woman to be admitted to the National Academy in 1944, when she was 42, for the work for which the Nobel committee honoured her almost forty years later in 1983. At the time of her election to the National Academy there were, despite the scale of the US scientific community, rather under 1,000 members; thus the distinction of recognition is considerable. An early recipient of the Association of American University Women's prestigious prize, she had no less than twelve honorary doctorates, from Rochester in 1947 to three in 1983, the year she won the Nobel prize. Such a biography speaks of McClintock's extraordinarily self-sufficiency as part of the small ultra-elite within science. Such people are rare—perhaps particularly so among women, for whom having sufficient privacy in which to be creative is more commonly a problem.[17] McClintock's isolation was not entirely self-chosen, for her work was not easy to communicate and her ideas on the mobility of genes within each chromosome ('transposition') commanded little support. Despite her early recognition, for many years she was relatively isolated in her Cold Spring Harbor laboratory, but—and it is an important but—never without research resources.

Keller interprets this isolation as a problem of language, of the difficulty that McClintock experienced in trying to communicate what she 'saw'. Keller argues that 'seeing' is crucial to many intensely creative scientists; the problem is that appealing to the 'seen' when there is no pre-existing understanding about what is out there to be 'seen' cannot provide empirical support. In this situation, when the geneticist Joshua Lederberg observed that 'the woman is mad or a genius', he was only articulating publicly what many geneticists more privately thought.

But while Keller lets the reader share the scientist's self-doubt at her failure to communicate her theories to her satisfaction, the outside world had the strong suspicion that she was a genius, and scientific honours continued to be bestowed on her, from a non-residential chair at Cornell in 1965 to the Kimber Genetics Medal of the National Academy in 1967 and, in 1970, the National Medal of Science. By the mid-seventies her ideas about transposition, which potentially challenge the central dogma of the fixity of the genome, began to be understood more widely and became influential in shaping the directions of new work. By this time, conventional molecular biological wisdom had already begun to question the earlier seemingly inviolable concept of the stability of the genome, not in the sense that there was a challenge to the understanding of genetic reproduction, but that the genome itself can, under a number of conditions, undergo rearrangement. There was considerable excitement about such 'jumping genes' as the flexibility they gave was seen to endow their bearer, whether the salmonella bacteria or maize, with a distinct evolutionary advantage. By transposition McClintock wished to draw attention to the general occurrence of cellular mechanisms which restructure the genome, mechanisms which are called into action by external or internal stress. DNA, far from being the stable macho molecule of the 1962 Watson–Crick prize story, becomes a structure of complex dynamic equilibrium. Such a complex dynamic structure has echoes of Laura Balbo's quilt-making metaphor to describe women's work in maintaining everyday life.[18]

A number of critics have suggested that Keller's account excessively celebrates McClintock's mysticism as if this was some undeclared dimension of femininity, or essentialist feminism, yet such criticism diminishes the very real difficulties in talking about the creative process, of understanding how an alternative vision is developed, how it is possible to 'see' something not seen before in nature. The brave attempt by Koestler with his book *The Sleepwalkers,* and the autobiographical accounts of scientists from Einstein to Richard Feynman, go some way towards discussing this process, but Keller attempts to make clearer what Dorothy Hodgkin spoke of when she thanked her colleagues for their 'eyes, brains and hands'. However, part of the charge of mysticism lies in McClintock's distinctive relationship with nature itself, for her conception constitutes a return to an earlier tradition when nature was seen as active, not passive. Vitalism, however discussed, in the context of the macho reductionist language of contemporary molecular biology, with a nature drained of all subjectivity, would be all too likely to sound like mysticism.

The detached style of McClintock's Nobel lecture makes no genuflections to the occasion, expressing neither pleasure nor gratitude; she neither notes the delay between the date of her work nor its subsequent recognition—yet this could be read as a matter of forty years. The nearest she gets to Yalow-like celebration of the certainty of her vision is when she reports offering 'my suggestion to the geneticists at Berkeley who then sent me an amused reply. My suggestion,' she says rather mildly, 'however, was not without logical support.' The lecture, essentially an overview of her work in genetics, describes the crucial experiments, almost entirely during the 1940s, showing how 'a genome may react to conditions for which it is unprepared, but to which it responds in a totally unexpected manner.' Her view of future research is that 'attention will undoubtedly be centred on the genome, and with greater appreciation of its significance as a highly sensitive organ of the cell, monitoring genomic activities and correcting common errors, sensing the unusual and unexpected events, and responding to them, often by restructuring the genome. We know nothing, however,' she concludes, 'about how the cell senses danger and initiates responses to it that are often truly remarkable.'[19] This activist conception of the cell is kin to Lovelock's Gaia, but where he seeks a popular audience, she is primarily concerned with her invisible college.[20]

McClintock's photographic portrait is of a piece with her prose. Despite the grandeur of the occasion her portrait shows her wearing the uniform of East Coast women intellectuals, a shirt collar over a woollen jersey making no concessions. She looks away from the camera as if she is really looking at something else; her lined face has a slight, detached smile.

RITA LEVI-MONTALCINI

Nothing could be more marked than the contrast with Rita Levi-Montalcini's portrait, which speaks of an agreement between photographer and subject—that this is to be an exceptional statement. And indeed she does cut an exceptional figure amongst women scientists. Dressed with silken elegance, she poses with her hand to her chin. On her wrist is a rich bracelet which acts, and has been chosen to act, as a foil to the eyes. Everything about her conveys a theatrical consciousness of her beauty and her presence. While the autobiography she writes does not begin, as did a rather earlier one, 'I was crawling out over the palace roof to rescue my kitten',[21] the world of high culture and wealth is evident in every aspect of her presentation of self and work.

She describes an intellectual dynasty of mutually admiring and affectionate people. Her father is described as a 'gifted mathematician,' her mother 'a talented painter and an exquisite human being'.[22] Her three siblings are all named and praised either for their achievements or, if these are not particularly evident, for their good taste. While she describes a domestic world governed by the father, not least in terms of secondary education, where he held strong views about the suitable subjects for girls, the larger context of the Italian university system had different and more liberal traditions of bourgeois women studying and researching from those of the Anglo-Saxon one. As a teenager Rita describes herself as isolated, directionless, uninterested in young men, and spending her time reading Selma Lagerlöf. From a very early age her construction of her own femininity excluded wifehood and motherhood: 'My experience in childhood and adolescence had convinced me that I was not cut out to be a wife. Babies did not attract me and I was altogether without the maternal sense so highly developed in small and adolescent girls.'

The death of a loved governess turned her towards medicine, and together with her cousin Eugenia she set about preparing herself for university admission. She gives a graphic account, not unlike a story from the eighteenth-century Edinburgh medical grave-snatchers Burke and Hare, of the means by which research students of the brain gained access to human material.[23] She describes travelling on a Rome bus with the corpse of a two-day old baby wrapped inadequately in newspaper. Her reflections as she sees that a small foot is sticking out are solely those of embarrassment from the construction that might be placed on the sight of a young woman carrying a dead baby. The lesson that she derives is not to carry such experimental material on public transport, but what is interesting is the confidence—not to say arrogance—that permits the retelling of this story, without any reflections on either the nature of the material, or how it had been secured.[24]

During the 1930s class privilege was only a partial protection from Italian fascism. Her increasingly tenuous place as a Jewish woman scientist in a developing fascistic context became non-viable once Mussolini's 1936 manifesto against Jewish scientists and professionals had been declared. Now the family was left with 'two alternatives . . . to emigrate to the States, or to pursue some activity which needed neither support nor connection with the outside Aryan world where we lived. My family chose this second alternative. I then decided to build a small research unit at home and installed it in my bedroom.' She then describes how the Jewish biologist Giuseppe Levi, who at university had taught both her (and also Salvador Luria and Renato Dulbecco, both Nobel Prize-winners and her lifelong friends), came to work with her as the universities gradually expelled the Jews.

As the situation became more stringent, even this existence, a scientific Garden of the Finzi Continis, could not be continued. After 1943, Italy was occupied by the German Army and the family went underground; where Italian political culture did not take anti-semitism entirely seriously, the German did. In 1945 Rita Levi-Montalcini and her family returned to Turin where she was restored to her university post. By 1947 she was involved in collaborative work with the St. Louis based Viktor Hamburger, a collaboration which lasted thirty years. During this period she held a professorship at the University of Washington from 1956 to her retirement in 1977. With the enthusiastic support of the Italian Science Research Council she established a research unit in Rome in 1962, and divided her time between the two continents. This engagement in the science of both countries may have cost her something at the US end, and certainly her biography, unlike McClintock's, lists few scientific honours, but it did ensure a strong Italian lobby for her Nobel award, and there was long and open discussion about how significant this would be for the morale of Italian science.[25] Undoubtedly *Unita*, the Italian Communist Party newspaper, long anticipated her Laureateship, referring to her as 'our Nobelist'.

The title of her Nobel lecture, 'The Nerve Growth Factor: Thirty Five Years Later', makes her scientific claim and political point rally. She then provides a historical perspective so that the audience may share the frustrations experienced by experimental embryologists of the 1940s, despite an earlier period, during the 1920s and 1930s, which had seemed to promise the early resolution of the paradoxes of development. Her work with Hamburger built from her earlier work with Levi, although she continued to suffer technical problems in resolving these immensely complex neurogenetic systems. She ushers in the next phase of the work with the subhead: 'The unexpected break: a gift from malignant tissues'. But as we read on we learn that the gift came from the imaginative experimental work of one of Hamburger's students; thus it was the created luck of science rather than the accident of fortune, but this is a scientific voice that enjoys story telling.

She explains how the development of the research work was initially blocked because the group lacked the expertise with tissue culture. This was, however, being developed in Brazil by Hertha Levi, working at the Rio de Janeiro institute directed by Carlos Chagas. In a passage which fuses images of science and femininity, Levi-Montalcini explains that she was invited by Chagas and so 'boarded a plane for Rio de Janeiro, carrying in my handbag two mice bearing transplants of mouse sarcomas'.[26]

Despite her vivid reporting that it was in Rio de Janeiro that the nerve growth factor 'revealed itself . . . in a grand and theatrical way', Levi-Montalcini and her colleagues had difficulty in convincing others. She does not report a story of results refused publication in prestige scientific journals, but infers this failure to convince from the evidence that few followed her down what she saw as an exciting path. Her problem in this respect was similar to that of McClintock during the fifties and sixties. Yet where

McClintock had a second immensely creative and communicating period in the 1970s, Levi-Montalcini's significant work was concentrated thirty-five years ago; the gap between achievement and recognition is in her case even harder to explain within the terms of the institution of the prize.

GERTRUDE ELION

The most recent woman to be honoured as a Nobel Laureate was Gertrude Elion[27] in 1988. Her parents were both first-generation US immigrants from Europe. Her father had qualified as a dentist, but was bankrupted through the stock-market crash in 1929. None the less her parents were able to help her financially within four years of the bankruptcy. She recalls a lost world of the Bronx as a good environment for childrearing, with good public schools and unrivalled opportunities for free tertiary education. She describes herself as 'a child with an insatiable thirst for knowledge and remember[s] enjoying all of [her] courses almost equally.'[28] She speculates that her affection for her grandfather, who died of cancer when she was 15, motivated her towards medical research, so that when she entered Hunter College she planned to major in science and especially chemistry. (Again, as with Yalow, the New York public educational system of the time showed its strength, demonstrating that it could be an effective substitute for the educational and cultural privilege of class.)

After college Elion had a bleak time searching for support to do graduate work or even merely to get a laboratory job. She describes a world of systematic and taken-for-granted discrimination in which progress was painfully slow. 'Jobs were scarce and the few positions that existed in laboratories were not available to women.' She describes one teaching job she had—biochemistry for nurses—which ran for three months out of the year. She then describes how a chemist offered to take her into his laboratory for no pay; she accepted for the experience. After eighteen months he was paying her 'the magnificent sum of $20 a week'. In 1933, some six years after entering undergraduate study, she was able, with the help of her parents, to enter graduate school at New York University. Having completed course work she trained as a teacher, then worked as a substitute teacher by day, researching at nights and weekends, completing her master's by 1941.

It was the outbreak of World War II with its demand for chemists by industrial laboratories which gave Elion, along with many of her generation and gender, the chance of a research job. From the inauspicious foothold of a job in a food industry laboratory she secured an assistantship with George Hitchens at the Burroughs Wellcome research laboratories. This was the first time, now almost ten years after entering Hunter, that Elion had a job where she could develop herself as a scientist. At the same time she also began a PhD at Brooklyn Polytechnic Institute, but the crunch came when she had to choose between going full time to complete the PhD, and abandoning it for her industrial research.

Elion tells us that after she had received three honorary doctorates from the Universities of George Washington, Brown and Michigan she felt that she had made the right choice. By carefully reciting this arduous story of getting into research, and of the fact that she has achieved so much without a PhD, she reminds us of just how exceptional her story is. For a man to get so far without a PhD would be surprising, for a woman it is little short of astonishing. It was the context of one of the most powerful US industrial laboratories, not academia with its passion for credentialism, which made this possible.

At Burroughs Wellcome she began that relationship to her work which enabled her to look back and characterize it as both 'my vocation and my avocation'. Although she began as an organic chemist she was never restricted to the single discipline. She became interested in microbiology and in the biological activities of the compounds she was synthesizing. Thus over the years she worked in biochemistry, pharmacology, immunology and eventually virology. In her Nobel address she sets about reporting forty years of work with no hint of complaint or criticism; instead she describes the research in which she and her colleagues have been engaged as a coherent set of scientific developments achieved over a period of time, which have consistently resulted in producing major therapeutic agents. One of these, Acyclovir, was a pioneering anti-viral for herpes, and also paved the way for other anti-virals, not least Retrovir or AZT, also produced by the Wellcome laboratories. It is a matter of some note that she describes this highly innovatory work, often developing drugs for patients with then fatal diseases, without using the language beloved of today's clinical researchers, in which they 'aggressively treat'. Elion's prose concerning her research, and one feels Elion's laboratory, goes capably on, not minimizing painful matters or glossing over clinical testing, but not glamourizing it with violent metaphor either. Her official portrait echoes this capable good sense.

Such a voice, describing the complex task of basic science directed very closely towards clinical objectives and in active collaboration with the clinical treatment of patients, is rare in the Nobel proceedings. More typically, research, even when it has a considerable pay-off for medicine, is described within the science and not hand-in-hand with its applications. It is often only when the joke is made that had the research not been carried out on such a socially significant compound, then the honour and recognition currently being enjoyed by the researcher would not have been forthcoming, that we can see the boundary line between social and scientific esteem being gently moved around. Elion is refreshing in that she ignores these delicate boundary games between social and scientific prestige systems, and talks about the nature of contemporary medical research when it is done by good scientists committed to patient care in the best industrial laboratories.

WHERE ARE THE FUTURE WOMEN PRIZE-WINNERS?

Perhaps it is not by chance that many women biomedical researchers say that it is easier to work and to be promoted in an industrial laboratory than in an academic setting. Maybe it is there that the Nobel committees should look for more potential women prize-winners, or among the observational sciences such as ethology or astronomy where numbers of women are currently eminent.[29] Can committees and procedures predominantly composed of men scientists under immense pressure to recognize other men scientists acknowledge the contribution of women unless they open their committee structures themselves to women, who are in an age of gender consciousness less likely to be gender blind? Otherwise it seems that the Nobel Prize system is unlikely to escape an even more age-linked construction of women of gold than operated in Plato's Republic. For today's Nobel committees it seems that women have to be at least 70, the age of the wise woman, the symbolic grandmother, to achieve recognition. Is there an unstated anxiety that, by recognizing women at the height of their creativity and with the social and political commitments of their generation, the committee might begin to disturb the networks of power? Perhaps women scientists in a period of feminist consciousness cannot be trusted to sustain the politics of prudential acquiescence which have become increasingly the hallmark of the scientific elite?

And in fifty years' time, when the descendants of today's feminists have access to the records of this past decade, how will the correspondence and debates of the 1980s compare with the unambiguous evidence of the double standard deployed (too late and unsuccessfully) against Marie Curie at the beginning of the century, or the manipulation of women's access to the Royal Society during the 1940s? Will they have been equally 'man'aged?

Notes

1. The award of the 1992 medicine and physiology Nobel Prize to two men biochemists in their seventies, E. Krebs and M. Fischer, caused considerable surprise and concern for just this reason.
2. Harriet Zuckerman's pioneering study covered five women Laureates. She notes that the interval between the work and its recognition is longer for women than men, yet those women Nobelists whose awards followed her study were older and the gap greater. Her study draws attention to the achievements of Jewish scientists who are strongly represented among the US Nobel Laureates. Both Zuckerman and her mentor Robert K. Merton, the pioneering sociologist of science, are Jewish and sensitive to the history of institutionalized anti-semitism in US academic life. Like many of his generation, Merton had found it necessary to change his name to one sounding more acceptably Anglo. Zuckerman, *Scientific Elite.*
3. Levi-Montalcini, *Le Prix Nobel,* 1986, p. 276 (hereafter as *LPN* plus date).
4. Zuckerman, *Scientific Elite,* p. 82.
5. For a sustained examination, see H. Rose and Rose, 'The Incorporation of Science', in H. Rose and Rose (eds), *Political Economy of Science.*
6. However, the papers of individuals not infrequently have fifty-year restrictions placed on them.
7. The biographies range from popular accounts, such as Opfell, *The Lady Laureates;* Phillips, *The Scientific Lady,* to scientific and biographical accounts written by feminist scientists and historians as part of a project to write women back into the 'his'tory of science, to bibliographic guides: Kohlstedt, 'In from the Periphery', *Signs,* 4 (1 1978); Schiebinger, 'The History and Philosophy of Women in Science', *Signs,* 12 (2 1987); Kass-Simon and Farnes (eds), *Women of Science,* Alic, *Hypatia's Heritage;* Amir-Am and Outram (eds), *Uneasy Careers and Intimate Lives;* Schiebinger *The Mind Has No Sex;* Searing (ed.), *The History of Women in Science, Technology and Medicine;* Ogilvie, *Women in Science;* Herzenberg, *Women Scientists from Antiquity to the Present;* Siegel and Finley, *Women in the Scientific Search.*
8. His stuffed horse and bloody clothes are displayed in the historical museum in Stockholm.
9. Senta Troemel-Ploetz draws attention to a little-known biography by Desamka Trbuhovic Gjuric, herself a mathematician acquainted with the Swiss milieu where the Einsteins lived and worked. This has been republished, but rather heavily edited, in German. 'Mileva Einstein Marić: The Woman Who Did Einstein's Mathematics', *W's Stud. Int. Forum,* 13 (5 1990).
10. Ibid., p. 418.
11. Walker, 'Did Einstein Espouse His Spouse's Ideas?' *Physics Today,* February (1980). However, more disturbingly, John Hackel, editor of *The Collected Papers of Albert Einstein,* Vols I and II, ignores this evidence. Despite my feeling that historians of science have recently been more willing to accept the contribution of women scientists, it seems that in the case of Einstein the myth of the unaided male genius must be preserved.
12. Aaron Klug, a crystallographer, a Nobel Laureate, and also Jewish, consistently wrote Franklin's contribution back into the scientific record.
13. Franklin was not, however, the only gifted woman in the Randall laboratory, a fact used by Maurice Wilkins to suggest that the laboratory was not hostile to women.
14. Perutz was complex. Though this action was no help to Franklin, he also lobbied the influential Swede Gunner Haag for Dorothy Hodgkin as a candidate for the Nobel Prize. Personal communication, C. Haag.
15. Biologist Richard Lewontin entertainingly deconstructs 'Honest Jim Watson's Big Thriller about DNA', in Stent (ed.), *James D. Watson.*
16. Keller, *A Feeling for the Organism.*

17. From Florence Nightingale to Virginia Woolf the plea for privacy is constant. Even today few women have a space within a family home which is exclusively theirs.
18. Balbo, 'Crazy Quilts', in Sassoon (ed.), *Women and the State.*
19. Barbara McClintock, *LPHN,* 1983, p. 192.
20. Her invisible college celebrated her achievements in the last year of her life. Fedora and Botstein (eds), *The Dynamic Genome.*
21. Levi-Montalcini in Knudsin (ed.), *Successful Women in Sciences.*
22. Levi-Montalcini, *LPN,* 1986, p. 277.
23. Levi-Montalcini, *In Praise of Imperfection.*
24. The culture of biomedical research in Italy has long been relatively unregulated by ethical debate. Even today 'smart' drugs are tested on Alzheimer patients by pharmacologists with industrial connections without reference to ethical committees or controls. Personal communication, Steven Rose.
25. Because the Italian highly educated elite is relatively small, women's participation in science has been acceptable as a cultural activity for upper-class women. Thus campaigning for a woman scientist created fewer problems than in other countries, although it unquestionably required much patience.
26. Levi-Montalcini, *LPN,* 1986, p. 283.
27. This is the only Nobel Laureate, caught perhaps by constructions of femininity, who does not give a birthdate.
28. Gertrude Elion is the least well documented of the women Nobel Prize-winners. As an industrial scientist she has a less public profile; for example she has published no books, unlike all the other women Laureates. The *LPN* 1988 publication is in this case particularly important.
29. There is a problem about the 'capturing' of an institution like the Nobel Prize by a discipline or even by a school, which then acts as a self-recruiting oligarchy. This latter is displayed to absurdity in the case of the Nobel Prize for Economics and Chicago Economics.

References

Alic, Margaret. *Hypatia's Heritage: A History of Women in Science from Antiquity through the Nineteenth Century.* Boston: Beacon Press, 1986.

Amir-Am, Pnina and Dorinda Outram, eds. *Uneasy Careers and Intimate Lives: Women in Science 1789–1989.* New Brunswick: Rutgers University Press, 1987.

Balbo, Laura. 'Crazy Quilts: Women's Perspectives on the Welfare State Crisis.' In *Women and the State,* ed. Ann Showstack Sassoon. London: Hutchinson, 1987.

Fedora, Nina and David Botstein, eds. *The Dynamic Genome: Barbara McClintock's Achievements in the Century of Genetics.* Cold Spring Harbor: Cold Spring Harbor Press, 1982.

Hackel, John, ed. *The Collected Papers of Albert Einstein.* Vols. I and II. Princeton, NJ: Princeton University Press, 1987, 1989.

Herzenberg, Caroline. *Women Scientists from Antiquity to the Present: An International Reference History and Biographical Directory of Some Notable Women Scientists from Ancient to Modern Times.* West Cornwall: Locust Hill Press, 1986.

Kass-Simon, G. and Patricia Farnes, eds, *Women of Science: Righting the Record.* Bloomington: Indiana University Press, 1990.

Keller, Evelyn Fox. *A Feeling for the Organism: The Life and Work of Barbara McClintock.* San Francisco: Freeman, 1983.

Kohlstedt, Sally. 'In from the Periphery': American Women in Science 1830–1880." *Signs: Journal of Woman in Culture and Society* 4 (1 1978): 81–96.

Levi-Montalcini, Rita. *In Praise of Imperfection: My Life and Work.* New York: Basic Books, 1988.

Levi-Montalcini, Rita. In *Successful Women in the Sciences,* ed. Ruth Kudsin. New York: New York Academy of Sciences, 1973.

Levi-Montalcini, Rita. *Le Prix Nobel.* Stockholm: Nobel Foundation, 1986.

Lewontin, Richard. 'Honest Jim Watson's Big Thriller about DNA.' In *James D. Watson: The Double Helix,* ed. Gunther Stent. London: Weidenfeld and Nicolson, 1981.

Ogilvie, Marilyn Bailey. *Women in Science: Antiquity through the Nineteenth Century: A Biographical Dictionary with Annotated Bibliography.* Cambridge, MA.: 1986.

Opfell, Olga. *The Lady Laureates: Women Who Have Won the Nobel Prize.* Metuchen, NJ: Scarecrow Press, 1986.

Phillips, Patricia. *The Scientific Lady: A Social History of Women's Scientific Interests 1580–1981.* London: St Martin's Press, 1990.

Rose, Hilary and Steven Rose, eds. *The Political Economy of Science.* London: Macmillan, 1976.

Schiebinger, Londa. *The Mind Has No Sex: Women in the Origins of Modern Science.* Cambridge, MA: Harvard University Press, 1989.

Schiebinger, Londa. 'The History and Philosophy of Women in Science: A Review Essay.' *Signs: Journal of Women in Culture and Society* 12 (2 1987): 305–32.

Searing, Susan, ed. *The History of Women in Science, Technology and Medicine: A Bibliographic Guide to the Disciplines and Professions.* Madison: University of Wisconsin Women's Studies Library, 1987.

Siegel, Patricia and Kay Thomas Finley. *Women in the Scientific Search: An American Bio-bibliography 1724–1979.* Metuchen, NJ: Scarecrow Press, 1985.

Troemel-Ploetz, Senta. 'Mileva Einstein Maríc: The Woman Who Did Einstein's Mathematics.' *Women's Studies International Forum* 13 (5 1990): 415–32.

Walker, Harris. 'Did Einstein Espouse His Spouse's Ideas?' *Physics Today* (February 1989): 9–10.

Zuckerman, Harriet. *The Scientific Elite: Nobel Laureates in the United States.* New York: Free Press, 1977.

THE CAREERS OF MEN AND WOMEN SCIENTISTS

Gender Differences in Career Attainments

Harriet Zuckerman

More than sixty years after its founding, the National Academy of Sciences elected its first women member: Florence Sabin, an anatomist and embryologist. But then Sabin's entire career was a succession of "firsts." In 1902 she was the first woman appointed to the faculty of the Johns Hopkins Medical School, then probably the most distinguished medical school in the United States. She was also the first woman full professor there (1917), the first woman elected president of the American Association of Anatomists (1924), and, upon leaving the Hopkins in 1925, the first woman to be made a full member of the Rockefeller Institute of Medical Research (now the Rockefeller University) (Breiger 1980; Rossiter 1982).

This array of posts makes it clear that Sabin became an insider and member of the scientific establishment. She was also an outsider and social pioneer, being not just the first, but often the only woman to be included in the circles in which she moved.[1] Sabin was atypical, if not unique, among women scientists of the time in the extent to which her work was recognized and rewarded by the scientific community. By contrast, the historical record shows that many accomplished women were either ignored or actively discouraged. Those honors which came to them at all came very late (Rossiter 1982). . . . men. Older cohorts of women scientists' differ from men in rank, salary, research performance, and reputation, with these differences being almost always in the direction of comparative disadvantage for women. However, there are also signs of growing parity in career attainments, particularly among younger scientists. It is not yet clear whether this trend will ultimately reduce disparities in men's and women's attainments as they grow older.

SOME EXPLANATIONS PROPOSED FOR GENDER DIFFERENCES IN CAREER ATTAINMENTS

There is little disagreement that women scientists' career attainments, on average, do not equal those of men. There is, however, much disagreement about the explanations for gender inequalities. In general, these fall into four classes and emphasize:

- Gender differences in scientific ability
- Gender differences arising from *social selection,* based on
  - a) gender discrimination
  - b) gender differences in role performance and the allocation of resources and rewards
- Gender differences arising from *self-selection,* including
  - a) marriage and motherhood and their consequences
  - b) gender differences in career commitment
- Outcomes of accumulation of advantage and disadvantage[2]

How well does the available evidence square with each of these explanations? Not well. The evidence on all is ambiguous, not because the theories are unclear but because the data are complex, often vexingly incoherent, and frequently partial.

Gender Differences in Scientific Ability

There is no support, as I noted earlier, for the view that the different career attainments of men and women scientists result from gender differences in ability or competence. To the extent that these can be measured by intelligence tests or academic performance, abilities of women scientists equal or surpass those of men. However, there is evidence that girls do less well than boys in mathematics (see Kahle and Matyas 1987) and also that girls turn up in disproportionately small numbers among youngsters with high scores on tests of mathematical ability. Benbow and Stanley (1980; 1983) conclude that superior male mathematical ability, "an expression of both endogenous and exogenous variables," accounts for this finding. However, there is also enough evidence for marked gender differences in socialization and exposure to mathematics to raise serious questions about this and to warrant further examination of these effects on variability in achievement scores of boys and girls. For our purposes, these conjectures are not entirely pertinent. Men and women who do science are a highly selected sample of all adult men and women. Data on youngsters, even highly selected ones, are not helpful in understanding field and specialty choice much less differences in career attainments. Yet women do, more often than men, select fields and specialties of science which are comparatively less demanding mathematically, but there is no systematic evidence indicating why this is so.

Processes of Social Selection

Explanations of gender differences in career attainments that emphasize gender discrimination, on the one hand, and women's poorer research performance, on the other, both rest on notions of social selection. Social selection processes involve decision making about individuals (here about their careers) over which they have no control. They contrast with processes of self-selection, in which decisions are controlled by individuals and are not, except perhaps indirectly, attributable to socially structured arrangements for selection.

Gender discrimination occurs when the unequal treatment of men and women is based on the functionally irrelevant criterion of gender. Discrimination can affect men's and women's career attainments when their opportunities for role performance are unequal, when their role performance is judged according to different standards, and when they are differently rewarded for the same quality of role performance. Gender discrimination, as with social discrimination generally, treats some social status "as relevant when intrinsically it is functionally irrelevant" (Merton 1972: 20). Proponents of the view that gender discrimination best explains the unequal career attainments of men and women point to instances of women having poorer facilities and resources for research, to their being judged by harsher standards, and to their being promoted and paid less than comparable men.

It is no easy matter, however, to assess the extent of gender discrimination and how it affects scientists' careers. Discrimination is often subtle and therefore difficult to identify, much less measure. It can be entangled with other forms of prejudice (based on age, for example), and because it appears throughout the career, a full accounting of its effects is hard to make. As a consequence, researchers have come to rely on indirect rather than direct measures of discrimination. They have assumed that differences in the career attainments of men and women which remain after differences has its problems, not least that it requires that appropriate evidence be available on all functionally relevant criteria which could account for gender differences in career attainment. (On "residualism" in its various guises in the law and in social science research, see Cole 1979: 36ff.)

When this mode of analysis is used, the evidence shows that gender discrimination affects promotions, tenure, and salary allocation among academic men and women with similar records of research performance. It also shows that discrimination is receding, especially for younger women. However, available data are limited only to position and to salary and do not register gender discrimination in informal social interaction or its subjective effects on women (see, for example, Briscoe 1984; Keller 1977).

There is also evidence suggesting gender discrimination may operate in different ways for different groups of women. Women who make important contributions to science may fare less well relative to comparable men than do the journeywomen of science relative to their performance peers. Cole's (1979: 120) studies show that women who have done important scientific work are less apt to be considered major contributors to their fields than are comparable men. Conversely, it has also been suggested that it is the journeywomen of science who fare poorly compared to men in the absence of clear-cut evidence of their role performance (Zuckerman and Cole 1974). Thus, the incidence and dynamics of gender discrimination in science have neither been satisfactorily described nor fully explained.

Discrimination can affect the career attainments of men and women, and it can also produce gender differences in the processes by which such attainments are reached. Reskin (1978) and Reskin and Hargens (1979) suggest that the connections between role performance and rewards for women are less consistent than those which apply in men's careers; women are more often rewarded for poor performance than men and less often for good performance. And, as noted, Cole (1979) observes that the processes of reputation building differ for men and women. If so, then women's incentives for high-level role performance are less clear than men's, and they may, as a result, perform less well.

Social selection, as I have indicated, also includes differential evaluation of men and women's role performance on functionally relevant criteria and differential treatment on this basis. Some believe that women are judged fairly and that gender differences in career attainments result from women performing less well than men. As I have repeatedly noted, we do not know how men and women do in their various roles as teachers, administrators, managers, and citizens of the scientific community. We do know that, on average, women publish less and are cited less than men. To the extent that these actually gauge research performance, then women's poorer performance is related to their lower career attainments, especially in those institutions which put a premium on publication. However, as we have seen, women's research performance does not explain all such differences; indeed, some remain after research performance and other relevant variables are taken into account. Moreover, the conclusion that women perform less well than men does not take into account unequal opportunities to do research. The sources of differential role performance may well reside in structured inequalities of opportunity. How much, we do not know.

Gender Differences as Outcomes of Self-Selection

Career attainments are of course shaped by decisions individuals make for themselves, by self-selection as well as by social selection. Women's decisions to marry and to have children, to take on their distinctive domestic and parental roles, are said to interfere with their scientific work and to lead to career decisions that benefit their families but damage their careers. The evidence here is mixed:

- Women scientists and engineers are more often employed part time, less often looking for work, and out of work longer than men. Women attribute these work patterns to their family obligations more often than men. However, actual family obligations (having young children) are a poor predictor of unemployment among women scientists and engineers.[3]

- Married and single women academics are less mobile geographically than men (Marwell, Rosenfeld and Spilerman 1979), and married women say that decisions to move are affected by their family obligations (Coggeshall 1981). Since promotion and pay increases are often tied to a change in employment, women's limited geographic mobility may, in part, account for gender differences in career attainments.
- Marriage and motherhood are widely believed to account for women scientists' lower rates of publication (Lester 1974: 42). However, on balance, the evidence suggests that this is not so. Married women Ph.D.'s in the sciences publish as much as single women, and having successive children is not associated with reduced rates of publication (see Astin and Bayer 1979; Ferber and Huber 1979; Helmreich, Spence *et al.* 1980; Wanner, Lewis and Gregorio 1981; Simon, Clark and Tifft 1966; Centra 1974; Cole 1979; Cole and Zuckerman 1987; Luukkonen-Gronow & Stolte-Heiskanen 1983; Toren 1989; Kyvik 1990; Joas 1990 but also see Hargens, McCann and Reskin 1978 for contradictory evidence).
- Moreover, marriage and parenthood are not uniformly associated with lower rank and salary among women. In some fields and classes of institutions, the correlations are positive and in others negative. Overall, however, they are not large (Ahern and Scott 1981, chap. 6). This is so in spite of the widespread belief that married women have poorer career opportunities than single women.

In short, women's domestic obligations are not *the* simple explanation of gender differences in career attainments since, in many respects, married women and women with children fare as well or better than single and childless women.

Gender Differences in Career Commitment

There are little or no systematic data on the career commitment of men and women scientists and engineers, especially those holding doctoral degrees. That is, there are no data bearing on whether women care less, more, or the same as men about rank, salary, responsibility, and recognition. There is indirect evidence that women are more apt than men to prefer teaching over research (or at least they did two decades ago [Bayer 1973]) and for living in urban as against less populous areas (Marwell, Rosenfeld and Spilerman 1979). But the connections between such career-related preferences and career commitment are not established nor are the ways these preferences are shaped by opportunities, perceived and real. This hypothesis lacks any support, pro or con.

Accumulation of Advantage and Disadvantage

The notion of the accumulation of advantage and disadvantage has been repeatedly used in studies of stratification in science (see Zuckerman 1989). It is plainly pertinent to the disparity observed in the attainments of men and women scientists. Accumulation of advantage occurs in science when certain groups receive greater opportunities to enlarge their contributions to knowledge and then are rewarded in accord with those contributions. Recipients are thereby enriched at an accelerating rate, and, conversely, nonrecipients become relatively impoverished (see Merton [1942] 1973; Zuckerman 1977: 59–60, 1989). The accumulation of advantage helps to account for the observed cross-sectional differences between men and women scientists in research performance, rewards, and recognition. It can also account for observed intra-gender variation (not all women are equally disadvantaged, nor are all men equally advantaged), and (not least) for the growing divergence in performance and attainments of men and women scientists as they grow older. It is also consistent with, or more precisely does not exclude, the third pattern we observed of growing parity in attainments of men and women, especially among the young.

To the extent that processes of accumulation of advantage and disadvantage are supplemented by self-selection, by women making decisions which they believe benefit their families but have the effect of damaging their careers, disparities between their attainments and those of men will be amplified and accentuated. The ideas of accumulation of advantage and disadvantage have been further elaborated and examined empirically not just in science but in a variety of other occupations (Zuckerman 1989: 169). But before we can conclude that accumulation of advantage and disadvantage and related processes of self-selection really do explain why the career attainments of men and women differ, more detailed data will be needed on how advantage and disadvantage actually accumulate.

A LIMITED RESEARCH AGENDA: DOMAINS OF SPECIFIED IGNORANCE[4]

Here is what we need to know, and why:

1. On the research performance of men and women scientists: We need to know why women publish less than men and the extent to which this results from discrimination, differential access to the means of scientific production, and women's preferences or choices. More specifically, we need to know the relative access men and women have to such important research resources as funds, space, time, appropriate co-workers, and instrumentation. How do women's organizational ranks and institutional affiliations, in combination, affect their resources for research and their research performance over the course of their careers? We also need to learn whether there are significant differences in the research strategies and practices of men and women scientists. Are there greater differences between men and women in these respects than among them? If so, do they affect how much research is done and its significance?
2. On disparities in career attainments of men and women: Why do these disparities grow as men and women get older? Does the accumulation of advantage explain this pattern fully, or is there evidence also for other explanations such as women's growing discouragement and reduced aspirations? (See Zuckerman and Cole [1975] on the "Triple Penalty" against women, which links discrimination to reduced aspirations.) Longitudinal studies on multiple age cohorts are needed to answer these questions.[5] Why do women fare better in certain sciences and less well in others? Is it the case, as Rossiter (1978) suggests, that women do better in new and growing fields? Are the "cultures" of some fields less consistent with feminine values than others, as Keller (1985) and Traweek (1984) imply?
3. On gender discrimination: its incidence, forms, and consequences: To what extent is discrimination, conditional, that is, targeted, or is it practiced against all women, regardless of their status characteristics? How does discrimination in its less blatant forms affect women's informal relations with their colleagues and their networks of associations? Rose (1985) observes that the networks of young men and women scientists differ not only in composition but also in how useful they are believed to be. More research attention needs to be paid to the consequences of informal associations for scientists' careers. And finally, how does the experience of gender discrimination

affect women's motivation and career commitment? Do men have equivalent experiences not associated with gender that have similar effects?

4. On changing labor markets: In what measure are the career attainments of men and women scientists and engineers determined by changing labor market conditions? Is the move toward gender parity likely to continue, or will it wane if jobs become scarce?
5. On the career consequences of marriage and parenthood: To what extent is women's limited geographic mobility (perceived and real) related to their poorer attainments? How do the complex arrangements dual career couples make affect their attainments? This is of no small moment given the fact that a majority of women scientists who are married are married to men scientists.
6. On commitment to careers: So little is known about the career commitment of men and women scientists (and other professionals) that this is a thoroughly uncharted area. It would indeed be useful to know whether men and women differ or are the same with respect to career aspirations, concern with promotion, income, and fame. Believing that they do, some attribute gender differences in career attainments to these attitudinal differences. Others contend that such differences are negligible and that structural barriers faced by women account for differences in career attainments. In either event, this domain of specified ignorance about attitudes requires further examination and needs to be linked to evidence on the behavior of men and women scientists.

So much for the future research agenda. Based on what is now known, how much have women scientists' careers changed since Florence Sabin's time? They have changed considerably, but change has been slow and uneven. Sabin's career, then a succession of "firsts," is now less atypical. It would have been inconceivable in 1925 that women scientists would be hired as faculty members by universities at about the rate they were getting Ph.D.s, and it would have been thought highly unlikely that women would be promoted into senior posts in all classes of universities at the rate they have. Still, their career attainments continue, on average, to be more modest than those of men in all sectors—in academia, industry, and government—and the gap in attainments grows as men and women age. Moreover, while some distinguished women scientists and engineers have become insiders and members of the scientific establishment, those who have often feel themselves to be outsiders and on the margin. It is not clear at this juncture whether parity will be achieved in the careers of men and women scientists and engineers and, if so, when.

Notes

1. On insiders and outsiders, see Merton 1972; on social pioneers, see Zuckerman 1987.
2. See Cole and Singer, Chapter 13 in Zuckerman et al. 1991, on the theory of limited differences, which brings together processes of self-selection, social selection, and cumulative advantage and disadvantage to help explain the "productivity puzzle."
3. Human capital economists emphasize that women's lower educational attainments, intermittent work histories, and part-time employment account in large measure for gender differences in attainments in the work force at large. Indeed, they may account, in part, for the gross cross-sectional differences observed here. They cannot be the whole explanation, however, since gender differences in career attainments appear in groups with the same human capital investments.
4. On the importance of specified ignorance in science and scholarship, see Merton 1987.
5. There is reason to believe that gender disparities in career attainments of lawyers and managers also grow as they age (Epstein 1987 [private communication]; Gallese 1985; White 1967). Comparative studies of other occupations are needed to establish the generality of this pattern.

References

Ahern, Nancy C. and Elizabeth L. Scott, Committee on the Education and Employment of Women in Science and Engineering. 1981. *Career Outcomes in a Matched Sample of Men and Women Ph.D.s: An Analytical Report.* Washington, D.C.: National Research Council, National Academy of Sciences.

Allison, Paul D. and John A. Stewart. 1974. "Productivity Differences among Scientists: Evidence for Accumulative Advantage." *American Sociological Review* 39: 596–606.

Astin, Helen S. 1969. *The Woman Doctorate in America.* New York: Russell Sage Foundation.

Astin, Helen S. and Alan E. Bayer. 1979. "Pervasive Sex Differences in the Academic Reward System: Scholarship, Marriage, and What Else?" In D. R. Lewis and W. E. Becker, eds., *Academic Rewards in Higher Education,* pp. 211–229. Cambridge, Mass.: Ballinger.

Bakanic, Von, Clark McPhail and Rita J. Simon. 1987. "The Manuscript Review and Decision-Making Process." *American Sociological Review* 52: 631–642.

Bayer, Alan E. 1973. "Teaching Faculty in Academe." *A.C.E. Research Reports* 8, no. 2.

Bayer, Alan E. and Helen S. Astin. 1975. "Sex Differentials in the Academic Reward System." *Science* 188: 796–802.

Bayer, Alan E. and John Folger. 1966. "Some Correlates of a Citation Measure of Productivity in Science." *Sociology of Education* 39: 381–390.

Benbow, C. P. and J. C. Stanley. 1980. "Sex Differences in Mathematical Ability: Factor or Artifact?" *Science* 212: 1262–1264.

———. 1983. "Sex Differences in Mathematical Ability: More Facts." *Science* 222: 1029–1031.

Breiger, G. H. 1980. "Florence Rena Sabin." In B. Sicherman, C. H. Green, I. Kantrov and H. Walker, eds., *Notable American Women: The Modern Period,* pp. 614–617. Cambridge: Belknap Press of Harvard University Press.

Briscoe, Anne M. 1984. "Scientific Sexism: The World of Chemistry." In V. B. Haas and C. C. Perrucci, eds., *Women in Scientific and Engineering Professions,* pp. 147–159. Ann Arbor: University of Michigan Press.

CEEWISE (Committee on the Education and Employment of Women in Science and Engineering). 1979. *Climbing the Academic Ladder; Doctoral Women Scientists in Academe.* Washington, D.C.: National Research Council, National Academy of Sciences.

———. 1980. *Women Scientists in Industry and Government: How Much Progress in the 1970s?* Washington, D.C.: National Research Council, National Academy of Sciences.

———. 1983. *Climbing the Ladder: An Update of the Status of Doctoral Women Scientists and Engineers.* Washington, D.C.: National Research Council, National Academy of Sciences.

Centra, John A. with Nancy M. Kuykendall. 1974. *Women, Men and the Doctorate.* Princeton, N.J.: Educational Testing Service.

Clark, S. M. and M. Corcoran. 1986. "Perspectives on the Professional Socialization of Women Faculty: A Case of Accumulative Disadvantage?" *Journal of Higher Education* 57: 20–43.

Coggeshall, Porter E. 1981. *Postdoctoral Appointments and Disappointments.* Washington, D.C.: National Academy Press.

Cole, Jonathan R. 1979. *Fair Science: Women in the Scientific Community.* New York: Free Press.

Cole, Jonathan R. and Stephen Cole. 1973. *Social Stratification in Science.* Chicago: University of Chicago Press.

Cole, Jonathan R. and Harriet Zuckerman. 1984. "The Productivity Puzzle: Persistence and Change in Patterns of Publication on Men and Women Scientists." In P. Maehr and M. W. Steinkamp, eds., *Advances in Motivation and Achievement,* pp. 217–256. Greenwich, Conn.: JAI Press.

———. 1987. "Marriage and Motherhood and Research Performance in Science." *Scientific American* 256(2): 119–125.

Cole, Stephen. 1970. "Professional Standing and the Reception of Scientific Discoveries." *American Sociological Review* 76: 286–306.

Douglass, Carl D. and John C. James. 1973. "Support of New Principal Investigators by N.I.H.: 1966–1972." *Science* 181: 241–244.

Edge, D. 1979. "Quantitative Measures of Communication in Science: A Critical Review." *History of Science* 17: 102–134.

Ferber, M. 1986. "Citations: Are They an Objective Measure of Work of Women and Men?" *Signs* 11: 381–389.

Ferber, M. and J. Huber. 1979. "Husbands, Wives, and Careers." *Journal of Marriage and the Family* 41: 315–325.

Fox, Mary Frank. 1985. "Location, Sex-Typing, and Salary Among Academics." *Work and Occupations* 12: 186–205.

Gallese, L. R., 1985. *Women Like Us: What Is Happening to the Women of the Harvard Business School Class of '75—The Women Who Had the First Chance To Make It To the Top.* New York: Morrow.

Garfield, Eugene. 1979. "Is Citation Analysis a Legitimate Evaluation Tool?" *Scientometrics* 1: 359–375.

———. 1982. "The 1,000 Most-Cited Contemporary Authors. Part 2A. Details on Authors in the Physical and Chemical Sciences and Some Comments about Nobels and Academy Memberships." *Current Contents* (March 1): 5–13.

Gaston, J. 1978. *The Reward System in British and American Science.* New York: Wiley.

Hargens, Lowell, James McCann and Barbara Reskin. 1978. "Productivity and Reproductivity: Marital Fertility and Professional Achievement Among Research Scientists." *Social Forces* 52: 129–146.

Harmon, L. R. 1978. *A Century of Doctorates: Data Analyses of Growth and Change.* Washington, D.C.: National Academy of Sciences.

Helmreich, R. L. and J. T. Spence. 1982. "Gender Differences in Productivity and Impact." *American Psychologist* 37: 1142.

Helmreich, R. L., J. T. Spence, W. E. Beane, G. W. Lucker and K. A. Matthews. 1980. "Making It in Academic Psychology: Demographic and Personality Correlates of Attainment." *Journal of Personality and Social Psychology* 39: 896–908.

Joas, Hans. 1990. "Das Deutsche Universitätssystem und die Karrieremöglichkeiten junger Wissenschaftler." In H. P. Hofschneider and K. U. Mayer, eds., *Generational Dynamics and Innovation in Science,* pp. 102–113. Munich: Wissenschaftlichen Rat der Max-Planck-Gesellschaft.

Kahle, Jane Butler and Marsha L. Matyas. 1987. "Equitable Science and Mathematics Education: A Discrepancy Model." In Linda S. Dix, ed., *Women: Their Underrepresentation and Career Differentials in Science and Engineering,* pp. 5–41. Washington, D.C.: National Academy Press.

Keller, Evelyn Fox. 1977. "The Anomaly of a Woman in Physics." In S. Ruddick and P. Daniels, eds., *Working It Out,* pp. 77–91. New York: Pantheon Books.

———. 1985. *Reflections on Gender in Science.* New Haven: Yale University Press.

Kyvik, Svein. 1990. "Motherhood and Scientific Productivity." *Social Studies of Science* 20: 149–60.

LeBold, William K., K. W. Linden, C. M. Jagacinski and K. D. Shell. 1983. *National Engineering Career Development Study: Engineers' Profiles of the Eighties.* West Lafayette, Ind.: Purdue University.

Lefkowitz, Mary R. 1979. "Education for Women in a Man's World." *The Chronicle of Higher Education* (August 6): 56.

Lester, Richard A. 1974. *Antibias Regulation of Universities; Faculty Problems and Their Solutions.* New York: McGraw-Hill.

Lewis, G. L. 1986. "Career Interruptions and Gender Differences in Salaries of Scientists and Engineers." Working paper prepared for the Office of Science and Engineering Personnel, National Research Council, National Academy of Sciences, Washington, D.C.

Long, J. Scott. 1978. "Productivity and Academic Position in the Scientific Career." *American Sociological Review* 43: 889–908.

———. 1987. "Problems and Prospects for Research on Sex Differences in the Scientific Career." In Linda S. Dix, ed., *Women: Their Underrepresentation and Career Differentials in Science and Engineering,* pp. 163–169. Washington, D.C.: National Academy Press.

Long, J. Scott, P. D. Allison and R. McGinnis. 1979. "Entrance Into the Academic Career." *American Sociological Review* 44: 816–830.

Long, J. Scott and R. McGinnis. 1981. "Organizational Context and Scientific Productivity." *American Sociological Review* 46: 422–442.

Luukkonen-Gronow, Terttu and Veronica Stolte-Heiskanen. 1983. "Myths and Realities of Role Incompatibility of Women Scientists." *Acta Sociologica* 26: 267–280.

Marwell, Gerald, Rachel Rosenfeld and Seymour Spilerman. 1979. "Geographic Constraints on Women's Careers in Academia." *Science* 205: 1225–1231.
Merton, Robert K. 1957. "Priorities in Scientific Discovery: A Chapter in the Sociology of Science." *American Sociological Review* 22: 635–659.
———. 1968. "The Matthew Effect in Science." *Science* 159: 156–163.
———. 1972. "The Perspectives of Insiders and Outsiders." *American Journal of Sociology* 77: 47.
———. [1942] 1973. "The Normative Structure of Science." In *The Sociology of Science,* pp. 267–278. Chicago: University of Chicago Press.
———. 1987. "Three Fragments from a Sociologist's Notebooks: Establishing the Phenomenon, Specified Ignorance, and Strategic Research Materials (SRMs)." *Annual Review of Sociology* 13: 1–28.
Mittermeir, R. and K. D. Knorr. 1979. "Scientific Productivity and Accumulative Advantage: Thesis Reassessed in the Light of International Data." *R&D Management* 9: 235–239.
National Institutes of Health, Special Programs Office, Office of Extramural Research and Training. 1981. *Women in Biomedical Research.* Publication No. 81–429. Washington, D.C.: NIH.
National Research Council, Commission on Human Resources. 1980. *Summary Report: 1979 Doctorate Recipients from United States Universities.* Washington, D.C.: National Academy Sciences.
National Science Board, National Science Foundation. 1977. *Science Indicators 1976.* NSB 77-1. Washington, D.C.: Government Printing Office.
———. 1982. *Science Indicators 1982.* NSB 83-1. Washington, D.C.: Government Printing Office.
———. 1985. *Science Indicators: The 1985 Report.* NSB 85–1. Washington, D.C.: Government Printing Office.
National Science Foundation. 1986. *Women and Minorities in Science and Engineering.* Washington D.C.: NSF.
Office of Economic Cooperation and Development (OECD). 1984. *Educational Trends in the 1970s: A Quantitative Analysis.* Paris: United Nations.
Perrucci, Carolyn Cummings. 1970. "Minority Status and the Pursuit of Professional Careers: Women in Science and Engineering." *Social Forces* 49: 245–259.
Price, Derek J. de S. 1976. "A General Theory of Bibliometric and Other Cumulative Advant Processes." *Journal of the American Society for Information Science* 27: 292–306.
Reskin, Barbara F. 1976. "Sex Differences in Status Attainment in Science: The Case of Postdoctoral Fellowships." *American Sociological Review* 41: 597–612.
———. 1977. "Scientific Productivity and the Reward System of Science." *American Sociological Review* 42: 491–504.
———. 1978. "Scientific Productivity, Sex and Location in the Institution of Science." *American Journal of Sociology* 83: 1235–1243.
Reskin, Barbara F. and Lowell L. Hargens. 1979. "Scientific Advancement of Male and Female Chemists." In R. Alvarez and K. Lutterman and associates, eds., *Discrimination in Organizations,* pp. 100–122. San Francisco: Jossey-Bass.
Rose, S. M. 1985. "Professional Networks of Junior Faculty in Psychology." *Psychology of Women Quarterly* 9: 533–547.
Rossiter, Margaret. 1978. "Sexual Segregation in the Sciences: Some Data and a Model." *Signs* 4: 146–151.
———. 1982. *Women Scientists in America: Struggles and Strategies to 1940.* Baltimore: Johns Hopkins University Press.
Russo, N. F. and A. N. O'Connell. 1980. "Models from Our Past—Psychology's Foremothers." *Psychology of Women Quarterly* 5: 11–54.
Sigelman, L. and F. P. Scioli, Jr. 1986. "Retreading Familiar Terrain—Bias, Peer Review and the NSF Political Science Program." Unpublished ms.
Simon, R. J., S. M. Clark and L. L. Tifft. 1966. "Of Nepotism, Marriage, and the Pursuit of an Academic Career." *Sociology of Education* 39: 344–358.
Syverson, P. D. 1980. *Summary Report 1979: Doctorate Recipients from United States Universities.* Washington, D.C.: National Academy of Sciences.
Toren, Nina. 1989. "The Nexus between Family and Work Roles of Academic Women: Reality Representation." Unpublished ms.

Traweek, Sharon. 1984. "High Energy Physics: A Male Preserve." *Technology Review* 87: 42–43.

Vetter, Betty M. 1981. "Women Scientists and Engineers: Trends in Participation." *Science* 214: 1313–1321.

Vetter, Betty M. and Eleanor R. Babco, eds. 1986. *Manpower Comments* (Commission on Professionals in Science and Technology) 23, no. 7.

Wanner, R. A., L. S. Lewis and D. I. Gregorio. 1981. "Research Productivity in Academia: A Comparative Study of the Sciences, Social Sciences, and Humanities." *Sociology of Education* 54: 238–253.

White, J. 1967. "Women in the Law." *Michigan Law Review* 65: 1051.

Zuckerman, Harriet. 1970. "Stratification in American Science." *Sociological Inquiry* 40: 235–257.

———. 1977. *Scientific Elite: Nobel Laureates in the United States.* New York: Free Press.

———. 1987. "Citation Analysis and the Complex Problem of Intellectual Influence." *Scientometrics* 12: 329–338.

———. 1989. "Accumulation of Advantage and Disadvantage: The Theory and Its Intellectual Biography." In Carlo Mongardini and Simonetta Tabboni, eds., *L'Opera de R. K. Merton e La Sociologia Contemporanea,* pp. 153–176. Genova: ECIG (Edizioni Culturali Internazionale).

Zuckerman, Harriet and Jonathan R. Cole. 1975. "Women in American Science." *Minerva* 13: 82–102.

Zuckerman, Harriet et al. 1991. *The Outer Circle: Women in the Scientific Community.* New York: Norton.

SECTION 2

SCIENCE, SEX, AND STEREOTYPES

CULTURAL IMAGES OF SCIENCE AND SCIENTISTS

Biographical and autobiographical accounts of women working as scientists, which we discussed in section 1, reveal the psychological costs for women of transgressing cultural norms. As their stories show, male colleagues ignored, discounted, and dismissed the commitments and achievements of the women scientists around them, to the detriment of science. Dispassionate and rational decision making about women's abilities was not possible in historical contexts in which women were presumed to be inferior to men by virtue of the natural order. But what of contemporary women in science and engineering? What are today's images of scientists and engineers? Have the years since the second wave of the women's movement provoked changes in cultural norms about women and men in scientific and engineering careers?

In 1983 a social scientist named David Wade Chambers published the results of his eleven-year study of the drawings of 4,807 children in 186 classes from kindergarten to grade five. The study's focus was on determining the age at which children reproduced the standard image of the American scientist, described by previous research as:

> a man who wears a white coat and works in a laboratory. He is elderly or middle aged and wears glasses . . . he may wear a beard . . . he is surrounded by equipment: test tubes, Bunsen burners, flasks and bottles, a jungle gym of blown glass tubes and weird machines with dials . . . he writes neatly in black notebooks. . . . One day he may straighten up and shout: "I've found it! I've found it!" . . . Through his work people will have new and better products . . . he has to keep dangerous secrets . . . his work may be dangerous . . . he is always reading a book.

This image, the essay reports, has remained stable since 1945.[1]

In his draw-a-scientist test, Chambers established that by the fourth and fifth grades a standard image of the scientist emerged in the drawings of most of the children in his sample. This scientist is a man of reason, driven by mind over body; he is someone who strains his eyes in intense observation, who works such long and unusual hours that he cannot find time to shave, and whose work is otherworldly and so requires "priestly white robes" (257). Even the deviations that Chambers encountered in the children's drawings were consistent in their representation of scientists as unconcerned with the ongoing matters of human life. Science is a one-gender world (only twenty-eight of the 4,807 drawings had a woman scientist in them) where tools of destruction, violence, and pain are created and morality is irrelevant. One hundred forty-five drawings (2.9 percent of the sample) clearly connected science with guns, bombs, and missiles, and a few included chemical and biological warfare, "such as the fifth grader who offered the following labels for the drawers of a filing cabinet: NEW GERMS FOR NEW DISEASES, NEW CHEMICALS FOR NEW POLUSHUN, and appropriately, NEW HEADS FOR NEW PEOPLE" (p. 263). Though such portrayals were offered by less than 10 percent of the children, Chambers speculates that a much larger proportion of the children were familiar with them via what he calls mythic images "of mankind's reaction to science" (p. 256):

> In one fourth grade class, the 24 pupils, after completing their drawings, were instructed to "draw another scientist." In the first set of drawings, no mythic stereotypes appeared and only one of the drawings incorporated elements of a morally dubious nature. The second set of drawings produced two Frankensteins along with nine pictures that included such clearly dangerous elements as bombs, poisons, and a scientist with test tube held high exclaiming: "With this I destroy the world!" This may indicate that nearly half the children in this class felt a certain ambivalence about the social value of science which did not emerge in their first drawing. (p. 263)

In all of these alternative images, not only is the scientist imagined as a man, but the work that he does is culturally constructed as work that only men can do—that is, work described as at once objective, obsessive, rational, and destructive. Girls are not socialized into the habits of mind and behavior that are necessary in this kind of work, it is often said, nor do the exigencies of most women's lives present them with experiences that might cause them to acquire such a mind-set. Women are associated in American culture with the ongoing details and moral ambiguities of daily life—work that involves taking care of children, teaching them "right and wrong," nurturing family relationships, and providing emotional support. This set of ideas about women and men, about their qualities and characteristics, is called symbolic gender, "a central organizing discourse of culture, one that not only shapes how we experience and understand ourselves as men and women but also interweaves with other discourses and shapes *them*."[2] Though symbolic gender reveals empirical information about the everyday lives of women and men only indirectly and partially, its historical durability speaks to its power to represent an enduring cultural fit between conceptions of men and those of science—a fit that discourages, if not precludes, the full participation of women in science. The popular-culture images of women who are active agents with power over others tend to be villains or psychotics, and if they are scientists, they behave within a conventionally feminine framework, such as the main character in the television series *Dr. Quinn, Medicine Woman* or the sexy and scantily clad scientist in the film *Medicine Man*.[3]

Given such conceptions, women who are earnest scientists are cultural aberrations, the exceptions that prove the rule. They are women who undertake, despite the odds, the demanding education and training required during doctoral education in the sciences. They may be aberrations because they are exceptionally talented and able, or because their parents are scientists, or because they are so independent of mind (or single-minded of purpose) as to ignore all of the social messages that proclaim science a male domain. But they are aberrations nonetheless. And so they make people uncomfortable, not because of any particular action on their part but because others are unsure how to behave around them.

There is some evidence that the image of the scientist as engaged in an amoral enterprise that requires the skills and zeal of a soldier at war is not restricted to the fantasies of children. It surfaces in literature ranging from college-level introductory textbooks to works on the philosophy of science and some of the earliest representations of the foundations of scientific study. And so a diligent student of the philosophy of science might learn that:

> the difference between common and scientific knowledge is roughly analogous to differences in standards of excellence which may be set up for handling firearms. Most men would qualify as expert shots if the standard of expertness were the ability to hit the side of a barn from a distance of a hundred feet. But only a much smaller number of individuals could meet the more rigorous requirement of consistently centering their shots upon a three-inch target at twice that distance. . . . The quest for systematic explanations requires that inquiry be directed to the relations of dependence between things irrespective of their bearing upon human values.[4]

A first-year college student contemplating a career in science could learn that:

> [a] career in science . . . serves the survival of the human species. . . . [Scientists] defend us all against the forces of extinction, and their dedication is that of the soldier in love with the battle. Often, they say they are the most blessed of human beings because they are paid for doing what they would do as a hobby if they had to.[5]

A budding biologist would learn that:

> scientists at work have the look of creatures following genetic instructions; they seem to be under the influence of a deeply placed human instinct. They are, despite their efforts at dignity, rather like young animals engaged in savage play. When they are near to an answer their hair stands on end, they sweat, they are awash in their own adrenalin. To grab the answer, and grab it first, is for them a more powerful drive than feeding or breeding or protecting themselves against the elements.[6]

All of these images share in common a portrayal of male scientists as engaged in activity within a culture where values are irrelevant and instincts prevail. If this is the culture of science, then it is a culture wherein its members set aside the constituent qualities of human relationships (morality, interdependence, agency, collective social life) in order to participate—in short, it is a "culture of no culture."[7]

ARE WOMEN OPTING OUT OF THE PIPELINE?

In the years since Chambers's essay was published, the effort to recruit women into mathematics and science promised to change the assumption that a scientist was necessarily a man. One result has been a series of articles on women's status in science, published in the general-interest science press and professional association newsletters. These articles summarize available data and/or present new data on women's presence at various stages in what has come to be called the educational "pipeline." In addition to providing empirical evidence for the continuing inequalities in opportunity, reward, and recognition between women and men in science, the authors often speculate about why the inequalities persist. A common thread among otherwise diverse analyses is the notion that men have certain qualities that are consistent with a scientific perspective and that women not only do not have these characteristics but also do not *want* to have them. So, for instance, at a 1963 conference on women in science at the Massachusetts Institute of Technology, psychologist Bruno Bettelheim explained, "We must start with the realization that, as much as women want to be good scientists or engineers, they want first and foremost to be womanly companions of men and to be mothers."[8]

We can perhaps never know precisely what the consequences for scientific knowledge are of pronouncements such as Bettleheim's. However, there is ample evidence of gender differences in the delivery of education and in educational achievement in primary and secondary schools in the United States. In 1992 the American Association of University Women issued a summary report on literally hundreds of studies on the ways students' gender influences the education they receive. The report, *How Schools Shortchange Girls,* concludes that "girls do not receive equitable amounts of teacher attention, that they are less apt than boys to see themselves reflected in the materials they study, and that they often are not expected or encouraged to pursue higher level mathematics and science courses."[9] In short, based on well-documented gender differences in the delivery of basic science and math education at primary and secondary levels, it seems a foregone conclusion that women would not seek careers in science and engineering. If women do not seek to become scientists and engineers, then there may be some truth in the stereotypes.

In a special issue of *Science* devoted to the subject of women and science, science reporter Joe Alper asked Camilla Benbow (an education researcher) for her explanation for why women would drop out of the pipeline:

> What we are measuring here is related to one of the biggest differences between genders, namely that of "people versus things. . . . Females tend to be more interested in the former, males in the latter." In some instances, this will lead women to specific fields. . . . "Females tend to go into more organic sciences, such as biology, medicine, and psychology, while males go for the more inorganic fields, such as physics and engineering." But in other cases these preferences can drive women out of science.[10]

In an article about the increasing participation of women in science, the authors report that women opt out at the graduate level because of lifestyle preferences:

> I have seen female graduate students come to this department who are exceptional, who did not leave because of academics whatsoever. Outshined many of the men by orders of magnitude, and they're gone. And I consider that such a waste. I look at these people as being excellent people who could go on and be in academia, and they leave with a master's because they say they don't want to live like this. They see what people have to do to succeed in academia. . . The women want to have another life; they want a family, [to] be able to socialize on the weekend.[11]

But is it true that women are not interested in scientific and engineering careers? Among undergraduates, the percentage of degree earners who were women has steadily increased between 1966 and 1997 in almost every area tracked by the National Science Foundation, including the physical sciences (from 14 percent to 38.5 percent), earth, atmospheric, and ocean sciences (from 9 percent to 34.5 percent), biological and agricultural sciences (from 25 percent to 51.6 percent), and engineering (from 0.4 percent to 18 percent). An important exception is in mathematical and computer sciences, where the percentage rose from 33 percent in 1966 to 39.5 percent in 1985 and then dropped off to 33.6 percent by 1997.[12]

Among graduate students, there has been a similar increase between 1966 and 1997 in the percentage of doctorates awarded to women, with increases in every field tracked by the National Science Foundation, including mathematical and computer sciences (from 6 percent to 20 percent). In 1997 women earned 22.6 percent of the doctorates in the physical sciences, 24 percent in earth, atmospheric, and ocean sciences, and 41 percent in the biological sciences. Indeed, a slightly higher percentage of doctorates was awarded to women in the biological sciences in 1997 (43 percent) than in the social sciences (39 percent).[13] Only in engineering have the percentages remained low, but even here professional organizations tout gains in recent years.

WOMEN IN A MAN'S WORLD

Articles about women's experiences in the general-interest science press sometimes portray the difficulties women have in negotiating a balance between being seen as serious about science and not appearing to be too serious about being a woman. In the widely distributed Association of American Colleges publication "Out of the Classroom: A Chilly Campus Climate for Women?" one student reports with dismay: "I've done everything I can to be taken seriously here. I never wear make-up, I never wear feminine clothes—in fact, I do everything I can to avoid looking attractive, but I'm still treated like a girl."[14] General-interest science press accounts of women in science are peppered with autobiographical accounts of the trials of being a woman in a man's world. These stories often describe encounters with a parent, adviser, or teacher who encouraged or discouraged them; a decision to postpone marriage and children; or accounts of struggles with balancing family and work, the difficulties of being among the few women scientists in the department, and the joys of the science itself which make it all worthwhile. The formula is a standard in storytelling, where the truly dedicated overcome all obstacles to accomplish their goals.

One of the ingredients in this formula is an epiphanic moment when the woman scientist realizes that the fact she is a woman matters to her male colleagues. Physicist Fumiko Yonezawa explains it this way:

> "I worked very hard. I had to bring [the three children] to nursery school; I had to do the shopping; I had to cook. My husband didn't help me in any way at all. He is a typical Japanese husband," she said. Furthermore, she says, one reason she stayed in academics is that the doors to industry were slammed in her face. Despite being consistently at the top of her university class, "when we tried to find jobs in companies, they all said, 'Only boys, no girls wanted.' Until then I didn't realize I was a girl."[15]

For Geri Richmond, a chemistry professor, this realization meant a major change in her appearance and in her relationships with her friends. She:

> spent her high school years as a cheerleader turning cartwheels on a basketball court and dating as much as possible. But in college, she did a complete turnaround. "I dug into science and enjoyed it so much that I didn't come up for air until I graduated," she recalls about her time at Kansas State University. To fit in with her male peers, she threw out her dresses, her pumps, her nail polish, her makeup. Even her hand lotion was jettisoned because its fragrance was a subtle evocation of her gender. "Socially, it was hard," she adds. "My girlfriends didn't understand what I was doing. I always had to struggle internally."[16]

Such stories highlight the moment of realizing that women in the social world of science are stigmatized by their gender—by, in Erving Goffman's sense, "abominations of the body," where one's difference is evident. Evelyn Fox Keller, in writing about her experiences as a graduate student in physics, describes the "sea of seats, you walk into a classroom early, and the classroom fills up, leaving a sea of empty seats around you. . . . What was wrong with me?"[17] Evelynn Hammonds, an African American writing about how her peers responded to her interests in science, puts it this way: "I was seen as weird and different, and *wrong!*—somehow not being a 'right kind of woman.'"[18] One woman explained how her adviser put it bluntly: "In my day we didn't have any contaminants," he said to her upon learning a woman was in his lab.[19]

A widely distributed MIT Artificial Intelligence Laboratory manuscript on women in computer science there gives paradigmatic examples of the expectation that women in engineering are ugly:

> When a female student at an engineering institute went home for vacation, her mother leafed through the book of photographs of the freshman class and exclaimed in surprise, "why some of these girls are pretty!"...
>
> "One of my friends was a genius who happened to be a pretty blonde girl. . . . [W]hile hunting around [Y] Hall, a man in his early 30s came up to her and asked if she needed help. She said that she was looking for her advisor's office. The man responded with a puzzled, 'What major are you?' When she answered, 'I'm in Electrical Engineering.' The man smiled at her and oozed, 'Oh, you're too pretty to be an EE major.'"[20]

These examples describe the forms that discrimination takes against women and confirm, for those who have had similar experiences, that indeed women are stigmatized by their gender. The author explains that such perspectives on women in science and engineering—that women are either too aberrant to sit near or too pretty to be taken seriously—leave women feeling uncomfortable and unwelcome:

> "When I was in graduate school, the professor in automata theory introduced the topic of decomposition by saying: 'Machines are a lot like women—many forms for the same function (wink wink).' As the only women in the class, you can imagine that I felt terrific."[21]

Another example from the MIT report ties this image of women as nonhuman to the process of dismissing them as colleagues altogether:

> "At a conference in France, a male speaker . . . who was speaking about the importance of testing, showed an overhead slide of a naked woman with a caption of the sort—'Would you buy this product without testing it first?' There were only 2 or 3 women in the audience (of about 150), but I had fleeting feelings of having accidentally walked into a stag party and wondering if he had either not expected any women to be there or had discounted the importance of directing his remarks to the women in the audience."[22]

Such accounts capture how treating women as sexual objects makes women feel uncomfortable; perhaps this is part of the reason why women might choose to opt out of computer science. These stories suggest how some men can play an active role in discouraging women from seeking careers in male-dominated fields. Some women have tried to avoid such treatment by playing down the fact that they are women. As one woman faculty member put it, "[T]o make it as a female scientist, you have to make it as a scientist and truly downplay the female."[23] The upshot is that in order to succeed, women have work to do in addition to their science. The work of suppressing all signs of one's gender—of ignoring the sexual attention and blunders of their male colleagues—is work that men do not have to do in science and engineering.

DIVERGING FROM THE NORM

Many of the readings in *Women, Science, and Technology* refer to the "culture of science and engineering" or "scientific culture." These common terms reduce the great diversity of practices across labs, departments, and individuals in science and engineering to a single "type" of culture that adheres to a common set of values, beliefs, and behaviors. It is important to remember that though there are important commonalities across fields and across time in the association between stereotypes about scientists' behavior and masculinity, there are also important differences. Many of these differences relate to the range of ways in which men can be "masculine."[24] Biologists can have stereotypes about chemists and vice versa, for instance.

Some differences between the cultures of disciplines relate to the historical presence and contributions of women within a discipline, where new subfields emerged because of their work. It was a collaboration between two women, Adrienne Zihlman and Nancy Tanner, that led to a challenge of the prevailing man-the-hunter model in human evolution. Empirical data from fossil, nonhuman primate, and ethnographic records led them to argue that the conventional model was an inaccurate portrayal of the organization of prehistoric human society. Though Zihlman denies that they offered their model as a feminist reinterpretation, she makes the point that the feminist movement created a context in which the question "Where are the women?" could be asked. The willingness of Zihlman and Tanner to look for the answer led to a reconsideration of the earlier model and still provides a touchstone in continuing debates about human origins.[25]

Similarly, Margaret Mead's interest in Ruth Benedict's work led her to explore the relationship between variations in sex roles across cultures, work that represents an early challenge to biological explanations for women's subordination to men. Their work broke new ground in anthropology, where, according to an interview with Benedict in *Time* (March 16, 1933), jobs were rare but jobs for women were rarer still.[26]

Historian Margaret Rossiter points to aggregate data from the first half of the twentieth century to suggest that a critical mass of women in a field, once it was reached, led to continuing high participation in the field by women. Her data show that 60 percent of women in science in 1921 were clustered in just three fields: botany, zoology, and psychology. These fields today continue to have uniquely high percentages of women participating at all levels, with 73 percent of bachelor's degrees 64 percent of doctorates in psychology awarded to women in 1995.[27]

GENDER AND POWER IN SCIENCE AND ENGINEERING

Perhaps the answer to the question "Do women opt out of science and engineering, or are they pushed out?" is that both processes contribute to the underrepresentation of women in science and engineering. The articles in this section examine the cultural backdrop against which these processes take place. This backdrop includes historical and biological information (or myth), language and vocabulary, and the social and psychological practice of "objectivity" in science. In her essay on nineteenth-century arguments against educating women to be scientists, Janice Law Trecker documents the ways in which the most scientific and "objective" authorities of the day concluded that the very future of the human race depended on the continued exclusion of women from scientific circles lest women cease to accept subordination to men and reject their family responsibilities. Carol Cohn's essay describes how twentieth-century notions of masculinity threaten the future of the human race, where the concept of "rationality" is used to mask the epitome of the irrational—weapons of mass destruction. Mary Barbercheck looks at the images in the advertising in the American Association for the Advancement of Science (AAAS) masthead journal, *Science*. She uncovers distinct patterns in the activities and characteristics of the people portrayed, ones that draw on cultural assumptions about science as a new frontier, women and people of color as the beneficiaries (and not creators) of scientific knowledge, and white men as figures of power and authority.

We close the section with excerpts from Evelyn Fox Keller's classic examination of the psychosocial dynamics that underwrite an association between masculinity and objectivity and thereby preclude the participation of women qua women in science and engineering. Her essay questions whether, given the importance of gender in our self-concepts, social arrangements, and professional cultures, science ever can be a world where "the matter of gender drops away."

NOTES

[1] David Chambers, "Stereotypic Images of the Scientist: The Draw the Scientist Test," *Science Education* 67, 2 (1983): 255–65, quote on 256. There is evidence that components of this image persist into the 1990s. See, e.g., Hilary M. Lips, "Gender- and Science-Related Attitudes as Predictors of College Students' Academic Choices," *Journal of Vocational Behavior* 40 (1992): 62–81, and Barbara L. Sherriff and Laura Binkley, "The Irreconcilable Images of Women, Science, and Engineering," *Journal of Women and Minorities in Science and Engineering* 3 (1997): 21–36.

[2] Carol Cohn, "War, Wimps, and Women," in Miriam Cooke and Angela Woollacott, eds., *Gendering War Talk* (Princeton, N.J.: Princeton University Press, 1993), quote on 228, emphasis in original.

[3] For a fuller account of these images, see "Fatal and Fetal Visions: The Backlash in the Movies," in Susan Faludi's *Backlash: The Undeclared War against American Women* (New York: Doubleday, 1991).

[4] Ernest Nagel, *The Structure of Science* (New York: Harcourt, Brace, 1979), 9–10.

[5] Thomas A. Easton, *Careers in Science* (Homewood, Ill.: Dow-Jones-Irwin, 1984), 5–6.

[6] From *The Lives of a Cell*, by Lewis Thomas, quoted in P. Raven and G. Johnson, *Biology* (New York: Worth, 1986), 283.

[7] Sharon Traweek, *Beamtimes and Lifetimes: The Culture of High Energy Physicists*, (Cambridge, Mass.: Harvard University Press, 1988), quote on 162.

[8] Jacquelyn Mattfield and Carol Van Aken, eds., *Women and the Scientific Professions: The MIT Symposium on American Women in Science and Engineering*, (Cambridge: MIT Press, 1965).

[9] American Association of University Women (AAUW), *How Schools Shortchange Girls* (Washington, D.C.: AAUW Educational Foundation and National Education Association, 1992); Myra Sadker and David Sadker, *Failing at Fairness: How America's Schools Cheat Girls* (New York: Charles Scribner's Sons, 1994).

[10] Joe Alper, "The Pipeline Is Leaking Women All the Way Along," *Science* 260 (1993): 409–11, quote on 409.

[11] Henry Etzkowitz et al., "The Paradox of Critical Mass for Women in Science," *Science* 266 (1994): 51–54, quote on 53.

[12] National Science Foundation (NSF), *Women, Minorities and Persons with Disabilities in Science and Engineering* (Washington, D.C.: U.S. Government Printing Office, 1999). See also Wendy Grossman, "Cyber View: Access Denied," *Scientific American*, August 1998, 38.

[13] NSF, *Women, Minorities*, Table 49, 61; Table 51, 63.

[14] Roberta Hall and Bernice Sandler, *Out of the Classroom: A Chilly Campus Climate for Women?* (Washington, D.C.: Project on the Status and Education of Women, Association of American Colleges, 1984), 5.

[15] Thomas Koppel, "No Girls Need Apply," *Science* 260 (1993): 422.

[16] Elizabeth Penisi, "Flexibility, Balance Draw Women to the University of Oregon," and "Close Up: Geri Richmond," *The Scientist* 4 (1990): 1, 7–9.

[17] Evelyn Fox Keller, "The Anomaly of a Woman in Physics," in Sara Ruddick and Pamela Daniels, eds., *Working It Out: Twenty-three Writers, Scientists and Scholars Talk about Their Lives* (New York: Pantheon, 1977), 77–91, quote on 86–87.

[18] Aimee Sands, "Never Meant to Survive: A Black Woman's Journey: An Interview with Evelynn Hammonds," in Sandra Harding, ed., *The Racial Economy of Science* (Bloomington: Indiana University Press, 1993), 239–48, quote on 242.

[19] Mary Fehrs and Roman Czujko, "Women in Physics: Reversing the Exclusion," *Physics Today,* August 1992, 33–40, quote on 38.

[20] Ellen Spertus, "Why Are There So Few Female Computer Scientists?" Artificial Intelligence Laboratory, Massachusetts Institute of Technology, Cambridge, Mass., 1991, 18.

[21] Ibid., 22.

[22] Ibid. It is tempting to argue that the climate has changed substantially in the last ten years, but current research indicates otherwise as the issues have become more complex. See, for example, two recent special issues: "Gender and Computer Technology," ed. Mary Wyer and Alison Adam, *Technology and Society* 18, 4 (1999–2000) and "Changing Perspectives on Woman and Technology," ed. David Morton, *Technology and Society* 19, 1 (2000).

[23] Gerhard Sonnert, *Who Succeeds in Science? The Gender Dimension* (New Brunswick, N.J.: Rutgers University Press, 1995), 178.

[24] See, for example, R. W. Connell, *Masculinities* (Los Angeles: University of California Press, 1995).

[25] Lori Hager, "Sex and Gender in Paleoanthropology," in Lori Hager, ed., *Women in Human Evolution* (New York: Routledge, 1997).

[26] Adam Kuper, *The Chosen Primate* (Cambridge, Mass.: Harvard University Press, 1994), 187; Margaret Rossiter, *Women Scientists in America: Struggles and Strategies to 1940* (Baltimore: Johns Hopkins University Press, 1982), 151.

[27] M. Rossiter, *Women Scientists to 1940,* 150–53; National Science Foundation, *Science and Engineering Indicators, 1998* (Washington, D.C.: U.S. Government Printing Office, 1998), appendix tables 2–20 and 2–30.

SEX, SCIENCE, AND EDUCATION

Janice Law Trecker

It was a widely held 19th century belief that science was a liberating intellectual force. The scientific method and the new scientific theories were not seen simply as means of exploring nature and matter, but as tools for approaching moral and social problems as well. The powers of the scientific method were believed sufficient to sweep away old prejudices and misconceptions while building up a new social and intellectual order. No social or even political problem was judged too great or too complex for this new approach and, especially in the last quarter of the century, scientists turned to their disciplines for the solution of a variety of vexing social problems. One of these harassing questions was the "Woman Problem," and rejecting old moral and theological data, scientific minds resolved to turn their expertise to a study of women and of women's place: "The question of woman's sphere, to use the modern phrase, is not to be solved by applying to it abstract principles of right and wrong. Its solution must be obtained from physiology, not from ethics and metaphysics. . . . The *quaestio vexata* of woman's sphere will be decided by her organization," wrote a prominent physician in 1874.[1] The *Quarterly Journal of Science* felt that Darwinism suggested a sound approach to the Woman Question: woman's role could be illuminated by applying the master's ideas of natural selection, differentiation and specialization to the study of social and sexual relationships.[2] While intellectuals might disagree on which scientific theory might best apply, there was never any doubt as to who would do the studying, examining and theorizing.

G. Stanley Hall wrote in his monumental *Adolescence* that woman was unable to solve her own problems or to be her own teacher, preacher or doctor: therefore, "she must be studied objectively and laboriously as we study children, and partly by men, because their sex must of necessity always remain objective and incommensurate with regard to woman and therefore more or less theoretical."[3]

This belief in the sovereign objectivity of science concealed certain difficulties which were to invalidate the scientific answers to the "Woman Question." These difficulties were, first, the tendency of inherited, nonscientific ideas to penetrate the scientists' social theories and, second, the fact that science, intellect and education were in themselves points of conflict between the new aspirations of the women's movement and the attitudes of the social order.

Perhaps it was the theoretician's very confidence in his own professionalism which permitted the easy transition from old stereotypes to "scientific" formulations. Hall's emphasis on masculine objectivity with regard to women too often became a purely theoretical stance. Despite their interest in the Woman Question, many of the thinkers who wrote about it had little interest in studying the feminine. Rather their interest was to fit woman into a variety of biological, evolutionary and anthropological theories. Most of these hypotheses were characterized by a dualistic bias which saw the female in all ways as the complement and contrary of the male. This pre-scientific habit of mind, combined with a belief in the objectivity of research and the purity of scientific study, permitted *conservative* 19th century doctors, scientists and educators to rework earlier theories about women's rights and place, without realizing that the origin of their ideas lay not in their empirical data, but in their cultural heritage. They ransacked the works of the evolutionists, comparative biologists, anthropologists and physicians. They measured skill, weighed brains, charted aptitudes for mathematics and tested memory; they figured out the average male consumption of food and studied the lives of individuals of genius. When they finished and made their recommendations for the proper role and education of women, however, they spoke with St. Paul and Rousseau about the complementary physical and psychological nature of the sexes and the subordination of women.

The new social and symbolic importance of science further complicated the situation and eventually made the scientists' quest for objectivity quixotic. This was especially true regarding theories about women and education, since science had succeeded theology and philosophy as knowledge "forbidden" to women and other inferiors. When classical languages and theological and philosophical studies had led to power and advancement within the masculine hierarchy, these studies had been believed too hard for the delicate structure of the female brain. In religious ages especially, tampering with theology had been considered inappropriate and "unfeminine." However, both the intellectual focus and the centers of social power had shifted by the 19th century. Whatever the pious might think, it was no longer theology or a mastery of Greek and Latin that prepared a young man for a brilliant career. Ancient verb forms and scholastic disputes could not match a knowledge of manufacturing, technology or engineering in an industrial era. Science and mathematics were displacing classical and philosophical studies, and with them came reasons why women should not be highly educated, at least not in such "difficult" disciplines as the sciences.

Nowhere is this shift in what constituted forbidden knowledge more clearly illustrated than in medicine. In the medieval world woman was the physician, and long after, the housewife's simples and potions and her nursing skill largely determined the health and safety of her family. At the dawn of the industrial era, women still dominated one medical specialty, obstetrics and gynecology, and the midwife was a respected figure in every American community. Once medicine became a science, however, attitudes changed, and even the midwife was driven from the field by professionally educated male practitioners. Suddenly medical matters were improper for women to know, and a decent, prudish ignorance plus a deferential confidence in the male physician became the correct female attitude.[4]

Science's new designation as "masculine" knowledge, and male fears of economic competition, made many of the theorists' arguments against female knowledge seem self-serving. No one could overlook the fact that science and the scientific method were potent as symbols as well as tools. The emotional connotations around the study of science and the belief in its great practical power made it almost impossible for scientists to be unbiased. Despite their confidence in their complete objectivity, the 19th century scientists' analysis of the Woman Problem forms a striking case study of the ways in which nonscientific ideas and social needs shape scientific thinking.

This is particularly true of the scientists' approach to women's education, the focus of much of their work on the woman problem. Education was a primary interest for several reasons. First, like other Americans, the 19th century scientific thinkers believed in its power. They tended to see the solution to many social problems in terms of education, and they had faith that the right sort of woman—or man—could be produced by the correct method of education. Second, they saw the growing body of educated women as direct professional and economic competition. While this was, of course, rarely advanced as a reason for desiring changes in women's education, the scientists' insistence that the "hard" sciences and medicine should not be a part of the feminine curriculum would, if followed, have kept many vital social, intellectual and industrial processes a masculine preserve.

Finally, education attracted attention as the most successful feminist challenge to the old ways of thinking. The 19th century women's movement potentially threatened great changes in education, in social and sexual mores and in politics. In the last quarter of the century, however, only the first of these really showed striking progress. It is significant that the scientists' analysis of and attacks on women's education came not when the pioneer academies were struggling for survival or when women were first integrating higher education. Rather, the scientific thinkers brought forward their new solutions to the Woman Question after women's education, including the study of the sciences, was well advanced and indubitably a success. No matter what their discipline or their initial approach, the scientific conservatives showed an interest in altering women's education. It is probable that this interest in education stemmed as much from the fact that feminist success was most evident in this field, as from a conviction as to the importance of education in shaping the feminine character.

Because they wrote after the development of higher education for women, the new theorists differed from older anti-feminist writers on women's schooling. The "scientific" arguments took account of women's new intellectual achievements—sometimes even conceded her intellectual equality—but they cautioned that these achievements were dangerous: for the woman's health, for the survival of the race, for the continued progress of the species. Furthermore, the new theorists against the intellectual female raised another, more subtle barrier to women's achievements and expectations. At the time when women were seeking to open professional and postgraduate education and to enter the learned professions, scientists brought forth evidence to indicate that woman was incapable of true excellence and that only a mediocrity of achievement and a supportive role in discovery could be her portion. Like Rousseau, these scientists believed that man was destined for discovery and innovation, woman for application and conservation.

The resulting arguments against the intellectual woman are difficult to classify, because they drew from an assortment of 19th century scientific ideas and because they were powered by a variety of 19th century obsessions. Evolution, the survival of the fittest, the racial supremacy of Caucasians, race suicide, the home, the dream of an orderly society—all these hopes and fears and cultural properties were mixed up with the role of woman, the psychology of the female and the proper ordering of the relations between the sexes.

A sexist and racist view of the world was at the heart of many 19th century scientific, as well as social, assumptions. Biology, anthropology and psychology were not immune to the idea that progress was rooted in the triumph and rule of superior species and beings. In scientific, as in popular understanding, the superior human being was identified with the white American or European male of a certain social standing, and anything which threatened the contemporary social order was seen as detrimental, not only to the status quo, but to the very progress of humanity.[5]

The first danger which women's education posed for stability and progress was the deterioration in health which rigorous intellectual work caused in female students. While not the first to advance this thesis, Dr. Clarke's *Sex in Education* was one of the most influential. His argument, and those of such contemporaries and successors as G. Stanley Hall, Henry Maudsley, T. Clouston and James Crichton-Browne, was based on two quite remarkable medical presumptions.[6] First, that woman's functional periodicity, i.e., menstruation, was the dominating fact of her life, and, second, that the mind-body linkage was such that the principle of conservation of energy should be applied. According to this view of mind and body, the brain withdrew nourishment from the rest of the body during intellectual activities. If the brain was overworked, often the body suffered and the individual's health decayed, frequently in the direction of hysteria and neuralgia.

Of course, such a mind-body linkage would apply to both sexes. However, because of menstruation and other facets of the female reproductive life, the withdrawal of "vital energy" by the brain was seen as more dangerous to women, especially at puberty, when the reproductive system was developing. Not only did menstruation cause women to be more susceptible to "derangement" and "instability," but neglect of rest and an excess of mental strain could permanently damage the constitution and the reproductive system.

Damage could follow directly from the brain's drawing too much blood from the reproductive organs, or indirectly through the evil effects of tension brought on by overly rigorous work. It could occur during a girl's school days, or after she finished school and was ready to begin her home and family. In either case, the ill effects were manifold. In 1892 Sir James Crichton-Browne, a British M.D., cited a host of ills including insomnia, neuralgia, chorea, anemia, hysteria and "general delicacy" among the effects of current methods of educating girls.[7] T.S. Clouston added warnings of stunted growth and nervousness, which was in turn related to headaches and hysteria.[8]

Considering the dangers these doctors saw in any activity which depleted the body's energies during adolescence, one would have thought they would have turned their primary attention to the severely overworked girls of the lower classes—to the factory children and the young domestics, seamstresses and farm workers. This, however, was not the case. It was intellectual, not physical application which interested this segment of the medical profession. Clarke, who was one of the few even to consider the plight of the young working woman, dismissed her dangers. The woman of the working class risked less since the real strains of physical labor typically didn't begin until after puberty (a dubious assumption in the 1870s) and in any case, she was not apt to be developed intellectually. What energy she had went entirely to the development of her physical organization instead of being frittered away in the study of Latin, Greek or advanced mathematics.[9]

The decay in health of intellectual, upper-middle-class female students was not, however severe, solely their own misfortune; it threatened their posterity as well. Because it was theorized that intellectual stimulation particularly affected and interrupted the reproductive system, education was thought to have a direct effect on the fecundity of graduates. Dr. Henry Maudsley wondered if highly educated women would have any children at all; Dr. Clarke predicted that in another generation American men would have to import wives. Hall, too, placed the blame on the college woman and not the college man: ". . . for she is far more liable than he to overdraw her reproductive power and consume in good looks, activity of mind and body, and other augmentations of her individuality, energy meant for the altruism of home and of posterity."[10]

Hall's use of the term "individuality" was significant. It was not only that the development of woman's individuality was threatening psychologically, but that individuality had a theoretical significance in contemporary biological theories. As Hall explained: "The batchelor woman is an interesting illustration of Spencer's law of the inverse relation of individuation and genesis. The completely developed individual is always a terminal representative in her line of descent. She has taken up and utilized in her own life all that was meant for her descendants and has so overdrawn her account with heredity that, like every perfectly developed individual, she is also completely sterile. . . . While the complete man can do and sometimes does this, woman has a far greater and very peculiar power of overdrawing her reserves."[11]

The segment of the scientific community represented by Crichton-Browne and Clarke was chiefly concerned with the individual woman and with the children they felt she wanted to bear (or should want to bear). The theoreticians of the science establishment, their popularizers and the social theorists were more concerned with the impact of low fecundity on the well-being of the community. British author Grant Allen, for one, was impressed with Darwinian ideas about the importance of an increasing population for the maintenance of animal vigor and for the selection of a superior stock. Since his own calculations convinced him that the British population would only remain stationary if each woman had four children, or if each marriage produced six, Allen was thoroughly alarmed by the declining birthrate. With rare boldness, he declared that married or not, women had to produce children; the alternative was the enfeeblement of the "cultivated classes," whose fertility had already declined sharply by 1889.[12]

While Allen's concern with the "cultivated classes" reflected the British situation, American writers were equally concerned that the "best" stock should remain dominant. Alarmists cited not only the high birthrates of the races of Africa and Asia, but the birthrates of immigrant stocks in America.[13] They saw the continued dominance, indeed existence, of their own group imperiled by the sudden shift in female attitudes, and with Allen, they agreed that women's "sexuality (which lies at the basis of everything) is enfeebled and destroyed." Education for women must therefore be shifted from the intellectual, masculine pattern to something new. As Allen wrote, ". . . instead of reform taking a rational direction—instead of women being educated to suckle strong and intelligent children, and to order well a wholesome, beautiful, reasonable household—the mistake was made of educating them like men—giving a like training for totally unlike functions."[14]

The idea that education was a detriment to female fertility was not the only 19th and early 20th century theory about women to draw support from evolutionary doctrines. There was another set of arguments placing limits on the attainments of the educated female which was also sustained by ideas drawn from the biological sciences. In this view, male superiority was a direct and inevitable consequence of greater genetic variability, which resulted in a greater possible range of masculine talent. This thesis was supported by a variety of arguments from comparisons of brain weights to complex evolutionary theories and subtle psychological investigation. Much of the research and speculation concentrated on the brain, as crude statements of female inferiority based on brain size gave way to consideration of the differences in intellectual and anatomical variations shown by each sex and of the possible significance of the differentials.

As Havelock Ellis pointed out in *Man and Woman*, few studies have more clearly shown the weight of unscientific prejudice than the study of the brain.[15] Indeed, to the probable discomfiture of those who based social arguments on male variability, it had at first been believed that female brains showed greater variability, a circumstance identified with the inferiority of woman's more primitive organ. Later, as it appeared that the male brain was the more variable, this interpretation changed. The newer view held that it was variability of intellect (suggested by variability in physical as well as mental abilities) which gave males the edge in human society. As the pioneer psychological tester Edward Thorndike wrote: "This one fundamental difference in variability is more important than all the differences between the average male and female capacities . . . a slight excess of male variability would mean that of one hundred of the most gifted individuals in this country not two would be women, and of the thousand most gifted, not one in twenty. . . . Not only the probability and desirability of marriage and the training of children as an essential feature of woman's career, *but also the restriction of women to the mediocre grades of ability and achievement should be reckoned with by our educational systems.*"[16]

Like a number of other scientific commentators on the education of women, Thorndike was forthright in drawing conclusions from his theoretical assumptions. "The education of women for such professions as administration, statesmanship, philosophy, or scientific research, where a very few gifted individuals are what society requires, is far less needed than education for such professions as nursing, teaching, medicine or architecture, where the average level is essential."[17] While high school and even college education was possible and acceptable for women, postgraduate education was socially a more "remunerative" investment for males.

This sort of social and educational conclusion was frequently drawn from ideas about male variability, a habit which one believer in the theory, Havelock Ellis, criticized on the grounds that the ability of the sexes was comparable, except at the furthest ends of the scale. Despite his caution about drawing sweeping educational prescriptions from variability, Ellis himself made use of the idea to account for the prevalence of male genius. Denying the existence of any social and cultural restrictions on feminine ability, Ellis theorized that while not totally restricted to males, genius was so rare among women as almost to be counted a masculine secondary sex characteristic.[18]

Ellis, Thorndike and other psychologists, biologists and physicians drew support from a variety of studies and statistical investigations, including relative numbers of male and female feebleminded, extensive measures of brain weights and cranial capacities, anatomical measurements of infants and studies of geniuses. Although their facts and figures were plentiful, their conclusions were hotly debated. Not only was the jump from greater male physical variability (even in such suggestive areas as brain weight) to greater mental variability questioned, but a variety of methodological objections were raised as well. Critics like Leta Hollingsworth cited social factors influencing crucial data and pointed to widely differing interpretations of terminology and statistical procedure.[19] Dr. Karl Pearson, who denied that the sexes differed in their degrees of variability, conducted a running battle with Havelock Ellis over methods of taking anatomical measurements and over what could legitimately be considered a variation.[20]

Considering the uncertainties surrounding the facts about male variability, it is surprising that this idea had such marked appeal. However, in addition to flattering old prejudices, the notion of variability was sustained by its role as a small but integral part of the theories of evolution.

One of the things which had interested Darwin and other biologists and evolutionists was the means by which new traits appeared. Among their objects of study were domestic animals, since selective breeding accelerated the production of new traits. Their observations led them to believe that new traits were more frequently introduced in males and transmitted through male offspring. Combined with the fact that in most feral mammal and bird species the adult male differs more from the young than does the adult female through such secondary sex characteristics as horns, brilliant plumage and manes, this evidence suggested that the male is the agent of variation in evolution. According to Darwin, there was both a psychological and a physiological basis for this tendency: "The greater eagerness of the males [*i.e.*, their sex drive] has thus indirectly led to their much more frequently developing secondary sexual characters than the females. But the development of such characters would be much aided, if the males were more liable to vary than the females—as I concluded they were. . . ."[21]

Darwin's idea of the variability of males, combined with his belief in stereotypical psychological characterizations of the sexes, was further elaborated by W.K. Brooks, who thought that males had a unique ability to store up variations within their reproductive cells through "gemmules."[22] Postulating gemmules did not really describe the genetic mechanism at work, but Brooks, at least in his popular articles, vigorously clarified what this mechanism might mean with regard to the Woman Problem. Believing that evolution was a combination of variation and heredity, Brooks advanced the idea that the ovum is "the material medium through which the law of heredity manifests itself, while the male element is the vehicle of new variations. The ovum is the conservative, the male element the progressive or variable factor in the process of evolution of the race as well as in the reproduction of the individual."[23] Furthermore, there was what Brooks called the "subjective side of evolution." For, he wrote, ". . . if the female organism is the conservative organism, to which is entrusted the keeping of all that has been gained during the past history of the race, it must follow that the female mind is the storehouse filled with the instincts, habits, intuitions, and laws of conduct which have been gained by experience. . . . The male mind must have the power of extending experience over new fields, and by comparison and generalization, of discovering new laws of nature. . . ."[24]

It is not too surprising that Brooks drew conservative conclusions about women's education. The proper education for women was general cultural knowledge to advance their role as the storehouses of past ideas. Only males should receive the technical and scientific training which is a prerequisite for new discoveries.

The female role as racial conservator strengthened the prevalent opinion that it was easier to describe (and prescribe for) the typical woman than the typical man. G. Stanley Hall's effusion on woman as "representative of the race" is instructive: "The male is the agent of variation and progress, and transmits variations best. . . . An ideal or typical male is hard to define, but there is a standard ideal woman. Because her mind is, more than that of man, essentially an organ of heredity, we find that, although she may seem volatile and desultory, the fact that her processes seem to be unconscious emancipates her from nature less than is the case with man. Her thought is a mode of thinking."[25]

In the terminology of the times, woman was anabolic—conservative and natural, while man was katabolic—variable, occasionally destructive, but able to go beyond nature, in thought as well as in physique. The Victorian stereotype of femininity was not, therefore, simply one cultural choice out of many, but the paradigm of the feminine role in the great drama of evolution. The woman who in some way challenged the stereotype was not only out of step with her culture, she was out of step with the very pattern of the universe. In the much quoted dictum, "The differences [between the sexes] may be exaggerated or lessened, but to obliterate them it would be necessary to have all the evolution over again on a new basis. What was decided among the prehistoric Protozoa cannot be annulled by Act of Parliament."[26]

Furthermore, it was not only a law of progress that there be sex differences, but that differentiation by sex steadily increase. This "law" was suggested by the discovery by comparative anatomists that the differences between the sexes in cranial capacity were more marked in "civilized" and "developed" stocks than in the "lower," more "primitive" races. Researchers pointed to new data which implied that there were greater differences in skull capacity between the sexes in European than in African stocks and greater differences between modern males and females than between the sexes in ancient stocks.[27] Since there was no doubt in the Western mind that the modern European or American represented the highest point of human development, the conclusions were clear. The noted "brain inferiority" of the female was a law of nature and the increasing differentiation and specialization of the sexes was an instrument of progress. Rather than striving to make women like men, a true social ordering and proper education would seek to accentuate the differences and to make the sexes mutually dependent and complementary—a process which would, incidentally, also increase sexual attraction.

The educational suggestions which these evolutionists drew from their theories were like those of the conservative medical men. The ideal female curriculum aimed at giving women the graces of a liberal, humanistic education without the intellectual tools or the spiritual hardiness to do much more than appreciate the productions of masculine genius. In the inimitable style of Dr. Hall, "Another principle [of female education] should be to broaden by retarding; to keep the purely mental back and by every method to bring the intuitions to the front; appeals to tact and taste should be incessant. . . ." If appeals to "tact and taste," emphasis on the heroic and spiritual elements in history and the encouragement of a sentimental imagination were not enough, girls were also to be burdened by an oversensitivity to their physical organization: ". . . perhaps the deepest law of the cosmos celebrates its highest triumphs in woman's life. For years everything must give way to its thorough and settled establishment. In the monthly sabbaths of rest the ideal school should revert to the meanings of the word leisure . . . then woman should realize that *to be* is greater than *to do*. . . ."[28]

Woman's education should be primarily "education for motherhood," and while the conservatives of the 19th century were willing to allow some intellectual training for females, they certainly did not want women who could enter their own intellectual preserve. "The *savante*—the woman of science—like the female athlete, is simply an anomaly, an exceptional being, holding a position more or less intermediate between the two sexes. In one case the brain, as in the other the muscular system, has undergone an abnormal development," declared the *Quarterly Journal of Science*.[29] Dismissing the idea that a previous denial of training had anything to do with the absence of first-rate female scientists, the *Journal* continued, "We would not seek to entice women into the observatory, the laboratory, or, above all, into the dissecting room, nor erect colleges for the training of female *savantes*. . . ."

However expressed, the underlying aim of the scientific conservatives was to suppress and to direct female individuality and talent into the socially acceptable channels of domestic, idealized womanhood and away from the disciplines which might increase her dangerous individuality and her knowledge of the crucial studies—i.e., the sciences. Having so recently secured the individuality of their own sex through such novelties as male suffrage, the 19th century rise in affluence, mass education and the escape from subsistence farming, conservative men were uncertain and frightened of the next step. In the new Faustian bargain, the masculine half of humanity would be given individuality and power through science, technology and abstract thought, while the feminine half of humanity would, in exchange, remain tied to nature, the race and reproduction.[30] No longer was his pattern the farmer, tied to home and soil, but the industrialist, the worker, the craftsman, the scientist, dependent not on nature but on the new mysteries of trade, capital and technology. This new masculine freedom would have to be purchased, and the price was the sacrifice of woman's individuality. Her willingness to be submerged in duties for the sake of the family, the state and the species was the condition of his emergence as the new man of the 19th century.

The conservatives elaborated their ideas with considerable imagination and however inaccurate and unscientific they may now appear, they were impressive in their union of the interests and fears and theories of their own day. By relating social and ethical questions to a supposedly impersonal science through evolution, these theorists could claim a consistent biological and philosophical foundation for their ideas about society and government. In the case of their ideas about women, a highly traditional formulation of women's proper role and education was seen as congruent with the feminine role in the family, the state, the species and even in the overall working out of the basic principle of the universe, the unfolding evolution of beings. Such a synthesis was not to be taken lightly.

Nonetheless, the speculations of the scientists were never allowed to dominate the field, and just as their analyses concentrated on education, so did the rebuttals of their opponents. Clarke's *Sex in Education* brought down a storm of protest, including the able volume of essays, *The Education of American Girls*, published specifically to counteract its influence. The conservatives were opposed on scientific, factual, methodological and philosophic grounds. To refute them, girls' health and academic records were scrutinized with the closest eye, records of fertility and health were kept, and the effects of a variety of educational practices detailed.[31] In spite of the diversity of the factual material assembled, however, the champions of women's education were united on their main objections. The women and men who wished to secure not only education, but real individuality for their female pupils rested their philosophic case on a dynamic conception of the female mind and on a new awareness of the social factors which influence the development of the human personality. For neither of these, but especially not for the latter, have they received adequate credit.

The arguments advanced by the moderate and progressive educators, the ideas of the feminists and the data on the health and achievement of American female students eventually destroyed fantastic fears about advanced mathematics causing sterility and science destroying the femininity of America's students. What is surprising is the tenacity of the "scientific" arguments, not their eventual defeat. Thomas Woody, the pioneer student of the history of American women's education, wrote: "It is strange, considering the immediate and very evident success of women in doing college work, that this belief in their mental inferiority and physical weakness continued as long as it did. Its persistence in the face of facts was one of the best proofs of the social prejudice that opposed women's collegiate education."[32]

In the case of the scientific and medical arguments, however, it is probable that they were sustained not only by the weight of antique prejudice, but also by the fact that prejudice was stated in the most modern and approved terms. While a priori statements of feminine limitations might have been laughed out of the journals and while religious sanctions were losing their power, arguments drawn from scientific research and especially from the data and theories of evolution had irresistible conviction. Modern researchers trying to account for the still powerful prejudices against the intellectual woman and against equal opportunity for women in education are often surprised at the strength of ideas ultimately derived from Genesis and the Epistles of St. Paul. The crucial point, however, is that those ideas saw a number of reincarnations—as medical cautions, as social theories and as appendages to evolution. A recent article on the history of American sociology has suggested that ideas about female inferiority in the work of pioneer American sociologists helped prepare the way for a rapid acceptance of similar ideas in the psychologies of Freud, his successors and popularizers.[33] An even stronger case can be made for the preservation of ideas about female inferiority within the educational and medical communities, and for the transmission of 19th century limits on women's individuality and intellect through the scientific and pseudo-scientific writings on women's education and "place."

While conservative scientists lost the battle against higher education for women, it is by no means clear that their influence was destroyed. Many of the problems of female education today—its reinforcement of sexual stereotypes, its subtle discouragement of the full range of feminine talent, the pressures on girls to avoid science, mathematics and technical subjects, and the well-documented bias against females in the upper levels of education—are indications that beliefs about the desirability of limitations on female education have not been totally destroyed, but have simply reappeared in different intellectual and social clothing.[34]

Notes

1. Edward H. Clarke, *Sex in Education* (Boston: Osgood, 1874), p. 12.
2. Anon., "Biology and Women's Rights," *Quarterly Journal of Science,* repr. in *Popular Science Monthly,* 14 (Dec. 1878), 201.
3. *Adolescence* (New York: Appleton, 1909), 2:634.
4. Alice Clark, *Working Life of Women in the Seventeenth Century* (London: Dutton, 1919), pp. 281 ff. for physicians' efforts to circumscribe midwives' work, knowledge and influence. Eleanor Flexner, *Century of Struggle* (New York: Atheneum, 1970), pp. 115–19, relates efforts to open medicine to women. For doctor-patient relations in 19th century America, see

Ann Wood, "The Fashionable Diseases," *Journal of Interdisciplinary History,* 3 (Summer 1973), pp. 25–52.

5. Other discussions of sex and race bias: Carroll Smith-Rosenberg and Charles Rosenberg, "The Female Animal: Medical and Biological Views of Woman and Her Roles in Nineteenth Century America," *Journal of American History,* 60 (Sept. 1973), pp. 350–52; Julia and Herman Schwendinger, "Sociology's Founding Fathers: Sexists to a Man," *Journal of Marriage and the Family,* 33 (Nov. 1971), 583 ff.
6. Other discussions: the Rosenbergs and Willystine Goodsell, *The Education of Women* (New York: Macmillan, 1923), pp. 63 ff. Interestingly, Goodsell was discussing these medical theories as still troubling questions.
7. "Sex in Education," *Popular Science Monthly,* 41 (Sept. 1892), 176.
8. "Female Education from a Medical Point of View," *Popular Science Monthly,* 24 (Dec. 1883), 214 ff. and 24 (Jan. 1884), 319 ff.
9. Clarke, p. 131.
10. Hall, 2:588.
11. Hall, 2:633.
12. Grant Allen, "Plain Words on the Woman Question," *Popular Science Monthly,* 36 (Dec. 1889), 170–81.
13. Nathan Allen, "Changes in New England Population," *Popular Science Monthly,* 23 (Aug. 1883), and "The Decay of the Family," *N.Y. Observer,* June 15, 1882. For later treatments: Arthur Newsholme, *The Declining Birthrate* (New York: Moffat Yard, 1911) and Sir Leo Chrozza Money, *The Peril of the White* (London: W. Collin's Sons, 1925). Also, John Higham, *Strangers in the Land: Patterns of American Nativism, 1860–1925.* rev. ed. (New York: Atheneum, 1971).
14. Grant Allen, p. 175.
15. *Man and Woman,* 6th ed. (London: A. C. Black, 1926), pp. 119 ff.
16. "Sex in Education," *Bookman* (1906), quoted in Leta Stetter Hollingsworth, "Variability as Related to Sex Differences in Achievement," *American Journal of Sociology,* 21 (Jan. 1914), 510 (Emphasis in original).
17. Thorndike, p. 510.
18. Ellis, pp. 430–31.
19. Hollingsworth, pp. 513–23; Goodsell, pp. 72–76.
20. Goodsell, pp. 69–71; Ellis, pp. 527–46.
21. Charles Darwin, *The Origin of Species and The Descent of Man* (New York: Modern Library, n.d.), p. 580.
22. Patrick Geddes and J. Arthur Thompson, *The Evolution of Sex,* ed. Havelock Ellis (New York: Scribner, n.d.), p. 267.
23. W. K. Brooks, "The Condition of Woman from a Zoological Point of View," *Popular Science Monthly,* 15 (June 1879), 150.
24. Brooks, p. 154.
25. Hall, 2:567.
26. Geddes and Thompson, p. 267.
27. M. A. Hardaker, "Science and the Woman Question," *Popular Science Monthly,* 20 (Mar. 1882), 577.
28. Hall, 2:639–40.
29. Anon., "Biology and Women's Rights," repr. *Popular Science Monthly,* 14 (Dec. 1878), 205.
30. This idea is implicit in the sharp 19th century demarcation of masculine and feminine spheres and the insistence on the greater closeness of the female to nature and to both mental and physical racial stereotypes.
31. For results of the survey done by the Association of Collegiate Alumnae (1884) and other studies, see Goodsell, pp. 86–89; also Lucinda H. Stone, "Effects of Mental Growth," *The Education of American Girls,* ed. Anna C. Brackett (New York: Putnam's, 1874); John Dewey, "Health and Sex in Education," *Popular Science Monthly,* 28 (Mar., 1886), 606–14; Charlotte W. Porter, "Physical Hindrances to Teaching Girls," *Forum,* 12 (Sept., 1891), 41 ff.; Mary T. Bissell, "Emotions vs. Health in Women," *Popular Science Monthly,* 32 (Feb., 1888), 504–10; Nellie Comins Whitaker, "The Health of American Girls," *Popular Science Monthly,* 71 (Sept.

1907), 234 ff.; Lucy M. Hall, "Higher Education of Women and the Family," *Popular Science Monthly,* 30 (Mar. 1887), 614 ff.

32. Thomas Woody, *A History of Women's Education in the United States* (New York: Science Press, 1929), 2:155.
33. Schwendingers, "Sociology's Founding Fathers," p. 789.
34. Sex bias against women in education has been exhaustively documented. For example, *Discrimination Against Women,* Parts 1 and 2 of Hearings Before the Special Subcommittee on Education regarding Section 805 of H.R. 16098, Washington, D.C. 1970; also, *A Matter of Simple Justice,* the Report of the President's Task Force on Women's Rights and Responsibilities, April 1970.

SEX AND DEATH IN THE RATIONAL WORLD OF DEFENSE INTELLECTUALS

Carol Cohn

. . . My close encounter with nuclear strategic analysis started in the summer of 1984. I was one of forty-eight college teachers (one of ten women) attending a summer workshop on nuclear weapons, nuclear strategic doctrine, and arms control, taught by distinguished "defense intellectuals." Defense intellectuals are men (and indeed, they are virtually all men) "who use the concept of deterrence to explain why it is safe to have weapons of a kind and number it is not safe to use."[1] They are civilians who move in and out of government, working sometimes as administrative officials or consultants, sometimes at universities and think tanks. They formulate what they call "rational" systems for dealing with the problems created by nuclear weapons: how to manage the arms race; how to deter the use of nuclear weapons; how to fight a nuclear war if deterrence fails. It is their calculations that are used to explain the necessity of having nuclear destructive capability at what George Kennan has called "levels of such grotesque dimensions as to defy rational understanding."[2] At the same time, it is their reasoning that is used to explain why it is not safe to live without nuclear weapons. In short, they create the theory that informs and legitimates American nuclear strategic practice.

For two weeks, I listened to men engage in dispassionate discussion of nuclear war. I found myself aghast, but morbidly fascinated—not by nuclear weaponry, or by images of nuclear destruction, but by the extraordinary abstraction and removal from what I knew as reality that characterized the professional discourse. I became obsessed by the question, How can they think this way? At the end of the summer program, when I was offered the opportunity to stay on at the university's center on defense technology and arms control (hereafter known as "the Center"), I jumped at the chance to find out how they could think "this" way.

. . . But as I learned their language, as I became more and more engaged with their information and their arguments, I found that my own thinking was changing. Soon, I could no longer cling to the comfort of studying an external and objectified "them." I had to confront a new question: How can *I* think this way? How can any of us? . . .

STAGE I: LISTENING

Clean Bombs and Clean Language

Entering the world of defense intellectuals was a bizarre experience—bizarre because it is a world where men spend their days calmly and matter-of-factly discussing nuclear weapons, nuclear strategy, and nuclear war. The discussions are carefully and intricately reasoned, occurring seemingly without any sense of horror, urgency, or moral outrage—in fact, there seems to be no graphic reality behind the words, as they speak of "first strikes," "counterforce exchanges," and "limited nuclear war," or as they debate the comparative values of a "minimum deterrent posture" versus a "nuclear war–fighting capability."

Yet what is striking about the men themselves is not, as the content of their conversations might suggest, their cold-bloodedness. Rather, it is that they are a group of men unusually endowed with charm, humor, intelligence, concern, and decency. Reader, I liked them. At least, I liked many of them. The attempt to understand how such men could contribute to an endeavor that I see as so fundamentally destructive became a continuing obsession for me, a lens through which I came to examine all of my experiences in their world.

In this early stage, I was gripped by the extraordinary language used to discuss nuclear war. What hit me first was the elaborate use of abstraction and euphemism, of words so bland that they never forced the speaker or enabled the listener to touch the realities of nuclear holocaust that lay behind the words.

Anyone who has seen pictures of Hiroshima burn victims or tried to imagine the pain of hundreds of glass shards blasted into flesh may find it perverse beyond imagination to hear a class of nuclear devices matter-of-factly referred to as "clean bombs." "Clean bombs" are nuclear devices that are largely fusion rather than fission and that therefore release a higher quantity of energy, not as radiation, but as blast, as destructive explosive power.[3]

"Clean bombs" may provide the perfect metaphor for the language of defense analysts and arms controllers. This language has enormous destructive power, but without emotional fallout, without the emotional fallout that would result if it were clear one was talking about plans for mass murder, mangled bodies, and unspeakable human suffering. Defense analysts talk about "countervalue attacks" rather than about incinerating cities. Human death, in nuclear parlance, is most often referred to as "collateral damage"; for, as one defense analyst said wryly, "The Air Force doesn't target people, it targets shoe factories."

Some phrases carry this cleaning-up to the point of inverting meaning. The MX missile will carry ten warheads, each with the explosure power of 300–475 kilotons of TNT: *one* missile the bearer of destruction approximately 250–400 times that of the Hiroshima bombing.[4] Ronald Reagan has dubbed the MX missile "the Peacekeeper." While this renaming was the object of considerable scorn in the community of defense analysts, these very same analysts refer to the MX as a "damage limitation weapon."

These phrases, only a few of the hundreds that could be discussed, exemplify the astounding chasm between image and reality that characterizes technostrategic language. They also hint at the terrifying way in which the existence of nuclear devices has distorted our perceptions and redefined the world. "Clean bombs" tells us that radiation is the only "dirty" part of killing people.

To take this one step further, such phrases can even seem healthful/curative/corrective. So that we not only have "clean bombs" but also "surgically clean strikes" ("counterforce" attacks that can purportedly "take out"—i.e., accurately destroy—an opponent's weapons or command centers without causing significant injury to anything else). The image of excision of the offending weapon is unspeakably ludicrous when the surgical tool is not a delicately controlled scalpel but a nuclear warhead. And somehow it seems to be forgotten that even scalpels spill blood.[5]

White Men in Ties Discussing Missile Size

Feminists have often suggested that an important aspect of the arms race is phallic worship, that "missile envy" is a significant motivating force in the nuclear build-up.[6] I have always found this an uncomfortably reductionist explanation and hoped that my research at the Center would yield a more complex analysis. But still, I was curious about the extent to which I might find a sexual subtext in the defense professionals' discourse. I was not prepared for what I found.

I think I had naively imagined myself as a feminist spy in the house of death—that I would need to sneak around and eavesdrop on what men said in unguarded moments, using all my subtlety and cunning to unearth whatever sexual imagery might be underneath how they thought and spoke. I had naively believed that these men, at least in public, would appear to be aware of feminist critiques. If they had not changed their language, I thought that at least at some point in a long talk about "penetration aids," someone would suddenly look up, slightly embarrassed to be caught in such blatant confirmation of feminist analyses of What's Going On Here.[7]

Of course, I was wrong. There was no evidence that any feminist critiques had ever reached the ears, much less the minds, of these men. American military dependence on nuclear weapons was explained as "irresistible, because you get more bang for the buck." Another lecturer solemnly and scientifically announced "to disarm is to get rid of all your stuff." (This may, in turn, explain why they see serious talk of nuclear disarmament as perfectly resistable, not to mention foolish. If disarmament is emasculation, how could any real man even consider it?) A professor's explanation of why the MX missile is to be placed in the silos of the newest Minuteman missiles, instead of replacing the older, less accurate ones, was "because they're in the nicest hole—you're not going to take the nicest missile you have and put it in a crummy hole." Other lectures were filled with discussion of vertical erector launchers, thrust-to-weight ratios, soft lay downs, deep penetration, and the comparative advantages of protracted versus spasm attacks—or what one military adviser to the National Security Council has called "releasing 70 to 80 percent of our megatonnage in one orgasmic whump."[8] There was serious concern about the need to harden our missiles and the need to "face it, the Russians are a little harder than we are." Disbelieving glances would occasionally pass between me and my one ally in the summer program, another woman, but no one else seemed to notice.

If the imagery is transparent, its significance may be less so. The temptation is to draw some conclusions about the defense intellectuals themselves—about what they are *really* talking about, or their motivations; but the temptation is worth resisting. Individual motivations cannot necessarily be read directly from imagery; the imagery itself does not originate in these particular individuals but in a broader cultural context.

Sexual imagery has, of course, been a part of the world of warfare since long before nuclear weapons were even a gleam in a physicist's eye. The history of the atomic bomb project itself is rife with overt images of competitive male sexuality, as is the discourse of the early nuclear physicists, strategists, and SAC commanders.[9] Both the military itself and the arms manufacturers are constantly exploiting the phallic imagery and promise of sexual domination that their weapons so conveniently suggest. A quick glance at the publications that constitute some of the research sources for defense intellectuals makes the depth and pervasiveness of the imagery evident.

Air Force Magazine's advertisements for new weapons, for example, rival *Playboy* as a catalog of men's sexual anxieties and fantasies. Consider the following, from the June 1985 issue: emblazoned in bold letters across the top of a two-page advertisement for the AV-8B Harrier II—"Speak Softly and Carry a Big Stick." The copy below boasts "an exceptional thrust to weight ratio" and "vectored thrust capability that makes the . . . unique rapid response possible." Then, just in case we've failed to get the message, the last line reminds us, "Just the sort of 'Big Stick' Teddy Roosevelt had in mind way back in 1901. . . ."[10]

Given the degree to which it suffuses their world, that defense intellectuals themselves use a lot of sexual imagery does not seem especially surprising. Nor does it, by itself, constitute grounds for imputing motivation. For me, the interesting issue is not so much the imagery's psychodynamic origins, as how it functions. How does it serve to make it possible for strategic planners and other defense intellectuals to do their macabre work? How does it function in their construction of a work world that feels tenable? Several stories illustrate the complexity.

During the summer program, a group of us visited the New London Navy base where nuclear submarines are homeported and the General Dynamics Electric Boat boatyards where a new Trident submarine was being constructed. At one point during the trip we took a tour of a nuclear powered submarine. When we reached the part of the sub where the missiles are housed, the officer accompanying us turned with a grin and asked if we wanted to stick our hands through a hole to "pat the missile." *Pat the missile?*

The image reappeared the next week, when a lecturer scornfully declared that the only real reason for deploying cruise and Pershing II missiles in Western Europe was "so that our allies can pat them." Some months later, another group of us went to be briefed at NORAD (the North American Aerospace Defense Command). On the way back, our plane went to refuel at Offut Air Force Base, the Strategic Air Command headquarters near Omaha, Nebraska. When word leaked out that our landing would be delayed because the new B-1 bomber was in the area, the plane became charged with a tangible excitement that built as we flew in our holding pattern, people craning their necks to try to catch a glimpse of the B-1 in the skies, and climaxed as we touched down on the runway and hurtled past it. Later, when I returned to the Center I encountered a man who, unable to go on the trip, said to me enviously, "I hear you got to pat a B-1."

What is all this "patting?" What are men doing when they "pat" these high-tech phalluses? Patting is an assertion of intimacy, sexual possession, affectionate domination. The thrill and pleasure of "patting the missile" is the proximity of all that phallic power, the possibility of vicariously appropriating it as one's own.

But if the predilection for patting phallic objects indicates something of the homoerotic excitement suggested by the language, it also has another side. For patting is not only an act of sexual intimacy. It is also what one does to babies, small children, the pet dog. One pats that which is small, cute, and harmless—not terrifyingly destructive. Pat it, and its lethality disappears.

Much of the sexual imagery I heard was rife with the sort of ambiguity suggested by "patting the missiles." The imagery can be construed as a deadly serious display of the connections between masculine sexuality and the arms race. At the same time, it can also be heard as a way of minimizing the seriousness of militarist endeavors, of denying their deadly consequences. A former Pentagon target analyst, in telling me why he thought plans for "limited nuclear war" were ridiculous, said, "Look, you gotta understand that it's a pissing contest—you gotta expect them to use everything they've got." What does this image say? Most obviously, that this is all about competition for manhood, and thus there is tremendous danger. But at the same time, the image diminishes the contest and its outcomes, by representing it as an act of boyish mischief. . . .

Domestic Bliss

Sanitized abstraction and sexual and patriarchal imagery, even if disturbing, seemed to fit easily into the masculinist world of nuclear war planning. What did not fit, what surprised and puzzled me most when I first heard it, was the set of metaphors that evoked images that can only be called domestic.

Nuclear missiles are based in "silos." On a Trident submarine, which carries twenty-four multiple warhead nuclear missiles, crew members call the part of the submarine where the missiles are lined up in their silos ready for launching "the Christmas tree farm." What could be more bucolic—farms, silos, Christmas trees?

In the ever-friendly, even romantic world of nuclear weaponry, enemies "exchange" warheads; one missile "takes out" another; weapons systems can "marry up"; "coupling" is sometimes used to refer to the wiring between mechanisms of warning and response, or to the psychopolitical links between strategic (intercontinental) and theater (European-based) weapons. The patterns in which a MIRVed missile's nuclear warheads land is known as a "footprint."[11] These nuclear explosives are not dropped; a "bus" "delivers" them. In addition, nuclear bombs are not referred to as bombs or even warheads; they are referred to as "reentry vehicles,"a term far more bland and benign, which is then shortened to "RVs," a term not only totally abstract and removed from the reality of a bomb but also resonant with the image of the recreational vehicles of the ideal family vacation.

These domestic images must be more than simply one more form of distancing, one more way to remove oneself from the grisly reality behind the words; ordinary abstraction is adequate to that task. Something else, something very peculiar, is going on here. Calling the pattern in which bombs fall a "footprint" almost seems a willful distorting process, a playful, perverse refusal of accountability—because to be accountable to reality is to be unable to do this work.

These words may also serve to domesticate, to *tame* the wild and uncontrollable forces of nuclear destruction. The metaphors minimize; they are a way to make phenomena that are beyond what the mind can encompass smaller and safer, and thus they are a way of gaining mastery over the unmasterable. The fire-breathing dragon under the bed, the one who threatens to incinerate your family, your town, your planet, becomes a pet you can pat.

Using language evocative of everyday experiences also may simply serve to make the nuclear strategic community more comfortable with what they are doing. "PAL" (permissive action links) is the carefully constructed, friendly acronym for the electronic system designed to prevent the unauthorized firing of nuclear warheads. "BAMBI" was the acronym developed for an early version of an antiballistic missile system (for Ballistic Missile Boost Intercept). The president's Annual Nuclear Weapons Stockpile Memorandum, which outlines both short- and long-range plans for production of new nuclear weapons, is benignly referred to as "the shopping list." The National Command Authorities choose from a "menu of options" when deciding among different targeting plans. The "cookie cutter" is a phrase used to describe a particular model of nuclear attack. Apparently it is also used at the Department of Defense to refer to the neutron bomb.[12]

The imagery that domesticates, that humanizes insentient weapons, may also serve, paradoxically, to make it all right to ignore sentient human bodies, human lives.[13] Perhaps it is possible to spend one's time thinking about scenarios for the use of destructive technology and to have human bodies remain invisible in that technological world precisely because that world itself now *includes* the domestic, the human, the warm, and playful—the Christmas trees, the RVs, the affectionate pats. It is a world that is in some sense complete unto itself; it even includes death and loss. But it is weapons, not humans, that get "killed." "Fratricide" occurs when one of your warheads "kills" another of your own warheads. There is much discussion of "vulnerability" and "survivability," but it is about the vulnerability and survival of weapons systems, not people.

Male Birth and Creation

There is one set of domestic images that demands separate attention—images that suggest men's desire to appropriate from women the power of giving life and that conflate creation and destruction. The bomb project is rife with images of male birth.[14] In December 1942, Ernest Lawrence's telegram to the physicists at Chicago read, "Congratulations to the new parents. Can hardly wait to see the new arrival."[15] At Los Alamos, the atom bomb was referred to as "Oppenheimer's baby." One of the physicists working at Los Alamos, Richard Feynman, writes that when he was temporarily on leave after his wife's death, he received a telegram saying, "The baby is expected on such and such a day."[16] At Lawrence Livermore, the hydrogen bomb was referred to as "Teller's baby," although those who wanted to disparage Edward Teller's contribution claimed he was not the bomb's father but its mother. They claimed that Stanislaw Ulam was the real father; he had the all important idea and inseminated Teller with it. Teller only "carried it" after that.[17]

Forty years later, this idea of male birth and its accompanying belittling of maternity—the denial of women's role in the process of creation and the reduction of "motherhood" to the provision of nurturance (apparently Teller did not need to provide an egg, only a womb)—seems thoroughly incorporated into the nuclear mentality, as I learned on a subsequent visit to U.S. Space Command in Colorado Springs. One of the briefings I attended included discussion of a new satellite system, the not yet "on line" MILSTAR system. The officer doing the briefing gave an excited recitation of its technical capabilities and then an explanation of the new Unified Space Command's role in the system. Self-effacingly he said, "We'll do the motherhood role—telemetry, tracking, and control—the maintenance."

In light of the imagery of male birth, the extraordinary names given to the bombs that reduced Hiroshima and Nagasaki to ash and rubble—"Little Boy" and "Fat Man"—at last become intelligible. These ultimate destroyers were the progeny of the atomic scientists—and emphatically not just any progeny but male progeny. In early tests, before they were certain that the bombs would work, the scientists expressed their concern by saying that they hoped the baby was a boy, not a girl—that is, not a dud.[18] General Grove's triumphant cable to Secretary of War Henry Stimson at the Potsdam conference, informing him that the first atomic bomb test was successful read, after decoding: "Doctor has just returned most enthusiastic and confident that the little boy is as husky as his big brother. The light in his eyes discernible from here to Highhold and I could have heard his screams from here to my farm."[19] Stimson, in turn, informed Churchill by writing him a note that read, "Babies satisfactorily born."[20] In 1952, Teller's exultant telegram to Los Alamos announcing the successful test of the hydrogen bomb, "Mike," at Eniwetok Atoll in the Marshall Islands, read, "It's a boy."[21] The nuclear scientists gave birth to male progeny with the ultimate power of violent domination over female Nature. The defense intellectuals' project is the creation of abstract formulations to control the forces the scientists created—and to participate thereby in their world-creating/destroying power.

The entire history of the bomb project, in fact, seems permeated with imagery that confounds man's overwhelming technological power to destroy nature with the power to create—imagery that inverts men's destruction and asserts in its place the power to create new life and a new world. It converts men's destruction into their rebirth.

William L. Laurence witnessed the Trinity test of the first atomic bomb and wrote: "The big boom came about a hundred seconds after the great flash—the first cry of a new-born world. . . . They clapped their hands as they leaped from the ground—earthbound man symbolising the birth of a new force."[22] Watching "Fat Man" being assembled the day before it was dropped on Nagasaki, he described seeing the bomb as "being fashioned into a living thing."[23] Decades later, General Bruce K. Holloway, the commander in chief of the Strategic Air Command from 1968 to 1972, described a nuclear war as involving "a big bang, like the start of the universe."[24]

God and the Nuclear Priesthood

The possibility that the language reveals an attempt to appropriate ultimate creative power is evident in another striking aspect of the language of nuclear weaponry and doctrine—the religious imagery. In a subculture of hard-nosed realism and hyper-rationality, in a world that claims as a sign of its superiority its vigilant purging of all nonrational elements, and in which people carefully excise from their discourse every possible trace of soft sentimentality, as though purging dangerous nonsterile elements from a lab, the last thing one might expect to find is religious imagery—imagery of the forces that science has been defined in *opposition to.* For surely, given that science's identity was forged by its separation from, by its struggle for freedom from, the constraints of religion, the only thing as unscientific as the female, the subjective, the emotional, would be the religious. And yet, religious imagery permeates the nuclear past and present. The first atomic bomb test was called Trinity—the unity of the Father, the Son, and the Holy Spirit, the male forces of Creation. The imagery is echoed in the language of the physicists who worked on the bomb and witnessed the test: "It was as though we stood at the first day of creation." Robert Oppenheimer thought of Krishna's words to Arjuna in the *Bhagavad Gita:* "I am become Death, the Shatterer of Worlds."[25]

Perhaps most astonishing of all is the fact that the creators of strategic doctrine actually refer to members of their community as "the nuclear priesthood." It is hard to decide what is most extraordinary about this: the easy arrogance of their claim to the virtues and supernatural power of the priesthood; the tacit admission (*never* spoken directly) that rather than being unflinching, hard-nosed, objective, empirically minded scientific describers of reality, they are really the creators of dogma; or the extraordinary implicit statement about who, or rather what, has become god. If this new priesthood attains its status through an inspired knowledge of nuclear weapons, it gives a whole new meaning to the phrase "a mighty fortress is our God."

STAGE 2: LEARNING TO SPEAK THE LANGUAGE

Although I was startled by the combination of dry abstraction and counter-intuitive imagery that characterizes the language of defense intellectuals, my attention and energy were quickly focused on decoding and learning to speak it. The first task was training the tongue in the articulation of acronyms.

Several years of reading the literature of nuclear weaponry and strategy had not prepared me for the degree to which acronyms littered all conversations, nor for the way in which they are used. Formerly, I had thought of them mainly as utilitarian. They allow you to write or speak faster. They act as a form of abstraction, removing you from the reality behind the words. They restrict communication to the initiated, leaving all others both uncomprehending and voiceless in the debate.

But, being at the Center, hearing the defense analysts use the acronyms, and then watching as I and others in the group started to fling acronyms around in our conversation revealed some additional, unexpected dimensions.

First, in speaking and hearing, a lot of these terms can be very sexy. A small supersonic rocket "designed to penetrate any Soviet air defense" is called a SRAM (for short-range attack missile). Submarine-launched cruise missiles are not referred to as SLCMs, but "slick'ems." Ground-launched cruise missiles are "glick'ems." Air-launched cruise missiles are not sexy but magical—"alchems" (ALCMs) replete with the illusion of turning base metals into gold.

TACAMO, the acronym used to refer to the planes designed to provide communications links to submarines, stands for "take charge and move out." The image seems closely related to the nicknames given to the new guidance systems for "smart weapons"—"shoot and scoot" or "fire and forget."

Other acronyms work in other ways. The plane in which the president supposedly will be flying around above a nuclear holocaust, receiving intelligence and issuing commands for the next bombing, is referred to as "kneecap" (for NEACP—National Emergency Airborne Command Post). The edge of derision suggested in referring to it as "kneecap" mirrors the edge of derision implied when it is talked about at all, since few believe that the president really would have the time to get into it, or that the communications systems would be working if he were in it, and some might go so far as to question the usefulness of his being able to direct an extended nuclear war from his kneecap even if it were feasible. (I never heard the morality of this idea addressed.) But it seems to me that speaking about it with that edge of derision is *exactly* what allows it to be spoken about and seriously discussed at all. It is the very ability to make fun of a concept that makes it possible to work with it rather than reject it outright.

In other words, what I learned at the program is that talking about nuclear weapons is fun. I am serious. The words are fun to say; they are racy, sexy, snappy. You can throw them around in rapid-fire succession. They are quick, clean, light; they trip off the tongue. You can reel off dozens of them in seconds, forgetting about how one might just interfere with the next, not to mention with the lives beneath them.

I am not describing a phenomenon experienced only by the perverse, although the phenomenon itself may be perverse indeed. Nearly everyone I observed clearly took pleasure in using the words. It mattered little whether we were lecturers or students, hawks or doves, men or women—we all learned it, and we all spoke it. Some of us may have spoken with a self-consciously ironic edge, but the pleasure was there nonetheless.

Part of the appeal was the thrill of being able to manipulate an arcane language, the power of entering the secret kingdom, being someone in the know. It is a glow that is a significant part of learning about nuclear weaponry. Few know, and those who do are powerful. You can rub elbows with them, perhaps even be one yourself.

That feeling, of course, does not come solely from the language. The whole setup of the summer program itself, for example, communicated the allures of power and the benefits of white male privileges. We were provided with luxurious accommodations, complete with young black women who came in to clean up after us each day; generous funding paid not only our transportation and food but also a large honorarium for attending; we met in lavishly appointed classrooms and lounges. Access to excellent athletic facilities was guaranteed by a "Temporary Privilege Card," which seemed to me to sum up the essence of the experience. Perhaps most important of all were the endless allusions by our lecturers to "what I told John [Kennedy]" and "and then Henry [Kissinger] said," or the lunches where we could sit next to a prominent political figure and listen to Washington gossip.

A more subtle, but perhaps more important, element of learning the language is that, when you speak it, you feel in control. The experience of mastering the words infuses your relation to the material. You can get so good at manipulating the words that it almost feels as though the whole thing is under control. Learning the language gives a sense of what I would call cognitive mastery; the feeling of mastery of technology that is finally *not* controllable but is instead powerful beyond human comprehension, powerful in a way that stretches and even thrills the imagination.

The more conversations I participated in using this language, the less frightened I was of nuclear war. How can learning to speak a language have such a powerful effect? One answer, I believe, is that the *process* of learning the language is itself a part of what removes you from the reality of nuclear war.

I entered a world where people spoke what amounted to a foreign language, a language I had to learn if we were to communicate with one another. So I became engaged in the challenge of it—of decoding the acronyms and figuring out which were the proper verbs to use. My focus was on the task of solving the puzzles, developing language competency—not on the weapons and wars behind the words. Although my interest was in thinking about nuclear war and its prevention, my energy was elsewhere.

By the time I was through, I had learned far more than a set of abstract words that refers to grisly subjects, for even when the subjects of a standard English and nukespeak description seem to be the same, they are, in fact, about utterly different phenomena. Consider the following descriptions, in each of which the subject is the aftermath of a nuclear attack:

> Everything was black, had vanished into the black dust, was destroyed. Only the flames that were beginning to lick their way up had any color. From the dust that was like a fog, figures began to loom up, black, hairless, faceless. They screamed with voices that were no longer human. Their screams drowned out the groans rising everywhere from the rubble, groans that seemed to rise from the very earth itself.[26]
>
> [You have to have ways to maintain communications in a] nuclear environment, a situation bound to include EMP blackout, brute force damage to systems, a heavy jamming environment, and so on.[27]

There are no ways to describe the phenomena represented in the first with the language of the second. Learning to speak the language of defense analysts is not a conscious, cold-blooded decision to ignore the effects of nuclear weapons on real live human beings, to ignore the sensory, the emotional experience, the human impact. It is simply learning a new language, but by the time you are through, the content of what you can talk about is monumentally different, as is the perspective from which you speak.

In the example above, the differences in the two descriptions of a "nuclear environment" stem partly from a difference in the vividness of the words themselves—the words of the first intensely immediate and evocative, the words of the second abstract and distancing. The passages also differ in their content; the first describes the effects of a nuclear blast on human beings, the second describes the impact of a nuclear blast on technical systems designed to assure the "command and control" of nuclear weapons. Both of these differences may stem from the difference of perspective: the speaker in the first is a victim of nuclear weapons, the speaker in the second is a user. The speaker in the first is using words to try to name and contain the horror of human suffering all around her; the speaker in the second is using words to ensure the possibility of launching the next nuclear attack. Technostrategic language can be used only to articulate the perspective of the users of nuclear weapons, not that of the victims.

Thus, speaking the expert language not only offers distance, a feeling of control, and an alternative focus for one's energies; it also offers escape—escape from thinking of oneself as a victim of nuclear war. I do not mean this on the level of individual consciousness; it is not that defense analysts somehow convince themselves that they would not be among the victims of nuclear war, should it occur. But I do mean it in terms of the structural position the speakers of the language occupy and the perspective they get from that position. *Structurally,* speaking technostrategic language removes them from the position of victim and puts them in the position of the planner, the user, the actor. From that position, there is neither need nor way to see oneself as a victim; no matter what one deeply knows or believes about the likelihood of nuclear war, and no matter what sort of terror or despair the knowledge of nuclear war's reality might inspire, the speakers of technostrategic language are positionally allowed, even forced, to escape that awareness, to escape viewing nuclear war from the position of the victim, by virtue of their linguistic stance as users, rather than victims, of nuclear weaponry.

Finally, then, I suspect that much of the reduced anxiety about nuclear war commonly experienced by both new speakers of the language and long-time experts comes from characteristics of the language itself: the distance afforded by its abstraction; the sense of control afforded by mastering it; and the fact that its content and concerns are that of the users rather than the victims of nuclear weapons. In learning the language, one goes from being the passive, powerless victim to the competent, wily, powerful purveyor of nuclear threats and nuclear explosive power. The enormous destructive effects of nuclear weapons systems become extensions of the self, rather than threats to it.

STAGE 3: DIALOGUE

It did not take very long to learn the language of nuclear war and much of the specialized information it contained. My focus quickly changed from mastering technical information and doctrinal arcana to attempting to understand more about how the dogma was rationalized. . . .

Since underlying rationales are rarely discussed in the everyday business of defense planning, I had to start asking more questions. At first, although I was tempted to use my newly acquired proficiency in technostrategic jargon, I vowed to speak English. I had long believed that one of the most important functions of an expert language is exclusion—the denial of a voice to those outside the professional community. I wanted to see whether a well-informed person could speak English and still carry on a knowledgeable conversation.

What I found was that no matter how well-informed or complex my questions were, if I spoke English rather than expert jargon, the men responded to me as though I were ignorant, simpleminded, or both. It did not appear to occur to anyone that I might actually be choosing not to speak their language.

A strong distaste for being patronized and dismissed made my experiment in English short-lived. I adapted my everyday speech to the vocabulary of strategic analysis. I spoke of "escalation dominance," "preemptive strikes," and, one of my favorites, "subholocaust engagements." Using the right phrases opened my way into long, elaborate discussions that taught me a lot about technostrategic reasoning and how to manipulate it.

I found, however, that the better I got at engaging in this discourse, the more impossible it became for me to express my own ideas, my own values. I could adopt the language and gain a wealth of new concepts and reasoning strategies—but at the same time as the language gave me access to things I had been unable to speak about before, it radically excluded others. I could not use the language to express my concerns because it was physically impossible. This language does not allow certain questions to be asked or certain values to be expressed.

To pick a bald example: the word "peace" is not a part of this discourse. As close as one can come is "strategic stability," a term that refers to a balance of numbers and types of weapons systems—not the political, social, economic, and psychological conditions implied by the word "peace." Not only is there no word signifying peace in this discourse, but the word "peace" itself cannot be used. To speak it is immediately to brand oneself as a soft-headed activist instead of an expert, a professional to be taken seriously.

If I was unable to speak my concerns in this language, more disturbing still was that I found it hard even to keep them in my own head. I had begun my research expecting abstract and sanitized discussions of nuclear war and had readied myself to replace my words for theirs, to be ever vigilant against slipping into the never-never land of abstraction. But no matter how prepared I was, no matter how firm my commitment to staying aware of the reality behind the words, over and over I found that I could not stay connected, could not keep human lives as my reference point. I found I could go for days speaking about nuclear weapons without once thinking about the people who would be incinerated by them.

It is tempting to attribute this problem to qualities of the language, the words themselves—the abstractness, the euphemisms, the sanitized, friendly, sexy acronyms. Then all we would need to do is change the words, make them more vivid; get the military planners to say "mass murder" instead of "collateral damage" and their thinking would change.

The problem, however, is not only that defense intellectuals use abstract terminology that removes them from the realities of which they speak. There *is* no reality of which they speak. Or, rather, the "reality" of which they speak is itself a world of abstractions. Deterrence theory, and much of strategic doctrine altogether, was invented largely by mathematicians, economists, and a few political scientists. It was invented to hold together abstractly, its validity judged by its internal logic. Questions of the correspondence to observable reality were not the issue. These abstract systems were developed as a way to make it possible to "think about the unthinkable"—not as a way to describe or codify relations on the ground.[28]

So the greatest problem with the idea of "limited nuclear war," for example, is not that it is grotesque to refer to the death and suffering caused by *any* use of nuclear weapons as "limited" or that "limited nuclear war" is an abstraction that is disconnected from human reality but, rather, that "limited nuclear war" is itself an abstract conceptual system, designed, embodied, achieved by computer modeling. It is an abstract world in which hypothetical, calm, rational actors have sufficient information to know exactly what size nuclear weapon the opponent has used against which targets, and in which they have adequate command and control to make sure that their response is precisely equilibrated to the attack. In this scenario, no field commander would use the tactical "mini-nukes" at his disposal in the height of a losing battle; no EMP-generated electronic failures, or direct attacks on command, and control centers, or human errors would destroy communications networks. Our rational actors would be free of emotional response to being attacked, free of political pressures from the populace, free from madness or despair or any of the myriad other factors that regularly affect human actions and decision making. They would act solely on the basis of a perfectly informed mathematical calculus of megatonnage.

So to refer to "limited nuclear war" is already to enter into a system that is de facto abstract and removed from reality. To use more descriptive language would not, by itself, change that. In fact, I am tempted to say that the abstractness of the entire conceptual system makes descriptive language nearly beside the point. In a discussion of "limited nuclear war," for example, it might make some difference if in place of saying "In a counterforce attack against hard targets collateral damage could be limited," a strategic analyst had to use words that were less abstract—if he had to say, for instance, "If we launch the missiles we have aimed at their missile silos, the explosions would cause the immediate mass murder of 10 million women, men, and children, as well as the extended illness, suffering, and eventual death of many millions more." It is true that the second sentence does not roll off the tongue or slide across one's consciousness quite as easily. But it is also true, I believe, that the ability to speak about "limited nuclear war" stems as much, if not more, from the fact that the term "limited nuclear war" refers to an abstract conceptual system rather than to events that might take place in the real world. As such, there is no need to think about the concrete human realities behind the model; what counts is the internal logic of the system.

This realization that the abstraction was not just in the words but also characterized the entire conceptual system itself helped me make sense of my difficulty in staying connected to human lives. But there was still a piece missing. How is it possible, for example, to make sense of the following paragraph? It is taken from a discussion of a scenario ("regime A") in which the United States and the USSR have revised their offensive weaponry, banned MIRVs, and gone to a regime of single warhead (Midgetman) missiles, with no "defensive shield" (or what is familiarly known as "Star Wars" or SDI):

> The strategic stability of regime A is based on the fact that both sides are deprived of any incentive ever to strike first. Since it takes roughly two warheads to destroy one enemy silo, an attacker must expend two of his missiles to destroy one of the enemy's. A first strike disarms the attacker. The aggressor ends up worse off than the aggressed.[29]

"The aggressor ends up worse off than the aggressed"? The homeland of "the aggressed" has just been devastated by the explosions of, say, a thousand nuclear bombs, each likely to be ten to one hundred times more powerful than the bomb dropped on Hiroshima, and the aggressor, whose homeland is still untouched, "ends up worse off"? How is it possible to think this? Even abstract language and abstract thinking do not seem to be a sufficient explanation.

I was only able to "make sense of it" when I finally asked myself the question that feminists have been asking about theories in every discipline: What is the reference point? Who (or what) is the *subject* here?

In other disciplines, we have frequently found that the reference point for theories about "universal human phenomena" has actually been white men. In technostrategic discourse, the reference point is not white men, it is not human beings at all; it is the weapons themselves. The aggressor thus ends up worse off than the aggressed because he has fewer weapons left; human factors are irrelevant to the calculus of gain and loss. . . .

The fact that the subjects of strategic paradigms are weapons has several important implications. First, and perhaps most critically, there simply is no way to talk about human death or human societies when you are using a language designed to talk about weapons. Human death simply *is* "collateral damage"—collateral to the real subject, which is the weapons themselves.

Second, if human lives are not the reference point, then it is not only impossible to talk about humans in this language, it also becomes in some sense illegitimate to ask the paradigm to reflect human concerns. Hence, questions that break through the numbing language of strategic analysis and raise issues in human terms can be dismissed easily. No one will claim that the questions are unimportant, but they are inexpert, unprofessional, irrelevant to the business at hand to ask. The discourse among the experts remains hermetically sealed.

The problem, then, is not only that the language is narrow but also that it is seen by its speakers as complete or whole unto itself—as representing a body of truths that exist independently of any other truth or knowledge. The isolation of this technical knowledge from social or psychological or moral thought, or feelings, is all seen as legitimate and necessary. The outcome is that defense intellectuals can talk about the weapons that are supposed to protect particular political entities, particular peoples and their way of life, without actually asking if weapons *can* do it, or if they are the best *way* to do it, or whether they may even damage the entities you are supposedly protecting. It is not that the men I spoke with would say that these are invalid questions. They would, however, simply say that they are separate questions, questions that are outside what they do, outside their realm of expertise. So their deliberations go on quite independently, as though with a life of their own, disconnected from the functions and values they are supposedly to serve.

Finally, the third problem is that this discourse has become virtually the only legitimate form of response to the question of how to achieve security. If the language of weaponry was one competing voice in the discussion, or one that was integrated with others, the fact that the referents of strategic paradigms are only weapons would be of little note. But when we realize that the only language and expertise offered to those interested in pursuing peace refers to nothing but weapons, its limits become staggering, and its entrapping qualities—the way in which, once you adopt it, it becomes so hard to stay connected to human concerns—become more comprehensible.

STAGE 4: THE TERROR

As a newcomer to the world of defense analysts, I was continually startled by likeable and admirable men, by their gallows humor, by the bloodcurdling casualness with which they regularly blew up the world while standing and chatting over the coffee pot. I also *heard* the language they spoke—heard the acronyms and euphemisms, and abstractions, heard the imagery, heard the pleasure with which they used it.

Within a few weeks, what had once been remarkable became unnoticeable. As I learned to speak, my perspective changed. I no longer stood outside the impermeable wall of technostrategic language and, once inside, I could no longer see it. Speaking the language, I could no longer really hear it. And once inside its protective walls, I began to find it difficult to get out. The impermeability worked both ways.

I had not only learned to speak a language: I had started to think in it. Its questions became my questions, its concepts shaped my responses to new ideas. Its definitions of the parameters of reality became mine. Like the White Queen, I began to believe six impossible things before breakfast. Not because I consciously believed, for instance, that a "surgically clean counterforce strike" was really possible, but instead because some elaborate piece of doctrinal reasoning I used was already predicated on the possibility of those strikes, as well as on a host of other impossible things.

My grasp on what *I* knew as reality seemed to slip. I might get very excited, for example, about a new strategic justification for a "no first use" policy and spend time discussing the ways in which its implications for our force structure in Western Europe were superior to the older version. And after a day or two I would suddenly step back, aghast that I was so involved with the military justifications for not using nuclear weapons—as though the moral ones were not enough. What I was actually talking about—the mass incineration caused by a nuclear attack—was no longer in my head.

Or I might hear some proposals that seemed to me infinitely superior to the usual arms control fare. First I would work out how and why these proposals were better and then work out all the ways to counter the arguments against them. But then, it might dawn on me that even though these two proposals sounded so different, they still shared a host of assumptions that I was not willing to make (e.g., about the inevitable, eternal conflict of interests between the United States and the USSR, or the desirability of having some form of nuclear deterrent, or the goal of "managing," rather than ending, the nuclear arms race). After struggling to this point of seeing what united both positions, I would first feel as though I had really accomplished something. And then all of a sudden, I would realize that these new insights were things I actually knew *before I ever entered* this community. Apparently, I had since forgotten them, at least functionally, if not absolutely.

I began to feel that I had fallen down the rabbit hole—and it was a struggle to climb back out.

CONCLUSIONS

Suffice it to say that the issues about language do not disappear after you have mastered technostrategic discourse. The seductions remain great. You can find all sorts of ways to seemingly beat the boys at their own game; you can show how even within their own definitions of rationality, most of what is happening in the development and deployment of nuclear forces is wildly irrational. You can also impress your friends and colleagues with sickly humorous stories about the way things really happen on the inside. There is tremendous pleasure in it, especially for those of us who have been closed out, who have been told that it is really all beyond us and we should just leave it to the benevolently paternal men in charge.

But as the pleasures deepen, so do the dangers. The activity of trying to out-reason defense intellectuals in their own games gets you thinking inside their rules, tacitly accepting all the unspoken assumptions of their paradigms. You become subject to the tyranny of concepts. The language shapes your categories of thought (e.g., here it becomes "good nukes" or "bad nukes," not, nukes or no nukes) and defines the boundaries of imagination (as you try to imagine a "minimally destabilizing basing mode" rather than a way to prevent the weapon from being deployed at all). . . .

Other recent entrants into this world have commented to me that, while it is the cold-blooded, abstract discussions that are most striking at first, within a short time "you get past it—you stop hearing it, it stops bothering you, it becomes normal—and you come to see that the language, itself, is not the problem."

However, I think it would be a mistake to dismiss these early impressions. They can help us learn something about the militarization of the mind, and they have, I believe, important implications for feminist scholars and activists who seek to create a more just and peaceful world.

Mechanisms of the mind's militarization are revealed through both listening to the language and learning to speak it. *Listening,* it becomes clear that participation in the world of nuclear strategic analysis does not necessarily require confrontation with the central fact about military activity—that the purpose of all weaponry and all strategy is to injure human bodies.[30] In fact, as Elaine Scarry points out, participation in military thinking does not require confrontation with, and actually demands the elision of, this reality.[31]

Listening to the discourse of nuclear experts reveals a series of culturally grounded and culturally acceptable mechanisms that serve this purpose and that make it possible to "think about the unthinkable," to work in institutions that foster the proliferation of nuclear weapons, to plan mass incinerations of millions of human beings for a living. Language that is abstract, sanitized, full of euphemisms; language that is sexy and fun to use; paradigms whose referent is weapons; imagery that domesticates and deflates the forces of mass destruction; imagery that reverses sentient and nonsentient matter, that conflates birth and death, destruction and creation—all of these are part of what makes it possible to be radically removed from the reality of what one is talking about and from the realities one is creating through the discourse.

Learning to speak the language reveals something about how thinking can become more abstract, more focused on parts disembedded from their context, more attentive to the survival of weapons than the survival of human beings. That is, it reveals something about the process of militarization—and the way in which that process may be undergone by man or woman, hawk or dove.

Most often, the act of learning technostrategic language is conceived of as an additive process: you add a new set of vocabulary words; you add the reflex ability to decode and use endless numbers of acronyms; you add some new information that the specialized language contains; you add the conceptual tools that will allow you to "think strategically." This additive view appears to be held by defense intellectuals themselves; as one said to me, "Much of the debate is in technical terms—learn it, and decide whether it's relevant later." This view also appears to be held by many who think of themselves as antinuclear, be they scholars and professionals attempting to change the field from within, or public interest lobbyists and educational organizations, or some feminist antimilitarists. Some believe that our nuclear policies are so riddled with irrationality that there is a lot of room for well-reasoned, well-informed arguments to make a difference; others, even if they do not believe that the technical information is very important, see it as necessary to master the language simply because it is too difficult to attain public legitimacy without it. In either case, the idea is that you add the expert language and information and proceed from there.

However, I have been arguing throughout this paper that learning the language is a transformative, rather than an additive, process. When you choose to learn it you enter a new mode of thinking—a mode of thinking not only about nuclear weapons but also, de facto, about military and political power and about the relationship between human ends and technological means.

Thus, those of us who find U.S. nuclear policy desperately misguided appear to face a serious quandary. If we refuse to learn the language, we are virtually guaranteed that our voices will remain outside the "politically relevant" spectrum of opinion. Yet, if we do learn and speak it, we not only severely limit what we can say but we also invite the transformation, the militarization, of our own thinking.

I have no solutions to this dilemma, but I would like to offer a few thoughts in an effort to reformulate its terms. First, it is important to recognize an assumption implicit in adopting the strategy of learning the language. When we assume that learning and speaking the language will give us a voice recognized as legitimate and will give us greater political influence, *we are assuming that the language itself actually articulates the criteria and reasoning strategies upon which nuclear weapons development and deployment decisions are made.* I believe that this is largely an illusion. Instead, I want to suggest that technostrategic discourse functions more as a gloss, as an ideological curtain behind which the actual reasons for these decisions hide. That rather than informing and shaping decisions, it far more often functions as a legitimation for political outcomes that have occurred for utterly different reasons. If this is true, it raises some serious questions about the extent of the political returns we might get from using technostrategic discourse, and whether they can ever balance out the potential problems and inherent costs.

I do not, however, want to suggest that none of us should learn the language. I do not believe that this language is well suited to achieving the goals desired by antimilitarists, yet at the same time, I, for one, have found the experience of learning the language useful and worthwhile (even if at times traumatic). The question for those of us who do choose to learn it, I think, is what use are we going to make of that knowledge?

One of the most intriguing options opened by learning the language is that it suggests a basis upon which to challenge the legitimacy of the defense intellectuals' dominance of the discourse on nuclear issues. When defense intellectuals are criticized for the cold-blooded inhumanity of the scenarios they plan, their response is to claim the high ground of rationality; they are the only ones whose response to the existence of nuclear weapons is objective and realistic. They portray those who are radically opposed to the nuclear status quo as irrational, unrealistic, too emotional. "Idealistic activists" is the pejorative they set against their own hard-nosed professionalism.

Much of their claim to legitimacy, then, is a claim to objectivity born of technical expertise and to the disciplined purging of the emotional valences that might threaten their objectivity. But if the surface of their discourse—its abstraction and technical jargon—appears at first to support these claims, a look just below the surface does not. There we find currents of homoerotic excitement, heterosexual domination, the drive toward competency and mastery, the pleasures of membership in an elite and privileged group, the ultimate importance and meaning of membership in the priesthood, and the thrilling power of becoming Death, shatterer of worlds. How is it possible to hold this up as a paragon of cool-headed objectivity?

I do not wish here to discuss or judge the holding of "objectivity" as an epistemological goal. I would simply point out that, as defense intellectuals rest their claims to legitimacy on the untainted rationality of their discourse, their project fails according to its own criteria. Deconstructing strategic discourse's claims to rationality is, then, in and of itself, an important way to challenge its hegemony as the sole legitimate language for public debate about nuclear policy.

I believe that feminists, and others who seek a more just and peaceful world, have a dual task before us—a deconstructive project and a reconstructive project that are intimately linked.[32] Our deconstructive task requires close attention to, and the dismantling of, technostrategic discourse. The dominant voice of militarized masculinity and decontextualized rationality speaks so loudly in our culture, it will remain difficult for any other voices to be heard until that voice loses some of its power to define what we hear and how we name the world—until that voice is delegitimated.

Our reconstructive task is a task of creating compelling alternative visions of possible futures, a task of recognizing and developing alternative conceptions of rationality, a task of creating rich and imaginative alternative voices—diverse voices whose conversations with each other will invent those futures.

Notes

1. Thomas Powers, "How Nuclear War Could Start," *New York Review of Books* (January 17, 1985), 33.
2. George Kennan, "A Modest Proposal," *New York Review of Books* (July 16, 1981), 14.
3. Fusion weapons' proportionally smaller yield of radioactive fallout led Atomic Energy Commission Chairman Lewis Strauss to announce in 1956 that hydrogen bomb tests were important "not only from a military point of view but from a humanitarian aspect." Although the bombs being tested were 1,000 times more powerful than those that devastated Hiroshima and Nagasaki, the proportional reduction of fallout apparently qualified them as not only clean but also humanitarian. Lewis Strauss is quoted in Ralph Lapp, "The 'Humanitarian' H-Bomb," *Bulletin of Atomic Scientists* 12, no. 7 (September 1956): 263.
4. "Kiloton" (or kt) is a measure of explosive power, measured by the number of thousands of tons of TNT required to release an equivalent amount of energy. The atomic bomb dropped on Hiroshima is estimated to have been approximately 12 kt. An MX missile is designed to carry up to ten Mk 21 reentry vehicles, each with a W-87 warhead. The yield of W-87 warheads is 300 kt, but they are "upgradable" to 475 kt.
5. Conservative government assessments of the number of deaths resulting from a "surgically clean" counterforce attack vary widely. The Office of Technology Assessment projects 2 million to 20 million immediate deaths. (See James Fallows, *National Defense* [New York: Random House, 1981], 159.) A 1975 Defense Department study estimated 18.3 million fatalities, while the U.S. Arms Control and Disarmament Agency, using different assumptions, arrived at a figure of 50 million (cited by Desmond Ball, "Can Nuclear War Be Controlled?" Adelphi Paper no. 169 [London: International Institute for Strategic Studies, 1981).
6. The phrase is Helen Caldicott's in *Missile Envy: The Arms Race and Nuclear War* (Toronto: Bantam Books, 1986).
7. For the uninitiated, "penetration aids" refers to devices that help bombers or missiles get past the "enemy's" defensive systems; e.g., stealth technology, chaff, or decoys. Within the defense intellectual community, they are also familiarly known as "penaids."

8. General William Odom, "C^3I and Telecommunications at the Policy Level," Incidental Paper, Seminar on C^3I: Command, Control, Communications and Intelligence (Cambridge, Mass.: Harvard University, Center for Information Policy Research, Spring 1980), 5.
9. This point has been amply documented by Brian Easlea, *Fathering the Unthinkable: Masculinity, Scientists and the Nuclear Arms Race* (London: Pluto Press, 1983).
10. *Air Force Magazine* 68, no. 6 (June 1985): 77–78.
11. MIRV stands for "multiple independently targetable re-entry vehicles." A MIRVed missile not only carries more than one warhead; its warheads can be aimed at different targets.
12. Henry T. Nash, "The Bureaucratization of Homicide," *Bulletin of Atomic Scientists* (April 1980), reprinted in E. P. Thompson and Dan Smith, eds., *Protest and Survive* (New York: Monthly Review Press, 1981), 159.
13. For a discussion of the functions of imagery that reverses sentient and insentient matter, that "exchange[s] . . . idioms between weapons and bodies," see Elaine Scarry, *The Body in Pain: The Making and Unmaking of the World* (New York: Oxford University Press, 1985), 60–157, esp. 67.
14. For further discussion of men's desire to appropriate from women the power of giving life and death, and its implications for men's war-making activities, see Dorothy Dinnerstein, *The Mermaid and the Minotaur* (New York: Harper & Row, 1977). For further analysis of male birth imagery in the atomic bomb project, see Evelyn Fox Keller, "From Secrets of Life to Secrets of Death" (paper delivered at the Kansas Seminar, Yale University, New Haven, Conn., November 1986); and Easlea (n. 15 above), 81–116.
15. Lawrence is quoted by Herbert Childs in *An American Genius: The Life of Ernest Orlando Lawrence* (New York: E. P. Dutton, 1968), 340.
16. Feynman writes about the telegram in Richard P. Feynman, "Los Alamos from Below," in *Reminiscences of Los Alamos, 1943–1945,* ed. Lawrence Badash, Joseph O. Hirshfelder, and Herbert P. Broida (Dordrecht: D. Reidel Publishing Co., 1980), 130.
17. Hans Bethe is quoted as saying that "Ulam was the father of the hydrogen bomb and Edward was the mother, because he carried the baby for quite a while" (J. Bernstein, *Hans Bethe: Prophet of Energy* [New York: Basic Books, 1980], 95).
18. The concern about having a boy, not a girl, is written about by Robert Jungk, *Brighter Than a Thousand Suns,* trans. James Cleugh (New York: Harcourt, Brace & Co., 1956), 197.
19. Richard E. Hewlett and Oscar E. Anderson, *The New World, 1939/46: A History of the United States Atomic Energy Commission,* 2 vols. (University Park: Pennsylvania State University Press, 1962), 1:386.
20. Winston Churchill, *The Second World War,* vol. 6., *Triumph and Tragedy* (London: Cassell, 1954), 551.
21. Quoted by Easlea, 130.
22. William L. Laurence, *Dawn over Zero: The Study of the Atomic Bomb* (London: Museum Press, 1974), 10.
23. Ibid., 188.
24. From a 1985 interview in which Holloway was explaining the logic of a "decapitating" strike against the Soviet leadership and command and control systems—and thus how nuclear war would be different from World War II, which was a "war of attrition," in which transportation, supply depots, and other targets were hit, rather than being a "big bang" (Daniel Ford, "The Button," *New Yorker Magazine* 61, no. 7 [April 8, 1985], 49).
25. Jungk, 201.
26. Hisako Matsubara, *Cranes at Dusk* (Garden City, N.Y.: Dial Press, 1985). The author was a child in Kyoto at the time the atomic bomb was dropped. Her description is based on the memories of survivors.
27. General Robert Rosenberg (formerly on the National Security Council staff during the Carter Administration), "The Influence of Policymaking on C^3I," Incidental Paper, Seminar on C^3I (Cambridge, Mass.: Harvard University, Center for Information Policy Research, Spring 1980), 59.
28. For fascinating, detailed accounts of the development of strategic doctrine, see Fred Kaplan, *The Wizards of Armageddon* (New York: Simon & Schuster, 1983); and Gregg F. Herken, *The Counsels of War* (New York: Alfred A. Knopf, 1985).

29. Charles Krauthammer, "Will Star Wars Kill Arms Control?" *New Republic,* no. 3,653 (January 21, 1985), 12–16.
30. For an eloquent and graphic exploration of this point, see Scarry (n. 23 above), 73.
31. Scarry catalogs a variety of mechanisms that serve this purpose (ibid., 60–157). The point is further developed by Sara Ruddick, "The Rationality of Care," in *Thinking about Women, War, and the Military,* ed. Jean Bethke Elshtain and Sheila Tobias (Totowa, N.J.: Rowman & Allanheld, in press).
32. Sandra Harding and Merrill Hintikka, eds., *Discovering Reality: Feminist Perspectives on Epistemology, Meta physics, Methodology and the Philosophy of Science* (Dordrecht: D. Reidel Publishing Co., 1983), ix–xix, esp. x.

MIXED MESSAGES
Men and Women in Advertisements in *Science*

Mary Barbercheck

Our culture is filled with messages that tell us not only how we should behave, but also who we should be. We receive these messages throughout our lives, and so their meaning seems natural. One of the most pervasive messages is that of the profound differences between men and women (Valian 1998). Most work in our culture is segregated by sex, and most professional fields in the sciences and engineering are traditionally male-dominated; it is only recently that women have entered the scientific workforce in appreciable numbers (Rossiter 1982, 1995). Although discrimination on the basis of sex has been outlawed in the United States since the 1970s, impediments for women scientists continue to exist, but in increasingly subtle patterns (Sonnert and Holton 1995; Valian 1998). Only a small fraction of the young men and women who receive their first academic degree in science, mathematics, or engineering will become research scientists. Research that tracks the flow of girls and women through the educational pipeline on their way to scientific careers reveals that women are awarded more than half of all undergraduate degrees. However, as aspiring scientists move through the training system, more women than men are diverted from the science career pipeline. Women currently account for about 38 percent of the graduate science and engineering degrees awarded in the United States, but only about 22 percent of employed scientists and engineers are women (National Science Foundation 1999).

There are two dominant models that explain why women are less likely to stay in science fields and, if awarded advanced degrees, are less likely than men to be successful in scientific careers (Sonnert and Holton 1995). The deficit model attributes the lower number of women scientists to their differential treatment. This model emphasizes structural barriers—legal, political, and social—that exist or existed in the social system of science. An assumption of the deficit model is that the goals of women and men are similar, but barriers to advancement keep women from accomplishing these goals at rates similar to those of men. Formal barriers (laws) have been removed, but subtle informal barriers remain: less access to resources such as space, equipment, and money; isolation from mentors, power brokers, key researchers and administrators, and "old-boy" networks (A Study on the Status of Women Faculty in Science at MIT, http://web.mit.edu/faculty/reports/, 1999; Wenneras and Wold 1997). In the deficit model it is assumed that women do not learn the "hidden" skills essential for a successful science career. Formal and informal structural barriers can directly affect the careers of women scientists but may also discourage women from choosing a science career. If women perceive that structural barriers in the social system of science will impede the potential rewards of a scientific career, they may choose another career in which the potential costs do not appear to outweigh the potential benefits. Interventions based on the deficit model include legal and policy changes, outreach programs to introduce young people to science and scientists, and mentoring programs.

The second model, the difference model, suggests that there are fewer women than men in science because women act differently (Sonnert and Holton 1995). The difference model assumes that there are fundamental differences in the outlook and goals of men and women. The obstacles of career achievement lie within women: they are innate or the result of gender-role socialization and cultural values. Particular attitudes about science may define it as a male field and therefore encourage male participation and discourage female participation. Even as rigid gender-role socialization declines, social practices still reinforce the image of the aggressive, successful man and the nurturing, supportive woman (Valian 1998). Whereas girls are socialized to interact in a style that deemphasizes aggressiveness and competitiveness, those characteristics are encouraged in boys and become embedded in a male interaction style. Culturally sanctioned typical female traits, in the current social system of science, are likely to put women at a disadvantage. These socialization patterns tend to distance women from the very characteristics that the social system of science rewards and reinforces: ambition, self-confidence, resilience, aggressiveness, and competitiveness. Interventions based on the difference model would seek to change the social norms of science to include qualities perceived as feminine. Instead of training women scientists to act more like men scientists, perhaps a social and epistemological reform of science is needed that will accommodate a wider range of behaviors and communication styles (Malcom 1999).

These two models take an either/or approach in that either obstacles are imposed on individuals by a system that constrains their choices or individuals place constraints on themselves that aggregate to social patterns. In this sense, then, neither model adequately takes into account the force of stereotypes, gender schemas, and images that surround us but do not seem to have the direct or concrete power to shape an individual's choices.

It is almost impossible not to know the difference between norms for masculinity and femininity in our society. Cultural beliefs about the masculine nature of scientists and science abound and may distance women from the field. The majority of Americans describe a scientist as a man who wears a white coat, works in a laboratory, and has facial hair and an "extravagant" hairdo (Mirsky 1997). In films, scientists are often portrayed as mad or overreaching, occasionally as heroic, although Ribalow (1999) has identified a new type of Hollywood scientist, the brainy babe. Scientific textbooks have reinforced the notion that science is a masculine endeavor by mentioning and picturing men almost exclusively and by showing the few women who do appear in gender-stereotypical roles. It is difficult to imagine that the constant pairing of "scientist" and "man" has no effect on women and men.

The mass media, especially advertising, sends strong cultural messages about desirable roles for women and men. The images of women and men in advertising are varied yet present a familiar range of stereotypes. The images of women are not self-reflective but describe women as they are ideally seen by men, and therefore the locus of power is with men (MacCurdy 1994). In advertisements and the mass media in general, male characters tend to be independent, assertive, athletic, important, technical, and responsible; they show ingenuity, leadership, bravery, or aggression. Female characters are more likely than men to be warm, emotional, romantic, affectionate, sensitive, frail, domestic, or helpless; they tend to need advice or protection, or serve others. It has been suggested that advertisements act as "achievement scripts" for women, providing them with models of appropriate behavior (Geis et al. 1984).

The task of the advertiser is to favorably dispose viewers to a product. Advertisements are intentionally designed to be unambiguous about a subject. The powerful ability of the advertiser to use a few models and props to evoke an understandable scene with just a quick glance is due not to art or technology, but to institutionalized arrangements in social life that allow us to understand the meanings of the images (Goffman 1976). The textual material outside of the picture also provides information about the product, but this is commonly redundant; the picture itself is often designed to tell a story without much textual assistance.

When people are shown in advertisements, we see the advertisers' views of how people of different sexes and ethnicities can be profitably pictured. Although the images shown in advertisements do not need to be representative of the social behavior of any particular person in real life, the pictures are usually not seen as peculiar or unnatural. For example, simply imagining a switch in the sex of the person in an advertisement often reveals the cultural stereotypes portrayed in them. Advertisers do not create the stereotypes they employ; they draw upon the cultural norms that are known to all who participate in social situations (Goffman 1976). Like movie images of scientists (Riballow 1999), print advertising images are a mirror that reflect the aspirations, hopes and beliefs of the audience.

> As advertising agencies compete among one another to influence us, we become the final referees in this contest and, in turn end up ourselves influencing in a significant way the content of the advertising page . . . the images and appeals that persuade us are by no means alien invasions into our psyche imposed from without, but rather welcomed reinforcements of our own original values. (Manca and Manca 1994)

The relationship between images of science and images of masculinity could reveal more than one model of masculinity, since the images of masculinity are varied (Lie & Sorensen 1996). Even if real individual men and women are different, there are fairly consistent ideas concerning masculinity and femininity. These stereotypes do not need to correspond to the personalities of real scientists, because the stereotypes are as real as living persons. Therefore, these stereotypes are not necessarily literally true, but they should not be devalued or ignored. Individuals are susceptible to stereotypes, and identification with a stereotype can influence performance (Steele 1997; Shih, Pittinsky, and Ambady 1999). Stereotypes may significantly impact decisions of great import in the lives of aspiring scientists, for example, in choosing to enter or remain in a field of study or on a career path, or in influencing those who make hiring, tenure, and promotion decisions (Valian 1998). In this essay I provide examples of messages that are sent to scientists—men and women, aspiring and established—during what one would assume to be a positive professional activity, reading a scientific journal.

Immersed in the broader culture and also in the culture of science, scientists are often not aware of biases that may arise from the stereotypes of men and women. A prevailing assumption is that gender is irrelevant in doing science, and therefore is irrelevant in the culture of science. But if gender is truly irrelevant, then one would expect that the images of people in professional publications would be quite different from those in the broader culture. I was curious to examine some current images of both men and women in science—more specifically, the images of people in the journal *Science*—to determine if the images there connect, either overtly or subtly, to gender stereotypes from the broader culture. *Science,* a weekly publication of the American Association for the Advancement of Science (AAAS), is one of the foremost scientific journals in the United States and is widely read across scientific disciplines. One of the missions of the AAAS is to promote diversity in the scientific workplace. In a news article entitled "Association Denounces Discrimination in the Workplace," the AAAS Board and Council issued a joint statement calling on the scientific community to be active in ensuring that discrimination "finds no comfort in our education and research institutions" (Pabst 1995). The joint statement was released to sensitize the scientific community to the fact that although discriminatory practices are illegal, they still exist in the sciences. AAAS's position is that discrimination is contrary to the very core of what it is to do science or be a scientist:

> The AAAS is committed to a work environment free from unlawful and unjust discrimination and condemns such discrimination in any form. . . . All scientific inquiry—from creative generation of ideas, through investigation, and to interpretation of

> findings—benefits from different points of view. . . . Discrimination creates an atmosphere that is not conducive to the advancement of science. It diverts attention from the rigors of science and undermines an individual's work or academic performance. . . . It also contributes to the loss of talent in science and engineering and to the alienation of capable individuals from the scientific and engineering professions. (Pabst 1995)

METHODS

To explore the extent of gender stereotypical content in *Science,* I examined the advertisements in all issues published from January 1995 through December 1997. I coded the frequency of each advertisement greater than a third of a page in size that carried a pictorial image in the following seven categories: (1)issue type: normal or with special focus/advertising supplement aimed at minorities or women; (2) people: with or without people in picture; (3) profession: scientist or not scientist; (4) sex: male, female, or both in the same picture; (5) race: white, African-American, Asian, other, or more than one race in the same picture; (6) image: authority/expert, athlete, nerd/nonconformist, or other; and (7) special qualities: the words *easy/simple* or *efficient/fast/reliable* emphasized in font size larger than bulk text. I scored the advertisements only in categories where I could unambiguously and immediately recognize the category; therefore, not all advertisements were coded in every category. I scored all advertisements regardless of the number of times a given advertisement appeared. Because my goal was to examine the use of stereotypical images rather than specific advertisements, each advertisement was considered a separate use.

A total of 141 issues of *Science* were examined. Nineteen (13.5 percent) of the issues were special issues that focused on women or people of color in science or contained advertising supplements aimed at women and people of color. In the 141 issues there were 4,070 pictorial advertisements greater than a third of a page in size. In 1,094 (26.8 percent) of the advertisements, bodies or body parts recognizable as belonging to either a man or a woman were depicted.

ADVERTISING RACE, GENDER, AND SCIENCE

The numbers of advertisements depicting women in regular issues was approximately half that of advertisements depicting men, whereas in special issues the numbers of advertisements depicting men and women were nearly equal. The proportion of advertisements depicting men, women, and both sexes in the same picture was different in the two types of issue (table 1). In regular issues men, women and both sexes together were portrayed in 63.5, 29.7, and 6.8 percent of the advertisements depicting people, respectively. In special issues the percentage of advertisements with men and women decreased to 30.5 percent and 28.2 percent, whereas advertisements depicting both sexes together increased to 41.2 percent. In 1995 women comprised approximately 50 percent of the U.S. population, and so were underrepresented in the advertisements (U.S. Bureau of the Census 1996).

The proportion of advertisements depicting people of color varied with issue type. In 1995 African Americans comprised about 14 percent of the U.S. population. In regular issues African Americans were underrepresented, comprising about 6.5 percent of the people depicted in the advertisements containing only one person. They were proportionately represented in special issues, comprising about 14 percent of the people shown in advertisements. Asians, who in 1995 comprised about 4 percent of the U.S.

TABLE 1 People in Advertisements in Regular and Special Issues of *Science*, 1995–1997

	Regular Issues (n = 122)			Special Issues (n = 19)		
	Males (n = 528, 63.5%)	Females (n = 247, 29.7%)	Both (n = 57, 6.8%)	Males (n = 80, 30.5%)	Females (n = 74, 28.2%)	Both (n = 108, 41.2%)
White	87.1%	80.9%	24.6%	82.5%	54.1%	39.8%
African-American	5.1%	9.3%	1.7%	10.0%	16.2%	0.9%
Asian	6.8%	8.9%	0%	6.3%	4.1%	0%
Multiple Races	0.9%	0.8%	73.6%	0.8%	25.7%	59.3%
Portrayed as Scientist	72.5%	63.5%	78.9%	66.3%	70.2%	59.3%

Figures are for percentage of advertisements portraying whites, African Americans, Asians, multiple races, and scientists calculated as percentages of total number of advertisements depicting men, women, or both sexes together.

population, were overrepresented in both special (5.9 percent) and regular (7.5 percent) issues of *Science.*

The proportion of advertisements depicting whites, African Americans, Asians, or multiple races in advertisements with men, women, or both sexes was different in regular and special issues of *Science.* The percentage of advertisements depicting white people was lower in special issues than in regular issues, where there was a slight decrease in the percentage of white men, from 87.1 percent in regular issues to 82.5 percent in special issues. However, most of the change in race was due to the decrease of the proportion of advertisements with white women, from 80.9 percent in regular issues to 54.1 percent in special issues. White men and women were more frequently shown together (24.6 and 39.8 percent of advertisements depicting white people in regular and special issues, respectively) than were Asian (0 percent) or African-American (<2 percent) men and women. African Americans occurred in a higher proportion of advertisements in special issues than in regular issues. This was due mainly to the increase of the percentage of African-American women, from 9.3 percent of advertisements depicting women in regular issues to 16.2 percent in special issues. There was a similar increase (from 5.5 to 11 percent of advertisements depicting men) in percentage of advertisements with African-American men between the regular and special issues.

Issue type and sex were related to the percentage of advertisements depicting multiple races together. When multiple races were depicted, it was most common for both women and men to be shown in the same advertisement (regular issues, 73.6 percent; special issues, 59.3 percent). Depiction of women in advertisements with multiple races increased from 0.8 percent in regular issues to 25.7 percent in special issues. Men and women of color were usually paired with white people. The depiction of only men in multiple-race groups was low in both types of issue (regular, 0.9 percent; special, 0.8 percent). The most acceptable way to portray diversity under the current social system of science may be through an increase in images of women of color rather than through an increase in images of men of color. The combination of the increased percentage of African-American females and the general absence of racially diverse male-only images suggests that diversity itself is a gendered image.

As *Science* is a scientific journal, it is interesting to look at the proportions of men and women portrayed as the scientific workforce. In the world of *Science* advertisements in regular issues, women make up about 18 percent of the total scientific workforce, which is slightly lower than the real percentage of 22 percent of women in the U.S. scientific workforce in 1995 (National Science Foundation 1999). In advertisements in special issues, women increased as members of the scientific workforce to about 20 percent, still lower, but more realistically reflecting the actual proportion in the United States.

THE STEREOTYPES

The Hero

Science is often mythologized in terms of the masculine hero ethic, and the advertisements in this study are no exception. The most common image was of the scientist as a hero or authority at the frontiers of progress. The word *discovery* often appears in a large font in these advertisements. The image is usually of a serious, lab-coat-clad scientist alone, often in quarter face, gazing at the object of his study, some type of apparatus, or into the unknown (fig. 1). He is unaware of and detached from the viewer. Exactly what the expert is gazing at is often unseen and remains a mystery to the viewer. Mastery of science bestows power in relation to others who lack this knowledge (Wacjman 1991). Sometimes the science and the scientist are one, with data or formulae projected onto the profile of a male head, an image of unity between the knowledge seeker and the knowledge—and perhaps a representation of the perfect flow of knowledge from nature through the scientist, without distortions of interpretation. The percentage of advertisements depicting the hero/authority image was related to sex and type of issue. When a woman was shown in the same advertisement with a man, she was more likely to be depicted as an authority than if she was shown alone. In the regular issues men, women, or both men and women in the same advertisements were depicted as heroes/authorities in 63.2, 44.5, and 56.2 percent of the ads, respectively. In the special issues the depiction of males as heroes/authorities decreased to 52.8 percent, whereas the depiction of females and both sexes as heroes/authorities increased to 55.6 and 68.7 percent, respectively. Thus one effect of the special issues was to equalize the representation of women and men as heroes.

The Nerd

A common portrayal in the advertisements is of the science nerd or its more benign variant, the social nonconformist. Nerds can be recognized by their unkempt hair, heavy-framed glasses, and pocket protectors. Unlike the experts, whose serious gaze is directed elsewhere, the nerd or nonconformist is smiling and looks directly out of the page at the viewer. The nerd displays just a little too much enthusiasm for his work, for example, jumping for joy. This is analogous to Seely's (1994) nonscientific "wild and crazy guy," which emphasizes a somewhat bizarre person free from the shackles of strict societal norms. Stemming from an antiscience theme in popular culture, the common stereotype of the nerd or egghead is depicted as an undersocialized person whose scientific pursuits leave him detached from the "real" world (Sonnert and

FIGURE 1 The hero/expert. This expert wears the signifiers of the scientist—gloves, lab coat, and face mask. His gaze and attention are focused away from the viewer, and he is totally absorbed by his research. © Microflex Corp. Used by permission.

Holton 1995). The nonconformist is a scientist but often is not associated with the stereotypical signifiers—a lab coat or heavy glasses. The nonconformist is often young, hip, and a rebel. One advertisement depicted an award-winning young male scientist wearing a flannel shirt and jeans, barefooted, and squatting (rather than sitting) on a stool. Males (18.6 percent) were depicted as nerds/nonconformists in a higher percentage of advertisements than were women (6.6 percent) or both sexes in the same advertisement (2.2 percent).

Women with scientific aspirations may face a double marginalization: entering the stigmatized subculture of nerds and then being an oddity among her colleagues because of her sex. Fortunately, the nerd image appears to be reserved largely for men.

However, one type of nonconformist image in which only females are depicted is the witch. The nerd or nonconformist is a social misfit because of his devotion to and enthusiasm for science and technology, which in this interpretation can be seen as a positive characterization. Technology is a medium of power, and technological competence is considered a valuable asset. In contrast, the witch is engaged in magic—an activity that is defined in opposition to science and technology. This association of gender with technological competence in the advertisements has a corollary in the sex-segregated workforce. For instance, women are more likely than men to work in jobs or careers that require little technical competence, and men tend to be found in a wide range of occupations that require technological training (Cockburn 1985).

Men at Work and Play

Several nonscientific images are employed for men in scientific advertisements, including construction workers, astronauts, businessmen, and technical representatives. However, the most common nonscientist image of men in advertisements is an athlete or explorer. This image in scientific advertising is analogous to Seely's (1994) characterization of the "man's man" in nonscientific advertising. In this image the masculine ideals of competition, rugged individualism, independence, strength, and quest for high quality are emphasized, and correspond well to characteristics valued in the current social culture of science. The man's man needs other men to validate his masculinity—he does manly stuff with other equally manly men. The man's man exists in an exclusive sphere, which affirms the belief that real men cannot enjoy serious challenges in the company of women. Indeed, in this stereotype the participation of women would devalue the achievement, so no true camaraderie can exist between men and women. In the *Science* advertisements, when men are not depicted as a hero or authority, they are most often (14.2 percent) depicted as being engaged in competitive sports or in physically challenging or risky recreational activities, alone or with other men. This image is used less frequently for women (2.8 percent) or in ads with both sexes (2.2 percent). Women are not portrayed with this image even when sports where females excel are depicted, such as gymnastics and track. Athletic activities of women or of both sexes together consisted of less strenuous, noncompetitive activities—for example, walking—and were depicted in an advertisement for life insurance rather than in advertisements for products used to do science.

SCIENCE MADE SIMPLE

As I proceeded with the content analysis of the advertisements, a striking pattern emerged regarding the large-font text that often accompanied the image and smaller bulk text. Words commonly appearing in large text included *accurate, fast, precise, economical, easy,* and *simple*. In regular issues women (13.3 percent) were more frequently associated with the words *easy* or *simple* than were men (6.7 percent) or both sexes (2.7 percent). Men (19.7 percent) were more frequently associated with the words *fast, reliable,* or *accurate* than were women (10.9 percent) or both sexes (12.8 percent). In special issues men were more frequently associated with *easy* (10.8 percent) than were women (4.8 percent) or both sexes together (1.7 percent), but women (4.8 percent) and men and women together (1.7 percent) were still less associated with *reliable, fast,* or *accurate* than men alone (22.9 percent).

In several advertisements, real or cartoon women are shown using equipment whose chief selling point appears to be ease of use (fig. 2). In one advertisement, a smiling blond woman is portrayed similarly to a "car model," merely pointing to, rather

FIGURE 2 Science made simple. Women portrayed as scientists are often paired with the message of ease-of-use of technical or analytical equipment. © Quiagen Corp. Reprinted with permission.

than using, a piece of equipment that is described as easy to use. In one advertisement that invites multiple interpretations, a soft-focus woman engaged in lab work provides the backdrop for a piece of equipment embedded in a puzzle shape, accompanied by an ambiguous phrase in large text: "The missing piece to simplify your day!" The double entendre implied by the sexual slang *piece* is clearly intended. We are left to guess at which piece is simplifying whose day. Whether the woman pictured is an instrument of simplification and objectification for the unseen (male) head of the lab or the advertised apparatus is simplifying a difficult technical task for the woman, neither interpretation has a positive meaning.

In contrast, in similar advertisements where a man is shown using a piece of scientific equipment, the word *easy* is generally not used. *Easy* is replaced by the words *fast*, *accurate*, or *reliable* in large text. Men are portrayed as having the ability to master technology and tackle the challenging problems in science, whereas women are portrayed as doing science with the aid of technology that makes the job easy. Perhaps this distinction allows the depiction of women's participation in science without devaluing the achievements of men.

WOMEN AT WORK AND NOT AT PLAY

Women were portrayed as nonscientists in 36.5 percent of the advertisements in which they occurred in the regular issues, and in 29.8 percent of the advertisements in the special issues of *Science.* Nonscientist images of men were dominated by sports images—men at play. The masculine sports images reflect activities largely engaged in for pleasure or thrill seeking. In contrast, the most common nonscientist depiction of women is as a beneficiary or consumer of science, often as a mother with a child or engaged in a domestic activity such as grocery shopping. This image is well described by MacCurdy's (1994) image category of the Virgin Mary, which depicts a nurturing, sexless, and selfless mother who exists primarily to care for others and who needs protection from the world outside the home. The women in these images are presented in ways that suggest vulnerability in an intimate setting, for example, wrapped in towels, wearing a bathrobe, or nude. She is often shown cheek to cheek with her child, smiling blissfully and gazing directly at the viewer or at her child. This is quite a contrast to the serious scientist, who, his attention and gaze focused elsewhere, is detached from the viewer.

Consumption has been defined as women's work (Bartel 1988), and since the 1920s the gender norm of division between production (male) and consumption (female) has been used by advertisers. The image of woman as a caregiver or as a consumer

FIGURE 3 The emotional woman. This portrayal conflicts with the notion that science requires the masculine attributes of intellectual objectivity and emotional detachment. © 2000 Pan Vera Corporation. Reprinted with permission.

rather than producer of scientific knowledge has also been commonly used in pharmaceutical advertising (Craig 1992; Mosher 1976). Whereas the role of caregiver is a real and worthwhile one for women (and men), are there any compelling reasons why these images should appear in a scientific journal? Unlike the sports images used for men, the characteristics culturally associated with caregiving and housekeeping are not the qualities usually deemed necessary for a successful career in science (teaching, perhaps, but not conducting research). These domestic images reinforce the idea that the appropriate activity for women is to stay at home and act as caregiver to her family, and affirm that a woman is dependent, which conflicts with the image of the independent scientist.

Even when depicted as scientists, women retain their stereotypical roles as nurturers. A recruitment advertisement for a prestigious midwestern university shows a female student with someone who is presumably her female adviser—both are wearing lab coats and standing in front of apparatus used in molecular biology research. In a large font over the picture are the words "It's much easier to learn from someone who cares that you are learning." Not only must the depicted female faculty member attend to all of her regular duties, it is assumed that she will mother her students and at the same time make science easy to learn.

In a series of advertisements that occurred only in special issues, a number of cleansers and cosmetics produced by the company are shown, accompanied by large text suggesting that of course women will want to work on these products, deemed to be of special interest to women. One may wonder what this means for women scientists who are not particularly nurturing or interested in working on or using the types of products that all women are supposed to be interested in—those associated with the "appropriate" roles for women. The message relayed is that if you can't be at home cleaning the house, you should want to work on products that other women can use to clean the house. Do these images of women as caregivers and housekeepers imply that male scientists don't care about students, or that men shouldn't be interested in domestic activities or do housework? The intellectual and detached aspects of the ideal scientist/hero image appear to be irreconcilable with the feminine caregiver images presented in the advertisements.

MOTHER NATURE

In the history and philosophy of science, nature has long been depicted as a woman, and science as the method by which to know and control nature. The notion that women are closer to nature and are more emotional, less analytical, and weaker than men is prevalent in Western culture. In the industrialized world, where scientific and technical rationality are highly valued, these associations play a powerful role in the ideological construction of women (nonscientists) as inferior (Plumwood 1993). The logical structure of dualism forms a major basis for the connection between nature and women, for example, man/woman, culture/nature, master/servant, reason/emotion, scientific/ignorant, civilized/primitive, public/private, independent/dependent, objective/subjective, competitive/nurturing, intellectual/intuitive. To read the first side of each pair is to read a list of stereotypical qualities traditionally attributed to men and to the human, while the second side presents qualities traditionally excluded from male ideals and associated with women. The stereotype is that scientists are white men who think objectively, rationally, and with suppressed emotions with the object of transcending and controlling nature. Women in real life and in advertisements can now be scientists (especially if the science is associated with caregiving or housekeeping), but the image of science itself and its orientation to masculine ideals and the domination of nature remains unchanged.

Although occurring infrequently, the image of women as a symbol of nature or as object of study is used to sell scientific products. In an image of the most overarching "mother" of all, we see a female hand with long, red-polished nails holding the earth. In another advertisement, we see only fragments of a woman—a made-up eye, a lipsticked and pursed mouth—interspersed with fragments of nature—flowers and seashells—accompanied by the word *discovery* in a large font (fig. 4). This image seems to suggest that, like nature, women can be fragmented, reduced, understood, and controlled by science. In what is perhaps the most explicit conflation of nature and woman in an adver-

FIGURE 4 **Woman as nature as object of scientific discovery. Here women and nature are reduced to fragments and identified with each other. Copyright 2000, Invitrogen Corporation. All rights reserved. Used by permission.**

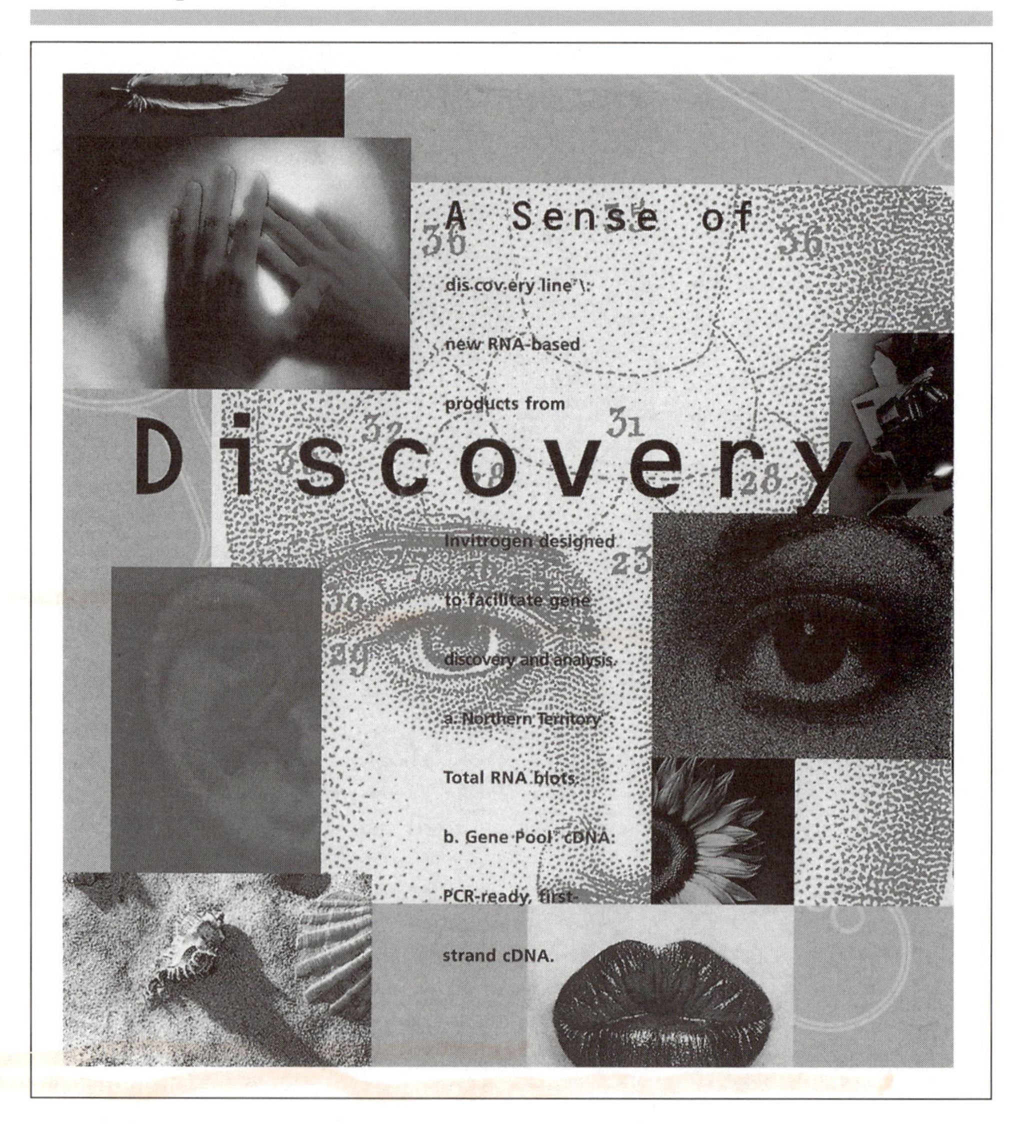

FIGURE 5 Women represented as nature and the unknown. Women, DNA, and Africa as territory to be explored and exploited. © New England Biolabs. Used by permission.

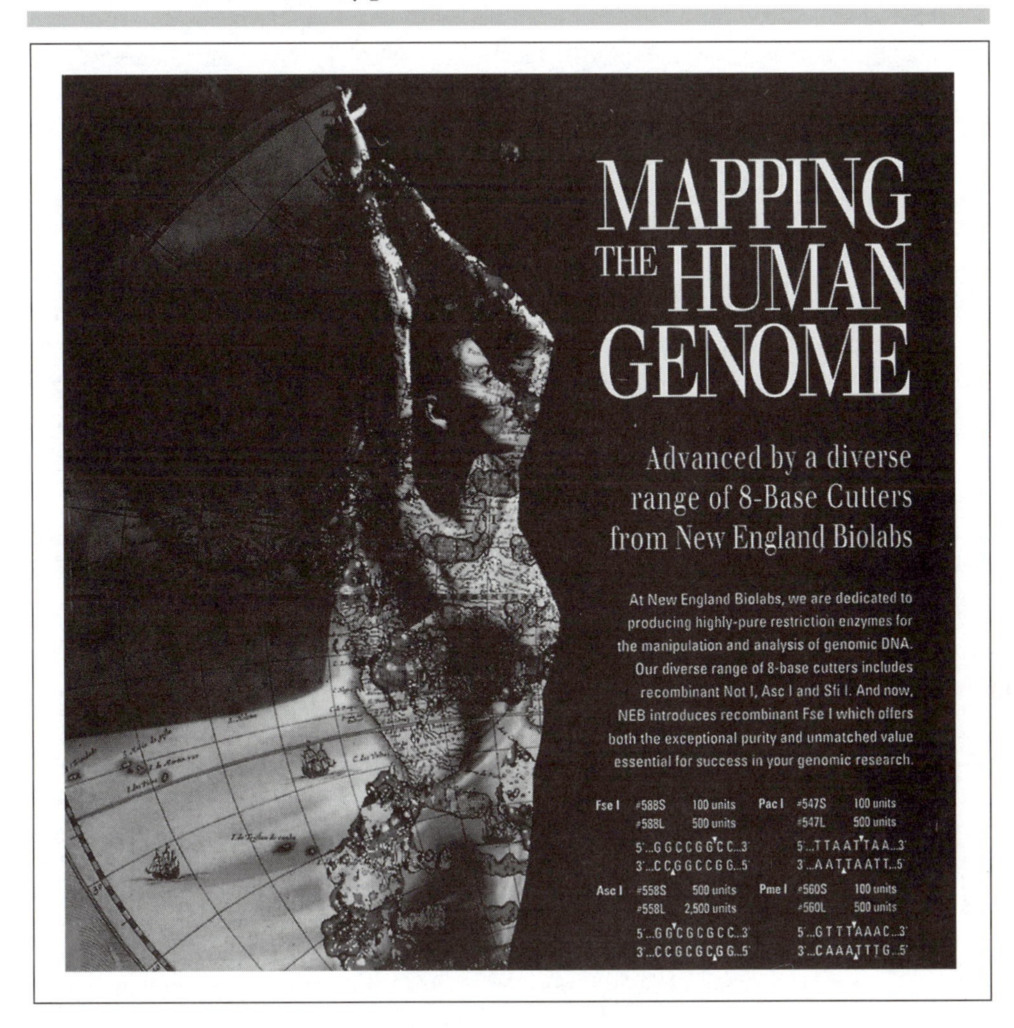

tisement for a biotechnology company, a nude woman, in profile, is overlaid by a representation of the double helix of DNA and an antique map of Africa (fig. 5). These are all images representing the unknown, ripe for exploitation—Freud's dark continent.

WHY WE SHOULD CARE

The point of examining the advertisements in *Science* is not to show that they are a problem per se. I am not necessarily advocating a sort of affirmative-action program for advertisers. The advertisements are most useful as a tool for revealing prevailing general attitudes and stereotypes about science and who can do science. We may hope, perhaps idealistically, that when our societal attitudes about people and their abilities become more equitable, the images described here will no longer appeal and sell products to us, and advertisers and advertising editors will provide images that reflect more equitable beliefs.

The stereotypes portrayed in the advertisements are not gender-neutral. Historically the mass media have portrayed a strongly negative image of women scientists as atypical women and atypical scientists, and increased numbers of women in the scientific workforce have not been matched by comparable improvements in the presentation of women (LaFollette 1988; Valian 1998). The advertisements in *Science* share biases similar to those in the popular media, where science is portrayed most often as an inappropriate activity for women. What is problematic is that such conventional stereotypes occur in the pages of *Science*, a prestigious and highly respected journal published by a scientific society whose goals include the active promotion of diversity and elimination of discrimination in science (Pabst 1995). What one would hope and expect to find in the pages of a journal with these stated goals would be images that reflect the goals that the members of the scientific society deem important. That advertisers and advertising editors are aware of gender and scientific stereotypes is evidenced by the greater proportion and more positive portrayals of women and people of color in the special issues compared with the regular issues of *Science*. Do editors and advertisers think that women and people of color read only the special issues of *Science*? Do they think that only women and people of color read the special issues?

The goal of the advertiser is to appeal to the conscious and subconscious desires and value systems of the consumer to create a need for a specific product, and that need must be translated into a badge of group membership. We live in a culture in which both men and women "know" that science is masculine. The emphasis on white men and stereotypes of masculinity in scientific advertising borrows from cultural assumptions about white male superiority to reaffirm the importance and superiority of science, and vice versa. At the same time this emphasis reinscribes the inferiority of the "other"—people of color and women—and underscores their outsider status and the inappropriateness of science as a career for them. In the current social system of science, to present an image of women and people of color as full participants in science would be to devalue science. The pervasiveness of links among cultural beliefs about men and women and science as portrayed by the advertisements suggests that the attainment of diversity in science still presents a considerable challenge.

My purpose here has been to alert hopeful and practicing scientists to some of the neglected social aspects of a science career. Once outsiders are aware of the potential problems, these issues can be counteracted, and individuals can make informed decisions that can increase chances for success and equity. Although I do not know how the advertisements in *Science* affect those who read them, we can be reasonably sure that these familiar images do little to challenge our stereotypes and biases. The images are devoid of any competing set of cultural messages and values that may be needed to change our stereotypes about science and scientists. The most significant message of this study may be that there is more cultural content between the covers of *Science* than we would care to acknowledge. The change of images in scientific advertising to more positive ones for women and people of color may help us slowly change our stereotypes about men, women, race, and science, and therefore make a contribution to the attainment of greater diversity in science.

References

Bartel, D. 1988. *Putting on Appearances: Gender and Advertising.* Temple Univ. Press, Philadelphia, 219 pp.

Cockburn, C. 1985. *Machinery of dominance: Women, Men, and Technical Know-how.* Northeastern Univ. Press, Boston, 282 pp.

Craig, R. S. 1992. Women as home caregivers: Gender portrayal in OTC drug commercials. *J. Drug Education* 22: 303–12.

Day, J. Cheeseman. 1995. US Bureau of Census. USGPO, P25–1104.
Geis, F., Brown, V., Jennings (Walstedt), J., and Porter, N. 1984. TV commercials as achievement scripts for women. *Sex Roles* 10: 513–25.
Goffman, E. 1976. Gender Advertisements. *Studies in the Anthropology of Visual Communication* 3(2): 65–154.
LaFollette, M. 1988. Eyes on the stars: Images of women scientists in popular magazines. *Science, Technol. And Human Values* 13: 262–75.
Lie, M., and Sorensen, K. 1996. *Making Technology Our Own? Domesticating Technology into Everyday Life.* Scandinavian Univ. Press, Oslo. 244 pp.
MacCurdy, M. 1994. The four women of the apocalypse: Polarized feminine images in magazine advertisements. Pp. 31–48 in *Gender and Utopia in Advertising,* L. Manca and A. Manca, eds. Procopian Press, Lisle, Ill., 168 pp.
Malcom, S. M. 1999. Fault lines. *Science* 284: 1271.
Manca, L., and Manca, A. 1994. Adam through the looking glass: Images of men in magazine advertisements of the 1980's. Pp. 111–31 in *Gender and Utopia in Advertising,* L. Manca and A. Manca, eds. Procopian Press, Lisle, Ill., 168 pp.
Mirsky, S. 1997. The big picture. *Scientific American,* November, p. 28.
Mosher, E. H. 1976. Portrayal of women in drug advertising: A medical betrayal. *J. Drug Issues* 6: 72–78.
National Science Foundation. 1999. *Women, Minorities, and Persons with Disabilities in Science and Engineering, 1998.* NSF 99-338. Washington, D.C.
Pabst, D. 1995. Association denounces discrimination in the workplace. *Science* 268: 590.
Plumwood, V. 1993. *Feminism and the Mastery of Nature.* Routledge, N.Y.
Ribalow, M. Z. 1999. Swashbucklers and brainy babes? *Science* 284: 2089–90.
Rossiter, M. W. 1982. *Women Scientists in America: Struggles and Strategies to 1940.* Johns Hopkins Univ. Press, Baltimore, 439 pp.
———. 1995. *The Women Scientist in America: Before Affirmative Action, 1940–1972.* Johns Hopkins Univ. Press, Baltimore, 584 pp.
Seely, P. 1994. The mirror and the window on the man of the nineties: Portrayals of males in television advertising. Pp. 95–110 in *Gender and Utopia in Advertising,* L. Manca and A. Manca, eds. Procopian Press, Lisle, Ill., 168 pp.
Shih, M., Pittinsky, T. L., and Ambady, N. 1999. Stereotype susceptibility: Identity salience and shifts in quantitiative performance. *Psychological Science* 10: 80–83.
Sonnert, G., and Holton G. 1995. *Who Succeeds in Science? The Gender Dimension.* Rutgers University Press, New Brunswick, N.J., 215 pp.
Steele, C. M. 1997. A threat in the air: How stereotypes shape intellectual identity and performance. *American Psychologist* 52: 613–29.
Thompson, E. L. 1979. Sexual bias in drug advertisements. *Soc. Sci. Med.* 13A: 187–91.
U.S. Bureau of the Census. 1996. *Population Projections of the United States by Age, Race, Sex, and Hispanic Origin: 1995–2050.* Document no. P25-1130. Government Printing Office, Washington, D.C.
Valian, V. 1998. *Why So Slow? The Advancement of Women.* MIT Press, Cambridge, Mass.
Wajcman, J. 1991. *Feminism Confronts Technology.* Pennsylvania State Univ. Press, University Park 184 pp.
Wajcman, J. 1991. The built environment: Women's place, gendered space. Pp. 110–36 in: *Feminism Confronts Technology,* Pennsylvania State University Press, University Park.
Wennerás, C., and Wold, A. 1997. Nepotism and sexism in peer review. *Nature* 387: 341–43.

GENDER AND SCIENCE
An Update

Evelyn Fox Keller

THE MEANING OF GENDER

Schemes for classifying human beings are necessarily multiple and highly variable. Different cultures identify and privilege different criteria in sorting people of their own and other cultures into groups: They may stress size, age, color, occupation, wealth, sanctity, wisdom, or a host of other demarcators. All cultures, however, sort a significant fraction of the human beings that inhabit that culture by sex. What are taken to be the principal indicators of sexual difference as well as the particular importance attributed to this difference undoubtedly vary, but, for fairly obvious reasons, people everywhere engage in the basic act of distinguishing people they call male from those they call female. For the most part, they even agree about who gets called what. Give or take a few marginal cases, these basic acts of categorization do exhibit conspicuous cross-cultural consensus: Different cultures will sort any given collection of adult human beings of reproductive age into the same two groups. For this reason, we can say that there is at least a minimal sense of the term "sex" that denotes categories given to us by nature.[1] One might even say that the universal importance of the reproductive consequences of sexual difference gives rise to as universal a preoccupation with the meaning of this difference.

But for all the cross-cultural consensus we may find around such a minimalist classification, we find equally remarkable cultural variability in what people have made and continue to make of this demarcation; in the significance to which they attribute it; in the properties it connotes; in the role it plays in ordering the human world beyond the immediate spheres of biological reproduction; even in the role it plays in ordering the nonhuman world. It was to underscore this cultural variability that American feminists of the 1970s introduced the distinction between sex and gender, assigning the term "gender" to the meanings of masculinity and femininity that a given culture attaches to the categories of male and female.[2]

The initial intent behind this distinction was to highlight the importance of non-biological (that is, social and cultural) factors shaping the development of adult men and women, to emphasize the truth of Simone de Beauvoir's famous dictum, "Women are not born, rather they are made." Its function was to shift attention away from the time-honored and perhaps even ubiquitous question of the meaning of sexual difference (that is, the meanings of masculine and feminine), *to* the question of how such meanings are constructed. In Donna Haraway's words, "Gender is a concept developed to contest the naturalization of sexual difference" (1991:131).

Very quickly, however, feminists came to see, and, as quickly, began to exploit, the considerably larger range of analytic functions that the multipotent category of gender is able to serve. From an original focus on gender as a cultural norm guiding the psychosocial development of individual men and women, the attention of feminists soon turned to gender as a cultural structure organizing social (and sexual) relations between men and women,[3] and finally, to gender as the basis of a sexual division of cognitive and emotional labor that brackets women, their work, and the values associated with that work from culturally normative delineations of categories intended as "human"—objectivity, morality, citizenship, power, often even, "human nature" itself. From this perspective, gender and gender norms come to be seen as silent organizers of the mental and discursive maps of the social and natural worlds we simultaneously inhabit and construct—*even of those worlds that women never enter.* This I call the symbolic work of gender; it remains silent precisely to the extent that norms associated with masculine culture are taken as universal.

The fact that it took the efforts of contemporary feminism to bring this symbolic work of gender into recognizable view is in itself noteworthy. In these efforts, the dual focus on women as subjects and on gender as a cultural construct was crucial. Analysis of the relevance of gender structures in conventionally male worlds only makes sense once we recognize gender not only as a bimodal term, applying symmetrically to men *and* women (that is, once we see that men too are gendered, that men too are made rather than born), but also as denoting social rather than natural kinds. Until we can begin to envisage the possibility of alternative arrangements, the symbolic work of gender remains both silent and inaccessible. And as long as gender is thought to pertain only to women, any question about its role can only be understood as a question about the presence or absence of biologically female persons.

This double shift in perception—first, from sex to gender, and second, from the force of gender in shaping the development of men and women to its force in delineating the cultural maps of the social and natural worlds these adults inhabit—constitutes the hallmark of contemporary feminist theory. Beginning in the mid 1970s, feminist historians, literary critics, sociologists, political scientists, psychologists, philosophers, and soon, natural scientists as well, sought to supplement earlier feminist analyses of the contribution, treatment, and representation of men and women in these various fields with an enlarged analysis of the ways in which privately held and publicly shared ideas about gender have shaped the underlying assumptions and operant categories in the intellectual history of each of these fields. Put simply, contemporary feminist theory might be described as "a form of attention, a lens that brings into focus a particular question: What does it mean to describe one aspect of human experience as 'male' and another as 'female'? How do such labels affect the ways in which we structure the world around us, assign value to its different domains, and in turn, acculturate and value actual men and women?" (Keller 1985:6).

With such questions as these, feminist scholars launched an intensive investigation of the traces of gender labels evident in many of the fundamental assumptions underlying the traditional academic disciplines. Their earliest efforts were confined to the humanities and social sciences, but by the late 1970s, the lens of feminist inquiry had extended to the natural sciences as well. Under particular scrutiny came those assumptions that posited a dichotomous (and hierarchical) structure tacitly modeled on the prior assumption of a dichotomous (and hierarchical) relation between male and female—for example, public/private; political/personal; reason/feeling; justice/care; objective/subjective; power/love, and so on. The object of this endeavor was not to reverse the conventional ordering of these relations, but to undermine the dichotomies themselves—to expose to radical critique a worldview that deploys categories of gender to rend the fabric of human life and thought along a multiplicity of mutually sanctioning, mutually supportive, and mutually defining binary oppositions.

FEMINISM AND SCIENCE

But if the inclusion of the natural sciences under this broad analytic net posed special opportunities, it also posed special difficulties, and special dangers, each of which requires special recognition. On the one hand, the presence of gender markings in the root categories of the natural sciences and their use in the hierarchical ordering of such categories (for example, mind and nature; reason and feeling; objective and subjective) is, if anything, more conspicuous than in the humanities and social sciences. At the same time, the central claim of the natural sciences is precisely to a methodology that transcends human particularity, that bears no imprint of individual or collective authorship. To signal this dilemma, I began my first inquiry into the relations between gender and science (Keller 1978) with a quote from George Simmel, written more than sixty years ago:

> The requirements of . . . correctness in practical judgments and objectivity in theoretical knowledge . . . belong as it were in their form and their claims to humanity in general, but in their actual historical configuration they are masculine throughout. Supposing that we describe these things, viewed as absolute ideas, by the single word "objective," we then find that in the history of our race the equation objective = masculine is a valid one (cited in Keller 1978:409).

Simmel's conclusion, while surely on the mark as a description of a cultural history, alerts us to the special danger that awaits a feminist critique of the natural sciences. Indeed, Simmel himself appears to have fallen into the very trap that we are seeking to expose: In neglecting to specify the space in which he claims "validity" for this equation as a *cultural or even ideological space,* his wording invites the reading of this space as a biological one. Indeed, by referring to its history as a "history of our race" without specifying "our race" as late-modern, northern European, he tacitly elides the existence of other cultural histories (as well as other "races") and invites the same conclusion that this cultural history has sought to establish; namely, that "objectivity" is simultaneously a universal value and a privileged possession of the male of the species.

The necessary starting point for a feminist critique of the natural sciences is thus the reframing of this equation as a conundrum: How is it that the scientific mind can be *seen* at one and the same time as both male and disembodied? How is it that thinking "objectively," that is, thinking that is defined as self-detached, impersonal, and transcendent, is also understood as "thinking like a man"? From the vantage point of our newly "enlightened" perceptions of gender, we might be tempted to say that the equation "objective = masculine," harmful though it (like that other equation woman = nature) may have been for aspiring women scientists in the past, was simply a descriptive mistake, reflecting misguided views of women. But what about the views of "objectivity" (or "nature") that such an equation necessarily also reflected (or inspired)? What difference—for science, now, rather than for women—might such an equation have made? Or, more generally, what sorts of work in the actual production of science has been accomplished by the association of gender with virtually all of the root categories of modern science over the three hundred odd years in which such associations prevailed? How have these associations helped to shape the criteria for "good" science? For distinguishing the values deemed "scientific" from those deemed "unscientific"? In short, what particular cultural norms and values has the language of gender carried into science, and how have these norms and values contributed to its shape and growth?

These, then, are some of the questions that feminist theory brings to the study of science, and that feminist historians and philosophers of science have been trying to answer over the last fifteen years. But, for reasons I have already briefly indicated, they are questions that are strikingly difficult to hold in clear focus (to keep distinct, for example, from questions about the presence or absence of women scientists). For many working scientists, they seem not even to "make sense."

One might suppose, for example, that once such questions were properly posed (that is, cleansed of any implication about the real abilities of actual women), they would have a special urgency for all practicing scientists who are also women. But experience suggests otherwise; even my own experience suggests otherwise. Despite repeated attempts at clarification, many scientists (especially, women scientists) persist in misreading the force that feminists attribute to gender ideology as a force being attributed to sex, that is, to the claim that women, for biological reasons, would do a different kind of science. The net effect is that, where some of us see a liberating potential (both for women *and* for science) in exhibiting the historical role of gender in science, these scientists often see only a reactionary potential, fearing its use to support the exclusion of women from science.[4]

The reasons for the divergence in perception between feminist critics and women scientists are deep and complex. Though undoubtedly fueled by political concerns, they rest finally neither on vocabulary, nor on logic, nor even on empirical evidence. Rather, they reflect a fundamental difference in mind-set between feminist critics and working scientists—a difference so radical that a "feminist scientist" appears today as much a contradiction in terms as a "woman scientist" once did[5]. . . .

THE MEANING OF SCIENCE

Although people everywhere, throughout history, have needed, desired, and sought reliable knowledge of the world around them, only certain forms of knowledge and certain procedures for acquiring such knowledge have come to count under the general rubric that we, in the late twentieth century, designate as science. Just as "masculine" and "feminine" are categories defined by a culture, and not by biological necessity, so too, "science" is the name we give to a set of practices and a body of knowledge delineated by a community. Even now, in part because of the great variety of practices that the label "science" continues to subsume, the term defies precise definition, obliging us to remain content with a conventional definition—as that which those people we call scientists do.

What has compelled recognition of the conventional (and hence social) character of modern science is the evidence provided over the last three decades by historians, philosophers, and sociologists of science who have undertaken close examination of what it is that those people we call (or have called) scientists actually do (or have done).[6] Careful attention to what questions get asked, of how research programs come to be legitimated and supported, of how theoretical disputes are resolved, of "how experiments end" reveals the working of cultural and social norms at every stage.[7] Consensus is commonly achieved, but it is rarely compelled by the forces of logic and evidence alone. On every level, choices are (must be) made that are social *even as* they are cognitive and technical. The direct implication is that not only different collections of facts, different focal points of scientific attention, but also different conceptions of explanation and proof, different representations of reality, different criteria of success, are both possible and consistent with what we call science.

But if such observations have come to seem obvious to many observers of science, they continue to seem largely absurd to the men and women actually engaged in the production of science. In order to see how cultural norms and values can, indeed have, helped define the success and shape the growth of science, it is necessary to understand how language embodies and enforces such norms and values. This need far exceeds the concerns of feminism, and the questions it gives rise to have become critical for anyone currently working in the history, philosophy, or sociology of science. That it continues to elude most working scientists is precisely a consequence of the fact that their world-views not only lack but actually preclude recognition of the force of language on what they, in their day-to-day activity as scientists, think and do. And this, I suggest, follows as much from the nature of their activity as it does from scientific ideology.

LANGUAGE AND THE DOING OF SCIENCE[8]

The reality is that the "doing" of science is, at its best, a gripping and fully absorbing activity—so much so that it is difficult for anyone so engaged to step outside the demands of the particular problems under investigation to reflect on the assumptions underlying that investigation, much less, on the language in which such assumptions can be said to "make sense." Keeping track of and following the arguments and data as they unfold, trying always to think ahead, demands total absorption; at the same time, the sense of discovering or even generating a new world yields an intoxication rarely paralleled in other academic fields. The net result is that scientists are probably less reflective of the "tacit assumptions" that guide their reasoning than any other intellectuals of the modern age.

Indeed, the success of their enterprise does not, at least in the short run, seem to require such reflectivity.[9] Some would even argue that very success demands abstaining from reflection upon matters that do not lend themselves to "clear and distinct" answers. Indeed, they might argue that what distinguishes contemporary science from the efforts of their forbears is precisely their recognition of the dual need to avoid talk *about* science, and to replace "ordinary" language by a technical discourse cleansed of the ambiguity and values that burden ordinary language, as the modern form of the scientific report requires. Let the data speak for themselves, these scientists demand. The problem is, of course, that data never do speak for themselves.

It is by now a near truism that all data presuppose interpretation. And if an interpretation is to be meaningful—if the data are to be "intelligible" to more than one person—it must be embedded in a community of common practices, shared conceptions of the meaning of terms and their relation to and interaction with the "objects" to which these terms point. In science as elsewhere, interpretation requires the sharing of a common language.

Sharing a language means sharing a conceptual universe. It means more than knowing the "right" names by which to call things; it means knowing the "right" syntax in which to pose claims and questions, and even more critically it means sharing a more or less agreed-upon understanding of what questions are legitimate to ask, and what can be accepted as meaningful answers. Every explicit question carries with it a complex of tacit (unarticulated and generally unrecognized) presuppositions and expectations that limit the range of acceptable answers in ways that only a properly versed respondent will recognize. To know what kinds of explanation will "make sense," what can be expected to count as "accounting for," is already to be a member of a particular language community.

But if there is one feature that distinguishes scientific from other communities, and that is indeed special to that particular discourse, it is precisely the assumption that the universe scientists study is directly accessible, that the "nature" they name as object of inquiry is unmediated by language and can therefore be veridically represented. On this assumption, "laws of nature" are beyond the relativity of language—indeed, they are beyond language, encoded in logical structures that require only the discernment of reason and the confirmation of experiment. Also on this assumption, the descriptive language of science is transparent and neutral; it does not require examination.

Confidence in the transparency and neutrality of scientific language is certainly useful in enabling scientists to get on with their job; it is also wondrously effective in supporting their special claims to truth. It encourages the view that their own language, because neutral, is absolute, and in so doing, helps secure their disciplinary borders against criticism. Language, assumed to be transparent, becomes impervious.

It falls to others, then, less enclosed by the demands of science's own self-understanding, to disclose the "thickness" of scientific language, to scrutinize the conventions of practice, interpretation, and shared aspirations on which the truth claims of that language depend, to expose the many forks in the road to knowledge that these very conventions have worked to obscure, and, in that process, finally, to uncover alternatives for the future. Under careful scrutiny, the hypothesized contrast between ordinary and scientific language gives way to a recognition of disconcerting similarity. Even the most purely technical discourses turn out to depend on metaphor, on ambiguity, on instabilities of meaning—indeed, on the very commonsense understanding of terms from which a technical discourse is supposed to emancipate us. Scientific arguments cannot begin to "make sense," much less be effective, without extensive recourse to shared conventions for controlling these inevitable ambiguities and instabilities. The very term "experimental control" needs to be understood in a far larger sense than has been the custom—describing not only the control of variables, but also of the ways of seeing, thinking, acting, and speaking in which an investigator must be extensively trained before he or she can become a contributing member of a discipline.

Even the conventional account scientists offer of their success has been shown by recent work in the history, philosophy, and sociology of science to be itself rooted in metaphor: The very idea, for example, of a one-to-one correspondence between theory and reality, or of scientific method as capable of revealing nature "as it is," is based on metaphors of mind or science as "mirror of nature." Simple logic, however, suggests that words are far too limited a resource, in whatever combinations, to permit a faithful representation of even our own experience, much less of the vast domain of natural phenomena. The metaphor of science as "mirror of nature" may be both psychologically and politically useful to scientists, but it is not particularly useful for a philosophical understanding of how science works; indeed, it has proven to be a positive barrier to our understanding of the development of science in its historical and social context. It is far more useful, and probably even more correct, to suppose, as Mary Hesse suggests, that "[s]cience is successful only because there are sufficient local and particular regularities between things in space-time domains where we can test them. These domains may be very large but it's an elementary piece of mathematics that there is an infinite gap between the largest conceivable number and infinity" (1989:E24).

In much the same sense, the idea of "laws of nature" can also be shown to be rooted in metaphor, a metaphor indelibly marked by its political and theological origins. Despite the insistence of philosophers that laws of nature are merely descriptive, not prescriptive, they are historically conceptualized as imposed from above and obeyed from below. "By those who first used the term, [laws of nature] were viewed as commands imposed by the deity upon matter, and even writers who do not accept this view often speak of them as 'obeyed' by the phenomena, or as agents by which the phenomena are produced."[10] In this sense, then, the metaphor of "laws of nature" carries into scientific practice the presupposition of an ontological hierarchy, ordering not only mind and matter, but theory and practice, and, of course, the normal and the aberrant. Even in the loosest (most purely descriptive) sense of the term *law,* the kinds of order in nature that laws can accommodate are restricted to those that can be expressed by the language in which laws of nature are codified. All languages are capable of describing regularity, but not all perceivable, nor even all describable, regularities can be expressed in the existing vocabularies of science. To assume, therefore, that all perceptible regularities can be represented by current (or even by future) theory is to impose a premature limit on what is "naturally" possible, as well as what is potentially understandable.

Nancy Cartwright (1990) has suggested that a better way to make sense of the theoretical successes of science (as well as its failures) would be to invoke the rather different metaphor of "Nature's Capacities." In apparent sympathy with Mary Hesse, as well as with a number of other contemporary historians and philosophers of science, she suggests that an understanding of the remarkable convergences between theory and experiment that scientists have produced requires attention not so much to the adequacy of the laws that are presumably being tested, but rather to the particular and highly local manipulation of theory and experimental procedure that is required to produce these convergences. Our usual talk of scientific laws, Cartwright suggests, belies (and elides) both the conceptual and linguistic work that is required to ground a theory, or "law," to fit a particular set of experimental circumstances and the material work required to construct an experimental apparatus to fit a theoretical claim. Scientific laws may be "true," but what they are true of is a distillation of highly contrived and exceedingly particular circumstances, as much artifact as nature.

TURNING FROM GENDER AND SCIENCE TO LANGUAGE AND SCIENCE

The questions about gender with which I began this essay can now be reformulated in terms of two separable kinds of inquiry: The first, bearing on the historical role of public and private conceptions of gender in the framing of the root metaphors of science, belongs to feminist theory proper, whereas the second, that of the role of such metaphors in the actual development of scientific theory and practice, belongs to a more general inquiry in the history and philosophy of science. By producing abundant historical evidence pertaining to the first question, and by exhibiting the in-principle possibility of alternative metaphoric options, feminist scholars have added critical incentive to the pursuit of the second question. And by undermining the realism and univocality of scientific discourse, the philosophical groundwork laid by Kuhn, Hesse, Cartwright, and many others, now makes it possible to pursue this larger question in earnest, pointing the way to the kind of analysis needed to show how such basic acts of naming have helped to shape the actual course of scientific development, and, in so doing, have helped to obscure if not foreclose other possible courses.

The most critical resource available for such an inquiry is the de facto plurality of organizing metaphors, theories, and practices evident throughout the history of science. At any given moment, in any given discipline, abundant variability can be readily identified along the following four closely interdependent axes: the aims of scientific inquiry; the questions judged most significant to ask; the theoretical and experimental methodologies deemed most productive for addressing these questions; and, finally, what counts as an acceptable answer or a satisfying explanation. Different metaphors of mind, nature, and the relation between them, reflect different psychological stances of observer to observed; these, in turn, give rise to different cognitive perspectives—to different aims, questions, and even to different methodological and explanatory preferences. Such variability is of course always subject to the forces of selection exerted by collective norms, yet there are many moments in scientific history in which alternative visions can survive for long enough to permit identification both of their distinctiveness, and of the selective pressures against which they must struggle.

The clearest and most dramatic such instance in my own research remains that provided by the life and work of the cytogeneticist, Barbara McClintock. McClintock offers a vision of science premised not on the domination of nature, but on "a feeling for the organism."[11] For her, a "feeling for the organism" is simultaneously a state of mind and a resource for knowledge: for the day-to-day work of conducting experiments, observing and interpreting their outcomes—in short, for the "doing" of science. "Nature," to McClintock, is best known for its largesse and prodigality; accordingly, her conception of the work of science is more consonant with that of exhibiting nature's "capacities" and multiple forms of order, than with pursuing the "laws of nature." Her alternative view invites the perception of nature as an active partner in a more reciprocal relation to an observer, equally active, but neither omniscient nor omnipotent; the story of her life's work (especially, her identification of genetic transposition) exhibits how that deviant perception bore fruit in equally dissident observations.

But history is strewn with such dissidents and deviants, often as persistent and perceptive but still less fortunate than McClintock. Normally, they are erased from the record, in a gesture readily justified by the conventional narrative of science. Without the validation of the dominant community, deviant claims, along with the deviant visions of science that had guided them, are dismissed as "mistakes," misguided and false steps in the history of science. What such a retrospective reading overlooks is that the ultimate value of any accomplishment in science—that which we all too casually call its "truth"—depends not on any special vision enabling some scientists to see directly into nature, but on the acceptance and pursuit of their work by the community around them, that is, on the prior existence or development of sufficient commonalities of language and adequate convergences between language and practice. Language not only guides how we as individuals think and act; it simultaneously provides the glue enabling others to think and act along similar lines, guaranteeing that our thoughts and actions *can* "make sense."

WHAT ABOUT "NATURE"?

Still, language does not "construct reality." Whatever force it may have, that force can, after all, only be exerted on language-speaking subjects—for our concerns here, on scientists and the people who fund their work. Though language is surely instrumental in guiding the material actions of these subjects, it would be foolhardy indeed to lose sight of the force of the material, nonlinguistic, substrata of those actions, that is, of that which we loosely call "nature." Metaphors work to focus our attention in particular ways, conceptually magnifying one set of similarities and differences while dwarfing or blurring others, guiding the construction of instruments that bring certain kinds of objects into view, and eclipsing others. Yet, for any given line of inquiry, it is conspicuously clear that not all metaphors are equally effective for the production of further knowledge. Furthermore, once these instruments and objects have come into existence, they take on a life of their own, available for appropriation to other ends, to other metaphoric schemes.

Consider, for example, the fate of genetic transposition. McClintock's search for this phenomenon was stimulated by her interest in the dynamics of kinship and interdependency; it was made visible by an analytic and interpretive system premised on "a feeling for the organism," on the integrity and internal agency of the organism. To McClintock, transposition was a wedge of resistance on behalf of the organism against control from without. But neither she herself nor her analytic and interpretive framework could prevent the ultimate appropriation of this mechanism, once exhibited, to entirely opposite aims—as an instrument for external control of organic forms by genetic engineers.

McClintock's vision of science was unarguably productive for her, and it has been seen to have great aesthetic and emotional appeal for many scientists. But it must be granted that her success pales before that of mainstream (molecular) biology. In the last few years (in part thanks to the techniques derived from genetic transposition itself), it is the successes and technological prowess of molecular biology rather than of McClintock's vision of science that have captured the scientific and popular imagination. These successes, and this prowess, cannot be ignored.

We may be well persuaded that the domain of natural phenomena is vastly larger than the domain of scientific theory as we know it, leaving ample room for alternative conceptions of science; that the accumulated body of scientific theory represents only one of the many ways in which human beings, including the human beings we call scientists, have sought to make sense of the world; even that the successes of these theories are highly local and specific. Yet, whatever philosophical accounts we might accept, the fact remains that science as we know it works exceedingly well. The question is, Can any other vision of science be reasonably expected to work as well? Just how plastic are our criteria of success?

Feminists (and others) may have irrevocably undermined our sense of innocence about the aspiration to dominate nature, but they/we have not answered the question of just what it is that is wrong with dominating nature. We know what is wrong with dominating persons—it deprives other subjects of the right to express their own subjectivities—and we may indeed worry about the extent to which the motivation to dominate nature reflects a desire for domination of other human beings.[12] But a salient point of a feminist perspective on science derives precisely from the fact that nature is not in fact a woman. A better pronoun for nature is surely "it," rather than "she." What then could be wrong with seeking, or even achieving, dominion over things per se?

Perhaps the simplest response is to point out that nature, while surely not a woman, is also not a "thing," nor is it even an "it" that can be delineated unto itself, either separate or separable from a speaking and knowing "we." What we know about nature we know only through our interactions with, or rather, our embeddedness in it. It is precisely because we ourselves are natural beings—beings *in* and *of* nature—that we *can* know. Thus, to represent nature as a "thing" or an "it," is itself a way of talking, undoubtedly convenient, but clearly more appropriate to some ends than to others. And just because there is no one else "out there" capable of choosing, we must acknowledge that these ends represent human choices, for which "we" alone are responsible. One question we need to ask is thus relatively straightforward: What are the particular ends to which the language of objectification, reification, and domination of nature is particularly appropriate, and perhaps even useful? And to what other ends might a different language—of kinship, embeddedness, and connectivity, of "feeling for the organism"—be equally appropriate and useful? But we also need to ask another, in many ways much harder, question: How do the properties of the natural world in which we are embedded constrain our social and technical ambitions? Just what is there in the practices and methods of science that permit the realization of certain hopes but not others?

Earlier in this essay, I attempted to describe the shift in mind-set from working scientist to feminist critic. But to make sense of the successes of science, however that success is measured, the traversal must also be charted in reverse: Feminist critics of science, along with other analysts of science, need to reclaim access to the mindset of the working scientist, to what makes their descriptions seem so compelling.

For this, we need to redress an omission from many of our analyses to date that is especially conspicuous to any working scientist: attention to the material constraints on which scientific knowledge depends, and correlatively, to the undeniable record of technological success that science as we know it can boast. If we grant the force of belief, we must surely not neglect the even more dramatic force of scientific "know-how." Although beliefs, interests, and cultural norms surely can, and do, influence the definition of scientific goals, as well as prevailing criteria of success in meeting those goals, they cannot in themselves generate either epistemological or technological success. Only where they mesh with the opportunities and constraints afforded by material reality can they lead to the generation of effective knowledge. Our analyses began with the question of where, and how, does the force of beliefs, interests, and cultural norms enter into the process by which effective knowledge is generated; the question that now remains is, Where, and how, does the nonlinguistic realm we call *nature* enter into that process? How do "nature" and "culture" interact in the production of scientific knowledge? Until feminist critics of science, along with other analysts of the influence of social forces on science, address this question, our accounts of science will not be recognizable to working scientists.

The question at issue is, finally, that of the meaning of science. Although we may now recognize that science neither does nor can "mirror" nature, to imply instead that it mirrors culture (or "interests") is not only to make a mockery of the commitment to the pursuit of reliable knowledge that constitutes the core of any working scientist's self-definition, but also to ignore the causal efficacy of that commitment. In other words, it is to practice an extraordinary denial of the manifest (at times even life threatening) successes of science. Until we can articulate an adequate response to the question of how "nature" interacts with "culture" in the production of scientific knowledge, until we find an adequate way of integrating the impact of multiple social and political forces, psychological predispositions, experimental constraints, and cognitive demands on the growth of science, working scientists will continue to find their more traditional mind-sets not only more comfortable, but far more adequate. And they will continue to view a mind-set that sometimes seems to grant force to beliefs and interests but not to "nature" as fundamentally incompatible, unintegrable, and laughable.

Notes

1. A somewhat different view is given by Tom Laqueur (1990).
2. See, for example, Gayle Rubin (1975).
3. See, for example, Rubin (1975) and Catherine MacKinnon (1988).
4. Of course, scientists are not the only ones who persist in such a mistranslation; it is also made by many others, and even by some feminists who are not themselves scientists. It is routinely made by the popular press. The significant point here is that this mistranslation persists in the minds of most women scientists even after they are alerted to the (feminist) distinction between sex and gender.
5. Indeed, a striking number of those feminist critics who began as working scientists have either changed fields altogether or have felt obliged to at least temporarily interrupt their work as laboratory or "desk" scientists (I am thinking, for example, of [the late] Maggie Benston, Ruth Hubbard, Marian Lowe, Evelynn Hammonds, Anne Fausto-Sterling, and myself).
6. In large part, stimulated by the publication of Thomas S. Kuhn's *The Structure of Scientific Revolutions,* in 1962.
7. See, for example, Galison (1988); Pickering (1984); Shapin and Schaffer (1985); Smith and Wise (1989).
8. The discussion that follows begins with a recapitulation of my remarks in Keller (1985: 129–32).
9. For an especially interesting discussion of this general phenomenon, see Markus (1987).
10. O. E. D., s.v. "law." The discussion here is adapted from the introduction to Part III, Keller (1985).
11. McClintock's own words, as well as the title of my book on this subject, Keller (1983).
12. See Keller (1985), Part II.

References

Cartwright, N. *Nature's Capacities.* Oxford: Oxford University Press, 1990.

Galison, P. "Between War and Peace." In *Science, Technology, and the Military,* edited by Everett Mendelsohn, Merritt Roe Smith, Peter Weingart. Dordrecht; Boston: Kluwer Academic Publishers, 1988. Mendelsohn, Smith & Weingart. (1988).

Haraway, D. *Simians, Cyborgs, and Women.* New York: Routledge, 1991.

Hesse, M. "Models, Metaphors and Myths." *N.Y. Times* October 22, 1989, p. E24.

Keller, E. F. *A Feeling for the Organism: The Life and Work of Barbara McClintock,* New York: W. H. Freeman, 1983.

Keller, E. F. "Gender and Science." *Psychoanalysis and Contemporary Thought* 1:409–33, 1978.

Keller, E. F. *Reflections on Gender and Science.* New Haven, CT: Yale Univ. Press, 1985.

Kuhn, T. S. *The Structure of Scientific Revolutions.* Chicago: Univ. of Chicago Press, 1962.

Laqueur, T. *The Making of Sexual Difference.* Cambridge: Harvard Univ. Press, 1990.

MacKinnon, C. *Feminism Unmodified.* Cambridge: Harvard Univ. Press, 1988.

Markus, G. "Why Is There No Hermeneutics of the Natural Sciences?" *Science in Context* 1 (1): 5–51, 1987.

Pickering, A. *Constructing Quarks.* Chicago: Univ. of Chicago Press, 1984.

Rubin, G. "The Traffic in Women: Notes on the 'Political Economy' of Sex." In *Toward an Anthropology of Women,* ed. R. R. Reiter. New York: Monthly Review Press, 1975.

Shapin, S. and S. Schaffer. *Leviathin and the Air-Pump.* Princeton: Princeton Univ. Press, 1985.

Smith, C. and N. Wise. *Energy and Empire: A Biographical Study of Lord Kelvin.* Cambridge: Cambridge Univ. Press, 1989.

CONSTRUCTING GENDER, CONSTRUCTING SCIENCE

HOW IDEAS ABOUT WOMEN AND MEN SHAPE SCIENCE AND TECHNOLOGY

In section 2, we examined how ideas about differences between men and women influence who can and cannot become a scientist. In this section we will explore how these ideas inform scientific knowledge itself. As we discussed in the introduction, how science is done is as important a question as what science is done. As illustrated in readings by Ruth Hubbard, Judy Wajcman, Suzanne Kessler, and Ruth Bleier, which research topics are deemed worthy of study, how research questions are formulated, and how the resulting data are gathered and interpreted often depend on when it is done, in what social, economic, and political environment it is done, and by whom it is done. In these readings, science is a social activity that is constructed and constrained by the shared practices of a community of highly trained specialists.

As Evelyn Fox Keller points out, these shared practices take place within the context of a shared language. "Sharing a language," she says, "means sharing a conceptual universe."[1] The language that scientists use thus is not transparent—it does not function simply as a passive vehicle through which scientists gather and relate knowledge of the natural world. Rather, language both represents and creates the shared meanings that a scientific community attaches to the concepts, metaphors, and images that scientists use. Specialized vocabularies develop in fields as a consequence of this process, but scientists (and all specialists) use concepts, metaphors, and images from the culture at large as well, as Carol Cohn's essay in the previous section so persuasively documents. The interpretation of any set of data thus necessarily involves tapping into the reservoir of shared meanings. A reliance on shared meanings, without which we would be unable to communicate, has important implications for understanding how science operates in our culture. As Dale Spender has observed:

> [G]iven that language is such an influential force in shaping our world, it is obvious that those who have the power to make the symbols and their meanings are in a privileged and highly advantageous position. . . . They have, at least, the potential to order the world to suit their own ends, the potential to construct a language, a reality, a body of knowledge in which they are the central figures, the potential to legitimate their own primacy and to create a system of beliefs which is beyond challenge (so that their superiority is "natural" and "objectively" tested).[2]

Understanding the language of science as socially embedded has provoked scholars to examine the degree to which scientific research and interpretation, like most other arenas of social life, are imbued with gender biases. What they have found is that concepts, metaphors, and images that rely on beliefs about women and men—and the differences between them—have a profound influence on definitions and interpretations of "natural" phenomena. In our review of feminist analyses of science, we have identified four general and interrelated areas where these influences have been shown to be apparent: conceptual premises, organization/classification of natural phenomena, constructions of research questions, and interpretations of data. This is not to say that all scientific research is distorted by gender biases. However, research documenting the influence of gender on scientific knowledge shows us the limitations of the scientific method in producing "objective" knowledge.

CONCEPTUAL PREMISES

Scientists identify a research question and develop a hypothesis within the context of a set of assumptions that are often unnamed and unannounced. These assumptions constrain the ability of researchers to respond to new evidence. One example is physical anthropologists' theories about women's and men's roles in human evolution.[3] In their reconstruction of early human life, most scientists have assumed since the 1950s that competition and sexual selection were the driving forces of evolution. Males fought with one another for food and for mates; they were the hunters. Females stayed close to home with the infants, foraging for nuts and berries; they were sexually receptive to whoever won the competition among men, and they were monogamous.

In the 1970s evidence emerged from several fields—primatology, anthropology, archaeology, and paleontology—that contradicted the idea that hunting by males was central to human evolution. Provoked in part by the feminist movement, researchers in these fields began to examine the role that women's activities may have played in early human activities. Nancy Tanner and Adrienne Zihlman, among others, challenged the assumptions of the sexual division of labor and monogamy upon which the hunting hypothesis was based. They argued that it was more likely that individuals shared a wide range of tasks, including both hunting and foraging. They also argued that women chose from among the men, rather than the reverse, and that contemporary Western notions of mating and marriage were too narrow to explain cross-cultural variation.[4]

Despite their efforts to consider a fuller account of human evolution, a male-centered paradigm reemerged. By the 1990s, and despite an increasing amount of genetic, paleontological, anatomical, behavioral, and archaeological evidence contradicting the hunting hypothesis, the theory that women as gatherers have played a role equal to men in human evolution has yet to gain wide acceptance. The male-as-hunter hypothesis, however, is securely embedded in the public mind through museum displays and television programs about human social evolution.[5]

Another example of how descriptions of the natural world can be constrained by cultural beliefs appears in introductory molecular biology and genetics textbooks. As Bonnie Spanier points out in "Gender Ideology in the Context of Molecular Biology," the exchange of genetic material in the ubiquitous single-celled bacteria, *Escherichia coli*, is explained with cultural and scientific terms consistent with the reproductive sex of higher organisms (such as humans). However, these terms are inappropriate and misleading. They describe the so-called "male" bacterium that replicates and donates a strand of genetic material (DNA) to the "female" bacterium through a narrow tube known as a pilus. The only difference between "male" and "female" bacteria is the presence or absence of this transferable piece of DNA, the F plasmid. An F^+ plasmid is denoted as male and an F^- plasmid as female. At the end of the transfer, both cells are F^+; thus in terms of the metaphor, both cells are male.

Why this exchange of genetic material is described as sex is a mystery. It is not an act of sexual reproduction, since the "male" and "female" bacterial cells do not fuse, as do the sperm and egg, to produce a new cell. The actual event is more like the donation of a kidney than an act of sex. It does not require designation of male and female cells in order to understand the event, and in fact, that designation makes the outcome of the event (two "males") difficult to explain logically within the initial heterosexual framework. Thus the use of the language of sexual reproduction to describe the replication and donation of the F plasmid from one bacterium to another not only is inaccurate, but also places constraints on how the phenomenon is further analyzed. Scientists may, for example, look only at how the "active male" bacterium initiates the event, when in fact it may be the so-called passive female bacterium that makes the transfer possible. With a biased and anthropomorphized view of "bacterial sex," the scientific questions that are pursued are limited by conventional understandings of an unrelated and complex human social behavior. Like the example of the inextinguishable hypothesis of man the hunter and the evolution of humankind, once a hypothesis is firmly rooted in the minds of both scientific experts and the public, it is difficult to reexamine, question, and modify, even when there is ample reason to do so.

ORGANIZATION/CLASSIFICATION OF THE NATURAL WORLD

Most people in the United States, even the youngest, know something basic about the natural world: that everything is classified into one of three categories—animal, vegetable, or mineral. Yet the specifics of these categories did not spring fully developed from nature; rather, they were created, defined, and defended by a series of scientists over centuries of work. Carolus Linnaeus, the eighteenth-century scientist who developed the scientific nomenclature still in use today, created the term *Mammalia* to describe one of the groups, humans, within the animal category. Linnaeus, it would seem, was celebrating the role of women in human reproduction by featuring a distinctive characteristic of females.

Historian Londa Schiebinger points out, however, that Linnaeus did not begin to use the term *Mammalia* in a cultural void.[6] The term arose within a historical moment in which social context and conflicts combined to lend credibility to his classification schema. By focusing on the breast as the physical trait that identified *Homo sapiens* as

Mammalia, Linnaeus drew on his culture's association of nursing with lower animals—women, cows, pigs, and sheep nurse their young. At the same time, his term emphasized and legitimized a sexual division of labor that assigned politics to men and the home to women. He did not do this arbitrarily, argues Schiebinger, since the physical evidence showed other characteristics that could have been emphasized, including hair, in order to distinguish the group he called Mammalia from other groups. In France in the late eighteenth century his new term provided a cultural fit between notions of women's close connection to nature and what should be considered "natural" in the social order. Because of prevailing social attitudes, the apparent emphasis on a trait of women reinscribed rather than challenged assumptions about men's superiority to women.

The drive to classify all human beings in a rank order from the highest (white European males) to the lowest (criminals, the lower classes, and children) fueled work in the nineteenth century that focused on brain size. Scientists assumed that brain size was indicative of brain power, that is, the larger the brain, the smarter the individual. (Indeed, this idea that mass equals intelligence circulates even today with slang insults such as "He's a pea brain" or "She's an airhead.") Paul Broca made a particularly well known contribution to this literature because of his stature as a prominent and respected scientist. Broca, after careful measurement of the size of the brains of 292 males and 140 females during autopsy, concluded that a pattern of difference was evident:

> We might ask if the small size of the female brain depends exclusively upon the small size of her body. . . . But we must not forget that women are, on the average, a little less intelligent than men, a difference which we should not exaggerate but which is, nonetheless, real. We are therefore permitted to suppose that the relatively small size of the female brain depends in part upon her physical inferiority and in part upon her intellectual inferiority.[7]

Broca's a priori classification of women as inferior to men constrained his ability to interpret his data as supporting any other conclusion. Though it may seem clear in retrospect that Broca presumed the inferiority of women and so found it in his data, at the time his work was widely accepted as factual. Moreover, it was applied directly to arguments that women should be excluded from higher education.[8]

Broca also tried to determine "the relative position of races in the human series" by measuring the ratio of the radius of the lower arm bone to the upper arm bone, reasoning that longer arms were indicated by a higher ratio, signifying a characteristic of apes. The closer a group was to apes, the less it had evolved. His hierarchical classification system fell apart, however, when his measurements found that darker-skinned groups had lower ratios than lighter-skinned groups. When his measurements of the brains of "yellow people" similarly contradicted the presumed hierarchy, he began to question not the value of the hierarchical classification system, but rather the interpretation of the data. Thus he argued that the brain-size classification system worked best to identify superior people, since some inferiors had large brains but no superiors had small brains.[9]

Though the theories about racial hierarchies that Broca developed have been dismissed by most of today's scientists, the cultural belief that groups can and should be distinguished from one another persists into contemporary U.S. society. The categories are familiar ones: there are only two sexes, male and female, and people fit into only one racial or ethnic category. An individual is either black, white, Asian, European, Native American, or Hispanic. Feminist scholars have pointed out that these categorizations belie the biological reality of diversity among human beings. Anne Fausto-Sterling argues that there are at least three other sexes in addition to male and female that deserve to be included in our sexual classification scheme.[10] Intersexed individuals are neither strictly male nor strictly female. Acknowledgments of their existence can be traced historically throughout human society and as early as the ancient Greeks, but a combination of legal and social practices has rendered them more or less invisible in contemporary society.

Evelynn Hammonds similarly questions the use of contemporary racial categorizations, pointing out that in the United States, characteristics that are associated with race are often conflated with those associated with ethnicity. Even celebrations of "racial diversity" in the popular press implicitly reinscribe racial boundaries and reinforce notions of male dominance by representing women of color as objects in white males' search for the perfect mate.[11]

CONSTRUCTION OF RESEARCH QUESTIONS

The effort to identify fundamental biological differences between women and men is not in and of itself necessarily biased, because medical knowledge about women's biology is critical to women's health care. However, when researchers begin with the assumption that there are important biological differences between women and men that can explain social arrangements, they are asking an already distorted research question, that is: How do the biological differences explain social arrangements? Today's sophisticated technologies and scientific methods cannot prevent biased interpretations of data that flow from biased questions.

In popular culture, too, the persistent common wisdom is that there are important natural differences that structure social life. Compare arguments made in 1879 to those made in 1992. In 1879 Gustav LeBon, an early social psychologist and supporter of Broca's work, argued that: "the day when, misunderstanding the inferior occupations which nature has given her, women leave the home and take part in our battles; on this day a social revolution will begin, and everything that maintains the sacred ties of the family will disappear."[12] A little over a hundred years later, Gordon Freeman, a chemist at the University of Alberta, claimed that women with children did not belong in the workforce because "the majority of women were equipped by nature to be nurturers, and most men were not." In an essay that originally appeared in the *Canadian Journal of Physics* (and then was featured in an article in the widely read *Science*) Freeman argued that half the children of working mothers suffer "serious psychological damage" because their mothers work. Without providing evidence to ground his arguments, Freeman claimed to understand why women work, explaining that they do so because they "distrust males' capacity to make a commitment to marriage," whereas men "fear commitment because of the threat of nuclear holocaust, the availability of birth control, and the socialist leanings of feminists."[13]

In Anne Fausto-Sterling's *Myths of Gender,* in the chapter entitled "A Question of Genius," she describes the history of efforts in the twentieth century to establish the biological bases of cognitive differences between women and men, with a focus on studying IQ and math ability. It is no accident that her chapter begins with the words "JOBS AND EDUCATION—that's what it's really all about." Most of the sex difference research, says Fausto-Sterling, "has been and continues to be used to avoid facing up to very real problems in our educational system and has provided a rationale for discrimination against women in the workplace."[14] What is remarkable about the sex difference research is how little difference has actually been found. Yet there is a clear effort in the publication and interpretation of research data to exaggerate and focus on the differences.

Paula Caplan and her colleagues write, in a critique of the work reporting sex-related differences in spatial (math) abilities that: "journal policies encourage the publication of studies in which sex differences *are* found and discourage the converse. Therefore, researchers who find no sex difference often do not submit their work for publications, and any real sex difference that might exist . . . are likely to be rather exaggerated."[15] Neurobiologist Ruth Bleier describes her experiences submitting a paper to

Science showing that there were no significant differences in spatial abilities between men and women. This "negative" data was rejected for publication, according to Bleier, because *Science* had been a major outlet for the very sex difference research she critiqued as methodologically flawed.[16]

Scientific work that appears to prove that women are less intelligent than men, because women have less innate mathematical ability than men, reinforces prevailing cultural stereotypes about women and men, so it persists relatively unchallenged in the mainstream. This remains so despite counterevidence that the differences arise from, and can be eliminated by, educational and/or social experiences.[17] Because scientific knowledge about sex differences has been used historically as evidence to deny educational and employment options to women, and because scientific researchers seldom address their background assumptions about social life, feminist scholars often are suspicious of research in this tradition. Indeed, since our culture is fundamentally organized around defining women as different from and inferior to men, it is hard to imagine "objective" or women-centered research in this area.

Biologist Ruth Hubbard sees sex difference research as emblematic of a more general issue in scientific research, arguing that true "objectivity" is difficult to achieve precisely because of the social arrangements surrounding the education, training, hiring, and promotion of scientists. Those who are "permitted" to make scientific facts share many social characteristics that have permeated their thought processes as part of the training to become scientists. These include a particular kind of education, the subject matter to which we are exposed, the history and culture of the European and North American upper class, and the rules of behavior that have been deemed acceptable for members of the academic workforce. Hubbard points out that the problem with "difference" research is not that differences may exist between groups of people, but rather that the distinguishing characteristics themselves come to be "valued differently and carry with them different amounts of prestige and power." Hubbard goes on to point out that research that makes sex differences appear "natural" and therefore unchanging is used to legitimate the segregation of women and men in the workplace, where women's labor is devalued. The economic disadvantage that confronts women can be supported by the weight of scientific authority, so that women are assigned by nature to jobs that are consistent with their innate abilities, skills, and interests.[18]

Moreover, the insistence that people fit neatly into either the male category or the female category, and the concurrent overemphasis on the reproductive role of women in human society, grounds the heterosexist and male-centered expectations for women's relations with men. Adrienne Rich puts it this way:

> In the mystique of the overpowering, all-conquering male sex drive, the penis-with-a-life-of-its own, is rooted the law of male sex right to women, which justifies prostitution as a universal cultural assumption on the one hand, while defending sexual slavery within the family . . . on the other. The adolescent male sex drive, which, as both young women and men are taught, once triggered cannot take responsibility for itself or take no for an answer, becomes . . . the norm and rationale for adult male sexual behavior: a condition of *arrested sexual development.* Women learn to accept as natural the inevitability of this "drive" because they receive it as dogma. Hence, marital rape; hence, the Japanese wife resignedly packing her suitcase for a weekend in the *kisaeng* brothels of Taiwan; hence, the psychological as well as economic imbalance of power between husband and wife, male employer and female worker, father and daughter, male professor and female student.[19]

Feminists are not critical of all work on sex differences, since there are compelling and meritorious reasons to study the differences between the biology of women and men. An important example is in medicine, where it is crucial that we understand how men and women differ in their physiological responses to medications, in how diseases affect them, and in how they age. Though this would be a logical context in which to study biological differences, research on how women and people of color diverge from the norms of white male biology has been noticeably absent in the medical community. As recently as the 1980s women were routinely excluded from clinical trials to determine drug efficacy and safety, and ethnic differences were (and still are) too seldom explored. Sometimes, then, dominant cultural assumptions underwrite research questions that as a result produce inadequate data, and sometimes dominant cultural assumptions mean that important research questions are not asked at all. We examine the consequences of both in the final section of the book.

INTERPRETATION OF DATA

Almost every step in scientific inquiry requires interpretation of some kind. A zoologist can look at the way an iguana slowly shuts its eyes when it is being petted and interpret that behavior as a sign that the iguana is enjoying itself. Another zoologist could see the same behavior and interpret it as a sign that the iguana is frightened.[20] One of these two scientists has an interpretation that is more consistent with the prevailing consensus about iguana responses to human touching.

In the case of gender there is consensus within the feminist community, derived from theory and research in a variety of fields, that the social, economic, and intellectual frameworks of Western culture have been influenced by beliefs about women and men and the differences between them. This includes "objective" scientific knowledge. When researchers interpret data through language filled with images and metaphors that evoke gender constructs, they are explaining the data based on social preconceptions that they bring to their work. They are tapping into what Carol Cohn has called "symbolic gender" in order to explain their data in terms that are shared by the wider community of scientists.[21]

Anthropologist Emily Martin has analyzed textbooks in molecular biology to examine how symbolic gender has influenced biologists' understanding of eggs and sperm. One of the primary tenets of theory about human evolution asserts that males (and thus sperm) are more important than females to understanding the process of human evolution. The evidence for this is derived from an interpretation of the relative value of eggs and sperm to reproduction. Martin argues that this evaluation is based on a male-centered interpretation rather than on the biological evidence:

> The texts have an almost dogged insistence on casting female processes in a negative light. The texts celebrate sperm production because it is continuous from puberty to senescence, while they portray egg production as inferior because it is finished at birth. This makes the female seem unproductive, but some texts will also insist that it is she who is wasteful. In a section heading for *Molecular Biology of the Cell,* a best-selling text, we are told that "Oogenesis is wasteful." The text goes on to emphasize that of the seven million oogonia, or egg germ cells, in the female embryo, most degenerate in the ovary. Of those that do go on to become oocytes, or eggs, many also degenerate, so that at birth only two million eggs remain in the ovaries. Degeneration continues throughout a women's life: by puberty 300,000 eggs remain, and only a few are present by menopause. "During the 40 or so years of a women's reproductive life, only 400 to 500 eggs will have been released," the authors write. "All the rest will have degenerated. It is still a mystery why so many eggs are formed only to die in the ovaries."
>
> The real mystery is why the male's vast production of sperm is not seen as wasteful. Assuming that a man "produces" 100 million (10^8) sperm per day (a conservative estimate), during an average reproductive life of sixty years, he would produce well over two trillion sperm in his lifetime. Assuming that a women "ripens" one egg per lunar

> month, or thirteen per year, over the course of her forty-year reproductive life, she would total five hundred eggs in her lifetime. But the word "waste" implies an excess, too much produced. Assuming two or three offspring, for every baby a women produces, she wastes only around two hundred eggs. For every baby a man produces, he wastes more than one trillion (10^{12}) sperm.[22]

Martin focuses on a specific example from a popular textbook. Feminist analyses of interpretive bias also extend beyond specific topics or interpretations within a subject area. Ruth Bleier has challenged the primary premises of the field of human sociobiology, deftly analyzed in this section in her essay "Sociobiology, Biological Determinism, and Human Behavior." E. O. Wilson, a highly regarded entomologist at Harvard University, has formed a school of sociobiological thought in which all human behaviors, social relationships, and organization are assumed to be genetically evolved adaptations. Wilsonian sociobiology takes as a primary premise that males and females have an unequal investment in reproduction, from subtle differences in the biological "cost" of producing eggs and sperm to the obvious differences in parental involvement in the birth of offspring. This unequal investment is hypothesized to lead inexorably to differences in behavior between males and females that maximize the "return" on investment for each. Bleier is unconvinced, however, since these behaviors are remarkably similar to the beliefs of nineteenth-century Western, privileged, white males about what is appropriate and "natural" in relations between women and men. Unfortunately, sociobiology cannot simply be dismissed as an old-fashioned idea. The arguments of Wilsonian sociobiology have reappeared recently as the cornerstone of evolutionary psychology, a newly defined field of research.[23]

Bonnie Spanier, herself a biologist, punctuates the importance to feminists, and to women in general, of continually applying a critical analysis of such work.

> One of the things feminists need to know to survive is not just that science can be dangerous to our health (indeed, what area of traditional masculinist knowledge isn't) but how to make sense, feminist sense, of scientific claims that affect our lives and the lives of all oppressed peoples. Whether or not we value masculinist notions of "reason" and "scientific evidence," feminists must understand scientific evidence within the norms of traditional science in order to critique it—speaking the language and using the methods of traditional science while transforming it at the same time. If we are successful in changing science sufficiently as a consequence of liberatory transformations, one day "traditional science" may well include—no, require—the tools and insights of feminist critique and experience. What do feminists need to know about science and technology? As much as possible and always within their social contexts.[24]

One needs only to read the title of a recent publication in evolutionary psychology by Randy Thornhill and Craig Palmer, *A Natural History of Rape: Biological Bases of Sexual Coercion,* to recognize the dangers of letting the premises of Wilsonian sociobiology and evolutionary psychology go unchallenged.

We have reviewed thus far feminist accounts of the intellectual pitfalls of scientific work that does not recognize how gender and language imbue research and analysis with social and cultural meanings. The resulting male-centered biases can take literal as well as analytic form. In "The Medical Construction of Gender: Case Management of Intersexed Infants," Suzanne Kessler examines physicians' and parents' surgical and socialization decisions in cases in which infants are born with ambiguous genitalia. Although the medical decisions are theoretically based on the results of diagnostic tests, Kessler's interviews with physicians reveal the overwhelming influence of cultural understandings of gender. Their primary assumption is that there are only two possible and biologically distinct sexes, and that the most important feature in each case is that the child be properly equipped to engage in heterosexual intercourse according to its gender. The greatest focus is on the penis and the male-centered understanding of sexuality. Infants without an adequate penis are defined as female by default. The "true sex" of the infant, insofar as that can be determined by genetic or hormonal profiles, is disregarded in the face of the parents' discomfort with the ambiguity. Surgical interventions attempt literally to construct the sex of the infant, and then parents consciously cultivate the child's gender identity accordingly. As the physicians and parents try to prepare the child for a life in heterosexual society, they disregard any forms of sexuality that might not involve vaginal intercourse, because of deeply held cultural beliefs about what is "natural" in human sexual relationships.

Because of the pervasiveness of beliefs about gender, and because science and technology are equally pervasive in our society, there are instances in which gender and science so mutually inform each other that they cannot be distinguished. Such is the case with architecture, where spatial arrangements literally shape our gender arrangements and, conversely, our gender arrangements shape our spaces. Judy Wajcman, in her essay "The Built Environment: Women's Place, Gendered Space," points out how architecture and urban planning are influenced by cultural beliefs about the separate roles of women and men. Buildings are designed in ways that arrange spaces at work and home according to those roles. Since biological research on sex differences supports the idea that these roles are "natural," prevailing designs are accepted as the designs of choice because they comply with social expectations. Men and women are separated daily by the physical realities of industrial centers, urban and suburban design, the presence or absence of public transportation, the location of affordable housing in relation to all of these, and the division of labor in the workplace, which distinguishes skilled and professional workers from unskilled workers.

Even our homes have been designed to reflect ideas about women and men, child-rearing, and domestic labor (who cooks, who cleans, who needs an office or a hobby room). Women have very little space allocated to them at home, especially space designed for leisure and rest from domestic chores. There is a playroom for the children, a "study" for the husband, and a bedroom for everyone except the wife and mother, who must sleep in the "master" bedroom. The kitchen is presumed to belong to women, but that is hardly a place of rest and domestic tranquility. The interrelationship between design and gender constructs physical barriers—tangible, concrete barriers—that perpetuate and strengthen the notions of women's separateness and difference, even as those notions about women promote the demand for such designs.

Increasing the participation of women and people of color in scientific and technological research is an important route to improving not only the dominant social world but also the dominant intellectual world. However, increasing diversity is a necessary but not sufficient step toward change. In the absence of a full appreciation of social influences on the creation of knowledge, scientific researchers can perpetuate social biases simply by practicing the conventions of their field. Feminist studies of science and technology have opened the door to reinventing science as a self-reflective and socially engaged enterprise. In sections 4 and 5 we have included essays that illustrate how feminist perspectives have enhanced and redirected research in several areas of research.

NOTES

[1] Evelyn Fox Keller, *Secrets of Life: Secrets of Death* (New York: Routledge, 1992), 28.

[2] Dale Spender, *Man Made Language* (New York: Routledge and Kegan Paul, 1980), 142.

[3] For a more detailed discussion, see Adrienne Zihlman, "The Paleolithic Glass Ceiling: Women in Human Evolution," in Lori D. Hager, ed., *Women in Human Evolution* (New York: Routledge, 1997).

[4] Nancy Tanner and Adriénne Zihlman, "Women in Evolution. Part I. Innovation and Selection in Human Origins," *Signs: Journal of Women in Culture and Society* 1, 3, pt. 1 (1976): 585–608; A. Zihlman, "Women in Evolution. Part II. Subsistence and Social Organization among Early Hominids," *Signs: Journal of Women in Culture and Society* 4, 1 (1978): 4–20.

[5] Autumn Stanley argues that the sexual division of labor in the man-the-hunter hypothesis by extension suggests that women must have been the major inventors of our most basic agricultural tools, the digging stick and carrying basket. Yet women's contributions to technological innovation are undervalued and underresearched. See Autumn Stanley, *Mothers and Daughters of Invention: Notes for a Revised History of Technology* (New Brunswick, N.J.: Rutgers University Press, 1995).

[6] Londa Schiebinger, "Why Mammals Are Called Mammals: Gender Politics in Eighteenth-Century Natural History," in Evelyn Fox Keller and Helen Longino, eds., *Feminism and Science* (New York: Oxford University Press, 1996).

[7] As quoted in Stephen J. Gould, "Women's Brains," in *The Panda's Thumb* (New York: Norton, 1980), 154.

[8] Ibid., 155.

[9] Steven J. Gould, "Measuring Heads," in *The Mismeasure of Man* (New York: Norton, 1981), 86–87. See also Nancy Stephan, "Race and Gender: The Role of Analogy in Science," in Sandra Harding, ed., *The "Racial" Economy of Science* (Bloomington: Indiana University Press, 1993).

[10] Anne Fausto-Sterling, "The Five Sexes: Why Male and Female Are Not Enough," *The Sciences,* March/April 1993, 20–25.

[11] Evelynn Hammonds, "New Technologies of Race," in Jennifer Terry and Melodie Calvert, eds., *Processed Lives: Gender and Technology in Everyday Life* (New York: Routledge, 1997).

[12] As quoted in Gould, "Women's Brains," 155.

[13] Robert Crease, "Canadian Chemist Takes on Working Women," *Science* 255 (1992): 1065–6.

[14] Anne Fausto-Sterling, *Myths of Gender* (New York: Basic Books, 1992 [1985]).

[15] P. J. Caplan, G. M. MacPherson, and P. Tobin, "Do Sex-Related Differences in Spatial Abilities Exist? A Multilevel Critique with New Data," *American Physiologist* 40, 7 (1985): 786–99, quote on 786. See also Paula Caplan and Jeremy Caplan, *Thinking Critically about Research on Sex and Gender* (New York: Harper Collins, 1994), esp. ch. 5, "Are Boys Better than Girls at Math?" 37–47.

[16] Ruth Bleier, "A Decade of Feminist Critiques in the Natural Sciences," *Signs: Journal of Women in Culture and Society* 14, 1 (1988): 182–95. Recent work points toward the influence of experience on neurophysiology. See Ingrid Wickelgran, "Nurture Helps Mold Able Minds," *Science* 283 (1999): 1832–4.

[17] Richard Devon, Renata Engel, and Geoffrey Turner, "The Effects of Spatial Visualization Skill Training on Gender and Retention in Engineering," *Journal of Women and Minorities in Science and Engineering* 4 (1998): 371–80.

[18] Girls and women are more likely than boys and men to value work related to reproduction and the home, because girls and women are taught to do so. For further discussion, see Virginia Valian, *Why So Slow? The Advancement of Women* (Cambridge, Mass.: MIT Press, 1999), esp. 23–46.

[19] Adrienne Rich, "Compulsory Heterosexuality and Lesbian Existence," in *Blood, Bread, and Poetry* (New York: Norton, 1986), 47.

[20] There is better evidence for the latter. See, for example, Philippe de Vosjoli, *The Green Iguana Manual* (Lakeside, Calif.: Advanced Vivarium Systems, 1992), 40.

[21] Carol Cohn, "Wars, Wimps, and Women: Talking Gender and Thinking War," in Miriam Cooke and Angela Woollacott, eds., *Gendering War Talk* (Princeton, N.J.: Princeton University Press, 1993).

[22] Emily Martin. "The Egg and the Sperm: How Science Has Constructed a Romance Based on Stereotypical Male-Female Roles," *Signs: Journal of Women in Culture and Society* 16, 3 (1991): 485–501, esp. 488–89.

[23] For examples of work in this tradition, see Edward O. Wilson, *Consilience: The Unity of Knowledge* (New York: Alfred A. Knopf, 1998); E. O. Wilson, *Sociobiology* (Cambridge, Mass.: Harvard University Press, 1980), esp. ch. 26; and Robert Wright, *The Moral Animal: Evolutionary Psychology and Everyday Life* (New York: Peter Smith, 1995).

[24] Bonnie Spanier, "Biological Determinism and Homosexuality," *NWSA Journal* 7, 1 (1995): 54–71.

SCIENCE, FACTS, AND FEMINISM

Ruth Hubbard

THE FACTS OF SCIENCE

The Brazilian educator, Paulo Freire, has pointed out that people who want to understand the role of politics in shaping education must "see the reasons behind facts" (Freire 1985,2). I want to begin by exploring some of the reasons behind a particular kind of facts, the facts of natural science. After all, facts aren't just out there. Every fact has a factor, a maker. The interesting question is: as people move through the world, how do we sort those aspects of it that we permit to become facts from those that we relegate to being fiction—untrue, imagined, imaginary, or figments of the imagination—and from those that, worse yet, we do not even notice and that therefore do not become fact, fiction, or figment? In other words, what criteria and mechanisms of selection do scientists use in the making of facts?

One thing is clear: making facts is a social enterprise. Individuals cannot just go off by themselves and dream up facts. When people do that, and the rest of us do not agree to accept or share the facts they offer us, we consider them schizophrenic, crazy. If we do agree, either because their facts sufficiently resemble ours or because they have the power to force us to accept their facts as real and true—to make us see the emperor's new clothes—then the new facts become part of our shared reality and their making, part of the fact-making enterprise.

Making science is such an enterprise. As scientists, our job is to generate facts that help people understand nature. But in doing this, we must follow rules of membership in the scientific community and go about our task of fact-making in professionally sanctioned ways. We must submit new facts to review by our colleagues and be willing to share them with qualified strangers by writing and speaking about them (unless we work for private companies with proprietary interests, in which case we still must share our facts, but only with particular people). If we follow proper procedure, we become accredited fact-makers. In that case our facts come to be accepted on faith and large numbers of people believe them even though they are in no position to say why what we put out are facts rather than fiction. After all, a lot of scientific facts are counter-intuitive, such as that the earth moves around the sun or that if you drop a pound of feathers and a pound of rocks, they will fall at the same rate.

What are the social or group characteristics of those of us who are allowed to make scientific facts? Above all, we must have a particular kind of education that includes graduate, and post-graduate training. That means that in addition to whatever subject matter we learn, we have been socialized to think in particular ways and have familiarized ourselves with that narrow slice of human history and culture that deals primarily with the experiences of western European and North American upper class men during the past century or two. It also means that we must not deviate too far from accepted rules of individual and social behavior and must talk and think in ways that let us earn the academic degrees required of a scientist.

Until the last decade or two, mainly upper-middle and upper class youngsters, most of them male and white, have had access to that kind of education. Lately, more white women and people of color (women and men) have been able to get it, but the class origins of scientists have not changed appreciably. The scientific professions still draw their members overwhelmingly from the upper-middle and upper classes.

How about other kinds of people? Have they no role in the making of science? Quite the contrary. In the ivory (that is, white) towers in which science gets made, lots of people are from working class and lower-middle class backgrounds, but they are the technicians, secretaries, and clean-up personnel. Decisions about who gets to be a faculty-level fact-maker are made by professors, deans, and university presidents who call on scientists from other, similar institutions to recommend candidates who they think will conform to the standards prescribed by universities and the scientific professions. At the larger, systemic level, decisions are made by government and private funding agencies which operate by what is called peer review. What that means is that small groups of people with similar personal and academic backgrounds decide whether a particular fact-making proposal has enough merit to be financed. Scientists who work in the same, or related, fields mutually sit on each other's decision making panels and whereas criteria for access are supposedly objective and meritocratic, orthodoxy and conformity count for a lot. Someone whose ideas and/or personality are out of line is less likely to succeed than "one of the boys"—and these days some of us girls are allowed to join the boys, particularly if we play by their rules.

Thus, science is made, by and large, by a self-perpetuating, self-reflexive group: by the chosen for the chosen. The assumption is that if the science is "good," in a professional sense, it will also be good for society. But no one and no group are responsible for looking at whether it is. Public accountability is not built into the system.

What are the alternatives? How could we have a science that is more open and accessible, a science *for* the people? And to what extent could—or should—it also be a science *by* the people? After all, divisions of labor are not necessarily bad. There is no reason and, indeed, no possibility, that in a complicated society like ours, everyone is able to do everything. Inequalities which are bad, come not from the fact that different people do different things, but from the fact that different tasks are valued differently and carry with them different amounts of prestige and power.

For historical reasons, this society values mental labor more highly than manual labor. We often pay more for it and think that it requires more specifically human qualities and therefore is superior. This is a mistake especially in the context of a scientific laboratory, because it means that the laboratory chief—the person "with ideas"—often gets the credit, whereas the laboratory workers—the people who work with their hands (as well as, often, their imaginations)—are the ones who perform the operations and make the observations that generate new hypotheses and that permit hunches, ideas, and hypotheses to become facts. . . .

WOMAN'S NATURE: REALITIES VERSUS SCIENTIFIC MYTHS

As I said before, to be believed, scientific facts must fit the world-view of the times. Therefore, at times of tension and upheaval, such as the last two decades, some researchers always try to "prove" that differences in the political, social, and economic status of women and men, blacks and whites, or poor people and rich people, are inevitable because they are the results of people's inborn qualities and traits. Such scientists have tried to "prove" that blacks are innately less intelligent than whites, or that women are innately weaker, more nurturing, less good at math than men. If, for the purposes of this discussion, we focus on sex differences, it is clear that the ideology of woman's nature can differ drastically from the realities of women's lives and indeed be antithetical to them. In fact, the ideology functions, at least in part, to obscure the ways women live and to make people look away from the realities or ask misleading questions about them. So, for example, the ideology that labels women as the natural reproducers of the species, and men as producers of goods, has not been used to exempt women from also producing goods and services, but to shunt us out of higher paying jobs, the professions, and other kinds of work that require continuity and provide a measure of power over one's own and, at times, other people's lives. Most women who work for pay do so in job categories, such as secretary or nurse, which often involve a great deal of concealed responsibility, but are underpaid. This is one reason why insisting on equal pay *within* job categories cannot remedy women's economic disadvantage. Women will continue to be underpaid as long as women's jobs are less well paid than men's jobs and as long as access to traditional men's jobs is limited by social pressures, career counseling, training and hiring practices, trade union policies, and various other subtle and not so subtle societal mechanisms, such as research that "proves" that girls are not as good as boys at spatial perception, mathematics and science. An entire range of discriminatory practices is justified by the claim that they follow from the limits that biology places on women's capacity to work. Though exceptions are made during wars and other emergencies, they are forgotten as soon as life resumes its normal course. Then women are expected to return to their subordinate roles, not because the quality of their work during the emergencies has been inferior, but because these roles are seen as natural.

A few years ago, a number of women employees in the American chemical and automotive industries were actually forced to choose between working at relatively well-paying jobs that had previously been done by men or remaining fertile. In one instance, five women were required to submit to sterilization by *hysterectomy* in order to avoid being transferred from work in the lead pigment department at the American Cyanamid plant in Willow Island, West Virginia to janitorial work at considerably lower wages and benefits (Stellman and Henifin 1982). Even though none of these women was pregnant or planning a pregnancy in the near future (indeed, the husband of one had had a vasectomy), they were considered "potentially pregnant" unless they could prove that they were sterile. This goes on despite the fact that exposure to lead can damage sperm as well as eggs and can affect the health of workers (male and female) as well as a "potential fetus." It is as though fertile women are at all times potential parents; men, never. But it is important to notice that this vicious choice is being forced only on women who have recently entered relatively well-paid, traditionally male jobs. Women whose work routinely involves reproductive hazards because it exposes them to chemical or radiation hazards, but who have traditionally female jobs such as nurses, X-ray technologists, laboratory technicians, cleaning women in surgical operating rooms, scientific laboratories or the chemical and biotechnology industries, beauticians, secretaries, workers in the ceramics industry, and domestic workers are not warned about the chemical or physical hazards of their work to their health or to that of a fetus, should they be pregnant. In other words, scientific knowledge about fetal susceptibility to noxious chemicals and radiation is used to keep women out of better paid job categories from which they had previously been excluded by discriminatory employment practices, but, in general, women (or, indeed, men) are not protected against health endangering work.

The ideology of woman's nature that is invoked at these times would have us believe that a woman's capacity to become pregnant leaves her always physically disabled by comparison with men. The scientific underpinnings for these ideas were elaborated in the nineteenth century by the white, university-educated, mainly upper class men who made up the bulk of the new professions of obstetrics and gynecology, biology, psychology, sociology and anthropology. These professionals used their theories of women's innate frailty to disqualify the girls and women of their own race and class who would have been competing with them for education and professional status. They also realized that they might lose the kinds of personal attention they were accustomed to get from mothers, wives, and sisters if women of their own class gained access to the professions. They did not invoke women's weakness when it came to poor women spending long hours working in the homes and factories belonging to members of the upper classes, nor against the ways black slave women were made to work on the plantations and in the homes of their masters and mistresses. . . .

During the past decade, feminists have uncovered this history. We have analyzed the self-serving theories and documented the absurdity of the claims as well as their class and race biases and their glaringly political intent (Hubbard and Lowe 1979; Lowe and Hubbard 1983; Bleier 1984; Fausto-Sterling 1985). But this kind of scientific mythmaking is not past history. Just as in the nineteenth century medical men and biologists fought women's political organizing for equality by claiming that our reproductive organs made us unfit for anything but childbearing and childrearing, just as Freud declared women to be intrinsically less stable, intellectually inventive and productive than men, so beginning in the 1970's, there has been a renaissance in sex differences research that has claimed to prove scientifically that women are innately better than men at home care and mothering while men are innately better fitted than women for the competitive life of the market place.

Questionable experimental results obtained with animals (primarily that prototypic human, the white laboratory rat) are treated as though they can be applied equally well to people. On this basis, some scientists are now claiming that the secretion of different amounts of so-called male hormones (androgens) by male and female fetuses produces life-long differences in women's and men's brains. They claim not only that these (unproved) differences in fetal hormone levels exist, but imply (without evidence) that they predispose women and men *as groups* to exhibit innate differences in our abilities to localize objects in space, in our verbal and mathematical aptitudes, in aggressiveness and competitiveness, nurturing ability, and so on (Money and Ehrhardt 1972; Goy and McEwen 1980; *Science* 1981). . . .

Sociobiologists have tried to prove that women's disproportionate contributions to child- and homecare are biologically programmed because women have a greater biological "investment" in our children than men have. They offer the following rationale: an organism's biological fitness, in the Darwinian sense, depends on producing the greatest possible number of offspring, who themselves survive long enough to reproduce, because this is what determines the frequency with which an individual's genes will be represented in successive generations. Following this logic a step further, sociobiologists argue that women and men must adopt basically different strategies to maximize opportunities to spread our genes into future generations. The calculus goes as follows: Eggs are larger than sperm and women can produce many fewer of them than men can sperm. Therefore each egg that develops into a child represents a much larger fraction of the total number of children a woman can produce, hence of her "reproductive fitness," than a sperm that becomes a child does of a man's "fitness." In addition, women "invest" the nine months of pregnancy in each child. Women must therefore be more careful than men to acquire well-endowed sex partners who will be good providers to make sure that their few investments (read, children) mature. Thus, from seemingly innocent biological asymmetries between sperm and eggs flow such major social consequences as female fidelity, male promiscuity, women's disproportional contribution to caring for home and children, and the unequal distribution of labor by sex. As sociobiologist, David Barash, says, "mother nature is sexist," so don't blame her human sons (Dawkins 1976; Barash 1979, esp. 46–90).

In devising these explanations, sociobiologists ignore the fact that human societies do not operate with a few superstuds; nor do stronger or more powerful men as a rule have more children than weaker ones. Men, in theory, could have many more children than women can, but in most societies equal numbers of men and women engage in producing children, though not in caring for them. These kinds of absurdities are useful to people who have a stake in maintaining present inequalities. They mystify procreation, yet have a superficial ring of plausibility and thus offer naturalistic justifications for discriminatory practices.

As the new scholarship on women has grown, a few anthropologists and biologists have tried to mitigate the male bias that underlies these kinds of theories by describing how females contribute to social life and species survival in important ways that are overlooked by scientists who think of females only in relation to reproduction and look to males for everything else (Lancaster 1975; Hrdy 1981, 1986; Kevles 1986). But, unless scientists challenge the basic premises that underlie the standard, male-centered descriptions and analyses, such revisions do not offer radically different formulations and insights. (For examples of more fundamental criticisms of evolutionary thinking and sociobiology, see Lowe and Hubbard 1979; Hubbard 1982; Lewontin, Rose and Kamin 1984).

SUBJECTIVITY AND OBJECTIVITY

I want to come back to Paulo Freire, who says: "Reality is never just simply the objective datum, the concrete fact, but is also people's [and I would say, certain people's] perception of it." And he speaks of "the indispensable unity between subjectivity and objectivity in the act of knowing" (Freire 1985, 51).

The recognition of this "indispensable unity" is what feminist methodology is about. It is especially necessary for a feminist methodology in science because the scientific method rests on a particular definition of objectivity, that we feminists must call into question. Feminists and others who draw attention to the devices that the dominant group has used to deny other people access to power—be it political power or the power to make facts—have come to understand how that definition of objectivity functions in the processes of exclusion I discussed at the beginning.

Natural scientists attain their objectivity by looking upon nature (including other people) in small chunks and as isolated objects. They usually deny, or at least do not acknowledge, their relationship to the "objects" they study. In other words, natural scientists describe their activities as though they existed in a vacuum. The way language is used in scientific writing reinforces this illusion because it implicitly denies the relevance of time, place, social context, authorship, and personal responsibility. When I report a discovery, I do not write, "One sunny Monday after a restful weekend, I came into the laboratory, set up my experiment and shortly noticed that . . ." No; proper style dictates, "It has been observed that . . ." This removes relevance of time and place, and implies that the observation did not originate in the head of a human observer, specifically my head, but out there in the world. By deleting the scientist-agent as well as her or his participation as observer, people are left with the concept of science as a thing in itself, that truly reflects nature and that can be treated as though it were as real as, and indeed equivalent to, nature.

A blatant example of the kind of context-stripping that is commonly called objectivity is the way E. O. Wilson opens the final chapter of his *Sociobiology: The New Synthesis* (Wilson 1975, 547). He writes: "Let us now consider man in the free spirit of natural history, as though we were zoologists from another planet completing a catalog of social species on earth." That statement epitomizes the fallacy we need to get rid of. There is no "free spirit of natural history," only a set of descriptions put forward by the mostly white, educated, Euro-American men who have been practicing a particular kind of science during the past two hundred years. Nor do we have any idea what "zoologists from another planet" would have to say about "man" (which, I guess is supposed to mean "people") or about other "social species on earth," since that would depend on how these "zoologists" were used to living on their own planet and by what experiences they would therefore judge us. Feminists must insist that subjectivity and context cannot be stripped away, that they must be acknowledged if we want to use science as a way to understand nature and society and to use the knowledge we gain constructively. . . .

The problem is that the context-stripping that worked reasonably well for the classical physics of falling bodies has become the model for how to do every kind of science. And this even though physicists since the beginning of this century have recognized that the experimenter is part of the experiment and influences its outcome. That insight produced Heisenberg's uncertainty principle in physics: the recognition that the operations the experimenter performs disturb the system so that it is impossible to specify simultaneously the position and momentum of atoms and elementary particles. So, how about standing the situation on its head and using the social sciences, where context stripping is clearly impossible, as a model and do all science in a way that acknowledges the experimenter as a self-conscious subject who lives, and does science, within the context in which the phenomena she or he observes occur? Anthropologists often try to take extensive field notes about a new culture as quickly as possible after they enter it, before they incorporate the perspective and expectations of that culture, because they realize that once they know the foreign culture well and feel at home in it, they will begin to take some of its most significant aspects for granted and stop seeing them. Yet they realize at the same time that they must also acknowledge the limitations their own personal and social backgrounds impose on the way they perceive the foreign society. Awareness of our subjectivity and context must be part of doing science because there is no way we can eliminate them. We come to the objects we study with our particular personal and social backgrounds and with inevitable interests. Once we acknowledge those, we can try to understand the world, so to speak, from inside instead of pretending to be objective outsiders looking in.

The social structure of the laboratory in which scientists work and the community and inter-personal relationships in which they live are also part of the subjective reality and context of doing science. Yet, we usually ignore them when we speak of a scientist's scientific work despite the fact that natural scientists work in highly organized social systems. Obviously, the sociology of laboratory life is structured by class, sex, and race, as is the rest of society. We saw before that to understand what goes on in the laboratory we must ask questions about who does what kinds of work. What does the lab chief—the person whose name appears on the stationery or on the door—contribute? How are decisions made about what work gets done and in what order? What role do women, whatever our class and race, or men of color and men from working class backgrounds play in this performance?

Note that women have played a very large role in the production of science—as wives, sisters, secretaries, technicians, and students of "great men"—though usually not as accredited scientists. One of our jobs as feminists must be to acknowledge that role. If feminists are to make a difference in the ways science is done and understood, we must not just try to become scientists who occupy the traditional structures, follow established patterns of behavior, and accept prevailing systems of explanation; we must understand and describe accurately the roles women have played all along in the process of making science. But we must also ask why certain ways of systematically interacting with nature and of using the knowledge so gained are acknowledged as science whereas others are not. . . .

I doubt that women as gendered beings have something new or different to contribute to science, but women as political beings do. One of the most important things we must do is to insist on the political content of science and on its political role. The pretense that science is objective, apolitical and value-neutral is profoundly political because it obscures the political role that science and technology play in underwriting the existing distribution of power in society. Science and technology always operate in somebody's interest and serve someone or some group of people. To the extent that scientists are "neutral" that merely means that they support the existing distribution of interests and power.

If we want to integrate feminist politics into our science, we must insist on the political nature and content of scientific work and of the way science is taught and otherwise communicated to the public. We must broaden the base of experience and knowledge on which scientists draw by making it possible for a wider range of people to do science, and to do it in different ways. We must also provide kinds of understanding that are useful and useable by a broad range of people. For this, science would have to be different from the way it is now. The important questions would have to be generated by a different social process. A wider range of people would have to have access to making scientific facts and to understanding and using them. Also, the process of validation would have to be under more public scrutiny, so that research topics and facts that benefit only a small elite while oppressing large segments of the population would not be acceptable. . . .

Of course it is difficult for feminists who, as women, are just gaining a toehold in science, to try to make fundamental changes in the ways scientists perceive science and do it. This is why many scientists who are feminists live double-lives and conform to the pretenses of an apolitical, value-free, meritocratic science in our working lives while living our politics elsewhere. Meanwhile, many of us who want to integrate our politics with our work, analyze and critique the standard science, but no longer do it. Here again, feminist health centers and counseling groups come to mind as efforts to integrate feminist inquiry and political praxis. It would be important for feminists, who are trying to reconceptualize reality and reorganize knowledge and its uses in areas other than health, to create environments ("outstitutes") in which we can work together and communicate with other individuals and groups, so that people with different backgrounds and agendas can exchange questions, answers, and expertise.

References

Barash, D. 1979. *The whispering within.* New York: Harper & Row.

Bleier, R. 1984. *Science and gender.* New York: Pergamon.

Boston Women's Health Book Collective. 1984. *The* new *our bodies, ourselves.* New York: Simon and Schuster.

Dawkins, R. 1976. *The selfish gene.* New York: Oxford University Press.

Fausto-Sterling, A. 1985. *Myths of gender.* New York: Basic Books.

Federation of Feminist Women's Health Centers. 1981. *A new view of a woman's body.* New York: Simon and Schuster.

Freire, P. 1985. *The politics of education.* South Hadley, MA: Bergin and Garvey.

Goy, R.W. and B.S. McEwen. 1980. *Sexual differentiation of the brain.* Cambridge, MA: M.I.T. Press.

Hrdy, S.B. 1981. *The woman that never evolved.* Cambridge, MA: Harvard University Press.

———. 1986. Empathy, polyandry, and the myth of the coy female. In *Feminist approaches to science,* ed. R. Bleier, 119–146. New York: Pergamon.

Hubbard, R. 1982. Have only men evolved? In *Biological woman—The convenient myth,* ed. R. Hubbard, M.S. Henifin and B. Fried, 17–46. Cambridge, MA: Schenkman.

Hubbard, R. and M. Lowe, eds. 1979. *Genes and gender II: Pitfalls in research on sex and gender.* Staten Island, NY: Gordian Press.

Kevles, B. 1986. *Females of the species.* Cambridge, MA: Harvard University Press.

Lancaster, J.B. 1975. *Primate behavior and the emergence of human culture.* New York: Holt, Rinehart and Winston.

Lewontin, R.C., S. Rose and L.J. Kamin. 1984. *Not in our genes.* New York: Pantheon.

Lowe, M. and R. Hubbard. 1979. Sociobiology and biosociology: Can science prove the biological basis of sex differences in behavior? In *Genes and gender II: Pitfalls in research on sex and gender,* ed. R. Hubbard and M. Lowe, 91–112. Staten Island, NY: Gordian Press.

Lowe, M. and R. Hubbard, eds. 1983. *Woman's nature: Rationalizations of inequality.* New York: Pergamon.

Money, J. and A.A. Ehrhardt. 1972. *Man & woman, boy & girl.* Baltimore: Johns Hopkins University Press.

Newman, L.M., ed. 1985. *Men's ideas/Women's realities: Popular science, 1870–1915.* New York: Pergamon.

Science. 1981. *211,* pp. 1263–1324.

Stellman, J.M. and M.S. Henifin. 1982. No fertile women need apply: Employment discrimination and reproductive hazards in the workplace. In *Biological woman—The convenient myth,* ed. R. Hubbard, M.S. Henifin and B. Fried, 117–145. Cambridge, MA: Schenkman.

Wilson, E.O. 1975. *Sociobiology: The new synthesis.* Cambridge, MA: Harvard University Press.

Woolf, V. 1928. *Orlando.* New York: Harcourt Brace Jovanovich; Harvest Paperback Edition.

THE MEDICAL CONSTRUCTION OF GENDER
Case Management of Intersexed Infants

Suzanne J. Kessler

The birth of intersexed infants, babies born with genitals that are neither clearly male nor clearly female, has been documented throughout recorded time. In the late twentieth century, medical technology has advanced to allow scientists to determine chromosomal and hormonal gender, which is typically taken to be the real, natural, biological gender, usually referred to as "sex."[1] Nevertheless, physicians who handle the cases of intersexed infants consider several factors beside biological ones in determining, assigning, and announcing the gender of a particular infant. Indeed, biological factors are often preempted in their deliberations by such cultural factors as the "correct" length of the penis and capacity of the vagina.

In the literature of intersexuality, issues such as announcing a baby's gender at the time of delivery, postdelivery discussions with the parents, and consultations with patients in adolescence are considered only peripherally to the central medical issues—etiology, diagnosis, and surgical procedures.[2] Yet members of medical teams have standard practices for managing intersexuality that rely ultimately on cultural understandings of gender. The process and guidelines by which decisions about gender (re)construction are made reveal the model for the social construction of gender generally. Moreover, in the face of apparently incontrovertible evidence—infants born with some combination of "female" and "male" reproductive and sexual features—physicians hold an incorrigible belief in and insistence upon female and male as the only "natural" options. This paradox highlights and calls into question the idea that female and male are biological givens compelling a culture of two genders.

Ideally, to undertake an extensive study of intersexed infant case management, I would like to have had direct access to particular events, for example, the deliveries of intersexed infants and the initial discussions among physicians, between physicians and parents, between parents, and among parents and family and friends of intersexed infants. The rarity with which intersexuality occurs, however, made this unfeasible.[3] Alternatively, physicians who have had considerable experience in dealing with this condition were interviewed. I do not assume that their "talk" about how they manage such cases mirrors their "talk" in the situation, but their words do reveal that they have certain assumptions about gender and that they impose those assumptions via their medical decisions on the patients they treat.

Interviews were conducted with six medical experts (three women and three men) in the field of pediatric intersexuality: one clinical geneticist, three endocrinologists (two of them pediatric specialists), one psychoendocrinologist, and one urologist. All of them have had extensive clinical experience with various intersexed syndromes, and some are internationally known researchers in the field of intersexuality. They were selected on the basis of their prominence in the field and their representation of four different medical centers in New York City. Although they know one another, they

---

I want to thank my student Jane Weider for skillfully conducting and transcribing the interviews for this article.

do not collaborate on research and are not part of the same management team. All were interviewed in the spring of 1985, in their offices, and interviews lasted between forty-five minutes and one hour. Unless further referenced, all quotations in this article are from these interviews.

THE THEORY OF INTERSEXUALITY MANAGEMENT

The sophistication of today's medical technology has led to an extensive compilation of various intersex categories based on the various causes of malformed genitals. The "true intersexed" condition, where both ovarian and testicular tissue are present in either the same gonad or in opposite gonads, accounts for fewer than 5 percent of all cases of ambiguous genitals.[4] More commonly, the infant has either ovaries or testes, but the genitals are ambiguous. If the infant has two ovaries, the condition is referred to as female pseudohermaphroditism. If the infant has two testes, the condition is referred to as male pseudohermaphroditism. There are numerous causes of both forms of pseudohermaphroditism, and although there are life-threatening aspects to some of these conditions, having ambiguous genitals per se is not harmful to the infant's health. Although most cases of ambiguous genitals do not represent true intersex, in keeping with the contemporary literature, I will refer to all such cases as intersexed.

Current attitudes toward the intersex condition are primarily influenced by three factors. First are the extraordinary advancements in surgical techniques and endocrinology in the last decade. For example, female genitals can now be constructed to be indistinguishable in appearance from normal natural ones. Some abnormally small penises can be enlarged with the exogenous application of hormones, although surgical skills are not sufficiently advanced to construct a normal-looking and functioning penis out of other tissue. Second, in the contemporary United States the influence of the feminist movement has called into question the valuation of women according to strictly reproductive functions, and the presence or absence of functional gonads is no longer the only or the definitive criterion for gender assignment. Third, contemporary psychological theorists have begun to focus on "gender identity" (one's sense of oneself as belonging to the female or male category) as distinct from "gender role" (cultural expectations of one's behavior as "appropriate" for a female or male). The relevance of this new gender identity theory for rethinking cases of ambiguous genitals is that gender must be assigned as early as possible in order for gender identity to develop successfully. As a result of these three factors, intersexuality is now considered a treatable condition of the genitals, one that needs to be resolved expeditiously.

According to all of the specialists interviewed, management of intersexed cases is based upon the theory of gender proposed first by John Money, J. G. Hampson, and J. L. Hampson in 1955 and developed in 1972 by Money and Anke A. Ehrhardt, which argues that gender identity is changeable until approximately eighteen months of age.[5] To use the Pygmalion allegory, one may begin with the same clay and fashion a god or a goddess."[6] The theory rests on satisfying several conditions: the experts must insure that the parents have no doubt about whether their child is male or female; the genitals must be made to match the assigned gender as soon as possible; gender-appropriate hormones must be administered at puberty; and intersexed children must be kept informed about their situation with age-appropriate explanations. If these conditions are met, the theory proposes, the intersexed child will develop a gender identity in accordance with the gender assignment (regardless of the chromosomal gender) and will not question her or his assignment and request reassignment at a later age.

Supportive evidence for Money and Ehrhardt's theory is based on only a handful of repeatedly cited cases, but it has been accepted because of the prestige of the theoreticians and its resonance with contemporary ideas about gender, children, psychology, and medicine. Gender and children are malleable; psychology and medicine are the tools used to transform them. This theory is so strongly endorsed that it has taken on the character of gospel. "I think we [physicians] have been raised in the Money theory," one endocrinologist said. Another claimed, "We always approach the problem in a similar way and it's been dictated, to a large extent, by the work of John Money and Anke Ehrhardt because they are the only people who have published, at least in medical literature, any data, any guidelines." It is provocative that this physician immediately followed this assertion with: "And I don't know how effective it really is." Contradictory data are rarely cited in reviews of the literature, were not mentioned by any of the physicians interviewed, and have not diminished these physicians' belief in the theory's validity.[7]

The doctors interviewed concur with the argument that gender be assigned immediately, decisively, and irreversibly, and that professional opinions be presented in a clear and unambiguous way. The psychoendocrinologist said that when doctors make a statement about the infant, they should "stick to it." The urologist said, "If you make a statement that later has to be disclaimed or discredited, you've weakened your credibility." A gender assignment made decisively, unambiguously, and irrevocably contributes, I believe, to the general impression that the infant's true, natural "sex" has been discovered, and that something that was there all along has been found. It also serves to maintain the credibility of the medical profession, reassure the parents, and reflexively substantiate Money and Ehrhardt's theory.

Also according to the theory, if operative correction is necessary, it should take place as soon as possible. If the infant is assigned the male gender, the initial stage of penis repair is usually undertaken in the first year, and further surgery is completed before the child enters school. If the infant is assigned the female gender, vulva repair (including clitoral reduction) is usually begun by three months of age. Money suggests that if reduction of phallic tissue were delayed beyond the neonatal period, the infant would have traumatic memories of having been castrated.[8] Vaginoplasty, in those females having an adequate internal structure (e.g., the vaginal canal is near its expected location), is done between the ages of one and four years. Girls who require more complicated surgical procedures might not be surgically corrected until preadolescence.[9] The complete vaginal canal is typically constructed only when the body is fully grown, following pubertal feminization with estrogen, although more recently some specialists have claimed surgical success with vaginal construction in the early childhood years.[10] Although physicians speculate about the possible trauma of an early childhood "castration" memory, there is no corresponding concern that vaginal reconstructive surgery delayed beyond the neonatal period is traumatic.

Even though gender identity theory places the critical age limit for gender reassignment between eighteen months and two years, the physicians acknowledge that diagnosis, gender assignment, and genital reconstruction cannot be delayed for as long as two years, since a clear gender assignment and correctly formed genitals will determine the kind of interactions parents will have with the child.[11] The geneticist argued that when parents "change a diaper and see genitalia that don't mean much in terms of gender assignment, I think it prolongs the negative response to the baby. . . . If you have clitoral enlargement that is so extraordinary that the parents can't distinguish between male and female, it is sometimes helpful to reduce that somewhat so that the parent views the child as female." Another physician concurred: parents "need to go home and do their job as child rearers with it very clear whether it's a boy or a girl."

DIAGNOSIS

A premature gender announcement by an obstetrician, prior to a close examination of an infant's genitals, can be problematic. Money and his colleagues claim that the primary complications in case management of intersexed infants can be traced to mishandling by medical personnel untrained in sexology.[12] According to one of the pediatric endocrinologists interviewed, obstetricians improperly educated about intersexed conditions "don't examine the babies closely enough at birth and say things just by looking, before separating legs and looking at everything, and jump to conclusions, because 99 percent of the time it's correct. . . . People get upset, physicians I mean. And they say things that are inappropriate." For example, he said that an inexperienced obstetrician might blurt out, "I think you have a boy, or no, maybe you have a girl." Other inappropriate remarks a doctor might make in postdelivery consultation with the parents include, "You have a little boy, but he'll never function as a little boy, so you better raise him as a little girl." As a result, said the pediatric endocrinologist, "the family comes away with the idea that they have a little boy, and that's what they wanted, and that's what they're going to get." In such cases parents sometimes insist that the child be raised male despite the physician's instructions to the contrary. "People have in mind certain things they've heard, that this is a boy, and they're not likely to forget that, or they're not likely to let it go easily." The urologist agreed that the first gender attribution is critical: "Once it's been announced, you've got a big problem on your hands." "One of the worst things is to allow [the parents] to go ahead and give a name and tell everyone, and it turns out the child has to be raised in the opposite sex."[13]

Physicians feel that the mismanagement of such cases requires careful remedying. The psychoendocrinologist asserted, "When I'm involved, I spend hours with the parents to explain to them what has happened and how a mistake like that could be made, *or not really a mistake but a different decision*" (my emphasis). One pediatric endocrinologist said, "[I] try to dissuade them from previous misconceptions, and say, 'Well, I know what they meant, but the way they said it confused you. This is, I think, a better way to think about it.'" These statements reveal physicians' efforts not only to protect parents from concluding that their child is neither male nor female but also to protect other physicians'decision-making processes. Case management involves perpetuating the notion that good medical decisions are based on interpretations of the infant's real "sex" rather than on cultural understandings of gender. . . .

The diagnosis of intersexed conditions includes assessing the chromosomal sex and the syndrome that produced the genital ambiguity, and may include medical procedures such as cytologic screening; chromosomal analysis; assessing serum electrolytes; hormone, gonadotropin, and steroids evaluation; digital examination; and radiographic genitography.[14] In any intersexed condition, if the infant is determined to be a genetic female (having an XX chromosome makeup), then the treatment—genital surgery to reduce the phallus size—can proceed relatively quickly, satisfying what the doctors believe are psychological and cultural demands. For example, 21-hydroxylase deficiency, a form of female pseudohermphroditism and one of the most common conditions, can be determined by a blood test within the first few days.

If, on the other hand, the infant is determined to have at least one Y chromosome, then surgery may be considerably delayed. A decision must be made whether to test the ability of the phallic tissue to respond to (HCG) androgen treatment, which is intended to enlarge the microphallus enough to be a penis. The endocrinologist explained, "You do HCG testing and you find out if the male can make testosterone. . . . You can get those results back probably within three weeks. . . . You're sure the male is making testosterone—but can he respond to it? It can take three months of waiting to see whether the phallus responds." If the Y-chromosome infant cannot make testosterone or cannot respond to the testosterone it makes, the phallus will not develop, and the Y-chromosome infant is not considered to be a male after all.

Should the infant's phallus respond to the local application of testosterone or a brief course of intramuscular injections of low-potency androgen, the gender assignment problem is resolved, but possibly at some later cost, since the penis will not grow again at puberty when the rest of the body develops.[15] Money's case management philosophy assumes that while it may be difficult for an adult male to have a much smaller than average penis, it is very detrimental to the morale of the young boy to have a micropenis.[16] In the former case the male's manliness might be at stake, but in the latter case his essential maleness might be. Although the psychological consequences of these experiences have not been empirically documented, Money and his colleagues suggest that it is wise to avoid the problems of both the micropenis in childhood and the still undersized penis postpuberty by reassigning many of these infants to the female gender.[17] This approach suggests that for Money and his colleagues, chromosomes are less relevant in determining gender than penis size, and that, by implication, "male" is defined not by the genetic condition of having one Y and one X chromosome or by the production of sperm but by the aesthetic condition of having an appropriately sized penis.

The tests and procedures required for diagnosis (and, consequently, for gender assignment) can take several months.[18] Although physicians are anxious not to make a premature gender assignment, their language suggests that it is difficult for them to take a completely neutral position and think and speak only of phallic tissue that belongs to an infant whose gender has not yet been determined or decided. Comments such as "seeing whether the male can respond to testosterone" imply at least a tentative male gender assignment of an XY infant. The psychoendocrinologist's explanation to parents of their infant's treatment program also illustrates this implicit male gender assignment. "Clearly this baby has an underdeveloped phallus. But if the phallus responds to this treatment, we are fairly confident that surgical techniques and hormonal techniques will help this child to look like a boy. But we want to make absolutely sure and use some hormone treatments and see whether the tissue reacts." The mere fact that this doctor refers to the genitals as an "underdeveloped" phallus rather than an overdeveloped clitoris suggests that the infant has been judged to be, at least provisionally, a male. In the case of the undersized phallus, what is ambiguous is not whether this is a penis but whether it is "good enough" to remain one. If at the end of the treatment period the phallic tissue has not responded, what had been a potential penis (referred to in the medical literature as a "clitoropenis") is now considered an enlarged clitoris (or "penoclitoris"), and reconstructive surgery is planned as for the genetic female.

The time-consuming nature of intersex diagnosis and the assumption, based on gender identity theory, that gender should be assigned as soon as possible thus present physicians with difficult dilemmas. Medical personnel are committed to discovering the etiology of the condition in order to determine the best course of treatment, which takes time. Yet they feel an urgent need to provide an immediate assignment and genitals that look and function appropriately. An immediate assignment that will need to be retracted is more problematic than a delayed assignment, since reassignment carries with it an additional set of social complications. The endocrinologist interviewed commented: "We've come very far in that we can diagnose eventually, many of the conditions. But we haven't come far enough. . . . We can't do it early enough. . . . Very frequently a decision is made before all this information is available, simply because it takes so long to make the correct diagnosis. And you cannot let a child go indefinitely, not in this society you can't. . . . There's pressure on parents [for a decision] and the parents transmit that pressure onto physicians." A pediatric endocrinologist agreed: "At times you may need to operate before a diagnosis can be made. . . . In one case parents were told to wait on the announcement while the infant was treated to see if the phallus would grow when treated with androgens. After the first month passed and there was some growth, the parents said they gave it a boy's name. They could only wait a month."

Deliberating out loud on the judiciousness of making parents wait for assignment decisions, the endocrinologist asked rhetorically, "Why do we do all these tests if in the end we're going to make the decision simply on the basis of the appearance of the genitalia?" This question suggests that the principles underlying physicians' decisions are cultural rather than biological, based on parental reaction and the medical team's perception of the infant's societal adjustment prospects given the way her/his genitals look or could be made to look. Moreover, as long as the decision rests largely on the criterion of genital appearance, and male is defined as having a "good-sized" penis, more infants will be assigned to the female gender than to the male.

THE WAITING PERIOD: DEALING WITH AMBIGUITY

During the period of ambiguity between birth and assignment, physicians not only must evaluate the infant's prospects to be a good male but also must manage parents' uncertainty about a genderless child. Physicians advise that parents postpone announcing the gender of the infant until a gender has been explicitly assigned. They believe that parents should not feel compelled to tell other people. The clinical geneticist interviewed said that physicians "basically encourage [parents] to treat [the infant] as neuter." One of the pediatric endocrinologists reported that in France parents confronted with this dilemma sometimes give the infant a neuter name, such as Claude or Jean. The psychoendocrinologist concurred: "If you have a truly borderline situation, and you want to make it dependent on the hormone treatment . . . then the parents are . . . told, 'Try not to make a decision. Refer to the baby as "baby." Don't think in terms of boy or girl.'" Yet, when asked whether this is a reasonable request to make of parents in our society, the physician answered: "I don't think so. I think parents can't do it." . . .

The geneticist explained that when directly asked by parents what to tell others about the gender of the infant, she says, "Why don't you just tell them that the baby is having problems and as soon as the problems are resolved we'll get back to you." A pediatric endocrinologist echoes this suggestion in advising parents to say, "Until the problem is solved [we] would really prefer not to discuss any of the details." According to the urologist, "If [the gender] isn't announced people may mutter about it and may grumble about it, but they haven't got anything to get their teeth into and make trouble over for the child, or the parents, or whatever." In short, parents are asked to sidestep the infant's gender rather than admit that the gender is unknown, thereby collaborating in a web of white lies, ellipses, and mystifications.

Even while physicians teach the parents how to deal with others who will not find the infant's condition comprehensible or acceptable, physicians must also make the condition comprehensible and acceptable to the parents, normalizing the intersexed condition for them. In doing so they help the parents consider the infant's condition in the most positive way. There are four key aspects to this "normalizing" process.

First, physicians teach parents normal fetal development and explain that all fetuses have the potential to be male or female. One of the endocrinologists explains, "In the absence of maleness you have femaleness. . . . It's really the basic design. The other [intersex] is really a variation on a theme." This explanation presents the intersex condition as a natural phase of every fetal development. Another endocrinologist "like[s] to show picture[s] to them and explain that at a certain point in development males and females look alike and then diverge for such and such reason." The professional literature suggests that doctors use diagrams that illustrate "nature's principle of using the same anlagen to produce the external genital parts of the male and female.[19]

Second, physicians stress the normalcy of the infant in other aspects. For example, the geneticist tells parents, "The baby is healthy, but there was a problem in the way the baby was developing." The endocrinologist says the infant has "a mild defect, just like anything could be considered a birth defect, a mole or a hemangioma." This language not only eases the blow to the parents but also redirects their attention. Terms like "hermaphrodite" or "abnormal" are not used. The urologist said that he advised parents "about the generalization of sticking to the good things and not confusing people with something that is unnecessary."

Third, physicians (at least initially) imply that it is not the gender of the child that is ambiguous but the genitals. They talk about "undeveloped," "maldeveloped," or "unfinished" organs. From a number of the physicians interviewed came the following explanations: "At a point in time the development proceeded in a different way, and sometimes the development isn't complete and we may have some trouble . . . in determining what the *actual* sex is. And so we have to do a blood test to help us" (my emphasis); "The baby may be a female, which you would know after the buccal smear, but you can't prove it yet. If so, then it's a normal female with a different appearance. This can be surgically corrected"; "The gender of your child isn't apparent to us at the moment"; "While this looks like a small penis, it's actually a large clitoris. And what we're going to do is put it back in its proper position and reduce the size of the tip of it enough so it doesn't look funny, so it looks right." Money and his colleagues report a case in which parents were advised to tell their friends that the reason their infant's gender was reannounced from male to female is that "the baby was . . . 'closed up down there' . . . when the closed skin was divided, the female organs were revealed, and the baby discovered to be, *in fact,* a girl" (emphasis mine). It was mistakenly assumed to be a male at first because "there was an excess of skin on the clitoris."[20]

The message in these examples is that the trouble lies in the doctor's ability to determine the gender, not in the baby's gender per se. The real gender will presumably be determined/proven by testing, and the "bad" genitals (which are confusing the situation for everyone) will be "repaired." The emphasis is not on the doctors creating gender but in their completing the genitals. Physicians say that they "reconstruct" the genitals rather than "construct" them. The surgeons reconstitute from remaining parts what should have been there all along. The fact that gender in an infant is "reannounced" rather than "reassigned" suggests that the first announcement was a mistake because the announcer was confused by the genitals. The gender always was what it is now seen to be.[21]

Finally, physicians tell parents that social factors are more important in gender development than biological ones, even though they are searching for biological causes. In essence, the physicians teach the parents Money and Ehrhardt's theory of gender development. In doing so, they shift the emphasis from the discovery of biological factors that are a sign of the "real" gender to providing the appropriate social conditions to produce the "real" gender. What remains unsaid is the apparent contradiction in the notion that a "real" or "natural" gender can be, or needs to be, produced artificially. The physician/parent discussions make it clear to family members that gender is not a biological given (even though, of course, their own procedures for diagnosis assume that it is), and that gender is fluid. The psychoendocrinologist paraphrased an explanation to parents thus: "It will depend, ultimately, on how everybody treats your child and how your child is looking as a person. . . . I can with confidence tell them that generally gender [identity] clearly agrees with the assignment." Similarly, a pediatric endocrinologist explained: "[I] try to impress upon them that there's an enormous amount of clinical data to support the fact that if you sex-reverse an infant . . . the majority of the time the alternative gender identity is commensurate with the socialization, the way that they're raised, and how people view them, and that seems to be the most critical."

The implication of these comments is that gender identity (of all children, not just those born with ambiguous genitals) is determined primarily by social factors, that the parents and community always construct the child's gender. In the case of intersexed infants, the physicians merely provide the right genitals to go along with the socialization. Of course, at normal births, when the infant's genitals are unambiguous, the parents are not told that the child's gender is ultimately up to socialization. In those cases, doctors do treat gender as a biological given.

SOCIAL FACTORS IN DECISION MAKING

Most of the physicians interviewed claimed that personal convictions of doctors ought to play no role in the decision-making process. The psychoendocrinologist explained: "I think the most critical factors [are] what is the possibility that this child will grow up with genitals which look like that of the assigned gender and which will ultimately function according to gender . . . That's why it's so important that it's a well-established team, because [personal convictions] can't really enter into it. It has to be what is surgically and endocrinologically possible for that baby to be able to make it . . . It's really much more within medical criteria. I don't think many social factors enter into it." While this doctor eschews the importance of social factors in gender assignment, she argues forcefully that social factors are extremely important in the development of gender identity. Indeed, she implies that social factors primarily enter the picture once the infant leaves the hospital.

In fact, doctors make decisions about gender on the basis of shared cultural values that are unstated, perhaps even unconscious, and therefore considered objective rather than subjective. Money states the fundamental rule for gender assignment: "Never assign a baby to be reared, and to surgical and hormonal therapy, as a boy, unless the phallic structure, hypospadiac or otherwise, is neonatally of at least the same caliber as that of same-aged males with small-average penises."[22] Elsewhere, he and his colleagues provide specific measurements for what qualifies as a micropenis: "A penis is, by convention, designated as a micropenis when at birth its dimensions are three or more standard deviations below the mean. . . . When it is correspondingly reduced in diameter with corpora that are vestigial . . . it unquestionably qualifies as a micropenis."[23] A pediatric endocrinologist claimed that although "the [size of the] phallus is not the deciding factor . . . if the phallus is less than 2 centimeters long at birth and won't respond to androgen treatments, then it's made into a female."

These guidelines are clear, but they focus on only one physical feature, one that is distinctly imbued with cultural meaning. This becomes especially apparent in the case of an XX infant with normal female reproductive gonads and a perfect penis. Would the size and shape of the penis, in this case, be the deciding factor in assigning the infant "male," or would the perfect penis be surgically destroyed and female genitals created? Money notes that this dilemma would be complicated by the anticipated reaction of the parents to seeing "their apparent son lose his penis."[24] Other researchers concur that parents are likely to want to raise a child with a normal-shaped penis (regardless of size) as "male," particularly if the scrotal area looks normal and if the parents have had no experience with intersexuality.[25] Elsewhere Money argues in favor of not neonatally amputating the penis of XX infants, since fetal masculinization of brain structures would predispose them "almost invariably [to] develop behaviorally as tomboys, even when reared as girls."[26] This reasoning implies, first, that tomboyish behavior in girls is bad and should be avoided; and, second, that it is preferable to remove the internal female organs, implant prosthetic testes, and regulate the "boy's" hormones for his entire life than to overlook or disregard the perfection of the penis.[27]

The ultimate proof to these physicians that they intervened appropriately and gave the intersexed infant the correct gender assignment is that the reconstructed genitals look normal and function normally once the patient reaches adulthood. The vulva, labia, and clitoris should appear ordinary to the woman and her partner(s), and the vagina should be able to receive a normal-sized penis. Similarly, the man and his partner(s) should feel that his penis (even if somewhat smaller than the norm) looks and functions in an unremarkable way. Although there is no reported data on how much emphasis the intersexed person, him- or herself, places upon genital appearance and functioning, the physicians are absolutely clear about what they believe is important. The clinical geneticist said, "If you have . . . a seventeen-year-old young lady who has gotten hormone therapy and has breast development and pubic hair and no vaginal opening, I can't even entertain the notion that this young lady wouldn't want to have corrective surgery." The urologist summarized his criteria: "Happiness is the biggest factor. Anatomy is part of happiness." Money states, "The primary deficit [of not having a sufficient penis]—and destroyer of morale—lies in being unable to satisfy the partner."[28] Another team of clinicians reveals their phallocentrism, arguing that the most serious mistake in gender assignment is to create "an individual unable to engage in genital [heterosexual] sex."[29]

The equation of gender with genitals could only have emerged in an age when medical science can create credible-appearing and functioning genitals, and an emphasis on the good phallus above all else could only have emerged in a culture that has rigid aesthetic and performance criteria for what constitutes maleness. The formulation "good penis equals male; absence of good penis equals female" is treated in the literature and by the physicians interviewed as an objective criterion, operative in all cases. There is a striking lack of attention to the size and shape requirements of the female genitals, other than that the vagina be able to receive a penis.[30]

In the late nineteenth century when women's reproductive function was culturally designated as their essential characteristic, the presence or absence of ovaries (whether or not they were fertile) was held to be the ultimate criterion of gender assignment for hermaphrodites. The urologist interviewed recalled a case as late as the 1950s of a male child reassigned to "female" at the age of four or five because ovaries had been discovered. Nevertheless, doctors today, schooled in the etiology and treatment of the various intersex syndromes, view decisions based primarily on gonads as wrong, although, they complain, the conviction that the gonads are the ultimate criterion "still dictates the decisions of the uneducated and uninformed."[31] Presumably, the educated and informed now know that decisions based primarily on phallic size, shape, and sexual capacity are right.

While the prospect of constructing good genitals is the primary consideration in physicians' gender assignments, another extramedical factor was repeatedly cited by the six physicians interviewed—the specialty of the attending physician. Although generally intersexed infants are treated by teams of specialists, only the person who coordinates the team is actually responsible for the case. This person, acknowledged by the other physicians as having chief responsibility, acts as spokesperson to the parents. Although all of the physicians claimed that these medical teams work smoothly with few discrepancies of opinion, several of them mentioned decision-making orientations that are grounded in particular medical specializations. One endocrinologist stated, "The easiest route to take, where there is ever any question . . . is to raise the child as female. . . . In this country that is usual if the infant falls into the hands of a pediatric endocrinologist. . . . If the decision is made by the urologists, who are mostly males, . . . they're always opting, because they do the surgery, they're always feeling they can correct anything." Another endocrinologist concurred: "[Most urologists] don't think in terms of dynamic processes. They're interested in fixing pipes and lengthening pipes, and not dealing with hormonal, and certainly not psychological issues. . . . 'What can I do with what I've got.'" Urologists were defended by the clinical geneticist: "Surgeons here, now I can't speak for elsewhere, they don't get into a situation where the child is a year old and they can't make anything." Whether or not urologists "like to make boys," as one endocrinologist claimed, the following example from a urologist who was interviewed explicitly links a cultural interpretation of masculinity to the medical treatment plan. The case involved an adolescent who had been assigned the female gender at birth but was developing some male pubertal signs and wanted to be a boy. "He was ill-equipped," said the urologist, "yet we made a very respectable male out of him. He now owns a huge construction business—those big cranes that put stuff up on the building."

POSTINFANCY CASE MANAGEMENT

After the infant's gender has been assigned, parents generally latch onto the assignment as the solution to the problem—and it is. The physician as detective has collected the evidence, as lawyer has presented the case, and as judge has rendered a verdict. Although most of the interviewees claimed that the parents are equal participants in the whole process, they gave no instances of parental participation prior to the gender assignment. After the physicians assign the infant's gender, the parents are encouraged to establish the credibility of that gender publicly by, for example, giving a detailed medical explanation to a leader in their community, such as a physician or pastor, who will explain the situation to curious casual acquaintances. Money argues that "medical terminology has a special layman's magic in such a context; it is final and authoritative and closes the issue." He also recommends that eventually the mother "settle [the] argument once and for all among her women friends by allowing some of them to see the baby's reconstructed genitalia."[32] Apparently, the powerful influence of normal-looking genitals helps overcome a history of ambiguous gender.

Some of the same issues that arise in assigning gender recur some years later when, at adolescence, the child may be referred to a physician for counseling.[33] The physician then tells the adolescent many of the same things his or her parents had been told years before, with the same language. Terms like "abnormal," "disorder," "disease," and "hermaphroditism" are avoided; the condition is normalized, and the child's gender is treated as unproblematic. One clinician explains to his patients that sex organs are different in appearance for each person, not just those who are intersexed. Furthermore, he tells the girls "that while most women menstruate, not all do . . . that conception is only one of a number of ways to become a parent; [and] that today some individuals are choosing not to become parents."[34] The clinical geneticist tells a typical female patient: "You are female. Female is not determined by your genes. Lots of other things determine being a woman. And you are a woman but you won't be able to have babies." . . .

Technically these physicians are lying when, for example, they explain to an adolescent XY female with an intersexed history that her "ovaries . . . had to be removed because they were unhealthy or were producing 'the wrong balance of hormones.'"[35] We can presume that these lies are told in the service of what the physicians consider a greater good—keeping individual/concrete genders as clear and uncontaminated as the notions of female and male are in the abstract. The clinician suggests that with some female patients it eventually may be possible to talk to them "about their gonads having some structures and features that are testicular-like."[36] This call for honesty might be based at least partly on the possibility of the child's discovering his or her chromosomal sex inadvertently from a buccal smear taken in a high school biology class. Today's litigious climate is possibly another encouragement.

In sum, the adolescent is typically told that certain internal organs did not form because of an endocrinological defect, not because those organs could never have developed in someone with her or his sex chromosomes. The topic of chromosomes is skirted. There are no published studies on how these adolescents experience their condition and their treatment by doctors. An endocrinologist interviewed mentioned that her adolescent patients rarely ask specifically what is wrong with them, suggesting that they are accomplices in this evasion. In spite of the "truth" having been evaded, the clinician's impression is that "their gender identities and general senses of well-being and self-esteem appear not to have suffered."[37]

CONCLUSION

Physicians conduct careful examinations of intersexed infants' genitals and perform intricate laboratory procedures. They are interpreters of the body, trained and committed to uncovering the "actual" gender obscured by ambiguous genitals. Yet they also have considerable leeway in assigning gender, and their decisions are influenced by cultural as well as medical factors. What is the relationship between the physician as discoverer and the physician as determiner of gender? Where is the relative emphasis placed in discussions with parents and adolescents and in the consciousness of physicians? It is misleading to characterize the doctors whose words are provided here as presenting themselves publicly to the parents as discoverers of the infant's real gender but privately acknowledging that the infant has no real gender other than the one being determined or constructed by the medical professionals. They are not hypocritical. It is also misleading to claim that physicians' focus shifts from discovery to determination over the course of treatment: first the doctors regard the infant's gender as an unknown but discoverable reality; then the doctors relinquish their attempts to find the real gender and treat the infant's gender as something they must construct. They are not medically incompetent or deficient. Instead, I am arguing that the peculiar balance of discovery and determination throughout treatment permits physicians to handle very problematic cases of gender in the most unproblematic of ways.

This balance relies fundamentally on a particular conception of the "natural."[38] Although the deformity of intersexed genitals would be immutable were it not for medical interference, physicians do not consider it natural. Instead they think of, and speak of, the surgical/hormonal alteration of such deformities as natural because such intervention returns the body to what it "ought to have been" if events had taken their typical course. The nonnormative is converted into the normative, and the normative state is considered natural.[39] The genital ambiguity is remedied to conform to a "natural," that is, culturally indisputable, gender dichotomy. Sherry Ortner's claim that the culture/nature distinction is itself a construction—a product of culture—is relevant here. Language and imagery help create and maintain a specific view of what is natural about the two genders and, I would argue, about the very idea of gender—that it consists of two exclusive types: female and male.[40] The belief that gender consists of two exclusive types is maintained and perpetuated by the medical community in the face of incontrovertible physical evidence that this is not mandated by biology. . . .

If physicians recognized that implicit in their management of gender is the notion that finally, and always, people construct gender as well as the social systems that are grounded in gender-based concepts, the possibilities for real societal transformations would be unlimited. Unfortunately, neither in their representations to the families of the intersexed nor among themselves do the physicians interviewed for this study draw such far-reaching implications from their work. Their "understanding" that particular genders are medically (re)constructed in these cases does not lead them to see that gender is always constructed. Accepting genital ambiguity as a natural option would require that physicians also acknowledge that genital ambiguity is "corrected" not because it is threatening to the infant's life but because it is threatening to the infant's culture.

Rather than admit to their role in perpetuating gender, physicians "psychologize" the issue by talking about the parents' anxiety and humiliation in being confronted with an anomalous infant. The physicians talk as though they have no choice but to respond to the parents' pressure for a resolution of psychological discomfort, and as though they have no choice but to use medical technology in the service of a two-gender culture. Neither the psychology nor the technology is doubted, since both shield physicians from responsibility. Indeed, for the most part, neither physicians nor parents emerge from the experience of intersex case management with a greater understanding of the social construction of gender. Society's accountability, like their own, is masked by the assumption that gender is a given. Thus, cases of intersexuality, instead of illustrating nature's failure to ordain gender in these isolated "unfortunate" instances, illustrate physicians' and Western society's failure of imagination—the failure to imagine that each of these management decisions is a moment when a specific instance of biological "sex" is transformed into a culturally constructed gender.

Notes

1. Suzanne J. Kessler and Wendy McKenna, *Gender: An Ethnomethodological Approach* (1978; reprint, Chicago: University of Chicago Press, 1985).
2. See, e.g., M. Bolkenius, R. Daum, and E. Heinrich, "Pediatric Surgical Principles in the Management of Children with Intersex," *Progressive Pediatric Surgery* 17 (1984): 33–38; Kenneth I. Glassberg, "Gender Assignment in Newborn Male Pseudohermaphrodites," *Urologic Clinics of North America* 7 (June 1980): 409–21; and Peter A. Lee et al., "Micropenis. I. Criteria, Etiologies and Classification," *Johns Hopkins Medical Journal* 146 (1980): 156–63.
3. It is impossible to get accurate statistics on the frequency of intersexuality. Chromosomal abnormalities (like XOXX or XXXY) are registered, but those conditions do not always imply ambiguous genitals, and most cases of ambiguous genitals do not involve chromosomal abnormalities. None of the physicians interviewed for this study would venture a guess on frequency rates, but all agreed that intersexuality is rare. One physician suggested that the average obstetrician may see only two cases in twenty years. Another estimated that a specialist may see only one a year, or possibly as many as five a year.
4. Mariano Castro-Magana, Moris Angulo, and Platon J. Collipp, "Management of the Child with Ambiguous Genitalia," *Medical Aspects of Human Sexuality* 18 (April 1984): 172–88.
5. John Money, J. G. Hampson, and J. L. Hampson, "Hermaphroditism: Recommendations concerning Assignment of Sex, Change of Sex, and Psychologic Management," *Bulletin of the Johns Hopkins Hospital* 97 (1955): 284–300; John Money, Reynolds Potter, and Clarice S. Stoll, "Sex Reannouncement in Hereditary Sex Deformity: Psychology and Sociology of Habilitation," *Social Science and Medicine* 3 (1969): 207–16; John Money and Anke A. Ehrhardt, *Man and Woman, Boy and Girl* (Baltimore: Johns Hopkins University Press, 1972); John Money, "Psychologic Consideration of Sex Assignment in Intersexuality," *Clinics in Plastic Surgery* 1 (April 1974): 215–22, "Psychological Counseling: Hermaphroditism," in *Endocrine and Genetic Diseases of Childhood and Adolescence*, ed. L. I. Gardner (Philadelphia:

Saunders, 1975): 609–18, and "Birth Defect of the Sex Organs: Telling the Parents and the Patient," *British Journal of Sexual Medicine* 10 (March 1983): 14; John Money et al., "Micropenis, Family Mental Health, and Neonatal Management: A Report on Fourteen Patients Reared as Girls," *Journal of Preventive Psychiatry* 1, no. 1 (1981): 17–27.

6. Money and Ehrhardt, 152.
7. Contradictory data are presented in Milton Diamond, "Sexual Identity, Monozygotic Twins Reared in Discordant Sex Roles and a BBC Follow-up," *Archives of Sexual Behavior* 11, no. 2 (1982): 181–86.
8. Money, "Psychologic Consideration of Sex Assignment in Intersexuality."
9. Castro-Magana, Angulo, and Collipp (n. 4 above).
10. Victor Braren et al., "True Hermaphroditism: A Rational Approach to Diagnosis and Treatment," *Urology* 15 (June 1980): 569–74.
11. Studies of normal newborns have shown that from the moment of birth the parent responds to the infant based on the infant's gender. Jeffrey Rubin, F. J. Provenzano, and Z. Luria, "The Eye of the Beholder: Parents' Views on Sex of Newborns," *American Journal of Orthopsychiatry* 44, no. 4 (1974): 512–19.
12. Money et al. (n. 5 above).
13. There is evidence from other kinds of sources that once a gender attribution is made, all further information buttresses that attribution, and only the most contradictory new information will cause the original gender attribution to be questioned. See, e.g., Kessler and McKenna (n. 1 above).
14. Castro-Magana, Angulo, and Collipp (n. 4 above).
15. Money, "Psychological Consideration of Sex Assignment in Intersexuality" (n. 5 above).
16. Technically, the term "micropenis" should be reserved for an exceptionally small but well-formed structure. A small, malformed "penis" should be referred to as a "microphallus" (Lee et al. [n. 2 above]).
17. Money et al., 26. A different view is argued by another leading gender identity theorist: "When a little boy (with an imperfect penis) knows he is a male, he creates a penis that functions symbolically the same as those of boys with normal penises" (Robert J. Stoller, *Sex and Gender* [New York: Aronson, 1968], 1:49).
18. W. Ch. Hecker, "Operative Correction of Intersexual Genitals in Children," *Pediatric Surgery* 17 (1984): 21–31.
19. Tom Mazur, "Ambiguous Genitalia: Detection and Counseling," *Pediatric Nursing* 9 (November/December 1983): 417–31; Money, "Psychologic Consideration of Sex Assignment in Intersexuality" (n. 5 above), 218.
20. Money, Potter, and Stoll (n. 5 above), 211.
21. The term "reassignment" is more commonly used to describe the gender changes of those who are cognizant of their earlier gender, e.g., transsexuals—people whose gender itself was a mistake.
22. Money, "Psychological Counseling: Hermaphroditism" (n. 5 above), 610.
23. Money et al. (n. 5 above), 18.
24. John Money, "Hermaphroditism and Pseudohermaphroditism," in *Gynecologic Endocrinology*, ed. Jay J. Gold (New York: Hoeber, 1968), 449–64, esp. 460.
25. Mojtaba Besheshti et al., "Gender Assignment in Male Pseudohermaphrodite Children," *Urology* (December 1983): 604–7. Of course, if the penis looked normal and the empty scrotum were overlooked, it might not be discovered until puberty that the male child was XX, with a female internal structure.
26. John Money, "Psychologic Consideration of Sex Assignment in Intersexuality" (n. 5 above), 216.
27. Weighing the probability of achieving a perfect penis against the probable trauma such procedures might involve is another social factor in decision making. According to an endocrinologist interviewed, if it seemed that an XY infant with an inadequate penis would require as many as ten genital operations over a six-year period in order to have an adequate penis, the infant would be assigned the female gender. In this case, the endocrinologist's practical and compassionate concern would override purely genital criteria.

28. Money, "Psychologic Consideration of Sex Assignment in Intersexuality," 217.
29. Castro-Magana, Angulo, and Collipp (n. 4 above), 180.
30. It is unclear how much of this bias is the result of a general, cultural devaluation of the female and how much the result of physicians' greater facility in constructing aesthetically correct and sexually functional female genitals.
31. Money, "Psychologic Consideration of Sex Assignment in Intersexuality," 215. Remnants of this anachronistic view can still be found, however, when doctors justify the removal of contradictory gonads on the grounds that they are typically sterile or at risk for malignancy (J. Dewhurst and D. B. Grant, "Intersex Problems," *Archives of Disease in Childhood* 59 [July–December 1984]: 1191–94). Presumably, if the gonads were functional and healthy their removal would provide an ethical dilemma for at least some medical professionals.
32. Money, "Psychological Counseling: Hermaphroditism" (n. 5 above), 613.
33. As with the literature on infancy, most of the published material on adolescents is on surgical and hormonal management rather than on social management. See, e.g., Joel J. Roslyn, Eric W. Fonkalsrud, and Barbara Lippe, "Intersex Disorders in Adolescents and Adults," *American Journal of Surgery* 146 (July 1983): 138–44.
34. Mazur (n. 19 above), 421.
35. Dewhurst and Grant, 1193.
36. Mazur, 422.
37. Ibid.
38. For an extended discussion of different ways of conceptualizing "natural," see Richard W. Smith, "What Kind of Sex Is Natural?" in *The Frontiers of Sex Research,* ed. Vern Bullough (Buffalo: Prometheus, 1979), 103–11.
39. This supports sociologist Harold Garfinkel's argument that we treat routine events as our due as social members and that we treat gender, like all normal forms, as a moral imperative. It is no wonder, then, that physicians conceptualize what they are doing as natural and unquestionably "right" (Harold Garfinkel, *Studies in Ethnomethodology* [Englewood Cliffs, N.J.: Prentice Hall, 1967]).
40. Sherry B. Ortner, "Is Female to Male as Nature Is to Culture?" in *Woman, Culture, and Society,* ed. Michelle Zimbalist Rosaldo and Louise Lamphere (Stanford, Calif.: Stanford University Press, 1974), 67–87.

SOCIOBIOLOGY, BIOLOGICAL DETERMINISM, AND HUMAN BEHAVIOR

Ruth Bleier

Because Wilsonian sociobiology is a particularly dramatic contemporary version of biological determinist theories of human behavior, because it is powerful and persuasive, because it is a particularly good example of bad science, because it provides "scientific" support for a dominant political ideology that directly opposes every goal and issue raised by the women's movement, and because it has been aggressively marketed and perceptibly incorporated into our culture, it seems a fitting area with which to begin the examination of science and scientific theories of biological determinism.

While the general field of sociobiology has a long and solid tradition of studying the social behavior of animals, in 1975 E. O. Wilson, whose area of expertise is insect behaviors, sought to establish sociobiology "as the systematic study of the biological basis of all social behavior." He stated his conviction that "It may not be too much to say that sociology and the other social sciences, as well as the humanities, are the last branches of biology waiting to be included in the Modern Synthesis" (Wilson, 1975b, p. 4). Thus, Wilson and those in his school of human sociobiology believe that all human behaviors, social relationships, and organization are genetically evolved adaptations, as I will describe below. Before proceeding, however, to a critique of the work of Wilsonian sociobiologists, it is important to distinguish it from the general field of sociobiology. There are many other scientists who study the social behaviors and characteristics of animals and are therefore sociobiologists but do not make reckless extrapolations to human social relationships and behaviors. Their observations and interpretations form an important part of the evidence I use to support my arguments concerning the inadequacies and distortions inherent in the "science" that Wilson and his followers popularize.

By reducing human behavior and complex social phenomena to genes and to inherited and programmed mechanisms of neuronal functioning, the message of the new Wilsonian Sociobiology becomes rapidly clear: we had best resign ourselves to the fact that the more unsavory aspects of human behavior, like wars, racism, and class struggle, are inevitable results of evolutionary adaptations based in our genes. And of key importance is the fact that the particular roles performed by women and men in society are also biologically, genetically determined; in fact, civilization as we know it, or perhaps any at all, could not have evolved in any other way. Thus the Sociobiologist and popular writer David Barash says, "There is good reason to believe that we are (genetically) primed to be much less sexually egalitarian than we appear to be" (Barash, 1979, p. 47)

But it is not only that the direct political and social statements and theories of Sociobiologists are dangerous to the interests and well being of women and minorities. If Sociobiology were a valid science, by even traditional standards, we should have to find ways to cope with the consequences of incontrovertible "truths." But this Sociobiology is deeply flawed conceptually, methodologically, and logically *as a science*. It is only *because* it concerns itself with the most complex aspects of human behaviors and social relationships, about which we suffer enormous depths of both ignorance and emotion, that Sociobiology achieves acceptance as a science. The same kinds of logical and methodological flaws in the sciences, say, of ant or camel behavior would be immediately obvious and unacceptable.

In this chapter I first review some basic postulates and assumptions of Sociobiological theory and outline the methodologies used for theory building. I then offer a detailed critique of Sociobiologists' theories and methods and indicate some alternative observations and interpretations that contradict their assumptions and conclusions. Finally, since the fundamental scientific issue is the validity of a theory based on the genetic determination of human behavior, I explore the relationship between genes and the fetal environment and between biology and learning.

SOME PREMISES AND APPROACHES OF SOCIOBIOLOGY

Natural Selection of Behaviors Through Gene Transmission

The basic premise of Sociobiology is that human behaviors and certain aspects of social organization have evolved, like our bodies, through adaptations based on Darwinian natural selection. It is important to understand Darwin's theory of evolution of the *physical forms* of animals by adaptation in order to understand its application by Sociobiologists to *behavior.* In its modern version, the theory assumes that by some genetic recombination or mutation, a particular anatomical characteristic appears anew in a species, let us say gray body color in a family of orange moths. If the gray color in the moths' particular ecological setting permits more gray than orange moths to survive predation and other causes of an early demise and therefore to reach sexual maturity so that more gray moths are reproduced than their relatives of the original orange color, then an increasing proportion of moths will be gray in successive generations. Over time, the genes for gray will be present in increasing numbers of moths and become a predominant feature of moths in *that* ecological setting. The new genetic feature for gray is then considered, in the language of Darwinian evolution, to be adaptive through natural selection, since it contributes to the maximum fitness of the moths, with *maximum fitness* being defined as the ability to leave many healthy descendants that are themselves able to reproduce and thus spread the genes for gray body color.

Sociobiologists suggest and assume that *behaviors* also evolve in similar ways so that "adaptive" and "successful" behaviors become based in our genes, and that certain genetic configurations became selected because they result in behaviors that are adaptive for survival. Our "innate" predispositions to display these behaviors constitute our human *nature.* It is important to note at this point that to be valid the theory requires that human behaviors be represented by a particular genetic configuration, because evolution through natural selection requires genetic variations (that is, mutant forms) from which to select. But Sociobiologists themselves, as well as geneticists, agree that it is not possible to link any specific human behavior with any specific gene or genetic configuration. The only evidence for such a link is that which is provided by Sociobiologists' circular logic. This logic makes a *premise* of the genetic basis of behaviors, then cites a certain animal or human behavior, constructs a speculative story to explain how the behavior (*if* it were genetically based) could have served or could serve to maximize the reproductive success of the individual, and this *conjecture* then becomes evidence for the *premise* that the behavior was genetically determined.

> This is the central principle of sociobiology: insofar as a behavior reflects at least some component of gene action, individuals will tend to behave so as to maximize their fitness. . . . The result is a very strange sort of purposefulness, in which a goal—maximization of fitness—appears to be sought, but without any of the participants necessarily having awareness of what they are doing, or why. (Barash, 1979, pp. 29 and 25)

Notice the *insofar* clause is key and serves to confuse the issue. All behavior of course reflects at least *some* component of gene action. Individuals of any species of animal behave within the limits of the broad range of biological capabilities defined by their genes. Humans walk rather than fly. Birds peck at their food. When we are frightened, our hearts beat faster. But what is really at issue in Sociobiological theory is not the physical capacity for behavior that biology provides but rather the genetic encoding of the entire range of complex human behaviors and characteristics that are expressed in a nearly infinite variety of ways by different individuals and cultures and often not expressed at all, such as altruism, loyalty, dominance, competitiveness, aggressivity. In addition, Sociobiology claims genetic encoding for such arbitrarily chosen and questionably sexually differentiated "traits" as coyness, fickleness, promiscuity, rapaciousness, or maternalism.

Sociobiologists make a passing attempt to acknowledge that learning, culture, or environment plays a role in human behavior, but it is clear that their hearts (and minds) are not engaged by this idea. David Barash clearly states his position on the contribution of learning to behavior:

> Core elements are the essential person, an entity bequeathed by evolution to each of us; they are the *us* upon which experience acts. The great strength of sociobiology is that its conception of the "core" is grounded in evolution. . . . (1979, p. 10)

> Biology and culture undoubtedly work together, but it is tempting to speculate that our biology is somehow more real, lying unnoticed within each of us, quietly but forcefully manipulating much of our behavior. Culture, which is overwhelmingly important in shaping the myriad details of our lives, is more likely seen as a thin veneer, compared to the underlying ground substance of our biology. (1979, p. 14)

Richard Dawkins, the Sociobiologist who coined the catchy anthropomorphic phrase, *selfish genes,* explains that genes and their expression are unaffected by environment:

> Now they swarm in huge colonies, safe inside gigantic lumbering robots, sealed off from the outside world, communicating with it by tortuous indirect routes, manipulating it by remote control. They are in you and in me; they created us, body and mind; and their preservation is the ultimate rationale for our existence. They have come a long way, those replicators. Now they go by the name of genes, and we are their survival machines. (1976, p. 21)

Mary Midgley, the British philosopher, suggests that "Dawkin's crude, cheap, blurred genetics is not just an expository device. It is the kingpin of his crude, cheap, blurred psychology" (1980a, p. 120). She further notes how the message of such "science" was transmitted to the general public by the cover of *Time* magazine's sociobiology number, which showed two puppets making love "while invisible genes twitch the strings above them . . ." (1980b, p. 26).

Sex Differences in Reproductive Strategies

Since a key concept for Sociobiological theory is that behaviors are programmed to maximize the ability of the body's genes to reproduce themselves, an important area for Sociobiological speculation is that of reproduction itself. The second key postulate, then, is that the two sexes have a different strategy for maximizing their fitness through the reproduction of the largest possible number of offspring, and it is to this difference that Sociobiologists are able to attribute what they consider to be differences in female and male *natures,* behaviors, and social roles. Sociobiologists believe that women and men have different strategies and behaviors for assuring the reproduction and survival of their genes because they have an "unequal" biological investment in each offspring. Their reasoning is that since human males produce millions of sperm a day and can theoretically "sire offspring with different women at hourly or at most daily intervals" (Van Den Berghe and Barash, 1977, p. 814), their investment in the future in terms of the maximum reproduction of their genes in offspring lies in inseminating as many women as possible. Also, their relative investment in any one offspring is small. The human female, however, has a much greater investment in each of her offspring because her egg is 85,000 times larger than a sperm (hence more "expensive" to produce), because she ordinarily produces but one egg at a time and only about 400 in her lifetime, and because she usually produces no more than one offspring a year. Furthermore, since she is the one who gestates the fetus in her body, her expenditure of energy for those months and for the subsequent year or two of lactation and infant care is considerably greater than the father's. Therefore, while the *genetic* contribution from each parent is equivalent (23 chromosomes), the mother contributes a larger proportion of her total reproductive potential and a larger investment of time and energy. These facts, according to Sociobiologists, result in different reproductive strategies in the two sexes: women are selective and choosy—they go for quality: men go for quantity. Thus, E. O. Wilson writes:

> It pays males to be aggressive, hasty, fickle, and undiscriminating. In theory it is more profitable for females to be coy, to hold back until they can identify males with the best genes. . . . Human beings obey this biological principle faithfully. (1978, p. 125)

And Barash explains further:

> The evolutionary mechanism should be clear. Genes that allow females to accept the sorts of mates who make lesser contributions to their reproductive success will leave fewer copies of themselves than will genes that influence the females to be more selective. . . . For males, a very different strategy applies. The maximum advantage goes to individuals with fewer inhibitions. A genetically influenced tendency to "play fast and loose"—"love 'em and leave 'em"—may well reflect more biological reality than most of us care to admit. (1979, p. 48)

The Leap to Sex Differences in Human Social Roles and Characteristics

Thus, we can see that Sociobiologists leap from some obvious facts such as the relative sizes and available numbers of eggs and sperm to sweeping and unwarranted generalizations about and explanations for presumed female and male *innate* characteristics: women are coy, choosy, and fussy; males are fickle and promiscuous. These characteristics then are used to ascribe a biological basis to such social phenomena and arrangements as marital fidelity for women and adultery, polygyny (harems), and rape by men. Sociobiologists explain that a woman stands to lose much less by her husband's sexual infidelity and by his fathering of children outside the marriage than a husband stands to lose by his wife's infidelity, since he would, in the latter case, be helping to rear children who do not bear his genes. It is for this reason, they claim, that there is a sexual double standard: a differential valuation of virginity and a differential condemnation of marital infidelity (Van Den Berghe and Barash, 1977).

Sociobiologists derive two other important postulates from the observation that the eggs and sperms that women and men contribute to the process of conception are different. The first is predictable: since a woman has a greater investment in terms of egg size and the time and energy spent in gestation, she also invests the major portion of total parental care in her offspring. She does this in order to protect her biological investment and her genes, since each of her offspring represents a greater proportion of her total reproductive capacity than it does for the father. An added factor is that women know with certainty that their genes have been passed on in their children; men have to take it on faith.

> Throughout their evolutionary history, males have generally been ill advised to devote themselves too strongly to the care of children, since the undertaking might turn out to be a wasted effort. (Barash, 1979, pp. 108–9)

There is a second important Sociobiological postulate derived from the fact that the total number of eggs available for fertilization is far fewer than the number of sperm available to fertilize them: competition among males for females is inevitable, since females, with their limited reproductive potential, are a scarce resource. Because of this competition on the time scale of evolution, the most reproductively successful males came to be those who were larger and more aggressive. It is this inherited male aggressivity that provides the biological basis for male dominance over females, male dominance hierarchies, competitiveness, territoriality, and war.

This, then, is how Sociobiology sees itself as replacing psychology and sociology. It is a social theory in the guise of biology; Sociobiologists provide the biological basis for all social phenomena and, in particular, for the social roles and the cultural representations of women and men. Thus Dawkins blandly declares:

> The female sex is exploited, and the fundamental evolutionary basis for the exploitation is the fact that eggs are larger than sperms. (1976, p. 158)

And Wilson explains:

> In hunter-gatherer societies, men hunt and women stay home. This strong bias persists in most agricultural and industrial societies and, on that ground alone, appears to have a genetic origin. (1975a, p. 47)

This quotation is particularly perplexing in view of Wilson's obvious and known familiarity with the renowned work of his Harvard colleagues, Richard Lee and Irven DeVore and their coworkers, on hunter-gatherer societies extensively documenting the exact opposite of this claim; that, in fact, women gatherers are away from "home" as much as the men. His knowledge of what women do in agricultural and industrial societies appears similarly based in mythic imagery rather than in modern anthropological scholarship let alone in the real world of agricultural and industrial economies where 50 to 100 percent of women may work outside the home. The most generous interpretation may be that extrapolations to human societies from insects is a hazardous (though not unrewarding) intellectual undertaking even for eminent entomologists. And, finally, to complete the unanimity of the Sociobiological voice, Barash speaks:

> . . . women have almost universally found themselves relegated to the nursery while men derive their greatest satisfaction from their jobs . . . such differences in male-female attachment to family versus vocation could derive in part from hormonal differences between sexes. . . . (1977, p. 301)

I should like to call attention to the last quotation as an example of Sociobiologists' tendency to play loose with both language and logic. Barash speaks of women being *relegated* (assigned, banished) to the nursery, while men *derive satisfaction* from their jobs, hardly equivalent states, conditions, or situations; he then proceeds to base them *both* in biology as though they *were* equivalent. It is like claiming that repeatedly jailed offenders have an innate attachment to their cells.

SOCIOBIOLOGICAL METHODOLOGY IN THEORY BUILDING

Having stated the basic postulates of their theory, Sociobiologists then go on to catalogue the behaviors they consider to be universal and characteristic of humans and thus to be either explainable by or supportive of their theory. These behaviors and characteristics are never defined so that we all can know that we are talking about the same thing, nor are they selected according to any agreed upon criteria from psychology, anthropology, or sociology. The behaviors and characteristics they choose to discuss and explain as universals of human societies are what upper/middle class white male North American and English scientists consider to be characteristic: male aggressivity, territoriality, and tribalism; indoctrinability and conformity; male competitiveness and entrepreneurship; altruism and selfishness. The existence of these supposedly genetically determined human characteristics ("traits") then obviously and logically explains such social phenomena as national chauvinism, xenophobia and war; slavery and capitalism; ethnocentrism and racism; dominance hierarchies and sexism.

In order to establish that these presumed universal human characteristics and social phenomena have evolved genetically, the next step in Sociobiological theory building is to demonstrate their existence throughout the animal world. The methodology consists essentially of flipping through the encyclopedic catalogue of animal behaviors and selecting particular behaviors of fishes, birds, insects or mammals that can be readily made to exemplify the various categories of human "traits" and social arrangements that Sociobiologists claim to be universal and genetically based. It is this step that introduces a number of methodological flaws into a theory already suffering from the conceptual ailments I have described.

But before discussing these flaws, I should like to place this critical next step within the context of the basic postulates and methodology of Sociobiology that I have described thus far. First, a picture is presented of human social organization and relationships. These are said to have universal elements that are based upon the existence of universal human behavioral traits that have evolved through natural selection because they were optimally adaptive; that is, the best alternative for survival from among several genetic variations. This assumes a specific genetic coding for specific behavioral "traits" and characteristics. It is not possible to adduce scientific proof for the presence or absence of specific behavioral traits in evolving hominids since traits leave no fossil record. Therefore, there is no way to identify the possible genetic variations from which current behavioral solutions have been selected. This forces Sociobiologists to demonstrate biological and evolutionary continuity by establishing similarities with other living nonhuman species that are viewed as representing an evolutionary continuum culminating in the human species. This is done by then describing carefully selected behaviors of particular species that represent and demonstrate some presumed human universal, such as female "coyness." But since we also do not know what the environmental, ecological, or reproductive problems were that such behaviors or characteristics were solving over the past several hundred million years, Sociobiologists attempt to reconstruct evolutionary history by inventing plausible stories that attempt to show how a particular behavior or social interaction in humans or other species *could* have or *would* have been adaptive and therefore favored by natural selection and genetically carried through subsequent generations. Basically, the aim is to establish the biological "innateness" and inevitability of present-day human behaviors and forms of social organization.

FLAWS IN SOCIOBIOLOGICAL THEORY AND METHODOLOGY

In the methodology and arguments used by Sociobiologists and other biological determinists, one can detect a number of recurring and interrelated flaws. The problems begin with the categories and definitions of behaviors that they consider characteristic of all people. When they proceed to draw analogies to animal behaviors, the problems are compounded by their selective use of particular animal models and by the language and concepts they apply to their descriptions of animal behaviors. We will find that these problems are intimately interrelated, but I shall try to analyze each, giving examples from important Sociobiological concepts, and then discuss two other kinds of methodological problems: the scientific tests one uses to validate hypotheses, and the classical and recurring issue of gene-environment, biology-culture interactions.

Ethnocentricity of Behavioral Description

The first problem lies in the Sociobiological descriptions of presumably universal human behaviors and social relationships, which are curiously similar to social organizations in the white Western industrial capitalist world. In this sense, Sociobiology is in fact an anachronism. It incorporates into its methodology the naive ethnocentric, androcentric, and anthropocentric fallacies discarded at least a decade or two ago by most competent and aware anthropologists and primatologists. Throughout Sociobiological writings there is a pervasive sense of the investigator's perception of his own self as a universal reference point, as equivalent to humanity, viewing all others—the other sex, other classes, races, cultures and civilizations, species, and epochs—in the light and language of his own experiences, values, and beliefs. He and his fraternity become the norm against which all *others* are measured and interpreted. (I use the male pronoun since Sociobiologists with few exceptions are male.) Thus, Sociobiologists make unwarranted generalizations about characteristic human behaviors, such as that "men would rather believe than know" (Wilson, 1975b, p. 561) or that women are coy and marry for upward social mobility. This means that much of the argument of Sociobiologists is devised to explain what *they* define as universal behavioral traits, the existence of which is, however, highly problematic to many students of human behavior. As the anthropologist Nancy Howell has said, ". . . they seem to be innocently ignorant of much of the complexity of human social life and cultures that sociobiology sets out to explain" (1979, p. 1295), though one wonders, when they see rape in the reproductive mechanism of flowers and war as a collective expression of individual male's innate aggressivity, just how "innocently ignorant" they can be. At the same time they seem also to be unconscious of any of the methodological problems that pervade attempts to describe human behavior, problems with which social scientists continue to struggle. As Richard Lewontin has pointed out, "anthropologists have long been acutely conscious of the difficulties of describing human behavior in such a way as not to dictate the analysis by the categories of description" (1976, p. 24). Sociobiologists simply declare what they consider to be categories of behavioral description, for example, entrepreneurship, territoriality, aggression, dominance, without relationship to any cultural or historical context, and then proceed to arbitrarily assign examples of human and animal behavior to that category to demonstrate its universality in the animal world.

The concept of dominance hierarchies is an example of both ethnocentrism of descriptions of human "traits" and the trap of dictating analysis by the use of arbitrary categorization of behavior. Barash asserts that we are "a species organized along distinct lines of dominance" (1979, p. 186). But as Ruth Hubbard points out:

> We in the industrialized countries have grown up in hierarchically structured societies, so that, to us, dominance hierarchies appear natural and inevitable. But it is a mistake to apply the same categories to societies that function quite differently and to pretend that differences between our society and theirs can be expressed merely as matters of degree. . . . To take widely and complexly different social manifestations and scale them along one dimension does violence to the sources and significances of human social behavior. Western technological societies have developed in their ways for their own historical reasons. Other societies have *their* histories that have led to *their* social forms. (1978, p. 134)

. . . Many anthropological studies suggest that dominance hierarchies have not uniformly characterized the organization of human societies either in the past or today. In order to prove both the universality and the evolutionary inevitability of male dominance and dominance hierarchies, Sociobiologists and other biological determinists cite the example of the prototypical primate troop with its chest-pounding leader that has become familiar to us all. I shall discuss the fallacies of this approach in a section to follow on anthropomorphism.

Another example of the ethnocentric and androcentric application of concepts of human behavior to animals can be found in Sociobiological explanations of polygyny (marriage of one man to many wives) and hypergamy (marriage for upward mobility). I have already alluded to the Sociobiological postulate that men, being producers of millions of sperm a day, maximize their fitness by impregnating as many women as possible and, therefore, have traditionally established systems of polygyny, and that women have evolved to be more selective. Van Den Berghe and Barash (1977) describe the fact that in some bird species the females "prefer" polygynous males (here used to mean males that mate with many females) over bachelors. Wondering why, biologists have concluded that it is because the polygynous males command better territory than bachelors, more land providing more food and more protection for the young. This leads Van Den Berghe and Barash (1977) then to another Sociobiological universal of female behavior, hypergamy, marrying males of higher socioeconomic status for upward social mobility:

> Extrapolating to humans, we suggest that men are selected for engaging in male-male competition over resources appropriate to reproductive success, and that women are selected for preferring men who are successful in that endeavor. Any genetically influenced tendencies in these directions will necessarily be favored by natural selection.
>
> It is true, of course, that social advantages of wealth, power, or rank need not, indeed often do not, coincide with physical superiority. Women in all societies have found a way of resolving this dilemma by marrying wealthy and powerful men while taking young and attractive ones as lovers: the object of the game is to have the husband assume parental obligations for the lover's children. Understandably, men in most societies do not take kindly to such female strategies on the part of their wives, though they are not averse to philandering with other men's wives. The solution to this moral dilemma is the double standard, independently invented in countless societies. In any case, ethnographic evidence points to different reproductive strategies on the part of men and women, and to a remarkable consistency in the institutionalized means of accommodating these biological predispositions. (pp. 814, 815)

In this way the authors postulate a genetic tendency and a "biological predisposition" for women to marry men of wealth, power, and rank. Yet it is perfectly obvious that this "predisposition" can govern the behavior of only a small percentage of the world's women, since only a tiny minority of men in all countries of the world have any wealth, power, or rank. Thus, the vast majority of women everywhere, who are in lower socioeconomic classes and marry within their class, are excluded from biological universality. Their "universal" hypergamy is what happens only in romantic fiction. Sociobiologists attempt to establish human *species universals* of behavior by using an extraordinarily ethnocentric and class-biased model based on the behavior of a relatively small group of people in their own countries and others where the sexual and marital exploits of the rich and powerful are familiar topics in the international press. Furthermore, they also imply that there exists a related biological predisposition that expresses itself in the sexual double standard "independently invented in countless societies" because of men's unwillingness to assume obligation for the offspring (genes) of their wives' lovers. There is no suggestion that the double standard could have social origins independent of genes, that it may be but one more reflection of the economic and political domination of men over women in "countless" patriarchal societies.

Since even biological determinists recognize that many so-called human characteristics or behaviors are *not* universal, they postulate "predispositions," that is, traits that are genetically determined but not always expressed. It is very difficult, however, to take seriously the existence of a "predisposition" if it is not manifested in the majority of human beings. Just as Sociobiologists claim territoriality to be an evolutionary predisposition even though it is not manifested in a large number, perhaps the majority, of species, one could use their reasoning to argue that the *sharing* of territory is based on a biological predisposition, since the majority of species do just that.

It is a remarkable feature of Sociobiologists' descriptions of human "traits" that there appears to be no recognition of the possibility that there may be something arbitrary, selective, or subjective in their characterizations of females and males; that if some other group, for example, women or black males or American Indian males, were to list what they consider to be characteristics of women and men, the lists would be quite different. There is no acknowledgment, for example, that there are many women who are *not* coy and would use other adjectives to describe women. Also my guess is that it would come as a surprise to Sociobiologists to know that many American women because of *their* experiences, would include in their list of male characteristics helplessness, impracticality, and dependence. One is then left to wonder why this kind of list is any less "scientific" than the list of "human" characteristics Sociobiologists have chosen to describe.

Lack of Definition of Behavioral Units

A further difficulty that one encounters in Sociobiological accounts of human behavioral categories is the absence of any precise description or definition of the behaviors Sociobiologists are seeking to explain. It is a requirement for any science to define the units or the phenomena that are the subjects of its investigations so as to ensure that different scientists, writers, and their readers are using the same terms to mean the same thing. Certainly a theory of social behavior needs to describe the behaviors it explains. But Sociobiologists do not describe or define what they mean, for example, by entrepreneurship or aggressivity. Is aggressivity fighting in bars, getting ahead in business, being creative, being a football star, a Don Juan, a war hero, a professor? Or is it being a mother who pursues City Hall and all of its politicians until a stoplight is installed where her children have to cross the street on their way to school?

Sociobiologists do not provide the answers to these questions. Every person who reads their literature has her/his own impression of what is being discussed, and perhaps that is precisely where Sociobiology's wide appeal and acceptance lies. Its statements can be interpreted in accordance with any person's subjective experiences, expectations, frame of reference, or prejudices rather than needing to be measured or judged against generally accepted standards of meaning or definition. This omission of a definition of the behavioral units that are being "explained" makes for further difficulty when we try to understand how Sociobiologists relate behaviors to genes. For example, if aggressivity is genetic and biological, what is it that is being inherited? Is it a physiological state of high energy; is it overactive adrenal glands with high levels of adrenalin in the blood; is it high intelligence and creativity; is it good body coordination; is it being "too" short and "therefore" insecure; is it "maternalism?" Or, as another example, what exactly do genes "encode" when they encode for hypergamy in females or entrepreneurship in males? Would biological determinists simply have to agree that what is biologically based is the perception of hunger and the drive for survival, and that both hypergamy and the different forms that entrepreneurship takes are simply those among an infinite variety of behavioral strategies that human beings *learn* and *select* as solutions to the problems of hunger and survival in their particular ecological and cultural niche? Or do they really mean that all females inherit a gene or a cluster of genes that drive them to look for and, of course, scheme to marry a rich man? Would they concede the possibility that, rather than genes for "entrepreneurship," the more successful gatherer-hunters may have been distinguished from the rest by their greater inventiveness (of tools), better memory (for plants and fertile sites), quicker intelligence, more energy or speed, or by superior ecological circumstances? Surely to understand the evolution of complex behaviors, a multiplicity of such characteristics can be considered and perhaps profitably analyzed, but invoking a murky concept like entrepreneurship seems useless, in contrast, except perhaps as a means of justifying the inevitability of our economic system.

Anthropomorphizing: The Choice of Animal Models and Use of Language

Following close on the heels of the first, large problems of Sociobiological methodology that I have just discussed—its subjective and fuzzy conceptualizations and categorizations of human behavioral "traits" and social relationships—is the next great problem: anthropomorphizing, the substitution of human "equivalents" for real or postulated animal behaviors. In efforts to uncover the biological origins of human behavior, some investigators select an animal model that reflects their image of relationships presumed to exist in human society and then impose the language and concepts ordinarily used to describe human behavior upon their observations and interpretations of animal behaviors. The conclusions are inevitable, for the entire structure is a self-fulfilling prophecy. It involves a method, long in disrepute, of reading human motivation and intent into animal behavior. This makes for poor science because it cannot lead to an understanding of an animal species' behaviors or how the behaviors have come to solve the animal's problems of survival in its particular environment; it is also a circular and ineffectual way to approach human behavior even if one could understand human behavior by extrapolating from animals. (For reasons I discuss later, I do not believe one can.) If you initially interpret an animal's behavior in terms of what you believe about human behavior, you cannot then use your interpretation of *that animal's* behavior to explain something about human behavior.

Anthropomorphizing makes for a poor science of animal behavior for several reasons. The one I have discussed is that applying to animals assumptions that one has about human behavior or relationships structures and distorts the actual observations that investigators make as well as those they fail to make, and, in so doing, biases the course and outcome of the research. A second related reason is that the technique makes the assumption that simply because an animal and a human behavior *look* alike, they *are* the same. But the two behaviors could have a superficial similarity and at the same time have a totally different significance for the body economy and represent different solutions to two completely different sets of problems of survival in their respective ecological circumstances. To apply human terminology to animals not only totally ignores these distinctions, but in the process circumvents or cancels out all the relevant questions and investigations that could lead one to understand either the animal or the human behavior. . . .

Flowers, Ducks and Rape

We can find a particularly extravagant use of human behavioral concepts and language in the descriptions of animals in Barash's second book, *The Whisperings Within.* He claims he does not want to be a "racy modern Aesop," but says he will, nonetheless, be telling many animal stories about "rape in ducks, adultery in bluebirds, prostitution in hummingbirds, divorce and lesbian pairing in gulls, even homosexual rape in parasitic worms" (p. 2). Noteworthy for its relevance to a key contemporary issue for women is Barash's view of the origins of rape. Among Sociobiologists, Barash in particular sees rape rampant in nature. First he cites the work of Daniel Janzen, "one of our most creative ecologists," who has pointed out that even plants "perform courtship displays, rape, promiscuity, and fickleness just as do animals." Barash goes on to describe what he evidently considers to be rape in flowers:

> For example, plants with male flowers will "attempt" to achieve as many fertilizations as possible. How is this done? Among other things, they bombard female flowers with incredible amounts of pollen, and some even seem to have specially evolved capacities to rape female flowers, by growing a pollen tube which forces its way to the ovary within each female. (1979, p. 30)

So by defining the insertion of a pollen tube into a female flower as a rape, Barash begins to set the scene for the naturalness and—yes—the innocence of rape:

> Plants that commit rape . . . are following evolutionary strategies that maximize their fitness. And, clearly, in neither case do the actors know what they are doing, or why. We human beings like to think we are different. We introspect, we are confident that we know what we are doing, and why. But we may have to open our minds and admit the possibility that our need to maximize our fitness may be whispering somewhere deep within us and that, know it or not, most of the time we are heeding these whisperings. (p. 31)

Barash here strongly suggests that rapists are simply unwitting tools of a blind genetic drive; that rape is an unconscious urge for reproductive success and hence, biologically speaking, both advantageous and inevitable. But he seems unaware that there may be a different definition of rape; that most women see it as an act of violence expressing hatred, contempt, and fear of women and also as a weapon of social control that keeps women from asserting autonomy and freedom of movement, and forces them to depend on male "protectors." If *that* is the definition of rape, and I would say women have the right and the knowledge to decide that, then it is not relevant to flowers. And *to name what flowers do as "rape" is specifically to deny that rape is a sexual act of physical violence committed by men against women,* an act embodying and enforcing the political power wielded by men over women.

Later in the book, Barash turns to rape among the birds and bees, especially mallard ducks. He explains that mallard ducks pair up for breeding, leaving some males unmated since there are usually more males than females. He then describes how one male or a group of unmated males may copulate with a mated female without the normal preliminary courtship rituals that mated couples engage in and "despite her obvious and vigorous protest. If that's not rape, it is certainly very much like it" (p. 54). But first of all, he gives no indication whether this is a frequent or a rare occurrence nor does he describe the circumstances of the observation. Secondly, there is again the problem of language, in the use of the word *protest.* Courtship rituals are complex behaviors set in motion as a result of complex interactions between the hormonal and nervous systems of the animal, usually the female, and certain environmental conditions, for example, season of year. The female's state stimulates the male and, in turn, sets in motion the courtship rituals between partners, which further sequentially prime the reproductive systems for biological readiness to mate, ovulate, and fertilize—an intricate, balanced interplay between sight, smell, the brain, hormones, and gonads.

Thus, we could accommodate Barash's description of resisted copulation within the concept of the female's being *biologically not primed* for mating at the time of the bachelor's intrusion, but to impute *rape* and *protest*—intent and motivation—to ducks is again to use words for some purpose other than the clarity and accuracy required of scientific description and analysis. And the next page provides us with a lead to his purpose:

> Rape in humans is by no means as simple, influenced as it is by an extremely complex overlay of cultural attitudes. Nevertheless mallard rape and bluebird adultery may have a degree of relevance to human behavior. Perhaps human rapists, in their own criminally misguided way, are doing the best they can to maximize their fitness. If so, they are not that different from the sexually excluded bachelor mallards. (p. 55)

So Barash completes his portrait of the pitiful rapist: a lonesome fellow, left out of the mainstream of socially acceptable ways to copulate and so spread his genes about, he must force himself upon an unwilling female for the purpose of ensuring their reproduction.

In these examples, then, Barash used the word *rape,* which has a specific connotation in human terms, to describe behavior of a plant and a bird. This serves two purposes for Sociobiology: to establish that rape is biological and hence *natural* and to defuse rape as an urgent political issue, which has at its heart a cultural tradition of misogyny and male violence directed against women.

Harems

Thus far in the discussion of methodology, the basic problem has been the projection of investigators' personal and cultural values and biases about human behavior in their society onto their observations and interpretations of animals' and other cultures' behaviors. Since what is involved in these anthropomorphic and ethnocentric descriptions is language, we see that words become burdened with heavy implications. Language can be used to mold reality to a particular "truth," to impose a particular perception of the world as reality. Sociobiologists use language to mold the truth when they say that courted females are *coy* or that insects have evolved *"rampant machismo"* (Wilson, 1975b, p. 320), or that *aggressivity* is a universal trait of males. When Barash and other Sociobiologists use the word *rape* to describe a male flower's act of pollinating a female flower, they appropriate the word in order to remove rape from its sociopolitical context of male violence against women, to make it an act of sexual desire and of reproductive *need*, and, finally, to claim for rape a biological basis and inevitability because of its universality in the animal world.

The traditional use of the word *harem* in primatology to describe a single-male troop of females is another example of biased language and androcentric fantasy that served to structure observations and conceptualizations concerning the social organization of such troops. In our culture, *harem* has a generally accepted connotation of a group of women who are dependent economically, socially, and presumably sexually on a powerful male whose bodily needs are their central concern and occupation.[1] When that word was then used to signify single-male troops of female primates and their offspring, it automatically carried with it the entire complex of meanings and assumptions stereotypically associated with humans. It was assumed that the male was of central importance, defending the troop, making decisions, having his choice of sex partners, and in return was groomed, fed, and sexed by his harem of dependent females. Language substituted for actual observations, but it served ideology and circular logic by "demonstrating" that human male dominance and polygyny are innate since they are rooted in our primate ancestors. While hierarchical organization around a central male exists for some primate species under some circumstances, for many species, the solitary male is peripheral, functions mainly as a stud, and remains only so long as the females want him (Lancaster, 1975).

The Omission of Unwelcome Animal Data

Another problem in Sociobiological writings is the omission of unwelcome data that confound the stereotype. For example, rather than being engaged by redwinged blackbirds that exhibit polygyny and hypergamy, Sociobiologists, in the true scientific spirit of inquiry, could find it challenging to try to understand the South American male rhea bird that incubates and tends the 50 or so eggs that are laid by several females in the nest he builds. Or they could find it fascinating to explore shared parenting by examining the phenomenon of "double clutching," a situation in which female shore birds produce two clutches of eggs in quick succession, one of which becomes her responsibility and the other the male's. Or there is the female South American jacana bird who has a territory where she keeps a "harem" of males. She fills with eggs the nest that each male builds in his own subterritory and leaves him to incubate them and tend the brood (Bonner, 1980). Many bonded sea bird pairs take turns sitting on the nest while the partner goes out to sea to bring back fish. Some penguins have an even more elaborate system whereby both partners fish together leaving the young in a huge crêche tended by a few adults. The emperor penguin father remains nearly immobile during the two months he incubates his offspring's egg in a fold of skin about his feet, while the mother hunts for food. Bonner notes that monogamy is the main mating system among animals in which both sexes share in parental care (p. 156), and I wonder why Sociobiologists do not use this phenomenon as a "natural" model for human social organization as much as they do examples of male promiscuity and female domesticity.

Other Problems with Language and Logic

There is another way in which writers can manipulate language and logic in order to reach a desired conclusion. This technique is to use words with different meanings as though they were equivalent. As previously described, Sociobiologists attribute mothers' major responsibility for child care to the greater maternal biological investment in conception, gestation and lactation. Two Sociobiologists explain the inevitability of the situation:

> For a woman, the successful raising of a single infant is essentially close to a fulltime occupation for a couple of years, and continues to claim much attention and energy for several more years. For a man, it often means only a minor additional burden. To a limited extent, sexual roles can be modified in the direction of equalization of parental load, but even the most "liberated" husband cannot share pregnancy with his wife. In any case, most societies make no attempt to equalize parental care; they leave women holding the babies.
>
> Among most vertebrates, female involvement with offspring is obligatory whereas male involvement is more facultative. For example, . . . among orangutans, males on Sumatra typically associate with a female and her young, whereas on Borneo they defend territories and limit their interactions to other adult males. . . . Significantly, predators and interspecific competitors are more abundant on Sumatra. In short, biology dictates that females bear the offspring, although environmental conditions can exert a powerful influence on the extent of male parental investment. Males and females are selected for differing patterns of parental care, and there is no reason to exempt Homo sapiens from this generalization. . . . (Van Den Berghe and Barash, 1977, pp. 813–184)

The authors show in this example that important, presumably genetic characteristics like the nature and quantity of parental care are actually determined by environmental conditions—but only for the male, since they consider the female still biologically committed to parental care. But this is where slippery language and logic intrude because they themselves reduce the mother's necessary or obligatory involvement in parenting to only the *pregnancy* itself, yet they skip from that fact to the conclusion that the mother's involvement in *child care* is biologically obligatory without in any way demonstrating the fact. Clearly the time that animals spend nursing offspring is obligatory but in most species consumes but a fraction of the mother's day. Among some species, for example, the siamang great ape, tamarins and marmosets, many fathers carry and care for the young all day and return it to the mother only for nursing (Snowdon and Suomi, 1982). Among many primate species studied it has been observed that adult male behavior toward infants is highly flexible and influenced by the particular social circumstances within the troop in any period of time (Parke and Suomi, 1981). Thus, whatever biological influences exist, parenting behaviors by both females and males are molded by social and ecological factos and learning as well. For most animal species, the amount of time the females invest in care of the young is also facultative, also related to ecological conditions and tends to be the reciprocal of the father's investment even in the example presented in the paragraph quoted above. Certainly, for humans, where even breast feeding is not obligatory, the authors have presented no argument for the natural selection of "differing patterns of parental care."

Nonetheless, Sociobiologists have no doubts about what is biologically right, as Barash expresses it:

> Because men maximize their fitness differently from women, it is perfectly good biology that business and profession taste sweeter to them, while home and child care taste sweeter to women. (1979, p. 114)

Once again, as in their treatment of rape, Sociobiologists select for their attention an issue of particular vital and current concern to women and try to establish with faulty methodology the genetic origins of the social arrangements our society provides for child care. But in the same discussion quoted above, Barash goes far beyond expressing his biological opinion about the naturalness of the predominant social order that sees woman's proper place to be in the home. He warns that in the recent efforts to find "alternative lifestyles," it is child-care practices that are frequently at issue and "predictably there is a cost in disregarding biology." He cites a study that describes children reared in the counterculture as being neglected, deprived, and emotionally disturbed, and says that women seeking such "liberation" from total responsibility for child care are adopting a male biological strategy and denying their own. Thus, Sociobiology provides its public with an important sociopolitical theory and program: many aspects of modern civilization, however undesirable, are unavoidable, being expressions of our genetic inheritance; if we attempt to eliminate certain obvious social injustices, we tamper with evolution and risk incalculable harm, as Barash warns, "to everyone concerned." What this may mean we can only guess.

The Search for Evolutionary Behavioral Continuity: Culture in Animals

Throughout this critique of the methodology of biological determinism, one underlying problem has been the particular animals that are chosen as models for human behavior. The reason for Sociobiologists' citing of examples from a variety of animal species is, as I have mentioned, to establish universality and therefore evolutionary continuity. At the outset it can be said that there is no necessary correlation between universality (even if it *could* be demonstrated and it cannot) and evolutionary continuity, since what are being examined are present-day representatives of species that have evolved independently of each other for the last 15 million to about 500 million years. That is, according to the fossil evidence, the first hominid lines split off from the apes either about 15 or 5 million years ago and continued their own evolutionary course; the apes and monkeys diverged into their independent evolutionary lines about 40 to 50 million years ago; the first primates radiated off from other mammals about 70 or more million years ago; mammals, from the other land vertebrates about 325 million years ago; and over the previous 200 million years the various water and amphibious vertebrate species were evolving in their niches (Pilbeam, 1972). Thus, with independent lines of development for every species over the last millions to hundreds of millions of years, we do not know what, if any, evolutionary relationships similar behaviors of different present-day species have to each other. But certainly no one can seriously maintain that either the behaviors or the brains of present-day species represent a "recapitulation" of the evolutionary pathway that humans have followed. All that we can assume is that each species has evolved in relationship to the series of ecological niches within which it has survived, and today's array of forms and behaviors represents the varied outcomes of those historical relationships. Related to this point is the fact that the kind of faulty use of animal examples being discussed here involves the implicit assumption of a "chain of being" and "ascent" of humans over more primitive animal "precursors." But since contemporary animals are not our precursors, it is no more logical to look at chimpanzees or mice to gain insight into our behavior that it would be to look at our behavior to gain insight into theirs.

A faulty premise underlying some of the studies or observations of animals, particularly primates, either in the laboratory or in the wild, is that such study will reveal basic biological mechanisms of behavior that have evolved genetically and are "uncontaminated" by culture. There are two questionable assumptions in this premise. The first is that there is such an entity as "basic biological mechanisms" of human behavior that can be *revealed* by stripping off layers of culture; that is, that there is any definition of human behavior that can conceptually or in reality exclude culture. But that is an issue of such importance and complexity that it requires its own chapter, Chapter 3. The other erroneous assumption is that animals themselves have no culture affecting their "basic biological" or genetically influenced mechanisms; that their behaviors express only genes and no learning. In his fine review and analysis of the behaviors of animals, Bonner (1980) describes the various manifestations of the capacity for learning, teaching, and culture among vertebrates. Related to differences in relative size and complexity of the organization of the brain are differences in complexity and flexibility of behavioral responses to environmental challenges and the ability of animals to learn new and adaptive behaviors from one another. It is this transmission of information by behavioral means that Bonner defines as culture and that plays an important role in social behaviors and relationships among animals and in their adaptation to their environments. Thus, we cannot look to most animal behaviors as *instinctual* or *innate* and, therefore, as providing peepholes into the pure genetic core and *nature* of the human species.

Validation by Prediction

One of the methodological techniques by which some Sociobiologists attempt to provide scientific validity or substance to their speculation is by making predictions. One criterion of a theory's value is its ability to predict what we will find under particular circumstances if we go and make the observations or conduct the proper experiment. Sociobiologists, Barash in particular, constantly "prove" the validity and predictive values of their theories by "predicting" what they and everyone else already know to be demonstrated fact; for example:

> Sociobiological theory would predict that adults with the most to gain and the least to lose would be the most eager adopters, and certainly this is true in the United States where childless couples are the predominant adopters. (1977, p. 313)

More relevant to this book is Barash's opinion about depression, which he sees as a "cry for help." Since males are genetically selected to be the *providers* of resources and females are those who are provided *for,*

> . . . in all societies, depression is significantly more common in women than in men. Their biology makes it more likely that women should be the sex to attempt care-eliciting behaviors. Males are supposed to be the care providers. Depression is also frequently associated with marital strife, a finding consistent with the suggestion that depression represents an unconscious effort to mobilize concern, attention and resources, in this case from an unresponsive or insufficiently responsive husband. (1979, p. 217)

Then Barash proceeds once again to address directly issues raised by the women's movement in his observation that, while depression is more common among married than among unmarried women, the opposite is true for men:

> The discovery that unmarried men are more likely to be depressed than are married men has been an important weapon for radical feminists, since it suggests that marriage itself is a male-designed phenomenon, tending to free men from depression while depressing women, presumably because of the emotionally stressful, sexist demands made upon married women in today's society. There may be much truth in this claim, but the male-female differences in depression associated with marriage also fit well with the sociobiological hypothesis. If men are the resource-providing sex and women are biologically predisposed to be resource receiving, and if depression is in fact a petition for resources (emotional, financial, etc.) it seems reasonable that unmarried men who showed depressive inclinations would be considered unattractive mates, while depressive tendencies in women would not be nearly as undesirable. (1979, pp. 217, 218)

We find in these passages a medley of methodological faults. First, there is the sarcastic dismissal of any suggestion that there may be a sociocultural context for depression among women, particularly among women who are married. Secondly, the explanation for depression is based upon acceptance of a sequence of unsubstantiated premises: "if men are the resource-providing sex," if women are "biologically predisposed to be resource receiving," "if depression is in fact a petition for resources," that depressed men are unattractive to women, and that depression in unmarried men is a cause rather than a result of their unmarried state. No one knows if any of these is true. Furthermore, other key Sociobiological premises posit quite the opposite—that women are the resource *providers* to their families, by *nature*, the nurturers, the givers. Even in an economic sense, so far as we know, women have historically always shared equally in providing material resources for their families through their labors both within and outside the home.

Barash than goes on to secure his argument by making a prediction: "We would also predict that if depression is a care-eliciting behavior, then it should be especially common following the birth of a child. . ." (1979, p. 218). As usual he claims a particular Sociobiological theory has been confirmed because it is able to "predict" a phenomenon that he, we, everyone already knows to exist; namely, postpartum depression.

If I were for the moment to accept Sociobiological premises, my predictions would be quite different from those proposed by Sociobiologists: Since women have a great biological investment in each pregnancy, which predisposes them to provide most of the parental care in order to protect optimally their genes in their offspring, I would predict:

1. A low incidence or absence of postpartum depression in women, since depression is *not* the optimal mental/physical state for the high energy requirements of postpartum lactation and infant care. In fact, I would further predict that the infants of depressed mothers do not fare as well physically or emotionally as infants of non-depressed mothers.
2. A high incidence of postpartum depression in fathers because they are deprived of a considerable portion of the parental care formerly invested in them by their wives, who, despite their high energy levels and resource-giving capacities, have finite limits and must share their resources equally. The father's depression is, of course, care-eliciting behavior, an unconscious effort to mobilize concern, attention, and resources.
3. A low incidence of depression in women in general, since most of them are fulfilling their biological predispositions to be mothers and nurturers. As Barash has said, life tastes "sweet" to them; in fact, I would predict that most women are manic most of the time. Furthermore, they are sensible enough to realize the futility of engaging in care-eliciting behavior directed toward men whose biological predisposition is toward aggressivity, activity, and competitiveness rather than nurturance.
4. In general, a high incidence of depression among both married and unmarried men. The vast majority of the men in the world in fact have very few resources, are not leaders, and rarely have an opportunity to hunt or go to war. In the face of the fact that they *cannot* provide resources as they are supposed to, are *not* fulfilling their genetic and evolutionary destinies, all that is left for them to do, in despair and frustration, is to cry for help.

Aside from the amusement of this exercise, I have wanted to illustrate two important fundamental flaws that make Sociobiology a very flimsy superstructure. First, premises in science are ordinarily expected to represent a generally accepted statement of current knowledge or at least a statement with some supporting evidence. But Sociobiological premises themselves are arbitrary, subjective, and conjectural even though they are stated as *givens.* Secondly, given any set of premises, whether conjectural or supported by evidence, *any number* of logical predictions or hypotheses may follow, not just the one a Sociobiologist or any particular scientist chooses to propose. The logical next step then is to recognize the importance of challenging the hypotheses by subjecting them to experimentation or to further observations that may tend to support or exclude one or another of the possible alternative hypotheses.

Sociobiologists predict what is already known to be true, then offer that known fact as proof of the validity of the premises from which they claim to be making the prediction. This method precludes the need either to test the prediction or to question the premises on which it was based.

SUMMARY AND CONCLUSION

Sociobiology, the modern version of biological determinist theories of human behavior, attempts to validate the belief that genes determine behaviors and that social relationships and cultures have evolved through the genetic transmission of behavioral traits and characteristics. Of central importance in Sociobiological theory, in keeping with the biological determinist tradition, are its efforts to explain in terms of *biology* the origins of the gender-differentiated roles and positions held by women and by men in modern as well as past civilizations. In so doing, Sociobiologists attempt to assign *natural* causes to phenomena of social origin. It is in part because Sociobiologists specifically address the very social issues that the women's movement has highlighted that Sociobiology functions as a political theory and program. Sociobiologists reinforce ancient stereotypes of women as coy, passive, dependent, maternal, and nurturant and base these temperaments in our genes. At the same time, and despite their liberal protestations, they explain and justify the existence of women's social and physical oppression by asserting the genetic origins, and hence inevitability, of rape, the sexual double standard, the relegation of women to the private world of home and motherhood, and other forms of the exploitation of women. Furthermore, its use of shoddy methodology and incorrect logic to support insupportable claims suggests a motive force other than the dispassionate pursuit of knowledge.

I have demonstrated a number of basic conceptual and methodological flaws in the work of Sociobiologists, which include faulty logic; unsupported assumptions and premises; inappropriate use of language; lack of definitions of the behaviors being explained; and ethnocentric, androcentric, and anthropocentric biases underlying the questions that are asked, the language used, the selection of animal models, and the interpretation of data. The more fundamental scientific problem, however, is the dichotomy that is drawn between genetic and environmental determinants of behavior. From the time of conception genes do *not* act in isolation from their environment, and even fairly stereotypical behaviors in animals, with few exceptions, represent interactions between experience or learning and biological mechanisms. What has evolved in response to environmental challenge is the brain and its capacities for learning and culture, not behaviors themselves. Behaviors are the *products* of the brain's functioning in interaction with the external world, and the innumerable patterns of social behaviors, relationships, and organization that characterize human societies have evolved through cultural transmission within specific historical contexts.

Note

1. For a different and multidimensional view of harems and the Muslim women who inhabit them, see Ahmed (1982).

References

Ahmed, L. Western ethnocentrism and perceptions of the harem. *Feminist Studies,* 1982, *8,* 521–534.
Barash, D. *Sociobiology and behavior.* New York: Elsevier, 1977.
Barash, D. *The whisperings within.* New York: Harper & Row, 1979.
Bonner, J. T. *The evolution of culture in animals.* Princeton: Princeton University Press, 1980.
Brown, J. L. *The evolution of behavior.* New York: W. W. Norton, 1975.
Dawkins, R. *The selfish gene.* New York: Oxford University Press, 1976.
Eaton, G. G. Male dominance and aggression in Japanese macaque reproduction. In W. Montagna and W. Sadler (Eds.), *Reproductive behavior.* New York: Plenum, 1974.
Herschberger, R. *Adam's rib.* New York: Harper & Row, 1970.
Hirsch, H. V. B., and Leventhal, A. G. Functional modification of the developing visual system. In M. Jacobson (Ed.), *Handbook of sensory physiology,* 1978, *9. Development of sensory systems.* New York: Springer-Verlag.
Howell, N. Sociobiological hypotheses explored. *Science,* 1979, *206,* 1294–1295.
Hrdy, S. B. *The woman that never evolved.* Cambridge: Harvard University Press, 1981.
Hubbard, R. From termite to human behavior. *Psychology Today,* 1978, *12,* 124–134.
Hubbard, R. The theory and practice of genetic reductionism—from Mendel's laws to genetic engineering. In S. Rose (Ed.), *Towards a liberatory biology.* London: Allison and Busby, 1982.
Kolata, G. B. Primate behavior: Sex and the dominant male. *Science,* 1976, *191,* 55–56.
Lancaster, J. B. *Primate behavior and the emergence of human culture.* New York: Holt, Rinehart & Winston, 1975.
Lappé, M. *Genetic politics.* New York: Simon & Schuster, 1979.
Leavitt, R. R. *Peaceable primates and gentle people: Anthropological approaches to women's studies.* New York: Harper & Row, 1975.
Leibowitz, L. *Perspectives in the anthropology of women.* In R. Reiter (Ed.). New York: Monthly Review Press, 1975.
Leibowitz, L. *Females, males, families: A biosocial approach.* North Scituate, MA: Duxbury Press, 1978.
Lewin, R. Seeds of change in embryonic development. *Science,* 1981, *214,* 42–44.
Lewontin, R. C. Sociobiology—a caricature of Darwinism. *Journal of Philosophy of Science,* 1976, *2,* 21–31.
Midgley, M. Gene-juggling. In A. Montagu (Ed.), *Sociobiology examined.* Oxford: Oxford University Press, 1980. (a)
Midgley, M. Rival fatalism: the hollowness of the sociobiology debate. In A. Montagu (Ed.), *Sociobiology examined.* Oxford: Oxford University Press, 1980. (b)
Parke, R. D., and Suomi, S. J. Adult male-infant relationships: human and nonhuman primate evidence. In K. Immelmann, G. Barlow, L. Petrinovich and M. Main (Eds.), *Early development in animals and man.* New York: Cambridge University Press, 1981.
Pilbeam, D. *The ascent of man.* New York: Macmillan, 1972.
Pilbeam, D. An idea we could live without: The naked ape. In A. Montagu (Ed.), *Man and aggression.* Oxford: Oxford University Press, 1973.
Rosenzweig, M. R., Bennett, E. L., and Diamond, M. C. Brain changes in response to experience. *Scientific American,* 1972, *226,* 22–30.
Rowell, T. *Social behavior of monkeys.* Baltimore: Penguin, 1972.
Rowell, T. The concept of social dominance. *Behavioral Biology,* 1974, *11,* 131–154.
Schaller, G. *The mountain gorilla: ecology and behavior.* Chicago: University of Chicago Press, 1963.
Snowdon, C. T., and Suomi, S. J. Paternal behavior in primates. In H. E. Fitzgerald, J. S. Mullins and P. Gage (Eds.), *Child nurturance,* 1982, New York: Plenum.
Van Den Berghe, P. L., and Barash, D. P. Inclusive fitness and human family structure. *American Anthropologist,* 1977, *79,* 809–823.
Wilson, E. O. Human decency is animal. *New York Times Magazine,* 1975, Oct. 12, 38–50. (a)
Wilson, E. O. *Sociobiology: The new synthesis.* Cambridge, MA: Harvard University Press, 1975. (b)
Wilson, E. O. *On human nature.* Cambridge, MA: Harvard University Press, 1978.
Winick, M. Nutritional disorders during brain development. In D. B. Tower (Ed.), *The clinical neurosciences.* New York: Raven Press, 1975.
Woolf, V. *Three guineas.* New York: Harcourt Brace & World, 1938.
Yerkes, R. M. *Chimpanzees.* New Haven, Conn.: Yale University Press, 1943.

THE BUILT ENVIRONMENT
Women's Place, Gendered Space

Judy Wajcman

> Whether the private home is a free-standing house in Frank Lloyd Wright's Broadacre City or a high tower flat in Le Corbusier's Radiant City, domestic work has been treated as a private, sex-stereotyped activity, and most architects continue to design domestic work spaces for isolated female workers. Hayden, *The Grand Domestic Revolution*

In every culture and historical epoch, domestic architecture is uniquely revealing about prevailing social relations and norms of household organization. The design of houses is imbued with values and ideas that both reflect and exert tremendous influence over the patterns and quality of our lives. In this chapter I want to broaden the discussion of household technology to include the house as a technological construct, and the built environment more generally. The built environment is taken to mean '. . . our created surroundings, including homes, their arrangement in relation to one another, to public spaces, transport routes, workplaces and the layout of cities.' (Matrix, 1984, p. 1)

In what follows, I will be arguing that the built environment reflects and reinforces a domestic ideal which emphasizes the importance of the home as a woman's place and a man's haven. Sexual divisions are literally built into houses and indeed the whole structure of the urban system. Architecture and urban planning have orchestrated the separation between women and men, private and public, home and paid employment, consumption and production, reproduction and production, suburb and city. While people do not actually live according to these dichotomies, the widespread belief in them does influence decisions and have an impact on women's lives.

The focus of much feminist literature has been housework and the implications of technological developments within the home. Postwar sociology has chiefly considered housing as an aspect of the distribution and transmission of social wealth and privilege, that is, as an aspect of social stratification. At an economic level, housing is a commodity and central to the generation of capitalist profits. It is only recently that the structure and shape of the house itself has been subjected to feminist analysis.

The physical form of buildings is usually taken to be the inevitable result of technological and engineering advances, for example, concrete and steel gave us the high-rise tower block of modernist architecture. Changes in the interior design of dwellings are likewise explained in terms of mechanical innovations. A classic example can be found in explanations of the changing location of the kitchen, which is often attributed to the invention of the Rumford stove. This combined stove for cooking and heating eliminated odour and pollution and is said to be thus responsible for the movement of the kitchen from the basement or rear of the house to its centre.[1]

Certainly innovations in building materials, engineering methods and domestic technologies are of major importance and make possible the development of new architectural forms. However, as with other technologies, the design of the built environment is stamped with wider social and economic relations. Historians of architecture provide many instances of physical structures and arrangements that incorporate explicit or implicit political purposes. One such example is the wide Parisian boulevard designed by Baron Haussmann to permit the movement of troops and thus prevent any recurrence of street fighting of the kind that took place during the revolution of 1848.

Michel Foucault's discussion of Bentham's Panopticon, an all-seeing architectural form designed to keep prisoners under constant surveillance, is a vivid illustration of how a building can itself embody techniques of control. Prisons though are not the only buildings that can be designed to institutionalize patterns of power and order. The new IBM headquarters in Sydney is curiously reminiscent of the Panopticon. Its open-plan offices and clear glass internal walls are intended to give the appearance of a 'status-free environment'. Hierarchies seem to be dissolved where even managers' offices have glass walls and are located close to their staff. In fact of course, what these arrangements achieve is the possibility for increased surveillance of staff, who must feel watched even when they are not. In this sense, the glass itself does the looking. Like the Panopticon, then, the structure of the building ensures that control is largely achieved through self-discipline.

Whilst domestic architecture may not provide us with such stark examples of the extent to which buildings incorporate techniques of social control, that women are constrained in particular ways by the form of the family dwelling is certain. The house both symbolizes patriarchal relations, and gives concrete expression to them. In the first part of this chapter I will chart the development of the modern house. In so doing, I will be arguing that architectural changes in the domestic arena are not simply driven by technological advances but are about expectations of women and men, and in particular are about the domestication of women. . . .

THE IDEAL HOME

Housing the Symmetrical Family

If the Second World War posed a challenge to traditional sex roles, this was to leave little trace on the design of houses. In fact the postwar period saw the revitalization of the ideology of separate spheres for women and men. The major housing construction programmes of the 1950s and 1960s coincided with women being pushed back into the home to tend their husbands and children.[2] The housing stock which predominates today dates from or bears the stamp of this period. With the rapid growth of owner-occupation, greater emphasis was placed on a more home-centred lifestyle for men as well as women. The idea of companionate marriage saw the family as increasingly sharing activities and cultivating intimate relationships in the comfort of a private home. Here 'good' communication, intimacy, awareness of the needs of others, shared leisure (often shared consumption) gained a prominence previously accorded to hygiene and nutrition. But for all these apparent changes, the continuity with Victorian middle-class domestic ideals was in many ways more profound than the discontinuities.

This new socio-psychological conception of familial relations found its main expression in the open-plan housing design that characterized the post-war period. The dark divided house gave way to a preference for light and open space, breaking down traditional divisions between formality and informality in behaviour. Architects promoted the idea of multi-function spaces and 'zoned' planning in houses became the norm. Spaces were demarcated for certain functions, but this was achieved without separate rooms. The 'activity area' of the living room, dining area, and kitchen had few walls, providing as much space and togetherness as possible. The lack of walls was thought to promote the modern ideology of marital equality. Famous for its open-plan interiors, Frank Lloyd Wright's domestic architecture was nevertheless faithful to the Victorian iconography of family life by placing a massive hearth at the very centre of his house designs.

Domestic servants had finally completely bowed out of the home and consequently the illusion that meals simply arrived in the dining room—as if from nowhere—could no longer be sustained. There was therefore less reason to have a separate kitchen and dining room and the kitchen was now enlarged and opened up to the rest of the house. This open design gave domestic work a more egalitarian appearance, as other members of the family shared the space, and by implication the tasks, hitherto allocated to women alone. As we know, the domestic division of labour was not transformed by these architectural changes! However, they did obscure the extent to which women continued to bear responsibility for servicing the family. Typically, there was now a table in the kitchen for eating at, again signifying a less formal lifestyle. The open-plan kitchen enabled mothers to supervise children while cooking the meal, as children were now seen as requiring constant attention and companionship. This partially explains the move of the kitchen to the back of the house with a picture window looking out on the garden.

To cater for this increased concern with children's needs, the multipurpose room, which later became known as the 'family room', came into existence. 'Although the family room most often served as a place where children could do as they pleased in the midst of clutter and noise, it was also an architectural expression of family togetherness.' (Wright, 1981, p. 255) Very little privacy is provided for individuals within the house, which becomes primarily a place for shared activities. The bedrooms now provided for the children are generally small, ensuring that they will spend most of their time in the larger family room. Adults in the house are assumed to need even less private space—especially women. Even the parents' bedroom belongs to 'the Master'. Women do not have a room of their own, their spatial needs being subsumed into the family's: if they have a domain it is the kitchen.

The last twenty years have witnessed major shifts in the social position of women and in the way women see themselves. Paradoxically, this period has also been characterized by a renewed rhetoric about women as soft, feminine and housebound which is increasingly at odds with reality. The white plastic, clinical kitchen has given way to a more cosy 'country kitchen' with pine-panelled walls and natural wood finishes. Laura Ashley patterned floral prints recall the cheerful simplicity of rural life. Although most new houses now have central heating, the fireplace remains the focal point of many living rooms, with furniture grouped around it.[3] It is still the place of the most expensive furniture, with faint echoes of the Victorian parlour.

The kitchen meanwhile has become the emotional centre of the home: it is from here that the relaxed, informal, symmetrical family lifestyle radiates. Power relations within the patriarchal family have become submerged by this ideology of togetherness. Thus the prototype for the modern house prescribed the form of household that would inhabit it, namely the white middle-class nuclear family. As such it was not only oppressive to most women, but also a markedly ethnocentric design, denying the existence and needs of other forms of family. The dominant modern housing design does not lend itself to satisfying the housing needs of the majority of households today, which are in fact no longer composed of nuclear families.

Symbolic values about domestic life are perhaps even more clearly expressed in the external appearance of houses. The exterior of houses is the prime indicator of people's social status and extremely important to their self-image. Houses are, after all, the major article of consumption and their exterior is what counts most when they are purchased. Architects' prime concern has always been with the public face of buildings and the current debate on the nature of post-modern architecture is reproducing this concern. The contrast between domestic and commercial architecture is interesting in this regard. While non-residential architecture has gone through massive transformations in style, building materials, and construction technology, the preference for Georgian and Victorian domestic architecture remains. The facades of old houses are retained while the interior is gutted and modernized. There is even a market for new houses that are replicas of these styles, or in America of colonial-style houses.

While state-of-the-art commercial buildings pride themselves on being energy efficient and maintenance-free, the house still uses traditional materials such as wood and bricks that are both expensive and laborious to maintain. The assumption that women will continue to do much of this domestic work for free no doubt explains the disregard for efficiency in domestic architecture. However, the explanation is clearly more complex: men too are involved in maintaining the exterior of the home, investing much of their spare time and money in do-it-yourself home improvements. Furthermore, the preference for traditional architecture reflects an attachment to traditional values and a desire that the home should be a haven, resembling the workplace as little as possible. High-rise towers have met with little objection as offices but have proved very unpopular as homes.

Semi-Detached in the Suburbs

For all that privacy within the house has diminished, the expectation is that families as a whole remain private from each other. (Matrix, 1984, p. 55) The Victorian ideal of the detached or semi-detached house in a suburban or semi-rural setting remains essentially unchanged. The one-family house with a garden was regarded by the middle class and working class alike as the best place to bring up children, offering a healthy environment away from the dirt, noise and danger of the city. Developers encouraged the massive post-war move to the suburbs, as low-density development meant more profit for the building industry as well as providing a mass market for consumer durables. Although women have paid a heavy price for suburban development, they shared men's dreams of home ownership, their disillusion with the city and hopes for a better life in the suburbs. It took several decades for the aridness and uniformity of modern suburban life, and especially the isolation and boredom it forced on the housewife, to become immortalized in Betty Friedan's account of 'the problem with no name'.

Consonant with this idea of the home as private space, the distinctiveness of the home became enshrined in state zoning policies, which were at the heart of post-war town planning. Cities and towns were to be geographically segregated into their various activities, each with its appropriate location and setting. Zoning '. . . closely approximated stereotypical ideas about *man's* use of the environment' (Matrix, 1984, p. 38). It was assumed that the home and the neighbourhood were the setting for most women's lives and that men would travel to work located elsewhere. The main function of transport would be to get men from home to work and back again.

The impact that this would have on women's mobility was not considered. As Susan Saegert (1980) has observed, the long-standing symbolic dichotomy between 'masculine cities and feminine suburbs' fundamentally shaped the actual organization of the urban environment, tying women more closely to their immediate locality. Residential areas were and still are physically separated from industrial/commercial sites, distancing women from the 'economy'. Zoning thus intensified the privatized nature of many women's lives and their exclusion from the public, socially organized productive life. Suburban zoning restrictions have also operated to separate different sorts of housing development, limiting moderately priced high-density buildings to inner-city sites. As such it has been an important tool in class and race segregation—most infamously in South African urban planning, where black people are expressly confined to certain parts of the city.

Since at least the mid-1970s employers have responded to the separation of the workplace and home by relocating certain kinds of activities to the suburbs in order to capture the potential labour of married women who reside there. This has required the rezoning of some suburban space, especially in middle-class suburbs because it is white middle-class wives that are wanted for office work. Urban space is once more being restructured as the demand for clerical work expands—work traditionally done by women. Developments in information and communication technologies greatly facilitate large scale shifts in the nature and location of employment, and the decentralization of workplaces. It is not only office work that is now being 'suburbanized'. Industrial zones on the urban periphery have become massive centres of development. And suburban sprawl has stimulated the development of regional retail complexes. Meanwhile, administrative and financial activities—head office functions—remain located in the central city area. Overall this represents at least a partial shift away from mono-functional zoning to a more mixed use of urban space.

There is currently much interest in the contemporary restructuring of cities around 'service' sector work, and the rapid restructuring of manufacturing. Some of these analyses focus on the spatial constitution of power, that is, how the spatial allocation of goods, services, and employment across a city act as hidden mechanisms for the unequal distribution of income among various groups in the urban population. In Los Angeles, for example, it has been pointed out that industrial restructuring has left the largely Chicano/Hispanic and black industrial working class cut off from the new workplaces.

While such studies recognize the spatial construction of class and race differences, they generally ignore the issue of gender relations—aside from the obligatory listing of women with other disadvantaged or oppressed 'minority' groups.[4] There is little attempt to explore the different implications of such developments for women and men, and the ways in which the contemporary restructuring of cities affects the social relations of reproduction as well as the relations of production.

FEMINIST ALTERNATIVES: WOULD WOMEN DO IT DIFFERENTLY?

If the built environment tends to institutionalize patriarchal relations, is this because it has been designed and constructed predominantly by men? Would women, then, produce a different physical environment?

Planning and architecture in Britain, North America and Australia are indeed white, male-dominated professions. This is mirrored through all stages of building; even the production of the physical built structure is done by an almost all-male workforce. As the feminist designers' collective known as Matrix (1984, p. 3) comments, 'women play almost no part in making decisions about or in creating the environment. It is a *man-made* environment.' In their critiques of modern architecture, urban planning and of public/private distinctions, feminists have drawn attention to the sexual politics of space. They have suggested that the inevitable outcome of a profession and an industry inhabited and controlled by men is a male-defined built space.

The domestic architecture often cited as the epitome of a masculinist approach is the multi-storey residential block. This functionalist architecture, which envisaged a vertical garden city with 'streets in the air', has been discredited by feminists amongst others.[5] The fact that housework and childcare might be made more oncrous and isolating for women stranded at dizzy heights, without safe and accessible outdoor space, did not occur to the pioneers of the Modern Movement. Apart from this obvious disregard for the quality of women's lives, these towers have also been seen as products of a specifically male vision. Modernism in architecture was obsessed with technological progress, adopting technology as both its instrument and symbol. The development of the high-rise form was a monument to technological innovation and a strikingly phallic symbol.

The underlying theme of such analyses is that women experience space differently from men and would therefore create different built environments. Margrit Kennedy, a Berlin-based architect, argues that 'there would be a significant difference between an environment shaped mainly by men and male values and an environment shaped mainly by women and female values' (1981, p. 76). Whereas men design a building from the outside in, women's greater preoccupation with interiors leads them to design buildings from the inside out. Kennedy suggests that there are the following male and female principles in architecture:

The Female Principles		**The Male Principles**
more user oriented	than	designer oriented
more ergonomic	than	large scale/monumental
more functional	than	formal
more flexible	than	fixed
more organically ordered	than	abstractly systematized
more holistic/complex	than	specialized/one-dimensional
more social	than	profit-oriented
more slowly growing	than	quickly constructed.

These ideas are echoed in many feminist critiques of architectural practice, which argue that whereas male subjectivity is expressed in tall phallic towers, female buildings are round, enclosing, curving and low-rise. Such views are not the prerogative of feminists alone.[6] In *The City in History*, Lewis Mumford proposed that in neolithic communities people lived in round dwellings, the house and the village being woman writ large: with the development of the city '[m]ale symbolisms and abstractions now become manifest: they show themselves in the insistent straight line, the rectangle, the firmly bounded geometric plan, the phallic tower and the obelisk . . .' (1961, p. 27).

Despite its initial appeal, there are a number of problems with this radical feminist position. To start with, the emphasis on universalized feminine and masculine traits in design cannot explain how it is that men as well as women have designed round and curving buildings. One need look no further than Gaudi's rippling architecture or the spiral shaped Guggenheim museum of Frank Lloyd Wright. Neither can it explain women's involvement in the design of highrise buildings. As Kennedy herself remarks, in countries such as the USSR that have a high proportion of women architects, the dominant Western models of architecture prevail. Even though there are an increasing number of women practising architecture in Western countries, their professional education and training means that the work of women architects is not qualitatively different from that of male architects. That women architects have traditionally been assumed to be best suited for the design of domestic architecture and interiors reflects their low status in the profession rather than a specifically female attribute. It is to do with the hierarchical relationship between what is considered to be great 'architecture' of the public realm as opposed to the mere 'building' of houses.

On closer inspection several of Kennedy's characteristics of 'male' design are features of architecture operating within the constraints set by commercial imperatives. Women architects working under the same market pressures tend to design like men. To see central city office towers solely as the product of masculinist, phallocentric design values is to present a very partial picture which ignores investment calculations, capital flows, global property markets and the private ownership of land. The appearance of high-rise office buildings is explained as much by economic processes which lead to overaccumulated capital being invested in the central business district. As Margo Huxley (1988, p. 41) points out, these investments depend on 'political actions to retain the primacy of the central city and on the perceptions of (male) corporate directors of the prestige and power that is reflected in taking occupancy of the latest high-rise, high-tech office tower'.

While an account in terms of capitalist investment demonstrates the material basis of high towers, we still need an explanation of the cultural forces at work which give towers an association with power and prestige. I would argue that the cultural association between high-rise towers and male power is not only or primarily about their physical shape but is also because they represent the triumph of advanced technology. Perhaps this is why the radical feminist preference for low-rise 'human scale' development presents a credible if under-articulated alternative.

The risks inherent in the formulation of a specifically feminist architecture lie in the temptation to regard women as a homogeneous group. As Matrix (1984) emphasizes, there is a tendency to simply reflect the approach of white, middle-class women in the profession. Women's experience is very diverse, especially in terms of class. This is one of the interesting issues that is raised in Dolores Hayden's (1982) extensive research on nineteenth-century American feminist plans for utopian communities. Alternative approaches to individualized housework in single-family homes were proposed by an earlier women's movement. This 'lost feminist tradition' identified the economic exploitation of women's labour by men as the most basic cause of women's inequality. The central object of their campaigning was to socialize household labour and childcare. Most significantly, they sought to do this by a complete transformation of the spatial form and material culture of American homes, neighbourhoods and cities. Recognizing that the exploitation of women's labour by men was embodied in the actual design of houses, these 'material feminists' believed that changing the entire physical framework of houses and neighbourhoods was the only way to free women from domestic drudgery. They therefore urged architects and urban planners to explore radically new types of residential building.[7]

Two of the more influential women were Melusina Fay Pierce and Charlotte Perkins Gilman. In 1868 Melusina Fay Pierce, a middle-class Massachusetts woman, outlined plans for cooperative residential neighbourhoods made up of kitchenless houses and a cooperative housekeeping centre. She suggested that women organize to perform their household tasks cooperatively, building communal kitchens, laundries, dining facilities and childcare centres as necessary. Freed from the domestic routine, they would then be able to develop other interests outside the home. Writing in 1898, the economist Charlotte Perkins Gilman recommended kitchenless houses of a similar sort, suggesting that they be linked in urban rows or connected by covered walkways in a suburban block. Like Pierce, Gilman favoured the construction of kitchenless apartments with collective dining facilities for women with families. For Gilman however, the socialization of domestic work, rather than cooperation in its execution, was the means to economic independence for women. She envisaged a completely professionalized system of housekeeping which would free women from the ties of cooking, cleaning and childcare.

Ultimately this domestic reform movement foundered on the difficulty of overcoming both sex and class divisions in their urban and suburban communities. The problem of domestic service versus domestic cooperation could not be resolved. Many cooperative housekeeping societies accepted hierarchical organizational structures which put educated, middle-class managers at the top and paid dishwashers and laundry workers rather poorly. 'Feminists with capital who could afford the new physical environment for collective domestic work never thought of voluntarily sharing that domestic work themselves' (Hayden, 1982, p. 201). Thus, the liberation of professional middle-class feminists from domestic drudgery involved exploiting women of a lower economic class. The failure of this experiment in architectural solutions to the problem of women's domestic oppression is instructive. It demonstrates the impossibility of divorcing gender from class and other relations of inequality. It also demonstrates that new, egalitarian architectural forms cannot simply be superimposed on a preexisting social order and be transformative in themselves.

AUTOMOBILES: TECHNOLOGY IN MOTION

So far I have discussed the gender dimensions of housing design and urban layout. However, any discussion of the physical built environment is incomplete without discussing the transport technology that binds these spaces together. In particular the automobile is now a preeminent feature of the urban environment.

The invention and mass production of the car has greatly influenced the shape of the modern city. One has only to think of cities like Los Angeles and new planned towns like Milton Keynes, to be reminded of this. From the beginning of the modern movement in architecture, architects like Le Corbusier and Frank Lloyd Wright saw cars as integral to the design of the city. In this section I will argue that the transport system, and in particular the dominance of the car, restricts women's mobility and exacerbates women's confinement to the home and the immediate locality. Women's and men's daily lives trace very different patterns of time, space and movement, and the modern city is predicated on a mode of transport that reflects and is organized around men's interests, activities and desires, to the detriment of women.

The manufacture of automobiles is the largest industry in the world economy. It is dominated by a handful of American, Japanese and European companies that control 80 per cent of global production. In 1987, a record 126,000 cars rolled off assembly lines each working day, and close to 400 million vehicles are currently on the world's streets.[8] The automobile and its infrastructure dominate most North American and Australian cities in the literal sense that vast tracts of land are required to accommodate them. Not only for the motorways, but also for roundabouts, bridges, service stations, and parking spaces—at home, work, the supermarket and everywhere that people are supposed to congregate. Small wonder that in American cities, close to half of all urban space is dedicated to the automobile; in Los Angeles, the figure reaches two-thirds.

For the individual, the mobility and convenience that the private car bestows are unparalleled by any other means of transportation. However, what appears to be an ideal solution to individual needs is increasingly illusory as more and more people choose, or are forced to make, similar decisions. In terms of individual mobility, the utility of the motor vehicle is diminishing as the number of cars on the road escalates. The prosperous 1950s and early 1960s were characterized by booming car ownership and, at least in the US and Australia, the car was expected to be the future of urban transport. The land use and transport planning procedures which emerged in the mid 1950s tended from the outset to be strongly associated with planning for roads and cars and pioneered the building of elaborate highway and freeway systems. However it transpired that freeways themselves spawned more and more traffic, becoming badly congested very soon after their completion. The obvious response to traffic congestion was to build more roads which were justified on technical grounds in terms of time, fuel and other perceived saving to the community from eliminating the congestion. 'This sets in motion a vicious circle or self-fulfilling prophecy of congestion, road building, sprawl, congestion and more road building.' (Newman, 1988, p. 15)

The net result is that London rush-hour traffic averages about 7 miles per hour; in Tokyo cars average 12 miles and in Paris 17. By comparison the average daily travel speed of 33 miles per hour in Southern California, where there are probably more miles of freeways than anywhere else in the world, may seem impressive. However as a result of a much lower population density than European cities, the advantage of speed is offset by the much longer distances required to travel to work. The irony is that a horse and buggy could cross downtown Los Angeles almost as fast in 1900 as an automobile can make this trip at 5pm today.

Motorway Madness

There is nothing inevitable about this rise and rise of the road. The state has played a major role in decisions about the extent to which transport investment is in roads as opposed to public transport. Again by comparison with Europe, American and Australian cities are characterized by a much heavier dependence on cars. Average Australian cities have four times, and US cities three times, more road supply per person than average European cities (Newman, 1988, p. 6). The politics of transport is dominated by conflict between road and rail lobbies, and technical discussions about efficient transport systems mask huge financial interests involved. The full extent of state subsidies to road transport are rarely exposed or documented. The expensive maintenance of motorways so heavily used by private road haulage companies is a case in point. The hidden subsidy to company car users via tax concessions and road maintenance is another. A Greater London Council study in 1986 found that the effective government contribution to company car users in London alone exceeded the revenue subsidy to London's public transport.

So far the story of the triumph of the car over other forms of transport technology may seem like another version of 'the paths not taken' argument, where people actively chose one type of technology in preference to others. However, in many cities that we now associate with the car, other forms of transport were not so long ago both preferred and extensively used. Contrary to popular impressions, Los Angeles is a sprawling metropolis not because of the automobile, but rather because it was built around the radial spurs of the electric railway system. It is almost forgotten today that in the United States there used to be a network of efficient and well-functioning urban and interurban rail systems in nearly every metropolitan area. By 1917, there were nearly 45,000 miles of trolley tracks which attracted billions of passengers. This transport system was not replaced by the motor car simply because of consumer choice. Rather, commercial interests joined forces at a key moment to close off all other options and ensure that henceforth investment would be channelled into automobile technology.

Beginning in the early 1930s, General Motors and other automobile tyre and oil interests, formed a holding company called National City Lines, whose sole objective was to purchase electric rail systems around the country and convert them to buses, which were manufactured and fuelled by members of the holding company. They acquired more than 100 rail systems in 45 cities, dismantled the electric lines and paved over the tracks. By the late fifties, about 90 per cent of the trolley network had been eliminated. The ultimate objective of this operation was to divert patrons of the earlier rail systems to General Motors cars. According to Snell, the reasons for this were clear: 'one subway car or electric rail car can take the place of from 50 to 100 automobiles'.[9] In 1949 General Motors, Standard Oil of California, and Firestone Tyres were found guilty of anti-trust conspiracy, but the damage had been done. By then, the political and economic power of the road lobby had succeeded in making American cities completely dependent upon the automobile. If there is a single force responsible for preventing the development of a diversified, balanced and ecologically-sound system of mass transportation, which was well within the bounds of the technologically feasible, it is the automotive and petroleum industries.

Women in the Slow Lane

If certain interests have conspired to make the motor car rule, the interests of certain social groups have been sacrificed to this end. The assumption of car ownership discriminates against the poor and the working class in general, and women constitute a disproportionate number of those affected. Older women and single mothers are among the poorest groups in society and have been literally left stranded in, or outside of, cities designed around the motor car. Although the automobile did not create suburbia, it certainly expanded and accelerated this process. The promotion of mass motor-car ownership has tended to exacerbate a greater dispersal of residential settlement often without any other mode of transport provided to service such areas.

These developments in transport policy have affected women and men differently.[10] Research on automobile use in Britain, North America and Australia indicates that proportionately more men than women have obtained drivers' licences, and that male car owners and drivers far outnumber female. Furthermore, while most women reside in car-owning households, evidence shows that women have considerably less access to the 'family car'. As a consequence of this, women are much more reliant than men on public transport to meet their travel requirements.

Despite women's low mobility, their travel needs are expanding as an increasing number of married women are entering the paid labour force and as the location of health care, educational resources and shopping facilities become more dispersed. Changes in patterns of consumption and service provision have increased the importance of transport access for women. For example, with the advent of the car, home-delivery services and corner stores gradually disappeared to be replaced by car-oriented supermarket complexes resulting in a significant increase in the proportion of time women spend on consumption activities. Even women who are not engaged in paid work must make frequent journeys to service the domestic needs of the household.

Although women are its primary users, in many ways public transport is not suitable for their needs and seems tailored to men's convenience. Recent work by geographers has drawn attention to the way the 'time-space maps' of the daily, weekly and overall life paths of individuals in their interactions with one another act as constraints on human activity. It has pointed to the major discrepancies between and within social communities in terms of fetters on mobility and communication. By emphasizing the critical connection between women's domestic roles and considerations of time and space, the time-geographic perspective adds a further dimension to our analysis of women's inequality. It has shown that the travel patterns of the two sexes are quite different and that, in response to domestic responsibilities, women elect to restrict the time spent on the journey to work. Given that family location is traditionally determined by its spatial relationship to the man's employment, women's opportunities are particularly restricted.

This is best illustrated by tracing the day-to-day activities of 'Jane', a single parent. 'Jane cannot leave home for work before a certain hour of the day because of her child's dependence on her for feeding and other needs, and because the sole accessible nursery is not yet open. Jane has no car and hence is faced with severe capability and coupling constraints in reaching the two 'stations' of the nursery and her place of work. Her choice of jobs is restricted by these constraints, and reciprocally the fact that she has little chance of acquiring or holding down a well-paid occupation reinforces the other constraints she faces in the trajectory of her path through the day. She has to collect her child in mid-afternoon, before the nursery closes, and is thus effectively restricted to part-time employment. Suppose she has a choice of two jobs, one better-paid and offering the chance to run a car, making it possible for her to take her child to a nursery further away from her home. On taking the more remunerative job, she finds that the time expended in driving to the nursery, to and from work and then back home again does not allow her time to do other necessary tasks, such as shopping, cooking and housework. She may therefore feel herself 'forced' to leave the job for a low-paid, part-time alternative nearer to home.[11]

This exposition of a mother's day emphasizes the role played by transport facilities in constraining women's access to employment, services and social life. In particular, whether women are employed part-time, full-time or at all is to a significant extent contingent on these spatial relations. Firstly, an increasing number of women work part-time and therefore travel more in off-peak periods when services are more erratic. Yet public transport is still overwhelmingly designed around the needs of full-time workers commuting to the central business district. Secondly, as Jane's story demonstrates, women's journeys have been shown to be more complex or multi-purpose than men's as a result of their roles as mothers, unpaid domestic workers and paid workers. This means that they do many more journeys of shorter duration than men and these journeys are across the city. Even if the journey can be accomplished by public transport it requires a number of changes and is therefore very time consuming and expensive. This is a major reason why the job market for women is much more geographically restricted than that for men.

Furthermore, more women than men travel with grocery bags, baby carriages and dependants. Waiting at bus stops, climbing up and down bus steps or worse still underground stairs is a nightmare for anyone who isn't young, able bodied and unencumbered. The dominance of the car has also made the city an alienating environment for women and pedestrians. To get under motorways that divide cities requires passing through often dark, dingy underground passages where again there are often many steps to negotiate. 'Urban motorways and rural trunk roads cut through women's lives, driving a noisy, polluting, dangerous wedge between their homes and workplaces, schools and health centres, causing them to walk roundabout routes, through hostile subways or over windy bridges, diverting and lengthening bus journeys, and creating unsafe, no-go areas of blank walls and derelict spaces' (Women and Transport Forum, 1988, p. 121). Women are more vulnerable to sexual harassment and male violence while using or waiting for public transport. The Greater London Council's (1985) survey on women and transport discovered that nearly a third of women in London never go out alone after dark, and for Asian women the figure is 40 per cent. Of those who do travel at night, black and ethnic minority women feel less safe than do white women as they have the additional fear of racist attack. As public transport becomes more automated, there are fewer staff on trains, buses and platforms so women feel even more at risk. Interestingly the most car-dominated cities are the most dangerous. Detroit has one of the highest per capita murder rates of any city in the West. In cities like these cars are used as much for protection as for transportation.

I have been emphasizing the way in which the organization of the transportation system compounds women's inequality, virtually locking them into a world of very limited physical space, and exacerbates the unequal allocation of resources within the city. Perhaps the most revealing illustration of the way reliance on public transport can restrict the access of certain groups to public amenities comes from an article called 'Do Artifacts Have Politics?' by Langdon Winner (1980). Winner tells us that anyone who has travelled the highways of America and has become used to the normal height of overpasses may well find something a little odd about some of the bridges over the parkways on Long Island, New York. Many of the overpasses are extraordinarily low, having as little as nine feet of clearance at the curb. Even those who notice this would not be inclined to attach any special meaning to it—we seldom give things like roads and bridges any consideration.

In fact, the two hundred low-hanging overpasses on Long Island were deliberately designed to achieve a particular social goal. Robert Moses, the master builder of roads, parks, bridges and other public works from the 1920s to the 1970s in New York, had these overpasses built to specifications that would discourage the presence of buses on his parkways. The reasons reflect Moses's class bias and racial prejudice. Affluent whites would be free to use their cars on the parkways for recreation and commuting. Poor people and blacks, who normally used public transport, were kept off the roads because the twelve-foot high buses could not get through the overpasses. One consequence was to limit access of racial minorities and low-income groups to Jones Beach, Moses's acclaimed public park. Although Winner does not mention women, women's dependence on public transport means that these physical arrangements also have a gender dimension.

This story illustrates that, far from being neutral, even seemingly innocuous technological forms such as roads and bridges embody and reinforce power relations. What is so significant about these vast technological projects is that they endure, such that for generations after Moses has gone, the highways and bridges he built to favour the use of the automobile over the development of mass transit continue to give New York much of its present form. 'Many of his monumental structures of concrete and steel embody a systematic social inequality, a way of engineering relationships among people that, after a time, becomes just another part of the landscape' (Winner, 1980, p. 124).

The Car Culture

Just as bridges may not be as innocent of political qualities as they may appear, so too cars have been shaped by a plethora of social and economic factors. Above I stressed that the dominance of the car was not simply about the efficient movement of people around cities but was ensured by economic forces. Means of travelling—whether by car, motorcycle or bicycle—are also consumer products charged with symbolic as well as economic and pragmatic meaning. The car is one of the central cultural commodities of the twentieth century: precisely because it is such a mass, commonplace technology, we often fail to appreciate its ideological significance. It is not simply technical efficiency that determines the design of cars but cultural forces that shape them.

Car manufacturers consciously design and style the appearance of their products to express consumer dreams, desires and aspirations. In turn, consumers purchase, along with their car, an image and a social identity. Cars are infused with powerful visual messages about the age, sex, race, social class and lifestyle of the user. Cars are a major feature of conspicuous consumption for men and have a central place in male culture. The masculine fantasies they represent take different forms, as can be seen by the contrasting designs of smooth, aerodynamic-style sports cars and the rugged, four-wheel-drive 'range rovers'. These have in common their symbolization of individual freedom and self-realization. Countless novels, films, popular songs and advertisements romanticize flight in a car and link cruising along the road with liberation. For men, cars afford a means of escape from domestic responsibilities, from family commitment, into a realm of private fantasy, autonomy and control.

Even more markedly than the car, the motorcycle is a symbolic object that represents physical toughness, virility, excitement, speed, danger and skill. Their conspicuous bodywork and mechanics resonate with their original military use, and speak of aggression and virility. Along with leather jackets, riders wear grease-stained jeans to express their technical competence. The experience of riding a bike encapsulates the outdoor, roving life of the wanderer with no ties. It also symbolizes a form of man's mastery of the machine; a powerful monster between his legs which he must tame. Trucks similarly are the giant iron horses of independent men who refer to themselves as 'cowboys' and boast of sexual encounters on the road. It is no accident that cars, trucks and motorcycles are usually personified as female and given women's names. They are after all the place where men feel most sexual, the vehicle for men's pursuit of sexual adventures, including their use of street prostitutes. In advertising their products, manufacturers associate these products with women's bodies and wild animals. Nubile women are draped over cars in advertisements. Men are the possessors and women the possessed. 'Manufacturers encourage the male user to perceive his machine as a temperamental woman who needs to be regularly maintained and pampered for high performance.' (Chambers, 1983, p. 308). Cars have long been a metaphor for sex and something wild in the already tamed urban environment. In recent years this imagery has become overlaid with new associations of the latest high tech computerization, bringing to the fore men's fascination with the power of technology—a theme further explored in the next chapter.

For all that I have been stressing that the car is a fetishized object for men, this is not the whole story nor the full extent of the gender relations embodied in the car. The design of the 'family car' reflects assumptions about the typical size of unit in which people wish to travel around. Furthermore, many cars are specifically designed with female drivers in mind. This is particularly explicit in the small hatchback car for 'running around town' and shopping. This is assumed to be the family's second car for the wife and mother to meet household needs. The powerful large car is destined for the male head of the household, although increasingly professional women are being targeted by manufacturers and advertisers as purchasers in their own right. Given the opportunity, women too enjoy driving fast and glamorous cars. However, for most women cars are a practical necessity to which they aspire for relief from drudgery and a release from home. They are also a relatively safe means of travel, given the violence and harassment to which women are subjected on public transport. And despite the prevalence of jokes about women drivers, in fact they are if anything more competent than men and much less likely to cause car accidents. Indeed the particular advantages that the car offers women sets up a tension for eco-feminism. While the car constitutes a major environmental hazard, for women, at least in the short term, demanding 'equal access' to the car is an important assertion of their right to independence, mobility and physical safety.

In this essay I have been concerned to establish the connections between the built environment and patriarchy. The development of the modern house and the organization of domestic space within it reflects cultural assumptions about family relationships, the home as women's place and women's place being in the home. Sexual divisions are not only physically built into houses, but into the whole urban structure. The modern city is, furthermore, constructed around a mode of transport that reflects and is organized in men's interests to the detriment of women. Once we recognize the gendered nature of the design and production of the built environment, once it is no longer seen as fixed, we can begin to make space for women.

Notes

1. According to W. and D. Andrews (1974, p. 316) the Rumford stove 'made possible the literal centralization of the woman to the activity of the house; technology, in short, placed the woman in the midst of things and not removed from them'.
2. Wright (1981, p. 256) notes that in the USA only 9 per cent of suburban women worked in 1950 compared with 27 per cent of the whole population.
3. To all intents and purposes of course the television is now the focal point of most living rooms, but it has not displaced the hearth, often being installed adjacent to the fireplace.
4. See D. Harvey (1989) and E. Soja (1989). One of the few articles that does attempt to draw out the implications of these changes for women is E. Harman (1983).
5. See A. Coleman (1985). For the classic critique, which is particularly interesting for its discussion of the consequences for bringing up children, see J. Jacobs (1962).
6. Indeed, some of these architectural principles have even gained royal approval! See The Prince of Wales (1989).
7. In England too there was much enthusiasm for cooperative housekeeping among the more socialist-inclined members of the Garden City Movement. Ebenezer Howard organized extensive experiments in cooperative housekeeping, building quadrangles of kitchenless units in the Garden Cities of Letchworth and Welwyn. According to Ravetz, however, the demise of domestic service was an important factor. 'It was perhaps this strong male interest in getting the housework done with minimum inconvenience to themselves that, more than any feminist inspiration, explains the interest of certain men or the garden city movement in collective housekeeping' (Ravetz, 1989, p. 192).
8. The source of information for this paragraph is M. Renner (1988) and the *New Internationalist* No. 195, May 1989, issue on 'Car Chaos'.
9. The elimination of the interurban rail systems is documented in detail by B. Snell, 'Report on American Ground Transport', Subcommittee on Antitrust and Monopoly, Senate Judiciary Committee, 26 February 1974.
10. The study of women and transportation is quite new and some interesting themes are emerging. See M. Cichocki (1980) and S. Fava (1980); L. Pickup (1988); Women and Transport Forum (1988) and V. Scharff (1988).
11. This summary of R. Palm and A. Pred (1978) is taken from A. Giddens (1984, pp. 114–15). In the original article, the authors make the important point that the daily prisms of women in various stages of the lifecycle and in various social classes are different.

References

Andrews, W. and D. 1974: 'Technology and the housewife in nineteenth-century America.' *Women's Studies*, 2, pp. 309–28.

Chambers, D. 1983: 'Symbolic equipment and the objects of leisure images.' *Leisure Studies*, 2, pp. 301–15.

Cichocki, M. 1980: 'Women's Travel Patterns in a Suburban Development' in G. Wekerle, R. Peterson, and D. Morley (eds): *New Space for Women*. Boulder, Colorado: Westview Press.

Coleman, A. 1985: *Utopia on Trial: Vision and Reality in Planned Housing*. London: Hilary Shipman.

Fava, S. 1980: 'Women's Place in the New Suburbia' in G. Wekerle, R. Peterson, and D. Morley (eds): *New Space for Women*. Boulder, Colorado: Westview Press.

Giddens, A. 1984: *The Constitution of Society*. Berkeley, California: University of California Press.

Harman, E. 1983: 'Capitalism patriarchy and the city' in C. Baldock and B. Cass (eds), *Women, Social Welfare and the State in Australia*. Sydney: Allen and Unwin.

Harvey, D. 1989: *The Condition of Postmodernity*. Oxford: Basil Blackwell.

Hayden, D. 1982: *The Grand Domestic Revolution: A History of Feminist Designs for American Homes, Neighborhoods, and Cities*. Cambridge, Massachusetts: MIT Press.

Huxley, M. 1988: 'Feminist Urban Theory: Gender, Class and the Built Environment'. *Transition*, 25, pp. 39–43.

Jacobs, J. 1962: *The Death and Life of Great American Cities.* London: Jonathan Cape.
Kennedy, M. 1981: 'Toward a Rediscovery of "Feminine" Principles In Architecture and Planning'. Women's Studies International Quarterly, 4, 1, pp. 75–81.
Kramarae, C. (ed.) 1988: *Technology and Women's Voices.* New York: Routledge & Kegan Paul.
Matrix (eds) 1984: *Making Space: Women and the Man-Made Environment.* London: Pluto Press.
Mumford, L. 1961: *The City in History.* New York: Harcourt, Brace and World..
Newman, P. 1988: 'Australian Cities at the Crossroads'. *Current Affairs Bulletin,* 65, 7, pp.4–15.
Palm, R. and Pred, A. 1978: 'The Status of American Women: A Time-Geographic View' in D. Lanegran and R. Palm (eds): *An Invitation to Geography.* New York: McGraw Hill.
Pickup, L. 1988: 'Hard to Get Around: A Study of Women's Travel Mobility' in J. Little, L. Peake, and P. Richardson (eds): *Women in Cities: Gender and the Urban Environment.* London: Macmillan.
The Prince of Wales 1989: *A Vision of Britain: A Personal View of Architecture.* London: Doubleday.
Ravetz, A. 1989: 'A View from the Interior' in Attfield, A. & Kirkham, P. (eds): *A View from the Interior: Feminism, Women and Design.* London: The Women's Press.
Renner, M. 1988: *Rethinking the Role of the Automobile.* Worldwatch Paper 84, Washington, June 1988.
Saegert, S. 1980: 'Masculine Cities and Feminine Suburbs: Polarized Ideas, Contradictory Realities'. *Signs,* 5, 3, pp. 96–111.
Scharff, V. 1988: 'Putting wheels on women's sphere' in Kramarae, C (ed.), 1988.
Soja, E. 1989: *Postmodern Geographies.* London: Verso.
Winner, L. 1980: 'Do Artifacts Have Politics?' *Daedalus,* 109, pp. 121–36.
Women and Transport Forum 1988: 'Women on the move: How public is public transport?' in Kramarae, C. (ed.) 1988.
Wright, G. 1981: *Building the Dream: A Social History of Housing in America.* New York: Pantheon.

SECTION 4

NEW SCIENCE, NEW KNOWLEDGE

BRINGING FEMINIST PERSPECTIVES INTO SCIENCE AND TECHNOLOGY STUDIES

In section 3 we argued that scientists and engineers hold preconceptions about gender differences that have influenced their choice of subjects, research methods, standards of evidence, interpretation of data, and conclusions about the natural and physical world. When these preconceptions are directed at research on human social life, they have particularly regressive implications, as Ruth Bleier pointed out in her critique of sociobiology in section 3. Nineteenth-century ideas about the "natural" limitations of women's intellectual capacities have been revived in the late twentieth century under the guise of evolutionary psychology. There are two consequences of this. One is that cultural ideas about women's incapacities and men's capabilities have great staying power, despite efforts to prove them inaccurate. Another consequence is that women of intellectual achievement make their way against a backdrop of assumptions about how exceptional they are—the exception that proves the rule that women do not belong in science.

When feminist critiques of science emerged in the 1970s, some women in science expressed fears that the feminist writings and critiques of science, in the effort to revalue women's accomplishments, implied that women scientists necessarily did science "differently," and "different" was not what they wanted to be.[1] "Women's science" would always be viewed as inferior science, and women in science did not want their work to be considered inferior to work done by their male colleagues. These women maintained that gender was irrelevant to the practice of science. As Evelyn Fox Keller puts it, their confidence "in the standards of scientific rigor was excessive."[2] Not only did the scientific method fail to eradicate social biases, it was sometimes used in the service of supporting them.

But is this inability to eliminate bias a flaw intrinsic in the scientific method or in those who use it? For an answer, some scholars point to the origins of modern Western science in the misogynist enclaves of Christian monasteries during the High Middle Ages, where the touchstone philosophies and methods of science emerged within the context of debates about the superiority of men over women.[3] In this view the scientific method is inescapably a product of its social, historical, and economic contexts, and since those reflected male-centered perspectives, so, too, does the scientific method. Thus nature is imagined as a female, to be conquered and dominated by the (male) scientist.[4] Others point to the specific psychodynamics involved in practicing objectivity, and the ways that the scientific method distinguishes scientific knowledge (and scientists) from other kinds of knowledge (and scholars).[5] One significant tenet of the scientific method is that the researcher is distant and separate from the subject of research, so that one may be an objective observer without influencing or being influenced by the observed phenomenon. This cognitive distance is understood to promote dispassionate, unbiased observation and control over experimental conditions, but it is also a form of rationality that is encouraged more often in men than women.[6]

The pursuit of scientific knowledge conventionally requires the practice of both the scientific method and objectivity. But because both are implicated in the marginalization of women in science, the question arises of whether there can be a "feminist science." Can there be a way to retain the goals of scientific research that focuses on using systematic methods to develop reproducible, reliable knowledge about the natural world without trying to "dominate" nature and perpetuate notions of gender inequality? There has certainly been excellent scientific work that did not embrace this method. Barbara McClintock, a Nobel laureate, was characterized as having a nontraditional approach to scientific study. She thought it was important to work with the whole organism, to know it well enough that she did not miss the subtle changes that occurred between generations in her corn crops. She also did not throw away data that challenged prevailing views in her field of research. Though McClintock did not think of this as feminist science, it was certainly not science as usual. Nevertheless, it was good science, outstanding science, and though it took some time for her work to be appreciated, Barbara McClintock's contributions will stand as some of the most remarkable work in her field for many years to come.

In certain fields, where much of the early research was conducted by a fairly homogeneous group of researchers (middle- to upper-class Western and/or European white men, for example), new perspectives from women and people of color have made clear changes to the dominant paradigms of those fields. In particular, the field of primatology is often cited as having been greatly influenced (and improved) by the presence of women. However, Linda Marie Fedigan, in her essay "Is Primatology a Feminist Science?" points out that while the field does in fact exhibit characteristics that conform to current ideas about feminist science, and does have a significant number of female scientists, it is not necessarily true that primatology was specifically informed by the women's movement or by the feminist critique of science. Though she concludes that primatology is indeed a "feminist science," she suggests that this may be due to the influence of other forces distinct from or in conjunction with feminist perspectives, rather than resulting primarily from the influx of women in the field and the development of a feminist critique of science. For example, the field may have come to a consensus that "feminist" scientific practices—such as factoring in sex and gender differences in research, developing a point of view that includes the female subject as well as the male one, viewing nature as a phenomenon that should be understood but not dominated, moving away from reductionism, and having a diverse community of researchers—may have been encouraged by the presence of women and by a scientific culture influenced by the women's movement, and may have improved primatological research.

Some feminist scholars in the social sciences have embraced the need for a "feminist science" both as a matter of improving our research and as an ethical imperative.[7] For example, in a recent paper Paige Smith and her colleagues described the research that they have been conducting about violence against women.[8] Specifically, they wanted to find a better method for characterizing, quantifying, and understanding the battering of women. Their idea was to begin by asking women in shelters what they thought battering was. Because they began with their subjects and attended to what these women thought, they were able to recognize and describe battering in an entirely new way.

Prior to the work of Smith and her colleagues, descriptions and surveys of battering had a focus on acute events covering a narrow time frame, such as a single assault taking place on one night, and there was an absence of any discourse on gender and on the specific personalities involved. Because the focus was so narrow, a significant percentage of battered women did not even identify themselves as battered when surveyed. Based on their interviews and documentation of the experiences of battered women, Smith and her colleagues developed a new framework by which to assess battering. This framework, called the Women's Experience with Battering (WEB) Scale, identifies ten items that are unique to and consistent among women who have been victims of battering. The list (see below) is striking because of its focus on the people involved, as well as on power dynamics. It also reveals the depth to which an abusive relationship can be ongoing and have both lasting and cumulative effects. The importance of research such as this cannot be overstated, especially because of its focus on women and its clear goal of improving women's lives. As Smith and her colleagues say: "This article [is] one way of using both qualitative methods and a feminist perspective to inform quantitative methods. A critical feminist concept that informed our research process was that battered women are the experts of their own lives."

The WEB Scale items ask participants to respond on a scale from "strongly agree" to "strongly disagree." The items are as follows:

1. He makes me feel unsafe even in my own home.
2. I feel ashamed of the things he does to me.
3. I try not to rock the boat because I am afraid of what he might do.
4. I feel like I am programmed to react a certain way to him.
5. I feel like he keeps me prisoner.
6. He makes me feel like I have no control over my life, no power, no protection.
7. I hide the truth from others because I am afraid not to.
8. I feel owned and controlled by him.
9. He can scare me without laying a hand on me.
10. He has a look that goes straight through me and terrifies me.

The insights of Smith and her colleagues resulted in the creation of new surveys and questionnaires that resonate with battered women and provide the researcher with a much richer and more accurate set of information. This woman-centered approach takes into account the subjective experiences of the battered women, providing a space in which they are valued and heard. It requires that the researchers see the women as active participants in the development of the research about them. They are not objects to be observed by and used for the benefit of a distant researcher. Again, this is not science as usual, but it is certainly systematic and reproducible research that has as a goal the improvement of women's lives. One could argue that as such, it is a good example of feminist science.

Sandra Harding has argued that there is no unique feminist method in the social sciences, but that feminist research nonetheless shares four characteristics: (1) the questions asked emerge from woman-centered concerns; (2) the purposes of the inquiry stem from the need to foster new and more acccurate knowledge for the benefit of women and society; (3) the hypotheses and evidence are not transparently unbiased and apolitical; and (4) the relationship between the researcher and the subject of study is a mutual and reflexive one.[9]

Feminist research in the sciences and in engineering could involve all of these characteristics as well. However, when the subject of study is the physical rather than the social world, new issues emerge. The sociological insight that scientific knowledge—indeed, all knowledge—is socially constructed poses a major challenge to a basic assumption of science: that scientists' explanations of natural phenomena mirror the natural world. For many, the notion that scientists' descriptions of the natural world can only be models of those phenomena is counter to their professional training. It also poses a challenge to those who would bring political issues into science, since their professional communities are likely to view their political commitments as a threat to objectivity.[10]

It is an underappreciated fact that there are many feminists in science and engineering, though their philosophical positions on issues of gender in science can vary greatly. There are at least four general stances that feminists in science take in thinking about science—professional equity, social equity, empiricist, and constructionist. Within a commitment to gender equity, there are two camps of feminist practice, one focusing on science and one focusing on society. Some women and men are committed to gender equity in education and employment in scientific and engineering professions, but they dismiss the notion that scientific research is itself tainted by gender biases. Others feel that the meritocracy in science and engineering rewards women and men equally, most of the time, and that gender differences in professional outcomes are a result of the different choices that women and men make about their work and family responsibilities; but at the same time, they support and participate in activist initiatives for the society as a whole, such as the National Abortion Rights Action League or the National Organization for Women.

Empiricist feminists take a position that includes an analysis of the contents of science as well as the equity positions of the first two. Empiricist feminists acknowledge that gender bias occurs in the formulation of questions and the interpretation of data, but they embrace the scientific method as a corrective because they see gender bias as producing "bad science."[11] A fourth stance is taken by what we term constructivist feminists, who accept the premise that all knowledge, including scientific knowledge, is socially constructed. For this group, the scientific method cannot eliminate bias, because it is the norms and values of the scientific community that determine what is considered adequate or inadequate research. If that community sustains and promotes gender biases (however unwittingly), then community values and research practices intertwine to sustain gender-biased science. Because social biases are unavoidable in research, scientific practice should include a recognition and evaluation of their impact as part of the research method.

One of the by-products of the concept of objectivity is that it is also employed as a way to structure the relationships among the people who practice science. It promotes a cognitive slippage that can conflate the evaluation of data with the evaluation of the researcher who produced the data. In academia, for instance, most scientists assume that the strengths and weaknesses of a data set can be determined by a set of standards that provide objective measures, just as the evaluation of a researcher's worth is measured by a set of standards. The standards in both cases are established by community consensus, sometimes in unspoken ways, but the standards can be and sometimes are inadequate or incomplete. When the topic is an experiment or an interpretation, the problem of inadequate or incomplete standards of evidence becomes part of the professional conversation about the usefulness of the research. However, when standards drive the structuring of social relations within science (that is, who is hired and promoted, who makes decisions about what), only measurable qualities are included in evaluations. Those who launch professional conversations about expanding the standards are met with the charge that they seek to lower the standards. Yet the evidence indicates that prevailing standards for achievement in science are meritocratic for men but not for women.[12]

Since no science is undertaken without organized social activity, a whole host of arrangements is influenced by commitments to objectivity. This includes the daily interactions among colleagues, the way that individual laboratories are structured and managed, the formation of nonoverlapping and largely noninteracting fields of research, and the unspoken but well-known ranking of these fields in terms of value and importance. Individuals are then ranked according to academic pedigree within their field. In fact, one can view the entire process of scientific training as an exercise in learning about or being indoctrinated in the system that maintains hierarchy: in status and rank, in the laboratory, in the department, and in the institution vis-à-vis claims to objective measures of worth.

The commitment to hierarchy as an organizing principle in professional life also has an influence on the areas of inquiry ranked as important and, in turn, on what students learn about the natural world. Bonnie Spanier argues, for instance, that an ideological commitment to hierarchy in science has led to an emphasis on techniques from recombinant DNA technology that privilege genetics over more holistic approaches to biology. Students in molecular biology are taught to understand the different subfields as hierarchically related, with molecular genetics at the top, supported by necessary but lesser fields and supplanting the wider focus of biology altogether. As a result, courses reduce life to the reproduction of genetic information, rather than seeing it as the consequence of the complex interactions among physiochemical reactions and organisms and environments. The gene carries the master code for life, and all else follows and is directed by it.[13]

Because of the influence of practices on content, then, answering the question: Can there be a feminist science? entails considering the possibilities for new organizational forms for science and engineering—in the workplace, in the evaluation and assessment processes, in educational arrangements, in funding practices, and in setting priorities for research directions. This is the point that Helen E. Longino makes in her essay "Can There Be a Feminist Science?"

Longino argues that, counter to the idea that good science must be value-free, we should attach feminist values to the process of doing science. Feminists in science who are committed to the conventions of science have taken the stance that science as usual is bad science, because the information about the world that it provides is partial at best, due to the historical lack of women in the development, practice, and concerns of research, and due to the male-centered perspectives that follow from the exclusion of women. Longino rejects this approach and argues that it is possible to be committed to particular values and still do good science. To demonstrate her argument, Longino examines how scientific assumptions have guided the interpretation of data on the influence of hormone exposure on gender-role behavior. She rejects determinist models that extrapolate from results gained from animal research, and promotes an alternative model that assumes and fully acknowledges human capacities for self-knowledge, self-reflection, and self-determination. Longino suggests that we do not restrict ourselves to eliminating bias, but that we trade one set of values for another in our assumptions, in order to reconstruct frameworks in science so that they are based on feminist ideals and principles. For Longino, this means not only a scientific revolution but a social revolution—totally reconstructing the social and political context in which science is done.

Rachel Maines, in her article "Socially Camouflaged Technologies: The Case of the Electromechanical Vibrator," takes us back to a different social and political context to show in historical relief how distorted science can affect women's lives. She examines the influence of cultural beliefs about female behavior and sexuality on the medical treatment of women for what the terminology of the day called "hysteria." The development of the electromechanical vibrator was in response to the needs of the medical community to reduce the cost and labor requirements of "treating" female disorders by physician-assisted masturbation. This is a particularly striking example of how a new technology, ostensibly developed for the care of women, was not developed in response to the needs or interests of women in sexual satisfaction, nor was its development woman-centered in any meaningful way. Rather, this is an instance where a medical tool was developed in order to relieve the male-dominated medical community of a task that was at once onerous and ethically questionable, especially for God-fearing physicians. The sexual desire of women was medicalized and treated as if it were a disease. As Maines explains in the article, because of the social taboos associated with masturbation in general and with female masturbation and sexuality in particular, physician-assisted masturbation was camouflaged, as were the associated technologies, by the authority and respectability of the medical profession. As a result, women were absent from the discourse, even as they were the topic of discussion.

We close this section with a study by Cynthia Kraus, "Naked Sex in Exile: On the Paradox of the 'Sex Question' in Feminism and in Science." Kraus examines the ways in which biological sex itself has been manipulated in *Drosophila* research as a standardized and routine laboratory practice. These manipulations are used in the service of studying not sex difference but rather the role of temperature in development. She points to feminist scientists' critiques of an overreliance on assumptions about sexual dimorphism in order to ask the question: "What is real/biological about biological sex?" Within the context of *Drosophila* research, even the biological can be socially constructed.

NOTES

[1] Helen E. Longino and Evelynn Hammonds, "Conflicts and Tensions in the Feminist Study of Gender and Science," in Marianne Hirsch and Evelyn Fox Keller, eds., *Conflicts in Feminism* (New York: Routledge, 1990).

[2] For an elaboration of this debate within the history of women in science, see Evelyn Fox Keller, "The Wo/Man Scientist: Issues of Sex and Gender in the Pursuit of Science," in Harriet Zuckerman, Jonathan Cole, and John Bruer, eds., *The Outer Circle: Women in the Scientific Community* (New York: Norton, 1991).

[3] David Noble, *A World without Women: The Christian Clerical Culture of Western Science* (New York: Oxford University Press, 1992). See also Londa Schiebinger, *The Mind Has No Sex? Women in the Origins of Modern Science* (Cambridge, Mass.: Harvard University Press, 1989).

[4] Genevieve Lloyd, "Reason, Science, and the Domination of Matter," in Evelyn Fox Keller and Helen Longino, eds., *Feminism and Science* (New York: Oxford University Press, 1996).

[5] Evelyn Fox Keller, "Dynamic Autonomy: Objects as Subjects," in *Reflections on Gender and Science* (New Haven, Conn.: Yale University Press, 1985); Susan Bordo, "The Cartesian Masculinization of Thought," *Signs: Journal of Women in Culture and Society* 11, 3 (1986): 439–56.

[6] For a discussion of object relations theory and gender in relation to scientific objectivity, see Evelyn Fox Keller, "Feminism and Science," *Signs: Journal of Women in Culture and Society* 7, 3 (1982): 589–602; see also Nancy Chodorow, *The Reproduction of Mothering* (Berkeley: University

of California Press, 1978); and Nancy Chodorow, "Gender as a Personal and Cultural Construction," *Signs: Journal of Women in Culture and Society* 20, 3 (1995): 516–44. For a different view that focuses on women's psychological development as driven by connections to others, see Judith Jordan et al., *Women's Growth in Connection* (New York: Guilford Press, 1991).

[7] See, for example, Mary Margaret Fonow and Judith A. Cook, *Beyond Methodology: Feminist Scholarship as Lived Research* (Bloomington: Indiana University Press, 1991); and Shulamit Reinharz, *Feminist Methods in Social Research* (New York: Oxford University Press, 1992).

[8] P. H. Smith, J. B. Smith, and J. A. L. Earp, "Beyond the Measurement Trap: A Reconstructed Conceptualization and Measurement of Woman Battering," *Psychology of Women Quarterly* 23 (1999): 177–93, esp. 189–90.

[9] Sandra Harding and Merrill Hintikka, eds., *Discovering Reality: Feminist Perspectives on Epistemology, Metaphysics, Methodology, and Philosophy of Science* (Dordrecht, Holland: D. Reidel, 1983).

[10] Sandra Harding, *Whose Science, Whose Knowledge? Thinking from Women's Lives* (Ithaca, N.Y.: Cornell University Press, 1991), 79.

[11] Sandra Harding, "The Instability of the Analytical Categories of Feminist Theory," *Signs: Journal of Women in Culture and Society* 11, 4 (1986): 645–64. For an extensive discussion of the various camps in feminist theory, see also Alison Jaggar and Paula Rothenberg, eds., *Feminist Frameworks* (New York: McGraw-Hill, 1992).

[12] Scott Long et al., "Rank Advancement in Academic Careers: Sex Differences and the Effects of Productivity," *American Sociological Review* 58, 5 (1993): 703–22.

[13] Bonnie Spanier, *Im/Partial Science: Gender Ideology in Molecular Biology* (Bloomington: Indiana University Press, 1995).

CAN THERE BE A FEMINIST SCIENCE?

Helen E. Longino

The question of this title conceals multiple ambiguities. Not only do the sciences consist of many distinct fields, but the term "science" can be used to refer to a method of inquiry, a historically changing collection of practices, a body of knowledge, a set of claims, a profession, a set of social groups, etc. And as the sciences are many, so are the scholarly disciplines that seek to understand them: philosophy, history, sociology, anthropology, psychology. Any answer from the perspective of some one of these disciplines will, then, of necessity, be partial. In this essay, I shall be asking about the possibility of theoretical natural science that is feminist and I shall ask from the perspective of a philosopher. Before beginning to develop my answer, however, I want to review some of the questions that could be meant, in order to arrive at the formulation I wish to address.

The question could be interpreted as factual, one to be answered by pointing to what feminists in the sciences are doing and saying: "Yes, and this is what it is." Such a response can be perceived as question-begging, however. Even such a friend of feminism as Stephen Jay Gould dismisses the idea of a distinctively feminist or even female contribution to the sciences. In a generally positive review of Ruth Bleier's book, *Science and Gender,* Gould (1984) brushes aside her connection between women's attitudes and values and the interactionist science she calls for. Scientists (male, of course) are already proceeding with wholist and interactionist research programs. Why, he implied, should women or feminists have any particular, distinctive, contributions to make? There is not masculinist and feminist science, just good and bad science. The question of a feminist science cannot be settled by pointing, but involves a deeper, subtler investigation.

The deeper question can itself have several meanings. One set of meanings is sociological, the other conceptual. The sociological meaning proceeds as follows. We know what sorts of social conditions make misogynist science possible. The work of Margaret Rossiter (1982) on the history of women scientists in the United States and the work of Kathryn Addelson (1983) on the social structure of professional science detail the relations between a particular social structure for science and the kinds of science produced. What sorts of social conditions would make feminist science possible? This is an important question, one I am not equipped directly to investigate, although what I can investigate is, I believe, relevant to it. This is the second, conceptual, interpretation of the question: what sort of sense does it make to talk about a feminist science? Why is the question itself not an oxymoron, linking, as it does, values and ideological commitment with the idea of impersonal, objective, value-free, inquiry? This is the problem I wish to address in this essay.

The hope for a feminist theoretical natural science has concealed an ambiguity between content and practice. In the content sense the idea of a feminist science involves a number of assumptions and calls a number of visions to mind. Some theorists have written as though a feminist science is one the theories of which encode a particular world view, characterized by complexity, interaction and wholism. Such a science is said to be feminist because it is the expression and valorization of a female sensibility or cognitive temperament. Alternatively, it is claimed that women have certain traits (dispositions to attend to particulars, interactive rather than individualist and controlling social attitudes and behaviors) that enable them to understand the true character of natural processes (which are complex and interactive).[1] While proponents of this interactionist view see it as an improvement over most contemporary science, it has also been branded as soft—misdescribed as non-mathematical. Women in the sciences who feel they are being asked to do not better science, but inferior science, have responded angrily to this characterization of feminist science, thinking that it is simply new clothing for the old idea that women can't do science. I think that the interactionist view can be defended against this response, although that requires rescuing it from some of its proponents as well. However, I also think that the characterization of feminist science as the expression of a distinctive female cognitive temperament has other drawbacks. It first conflates feminine with feminist. While it is important to reject the traditional derogation of the virtues assigned to women, it is also important to remember that women are *constructed* to occupy positions of social subordinates. We should not uncritically embrace the feminine.

This characterization of feminist science is also a version of recently propounded notions of a 'women's standpoint' or a 'feminist standpoint' and suffers from the same suspect universalization that these ideas suffer from. If there is one such standpoint, there are many: as Maria Lugones and Elizabeth Spelman spell out in their tellingly entitled article, "Have We Got a Theory for You: Feminist Theory, Cultural Imperialism, and the Demand for 'The Woman's Voice,'" women are too diverse in our experiences to generate a single cognitive framework (Lugones and Spelman 1983). In addition, the sciences are themselves too diverse for me to think that they might be equally transformed by such a framework. To reject this concept of a feminist science, however, is not to disengage science from feminism. I want to suggest that we focus on science as practice rather than content, as process rather than product; hence, not on feminist science, but on doing science as a feminist.

The doing of science involves many practices: how one structures a laboratory (hierarchically or collectively), how one relates to other scientists (competitively or cooperatively), how and whether one engages in political struggles over affirmative action. It extends also to intellectual practices, to the activities of scientific inquiry, such as observation and reasoning. Can there be a feminist scientific inquiry? This possibility is seen to be problematic against the background of certain standard presuppositions about science. The claim that there could be a feminist science in the sense of an intellectual practice is either nonsense because oxymoronic as suggested above or the claim is interpreted to mean that established science (science as done and dominated by men) is wrong about the world. Feminist science in this latter interpretation is presented as correcting the errors of masculine, standard science and as revealing the truth that is hidden by masculine 'bad' science, as taking the sex out of science.

Both of these interpretations involve the rejection of one approach as incorrect and the embracing of the other as the way to a truer understanding of the natural world. Both trade one absolutism for another. Each is a side of the same coin, and that coin, I think, is the idea of a value-free science. This is the idea that scientific methodology guarantees the independence of scientific inquiry from values of value-related considerations. A science or a scientific research program informed by values is *ipso facto* "bad science." "Good science" is inquiry protected by methodology from values and ideology. This same idea underlies Gould's response to Bleier, so it bears closer scrutiny. In the pages that follow, I shall examine the idea of value-free science and then apply the results of that examination to the idea of feminist scientific inquiry.

. . . .

In earlier articles (Longino 1981, 1983b; Longino and Doell 1983), I've used similar considerations to argue that scientific objectivity has to be reconceived as a function of the communal structure of scientific inquiry rather than as a property of individual scientists. I've then used these notions about scientific methodology to show that science displaying masculine bias is not *ipso facto* improper or 'bad' science; that the fabric of science can neither rule out the expression of bias nor legitimate it. So I've argued that both the expression of masculine bias in the sciences and feminist criticism of research exhibiting that bias are—shall we say—business as usual; that scientific inquiry should be expected to display the deep metaphysical and normative commitments of the culture in which it flourishes; and finally that criticism of the deep assumptions that guide scientific reasoning about data is a proper part of science.

The argument I've just offered about the idea of a value-free science is similar in spirit to those earlier arguments. I think it makes it possible to see these questions from a slightly different angle.

There is a tradition of viewing scientific inquiry as somehow inexorable. This involves supposing that the phenomena of the natural world are fixed in determinate relations with each other, that these relations can be known and formulated in a consistent and unified way. This is not the old "unified science" idea of the logical positivists, with its privileging of physics. In its "unexplicated" or "pre-analytic" state, it is simply the idea that there is one consistent, integrated or coherent, true theoretical treatment of all natural phenomena. . . .

It's no longer possible, in a century that has seen the splintering of the scientific disciplines, to give such a unified description of the objects of inquiry. But the belief that the job is to discover fixed relations of some sort, and that the application of observation, experiment and reason leads ineluctably to unifiable, if not unified, knowledge of an independent reality, is still with us. It is evidenced most clearly in two features of scientific rhetoric: the use of the passive voice as in "it is concluded that . . ." or "it has been discovered that . . ." and the attribution of agency to the data, as in "the data suggest. . . ." Such language has been criticized for the abdication of responsibility it indicates. Even more, the scientific inquirer, and we with her, become passive observers, victims of the truth. The idea of a value-free science is integral to this view of scientific inquiry. And if we reject that idea we can also reject our roles as passive onlookers, helpless to affect the course of knowledge.

Let me develop this point somewhat more concretely and autobiographically. Biologist Ruth Doell and I have been examining studies in three areas of research on the influence of sex hormones on human behavior and cognitive performance: research on the influence of pre-natal, *in utero,* exposure to higher or lower than normal levels of androgens and estrogens on so-called 'gender-role' behavior in children, influence of androgens (pre- and post-natal) on homosexuality in women, and influence of lower than normal (for men) levels of androgen at puberty on spatial abilities (Doell and Longino, forthcoming).

The studies we looked at are vulnerable to criticism of their data and their observation methodologies. They also show clear evidence of androcentric bias—in the assumption that there are just two sexes and two genders (us and them), in the designation of appropriate and inappropriate behaviors for male and female children, in the caricature of lesbianism, in the assumption of male mathematical superiority. We did not find, however, that these assumptions mediated the inferences from data to theory that we found objectionable. These sexist assumptions did affect the way the data were described. What mediated the inferences from the alleged data (i.e., what functioned as auxiliary hypotheses or what provided auxiliary hypotheses) was what we called the linear model—the assumption that there is a direct one-way causal relationship between pre- or post-natal hormone levels and later behavior or cognitive performance. To put it crudely, fetal gonadal hormones organize the brain at critical periods of development. The organism is thereby disposed to respond in a range of ways to a range of environmental stimuli. The assumption of unidirectional programming is supposedly supported by the finding of such a relationship in other mammals; in particular, by experiments demonstrating the dependence of sexual behaviors—mounting and lordosis—on perinatal hormone exposure and the finding of effects of sex hormones on the development of rodent brains. To bring it to bear on humans is to ignore, among other things, some important differences between human brains and those of other species. It also implies a willingness to regard humans in a particular way—to see us as produced by factors over which we have no control. Not only are we, as scientists, victims of the truth, but we are the prisoners of our physiology.[2] In the name of extending an explanatory model, human capacities for self-knowledge, self-reflection, self-determination are eliminated from any role in human action (at least in the behaviors studied).

Doell and I have therefore argued for the replacement of that linear model of the role of the brain in behavior by one of much greater complexity that includes physiological, environmental, historical and psychological elements. Such a model allows not only for the interaction of physiological and environmental factors but also for the interaction of these with a continuously self-modifying, self-representational (and self-organizing) central processing system. . . . We argue that a model of at least that degree of complexity is necessary to account for the human behaviors studies in the sex hormones and behavior research and that if gonadal hormones function at all at these levels, they will probably be found at most to facilitate or inhibit neural processing in general. The strategy we take in our argument is to show that the degree of intentionality involved in the behaviors in question is greater than is presupposed by the hormonal influence researchers and to argue that this degree of intentionality implicates the higher brain processes.

To this point Ruth Doell and I agree. I want to go further and describe what we've done from the perspective of the above philosophical discussion of scientific methodology.

Abandoning my polemical mood for a more reflective one, I want to say that, in the end, commitment to one or another model is strongly influenced by values or other contextual features. The models themselves determine the relevance and interpretation of data. The linear or complex models are not in turn independently or conclusively supported by data. I doubt for instance that value-free inquiry will reveal the efficacy or inefficacy of intentional states or of physiological factors like hormone exposure in human action. I think instead that a research program in neuro-science that assumes the linear model and sex-gender dualism will show the influence of hormone exposure on gender-role behavior. And I think that a research program in neuro-science and psychology proceeding on the assumption that humans do possess the capacities for self-consciousness, self-reflection, and self-determination, and which then asks how the structure of the human brain and nervous system enables the expression of these capacities, will reveal the efficacy of intentional states (understood as very complex sorts of brain states).

While this latter assumption does not itself contain normative terms, I think that the decision to adopt it is motivated by value-laden considerations—by the desire to understand ourselves and others as self-determining (at least some of the time), that is, as capable of acting on the basis of concepts or representations of ourselves and the world in which we act. (Such representations are not necessarily correct, they are surely mediated by our cultures; all we wish to claim is that they are efficacious.) I think further that this desire on Ruth Doell's and my part is, in several ways, an aspect of our feminism. Our preference for a neurobiological model that allows for agency, for the efficacy of intentionality is partly a validation of our (and everyone's) subjective experience of thought, deliberation, and choice. One of the tenets of feminist research is the valorization of subjective experience, and so our preference in this regard conforms to feminist research patterns. There is, however, a more direct way in which our feminism is expressed in this preference. Feminism is many things to many people, but it is at its core in part about the expansion of human potentiality. When feminists talk of breaking out and do break out of socially prescribed sex-roles, when feminists criticize the institutions of domination, we are thereby insisting on the capacity of humans—male and female—to act on perceptions of self and society and to act to bring about changes in self and society on the basis of those perceptions. (Not overnight and not by a mere act of will. The point is that we act.) And so our criticism of theories of the hormonal influence or determination of so-called gender-role behavior is not just a rejection of the sexist bias in the description of the phenomena—the behavior of the children studied, the sexual lives of lesbians, etc.—but of the limitations on human capacity imposed by the analytic model underlying such research.[3]

While the argument strategy we adopt against the linear model rests on a certain understanding of intention, the values motivating our adoption of that understanding remain hidden in that polemical context. Our political commitments, however, presuppose a certain understanding of human action, so that when faced with a conflict between these commitments and a particular model of brain-behavior relationships we allow the political commitments to guide the choice.

The relevance of my argument about value-free science should be becoming clear. Feminists—in and out of science—often condemn masculine bias in the sciences from the vantage point of commitment to a value-free science. Androcentric bias, once identified, can then be seen as a violation of the rules, as "bad" science. Feminist science, by contrast, can eliminate that bias and produce better, good, more true or gender free science. From that perspective the process I've just described is anathema. But if scientific methods generated by constitutive values cannot guarantee independence from contextual values, then that approach to sexist science won't work. We cannot restrict ourselves simply to the elimination of bias, but must expand our scope to include the detection of limiting and interpretive frameworks and the finding or construction of more appropriate frameworks. We need not, indeed should not, wait for such a framework to emerge from the data. In waiting, if my argument is correct, we run the danger of working unconsciously with assumptions still laden with values from the context we seek to change. Instead of remaining passive with respect to the data and what the data suggest, we can acknowledge our ability to affect the course of knowledge and fashion or favor research programs that are consistent with the values and commitments we express in the rest of our lives. From this perspective, the idea of a value-free science is not just empty, but pernicious.

Accepting the relevance to our practice as scientists of our political commitments does not imply simple and crude impositions of those ideas onto the corner of the natural world under study. If we recognize, however, that knowledge is shaped by the assumptions, values and interests of a culture and that, within limits, one can choose one's culture, then it's clear that as scientists/theorists we have a choice. We can continue to do establishment science, comfortably wrapped in the myths of scientific rhetoric or we can alter our intellectual allegiances. While remaining committed to an abstract goal of understanding, we can choose to whom, socially and politically, we are accountable in our pursuit of that goal. In particular we can choose between being accountable to the traditional establishment or to our political comrades.

Such accountability does not demand a radical break with the science one has learned and practiced. The development of a "new" science involves a more dialectical evolution and more continuity with established science than the familiar language of scientific revolutions implies.

In focusing on accountability and choice, this conception of feminist science differs from those that proceed from the assumption of a congruence between certain models of natural processes and women's inherent modes of understanding.[4] I am arguing instead for the deliberate and active choice of an interpretive model and for the legitimacy of basing that choice on political considerations in this case. Obviously model choice is also constrained by (what we know of) reality, that is, by the data. But reality (what we know of it) is, I have already argued, inadequate to uniquely determine model choice. The feminist theorists mentioned above have focused on the relation between the content of a theory and female values or experiences, in particular on the perceived congruence between interactionist, wholist visions of nature and a form of understanding and set of values widely attributed to women. In contrast, I am suggesting that a feminist scientific practice admits political considerations as relevant constraints on reasoning, which, through their influence on reasoning and interpretation, shape content. In this specific case, those considerations in combination with the phenomena support an explanatory model that is highly interactionist, highly complex. This argument is so far, however, neutral on the issue of whether an interactionist and complex account of natural processes will always be the preferred one. If it is preferred, however, this will be because of explicitly political considerations and not because interactionism is the expression of "women's nature."

The integration of a political commitment with scientific work will be expressed differently in different fields. In some, such as the complex of research programs having a bearing on the understanding of human behavior, certain moves, such as the one described above, seem quite obvious. In others it may not be clear how to express an alternate set of values in inquiry, or what values would be appropriate. The first step, however, is to abandon the idea that scrutiny of the data yields a seamless web of knowledge. The second is to think through a particular field and try to understand just what its unstated and fundamental assumptions are and how they influence the course of inquiry. Knowing something of the history of a field is necessary to this process, as is continued conversation with other feminists.

The feminist interventions I imagine will be local (i.e., specific to a particular area of research); they may not be exclusive (i.e., different feminist perspectives may be represented in theorizing); and they will be in some way continuous with existing scientific work. The accretion of such interventions, of science done by feminists as feminists, and by members of other disenfranchised groups, has the potential, nevertheless, ultimately to transform the character of scientific discourse.

Doing science differently requires more than just the will to do so and it would be disingenuous to pretend that our philosophies of science are the only barrier. Scientific inquiry takes place in a social, political and economic context which imposes a variety of institutional obstacles to innovation, let alone to the intellectual working out of oppositional and political commitments. The nature of university career ladders means that one's work must be recognized as meeting certain standards of quality in order that one be able to continue it. If those standards are intimately bound up with values and assumptions one rejects, incomprehension rather than conversion is likely. Success requires that we present our work in a way that satisfies those standards and it is easier to do work that looks just like work known to satisfy them than to strike out in a new direction. Another push to conformity comes from the structure of support for science. Many of the scientific ideas argued to be consistent with a feminist politics have a distinctively nonproduction orientation.[5] In the example discussed above, thinking of the brain as hormonally programmed makes intervention and control more likely than does thinking of it as a self-organizing complexly interactive system. The doing of science, however, requires financial support and those who provide that support are increasingly industry and the military. As might be expected they support research projects likely to meet their needs, projects which promise even greater possibilities for intervention in and manipulation of natural processes. Our sciences are being harnessed to the making of money and the waging of war. The possibility of alternate understandings of the natural world is irrelevant to a culture driven by those interests. To do feminist science we must change the social and political context in which science is done.

So: can there be a feminist science? If this means: is it in principle possible to do science as a feminist?, the answer must be: yes. If this means: can we in practice do science as feminists?, the answer must be: not until we change present conditions.

Notes

I am grateful to the Wellesley Center for Research on Women for the Mellon Scholarship during which I worked on the ideas in this essay. I am also grateful to audiences at UC Berkeley, Northeastern University, Brandeis University and Rice University for their comments and to the anonymous reviewers for *Hypatia* for their suggestions. An earlier version appeared as Wellesley Center for Research on Women Working Paper #63.

1. This seems to be suggested in Bleier (1984), Rose (1983) and in Sandra Harding's (1980) early work.
2. For a striking expression of this point of view see Witelson (1985).
3. Ideological commitments other than feminist ones may lead to the same assumptions and the variety of feminisms means that feminist commitments can lead to different and incompatible assumptions.
4. Cf. note 1, above.
5. This is not to say that interactionist ideas may not be applied in productive contexts, but that, unlike linear causal models, they are several steps away from the manipulation of natural processes immediately suggested by the latter. See Keller (1985), especially Chapter 10.

References

Addelson, Kathryn Pine. 1983. The man of professional wisdom. In *Discovering reality,* ed. Sandra Harding and Merrill Hintikka. Dordrecht: Reidel.

Bleier, Ruth. 1984. *Science and gender.* Elmsford, NY: Pergamon.

Doell, Ruth, and Helen E. Longino. N.d. *Journal of Homosexuality.* Forthcoming.

Edelman, Gerald and Vernon Mountcastle. 1978. *The mindful brain.* Cambridge, MA: MIT Press.

Gould, Stephen J. 1984. Review of Ruth Bleier, *Science and gender. New York Times Book Review,* VVI, 7 (August 12): 1.

Harding, Sandra. 1980. The norms of inquiry and masculine experience. In *PSA 1980,* Vol. 2, ed. Peter Asquith and Ronald Giere. East Lansing, MI: Philosophy of Science Association.

Keller, Evelyn Fox. 1985. *Reflections on gender and science.* New Haven, CT: Yale University Press.

Longino, Helen. 1979. Evidence and hypothesis. *Philosophy of Science* 46 (1) 35–56.

———. 1981. Scientific objectivity and feminist theorizing. *Liberal Education* 67 (3): 33–41.

———. 1983a. The idea of a value free science. Paper presented to the Pacific Division of the American Philosophical Association, March 25. Berkeley, CA.

———. 1983b. Scientific objectivity and logics of science. *Inquiry* 26 (1): 85–106.

———. 1983c. Beyond "bad science." *Science, Technology and Human Values* 8 (1): 7–17.

Longino, Helen and Ruth Doell. 1983. Body, bias and behavior. *Signs* 9 (2): 206–227.

Lugones, Maria and Elizabeth Spelman. 1983. Have we got a theory for you! Feminist theory, cultural imperialism and the demand for "the woman's voice." *Hypatia 1,* published as a special issue of *Women's Studies International Forum* 6 (6): 573–581.

Rose, Hilary. 1983. Hand, brain, and heart: A feminist epistemology for the natural sciences. *Signs* 9 (1): 73–90.

Rossiter, Margaret. 1982. *Women scientists in America: Struggles and strategies to 1940.* Baltimore, MD: Johns Hopkins University Press.

Witelson, Sandra. 1985. An exchange on gender. *New York Review of Books* (October 24).

SOCIALLY CAMOUFLAGED TECHNOLOGIES
The Case of the Electromechanical Vibrator

Rachel Maines

Certain commodities are sold in the legal marketplace for which the expected use is either illegal or socially unacceptable. Marketing of these goods, therefore, requires camouflaging of the design purpose in a verbal and visual rhetoric that conveys to the knowledgeable consumer the item's selling points without actually endorsing its socially prohibited uses. I refer not to goods that are actually illegal in character, such as marijuana, but to their grey-market background technologies, such as cigarette rolling papers. Marketing efforts for goods of this type have similar characteristics over time, despite the dissimilarity of the advertised commodities. I shall discuss here an electromechanical technology that addresses formerly prohibited expressions of women's sexuality—the vibrator in its earliest incarnation between 1870 and 1930. Comparisons will be drawn between marketing strategies for this electromechanical technology, introduced between 1880 and 1903, and that of emmenagogues, distilling, burglary tools, and computer software copying, as well as the paradigm example of drug paraphernalia.

I shall argue here that electromechanical massage of the female genitalia achieved acceptance during the period in question by both professionals and consumers not only because it was less cumbersome, labor-intensive and costly than predecessor technologies, but because it maintained the social camouflage of sexual massage treatment through its associations with modern professional instrumentation and with prevailing beliefs about electricity as a healing agent.[1]

The case of the electromechanical vibrator, as a technology associated with women's sexuality, involves issues of acceptability rather than legality. The vibrator and its predecessor technologies, including the dildo, are associated with masturbation, a socially prohibited activity until well into the second half of this century.[2] Devices for mechanically-assisted female masturbation, mainly vibrators and dildoes, were marketed in the popular press from the late nineteenth century through the early thirties in similarly camouflaged advertising. Such advertisements temporarily disappeared from popular literature after the vibrator began to appear in stag films, which may have rendered the camouflage inadequate, and did not resurface until social change made it unnecessary to disguise the sexual uses of the device.[3]

For purposes of this discussion, a vibrator is a mechanical or electromechanical appliance imparting rapid and rhythmic pressure through a contoured working surface usually mounted at a right angle to the handle. These points of contact generally take the form of a set of interchangeable vibratodes configured to the anatomical areas they are intended to address. Vibrators are rarely employed internally in masturbation; they thus differ from dildoes, which are generally straight-shafted and may or may not include a vibratory component. Vibrators are here distinguished also from massagers, the working surfaces of which are flat or dished.[4] It should be noted that this is a historian's distinction imposed on the primary sources; medical authors and appliance manufacturers apply a heterogeneous nomenclature to massage technologies. Vibrators and dildoes rarely appeared in household advertising between 1930 and 1955, massagers continued to be marketed, mainly through household magazines.[5]

The electromechanical vibrator, introduced as a medical instrument in the 1880s and as a home appliance between 1900 and 1903, represented the convergence of several older medical massage technologies, including manual, hydriatic, electrotherapeutic and mechanical methods. Internal and external gynecological massage with lubricated fingers had been a standard medical treatment for hysteria, disorders of menstruation and other female complaints at least since the time of Aretaeus Cappadox (circa 150 A.D.), and the evidence suggests that orgasmic response on the part of the patient may have been the intended therapeutic result.[6] Douche therapy, a method of directing a jet of pumped water at the pelvic area and vulva, was employed for similar purposes after hydrotherapy became popular in the eighteenth and nineteenth centuries.[7] The camouflage of the apparently sexual character of such therapy was accomplished through its medical respectability and through creative definitions both of the diseases for which massage was indicated and of the effects of treatment. In the case of the electromechanical vibrator, the use of electrical power contributed the cachet of modernity and linked the instrument to older technologies of electrotherapeutics, in which patients received low-voltage electricity through electrodes attached directly to the skin or mucous membranes, and to light-bath therapy, in which electric light was applied to the skin in a closed cabinet. The electrotherapeutic association was explicitly invoked in the original term for the vibrator's interchangeable applicators, which were known as "vibratodes." Electrical treatments were employed in hysteria as soon as they were introduced in the eighteenth century, and remained in use as late as the 1920s.

Hysteria as a disease paradigm, from its origins in the Egyptian medical corpus through its conceptual eradication by Amèrican Psychological Association fiat in 1952, was so vaguely and subjectively defined that it might encompass almost any set of ambiguous symptoms that troubled a woman or her family. As its name suggests, hysteria as well as its "sister" complaint chlorosis were until the twentieth century thought to have their etiology in the female reproductive tract generally, and more particularly in the organism's response to sexual deprivation.[8] This physiological condition seems to have achieved epidemic proportions among women and girls, at least in the modern period.[9] Sydenham, writing in the seventeenth century, observed that hysteria was the most common of all diseases except fevers.[10]

In the late nineteenth century, physicians noted with alarm that from half to three-quarters of all women showed signs of hysterical affliction. Among the many symptoms listed in medical descriptions of the syndrome are anxiety, sense of heaviness in the pelvis, edema (swelling) in the lower abdomen and genital areas, wandering of attention and associated tendencies to indulge in sexual fantasy, insomnia, irritability, and "excessive" vaginal lubrication.[11]

The therapeutic objective in such cases was to produce a "crisis" of the disease in the Hippocratic sense of this expression, corresponding to the point in infectious diseases at which the fever breaks. Manual massage of the vulva by physicians or midwives, with fragrant oils as lubricants, formed part of the standard treatment repertoire for hysteria, chlorosis and related disorders from ancient times until the post-Freudian era. The crisis induced by this procedure was usually called the "hysterical paroxysm." Treatment for hysteria might comprise up to three-quarters of a physician's practice in the nineteenth century. Doctors who employed vulvular massage treatment in hysteria thus required fast, efficient and effective means of producing the desired crisis. Portability of the technology was also a desideratum, as physicians treated many patients in their homes, and only manual massage under these conditions was possible until the introduction of the portable battery-powered vibrator for medical use in the late 1880s.

Patients reported experiencing symptomatic relief after such treatments, and such conditions as pelvic congestion and insomnia were noticeably ameliorated, especially if therapy continued on a regular basis. A few physicians, including Nathaniel Highmore in the seventeenth century and Auguste Tripier, a nineteenth century electrotherapist, clearly recognized the hysterical paroxysm as sexual orgasm.[12] That many of their colleagues also perceived the sexual character of hysteria treatments is suggested by the fact that, in the case of married women, one of the therapeutic options was intercourse, and in the case of single women, marriage was routinely recommended.[13] "God-fearing physicians," as Zacuto expressed it in the seventeenth century, were expected to induce the paroxysm with their own fingers only when absolutely necessary, as in the case of very young single women, widows and nuns.[14]

Many later physicians, however, such as the nineteenth century hydrotherapist John Harvey Kellogg, seem not to have perceived the sexual character of patient response. Kellogg wrote extensively about hydrotherapy and electrotherapeutics in gynecology. In his "Electrotherapeutics in Chronic Maladies," published in *Modern Medicine* in 1904, he describes "strong contractions of the abdominal muscles" in a female patient undergoing treatment, and similar reactions such that "the office table was made to tremble quite violently with the movement."[15] In their analysis of the situation, these physicians may have been handicapped by their failure to recognize that penetration is a successful means of producing orgasm in only a minority of women; thus treatments that did not involve significant vaginal penetration were not morally suspect. In effect, misperceptions of female sexuality formed part of the camouflage of the original manual technique that preceded the electromechanical vibrator. Insertion of the speculum, however, since it travelled the same path as the supposedly irresistible penis during intercourse, was widely criticized in the medical community for its purportedly immoral effect on patients.[16] That some questioned the ethics of the vulvular massage procedure is clear; Thomas Stretch Dowse quotes Graham as observing that "Massage of the pelvic organs should be intrusted to those alone who have 'clean hands and a pure heart'."[17] One physician, however, in an article significantly titled "Signs of Masturbation in the Female," proposed the application of an electrical charge to the clitoris as a test of salacious propensities in women. Sensitivity of the organ to this type of electrical stimulation, in his view, indicated secret indulgence in what was known in the nineteenth century as "a bad habit."[18] Ironically, such women were often treated electrically for hysteria supposedly caused by masturbation.

However they construed the benefits, physicians regarded the genital massage procedure, which could take as long as an hour of skilled therapeutic activity, as something of a chore, and made early attempts to mechanize it. Hydrotherapy, in the form of what was known as the "pelvic douche" (massage of the lower pelvis with a jet of pumped water), provided similar relief to the patient with reduced demands on the therapist. Doctors of the eighteenth and nineteenth centuries frequently recommended douche therapy for their women patients who could afford spa visits. This market was limited, however, as both treatment and travel were costly.[19] A very small minority of patients and doctors could afford to install hydrotherapeutic facilities in convenient locations; both doctor and patient usually had to travel to the spa. Electrically-powered equipment, when it became available, thus had a decentralizing and cost-reducing effect on massage treatment.

In the 1860s, some spas and clinics introduced a coal-fired steam powered device invented by a Dr. George Taylor, called the "Manipulator," which massaged the lower pelvis while the patient either stood or lay on a table.[20] This too required a considerable expenditure either by the physician who purchased the equipment or by the patient who was required to travel to a spa for treatment. Thus, when the electromechanical vibrator was invented two decades later in England by Mortimer Granville and manufactured by Weiss, a ready market already existed in the medical community.[21] Ironically, Mortimer Granville considered the use of his instrument on women, especially hysterics, a morally indefensible act, and recommended the device only for use on the male skeletal muscles.[22] Although his original battery-powered model was heavy and unreliable, it was more portable than water-powered massage and less fatiguing to the operator than manual massage (fig. 1).

Air-pressure models were introduced, but they required cumbersome tanks of compressed air, which needed frequent refilling. When line electricity became widely available, portable plug-in models made vibratory house calls more expeditious and cost effective for the enterprising physician. The difficulty of maintaining batteries in or out of the office was noted by several medical writers of the period predating the introduction of plug-in vibrators.[23] Batteries and small office generators were liable to fail at crucial moments during patient treatment, and required more engineering expertise for their maintenance than most physicians cared to acquire. Portable models using dc or ac line electricity were available with a wide range of vibratodes, such as the twelve-inch rectal probe supplied with one of the Gorman firm's vibrators.

Despite its inventor's reservations, the Weiss instrument and later devices on the same principle were widely used by physicians for pelvic disorders in women and girls. The social camouflage applied to the older manual technology was carefully maintained in connection with the new, at least until the 1920s. The marketing of medical vibrators to physicians and the discussion of them in such works as Covey's *Profitable Office Specialties* addressed two important professional considerations: the respectability of the devices as medical instruments (including their reassuringly clinical appearance) and their utility in the fast and efficient treatment of those chronic disorders, such as pelvic complaints in women, that provided a significant portion of a physician's income.[24] The importance of a prestige image for electromechanical instrumentation, and its role in the pricing of medical vibrators is illustrated by a paragraph in the advertising brochure for the "Chattanooga," (fig. 2), at $200 in 1904 the most costly of the physicians' office models:

> The Physician can give with the "Chattanooga" Vibrator a thorough massage treatment in three minutes that is extremely pleasant and beneficial, but this instrument is neither designed nor sold as a "Massage Machine." It is sold only to Physicians, and constructed for the express purpose of exciting the various organs of the body into activity through their central nervous supply.[25]

FIGURE 1 Joseph Mortimer Granville's "percuteur" of 1883, manufactured by the Weiss Instrument Company.

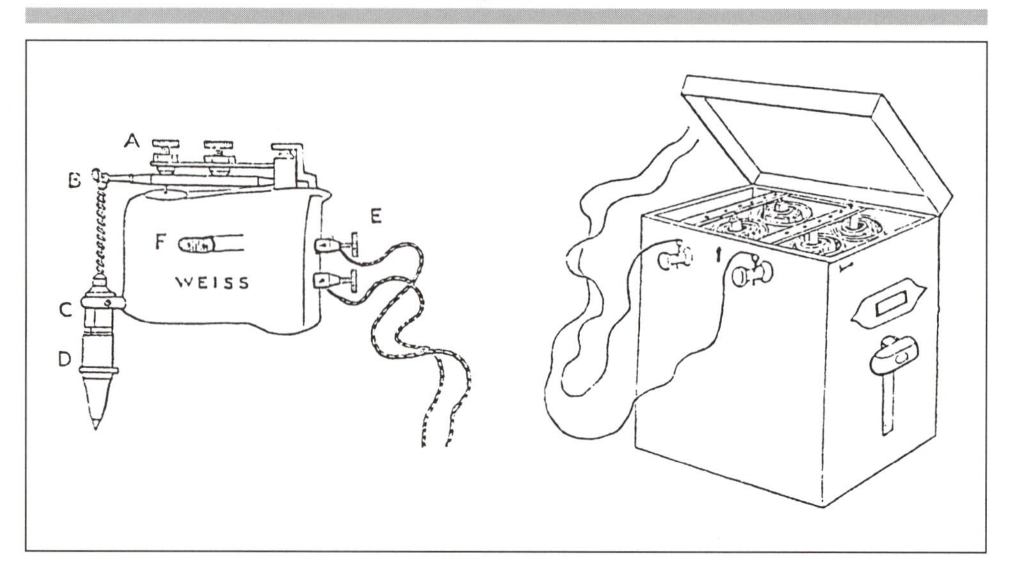

FIGURE 2 (A) The Chattanooga, at $200 the most expensive medical vibrator available in 1904, could be wheeled over the operating table and its vibrating head rotated for the physician's convenience. (B) Chattanooga Vibrator parts.

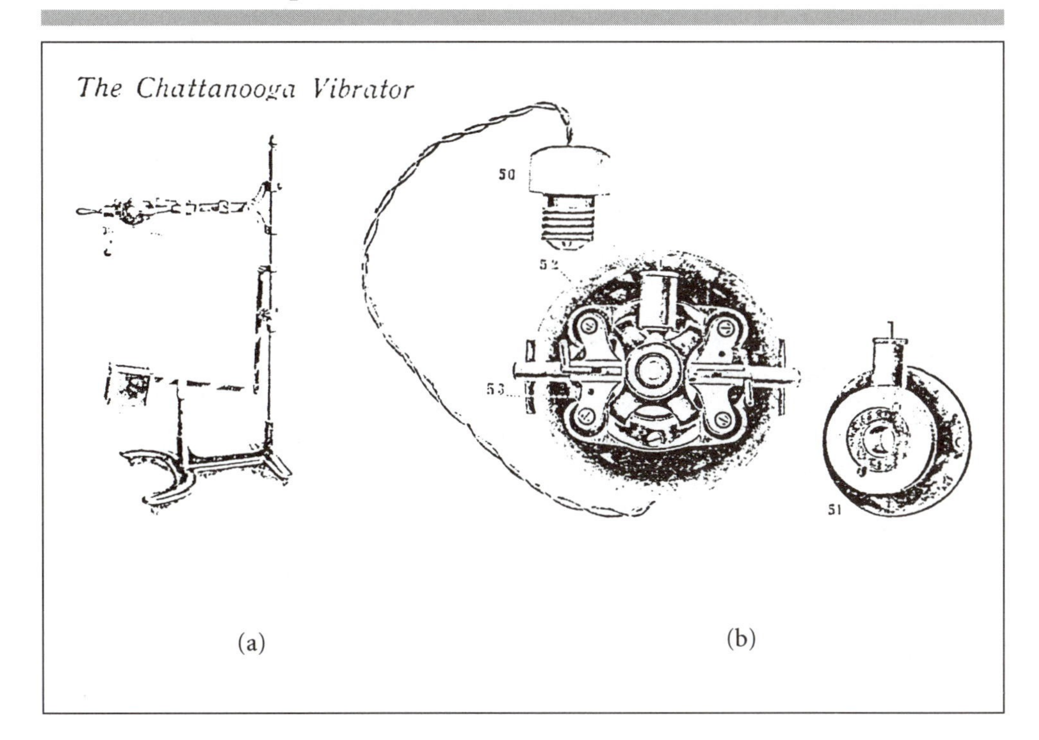

I do not mean to suggest that gynecological treatments were the only uses of such devices, or that all physicians who purchased them used them for the production of orgasm in female patients, but the literature suggests that a substantial number were interested in the new technology's utility in the hysteroneurasthenic complaints. The interposition of an official-looking machine must have done much to restore clinical dignity to the massage procedure. The vibrator was introduced in 1899 as a home medical appliance, and was by 1904 advertised in household magazines in suggestive terms we shall examine later on. It was important for physicians to be able to justify to patients the expense of $2–3 per treatment, as home vibrators were available for about $5.

The acceptance of the electromechanical vibrator by physicians at the turn of this century may also have been influenced by their earlier adoption of electrotherapeutics, with which vibratory treatment could be, and often was, combined.[26] Vibratory therapeutics were introduced from London and Paris, especially from the famous Hôpital Salpêtrière, which added to their respectability in the medical community.[27] It is worth noting as well that in this period electrical and other vibrations were a subject of great interest and considerable confusion, not only among doctors and the general public, but even among scientists like Tesla, who is reported to have fallen under their spell. ". . . [T]he Earth," he wrote, "is responsive to electrical vibrations of definite pitch just as a tuning fork to certain waves of sound. These particular electrical vibrations, capable of powerfully exciting the Globe, lend themselves to innumerable uses of great importance . . ."[28] In the same category of mystical reverence for vibration is

Samuel Wallian's contemporaneous essay on "The Undulatory Theory in Therapeutics," in which he describes "modalities or manifestations of vibratory impulse" as the guiding principle of the universe. "Each change and gradation is not a transformation, as mollusk into mammal, or monkey into man, but an evidence of a variation in vibratory velocity. A certain rate begets a *vermis,* another and higher rate produces a *viper,* a *vertebrate,* a *vestryman.*"[29]

In 1900, according to Monell, more than a dozen medical vibratory devices for physicians had been available for examination at the Paris Exposition. Of these, few were able to compete in the long term with electromechanical models. Mary L. H. Arnold Snow, writing for a medical readership in 1904, discusses in some depth more than twenty types, of which more than half are electromechanical. These models, some priced to the medical trade as low as $15, delivered vibrations from one to 7,000 pulses a minute. Some were floor-standing machines on rollers; others could be suspended from the ceiling like the modern impact wrench.[30] The more expensive models were adapted to either ac or dc currents. A few, such as those of the British firm Schall and Son, could even be ordered with motors custom-wound to a physician's specifications. Portable and battery-powered electromechanical vibrators were generally less expensive than floor models, which both looked more imposing as instruments and were less likely to transmit fatiguing vibrations to the doctor's hands.

Patients were treated in health spa complexes, in doctor's offices or their own homes with portable equipment. Designs consonant with prevailing notions of what a medical instrument should look like inspired consumer confidence in the physician and his apparatus, justified treatment costs, and, in the case of hysteria treatments, camouflaged the sexual character of the therapy. Hand or foot-powered models, however, were tiring to the operator; water-powered ones became too expensive to operate when municipalities began metering water in the early twentieth century. Gasoline engines and batteries were cumbersome and difficult to maintain, as noted above. No fuel or air-tank handling by the user was required for line electricity, in contrast with compressed air, steam and petroleum as power sources. In the years after 1900, as line electricity became the norm in urban communities, the electromechanical vibrator emerged as the dominant technology for medical massage.

Some physicians contributed to this trend by endorsing the vibrator in works like that of Monell, who had studied vibratory massage in medical practice in the United States and Europe at the turn of this century. He praises its usefulness in female complaints:

> . . . pelvic massage (in gynecology) has its brilliant advocates and they report wonderful results, but when practitioners must supply the skilled technic with their own fingers the method has no value to the majority. But special applicators (motor-driven) give practical value and office convenience to what otherwise is impractical.[31]

Other medical writers suggested combining vibratory treatment of the pelvis with hydro- and electrotherapy, a refinement made possible by the ready adaptability of the new electromechanical technology.

At the same period, mechanical and electromechanical vibrators were introduced as home medical appliances. One of the earliest was the Vibratile, a battery-operated massage device advertised in 1899. Like the vibrators sold to doctors, home appliances could be handpowered, water-driven, battery or street-current apparatus in a relatively wide range of prices from $1.50 to $28.75. This last named was the price of a Sears, Roebuck model of 1918, which could be purchased as an attachment for a separate electrical motor, drawing current through a lamp socket, which also powered a fan, buffer, grinder, mixer and sewing machine. The complete set was marketed in the catalogue under the headline "Aids that Every Woman Appreciates." (fig. 3). Vibrators were mainly marketed to women, although men were sometimes exhorted to purchase the devices as gifts for their wives, or to become door-to-door sales representatives for the manufacturer.[32]

The electromechanical vibrator was preceded in the home market by a variety of electrotherapeutic appliances which continued to be advertised through the twenties, often in the same publications as vibratory massage devices. Montgomery Ward, Sears Roebuck and the Canadian mail order department store T. Eaton and Company all sold medical batteries by direct-mail by the end of the nineteenth century. These were simply batteries with electrodes that administered a mild shock. Some, like Butler's Electro-Massage Machine, produced their own electricity with friction motors. Contemporaneous and later appliances sometimes had special features, such as Dr. H. Sanche's Oxydonor, which produced ozone in addition to the current when one electrode was placed in water. "Electric" massage rollers, combs and brushes with a supposedly permanent charge retailed at this time for prices between one and five dollars. Publications like the *Home Needlework Magazine* and *Men and Women* advertised these devices, as well as related technologies, including correspondence courses in manual massage.

Vibrators with water motors, a popular power source, as noted above, before the introduction of metered water, were advertised in such journals as *Modern Women*, which emphasized the cost savings over treatments by physicians and further emphasized the advantage of privacy offered by home treatment. Such devices were marketed through the teens in *Hearst's* and its successors, and in *Woman's Home Companion.*[33] Electromechanical vibrators were sold in the upper middle class market, in magazines typically retailing for between ten and fifteen cents an issue. As in the case of medical vibrators, models adapted to both ac and dc current were more expensive than those for use with dc only; all were fitted with screw-in plugs through the twenties.[34]

All types of vibrators were advertised as benefiting health and beauty by stimulating the circulation and soothing the nerves. The makers of the electromechanical American vibrator, for example, recommended their product as an ". . . alleviating, curative and beautifying agent . . . It will increase deficient circulation—develop the muscles—remove wrinkles and facial blemishes, and beautify the complexion."[35] Advertisements directed to male purchasers similarly emphasized the machine's advantages for improving a woman's appearance and disposition. And ad in a 1921 issue of *Hearst's* urges the considerate husband to "Give 'her' a Star for Christmas" on the grounds that it would be "A Gift That Will *Keep* Her Young and Pretty." The same device was listed in another advertisement with several other electrical appliances, and labelled "Such Delightful Companions!"[36] A husband, these advertisements seem to suggest, who presented his wife with these progressive and apparently respectable medical aids might leave for work in the morning secure in the knowledge that his spouse's day would be pleasantly and productively invested in self-treatment. Like other electrical appliance advertising of the time, electromechanical vibrator ads emphasized the role of the device in making a woman's home a veritable Utopia of modern technology, and its utility in reducing the number of occasions, such as visiting her physician, on which she would be required to leave her domestic paradise.[37]

Advertisements for vibrators often shared magazine pages with books on sexual matters, such as Howard's popular *Sex Problems in Worry and Work* and Walling's *Sexology*, handguns, cures for alcoholism and, occasionally, even personals, from both men and women, in which matrimony was the declared objective. Sexuality is never explicit in vibrator advertising; the tone is vague but provocative, as in the Swedish

FIGURE 3 The vibratory attachments for the 1918 Sears Roebuck home motor were only one of many electromechanical possibilities.

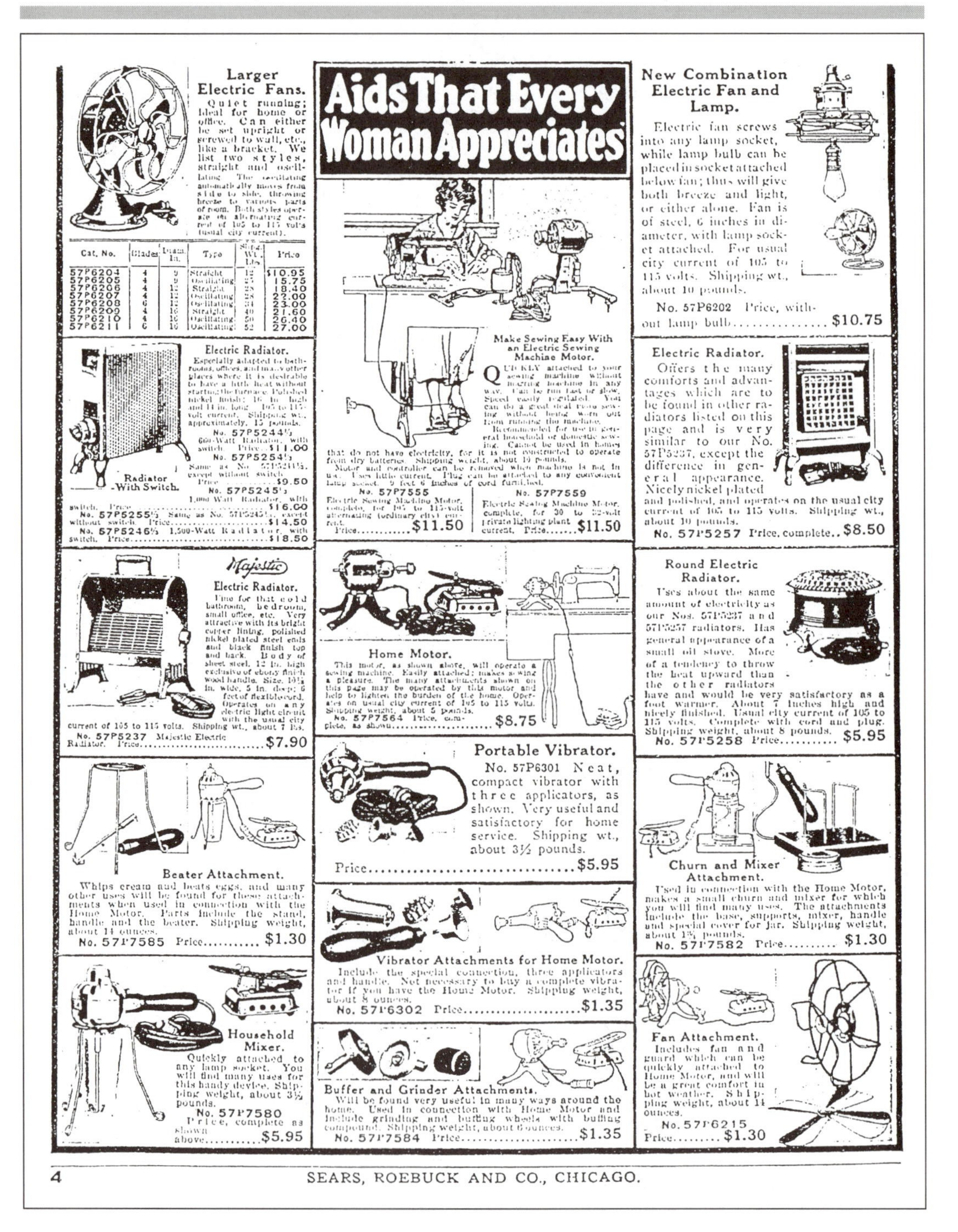

Larger Electric Fans.
Quiet running; ideal for home or office. Can either be set upright or screwed to wall, etc., like a bracket. We list two styles, straight and oscillating. The oscillating automatically moves from side to side, throwing breeze to various parts of room. Both styles operate on alternating current of 105 to 115 volts (usual city current).

Cat. No.	Blades	Diam. In.	Type	Shpg. Wt., Lbs.	Price
57P6204	4	9	Straight	12	$10.95
57P6205	4	9	Oscillating	25	15.75
57P6206	4	12	Straight	28	18.40
57P6207	4	12	Oscillating	28	22.00
57P6208	6	12	Oscillating	34	23.00
57P6209	4	16	Straight	40	21.60
57P6210	4	16	Oscillating	50	26.40
57P6211	6	16	Oscillating	52	27.00

Electric Radiator.
Especially adapted to bathrooms, offices, and many other places where it is desirable to have a little heat without starting the furnace. Polished nickel finish; 16 in. high and 14 in. long. 105 to 115-volt current. Shipping wt., approximately, 15 pounds.
No. 57P5244⅓ 600-Watt Radiator, with switch. Price..$11.00
No. 57P5254⅓ Same as No. 57P5244⅓, except without switch. Price..............$9.50
No. 57P5245⅓ 1,000 Watt Radiator, with switch. Price..............................$16.00
No. 57P5255⅓ Same as No. 57P5245⅓, except without switch. Price......................$14.50
No. 57P5246⅓ 1,500-Watt Radiator, with switch. Price..............................$18.50
Radiator -With Switch.

Majestic Electric Radiator.
Fine for that cold bathroom, bedroom, small office, etc. Very attractive with its bright copper lining, polished nickel plated steel ends and black finish top and back. Body of sheet steel. 12 in. high exclusive of ebony finish wood handle. Size, 10½ in. wide, 5 in. deep; 6 feet of flexible cord. Operates on any electric light circuit with the usual city current of 105 to 115 volts. Shipping wt., about 7 lbs.
No. 57P5237 Majestic Electric Radiator. Price..............................$7.90

Beater Attachment.
Whips cream and beats eggs, and many other uses will be found for these attachments when used in connection with the Home Motor. Parts include the stand, handle and the beater. Shipping weight, about 14 ounces.
No. 57P7585 Price.......... $1.30

Household Mixer.
Quickly attached to any lamp socket. You will find many uses for this handy device. Shipping weight, about 3½ pounds.
No. 57P7580 Price, complete as shown above..........$5.95

Aids That Every Woman Appreciates

Make Sewing Easy With an Electric Sewing Machine Motor.
QUICKLY attached to your sewing machine without marring machine in any way. Can be run fast or slow. Speed easily regulated. You can do a great deal more sewing without being worn out from running the machine.
Recommended for use in general household or domestic sewing. Cannot be used in homes that do not have electricity, for it is not constructed to operate from dry batteries. Shipping weight, about 10 pounds.
Motor and controller can be removed when machine is not in use. Uses little current. Plug can be attached to any convenient lamp socket. 9 feet 6 inches of cord furnished.
No. 57P7555 Electric Sewing Machine Motor, complete, for 105 to 115-volt alternating (ordinary city) current. Price............$11.50
No. 57P7559 Electric Sewing Machine Motor, complete, for 30 to 32-volt private lighting plant current. Price.......$11.50

Home Motor.
This motor, as shown above, will operate a sewing machine. Easily attached; makes sewing a pleasure. The many attachments shown on this page may be operated by this motor and help to lighten the burden of the home. Operates on usual city current of 105 to 115 volts. Shipping weight, about 5 pounds.
No. 57P7564 Price, complete, as shown.......................$8.75

Portable Vibrator.
No. 57P6301 Neat, compact vibrator with three applicators, as shown. Very useful and satisfactory for home service. Shipping wt., about 3½ pounds.
Price..............................$5.95

Vibrator Attachments for Home Motor.
Include the special connection, three applicators and handle. Not necessary to buy a complete vibrator if you have the Home Motor. Shipping weight, about 8 ounces.
No. 57P6302 Price......................$1.35

Buffer and Grinder Attachments.
Will be found very useful in many ways around the home. Used in connection with Home Motor and include grinding and buffing wheels with buffing compound. Shipping weight, about 6 ounces.
No. 57P7584 Price......................$1.35

New Combination Electric Fan and Lamp.
Electric fan screws into any lamp socket, while lamp bulb can be placed in socket attached below fan; thus will give both breeze and light, or either alone. Fan is of steel, 6 inches in diameter, with lamp socket attached. For usual city current of 105 to 115 volts. Shipping wt., about 10 pounds.
No. 57P6202 Price, without lamp bulb.............. $10.75

Electric Radiator.
Offers the many comforts and advantages which are to be found in other radiators listed on this page and is very similar to our No. 57P5237, except the difference in general appearance. Nicely nickel plated and polished, and operates on the usual city current of 105 to 115 volts. Shipping wt., about 10 pounds.
No. 57P5257 Price, complete.. $8.50

Round Electric Radiator.
Uses about the same amount of electricity as our Nos. 57P5237 and 57P5257 radiators. Has general appearance of a small oil stove. More of a tendency to throw the heat upward than the other radiators have and would be very satisfactory as a foot warmer. About 7 inches high and nicely finished. Usual city current of 105 to 115 volts. Complete with cord and plug. Shipping weight, about 8 pounds.
No. 57P5258 Price.......... $5.95

Churn and Mixer Attachment.
Used in connection with the Home Motor, makes a small churn and mixer for which you will find many uses. The attachments include the base, supports, mixer, handle and special cover for jar. Shipping weight, about 1¾ pounds.
No. 57P7582 Price......... $1.30

Fan Attachment.
Includes fan and guard which can be quickly attached to Home Motor, and will be a great comfort in hot weather. Shipping weight, about 14 ounces.
No. 57P6215 Price........ $1.30

4 SEARS, ROEBUCK AND CO., CHICAGO.

Vibrator advertisement in *Modern Priscilla* of 1913, offering "a machine that gives 30,000 thrilling, invigorating, penetrating, revitalizing vibrations per minute . . . Irresistible desire to own it, once you feel the living pulsing touch of its rhythmic vibratory motion." Illustrations in these layouts typically include voluptuously proportioned women in various states of *déshabillé.* The White Cross vibrator, made by a Chicago firm that manufactured a variety of small electrical appliances, was also advertised in *Modern Priscilla,* where the maker assured readers that "It makes you fairly tingle with the joy of living."[38] It is worth noting that the name "White Cross" was drawn from that of an international organization devoted to what was known in the early twentieth century as "social hygiene," the discovery and eradication of masturbation and prostitution wherever they appeared. The Chicago maker of White Cross appliances, in no known way affiliated with the organization, evidently hoped to trade on the name's association with decency and moral purity.[39] A 1916 advertisement from the White Cross manufacturer in *American Magazine* nevertheless makes the closest approach to explicit sexual claims when it promises that "All the keen relish, the pleasures of youth, will throb within you."[40] The utility of the product for female masturbation was thus consistently camouflaged.

Electromechanical vibrator advertising almost never appeared in magazines selling for less than 5 cents an issue (10 to 20 cents is the median range) or more than 25 cents. Readers of the former were unlikely to have access to electrical current; readers of the latter, including, for example, *Vanity Fair,* were more likely to respond to advertising for spas and private manual massage. While at least a dozen and probably more than twenty U.S. firms manufactured electromechanical vibrators before 1930, sales of these appliances were not reported in the electrical trade press. A listing from the February 1927 *NELA Bulletin* is typical; no massage equipment of any kind appears on an otherwise comprehensive list that includes violet-ray appliances.[41] A 1925 article in *Electrical World,* under the title "How Many Appliances are in Use?", lists only irons, washing machines, cleaners, ranges, water heaters, percolators, toasters, waffle irons, kitchen units and ironers.[42] *Scientific American* listed in 1907 only the corn popper, chafing dish, milk warmer, shaving cup, percolator and iron in a list of domestic electrical appliances.[43] References to vibrators were extremely rare even in popular discussions of electrical appliances.[44] The U.S. Bureau of the Census, which found 66 establishments manufacturing electro-therapeutic apparatus in 1908, does not disaggregate by instrument type either in this category or in "electrical household goods." The 1919 volume, showing the electromedical market at a figure well over $2 million, also omits detailed itemization. Vibrators appear by name in the 1949 *Census of Manufactures,* but it is unclear whether the listing for them, aggregated with statistics for curling irons and hair dryers, includes those sold as medical instruments to physicians.[45] This dearth of data renders sales tracking of the electromechanical vibrator extremely difficult. The omissions from engineering literature are worth noting, as the electromechanical vibrator was one of the first electrical appliances for personal care, partly because it was seen as a safe method of self-treatment.[46]

The marketing strategy for the early electromechanical vibrator was similar to that employed for contemporaneous and even modern technologies for which social camouflage is considered necessary. Technologically, the devices so marketed differ from modern vibrators sold for explicitly sexual purposes only in their greater overall weight, accounted for by the use of metal housings in the former and plastic in the latter. The basic set of vibratodes is identical, as is the mechanical action. The social context of the machine, however, has undergone profound change. Liberalized attitudes toward masturbation in both sexes and increasing understanding of women's sexuality have made social camouflage superfluous.

In the case of the vibrator, the issue is one of acceptability, but there are many examples of similarly marketed technology of which the expected use was actually illegal. One of these, which shares with the vibrator a focus on women's sexuality, was that of "emmenagogues" or abortifacient drugs sold through the mail and sometimes even off the shelf in the first few decades of this century. Emmenagogues, called in pre-FDA advertising copy "cycle restorers," were intended to bring on the menses in women who were "late." Induced abortion by any means was of course illegal, but late menses are not reliable indicators of pregnancy. Thus, women who purchased and took "cycle restorers" might or might not be in violation of antiabortion laws; they themselves might not be certain without a medical examination. The advertising of these commodities makes free use of this ambiguity in texts like the following from *Good Stories* of 1933:

> Late? End Delay—Worry. American Periodic Relief Compound double strength tablets combine Safety with Quick Action. Relieve most Stubborn cases. No Pain. New discovery. Easily taken. Solves women's most perplexing problem. RELIEVES WHEN ALL OTHERS FAIL. Don't be discouraged, end worry at once. Send $1.00 for Standard size package and full directions. Mailed same day, special delivery in plain wrapper. American Periodic Relief Compound Tablets, extra strength for stubborn cases, $2.00. Generous Size Package. New Book free.[47]

The rhetoric here does not mention the possibility of pregnancy, but the product's selling points would clearly suggest this to the informed consumer through the mentions of safety, absence of pain, and stubborn cases. The readers of the pulp tabloid *Good Stories* clearly did not require an explanation of "women's most perplexing problem."

Distilling technology raises similar issues of legality. During the Prohibition period, the classified section of a 1920 *Ainslee's* sold one and four gallon copper stills by mail, advising the customer that the apparatus was "Ideal for distilling water for drinking purposes, automobile batteries and industrial uses."[48] Modern advertisements for distilling equipment contain similar camouflage rhetoric, directing attention away from the likelihood that most consumers intend to employ the device in the production of beverages considerably stronger than water.[49]

Although changes in sexual mores have liberated the vibrator, social camouflage remains necessary for stills and many other modern commodities, including drug paraphernalia. The Deering Prep Kit, for example, is advertised at nearly $50 as a superlative device for grinding and preparing fine powders, "such as vitamin pills or spices."[50] Burglary tools are marketed in some popular (if lowbrow) magazines with the admonition that they are to be used only to break into one's own home or automobile, in the event of having locked oneself out. The camouflage rhetoric seems to suggest that all prudent drivers and homeowners carry such tools on their persons at all times. Most recently, we have seen the appearance of computer software for breaking copy protection, advertised in terms that explicitly prohibit its use for piracy, although surely no software publisher is so naive as to believe that all purchasers intend to break copy protection only to make backup copies of legitimately purchased programs and data.[51] As in vibrator advertising, the product's advantages are revealed to knowledgeable consumers in language that disclaims the manufacturers' responsibility for illegal or immoral uses of the product.

The marketing of socially camouflaged technologies is directed to consumers who already understand the design purpose of the product, but whose legally and/or culturally unacceptable intentions in purchasing it cannot be formally recognized by the seller. The marketing rhetoric must extoll the product's advantages for achieving the purchaser's goals—in the case of the vibrator, the production of orgasm—by indirection and innuendo, particularly with reference to the overall results, i.e., relaxation and relief from tension. The same pattern emerges in the advertisement of emmenagogues: according to the manufacturer, it is "Worry and Delay" that are ended, not pregnancy. In the case of software copyright protection programs, drug paraphernalia and distilling equipment, the expected input and/or output are simply misrepresented, so that an expensive finely-calibrated scale with its own fitted carrying case may be pictured in use in the weighing of jelly beans. As social values and legal restrictions shift, the social camouflaging of technologies may be expected to change in response, or to be dispensed with altogether, as in the case of the vibrator.

References

1. Various versions of this paper have benefitted from comments and criticism from John Senior at the Bakken, Joel Tarr of Carnegie-Mellon University, Shere Hite of Hite Research, Karen Reeds of Rutgers University Press, my former students at Clarkson University, and participants in the Social and Economic History Seminar, Queens University (Canada), the Hannah Lecture series in the History of Medicine at the University of Ottawa, and the 1986 annual meeting of the Society for the History of Technology with the Society for the Social Study of Science. Anonymous referees of this and other journals have also provided valuable guidance in structuring the presentation of my research results.
2. Sokolow, Jayme A., *Eros and Modernization: Sylvester Graham, Health Reform and the Origins of Victorian Sexuality in America.* Rutherford, NJ: Fairleigh Dickinson University Press, 1983, pp. 77–99; Haller, John S., and Robin Haller, *The Physician and Sexuality in Victorian America.* Urbana: University of Illinois Press, 1973, pp. 184–216; Greydanus, Donald E., "Masturbation; Historic Perspective," *New York State Journal of Medicine,* November 1980, vol. 80, no. 12, pp. 1892–1896; Szasz, Thomas, *The Manufacture of Madness.* New York: Harper and Row, 1977, pp. 180–206; Hare, E. H., "Masturbatory Insanity: The History of an Idea," *Journal of Mental Sciences,* 1962, vol. 108, pp. 1–25; and Bullough, Vern, "Technology for the Prevention of 'Les Maladies Produites par la Masturbation,'" *Technology and Culture,* October 1987, vol. 28, no. 4, pp. 828–832.
3. On the vibrator in stag films, see Blake, Roger, *Sex Gadgets.* Cleveland: Century, 1968, pp. 33–46. An early postwar reference to the vibrator as an unabashedly sexual instrument is Ellis, Albert, *If This Be Sexual Heresy.* New York: Lyle Stuart, 1963, p. 136.
4. Vibrators and dildoes are illustrated in Tabori, Paul, *The Humor and Technology of Sex.* New York: Julian Press, 1969; the dildo is discussed in a clinical context in Masters, William H., *Human Sexual Response.* Boston: Little, Brown, 1966. Vibrators of the period to which I refer in this essay are illustrated in Gorman, Sam J., *Electro Therapeutic Apparatus.* 10th ed. Chicago: Sam J. Gorman, c1912; Wappler Electric Manufacturing Co. Inc. *Wappler Cautery and Light Apparatus and Accessories.* 2nd ed. New York: Wappler Electric Manufacturing, 1914, pp. 7 and 42–43; Manhattan Electrical Supply Co., *Catalogue Twenty-Six: Something Electrical for Everybody.* New York: MESCO, n.d.; and Snow, Mary Lydia Hastings Arnold, *Mechanical Vibration and Its Therapeutic Application.* New York: Scientific Author's Publication Company, 1904 and 1912. For modern vibrators, see Kaplan, Helen Singer, "The Vibrator: A Misunderstood Machine," *Redbook,* May 1984, p. 34; and Swarz, Mimi, "For the Woman Who Has Almost Everything," *Esquire,* July 1980, pp. 56–63.
5. See, for examples of such advertising, which in fact included a persistent abdominal emphasis, "Amazing New Electric Vibrating Massage Pillow," Niresk Industries (Chicago, IL) advertisement in *Workbasket,* October 1958, p. 95; "Don't be Fat," body massager (Spot Reducer) advertisement in *Workbasket,* September 1958, p. 90; and "Uvral Pneumatic Massage Pulsator," in *Electrical Age for Women,* January 1932, vol. 2, no. 7, pp. 275–276.
6. This therapy is extensively documented but rarely noted by historians. For only a few examples of medical discussions of vulvular massage in the hysteroneurasthenic disorders, see Aretaeus Cappadox, *The Extant Works of Aretaeus the Cappadocian,* ed. and transl. by Francis

Adams. London: Sydenham Society, 1856, pp. 44–45, 285–287, and 449–451; Forestus, Alemarianus Petrus (Pieter van Foreest), *Observationem et Curationem Medicinalium ac Chirurgicarum Opera Omnia.* Rothomagi: Bertherlin, 1653, vol. 3, book 28, pp. 277–340; Galen of Pergamon, *De Locis Affectis,* transl. by Rudolph Siegel. Basel and New York: S. Karger, 1976, book VI, chapter II: 39; and Weber, A. Sigismond, *Traitement par l'Electricité et le Massage.* Paris: Alex Coccoz, 1889, pp. 73–80. Of modern scholars, only Audrey Eccles discusses this therapy in detail in her *Obstetrics and Gynaecology in Tudor and Stuart England.* London and Canberra: Croom Helm, 1982, pp. 76–83.

7. Baruch, Simon, *The Principles and Practice of Hydrotherapy: A Guide to the Application of Water in Disease.* New York: William Wood and Company, 1897, pp. 101, 211, 248 and 365; Dieffenbach, William H., *Hydrotherapy.* New York: Rebman, 1909, pp. 238–245; Good Health Publishing Company. *20th Century Therapeutic Appliances.* Battle Creek, MI: Good Health Publishing, 1909, pp. 20–21; Hedley, William Snowdon. *The Hydro-Electric Methods in Medicine.* London: H. K. Lewis, 1892; Hinsdale, Guy, *Hydrotherapy.* Philadelphia and London: W. B. Saunders Company, 1910, p. 224; Kellogg, John Harvey, *Rational Hydrotherapy.* Philadelphia: Davis, 1901; Irwin, J. A., *Hydrotherapy at Saratoga.* New York: Casell, 1892, pp. 85–134 and 246–248; Pope, Curran, *Practical Hydrotherapy: A Manual for Students and Practitioners.* Cincinnati, OH: Lancet-Clinic Publishing Co., 1909, pp. 181–192 and 506–538; and Trall, Russell Thacher, *The Hydropathic Encyclopedia.* New York: Fowlers and Wells, 1852, pp. 273–295. Women were reportedly in the majority as patients at spas, and some were owned by women entrepreneurs and/or physicians. See Whyman, T., "Visitors to Margate in the 1841 Census Returns," *Local Population Studies,* vol. 8, 1972, p. 23. Since at least the time of Jerome, baths and watering places have had a reputation for encouraging unacceptable expressions of sexuality. For female masturbation with water, see Aphrodite, J. [pseud.], *To Turn You On: 39 Sex Fantasies for Women.* Secaucus, NJ: Lyle Stuart, Inc., 1975, pp. 83–91; and Halpert, E., "On a Particular Form of Masturbation in Women: Masturbation with Water," *Journal of the American Psychoanalytic Association,* 1973, vol. 21, p. 526.
8. A bibliography of nineteenth century American works on women and sexuality in relation to hysteria is available in Sahli, Nancy, *Women and Sexuality in America: A Bibliography.* Boston: Hall, 1984. See also Shorter, Edward, "Paralysis: The Rise and Fall of the 'Hysterical' Symptom," *Journal of Social History,* Summer 1986, vol. 19, no. 4, pp. 549–582; Satow, Roberta, "Where Has All the Hysteria Gone?" *Psychoanalytic Review,* 1979–80, vol. 66, pp. 463–473; Bourneville, Désiré Magloire and P. Regnard, *Iconographie Photographique de la Salpêtrière.* Paris: Progres-Medical, 1878, vol. 2, pp. 97–219; Charcot, Jean-Martin. *Clinical Lectures on Certain Diseases of the Nervous System,* transl. by E. P. Hurd. Detroit: G. S. Davis, 1888, p. 141; Ellis, Havelock, *Studies in the Psychology of Sex,* vol. 1, New York: Random House, 1940, p. 270; Krohn, Alan, *Hysteria: The Elusive Neurosis.* New York: International Universities Press, 1978, pp. 46–51; McGrath, William J., *Freud's Discovery of Psychoanalysis: the Politics of Hysteria.* Ithaca, NY: Cornell University Press, 1986, pp. 152–172; Veith, Ilza, *Hysteria: The History of a Disease.* Chicago: University of Chicago Press, 1965; Wittels, Franz, *Freud and His Time.* New York: Grosset and Dunlap, 1931, pp. 215–242; and Ziegler, Dewey and Paul Norman, "On The Natural History of Hysteria in Women," *Diseases of the Nervous System,* 1967, vol. 15, pp. 301–306.
9. Bauer, Carol, "The Little Health of Ladies: An Anatomy of Female Invalidism in the Nineteenth Century," *Journal of the American Medical Woman's Association,* October 1981, vol. 36, no. 10, pp. 300–306; Ehrenreich, Barbara and D. English, *Complaints and Disorders: The Sexual Politics of Sickness.* Old Westbury, NY: Feminist Press, 1973, pp. 15–44; and Trall, Russell Thacher, *The Health and Diseases of Women.* Battle Creek, MI: Health Reformer, 1873, pp. 7–8.
10. Sydenham Thomas, "Epistolary Dissertation on Hysteria," in *The Works of Thomas Sydenham,* transl. by R. G. Latham. London: Printed for the Sydenham Society, 1848, vol. 2, pp. 56 and 85: and Payne, Joseph Frank, *Thomas Sydenham.* New York: Longmans, Green and Co., 1900, p. 143.
11. Only a minority of writers on hysteria associated the affliction with paralysis until Freud made this part of the canonical disease paradigm in the twentieth century.

12. Gall, Franz Josef, *Anatomie et Physiologie du Systéme Nerveux en Génèral.* Paris: F. Schoell, 1810–1819, vol. 3, p. 86; Tripier, Auguste Élisabeth Philogene, *Leçons Cliniques sur les Maladies de Femmes.* Paris: Octave Doin, Editeur, 1883, pp. 347–351; Highmore, Nathaniel, *de Passione Hysterica et Affectione Hypochondriaca.* Oxon.: Excudebat A. Lichfield impensis R. Davis, 1660, pp. 20–35; and Ellis, *Studies in the Psychology of Sex,* vol. 1, p. 225; see also Briquet, Pierre, *Traitè Clinique et Thérapeutique de l'Hystèrie.* Paris: J. B. Baillière et Fils, 1859, pp. 137–138, 570 and 613.
13. Cullen, William, *First Lines in the Practice of Physic.* Edinburgh: Bell, Bradfute, etc., 1791, pp. 43–47; Burton, Robert, *The Anatomy of Melancholy,* Floyd Dell and Paul Jordan Smith, eds. New York: Farrar and Rinehart, 1927, pp. 353–355; Horst, Gregor, *Dissertationem . . . inauguralem De Mania. . . . Gissae: typis Viduae Friederici Kargeri,* 1677, pp. 9–18; King, A. F. A., "Hysteria," *American Journal of Obstetrics,* May 18, 1891, vol. 24, no. 5, pp. 513–532; *Medieval Woman's Guide to Health,* transl. by Beryl Rowland. Kent, OH: Kent State University Press, 1981, pp. 2, 63 and 87; Pinel, Philippe, *A Treatise on Insanity,* transl. by D. D. Davis. Facsimile edition of the London 1806 edition; New York: Hafner, 1962, pp. 229–230; and Reich, Wilhelm, *Genitality in the Theory and Therapy of Neurosis,* transl. by Philip Schmitz. New York: Farrar, Straus and Giroux, 1980 (reprint of 1927 edition), pp. 54–55 and 93.
14. Zacuto, Abraham, *Praxis Medica Admiranda.* London: Apud Ioannem—Antonium Huguetan, 1637, p. 267. Zacuto is at pains to point out that some physicians regard vulvular massage as indecent: "Num autem ex hac occasione, liceat Medico timenti Deum, sopitis pariter cunctis sensibus, & una abolita respiratione in foeminis quasi animam agentibus, seu in maximo vitae periculo constitutus, veneficium illud semen, foras ab utero, titillationibus, & frictionbius partium obscoenarium elidere, different eloquenter . . ."
15. October-November, p. 4. Kellogg's background is described in detail in Schwarz, Richard W., *John Harvey Kellogg, MD.* Nashville: Southern Publishing Association, c1970.
16. Women who regularly undergo the discomfort of gynecological examination with this instrument are justifiably amused by its nineteenth century mythology. For an example of conservative views on the speculum, see Griesinger, Wilhelm, *Mental Pathology and Therapeutics,* transl. by C. Lockhart Robinson and James Rutherford. London: New Sydenham Society, 1867, p. 202. On the inefficiency of penetration as a means to female orgasm, the standard modern work is of course Hite, Shere, *The Hite Report on Female Sexuality.* New York: MacMillan Company, 1976, but the phenomenon was widely noted by progressive physicians and others before the seventies. Most of these latter, however, regarded the failure of penetration to fully arouse about three-quarters of the female population as either a pathology on the women's part or as evidence of a natural diffidence in the female. Hite is the first to point out that the experience of the majority constitutes a norm, not a deviation. For examples of various male views on this subject, see Hollender, Marc H., "The Medical Profession and Sex in 1900,' *American Journal of Obstetrics and Gynecology,* vol. 108, no. 1, 1970, pp. 139–148; Degler, Carl, "What Ought to be and What Was," *American Historical Review,* vol. 79, 1974, pp. 1467–1490; and his *At Odds: Women and the Family in America from the Revolution to the Present.* New York: Oxford University Press, 1980, pp. 249–278; and Tourette, Gilles de la., *Traité Clinique et Thérapeutique de l'Hystèrie Paroxystique.* Paris: Plon, 1895, vol. 1, p. 46. Feminine views are seldom recorded before this century; a few examples are those reported by Katherine B. Davis, summarized in Dickson, Robert L. and Henry Pierson, "The Average Sex Life of American Women," *Journal of the American Medical Association,* vol. 85, 1925, pp. 113–117; Lazarsfeld, Sofie, *Woman's Experience of the Male.* London: Encyclopedic Press, 1967, pp. 112, 181, 271 and 308. It has also been noted that few women have difficulty achieving orgasm in masturbation, and that the median time to orgasm in masturbation is substantially the same in both sexes: Kinsey, Alfred Charles, *Sexual Behavior in the Human Female.* Philadelphia: Saunders, 1953, p. 163.
17. Dowse, Thomas Stretch, *Lectures on Massage and Electricity in the Treatment of Disease.* Bristol: John Wright and Co., 1903, p. 181.
18. Smith, E. H., in *Pacific Medical Journal,* February 1903.
19. For examples of spa expenses in the United States, see Cloyes, Samuel A., *The Healer; the Story of Dr. Samantha S. Nivison and Dryden Springs, 1820–1915.* Ithaca, NY: DeWitt Historical

Society of Tompkins County, 1969, p. 24; Karsh, Estrellita, "Taking the Waters at Stafford Springs," *Harvard Library Bulletin*, July 1980, vol. 28, no. 3, pp. 264–281; McMillan, Marilyn, "An Eldorado of Ease and Elegance: Taking the Waters at White Sulphur Springs," *Montana*, vol. 35, Spring 1985, pp. 36–49; and Meeks, Harold, "Smelly, Stagnant and Successful: Vermont's Mineral Springs," *Vermont History*, 1979, vol. 47, no. 1, pp. 5–20.

20. Taylor wrote indefatiguably on the subject of physical therapies for pelvic disorders, and devoted considerable effort to the invention of mechanisms for this purpose. See Taylor, George Henry, *Diseases of Women*. Philadelphia and New York: G. McClean, 1871; *Health for Women*. New York: John B. Alden, 1883 and eleven subsequent editions; "Improvements in Medical Rubbing Apparatus," U.S. Patent 175,202 dated March 21, 1876; *Mechanical Aids in the Treatment of Chronic Forms of Disease*. New York: Rodgers, 1893; *Pelvic and Hernial Therapeutics*. New York: J. B. Alden, 1885; and "Movement Cure," U.S. Patent 263,625 dated August 29, 1882.
21. An example of the early Weiss model is available for study at the Bakken (Library and Museum), Minneapolis, MN, accession number 82.100.
22. Mortimer Granville, Joseph, *Nerve-Vibration and Excitation as Agents in the Treatment of Functional Disorders and Organic Disease*. London: J.&A. Churchill, 1883, p. 57; his American colleague Noble Murray Eberhart advises against vibrating pregnant women "about the generative organs" for fear of producing contractions. See his *A Brief Guide to Vibratory Technique*. 4th ed. rev. and enl. Chicago: New Medicine Publication, c1915, p. 59. For examples of enthusiastic endorsements of the new technology, see Gottschalk, Franklin Benjamin, *Practical Electro-Therapeutics*. Hammond, IN: F. S. Betz, 1904; the same author's *Static Electricity, X-Ray and Electro-Vibration: Their Therapeutic Application*. Chicago: Eisele, 1903; International Correspondence Schools, *A System of Electrotherapeutics*. Scranton, PA: International Textbook Company, 1903, vol. 4; Matijaca, Anthony, *Principles of Electro-Medicine, Electro-Surgery and Radiology*. Tangerine, FL, Butler, NJ and New York, NY: Benedict Lust, 1917; Monell, Samuel Howard, *A System of Instruction in X-Ray Methods and Medical Uses of Light, Hot-Air, Vibration and High Frequency Currents*. New York: E. R. Pelton, 1902; Pilgrim, Maurice Riescher, *Mechanical Vibratory Stimulation; Its Theory and Application in the Treatment of Disease*. New York City: Lawrence Press, c1903; Rice, May Cushman, *Electricity in Gynecology*. Chicago: Laing, 1909; Rockwell, Alphonse David, *The Medical and Surgical Uses of Electricity*. New ed. New York: E. G. Treat, 1903; Snow, *Mechanical Vibration and its Therapeutic Application;* Waggoner, Melanchthon R. *The Note Book of an Electro-Therapist*. Chicago: McIntosh Electrical Corporation, 1923; Wallian, Samuel Spencer, *Rhythmotherapy*. Chicago: Ouellette Press, 1906; and the same author's "Undulatory Theory in Therapeutics," *Medical Brief*, May and June, 1905.
23. See for example, Smith, A. Lapthorn, "Disorders of Menstruation," in *An International System of Electro-Therapeutics*, Horatio Bigelow, ed. Philadelphia: F. A. Davis, 1894, p. G163.
24. Covey, Alfred Dale, *Profitable Office Specialities*. Detroit: Physicians Supply Co., 1912, pp. 16, 18, and 79–95; Bubier, Edward Trevert, *Electro-Therapeutic Hand Book*. New York: Manhattan Electric Supply Co., 1900; Duck, J. J. Co., *Anything Electrical: Catalog No. 6*. Toledo, OH: J. J. Duck, 1916, p. 162; Golden Manufacturing Co., *Vibration: Nature's Great Underlying Force for Health, Strength and Beauty*. Detroit, MI: Golden Manufacturing Co., 1914; Gorman, Sam J. Co. *Physician's Vibragenitant*. Chicago: Sam J. Gorman and Co., n.d.; Keystone Electric Co., *Illustrated Catalogue and Price List of Electro-Therapeutic Appliances . . . etc.* Philadelphia: Keystone Electric Company, c1903, pp. 63–66; Schall and Son, Ltd., *Electro-Medical Instruments and Their Management . . .* 17th ed. London and Glasgow: Schall and Son, 1925; Vibrator Instrument Co., *A Treatise on Vibration and Mechanical Stimulation*. Chattanooga, TN: Vibrator Instrument, 1902; Vibrator Instrument Co. Clinical Dept., *A Course on Mechanical Vibratory Stimulation*. New York City: Vibrator Instrument, 1903; "Vibratory Therapeutics," *Scientific American*, vol. 67, October 22, 1892, p. 265. Most of these manufacturers were quite respectable instrument firms; see Davis, Audrey B., *Medicine and Its Technology: An Introduction to the History of Medical Instrumentation*. Westport, CT: Greenwood Press, 1981, p. 22.

25. Vibrator Instrument Company, *Chattanooga Vibrator.* Chattanooga, TN: Vibrator Instrument, 1904, pp. 3 and 26.
26. Vigouroux, Auguste, *Ètude sur la Rèsistance Èlectrique chez les Melancoliques.* Paris: J. Rueff et Cie, Èditeurs, 1890; Cowen, Richard J., *Electricity in Gynecology.* London: Bailière, Tindall and Cox, 1900; Engelmann, George J., "The Use of Electricity in Gynecological Practice," *Gynecological Transactions,* vol. 11, 1886; Reynolds, David V., "A Brief History of Electrotherapeutics," in *Neuroelectric Research,* D. V. Reynolds and A. Sjoberg, eds. Springfield, IL: Thomas, 1971, pp. 5–12; and Shoemaker, John V., "Electricity in the Treatment of Disease," *Scientific American Supplement,* January 5, 1907, vol. 63, pp. 25923–25924.
27. "Vibratory Therapeutics," *Scientific American,* vol. 67, October 22, 1892, p. 265.
28. O'Neill, John J., *Prodigal Genius: The Life of Nikola Tesla.* New York: Ives Washburn, Inc., 1944, p. 210.
29. *Medical Brief,* May 1905, p. 417. See also the theory of light vibrations employed in the Master Electric Company's advertising brochure *The Master Violet Ray.* Chicago: n.d.
30. Monell, *A System of Instruction . . .*, p. 595; Snow, *Mechanical Vibration.*
31. Monell, *A System of Instrumentation . . .*, p. 591.
32. See for example, "Wanted, Agents and Salesman . . ." Swedish Vibrator Company, *Modern Priscilla,* April 1913, p. 60.
33. "Agents! Drop Dead Ones!" Blackstone Water Power Vacuum Massage Machine, *Hearst's,* April 1916, p. 327; and "Hydro-Massage" Warner Motor Company, *Modern Women,* vol. 11, no. 1, December 1906, p. 190.
34. Wall receptacles are a relatively late introduction. See Schroeder, Fred E., "More 'Small Things Forgotten:' Domestic Electrical Plugs and Receptacles, 1881–1931," *Technology and Culture,* July 1986, vol. 27, no. 3, pp. 525–543.
35. "Massage is as old as the hills . . .," American Vibrator Company, *Woman's Home Companion,* April 1906, p. 42.
36. "Such Delightful Companions!" Star Electrical Necessities, 1922, reproduced in Jones, Edgar R., *Those Were the Good Old Days.* New York: Fireside Books, 1959, unpaged; and "A Gift that Will Keep Her Young and Pretty," Star Home Electric Massage, *Hearst's International,* December 1921, p. 82.
37. See for example, the Ediswan advertisement in *Electrical Age for Women,* January 1932, vol. 2, no. 7, p. 274, and review on page 275 of the same publication.
38. "Vibration Is Life," Lindstrom-Smith Co., *Modern Priscilla,* December 1910, p. 27.
39. Pivar, David J. *Purity Crusade: Sexual Morality and Social Control, 1868–1900.* Westport, CT: Greenwood Press, 1973, pp. 110–117.
40. See also *American Magazine,* December 1912, vol. 75, no. 2, January 1913; vol. 75, no. 3, May 1913; vol. 75, no. 7, p. 127; *Needlecraft,* September 1912, p. 23; *Home Needlework Magazine,* October 1908, p. 479, October 1915, p. 45; *Hearst's,* January 1916, p. 67, February 1916, p. 154, April 1916, p. 329; June 1916, p. 473, and *National Home Journal,* September 1908, p. 15.
41. Davidson, J. E., "Electrical Appliance Sales During 1926," *NELA Bulletin,* vol. 14, no. 2, pp. 119–120.
42. December 5, 1925, vol. 86, p. 1164. See also Hughes, George A. "How the Domestic Electrical Appliances Are Serving the Country," *Electrical Review,* June 15, 1918, vol. 72, p. 983; Edkins, E. A., "Prevalent Trends of Domestic Appliance Market," *Electrical World,* March 30, 1918, pp. 670–671; and "Surveys Retail Sale of Electrical Appliances," *Printer's Ink,* vol. 159, May 19, 1932, p. 35.
43. "Electrical Devices for the Household," *Scientific American,* January 26, 1907, vol. 96, p. 95.
44. The vibrator is not included in extensive lists of appliances in Lamborn, Helen, "Electricity for Domestic Uses," *Harper's Bazaar,* April 1910, vol. 44, p. 285; and Knowlton, H. S., "Extending the Uses of Electricity," *Cassier's Magazine,* vol. 30, June 1906, pp. 99–105.
45. U.S. Bureau of the Census. *Census of Manufactures,* 1908, 1919, and 1947, pp. 216–217, 203, and 734 and 748 respectively.

46. On the early history of appliances, see Lifshey, Earl, *The Housewares Story.* Chicago: Housewares Manufacturers' Association, 1973. For the safety issue, see "Electromedical Apparatus for Domestic Use," *Electrical Review,* October 22, 1926, p. 682.
47. *Good Stories,* October 1933, p. 2; see also similar advertisement in the same issue for Dr. Roger's Relief Compound, p. 12.
48. "Water Stills," *Ainslee's Magazine,* October 1920, p. 164.
49. See for example, Damark International, Inc., *Catalog B-330.* Minneapolis, MN: Damark International, 1988, p. 7, which emphasizes the "Alambiccus Distiller's" usefulness for distilling herbal extracts.
50. *Mellow Mail Catalogue.* Cooper Station, New York City: 1984, pp. 32–39.
51. Levy, Steven, *Hackers: Heroes of the Computer Revolution.* Garden City, NY: Anchor Press/Doubleday, 1984, p. 377.

IS PRIMATOLOGY A FEMINIST SCIENCE?

Linda Marie Fedigan

Primatology appears to have come of age. Historical analyses of our field are now being written. But exactly what sort of discipline has primatology grown up to be? Not for the first time, I found myself pondering this question recently as I spent a day reading some forty of the many reviews of Donna Haraway's 1989 book, *Primate Visions.* Most primatologists are aware of Haraway's nearly 500-page analysis of the history of ideas and practices in the science of primatology; some will have read the book, and many more will have read the reviews of the book that appeared in biological and anthropological journals. Thus, they will be aware that *Primate Visions* was almost universally panned by primatologists (e.g., Cachel 1990; Cartmill 1991; Dunbar 1990, cf., Stanford 1991; Jolly and Jolly 1990; Rodman 1990; Reynolds 1991; Small 1990). However, they may not know that the same book was greeted with much fanfare and the highest praise in a range of journals, from history to science to feminist periodicals (e.g., Fausto-Sterling 1990; Harding 1990; Hubbard 1989; Marcus 1990; Masters 1990; Nyhart 1992; Rossiter 1990; Scheich 1991). For example, one of the latter reviewers stated that *Primate Visions* "changed her life" and was the "most important book to come along in twenty years" (Fausto-Sterling 1990). Although there were exceptions, one can generalize that practicing animal-watchers did not like the book ("infuriating" was an adjective that appeared repeatedly in their reviews), whereas those who study the process of science, especially those feminists who study science, found it brilliant and stunning. A perfect example of this dichotomized reaction is the joint review by Alison Jolly and her daughter Margaretta in the *New Scientist* (1990): the primatologist mother found the book incomprehensible and wrong-headed, whereas the feminist, postmodernist daughter thought it noble and provocative.

It is possible to suggest several reasons why primatologists, male and female, younger and older alike, reacted so negatively to the book. First of all, as noted by Callan (1990) and Cartmill (1991), the deconstructionist analysis practiced by Haraway can be seen as a hostile act that challenges the authority of the scientist. Her fundamental assertions that facts are relative, that science is a form of story-telling, that sociopolitical forces have a major impact on how science is done, are deeply disturbing to many scientists. Secondly, Haraway is an "outsider," who, like a journalist with an agenda, reported a version of the history of primatology with which many of the people who lived that history cannot concur (e.g., Dunbar 1990; Rodman 1990; Small 1990). Thirdly, *Primate Visions* frustrated many readers because it is written in a prose that is inaccessible to them, a writing style referred to by Alison Jolly as "armor-plated, post-modern, feminist jargon." Haraway herself did not intend her analysis to be hostile to primatologists (1989: 366), and she may well have been surprised by the extent and depth of negative response she received from its practitioners. Indeed, it could be argued that Haraway's depiction of the history of primatology is that of a science becoming increasingly enlightened over time, especially, she implied, as more women entered the discipline. A thorough analysis of Donna Haraway's *Primate Visions* and the reactions to it is beyond the scope of this chapter, but I would like to pursue here the point that feminist scholars liked and approved of this book, and, in fact, many of them look very favorably on the discipline of primatology. Primatologists should be aware that Haraway is only one of a group of "science studies" scholars who are out there watching and evaluating scientists; turning the tables by following *us* around with tape recorders and notebooks.

A review of the literature on gender and science shows that feminist scholars often single out primatology as a discipline in which women have made a greater than average impact (see Fedigan 1994; Strum and Fedigan, in press), and one in which women have had a marked influence for the betterment of their science. Although such scholars may disagree as to whether women have always, or only recently, played an important role in primatology, and they may dispute the precise nature of this role, it is clear that primatology is often singled out for praise by feminists. Indeed, it is sometimes interpreted as a feminist science itself. For example, Rosser (1986: 175) said: "Primatology is the field within the sciences where the research has been most transformed by the feminist perspective." And Bleier (1986: 10) concluded that:

> Primatology thus serves as an example of the correction that a feminist perspective can effect in a field of knowledge . . . primatology is a lone example in the natural sciences of dramatic changes made under feminist viewpoints. This is related, in part, to the presence of a critical mass of women and feminists within the field . . .

Similarly, Keller (1987a: 235) commented that:

> Over the past 15 years, women working in the field [of primatology] have undertaken an extensive re-examination of theoretical concepts, often using essentially the same methodological tools. These efforts have resulted in some radically different formulations.

What strikes me as curious about such accolades from feminist science scholars is the possibility that theirs is an unrequited love affair, because there are so few primatologists who acknowledge that they are feminists or admire, much less pursue, feminist goals. Obviously, one may counter that it is not common scientific practice to declare one's sociopolitical allegiances, and that we have no objective data on the proportion of primatologists who could be considered feminists. Further, it is possible that some primatologists wish to disassociate themselves from the implications and repercussions of being labeled feminists, while at the same time adhering to principles congruent with those of feminism. Has primatology quietly, and without announcement, become a genre of feminist science? Or is this a case of mistaken identity? Is it possible that primatologists are doing things of which feminists approve for reasons not directly related to feminism? In order to consider this question, it is necessary to first address a set of prior issues. What *do* feminists approve of in science—what is the feminist critique of science? What are the criteria for a feminist science? Is primatology a discipline influenced by the woman's point of view? Is primatology a discipline influenced by the feminist point of view, indeed, a feminist science? I do not claim to give a definitive answer to the last question, but I will lay out the issues, offer an opinion, and make suggestions for how we might develop a better sense of primatology's place in science.

FEMINIST CRITIQUES OF SCIENCE

It took some time for feminist scholars to turn their critical eye on the natural sciences, and even today there is not a unified challenge to the conceptual framework of science or one coherent strategy for alleviating what feminists see to be the problems with the scientific enterprise. According to Fee (1986), feminists in the early stages of the women's movement saw science and technology as located in the (public) male world and having little to do with the politics of personal relationships, sexuality, and reproduction that were the focus of their concerns. Beginning in the mid-1970s and early 1980s, however, the growing issues of reproductive engineering, and the relationship between science and the technologies affecting the lives of women around the world, led feminist scholars to turn their analytical skills to addressing the production and application of scientific knowledge. In particular, many of these writers developed critiques of specific theories in the biological sciences, ranging from models of human evolution to deterministic explanations of differences between the sexes to endocrinological constructions of ontogeny (e.g., Birke 1986; Bleier 1984; Fausto-Sterling 1985; Haraway 1978, 1981; Hubbard *et al.* 1982; Keller 1992; Leibowitz 1983; Longino and Doell 1983; Lowe and Hubbard 1983; Sayers 1982; Tanner 1981; Tuana 1989; Zihlman 1978, 1981). Usually these critiques sought to expose the androcentric language and concepts seen as inherent in the theories, and sometimes they offered an alternative explanation—one from the female point of view.

As well, feminist scholars in the 1980s and 1990s turned their attention to critiquing the entire scientific enterprise as it has been traditionally conceptualized and conducted in the Western world (e.g., Harding 1986; Keller 1985, 1992; Longino 1990; Merchant 1980; Tuana 1993). These analysts concluded that the history of science in the West is founded on assumptions of male domination and patriarchal power. Keller and others have argued that, at least since the Renaissance, the language and metaphors of science have been those of domination and sexuality. The mind is male and nature is female, men gain knowledge (power) by conquering and penetrating nature. Although these metaphors may no longer be so overt as in the writings of Francis Bacon, the fundamental dualities of mind/body, objectivity/subjectivity, active/passive, detachment/attachment, dominance/subordinance, subject/object, rationality/emotionality have become fundamental in Western thinking, and in all cases the former are associated with men, and with science. This association is believed by some to be the reason why women, even today, are less attracted to, and comfortable in, science. According to this argument, the men who brought about the scientific revolution created an enterprise in their own idealized image. Keller (1985 but cf. 1992), Chodorow (1978), Dinnerstein (1976), and Merchant (1980) have offered psychoanalytic theories to explain why men in Western societies wish to associate themselves with characteristics such as detachment, objectivity and rationality, and to accord them higher value than their opposites.

Women have reacted to this model of science in various ways. Most have simply steered clear of the enterprise. Others have attempted to enter science, but, according to Fee (1986), found it strategic to deny that gender attributes play any role in science. Often women scientists have found it necessary to be "nonfeminine" in order to be accorded authority. However, others have argued that women should not have to remake themselves in a masculine manner in order to be scientists; rather, science itself should change.

Harding (1986) has identified five different types of feminist critique of science. The first are equity studies which document the obstacles that women face in obtaining the educational and employment opportunities available to similarly talented men. The second are studies of the sexist uses and abuses of science and technology in various fields such as reproductive technologies. The third line of feminist critique questions the concept and possibility of scientific objectivity by demonstrating that all steps in the process are value-laden, from the original selection of phenomena to be studied to the final interpretation of results. A fourth type of critique uses techniques from psychoanalysis, literary criticism, and historical interpretation to find hidden symbolic and structural meanings in scientific claims and practices. And the fifth area of feminist criticism involves the development of feminist epistemologies (e.g., feminist empiricism, standpoint, and postmodernism) to lay the foundation for an alternative understanding of how knowledge and beliefs are grounded in social experience.

Keller characterized the feminist critique of science as occurring along a political spectrum. Slightly left of center is the liberal critique that almost all scientists are men because of unfair employment practices. Compared to other criticisms, this critique would be relatively easy to address and correct. Further to the left is the radical critique that the predominance of men in science has led to bias in the choice of problems with which scientists have concerned themselves. In several sciences, such as the health sciences (and, I would argue, primatology), this criticism has begun to be addressed. Slightly more radical is the claim of bias in the design and interpretation of experiments. Finally, the most radical critique is to question the very assumptions of objectivity and rationality that underlie the scientific enterprise itself. Keller has cautioned against a view of science as pure social product and outlined the dangers of an intellectual descent into total relativity. In her opinion, we should reformulate and maintain the objective effort but abandon the objectivist illusion. "In short, rather than abandon the quintessentially human effort to understand the world in rational terms, we need to refine that effort" (Keller 1987a: 238).

Harding (1986) has also noted that the ultimate objective of feminist critiques should be to bring an end to androcentrism, not to systematic inquiry, even though an end to androcentrism will require far-reaching transformations of that inquiry. Although the feminist critiques are obviously diverse, it seems to me that they share two fundamental commonalties: (1) the assertion that the inferior status of women in science is related to the inferior status of women in society at large, and one will not change without reform in the other; and (2) the attempt to document and bring an end to androcentric bias in science.

FEMINIST MODELS OF SCIENCE

Just as there are various feminist critiques and many types of feminists, so there are a number of different models for feminist science. Some theorists have observed that the sciences are so diverse, it is unreasonable to expect them all to be transformed by one feminist framework, and that the search for one "correct" feminist approach is misplaced and runs the dangers of introducing a new orthodoxy (e.g., Longino 1989, 1990; Stanley and Wise 1983). Others have argued that it is not possible to even begin to design a feminist science until we have a more feminist and egalitarian society (Birke 1986; Bleier 1986; Fee 1983), or that asking us to envision a feminist science today is like asking a medieval peasant to design a space capsule (Fee 1983).

Nonetheless, a number of scholars have outlined their vision of what science would look like in a future, more feminist society, or how science might be, and indeed is, practiced by feminists today (e.g., Birke 1986; Bleier 1986; Fee 1986; Harding 1986; Longino 1990; Rosser 1989; Wylie 1992). Rather than describe each of these models in turn, I will attempt to extract the features that many of the descriptions have in common. Although I recognize that this risks oversimplification and the implication of one limiting orthodoxy, when in fact many views prevail, it does allow us to distill the elements of feminist ideology that have been applied specifically to the transformation of the practices of science. And such a distillation of the literature on feminist science is necessary before we can assess its application to the field of primate studies.

There are at least six features commonly outlined in models of feminist science. The first may be referred to as reflexivity, or the acknowledgement of the contextual values that influence everyone, including the scientists among us. Such contextual values are believed to act as constraints on the reasoning and interpretations that affect our world view, and usually are seen to be related to race, class, gender, and nationality, among other factors. In a feminist science, it is often proposed that practitioners would seek to understand their fundamental assumptions and how these affect their science; they would see themselves as people whose background and experiences are involved in the process of doing science. Such an acknowledgement of biases and of the role that sociopolitical considerations play in the scientific enterprise would clearly require a rethinking of the traditional concept of scientific objectivity.

In particular, feminists have been concerned that scientists acknowledge the role that gender plays in how they perceive the world, and that scientists explicitly factor gender into their research. This leads to the second feature common to many models of feminist science: the goal of empowering women by developing a way of understanding the world from the woman's point of view. As noted by Wylie (1992), such research would assist scientists to critically reassess the theory that distorts or devalues the lives and experiences of women, and would allow us to evaluate and understand the gendered dimensions of life that conventional categories of analysis ignore.

A third common feature of feminist models involves a reconceptualization of nature. In many models of feminist science, nature would be conceptualized not as passive and subject to human control, domination and manipulation, but rather as active, complex, and holistic. Science would be committed to understanding and working in cooperation with nature; and the language of scientists would shift away from metaphors of hierarchy and domination to those of comprehension and "empowerment." Related to this is a fourth feature suggested in many models; the move away from dualisms and reductionism. Many feminist scientists have argued for the lessening of boundaries between the scientist as knower, and the object of knowledge, between objectivity and subjectivity, dispassion and empathy, and a move toward seeing the elements of nature on a continuum rather than in binary opposition.

Fifth, scientific knowledge would be seen and used as a liberating tool rather than one of domination and nationalism; it would be geared to humanitarian values, and to the solution of world problems. Many models of feminist science speak of an enterprise that would serve humanity rather than the military-industrial complex of western nations ("human need rather than corporate greed": Birke 1986: 143). And finally, in feminist models, the scientific community itself would change; it would become less elitist and more accessible, egalitarian, diverse in make-up and background, and humble in the face of the complexity of life.

Clearly these are utopian goals, and perhaps we can understand now why many feminists argue that a feminist science is not possible in our present world. A more pragmatic approach is taken by Harding (1989, 1991), who concludes that there *are* feminist sciences already in existence today, and that we can recognize them by observing what feminist scientists *do* in fields such as anthropology and psychology, where feminist efforts are already a force with which to reckon. According to Harding, feminist scientists are characterized by being strongly reflexive, by focusing on gender as a variable that infuses behavior, views and society, and by "thinking from women's lives," thereby providing some of the crucial resources needed to develop science for the many, rather than for the elitist few.

FEMALE, FEMININE, AND FEMINIST SCIENCE

One of the confusing issues for nonfeminists and feminists alike is precisely what it means to "think from women's lives." Some have taken this to mean that women might possess a unified cognitive framework that can be brought to bear on the practices of science, and that women may thus do science differently from their male counterparts.

Those adhering to this view can be broken into two categories. A very small minority of feminists have argued that women have biologically based traits which are superior to those of men, and that these traits should be espoused in science (e.g., Elshtain 1981; MacMillan 1982). This might be characterized as the argument for a "female science" based on biological sex differences. More commonly, theorists have suggested that the behavior and beliefs of women are *socially* constructed, and that it is the differential history, status, and socialization of women which provide them with a perspective on life and on science that is different from that of their male colleagues. This can be characterized as the argument for a "feminine science" based on socialized gender differences. Scattered through the literature on gender and science (see references in Fee 1983, 1986; Harding 1986; Longino 1990; Rosser 1986, 1989) are suggestions that, as a result of their experiences and position in life, women are more likely than men to possess certain characteristics that enable them to better understand the complexities of natural processes, or at least to develop an alternative world view to the traditional dualistic, hierarchical, "masculine view" of science. A short list of proposed "feminine characteristics" are: a sense of connectedness to nature, an integrative, holistic, contextual world view, a disposition to attend to details, complexities and interactions, a sense of patience and empathy, and a high valuation of pragmatic, experiential knowledge. Fee (1986), for example, has argued that, whether consciously articulated or not, women carry the seeds of an alternative epistemology, and several notable works in psychology (e.g., Belenky *et al.* 1986; Gilligan 1982) have pursued this argumentation.

Some theorists have implied that a feminist science, that is a science based on a theoretical/political stance, would incorporate these presumed feminine characteristics, but there have been objections to this conflation of feminine traits and feminist goals on several grounds. For example, Longino (1990) noted that some women scientists object to such a characterization of feminist science simply as "soft" science, as a new guise for the old argument that women cannot do real, quantitative, hard science. A related objection to the thesis that women scientists will exhibit socialized "feminine traits" is the counterargument that both women and men scientists have been strongly socialized as scientists, and thus gender differences should be minimized. And some feminists (e.g., Harding 1986; Keller 1987b; Longino 1990) have argued that these very traits ascribed to women are socially constructed categories that originated in the historical subordination of women, and are merely the converse of the culturally dominant "masculine" traits. As such, they may be as much characteristics of "outsiders" of the scientific mainstream as characteristics of women. At the very least, it would surely be an oversimplification to suggest that these "feminine" traits reflect the temperaments and world view of all women.

Thus, it is important to distinguish the concept of a feminist science from that of a feminine science: feminism is a theoretical/political stance, and thus the characteristics of *feminists* doing science may well be distinctive from those of *women* doing science (see also Keller 1987b, 1992 on the distinction between gender ideology and women doing science). Feminist theorists, such as Harding, Keller and Longino, are not proposing that feminine biases should replace masculine biases in science, rather they are proposing that an acknowledgement of biases (i.e., contextual values) and a greater diversity of contextual values through the inclusion of people of different backgrounds will result in better science.

In practice, however, it is not always easy to separate the idea of a feminine from a feminist science, since many feminists do see those values thought to be more characteristic of women as essential to a feminist science. As Schiebinger (1987) has noted, traditional feminine values alone may not serve well as an epistemological base for new philosophies of science, but feminist critiques do promote feminine values as an essential part of the human experience, and envision a science that would integrate all aspects of the human experience.

WOMEN AND PRIMATOLOGY

Having summarized the feminist critique of science and distilled the common features of feminist models of science, we are now in a better position to address the questions about primatology raised at the beginning of this chapter. Is primatology a discipline influenced by the woman's point of view? There are several levels at which this question may be addressed. First, there is the presence of a "critical mass of women" in primatology referred to by Bleier (1986) in the statement quoted earlier. A common perception among many observers of science is that there are more women in primatology than in similar fields. My recent analysis of proportions of women and men in professional societies in 1991–2 established that there *is* a significantly higher proportion of women in primatology than in analogous biological sciences, such as ornithology, mammalogy, and benthology (Fedigan 1994). However, there are *not* significantly more women primatologists than there are women anthropologists, psychologists and animal behaviorists, the latter being the three parental disciplines that gave rise to primatology. In 1991, women made up 48 per cent of the membership of the American Society of Primatologists and 38 per cent of the International Primatological Society. By 1992, French (1993) reported that women made up 52 per cent of the American Society of Primatologists. There has been a significant increase in the proportion of women members of primatological societies over the past decade. Thus, the perception that there is a critical mass of women in primatology is likely valid in a comparison across the biological sciences, but not particularly striking from the perspective of the behavioral sciences, such as anthropology and psychology.

Secondly, does the presence of relatively more women, or near gender parity, in a given science influence that discipline? As noted earlier, it has sometimes been argued that women may practice science differently from men, that is, they may tend to choose different topics, frame different questions, prefer different theories and hypotheses, select different methods, and favor different interpretations of scientific findings than do their male counterparts. There has been as yet little research into what male and female primatologists actually do, so there is not much evidence to support or reject the argument of gender differences in scientific practice. The primary assumption is that women scientists focus more on female animals, and there has been some, mainly indirect, evidence that this is the case (e.g., Adams and Burnett 1991; Burk 1986; Haraway 1989; Small 1984; cf. Holmes and Hitchcock 1992). It has also been suggested that women are more likely to try to see the social and physical environment from the female animal's point of view (Haraway 1989; Hrdy 1984; Rowell 1984). I have argued elsewhere (Strum and Fedigan, in press) that over the past two decades the image of female primates has been fleshed out to include much more than just their roles as mothers and sexual partners of males, the two primary descriptors used in earlier studies of primate behavior. In the past twenty years there have been many studies of the significance of female bonding through matrilineal networks, as well as analyses of female sexual assertiveness, female long-term knowledge of the group's local environment, female social strategies, female cognitive skills, and female competition for reproductive success. That women have been more responsible than men for developing our present model of the female primate has been suggested, but not documented. A quantitative scientist might examine whether there is a significant relationship between the relative proportions of women in primatology over the past four decades and the proportions of published papers written "from the female animal's point of view." This has not yet been done.

Finally, there is the possibility that primatology has been influenced by a distinctive cognitive and emotional framework or worldview of women described earlier as the "feminine" approach to science. Although there have been many criticisms of this suggestion, others have argued that women scientists are more likely than men to be patient and empathetic, to take a holistic, contextual approach, to attend to complexities and details, to favor pragmatic, empirical evidence, and integrative interpretations. Is this true of women primatologists? I think that this would be almost impossible to establish on any global scale. However, I have argued elsewhere (Fedigan and Fedigan 1989) that the women who were primarily responsible for transforming our model of baboon behavior in the 1970s and 1980s exhibited all of the characteristics just cited, albeit as did several of the men.

FEMINISM AND PRIMATOLOGY

Has primatology been influenced by the sociopolitical movement known as the women's movement and the theoretical/political stance known as feminism? Some scholars (e.g., Haraway 1989; Hrdy 1986; Sperling 1991) have argued it cannot be a coincidence that a strong shift in the perception of female primates began to occur in the mid-1970s, during the same years as those in which the second wave of western feminism urged scientists to take account of the female point of view. Apart from noting this apparent synchrony of historical events, how might we document the impact of feminism on primatology? Few primatologists, other than Hrdy (1986) and Smuts (in Rosenthal, 1991) have identified themselves in print as feminists, which does not mean that others were not influenced by feminism. It would be possible to ask those primatologists who focused on females and the female point of view, what influenced them to do so. However, this method would also run the risks of any self-reporting study (e.g., revisionist history).

Another approach would be to build a circumstantial case by showing that primatology in the past twenty years has shifted toward the values and practices of feminist science. One of the "science studies" scholars (Rosser 1986) has already made such an argument about primatology, and I will briefly outline her logic here, as well as offering my own examples for clarity.

Rosser modified a scheme originally developed to track the changes in curricula in the liberal arts and applied it to the feminist transformation of research and teaching in the sciences. Her scheme consists of six stages in the feminist transformation of science. Stage 1 is characterized by the failure to even note absence of women (or females). I would say that this stage would encompass the first wave of field studies following World War II (approximately 1950–65), during which time the male dominance hierarchy was often assumed to represent the entire social system of primates (see Strum and Fedigan, in press). Stage 2 begins the search for the missing females. Still working within the on-going paradigms of the science, the research that was formerly carried out on the males of the species was now conducted on the females as well. My interpretation is that in primatology, this stage was characterized by the deliberate attempt to collect more data on females and the publication of books such as *Female Primates* (Small 1984) and *Social Behavior of Female Vertebrates* (Wasser 1983). Stage 3 is characterized by a growing awareness that females have been a disadvantaged, subordinate group, and a questioning about why this is the case. Examples of this stage in primatology might be Hrdy and Williams (1983) and Fedigan (1982), both of which critiqued the past biases against females in primatological theory and data collection.

Stage 4 in Rosser's scheme represents the transition from questioning within the traditional paradigm of the given science, to a breaking free to study females on their own terms, that is, to develop a female point of view which may be outside the prevailing paradigm. This stage includes a rise in feminist consciousness on the part of the researcher. Rosser takes her example of this stage from Hrdy's description (1981, 1986) of how she (Hrdy) realized that the theories she had learned in graduate school did not apply to the female langurs she was studying. Hrdy noted that her shifting perception of female langurs was linked to her dawning awareness of male—female power relationships in her own life, and her attempts to understand and articulate the general experience of female primates. Stage 5 is characterized by the use of the newly discovered female point of view to challenge the traditional theories and models of the science. Gender is used as a category of analysis to test the traditional paradigms. Again, Rosser uses Hrdy's research as an example, and interprets Hrdy's studies of female competition, sexual assertiveness, and infanticide as examples of testing the established paradigms of sociobiology in the science of primatology. Other examples of testing and challenging established sociobiological theories using gender as a category of analysis would be Small (1993) and Smuts (1992; see also Smuts and Smuts 1992). Stage 6 represents a transformed, "balanced" view in which both female and male perspectives and experiences are included and integrated.

Thus, based largely on her reading of Sarah Hrdy's research, Rosser finds that primatology is the field within the sciences which has been most transformed by the feminist perspective. While it is certainly true that Rosser's interpretation would be strengthened had she read more widely in primatology, can we nonetheless concur with her general conclusion that our discipline has moved through the stages as outlined? I would argue, and have done so elsewhere (Fedigan 1994), that primatology has shown itself to be very responsive to criticisms of androcentric language and interpretations, and quite willing to redress the past focus on male behavior with a present focus on both sexes and on the relationship between the sexes. As primatologists, we have certainly seen more and more efforts to collect information on female lives and behaviors, and to develop equivalent understandings of how female and male primates perceive, behave, and interact in their worlds. If this is a feminist transformation, then it has happened in primatology. Below I will consider alternative explanations for why primatology in the past twenty years has better developed its knowledge and understanding of female primates.

A more generalized, if still circumstantial, case might be built by examining trends in primatology, especially changing trends over the past twenty years, in light of the six common characteristics of feminist models of science described earlier. Although I cannot pretend to a quantitative analysis or even a profound qualitative analysis here, I will offer my opinions as to whether or not primatology exhibits any or all of these six characteristics, as a vehicle for further discussion.

The most commonly mentioned feature of feminist science is "reflexivity," which, as noted above, refers to an awareness and acknowledgement of the contextual values that constrain our perception of the world, especially our views of our scientific subject-matter. Nothing in the published work of primatologists indicates that they are particularly reflexive about the role of race, class, or national biases in their work. However, there is one fundamental tenet in primatology which is highly reflexive and that is the awareness of the dangers of anthropomorphism. Primatologists work with animals that look and often seem to behave in ways familiar to humans, and one of the principles that is drilled into new recruits is that we must avoid ascribing human motivations, value's and understandings to our animal subjects. As scientists, primatologists are constantly reminded that we are limited by our human world view, and that this affects our understanding of our subjects, even as we strive to understand the animals in their own right. Further, most primatologists in North America are trained in anthropology departments (French 1993), and will be familiar with the taboo against ethnocentrism, the latter being the often unconscious view that one's cultural patterns are the only acceptable form of behavior. Although primatologists, like other scientists, strive for objectivity in their research, they have been made well aware that scientists come to their subject-matter with certain preconceptions.

A second feature common to feminist models of science is the factoring of sex and gender differences into research and the development of the female point of view. I would say that primatology has definitely developed a strong female point of view over the past fifteen years, and it may well be this attention paid to female primates on the part of scientists that drew the attention of feminist scholars in the first place. Why have primatologists developed a strong female point of view? As noted above, it may be the result of feminist ideology. It may also be that the nature of the subject-matter lends itself to a female-centered "world view" in primatologists. Many primate societies are female-bonded; thus kin-related females are the permanent core of the social group, competing with conspecifics for resources, defending themselves against predators, and finding enough food to feed themselves and their suckling young. This was not immediately recognized by primatologists, but it has now forced itself on the consciousness of these scientists, and possibly facilitated a strong focus on females as well as attracting more women to the discipline.

A third feature in feminist models is a reconceptualization of nature as a complex phenomenon with which humans would best attempt to cooperate rather than dominate. Does primatology exhibit this trait? I would answer a cautious yes, and suggest that the primatologists' conceptualization of nature, like the primatologist's concept of female primates, is based largely on their subject-matter—the primates. Primates are complex, long-lived animals who exist in a multi-layered web of environmental and social interactions. In order to observe them in the wild, many months, even years, of patient observation are necessary. One develops a very different attitude in this type of study than that developed, for example, when studying thousands of short-lived creatures whose populations are easily manipulated. Without belittling the laboratory work and experimental field work that does take place in primatology, I would say that the goal of most field observation is to better understand the subject-matter, rather than to manipulate or control it. Furthermore, all primatologists are concerned about the increasingly endangered populations of primates in the wild, and the destruction of their habitats. This renders almost all primatologists environmentalists, the latter being a group that is certainly dedicated to working with and not against nature.

Has primatology exhibited the fourth feature common to many models of feminist science, that is, a move away from reductionism and dualisms? Again, I would answer a qualified yes. I would not argue that most primatologists have lessened the boundaries between themselves as scientists and their subjects, nor do they usually have the ability or desire to let the "subject" speak for her or his self, as is recently the case in the human behavioral sciences. However, a very important trend in the past twenty years of primatology is to increasingly portray our subjects as cognizant, sentient, socially intelligent creatures, who are not simply automatons responding to genetic or hormonal directives. A good example is the study of social dominance relations. At first it was assumed by many primatologists that the bigger, stronger, tougher individuals would be socially dominant over their conspecifics. Now we realize the enormous role played by individual intelligence, social traditions, and social strategies in determining power relationships among nonhuman primates. We have moved from an oversimplified concept of "brute" force to a more complex one of "social finesse" (e.g., Strum 1987). I would say that a move from reductionist understandings of primate behavior to more sophisticated ones is characteristic of many areas of primatological research in the past couple of decades.

Fifth, is primatology geared to humanitarian values and to the solution of world problems rather than to serving nationalistic interests? Clearly, unlike such fields as physics and engineering, primatology does not lend itself particularly well to serving nationalistic, military—industrial interests. However, as pointed out by Haraway (1989), primatological research has sometimes been carried out by and for military interests. I do not know if this is any less true today than in the past. I do know, however, that primates are often used as models for human problems, both behavioral and biological, and in that respect primatology does serve humanitarian ends. The study of primates allows us to put humans into a larger, cross-specific comparative perspective, and one of the ultimate rewards of studying our primate relatives is a better understanding of what it means to be human.

Finally, there is the question of the primatological community; has it become more diverse, accessible and egalitarian over time, as postulated in feminist models of science? Certainly, more and more women are entering the discipline, but there is little evidence in North America and Europe that people of diverse races and classes are pouring into this science. However, there is an increasingly good representation of different nationalities at international primatological meetings, and there have been attempts on the part of many primatologists working in Third World countries to train local people to become scientists. Furthermore, the two major primatological societies (the International Primatological Society and the American Society of Primatologists) have recently made available scholarships specifically targeted for Third World students and scholars. But clearly more could be done to encourage accessibility and diversity of background in this science.

CONCLUSION

In sum, primatology does exhibit several of the features that have been described in feminist models of science. Also, more and more women have entered the discipline over the past decade, and recently there are nearly equal proportions of women and men primatologists. Over the past twenty years, primatology has produced a strong, well-developed focus on the female as well as the male primate. Has primatology become a genre of feminist science? According to the published criteria available on feminist science, I would say, yes. But whether by design or not is a different question. Some primatologists are no doubt feminists. Others may subscribe to values and practices approved of by feminists for reasons that they do not directly relate to feminism.

If the correlation between feminist science and trends in primatology that has been suggested in this chapter were substantiated, at least two alternative explanations should be considered. The first is that the objectives of a feminist science may be similar to those of other alternative approaches to the scientific enterprise. For example, Fee (1986), Haraway (1989) and Montgomery (1991) have noted the similarities between the feminist critique of science and other epistemologies of science, such as the African, Indian, Chinese, Japanese and Marxist perspectives on natural knowledge. There may not be that many different ways to do science. The women's movement in the 1970s can also be seen as part of a larger liberation movement growing out of the "counter-culture" of the 1960s in North American and Europe. A thorough analysis would consider the possible influences of many social forces, and not just feminism, on the development of the discipline of primatology in North America and Europe.

Secondly, some of the trends in primatology that have been identified in this chapter, such as the development of a female as well as male perspective, and the move from reductionism and dualisms to increasingly complex, sophisticated explanatory models, could arguably result from the processes intrinsic to the maturation of all scientific disciplines. It is possible that any new science would go through initial stages of being relatively mechanistic and making simplifying assumptions. As the science matures, it would be expected to graduate to sophisticated models that are more complex, dynamic, and multi-factorial. Thus, the goals of those who try to develop a better, more mature science of primatology may sometimes dovetail with the goals of those aspiring to a feminist science.

Nonetheless, a good circumstantial case can be made that primatology has been influenced, if not transformed, by feminist perspectives and objectives, and I have suggested ways that this influence might be more directly documented. At the very least, we should give credit to the feminist critique for drawing our attention to androcentric bias in science, and for challenging us to develop a more balanced view in which both female and male perspectives and experiences are taken fully into account.

However, the reception of the feminist critique by practicing scientists, including women scientists, has often been less than positive, and Hammonds reviews the reasons for this lack of enthusiasm (Longino and Hammonds 1990). She suggests that a primary reason for the negative response is the perception by scientists that the feminist critique of science is a political rather than a scholarly enterprise. She also argues that scientists and feminists cast the "women in science" problem differently: scientists ask "what is it about women's lives that keep them from doing science?", whereas feminists ask "what is it about science that keeps women from participating?" The former question locates the problem with women; the latter formulation situates the problem in science.

Do these general observations on the chasm between many practicing scientists and feminist critics of science help us to understand the negative reaction to Haraway's history of primatology on the part of its practitioners? Longino (in Longino and Hammonds 1990) states that scientists may misread Haraway as an anti-realist who licenses any claim so long as it is in opposition to the mainstream discourse, and who sees primatology as nothing more than self-serving stories. Longino argues on the contrary that Haraway sees the production of primate knowledge as rule-governed (although the rules may change over time), and Haraway acknowledges that scientific representations, produced according to the rules of inquiry in given fields, have made it possible to interact with our material surroundings in reliable ways. However, she believes that scientists cannot inform us about human values and justice. According to Longino, Haraway does not dispute the role of science as representer of natural processes, but she does contest primatology's claim to hold objective blueprints for the transition from nature to culture and for the original form of human society and justice. Thus, Haraway has tried to convince her readers that "primatology is politics" and "political," as noted by Hammonds, is precisely what most practicing scientists do not wish to be. One of primatology's self-avowed tasks is to help us understand the evolution of primate and human sociality, and even those primatologists who would agree with many of the goals of feminist science may not be able to accept Haraway's fundamental questioning of their authority in this endeavor.

ACKNOWLEDGEMENTS

My research is supported by an on-going grant from the Natural Sciences and Engineering Research Council of Canada (NSERCC, Operating Grant no. A7723). Long walks and lively conversations with Shirley Strum over the past several years stimulated me to address the issues in this chapter, and I thank Shirley for her probing, but always courteous, questions about my assumptions. I also thank Pam Asquith, Mary Pavelka, Sandra Zohar and Lori Hager for their critical reading of the manuscript, and Meg Conkey for sharing her list of reviews of Donna Haraway's *Primate Visions.*

Bibliography

Adams, E. R. and Burnett, G. W. (1991) "Scientific Vocabulary Divergence among Female Primatologists Working in East Africa," *Social Studies of Science* 21:547–60.

Belenky, M. E., Clinchy, B. M., Goldberger, N. R., and Tarule, J. M. (1986) *Women's Ways of Knowing. The Development of Self, Voice, and Mind,* New York: Basic Books, Inc.

Birke, L. (1986) *Women, Feminism and Biology. The Feminist Challenge,* New York: Metheun.

Bleier, R. (1984) *Science and Gender. A Critique of Biology and Its Theories on Women,* New York: Pergamon Press.

——— (1986) "Introduction," in R. Bleier (ed.) *Feminist Approaches to Science,* New York: Pergamon Press.

Burk, T. (1986) "Sexual Selection, Feminism and the Behavior of Biologists: Changes in the Study of Animal Behavior, 1953–85," *Creighton University Faculty Journal* 5: 1–16.

Cachel, S. (1990) "Partisan Primatology," *American Journal of Primatology* 22: 139–142.

Callan, H. (1990) "Writing Primates," *Anthropology Today* 6: 13–15

Cartmill, M. (1991) "Review of *Primate Visions,*" *International Journal of Primatology* 12: 67–75.

Chodorow, N. (1978) *The Reproduction of Mothering: Psychoanalysis and the Sociology of Gender,* Berkeley: University of California Press.

Dinnerstein, D. (1976) *The Mermaid and the Minotaur: Sexual Arrangements and the Human Malaise,* New York: Harper and Row.

Dunbar, R. (1990) "The Apes as We Want to See Them," *New York Times Book Review* January 10: 30.

Elshtain, J. B. (1981) *Public Man, Private Woman: Woman in Social and Political Thought,* Princeton, NJ: Princeton University Press.

Fausto-Sterling, A. (1985) *Myths of Gender,* New York: Basic Books.

——— (1990) "Essay Review: Primate Visions, a Model for Historians of Science?" *Journal of the History of Biology* 23: 329–333.

Fedigan, L. M. (1982) *Primate Paradigms. Sex Roles and Social Bonds.* Chicago: University of Chicago Press.

——— (1994) "Science and the Successful Female: Why There Are So Many Women Primatologists," *American Anthropologist* 96: 529–40.

——— and Fedigan, L. (1989) "Gender and the Study of Primates," in S. Morgan (ed.) *Gender and Anthropology. Critical Reviews for Teaching and Research,* Washington DC: American Anthropological Association, pp. 41–64.

Fee, E. (1983) "Women's Nature and Scientific Objectivity," in M. Lowe and R. Hubbard (eds) *Woman's Nature. Rationalizations of Inequality,* New York: Pergamon Press.

——— (1986) "Critiques of Modern Science: the Relationship of Feminism to other Radical Epistemologies," in R. Bleier (ed.) *Feminist Approaches to Science,* New York: Pergamon Press.

French, J. A. (1993) "A Demographic Analysis of the Membership of the American Society of Primatologists: 1992," *American Journal of Primatology* 29: 159–165.

Gilligan, C. (1982) *In a Different Voice. Psychological Theory and Women's Development,* Cambridge, Mass.: Harvard University Press.

Haraway, D. (1978) "Animal Sociology and a Natural Economy of the Body Politic," *Signs* 4: 21–60.

——— (1981) "In the Beginning Was the Word: The Genesis of Biological Theory," *Signs* 6: 469–481.

——— (1989) *Primate Visions. Gender, Race and Nature in the World of Modern Science,* New York: Routledge, Chapman, and Hall.

Harding, S. (1986) *The Science Question in Feminism,* Ithaca: Cornell University Press.

——— (1989) "Is There a Feminist Method?" in N. Tuana (ed.) *Feminism and Science,* Bloomington: Indiana University Press.

——— (1990) "Review of *Primate Visions*," *National Women's Studies Association Journal* 2: 295–298.
——— (1991) *Whose Science? Whose Knowledge?* Ithaca: Cornell University Press.
Holmes, D. J. and Hitchcock, C. L. (1991) "Gender as a Predictor of Research Topic in Animal Behavior," Paper presented at the Annual National Meetings of the Animal Behavior Society, University of North Carolina at Wilmington.
Hubbard, R. (1989) "Planet of the Apes, Dismantling the Empire of Science," *The Village Voice*, October 3: 63.
———, Henefin, M. S. and Fried, B. (eds) (1982) *Biological Woman: The Convenient Myth*, Cambridge, Mass.: Schenkman Press.
Hrdy, S. B. (1981) *The Woman That Never Evolved*, Cambridge, Mass.: Harvard University Press.
——— (1984) "Introduction," in M. Small (ed.) *Female Primates. Studies by Women Primatologists*, New York: Alan R. Liss.
——— (1986) "Empathy, Polyandry, and the Myth of the Coy Female," in R. Bleier (ed.) *Feminist Approaches to Science*, New York: Pergamon Press.
——— and Williams, G. C. (1983) "Behavioral Biology and the Double Standard," in S. K. Wasser (ed.) *Social Behavior of Female Vertebrates*, New York: Academic Press.
Jolly, A. and Jolly, M. (1990) "A View from the Other End of the Telescope," *New Scientist* 21: 58.
Keller, E. F. (1985) *Reflections on Gender and Science*, New Haven, CT: Yale University Press.
——— (1987a) "Feminism and Science," in S. Harding and J. F. O'Barr (eds) *Sex and Scientific Inquiry*, Chicago: University of Chicago Press.
——— (1987b) "Women Scientists and Feminist Critics of Science," *Daedalus* 116: 77–91.
——— (1992) *Secrets of Life. Secrets of Death. Essays on Language, Gender and Science*, New York: Routledge.
Leibowitz, L. (1983) "Origins of the Sexual Division of Labor," in M. Lowe and R. Hubbard (eds) *Woman's Nature: Rationalizations of Inequality*, New York: Pergamon Press.
Longino, H. (1989) "Can There Be a Feminist Science?", in N. Tuana (ed.) *Feminism and Science*, Bloomington: Indiana University Press.
——— (1990) *Science as Social Knowledge*, Princeton: Princeton University Press.
——— and Doell, R. (1983) "Body, Bias and Behavior: a Comparative Analysis of Reasoning in Two Areas of Biological Science," *Signs* 9: 206–227.
——— and Hammonds, E. (1990) "Conflicts and Tensions in the Feminist Study of Gender and Science," in M. Hirsch and E. Fox Keller (eds) *Conflicts in Feminism*, New York: Routledge.
Lowe, M. and Hubbard, R. (eds) (1983) *Woman's Nature. Rationalizations of Inequality*, New York: Pergamon Press.
MacMillan, C. (1982) *Woman, Reason, and Nature*, Princeton, NJ: Princeton University Press.
Marcus, G. E. (1990) "The Discourse of Primatology," *Science* 248: 886–887.
Masters, J. (1990) "Natural Selection, Cultural Construction," *The Women's Review of Books* VII (January): 18–19.
Merchant, C. (1980) *The Death of Nature: Women, Ecology and the Scientific Revolution*, New York: Harper and Row.
Montgomery, S. (1991) *Walking with the Great Apes*, Boston: Houghton Mifflin Co.
Nyhart, L. K. (1992) "Review of *Primate Visions*," *Signs* 17: 481–484.
Reynolds, V. (1991) "Review of *Primate Visions*," *Man* 26: 167–168.
Rodman, P. S. (1990) "Flawed Vision: Deconstruction of Primatology and Primatologists," *Current Anthropology* 31: 484–486.
Rosenthal, E. (1991) "The Forgotten Female," *Discover* 12: 22–27.
Rosser, S. (1986) "The Relationship between Women's Studies and Women in Science," in R. Bleier (ed.) *Feminist Approaches to Science*, New York: Pergamon Press.
——— (1989) "Feminist Scholarship in the Sciences: Where Are We Now and When Can We Expect a Theoretical Breakthrough?", in N. Tuana (ed.) *Feminism and Science*, Bloomington: Indiana University Press.
Rossiter, M. W. (1990) "Review of *Primate Visions*," *The Journal of American History* 77: 712–713.
Rowell, T. E. (1984) "Introduction," in M. F. Small (ed.) *Female Primates. Studies by Women Primatologists*, New York: Alan R. Liss.

Sayers, J. (1982) *Biological Politics: Feminist and Anti-feminist Perspectives,* New York: Tavistock Publications.
Scheich, E. (1991) "Review of *Primate Visions,*" *American Historical Review* 96: 829–830.
Schiebinger, L. (1987) "The History and Philosophy of Women in Science: A Review Essay," in S. Harding and J. O'Barr (eds) *Sex and Scientific Inquiry,* Chicago: University of Chicago Press.
Small, M. F. (ed.) (1984) *Female Primates. Studies by Women Primatologists,* New York: Alan R. Liss.
——— (1990) "Review of *Primate Visions,*" *American Journal of Physical Anthropology* 82: 527–532.
——— (1993) *Female Choices. Sexual Behavior of Female Primates,* Ithaca: Cornell University Press.
Smuts, B. B. (1992) "Male Aggression against Women," *Human Nature* 3: 1–44.
——— and Smuts, R. W. (1992) "Male Aggression and Sexual Coercion of Females in Non-human Primates and Other Mammals: Evidence and Theoretical Implications," in P. J. B. Slater, M. Milinski, J. S. Rosenblatt, and C. T. Snowdon (eds) *Advances in the Study of Behavior* (vol. 22), New York: Academic Press.
Sperling, S. (1991) "Baboons with Briefcases vs. Langurs in Lipstick. Feminism and Functionalism in Primate Studies," in M. di Leonardo (ed.) *Gender at the Crossroads of Knowledge: Feminist Anthropology in the Postmodern Era,* Berkeley: University of California Press.
Stanford, C. B. (1991) "Review of *Primate Visions,*" *American Anthropologist* 93: 1031–32.
Stanley, L. and Wise, S. (1983) *Breaking Out: Feminist Consciousness and Feminist Research,* London: Routledge and Kegan Paul.
Strum, S. C. (1987) *Almost Human. A Journey into the World of Baboons,* New York: Random House.
——— and Fedigan, L. M. (forthcoming) "Theory, Methods and Women Scientists: What or Who Changed Our Views of Primate Society?," in S. C. Strum and D. G. Lindburg (eds) *The New Physical Anthropology,* Englewood Cliffs, NJ: Prentice Hall.
Tanner, N. (1981) *On Becoming Human,* Cambridge: Cambridge University Press.
Tuana, N. (1989) "The Weaker Seed: The Sexist Bias of Reproductive Theory," in N. Tuana (ed.) *Feminism and Science,* Bloomington: Indiana University Press.
——— (1993) *The Less Noble Sex. Scientific, Religious, and Philosophical Conceptions of Woman's Nature,* Bloomington: Indiana University Press.
Wasser, S. K. (ed.) (1983) *Social Behavior of Female Vertebrates,* New York: Academic Press.
Wylie, A. (1992) "Reasoning about Ourselves: Feminist Methodology in the Social Sciences," in E. D. Harvey and K. Okruhlik (eds) *Women and Reason,* Ann Arbor: University of Michigan Press.
Zihlman, A. (1978) "Women in Evolution. Part II: Subsistence and Social Organization among Early Hominids," *Signs* 4(1): 4–20.
——— (1981) "Women as Shapers of the Human Adaptation," in F. Dahlberg (ed.) *Woman the Gatherer,* New Haven, Conn.: Yale University Press, pp. 75–120.

NAKED SEX IN EXILE
On the Paradox of the "Sex Question" in Feminism and in Science[1]

Cynthia Kraus

In the American scene, according to Sandra Harding (1986), the nature of feminist critiques of science has evolved since the mid-1970s from a reformist to a revolutionary position. This critical history began with the "woman question" in science, which problematizes the exclusion of women from science and the "unscientific" androcentrism that resulted from this underrepresentation. It subsequently moved on to the "science question" in feminism, to interrogate the androcentrism structuring the very standards of scientific investigation, notably the equation of "objectivity" with the Western attributes of masculinity (see also Fox Keller 1987, 1992). For Harding, this evolution from the critique of bad science to that of science as usual emerged out of the paradoxical grounds from which feminist scholars articulated their claims about androcentrism in science:

> Clearly, more scientifically rigorous and objective inquiry has produced the evidence supporting specific charges of androcentrism—but that same inquiry suggests that this kind of rigor and objectivity is androcentric! It is this paradox that raises the Science Question in feminism. (1986, 110)

This paper tries to take the science question in feminism one step further, from the critique of the androcentric methodological discourse of rigor and objectivity to the critique of a substantive construct, indeed, to the questioning of substance as construct itself. More specifically, it addresses a new paradox emerging out of the still-pervasive assumption that one part of sex—what I call "naked sex"—is prior to gender construction, wherein naked sex's resistance to constructivist analysis would derive from the "thingness" or the "stuff" composing sex, namely, from the *matter* of sexual difference (see, e.g., Hausman 1995). As you are no doubt aware, this issue has already been addressed, in a provocative manner, by Judith Butler in *Bodies that Matter* (1993). As an extension of this critical endeavor, I suggest here that conceiving of matter as the substance of sexual difference can be considered a naturalized effect produced by the very gesture of denaturalizing boundaries that are usually posited as themselves natural divides—for example, between nature and culture, sex and gender, women and men, or even female and male.

FROM THE FEMINIST THEORY ROOM TO THE FLY LABORATORY

The present discussion begins by analyzing—as a typical example of this paradoxical gesture—the terms in which feminist biologists have fleshed out sex from the body-as-biology by problematizing the divide between sex and gender, and nonetheless reinscribed the sex-determining genes as the "natural preserve" of gender construction.[1] Along the same lines, I will show that naked sex can be likewise considered the problematic remainder of both the feminist critical focus on biological determinism and the "master narrative" in feminist critiques of science—the critique of gender (androcentric/

sexist) biases—that has remained prevalent from the woman question in science to the science question in feminism. I will thus explain why the epistemological framework of the critique of gender biases fails to provide any analytical insight into the experimental life of sex, and in particular into the odd life of sexual difference in sex-determination research in the fruit fly, *Drosophila melanogaster.*

From this perspective, it is precisely because *Drosophila* sex-determination research does *not* provide a good example of androcentrism—but, rather, a counterexample—that this scientific field is of particular interest for exploring a new critical entry into the allegedly material foundation of sexual difference in feminism and in science. We will thus move from the feminist theory room to the fly laboratory, from where I propose to recount an experimental history of the sex-determining gene in the fruit fly, *Sex-lethal (Sxl).* I will focus on a three-year time frame, from 1976 to 1979, during which the basis for a genetic model for sex determination was built up. My discussion is based on the scientific papers published in 1976, 1978, and 1979 by Thomas W. Cline that paved the way for isolating *Sex-lethal* and mapping out the sex-determination system in this organism. It also draws on my ongoing fieldwork in Cline's laboratory on sex determination in *Drosophila* at the University of California, Berkeley, as well as on the first series of interviews I conducted with him and his research team in 1999.[2]

I will here argue that the same working process that brings sex into existence simultaneously unmakes sex as a biological given by remaking it into an experimental tool. Further, we will see that the entire research process from 1976 to 1979 has centrally been organized around the distinctions between the sexes, a process that also involved unsexing sex as a nonsexual aspect of development. To put it differently, my selective experimental history of *Sex-lethal* focuses on the sexing and unsexing practices specifically engaged in knowing sex in the fruit fly, and seeks to underscore that sex never emerges as naked sex in this particular process of knowledge production. It is this analytical surprise at the heart of *Drosophila* sex determination that poses what might be called the sex question in feminism and in science.

BORDER CROSSING IN THE EPISTEMOLOGY OF GENDER: NAKED SEX IN EXILE

Denaturalizing the Natural by Border Crossing

The critical endeavors of feminist biologists to "fight with science's own tools" (Hubbard, Henifin, and Fried 1979, xxi) have been repeatedly relegated to a mere refutation of "bad science," leaving "good science" or "science as usual" unchallenged.[3] This view tends, however, to overlook the analytical displacement they effectuated in their critical analyses of the scientific construction of sex. As I have earlier suggested, this analytical displacement has consisted of denaturalizing purported natural borderlines through the critical gesture of crossing over allegedly impassable boundaries, in particular those between sex and gender, along with the related dichotomies of nature/culture, woman/man, and even female/male.

Feminist biologists have, according to Evelyn Fox Keller (1992), tended to "put a wedge, between science and nature rather than between sex and gender" (45), partly because "in biological terms, there is no language for distinguishing sex and gender" (44). In my view, the critical gesture of feminist biologists has, quite on the contrary, amounted to analytically dissociating the (un)scientific convergence between sex and gender. To be more specific, they have challenged the belief that sex determines gender by arguing that the naturalization of sex by the biological sciences precisely proceeds from the analytical confusion between sex and gender:

> I have used the term *sex differences* [emphasis in original] since that is the name by which this area of biological and social science research is known. *In actuality, what is at issue are gender differences* [emphasis added]; . . . gender is, in fact, a social construction or accomplishment, and gender attributions differ across cultures. *Science, however, in the form of gender-difference and gender-role (sex-difference and sex-role) research* [emphasis added], views these gender attributions as *natural* categories [emphasis in original] for which biological explanations are appropriate and even necessary. (Bleier 1984, 80 n.1)[4]

It is hence sex-difference research (in sociobiology, behavioral biology, and neuroendocrinology, inter alia), and not its critics, that fundamentally mistakes gender difference for sexual difference. This claim resignifies the 1970s sex/gender system, wherein gender was understood as "the social construction of sex" (see fig. 1). It moves the critical focus from the belief that sex determines gender toward a questioning of the assumption that biology determines sexual dimorphism itself; in short, toward an inquiry into sex as "the gender construction of biology"—the scientific construction of biology along the axis of gender—whereby the comparison between gender and sex now relates "something social to something that is social *again*."[5]

To question the biological foundation of sex, and not only of gender, feminist biologists have not merely underscored that sexual dimorphism bears the mark of gender dichotomies. They have even reverted the characterization of gender against itself, for all that is true of gender—notably its cultural variability—turns out to be doubly relevant to sex. As a matter of fact, *it is the biology of sex that appears far more plastic than the politics of gender.*

This line of argument has centrally involved crossing over the distinctions—the feminist analytical one included—between sex and gender, troubling the clear-cut lines between woman and man, female and male, in the same gesture. In this respect, just as population genetics has shown that the multiple overlapping variations in gene frequencies undermine any racial classification for humans (e.g., Langaney 1977), feminist biologists have brought to the fore that the observable differences between the sexes, if any, are minute and statistically insignificant, because variations among a single sex may be as great, if not greater, than those between the two sexes.[6]

Through the critical gesture of passing over these lines, it is not only gender passing for sex that is uncovered, but the more general feat of the social passing for biology, hence extending the border crossing over all of the nature/culture oppositions. For feminist biologists, cultural variations in sexual dimorphism at the level of anatomy

FIGURE 1 Caricature of the 1970 Sex/Gender System

Sex	Gender
Biological Sex Female/Male Nature Recipient (of culture) Immutable (through time, space)	Social Sex Woman/Men Culture Content (of culture) Variable (through time, space)

(including the skeleton), physiology, or metabolism are evidence that differences between the sexes are not transcultural universals; they even vary in a single individual over the course of her/his life, with age, diet, or sustained physical exercise, to name only a few factors.[7] Nor can it be assumed a priori that these differences have a biological origin, for there is no consistent way of "stripping" biology from the socialization of bodies to uncover an immutable core, a "naked human essence" (Bleier 1984, 198). Is there any room left for naked sex?

Redoubling Sex

As a matter of fact, what sex has undergone in the course of border crossing is better understood as a "redoubling," resulting in a splitting of the category of sex along lines parallel to those previously separating biological sex and social gender (compare figs. 1 and 2). In other words, the critical gesture of denaturalizing the natural by border crossing can be figured as a partial colonization of sex by gender, producing a trilogy, where naked sex plays the excluded third: gender plus "gender difference mistaken for sexual difference" versus "naked sex" (see fig. 2).

If science is not a mirror of nature, if most of sex is not a reflection of biology, what is this part of sex that is preserved? Despite the variety of approaches promulgated by different tendencies in feminist scholarship, the critical concept of gender was taken up by all to challenge determinist assumptions about the presumed biological origin of *gender* dimorphism, assumptions that were embedded in terms such as *sex* or *sexual difference* (e.g., Scott 1986). As we have earlier seen, this challenge has been taken one step downstream by feminist biologists: they have brought to the fore the non-dimorphic plasticity of sex to undermine the assumption that the biological mandate of gender originates in sexual dimorphism. Naked sex has, however, been haunting the displacement from a critique of the biological origin of gender to that of sex, producing an unsought alliance: my enemy's friend is my friend, too. The feminist critical focus on biological determinism, from which the critique of sexual dimorphism derives, paradoxically rejoins biological determinism at "the last sex station": both protagonists eventually assume the existence of two "natural" human groups, which are materially specific in the genetic constitution of their bodies.[8] That the partition between the sex-determining genes that initiate the sexing of the soma in the developing organism would draw the material line between the male and the female can be inferred from the fact that this part of sex is precisely left unquestioned, even in the feminist critiques of sex-determination research.

Compared to other areas of sex-difference research, sex determination has received little attention from feminist scholars. Moreover, the few critics who have inquired into this field have scrutinized research carried out on the human only. But all frame their

FIGURE 2 Redoubling Sex

Naked Sex	"Gender Difference Mistaken for Sexual Difference"	Gender
Natural preserve of gender or minimal ontology of sex	The social *passing for* biology	Making two social classes of humans

analysis as a critique of gender biases and locate the operation of these biases in the asymmetrical—male/testis/active-centered—mapping of the human sex-determination pathway: the induction of the first sexual dimorphism in the developing embryo is equated with the determination of the male sex, and depends on the activation of a gene usually carried by the Y chromosome, the testis-determining factor (or TDF);[9] in this picture, the female sex is defined as the negative and privative counterpart of the male, since an ovary would develop passively, that is, in the TDF default mode.[10] This model of the human sex-determination pathway has barely been revisited, though X-linked and autosomal loci have been, more recently, implicated with inducing ovarian tissue.[11]

The specific charges addressed to human sex-determination research give us a clue about the nature of the core argument establishing the critique of gender biases, a point that will be taken up again below. It now suffices to say that this critique grounds itself in disclosing that presumed biological divides, such as active/passive, that are embedded in the deep layers of sex are actually cultural lines drawn along traditional gender dichotomies. Once again, it is is the passing of social gender for biological sex that is the matter of a bias. Against the alleged sexual dimorphism, feminist critics have underscored incremental variations and overlappings between the two sexes at all the biological levels of sex—hormones, testis, ovary, internal and external morphology. Likewise, the many chromosomal variants to the standard 46,XX for females and 46,XY for males complicate any dichotomous classification. Critics have nonetheless reclaimed a qualitative difference for the sex-determining genes, and only for this "biological level." They have called for two symmetric accounts of the male and female sex-determination pathways, arguing that the current androcentric model passing for a general model is irrelevant for thinking the determination of the female sex.[12] They have thus maintained the very partition between the sex-determining genes as the part of sex that does not fall within "gender mistaken for sex," while they have otherwise challenged the making of two and only two sexes.[13]

Naked Sex: The Dustbin of Gender Constructivism

If gender's minimal ontology of sex refers to the sex-determining genes, what is fully conceded to naked sex varies within the heterogeneous space of gender scholarship. As we have seen, for feminist biologists it tends to be confined to the sex-determining genes. For those who take the male/testis/active-centered model of human sex determination at face value, naked sex would include these gender biases.[14] Other scholars resuscitate, without blinking, the undeniability of "obvious" differences between the sexes.[15] No one, it seems, gives up the ontological commitment to one part of sex that would be transcultural and biological, to what Evelyn Fox Keller (1989) has contended is an "observational core" (313) "that has thus far defied modulation" (316).

The very variability in the content of naked sex indicates that this "last sex station" can be understood as a theoretical effect of the concept of gender. It functions like the dustbin of anything that is rejected from models of gender construction. Fox Keller has even announced this "left-over of sex" as gender constructivism's happy ending: "what is left to both 'sex' and 'nature' is now little enough. But it is not yet nothing" (1989, 316). I see this not-nothing, here renamed "naked sex," as a placeholder that has enabled the critical gesture of denaturalizing the natural by border crossing. At the same time, this gesture has been secured by positing naked sex as an epistemological fetish for the epistemology of gender. More specifically, it stands for gender's minimal ontology of sex supporting feminist critical knowledge practices in deconstructing sex as "the gender construction of biology."

RETHINKING SEX WITH THE FRUIT FLY: AN EXPERIMENTAL HISTORY (1976–1979) OF THE ISOLATION OF THE *DROSOPHILA* SEX-DETERMINING GENE, *SEX-LETHAL (SXL)*

Beyond the Feminist Master Narrative of Gender Biases in Science

We have seen that the critiques of sexual dimorphism by feminist biologists have been centrally organized around the demonstration that the process of making gender constructs into biological facts consists in confounding sex with gender. The convergence between sex and gender has been taken as evidence for this fallacy. The critiques of gender biases in the field of sex determination in the human have been structured along the same lines. Gender operates as a bias, because the activity and the presence of the human sex-determining gene are duly conferred to the male sex, while the "opposite sex" is allocated to what best suits the feminine, that is, passivity and absence—here of the TDF. Feminist critics have pinned down the scientific confusion between sex and gender by redeploying in the opposite direction the analytical independence of sex and gender in the specific terms discussed earlier.

The fruit fly, it seems, has not been invited to join the feminist banquet. The second part of my discussion stars *Drosophila,* because it brings some "gender trouble" (Butler 1990) into the anthropocentric feminist master narrative of gender biases in science. Contrary to the human sex-determination pathway regulated by the testis-determining factor (TDF) on the Y chromosome, the primary event of *Drosophila* sex determination is initiated by the activation of the master switch gene, *Sex-lethal,* located on the X chromosome (see fig. 3). It consists in counting the number of X chromosome in its ratio with nonsexual chromosomes or autosomes (A), regardless of the Y chromosome (e.g., Cline 1993). In the standard—and here simplified—scenarios, *Sex-lethal* is activated in XX/AA cells, and its products induce them to develop as female; the gene is off in XY/AA cells, which thus develop into male cells. In the account of *Drosophila* sex determination, the same gender dichotomies of active/passive, on/off, absent/present, and induced versus noninduced sex are distributed between the two sexes in an exactly reverse fashion to the human: in the fruit fly, the female sex is paired with the presence and the activity of *Sex-lethal,* as well as the induction of ovarian tissue, while the male sex is characterized by its absence, testic-

FIGURE 3 Of Flies and Men: "Gender Trouble"

Sexed as	**Human sex-determining gene:** ***Testis-determining factor (TDF)*** on the **Y** chromosome	**Cross-distribution** of gender dichotomies between the Human and *Drosophila*	***Drosophila*** **sex-determining gene:** ***Sex-lethal (Sxl),*** on the **X** chromosome
Female	**off/passive** in XX cells → ovary	(X)	**on/active** in XX/AA cells → ovary **induced** sex
Male	**on/active** in XY cells → testis **induced** sex		**off/passive** in X(Y)/AA cells → testis

ular tissue forming passively, without induction. In short, we have a gynocentric—female/ovary/active-centered—mapping of the *Drosophila* sex-determination pathway, whereby the male is regendered with feminine gender attributes, and conversely.

Since the critique of gender biases is framed as a critique of the unscientific convergence between sex and gender, their divergence in *Drosophila* research and the cross distribution of gender between this organism and the human remain outside of its analytical scope. These displacements in the language of gender might warrant, in this case, a stamp of approval, and be turned into the critical equivalent of woman the gatherer for displacing man the hunter. Along the same lines, we might decenter universal man from human sex-determination research. However, this would overlook the fact that, beyond the issue of gender, dichotomies such as active/passive do not seem to pass the test of science, either. Interestingly enough, some women scientists have pinpointed the fact that such dichotomies are misnomers, waiving a basic understanding of gene regulation: they contradict available experimental data (e.g., Eicher and Washburn 1986) or can be put the other way round, for example, turning off a chromosome may be considered a more active biological event that leaving it on.[16] In my view, the *Drosophila* case rather indicates that we need to do more than just tune the critique of gender biases in science. The main problem lies in its very epistemological ground, namely (and as we have already seen), in the critical gesture of identifying gender biases in the passing of social gender for biological sex.

More specifically, I suggest here that this gesture, which has fostered a broader questioning of the social constructedness of biological sex itself since the 1980s, has simultaneously exacerbated analytical antagonisms between sex and gender, and between feminism and science: on the one hand, sex emerges as a symptom of gender, whereby gender operates in the disguise of sex, leaving apparently nothing left to sex that is not the "gender construction of biology"; on the other hand, the same critique preserves the sex-determining genes—the minimal package for naked sex, as already said—apart from "gender mistaken for sex." As a paradoxical result, the critique of gender biases in science subsumes most of sex under the category of gender, the analytical toolbox of feminist scholarship, while delegating to science the cultural privilege of telling the remaining story of sex, the one escaping the narrative of gender biases. The latter unwittingly continues to subscribe to a scientistic ideal of both scientific inquiry and feminist analysis by ultimately enforcing the "neutralization" of sex. Not surprisingly, the epistemological framework of the critique of gender biases fails to articulate the specific ways in which sex becomes scientifically performative, not as a pitfall or a blind spot, but as the most meaningful "experimental operator" to be tackled in particular research systems, as we will see is the case with the *Drosophila* sex-determination system.

The experimental history of the *Drosophila* sex-determining gene, *Sex-lethal (Sxl),* I propose to recount now seeks to revisit naked sex—the dustbin of gender constructivism that functions like a black box. It will suggest that what is the matter of biological sex is not delineated once and for all, but depends on the peculiar practices involved, from making sex a research object for *Drosophila* developmental genetics to the isolation of *Sex-lethal* (1976–78) and eventually the mapping of the sex-determination system (1978–79) in this organism. My analytical focus on the singular system of practices engaged in this research process tries to depart from the "double blackmail" wherein one part of sexual difference is ultimately posited as either "out there" or a mere object of the mind.[17] While the returning question of what is real/biological about biological sex has been haunting the feminist theory room, my approach seeks to displace this question toward an inquiry into the "realization" of sex, that is, into the performativity of sex in science beyond a performativity of gender biases. From this perspective, tracing the experimental realization of sex opens up the possibility of reconsidering biological sex as one instantiation of sex among others.

Sex in a Detective Story

The isolation of the sex-determining gene, *Sex-lethal*, can be considered an "unprecedented event" (Rheinberger 1997), i.e., contingent and unforeseen, and yet produced by a singular experimental trajectory. Chromosomal sex determination was already reported, in 1921, to depend on the balance between X chromosomes and autosomes, irrespective of the Y (Bridges 1921, 1925). While the cloning of *Sex-lethal* required recombinant DNA, available only in the 1980s, the absence of these technical tools appears inadequate to explain why sex determination has remained one of the most impracticable objects of inquiry for more than fifty years. The eventual elucidation of its genetic basis has involved research practices available long before, specifically the use of sex mosaics and temperature-sensitive mutations. Sex mosaics have been prepared as genetic tools for the study of chromosomal inheritence patterns as early as 1914 (Morgan 1914). Temperature-sensitive mutations—a common tool in biochemical studies on bacteria—have also been in use since the mid-1960s for understanding development.[18]

However, it seems, little has been advanced about sex determination in the fruit fly up till the late 1970s. I suggest that the experimental exploration and resolution of the genetics of sex determination, from 1976 to 1979, have become "doable" (Fujimura 1987) through the specific convergence of sexing and unsexing research practices. The latter attained full "resonance" (Rheinberger 1997) when they mapped out a new space of investigation for developmental genetics, namely, the sex-determination system. This resonance itself depended on the particular nature of the experimental system that, unexpectedly, provided the key entry into the genetics of sex determination. The sex-determining gene emerged as an "epistemic thing" (ibid.)—an unknown thing to be known—through a set of practices entirely organized from within a maternal-effect system, the *daughterless* system, first reported in 1954, but at the time *not* related to sex determination (*da;* Bell 1954). The experimental history of *Sex-lethal* begins with a 1976 study about the effects of temperature on the *daughterless* mutant phenotype, and presents itself as the unanticipated plot of a detective story.

A Forensics of Sex: Tackling the Killer's Modus Operandi

Sexing Life and Death, Unsexing Sex. What kind of crime scene is the *daughterless* system? Females with two normal X chromosomes, but carrying two copies of the maternal-effect mutation located on the second chromosome and named *daughterless (da)*, produce only male progeny (see fig. 4). More precisely, this mutation is lethal to all daughters; a small number of sons die too, but most survive and develop normally. It is an unusual maternal effect, because its action depends on the sex of the progeny: the eggs of mothers mutant for *daughterless* cannot support female development.

The most striking aspect of the *daughterless* mutation—the unisexual progeny—appears to tell something about sex, but what it says exactly remains unclear. Early work on *daughterless* had indicated that the unisexual progeny was not a function of sexual difference per se—a female or male phenotype. Sex-transforming mutations such as *transformer* or *doublesex* that can usually masculinize the phenotype of a chromosomal female had proven ineffectual in rescuing female embryos from the maternal lethal effect (e.g., Bell 1954). In actuality, there is no sexual phenotype to be observed for more than half of the *daughterless* progeny, since embryos die long

FIGURE 4 The Criminal Profile of the *daughterless (da)* System prior to 1976

da/da Mothers		
***da/da* daughters**	**Sons**	
All die as embryos	Some die	Majority survives and develops normally
XX/AA embryos = **2X**	**XY/AA** embryos = **1X**	

before any sexual dimorphism has developed. The cause of death would better be traced back to a difference between chromosomal males and females, more precisely to a difference between a 1X and a 2X embryo.

While sexing life and death was bringing the distinctions between the sexes down to the chromosomal level, sex itself was being unsexed in the same process, having the terms *female* and *male* stand for something other than sex. They are convenient short-cuts to refer to a chromosomal difference—1X versus 2X. It was known for decades that the sexual phenotype in the fruit fly depends on the balance between X chromosomes and autosomes (A). But it is precisely this state of the art that obscured any possible involvement of sex determination in the criminal action of *daughterless.* It did not help the scientist make sense of lethality, since the phenotype resulting from disruptions in the sex-determination pathway was expected to be sex transformation, wherein a chromosomal female is transformed into a phenotypic male, and conversely. Lethality could become legible within the *daughterless* system by suspending the established facts of sex and by involving chromosomal difference in a general aspect of cell growth and viability. Sex determination would indeed walk in through the main entrance as just another *nonsexual* developmental difference, identical in nature to "eye versus wing" or "leg versus tail." In other words, sex chromosome difference was being banalized as a difference in the expression of the same genetic information at the level of basic cell functions in the developing embryo, a process that simultaneously appeared highly specialized in killing 2X embryos over 1X embryos.

Sexing Flies, Tooling Sex. While the experimental signs of the *daughterless* system have required that we rework sex in many respects, the sexual diagnosis of the dead embryos as females and of the viable flies as males has simultaneously been carried out with ease. In this case, the very distinctions between the two sexes stand out as immediately present and transparent. What enables the researcher to distinguish them in the first place? Not surprisingly, the problem gives rise to practical guides designed to instruct the apprentice drosophilist in the art of "fly pushing"—the practice of sorting out males from females with a brush under the microscope:

> While this distinction is easy to make with practice, care must be taken at the beginning.
>
> (i) The females are generally larger.
>
> (ii) They have a pointed abdomen which becomes expanded prior to egg laying and is somewhat concave immediately after.
>
> (iii) The tip of the male abdomen is more rounded and is dark compared with the striped tip of the female abdomen. Both shape and color may be deceptive in newly eclosed flies and in some body color mutants.
>
> (iv) The genitalia of the two sexes are very different; *learn to know these differences by examining the genitalia of flies of known sex.*

(v) D. melanogaster can be sexed unambiguously by looking for the presence of sex combs, a row of thick dark bristles on the tarsus of the first pair of legs. These are found only in males. (Roberts 1986, 23, emphasis added)

The distinctions between the sexes explicitly emerge in relation to a set of sexing practices that mobilize at least three registers of difference, making sex a composite: first, comparisons (i–iii); second, the use of intensive superlativity emphasizing oppositeness (iv); and third, the language of presence and absence (v). Of particular interest is the practical injunction "learn to know these differences by examining the genitalia of flies of known sex," indicating that the difference between male and female genitalia depends on comparing "known sex" with "sex to be determined." As a matter of fact, all the listed distinctions between the sexes are a function of this comparison, as they equally presuppose prior normative decisions about what sex is and about which sex is which. Sexual difference does not precede the practice of sexing flies as some material substance inscribed in "prescientific" flies, but is carried along through an antecedent set of materializing epistemic practices, those of earlier experiments in the history of *Drosophila* biology made "nature."

In this respect, the know-how engaged in the practice of sexing flies reenacts what Thomas Laqueur (1990) calls the "two-sex/flesh model." While historians trace the inscription of sexual difference in the body and the invention of two incommensurable sexes to the eighteenth century (e.g., ibid.), it seems nonetheless extremely difficult to single out a primary origin of sexual dimorphism, even if it can be ascribed to specific sexing practices that refer back to other, earlier systems of practices and knowledge. Scholars studying science itself have suggested that the open-ended nature of scientific inquiry calls into question the very idea of an "assignable origin" (Rheinberger 1997, 105), as black boxes might be reopened and reworked anew in the research process. The experimental history of the sex-determining gene is indeed a story wherein sex that has never left the experimental scene returns undefined.

Interestingly, within the particular research process organized from within the *daughterless* system, sex emerges as an object that simultaneously bears a nature-made facticity and the technique of a tool, much like temperature-sensitive mutations and sex mosaics. The dehistoricization of sex does not simply mask the experimental genealogy of the operational distinctions between the sexes. It is simultaneously the very working process through which sex itself is transformed into an experimental tool, because it has already been black-boxed and standardized into a routine laboratory practice,[19] along with other basic *Drosophila* techniques such as anesthetizing and transferring flies, collecting virgins, and setting up a cross.[20] Temperature shifts and sex mosaics could be redeployed as genetic tools onto the still-undefined research object emerging from the *daughterless* system, as they had been shifted from the status of "epistemic things" to that of (ap)proved technical devices long before 1976–79. As for sex, the erasure of its conditions of emergence and intelligibility is the same temporal process that brings sex into experimental existence and remakes it into a tool.

"The Game of Playing off One Sex against the Other": Unboxing Sex's Black Box. What kind of tools are the distinctions between the sexes? They are the performative tools of a singular system of practices on its way of becoming the distinctive experimental style of sex-determination research, namely (to borrow Cline's phrase), "the game of playing off one sex against the other" (1999).[21] While the historicity of these distinctions is black-boxed in the practice of sexing flies—thereby securing their operationality as a tool—the system of epistemic practices engaged in the research process has been entirely organized around the distinctions between the sexes in response to the unusual specificities of the *daughterless* system. As we have seen earlier, these unusual experimental signs have been deciphered through sexing life and death, while simultaneously redefining the understanding of sex as sexual difference toward sex chromosomes. Most important, the chromosomal difference between 1X and 2X has eventually emerged as just another nonsexual developmental difference interfering with cell growth and differentiation. In response to this, the entire research process has consistently amounted to tackling the distinctions between the sexes by exhausting their combinational along the experimental lines of the *daughterless* system, wherein what is beneficial—in the developmental sense—to one sex is detrimental to the other. Moreover, we will see that the same combinational of sex simultaneously unboxes sex's black box, as sex also emerges as an object whose very definition is suspended and in suspense in the experimental process.

Profiling the Lethal Focus by Breaking Down Sex: 1976

The lethal effects of the *daughterless* mutation have precluded direct genetic analysis, since the death of all female progeny prevents the propagation of successive generations of mutant flies. These complications have been overcome by using heat treatment—including temperature shifts—and sex mosaics. These two genetic tools involved in the research process from 1976 to 1979 fully take advantage of the distinctions between the sexes as experimental operators to be broken down and recombined. By testing whether the complex phenotype of the *daughterless* mutation might be temperature-sensitive, Cline's 1976 study redeployed a tool that had already been used as a rescuing device in earlier work on lethal mutations in *Drosophila* (e.g., Suzuki et al. 1967). The particular 1976 experimental design first inquired into the effects of heat treatment with respect to the maternal genotype (*da/da* or *da/da*$^{+}$[22]) on female and male progeny, by exposing them at the different but constant temperatures of 18°, 22°, 25°, and 29°.[23] While 18°-conditioned female progeny could be rescued from the otherwise lethal maternal effect, no progeny of either sex survived at 29°, a temperature at which eggs were sterile. The combined use of temperature shifts—useful in defining the developmental stages at which temperature affects the mutant's phenotype—enabled workers to sort out three separate aspects in the action of *daughterless.*[24] Two maternal effects during maternal oogenesis (egg formation) were identified (see fig. 5): the first maternal effect acts as a sterility effect that results in no progeny of either sex; the second maternal effect acts as a sex-specific lethal effect that kills all 2X embryos. In addition, during early embryogenesis, a third and zygotic effect is superimposed on the female-specific lethal maternal effect.[25] This third effect acts on both sexes as a differential lethal effect and accounts for the non-sex-specific action of the *daughterless* mutation in killing some 1X embryos.

Breaking down the *daughterless* lethal effects with respect to chromosomal sex enabled workers to single out sex-specific lethality as the lethal focus among other lethal effects. It is for this reason that sex-specific lethality emerged as the most meaningful experimental sign from within the *daughterless* system. The sterility effect does not discriminate between the sexes at all and thus provides no clear entry into the unusual progeny sex ratio. The sex-differential effect appears less straightforward in its action than the absolute female-specific lethal effect. While the female-sterile and sex-differential effects might be considered "noise" for the sake of experimental exploration, the absolute action on sex defined the distinctive criminal modus operandi of the *daughterless* mutation, and thus what needed to be experimentally tackled.

The second experimental design presented in the 1976 paper investigated the genes functioning in the 2X zygote that enabled female progeny to survive the maternal lethal effect when conditioned at 18°. It tried to trace its genetic basis "backward" by focusing on the part played by the genotype of the progeny. For this purpose, sex

FIGURE 5 Profiling the Lethal Focus by Breaking down Sex: 1976

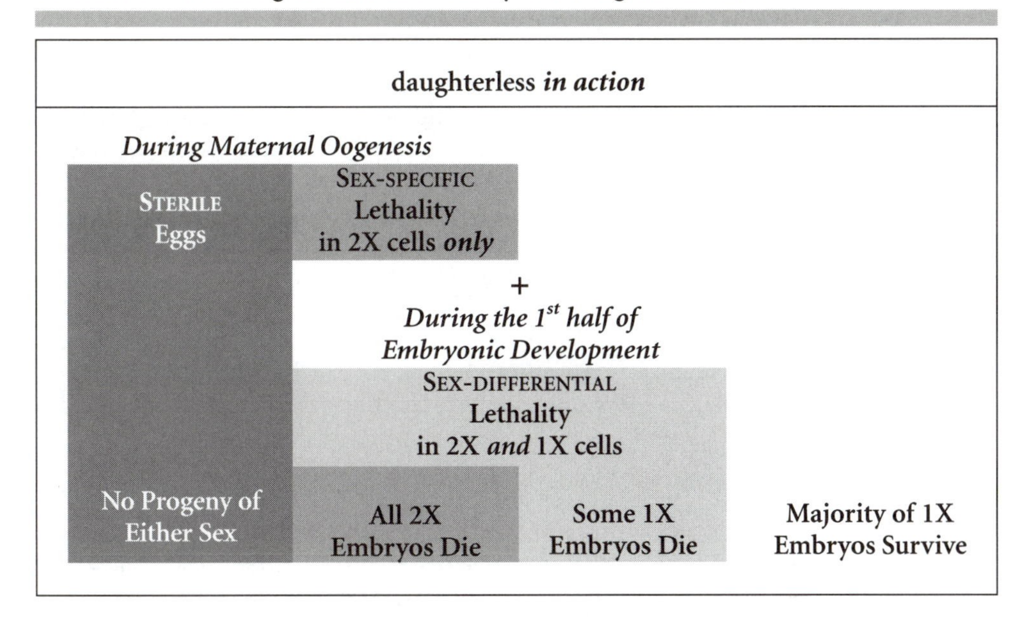

mosaics were manufactured, that is, embryos that were various combinations of 2X and 1X cells. Sex mosaics work as a trick to construct an overall viable embryo, by having a 2X embryo be more like a 1X embryo. The differential expression in X-chromosome doses become observable and comparable at the level of the individual cells in a single organism. The 1976 sexual mosaics proved an efficient rescuing device, since they could be recovered at 25°, while whole-body females died at this temperature. Their recovery was primarily a function of the lesser amount of 2X tissue they possessed, and secondarily of their distribution in the embryo. Moreover, these mosaics enabled workers to highlight the fact that the 2X tissue presented signs of cell death. However, unlike cell death—a process constitutive of development—the effects in the morphology of 2X cells were sex-specific, since 1X cells right next to them developed normally.[26] This suggested that a gene product missing in mutant zygotes was vital to the development of 2X cells but not required by 1X cells—a gene whose action was dependent on the dose of X chromosomes. The question of whether this putative gene might be linked to the vital process of X-chromosome dosage compensation—wherein 1X cells need to produce twice the amount of X-linked products as 2X cells—is addressed in the discussion section of the paper. While this question could not be settled at that point, sex determination was not yet implicated in the experimental narrative, as the dead 2X cells in the 1976 sexual mosaics obscured the issue by masking whether these cells tried to develop as male.

Unsuspected Suspects: 1978

In 1978 the game unexpectedly took an interesting turn with the appearance of a spontaneous mutation in a stock of mutant females, rescued in the earlier experimental setup at 18°. This new mutation on the X chromosome and named *Sex-lethal, Male-specific #1* (Sxl^{M1}) in Cline's 1978 paper, was able to rescue 2X progeny from the *daughterless* maternal lethal effect. While the search for a mutation capable of counteracting this effect had remained unsuccessful until then, the real interest came from the fact that this mutation had exactly opposite effects on the two sexes with regard to *daughterless:* it rescued daughters but was dominantly lethal to male progeny. The reiterated use of heat treatment and temperature shifts produced additional results indicating that the two opposite functions of *Sxl^{M1}*—female-rescuing and male-lethal—were alternative forms of a single mutation. A most significant turn was taken when this new mutation was mapped at the region where an opposite kind of mutation had been isolated in 1960: a female-specific mutation, *Female-lethal,* renamed *Sex-lethal, Female-specific #1 (Sxl^{F1})* in Cline's 1978 paper.[27] The game could be played on.

By recombining the variables involved up till now—1X, 2X, *da, da^{+}*, the egg, the zygote, generational classes, and so on—with *Sxl^{M1}* and *Sxl^{F1}*, as well as with the wild-type locus *Sex-lethal (Sxl^{+}),* it appears that *Sex-lethal, Male-specific #1* counteracted both *daughterless* and *Sex-lethal, Female-specific #1* (see fig. 6). Conversely, *Sxl^{M1}* was lethal to 1X embryos from *da/da* mothers. As for the two female lethals, *daughterless* and *Sxl^{F1}*, they enhanced each other's lethal effects, which implicated them as accomplices in the same vital developmental process that depended on the X/A balance.

Sex Determination: From Suspicion (1978) to Arrest (1979)

The emergence of a new epistemic object—*Sex-lethal, Male-specific #1*—that brought a formerly isolated female lethal into a new web of interactions was already reorganizing the initial knowledge space of the *daughterless* system. Though it was only later, in 1979, that the *Sex-lethal* locus was implicated in the process of sex determination, the state of the art was advanced enough in 1978 to map a *daughterless/Sex-lethal* system.[28] Its epistemic web is constituted of the genetic and developmental interactions between *daughterless,* the *Sex-lethal* loci, and the dose of X chromosomes indicated by the X/A bracket (see fig. 7). It figures a regulatory model where genes control other genes, a model on its way to superseding, during the 1970s, the old paradigm that one gene controls one enzyme. In the 1978 model, the wild-type *daughterless* locus on the mother's second chromosome controls the synthesis of a cytoplasmic factor during egg formation. This maternal factor is later required for the activation of the *Sex-lethal* locus, through its "control region," which works as an "interface" between the maternal factor and the wild-type *Sex-lethal* product that is vital for female development but lethal to males.

FIGURE 6 Unsuspected Suspects

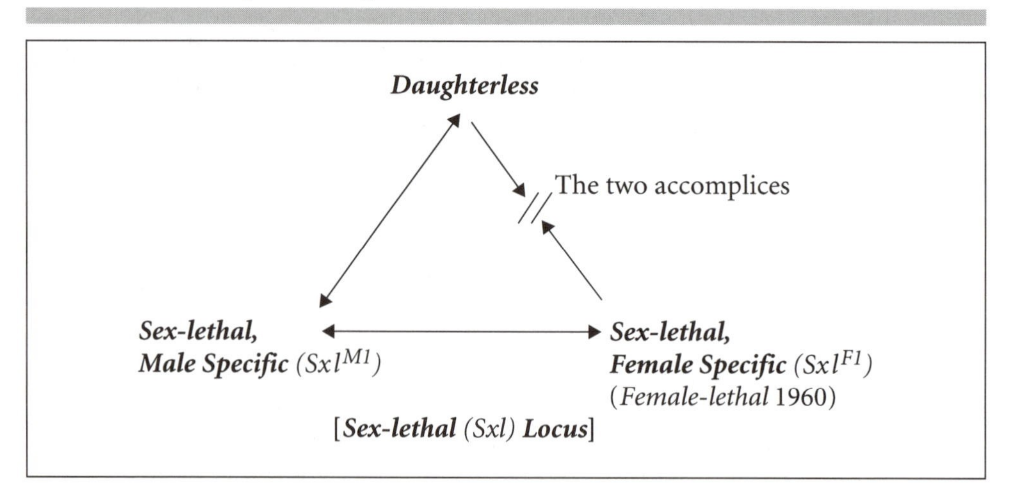

FIGURE 7 Mapping the 1978 Knowledge Space: Sex Determination under Suspicion

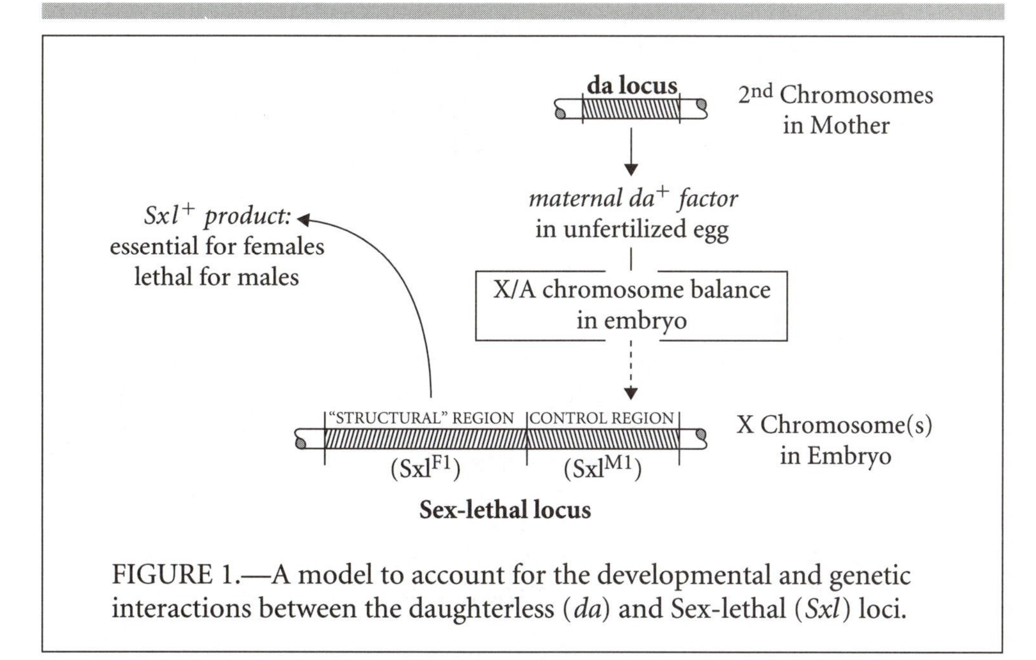

FIGURE 1.—A model to account for the developmental and genetic interactions between the daughterless (*da*) and Sex-lethal (*Sxl*) loci.

Cline (1978, 693). Figure reproduced with permission of the author

This tentative model maps the 1978 knowledge space and simultaneously redistributes the experimental roles between the different epistemic objects. The 1979 experiments targeted right away the role of the *Sex-lethal* locus in development, as the experimental problem had been reformulated as "what kind of developmental system might specifically require a gene or its product to be active in females, but be inactive or absent in males?" (Cline 1978, 695). The genetic mosaics manufactured this time, in order to study the effects of Sxl^{M1} on tissue growth and differentiation, enabled workers to observe, for the first time, developmental sex reversal in the somatic cells, thus implicating the *Sex-lethal* locus in the sex-determination pathway: 1X cells carrying the mutant allele *Sex-lethal, Male-specific #1* tried to develop into female tissue; concurring results indicated that *Sex-lethal, Female-specific #1* was capable of inducing male-specific morphological changes in 2X cells. While *Sex-lethal* has emerged from within the 1976 *daughterless* system, the 1979 experiments displaced it one step further—from the 1978 *daughterless/Sex-lethal* system toward the *Drosophila* sex-determination system organized around the *Sex-lethal* locus as the female-specific developmental signal.

BY WAY OF CONCLUSION: HOW TO DO SCIENTIFIC THINGS WITH SEX

The experimental history of the sex-determining gene, *Sex-lethal,* continues beyond the mapping of the genetic basis for the *Drosophila* sex-determining system in 1979. The observation of sex reversal—that is, sex-specific and not intrasexual or mixed-sex transformation—was not yet enough evidence to establish that *Sex-lethal* controlled both sex determination and the vital process of X-chromosome dosage compensation. Interestingly, dosage compensation was elucidated in 1934 by Herman Muller, the same scientist who reported the *Female-lethal* mutation in 1960. What he had isolated as the *Female-lethal* locus would be shown to control dosage compensation by the beginning of the 1980s (e.g., Cline 1983, 260–74), a link made possible after a *Male-specific lethal* (Sxl^{M1}) had been mapped at the same region of the X chromosome in 1979. That sex determination and dosage compensation are coordinately controlled by the *Sex-lethal* locus and that the *daughterless* maternal factor is required for *Sxl* to respond to the X-chromosome dose will eventually explain why the observable phenotype resulting from disruptions in the process of sex determination is not sex transformation, as expected, but sex-specific lethality.

While the present history telling ends earlier, I hope to have shown in the scope of this paper that making sex an object of research and knowledge from within the *daughterless* system toward the mapping of the *Drosophila* sex-determination system involved remaking sex into an experimental tool and unmaking it as a "natural fact." As the laboratory ontology of sex has, unexpectedly, appeared less heavy and black-boxed than in most radical feminist critiques of the scientific construction of sex, reconstituting the experimental history of sex-determination research with a focus on the sexing and unsexing dynamic may be as challenging to feminist scholars and science studies scholars as the *daughterless* system has been to drosophilists. It can become a good place to rethink the issue of sexual difference by opening up alternative feminist analyses of science. Indeed, we have seen that the sexing and unsexing practices engaged throughout the entire research process have been specifically structured around "the game of playing off one sex against the other" in response to the unusual specificities of the *daughterless.* These specificities have brought about unusual experimental resignifications of sex: (a) sexing death and life into the measures for a female or a male embryo, respectively; (b) resexing the distinctions between the sexes apart from sexual difference toward sexual chromosomes; and (c) unsexing chromosomal sex into a nonsexual developmental difference. The performativity of sex enacted through this forensics of sex to tackle the killer's modus operandi has thus been constitutive of the practicability of sex-determination research and the condition of possibility of knowing sex in a developmental sense. As such, "the game of playing off one sex against the other" cannot be easily collapsed into a performativity of gender biases. In the case of the *daughterless* system, it had enabled workers to explore how to do scientific things with sex.

Notes

This paper draws on earlier presentations (see Kraus 2000b, 2000c, 1999a, 1999b) and presents work in progress for a Ph.D. in philosophy (University of Lausanne, Switzerland) that has been conducted since summer 1997 at the University of California, Berkeley, on research fellowships granted by the Swiss National Science Foundation, the Foundation of the 450th Anniversary of the University of Lausanne, and the Rectorate of the University of Lausanne. My thanks go to Donna Haraway and her seminar members for their comments and criticisms on an early draft. Special thanks also to Judith Butler and Ellen Hertz for their stimulating supervision and feedback on my ongoing research, and to Dina Al-Kassim, Bruno Latour, Francesco Panese, Paul Rabinow, and James Salazar for their generous engagement with my work and their most appreciated critical readings, as well as to the two anonymous reviewers of the manuscript of this essay for their helpful comments and suggestions for revision.

1. In actuality, it is mostly, but not exclusively, feminist biologists who have questioned the scientific construction of biological sex. This critical endeavor is associated with the woman question in science and feminist empiricism by Harding (1986, 1989), while it historically belongs to the first of the two feminist programs for Fox Keller (1987, 1992).
2. My special thanks go here to Thomas W. Cline for giving me the opportunity to do my fieldwork in his laboratory and for training me in the art of fly genetics. My warmest thanks to all the scientists of this lab, who graciously answered my questions in interviews (in this paper I quote only Cline), had me visit the laboratory, and introduced me to experiments. They all continue to help me navigate in the world of the flies, and their generous collaboration does not imply that they agree with my arguments and interpretations.
3. See, for example, Harding 1986, 1989; Fox Keller 1992.
4. See also Bleier 1986, 147; Fausto-Sterling 1992a, 249.
5. I borrow this phrase from the French sociologist Christine Delphy (1991, 95). This refers to the relationship between gender and sex, when she calls for postulating the analytical precedence of gender over sex, wherein sex refers to "something social *again,* this time the representations that a given society has of what is 'biology'" (ibid., emphasis in original). In my view, this definition of sex's sociality effects the redoubling of sex that will be discussed in more detail below.
6. See, e.g., Bleier 1984, 94, 109; Fausto-Sterling 1992a, 26, 51, 218, 221; Lambert 1987.
7. See, e.g., Bleier 1984; Fausto-Sterling 1992a; Birke 1992.
8. The French sociologist Colette Guillaumin (1977, 1981) has raised the issue of the presumed material specificity in relation to the making of "human races" into biologically distinct entities.
9. During the thirty-year pursuit for the human sex-determining gene, the TDF locus was originally mapped on the short arm (Yp) of the Y chromosome (1959–66), then as the male-specific histocompatibility antigen (H-Y) (1975–84), then in interval 1 of Yp (1986–87), then as the zinc finger protein (ZFY) in interval 1A2 (1987–89), and eventually as the Sex-determining Region of the Y (SRY) in interval 1A1 (1990–). For a review, see for example, McLaren 1990.
10. See Fausto-Sterling 1987, 1989, 1992a, 1992b, 1997; Birke 1992.
11. Before the mid-1980s, when the current candidate to the role of TDF was H-Y, a few researchers tentatively suggested an ovary-determining pathway, symmetric to testis induction. Wachtel proposed an "Ovary-Inducing Molecule" (1983, 200–1); Eicher and Washburn formulated, on the basis of their experiments in mice, two differential sex-determining pathways, one inducing the ovary, the other the testis (1986, 342). It was only in the mid-1990s that this idea received some credit with the implication of an X-linked locus—the Dosage-sensitive Sex-reversal locus (DSS)—in male-to-female sex reversal (Bardoni et al. 1994). A smaller locus (DAX-1) was subsequently mapped in the DSS region (Zanaria et al. 1994). Nonsexual chromosomes, that is autosomal loci, have also been implicated in male-to-female sex reversal: WT-1 on chromosome 11 (e.g., Kreidberg et al. 1993), *SRA1* (e.g., Haqq et al. 1994), later included in SOX9 on chromosome 17 (e.g., Foster et al. 1994; Wagner et al. 1994), an interval of the short arm of chromosome 9, of the long arm of chromosome 10 (e.g., Bennett et al. 1993), and so on.
12. See Fausto-Sterling 1987, 1989, 1992a, 1992b, 1997; Birke 1992.
13. I have shown elsewhere that the presence or absence of a functional TDF (in the form of any of the various candidates, including the latest, SRY) does not enable the stabilization of any boundary between male and female with respect to the sex-determining genes. The TDF locus may be present but inactivated or absent in some 45,XX males (e.g., North, Affara, and Ferguson-Smith 1991), while it may be present and functional in some 46,XY females (e.g., Hawkins et al. 1992). Similarly, testicular tissue can be formed in its absence, as is the case with true 46,XX hermaphrodites, who carry no detectable Y-specific DNA (e.g., Waibel et al. 1987). For more details, see Kraus (2000a, 1996).
14. See, for example, Longino and Doell 1987, 179; Hubbard and Wald 1993, 45–46.
15. See, for example, Harding 1998, 97; 1997, 192.
16. Comment offered by the second anonymous reviewer.
17. I borrow this phrase from Slavoj Zizek (1999).

18. See, for example, Suzuki et al. 1967; Tarsoff and Suzuki 1970; Holden and Suzuki 1973.
19. See, for example, Latour 1989, 109, fig. 1.4.
20. See Roberts 1986, 1–38.
21. My thanks to Cline for permission to quote.
22. *Da/da* stands for two alleles (copies) carrying the daughterless mutation, while da/da^{+} stands for one mutant and one wild-type [$^{+}$] allele.
23. All temperature measures are in Celsius.
24. For a review, see Suzuki 1970.
25. Maternal-effect mutations have proven the most useful systems to genetically separate the factors in the egg cytoplasm from those in the zygote (fertilized egg) and their respective influence on developmental processes. Their study in *Drosophila* embryos has precisely provided the key access into the genes controlling the earliest stage of embryonic development for developmental genetics, a new field in the making by the mid-1970s. See, e.g., Gilbert 1991; Kohler 1994; Fox Keller 1996.
26. For more details about the sex-specific nature of the effects on the morphology of 2X cells, see Cline 1976, 732–38.
27. Muller and Zimmering 1960.
28. See also Cline 1979a, 274.

References

Bardoni, Barbara, et al. 1994. "A dosage sensitive locus at chromosome Xp21 is involved in male to female sex reversal." *Nature Genetics* 7: 497–501.

Bell, A. Earl. 1954. "A gene in Drosophila melanogaster that produces all male progeny" [abstracts of papers presented at the 1954 Meetings of the Genetics Society of America]. *Genetics* 39 (November): 958–59.

Bennett, C. P., et al. 1993. "Deletion 9p and sex reversal." *J. Med. Genet.* 30: 518–520.

Birke, Lynda. 1992. "In pursuit of difference: Scientific studies of women and men." In *Inventing Women. Science, Technology and Gender,* eds. Gill Kirkup and Laurie Smith Keller, 81–102. Cambridge: Polity Press.

Bleier, Ruth. 1986. "Sex differences research: Science or belief?" In *Feminist Approaches to Science,* ed. Ruth Bleier, 147–95. New York: Pergamon Press.

———. 1984. *Science and Gender: A Critique of Biology and Its Theories on Women.* New York: Pergamon Press.

Bridges, Calvin A. 1925. "Sex in relation to chromosomes and genes." *Am. Nat.* 59: 127–37.

———. 1921. "Triploid intersexes in Drosophila melanogaster." *Science* 54: 252–54.

Butler, Judith. 1993. *Bodies that Matter: On the Discursive Limits of "Sex."* New York: Routledge.

———. 1990. *Gender Trouble: Feminism and the Subversion of Identity.* New York: Routledge.

Cline, Thomas W. 1999. Tape-recorded interview with author, May 17.

———. 1993. "The Drosophila sex determination signal: How do flies count to two?" *Trends in Genetics* 9, 11 (November): 385–90.

———. 1983. "The interaction between Daughterless and Sex-lethal in triploids: A lethal sex-transforming maternal effect linking sex determination and dosage compensation in *Drosophila melanogaster.*" *Dev. Biol.* 95: 260–74.

———. 1979a. "A male-specific lethal mutation in *Drosophila melanogaster* that transforms sex." *Dev. Biol.* 72: 266–75.

———. 1979b. "A product of the maternally influenced Sex-lethal gene determines sex in Drosophila melanogaster" [abstracts of papers presented at the 1979 meetings of the Genetics Society of America]. *Genetics* 91 (suppl.): s22.

———. 1978. "Two closely linked mutations in Drosophila melanogaster that are lethal to opposite sexes and interact with daughterless." *Genetics* 90 (December): 683–98.

———. 1976. "A sex-specific, temperature-sensitive maternal effect of the daughterless mutation of Drosophila melanogaster." *Genetics* 84 (December): 723–42.

Delphy, Christine. 1991. "Penser le genre: quels problèmes?" In *Sexe et genre. De la hiérarchie entre les sexes,* ed. Marie-Claude Hurtig, Michèle Kail, and Hélène Rouch, 89–102. Paris: Editions du CNRS.

Eicher, Eva M., and Linda L. Washburn. 1986. "Genetic Control of Primary Sex Determination in Mice." *Ann. Rev. Genet.* 20: 327–60.

Fausto-Sterling, Anne. 1997. "How to build a man." In *Science and Homosexualities,* ed. Vernon Rosario, 219–25. New York, London: Routledge.

———. (1985) 1992a. *Myths of Gender: Biological Theories about Women and Men.* New York: Basic Books.

———. 1992b. "Why do we know so little about human sex?" *Discover* (June): 28–30.

———. 1989. "Life in the XY corral." *Women's Studies International Forum* 12, 3: 319–31.

———. 1987. "Society writes biology/biology constructs gender." *Daedalus* 116, 4 (fall): 61–76.

Foster, J. W., et al. 1994. "Campomelic dysplasia and autosomal sex reversal caused by mutations in an *SRY*-related gene." *Nature* 372: 525–29.

Fox Keller, Evelyn. 1996. "*Drosophila* embryos as transitional objects: The work of Donald Poulson and Christiane Nüsslein-Volhard." *Historical Studies in the Physical and Biological Sciences* 26: 313–46.

———. 1992. "How gender matters, or why it's so hard for us to count past two." In *Inventing Women: Science, Technology and Gender,* eds. Gill Kirkup and Laurie Smith Keller, 42–56. Cambridge: Polity Press.

———. 1989. "Holding the center of feminist theory." *Women's Studies International Forum* 12, 3: 313–18.

———. 1987. "Feminism and science." In *Sex and Scientific Inquiry,* ed. Sandra Harding and Jean F. O'Barr, 233–46. Chicago and London: University of Chicago Press.

Fujimura, Joan. 1987. "Constructing doable problems in cancer research: Where social worlds meet." *Social Studies of Science* 17:257–93.

Gilbert, Scott F. 1991. "Induction and the origin of developmental genetics." In *A Conceptual History of Modern Biology,* vol. 7, *Developmental Biology: A Comprehensive Synthesis,* ed. Scott F. Gilbert. New York and London: Plenum Press.

Guillaumin, Colette. 1981. "Je sais bien mais quand même' ou les avatars de la notion de 'race,'" *Le Genre Humain* 1 *(La Science face au racisme).*

———. 1977. "Race et nature: Système des marques, idées de groupes naturels et rapports sociaux." *Pluriel* 11.

Haqq, Christopher M., et al. 1994. "Molecular basis of mammalian sexual determination: Activation of Müllerian inhibiting substance gene expression by SRY." *Science* 266: 1494–500.

Harding, Sandra. 1998. *Is Science Multicultural? Postcolonialisms, Feminisms, and Epistemologies.* Bloomington and Indianapolis: Indiana University Press.

———. 1997. "Women's standpoints on nature: What makes them possible?" *Osiris* 12: 186–200.

———. 1989. "How the women's movement benefits science: Two views." *Women's Studies International Forum* 12, 3: 271–83.

———. 1986. *The Science Question in Feminism.* Ithaca, N.Y.: Cornell University Press.

Hausman, Bernice L. 1995. *Changing Sex: Transsexualism, Technology and the Idea of Gender.* Durham and London: Duke University Press.

Hawkins, J. R., et al. 1992. "Mutational analysis of SRY: Nonsense and missense mutations in XY sex reversal." *Hum. Genet.* 88: 471–74.

Holden, Jeanette J., and David T. Suzuki. 1973. "Temperature-sensitive mutations in Drosophila melanogaster XII. The genetics and developmental effects of dominant lethals on chromosome 31,2,3," *Genetics* 73 (March): 445–58.

Hubbard, Ruth, Marie Sue Henifin, and Barbara Fried, eds. 1979. *Women Look at Biology Looking at Women: A Collection of Feminist Critiques.* Cambridge, Mass.: Schenkman.

Hubbard, Ruth, and Elijah Wald. 1993. *Exploding the Gene Myth: How Genetic Information Is Produced and Manipulated by Scientists, Physicians, Employers, Insurance Companies, Educators, and Law Enforcers.* Boston: Beacon Press.

Knorr Cetina, Karin D. 1999. "Postsocial (knowledge) societies: Objectualization, individualization, and the idea of an object-centered sociality." Paper presented at the History of Consciousness Department, April 15, 1999, University of California, Santa Cruz.

Kohler, Robert E. 1994. *Lords of the Fly: Drosophila Genetics and the Experimental Life.* Chicago and London: University of Chicago Press.

Kraus, Cynthia. 2000a. "La bicatégorisation par sexe 'à l'épreuve de la science': Le cas des recherches en biologie sur la détermination du sexe chez les humains." In *L'Invention du naturel—Les sciences et la fabrication du féminin et du masculin,* eds. Delphine Gardey and llana Löwy, 187–213. Paris: Editions des archives contemporaines.

———. 2000b. "Knowing sex in the fruit fly (1976–1979), or 'how to do scientific things with sex."' Paper presented at Beyond Understanding: Re-considering Knowledge and Belief, April 14–15, Doreen B. Townsend Center for the Humanities, University of California, Berkeley.

———.2000c. "Rethinking sex: Beyond the feminist 'master narrative' of gender biases in science." Paper presented at Thinking Gender: The Tenth Annual Graduate Student Research Conference, March 10, 2000, University of California, Los Angeles.

———. 1999a. "Revisiting feminist theory and the history of developmental genetics with the fruitfly: A short story about the isolation of the *Drosophila* sex-determining gene, *Sex-lethal (Sxl).*" Paper presented at Sex, Gender, Culture: The Third Annual History and Theory Conference, November 13–14, 1999, University of California, Irvine.

———. 1999b. "Sex-in-the-making: The odd life of 'sexual difference' in *Drosophila* sex-determination research." Paper presented at the Department of Rhetoric, October 28, 1999, University of California, Berkeley (sponsored by the Townsend Center Material Culture Working Group).

———. 1996. "La bicatégorisation par 'sexe': Problèmes et enjeux des recherches en biologie sur la détermination du sexe chez les humains." Master's thesis, University of Lausanne, Switzerland, 1996.

Kreidberg, J. A., et al. 1993. "WT-1 is required for early kidney development." *Cell* 74: 679–91.

Lambert, Helen H. 1987. "Biology and equality: A perspective on sex differences." In *Sex and Scientific Inquiry,* ed. Sandra Harding and Joan F. O'Barr, 125–45. Chicago and London: University of Chicago Press.

Langaney, André. 1977. "La résurrection de l'anthropologie." *Science et Vie: Génétique et Anthropologie,* hors-série, no. 120: 4–11.

Laqueur, Thomas. 1990. *Making Sex: Body and Gender from the Greeks to Freud.* Cambridge, Mass.: Harvard University Press.

Latour, Bruno. 1989. *La science en action: Introduction à la sociologie des sciences* (trad. M. Biezunski). Paris: Gallimard.

Longino, Helen, and Ruth Doell. 1987. "Body, bias, and behavior: A comparative analysis of reasoning in two areas of biological science." In *Sex and Scientific Inquiry,* ed. Sandra Harding and Jean F. O'Barr, 165–86. Chicago and London: University of Chicago Press.

McLaren, Anne. 1990. "What makes a man a man?" *Nature* 346: 216–17.

Morgan, Thomas H. 1914. "Mosaics and gynandromorphs in Drosophila." *Proc. Soc. Exper. Biol. Med.* 11: 171.

Muller, Herman J., and Stanley Zimmering. 1960. "A sex-linked lethal without evident effect in Drosophila males but partially dominant in females." *Genetics* 45 (September): 1001–2.

North, M., N. Affara, and M. A. Ferguson-Smith. 1991. "Analysis of SRY, the present candidate testis determining factor (TDF), in sex reversed patients and evidence for novel regulation finger gene ZFY (abstract)." *J. Med. Genet.* 28: 550.

Rheinberger, Hans-Jörg. 1997. *Towards a History of Epistemic Things: Synthesizing Proteins in the Test Tube.* Stanford, Calif.: Stanford University Press.

Roberts, David B., ed. 1986. *Drosophila: A Practical Approach.* Oxford and Washington, D.C.: IRL Press.

Scott, Joan W. 1986. "Gender: A useful category of historical analysis." *American Historical Review* 91 (December).

Suzuki, David T. 1970. "Temperature-sensitive mutations in Drosophila melanogaster." *Science* 170: 695–706.

Suzuki, David T., et al. 1967. "Temperature-sensitive mutations in Drosophila melanogaster. I. Relative frequencies among gamma-ray and chemically induced sex-linked recessive lethals and semilethals." *Proc. Natl. Acad. Sci., U.S.,* 57: 907–12.

Tarsoff, M., and D. T. Suzuki. 1970. "Temperature-sensitive mutations in Drosophila melanogaster. VI. Temperature effects on development of sex-linked recessive lethals." *Dev. Biol.* 23: 492–509.

Wachtel, Stephen S. 1983. *H-Y Antigen and the Biology of Sex Determination.* New York: Grune and Stratton.
Wagner, T., et al. 1994. "Autosomal sex reversal and compomelic dysplasia are caused by mutations in and around the SRY-related gene SOX9." *Cell* 79: 1111–20.
Waibel, F., et al. 1987. "Absence of Y-specific DNA sequences in human 46,XX true hermaphroditism and in 45,X mixed gonadal dysgenesis." *Hum. Genet.* 76: 332–36.
Zanaria, Elena, et al. 1994. "An unsual member of the nuclear hormone receptor superfamily responsible for X-linked adrenal hyposplasia congenita." *Nature* 372: 635–41.
Zizek, Slavoj. 1999. "Against the Double Blackmail" [forwarded e-mail], April 22.

SECTION 5

REPRODUCIBLE INSIGHTS

WOMEN CREATING KNOWLEDGE, SOCIAL POLICY, AND CHANGE

In the introduction to section 4 we reviewed feminist theory that extends and redefines scientific theories and methods so that women's lives and experiences are fully included. The absence of women, as embodied subjects and as objective researchers, has fundamentally limited the scope and accuracy of much of what is known in Western science. Some argue that the development of modern science depended on and reinscribed notions of women's intellectual and physical inferiority to men.[1] Contemporary scientists, too, sometimes sift their ideas through a sociopolitical filter that reinforces rather than challenges assumptions about fundamental physiological and psychological differences between the sexes.[2]

In the last decade some feminist scientists have argued that the root of women's subordination is located in broad acceptance of biological explanations for gender-based social arrangements.[3] Their efforts seek to develop a fuller account, a better explanation of if, how, and under what conditions there are demonstrably meaningful biological and behavioral differences between women and men. But feminist scientists cannot by themselves undo the centuries of misinformation that inform ideologies of sex differences. We can critique canonical knowledge, we can offer alternative interpretations and hypotheses of existing data, we can generate new research that challenges old ideas, and we can develop new models of social organization and interpersonal relations. But unless those critiques, new ideas, and new social organizations are woven into the scientific community and society in general, they will have little impact.

Thus no effort in feminist education would be complete without a focus on the process of implementing the new perspectives offered by feminist studies of science.

In feminist education, the bridge between theory and practice is a thoroughgoing concern. It is a central goal of feminist initiatives to improve and enrich the health, well-being, and happiness of all women (and men) through fighting the oppressions that privilege the few at the expense of many.[4] Scientific research has sometimes played a role in legitimating these oppressions.[5] Nevertheless, precisely because scientific research cannot be neutral, because it is informed by and informs contemporary social, historical, and economic academic and public policy debates, and because scientific research can be used persuasively, those who are scientifically literate emerge as key players in public debates about the policy issues that shape the conditions of women's (indeed, everyone's) daily lives.

We have in multiple ways made the point that it matters that women have been excluded and/or marginalized from the mainstream of scientific and technological education, research, and development. It matters for a number of reasons, the most practical of which is that exclusion and marginalization have denied women equal access to well-paying and satisfying careers in the fields of their choice. It matters because the contents of scientific research, where inquiry begins with assumptions of male as norm, present an incomplete and inaccurate picture of the natural world. It also matters because where women are present, there is a higher probability that someone will notice and question research assumptions and directions that reinforce cultural biases against women (though women's presence alone is no guarantee of this). It matters, too, because scientific and technological research and innovations make critical contributions to contemporary social and economic life. Wherever women and their lives and experiences are absent from decision-making processes about the research, funding, and promoting of new developments, there is a lost opportunity for innovative thinking that improves everyone's lives. Instead we confront replaced, revised, and reinforced versions of nineteenth-century ideas that celebrated the great wonders of *man*kind's intellect.[6] So it does matter that the science and technology of today's world have been constructed by and for the benefit of (with important exceptions) a small group of men trained in the Western scientific tradition.

In the governmental arena, where policy-making power resides at state and federal levels, women are only just beginning to gain a foothold. Despite the fact that most of the world's governments claim to be formally committed to full equality for women, in no country of the world are women represented in government in proportion to the population.[7] In the United States recent elections have brought the percentage of women holding seats in state houses to an average of about 15 percent. In a few states voters have succeeded in electing higher percentages of women to their state legislatures, but only six (Washington, Nevada, Colorado, Arizona, Vermont, and New Hampshire) have over 30 percent, and none has over 40 percent women among their legislators.[8] Among state and federal legislators, men and women, those who seek to develop public policy about science and technology from a woman-centered and feminist perspective are few and far between.[9] Among those few there is but a handful nationally who have scientific expertise. This should be no surprise. How could it be any different, with the history of exclusion from both the institutions of scientific/technological expertise *and* the institutions of political power and practice?

If change is our goal, but we have limited access to the institutions and leadership positions through which change is promoted, then how can we accomplish anything? We can teach ourselves and one another. We can pay attention. We can learn how to speak out, how to make the argument, how to think critically about the issues at hand. We can take comfort in the fact that the process of moving new ideas into the mainstream is neither orderly nor predictable. Unintended consequences can work to our benefit, just as they may work to our disadvantage. The need is to pay attention, to monitor, to stay in the struggle, to understand what is happening, and always to keep women at the center of the frame.

For instance, in the conventional paradigm for the emergence and development of new technologies, researchers develop a potentially important idea to address an identified need. The idea is the subject of a series of experiments, to be tested, elaborated, retested, and eventually shaped into a marketable idea or material product. Research and development take place within the world of "objective" science, where each step along the way is directed by apparently unbiased decisions dictated not by the researchers but by the outcome of each experiment. The success of an innovation, likewise, is determined not by human actors but by a faceless "marketplace" where competitive forces promote the survival of the products that best fit the market's needs. In this model, social changes necessarily follow as the new product (if it is an important one, such as the computer) is incorporated into social life.[10]

But as historical and social studies of technoscience have amply demonstrated, this conventional linear model for the development of innovations captures neither the more dynamic processes that influence their emergence and use nor the social changes that influence and transpire from the innovations.[11] By abandoning an understanding of innovation and social change as driven by a linear, rational, value-neutral, and inevitable scientific process, we acquire a more accurate vision of social change and can reject powerlessness and marginalization. Opportunities for promoting or, alternatively, discouraging a technological innovation become visible at many (sometimes simultaneous) points within systems of research and development that do not conform to simplistic linear models.

A recent example of political activity to discourage a new technology is the controversy surrounding Terminator technology. This patented technology alters plants to keep them from producing viable seed. The product is intended to prevent farmers from saving seeds from their harvests for replanting, thus requiring them to purchase new seed each season. Critics maintain that Terminator technology will economically and socially impoverish farming communities by disrupting farmers' ability to develop locally adapted seed strains. In addition, according to Neth Dano of the Philippines-based South East Asian Regional Institute for Community Education, the new seed technology will disproportionately impact women, since they tend to be the ones who share and exchange seeds. In response to such concerns, the Rural Advancement Fund International has initiated an international effort to encourage national patent offices around the world to reject patent applications for engineered seed sterility.[12]

Donna Haraway argues that such a response is a necessary component of a critical, multisided, public, and democratic science. Her vision of what she calls technoscientific democracy "does not necessarily mean an antimarket politics and certainly not an antiscience politics. But such a democracy does require a critical science politics at the national, as well as at many other kinds of local, level. "Critical" means evaluative, public, multiactor, multiagenda, oriented to equality and heterogeneous well-being."[13] She argues that "situated knowledge" is an untapped and yet essential component of democratic science, one that recognizes the limitations of any individual's capacity to "know reality" and that offers an antidote—a conception of diverse, informed participants engaged in a fully democratic process of creating public policy that serves the public interest. Yet implementing such a vision will not be easy. Even the definition of "public interest" is contested territory. The United States is a culturally heterogeneous country with a capitalist economy. Which public? Whose interests?

Nowhere are these issues more in evidence than in the development and delivery of medical knowledge and heath care specific to women. In her book *Women's Health—Missing from U.S. Medicine,* Sue Rosser catalogues the ways in which research about women's bodies suffers from the biases and distortions identified by feminist studies of science and technology. Research directions, standards of evidence, interpretation of data, and the implementation of research findings—all of these have been influenced by the inadequate incorporation of women into all aspects of scientific research and development. Women have been absent from studies that were expressly focused on issues in women's health, so that, for instance, drug trials on the role of estrogen in protecting against heart attacks included only male participants.[14]

Alternatively, women have been included in high-risk or poorly researched studies when there was potential for large profits, for instance in the case of contraceptives. The Dalkon Shield is a notorious example. It was an intrauterine contraceptive device developed by Hugh Davis, M.D., a faculty member of the Johns Hopkins University Medical, School, who stood to profit from its manufacture and sale. Based on one small study of six hundred women for one year, and ignoring the advice of scientists who had concerns about the shortage of reliable data, A. H. Robins purchased the device and introduced it to the market in 1970. They stopped sales of the Dalkon Shield just four years later but did not recall those already sold and in use. About 235,000 American women suffered injuries (most of which involved life-threatening pelvic infections, and many of which left women infertile), and twenty women died. A. H. Robins filed for bankruptcy in reaction to a class action suit. The litigation ended when a trust fund was set up to compensate the injured women, but the majority received $725 or less. Final payments from the company were not completed until 1996.[15]

The controversy surrounding the Dalkon Shield case led to legislation that required companies to show their medical products to be safe and effective before they could be approved by the Food and Drug Administration for marketing.[16] Yet controversies continue to surround currently available medical products for women's bodies. For instance, approximately four hundred thousand women have brought a class action lawsuit against manufacturers of silicone breast implants, claiming that the implants cause a variety of autoimmune diseases.[17] The safety of conventional medical practices such as routinely scheduled mammograms for women over forty and estrogen replacement therapy for menopause have also come into question.[18]

Because the physiological processes of women's bodies are underresearched relative to men, women are underdiagnosed for some diseases (such as heart disease and AIDS) and overdiagnosed for others relative to men (such as mental illnesses). Women also are subjected to surgical and drug regimens that may not be as effective for women as men (i.e., women are less likely than men to survive coronary bypass surgery).[19] To complicate the picture still further, women have different health concerns depending on their racial/ethnic families of origin. Research and treatment are particularly underdeveloped for diseases linked to racial/ethnic groups, including sickle cell anemia and systemic lupus erythematosus among African Americans, alcoholism among Native Americans, and hemoglobin E disease and hepatitis B among Asian Americans.[20] Cervical cancer rates are twice as high among Hispanic women as non-Hispanic women, and African-American women have higher rates of hypertension than European-American women. Japanese- and Chinese-American women are less likely than Filipina women to suffer from hypertension.[21]

Indeed, even the components of women's physiology that are reputed to be at the heart of femininity itself, our "hormonal hurricanes," as Anne Fausto-Sterling dubbed them, are sometimes wildly misunderstood.[22] Yet understanding how hormone cycles work is critical to understanding how the immune system works, which is critical to women's health in particular, since an estimated 75 percent of autoimmune disease patients are women. It is also critical to the general science of medicine, since the relationship between hormones and the immune system has implications for areas as diverse as drug testing, the timing of vaccinations, infertility problems, and administering chemotherapy.[23]

Critiques of the limitations of conventional medical research related to women emerged in the scholarly literature in the 1980s, along with feminist studies of science more generally and the women's health movement. However, it was women in Congress, sparked by activist communities, who worked together across conventional political lines to begin efforts toward a more inclusive national research agenda. Among these were Democrats Patricia Schroeder and Barbara Mikulski and Republicans Constance Morella and Olympia Snowe, whose lobbying efforts eventually led to the establishment of the Office of Research on Women's Health within the National Institutes of Health (NIH), the Women's Health Initiative, and the NIH Revitalization Act of 1993.[24] The NIH Revitalization Act requires that women and people of color be explicitly included in all grant proposals using human subjects (or else the proposal must explain why they are not). The Women's Health Initiative funds a national network of Centers of Excellence in Women's Health through which federally sponsored research is organized. It is designed to collect baseline data on cardiovascular diseases, cancer, and osteoporosis, the three leading major health threats among women over forty-five. That the initiative is collecting *baseline* data underscores the degree of impoverishment of our knowledge. The extent to which such efforts on the part of mainstream institutions will lead to the recentering of our knowledge base, so that it fully includes women's lives (in all their variety) to the same degree that it includes men's lives, remains to be seen.[25] It will depend on how much public support there is, and how much support in Congress.

Grassroots women's health initiatives have also contributed to the currents of change. They most often emphasize community-based empowerment, health delivery, and disease prevention within the context of the biological or genetic elements of health. These organizations sponsor educational efforts to support a wide variety of health care issues for women, including parent and child health care, breast cancer and cervical cancer examinations, blood pressure monitoring, nutrition needs, and childbirth. Though each has its own goals, projects, and community strategies, they share a focus on how social factors influence patterns of risk and access to adequate treatment. Among the best known national efforts are the National Black Women's Health Project (NBWHP), founded by Byllye Avery in 1984; the Boston Women's Health Book Collective, which has published *Our Bodies, Ourselves* since 1970; and the National Women's Health Network. The last of these is an advocacy organization that lobbies Congress and other government agencies as well as serving as a clearinghouse of women's health information. The National Black Women's Health Project (NBWHP) promotes collective political action on behalf of black women in particular, but its goals statement is a good model for women's health initiatives in general:

> The following goals of NBWHP's Self-Help Groups reflect our basic beliefs about defining, promoting and maintaining our health;
>
> 1. To raise the consciousness of Black women, particularly Black women in low income communities, about the severity and pervasiveness of our health problems within the context of racism, sexism, classism and heterosexism in our society.
> 2. To provide a comfortable and safe atmosphere in which Black women can explore health issues.
> 3. To provide opportunities for Black women to become knowledgeable health advocates for ourselves and our communities.
> 4. To increase Black women's well-being through knowledge of the availability and use of health services and resources.
> 5. To participate in a national network linking Black women together to address key health problems in our communities.

> By working toward these goals, Black women can help not only themselves and their sisters within groups, but can create a conscious activist network between groups and communities. This "ripple effect" can result in massive numbers of Black women across varied communities increasing their awareness and knowledge of health and wellness. Fostering such discussions and exchanging information are necessary for Black women to feel comfortable discussing health issues with one another, wherever we are in our communities.[26]

As the NBWHP model suggests, these organizations and initiatives are committed to both critiquing the status quo of medical knowledge and treatment and developing an understanding of the political and social processes involved in using the knowledge and accessing the treatment. All are aimed at improving, enriching, and expanding the conditions of women's lives within the larger social, political, and economic context.

Similarly, the readings we feature in this section of the book explore the ways in which science and politics are complicit and implicit partners in controlling the conditions in which women live. Emily Martin, in her essay "Premenstrual Syndrome, Work Discipline, and Anger," looks at nineteenth- and twentieth-century debates about white middle- and upper-class women in the paid workforce. She points to the history of medical ideas about menstruation as a case in point, where male physicians' beliefs about women's mental and physical abilities lent the weight of scientific authority to arguments against women in the workplace. Though prototypical feminist research by psychologist Leta Hollingworth in 1914 documented that women were no less capable of manual and mental work when they were menstruating than when they were not, her findings were swamped by those more conveniently aligned with conventional attitudes that saw women as perpetually diseased and disabled. Martin does not dismiss the experiences of menstruation as unimportant, but she argues that instead of understanding our bodies in negative terms we should challenge the conditions and descriptions that mark us as unhealthy by nature.

The Western cultural belief that women are closer to nature than men has a long history.[27] Though this cultural belief might account for the ways in which women and nature alike are dismissed and exploited, Ruth Perry argues for a more complicated perspective on the women-and-nature link. As she points out in her essay, "Engendering Environmental Thinking: A Feminist Analysis of the Present Crisis," it is multinational corporations, increasingly empowered by state and national legislation, that pose the greatest threat to our environment. Women make up the majority of unpaid environmental activists around the world, because women more often than men take seriously "the labor of reproducing the conditions for life" so critical to the survival of the earth. If public policy makers likewise took this labor seriously, environmental pollution would be inconceivable. Instead, policy makers and environmental engineers can argue that "dilution is the solution" when there is potential for environmental degradation from all sorts of landfills, factories, power plants, agrichemicals, or even home cleaning products.

When reproduction *is* at the center of public discussion in the contemporary United States, the topics—alcohol and drug use, for instance—are exclusive to women, as if men had no role in the reproduction of human life and the conditions thereof. In "Between Fathers and Fetuses: The Social Construction of Male Reproduction and the Politics of Fetal Harm," Cynthia Daniels maps a social terrain in which women are much *too* central, because public policy initiatives are directed at controlling what we do with our bodies. That is, the struggle is not simply to ensure that women are the focus of interest. We also have to ask whose focus and whose interests are served by the policies and patterns that emerge.

These questions are not only central ones to ask about local, state, and national policies and practices. Individual behaviors and old habits can perpetuate inequalities even in the context of apparent changes, since some changes are superficial. So, for instance, the average contemporary U.S. kitchen contains between twelve and twenty appliances with electric motors in them. These devices and their prototypes have been researched, developed, and marketed since the nineteenth century as time-saving, but research finds that the amount of time women spend working in the home has changed little in the last century, while the type of work has changed dramatically.[28] The drive to motorize all household tasks (including squeezing lemons, chopping vegetables, brushing teeth, and stirring batters) is thus less a response to a need among women to reduce their workload "than a reflection of the economic and technical capacity for making motors."[29]

To take another example, the economic and technical capacity for making computers is at an all-time high to meet the growing demand in the United States. Nearly 37 percent of U.S. households in 1997 owned a personal computer, and 26 percent had modems as well, with 17 percent using e-mail at home. These figures show dramatic increases over 1994 figures, with growth in computer ownership up 52 percent, modem ownership up 139 percent, and e-mail use up 397 percent.[30] Educators are beginning to debate the rush to develop computer-based learning practices in the schools, where a "digital divide" based on race, gender, and class threatens to undermine the democratic commitments of public education.[31] Recent data show that there are marked inequalities in home ownership of computers, and those inequalities seem to translate into choices and performance in the schools. Twice the percentage of white households (41 percent) as African-American (19 percent) or Hispanic (19 percent) households include a computer. A similar gap appears in the percentage of white (21 percent) compared to African-American (8 percent) or Hispanic (9 percent) households who have online access. Moreover, these gaps seem to be growing at all income levels, including among those earning above $75,000. The rural poor are the least likely to have a computer, with only 8 percent of households owning computers and only 2 percent having online access.[32]

Some have argued that new technologies have seldom fundamentally challenged social inequalities.[33] Indeed, it is tempting to see science and technology as irretrievably enmeshed in the politics and practices of misogynist, male-centered professions. We would argue against a counsel of despair, reminding readers that feminist movements inside and outside the academy in the last decade have created opportunities to direct scientific and technological change toward better politics and practices. As tempting as it might be to retire from the challenge, a more effective strategy would be to reclaim and reenvision science and technology for alternative and liberatory purposes. This is the project that Alison Adam maps out in the closing essay here, "Feminist AI Projects and Cyberfutures," complete with hesitations and imaginative leaps. Adam argues from a practical perspective, pointing out that the Internet and cyberspace are new territory for misogynist colonization. But she is not promoting an uncritical embrace of information and computer technologies for feminist action. Quite the contrary: she warns that the current forms of cyberfeminism are but a starting point in the more significant project of infusing the development of those technologies with perspectives that include and benefit women.

We have tried throughout this book to present feminist science studies in such a way as to make the general point that scientists and a science-literate public can enrich and enlarge their research and perspectives on the social and natural world by including women. This is not a new idea, but it bears repeating, because the mother field of feminist science studies, women's studies, is one of the great educational innovations of the twentieth century. In less than thirty years interest in scholarship by, about, and for women has grown from a few isolated courses offered informally on and off campus to over five hundred women's studies programs enrolling more than a million students in courses in the United States alone. Internationally, the story is even more dramatic, since scholarship on women has emerged within universities and research centers all over the world. This is a profound accomplishment, and we tip our bonnets to the early pioneers, especially those brave women who first critiqued science. As new struggles emerge in the effort to institutionalize and implement what has been learned about the social and political processes that can either encourage or dismiss women as educators, researchers, and subjects of study, it is easy to forget how much ground has been gained. So we end with a quote from today's young women to remind our readers that new generations will carry on the work of researching, learning, teaching, and acting on behalf of women's futures.

The quote comes from the band Bikini Kill, and it outlines the Riot Grrrl philosophy. Riot Grrrl is a community of young feminists who, among other activities, publish "zines" and create websites for the exchange of political comment and personal support and encouragement. The philosophy eerily echoes in tone the "Excerpts from the Diaries of All Oppressed Women" by the Women's Collective of the New York High School Student Union, which appeared in the 1970 feminist classic *Sisterhood Is Powerful*. Riot Grrrls have a no-nonsense attitude toward inequality:

> BECAUSE us girls crave records and books and fanzines that speak to US that WE feel included in and can understand in our own ways. . . .
> BECAUSE viewing our work as being connected to our girlfriends–politics–real lives is essential if we are gonna figure out how [what] we are doing impacts, reflects, perpetuates, or DISRUPTS the status quo. . . .
> BECAUSE we don't wanna assimilate to someone else's (boy) standards of what is or isn't. . . .
> BECAUSE we are angry at a society that tells us Girl=Dumb, Girl=Bad, Girl=Weak. . . .
> BECAUSE I believe with my wholeheartmindbody that girls constitute a revolutionary soul force that can, and will, change the world for real.[34]

We can only hope that Riot Grrrls will decide to become scientists and engineers.

NOTES

[1] David Noble, *A World without Women: The Clerical Culture of Western Science* (New York: Knopf, 1992); Londa Schiebinger, *The Mind Has No Sex? Women in the Origins of Modern Science* (Cambridge, Mass.: Harvard University Press, 1989).

[2] For an overview, see Helen Longino, *Science as Social Knowledge* (Princeton, N.J.: Princeton University Press, 1990), in particular ch. 6, "Research on Sex Differences," 103–32. See also Alice Eagly, "Sex Differences in Social Behavior: Comparing Social Role Theory and Evolutionary Psychology," *American Psychologist* 52, 12 (1997):1380–83.

[3] This is not a new critique by feminists. Mary Putnam Jacobi, in her 1877 book *The Question of Rest for Women during Menstruation,* argued that biological sex differences were a myth. Leta Stetter Hollingworth in 1916 directly challenged assertions by social Darwinists that women were innately inferior to men, pointing to the inadequacy of the evidence upon which their interpretations relied. For a discussion of these foremothers, see Florence Denmark and Linda Fernandez, "Historical Development of the Psychology of Women," in Florence Denmark and Michele Paludi, eds., *Psychology of Women: A Handbook of Issues and Theories* (Westport, Conn.: Greenwood Press, 1993). For recent critiques of biological arguments, see Longino, *Science as Social Knowledge;* Anne Fausto-Sterling, *Myths of Gender* (New York: Basic Books, 1992); and Londa Schiebinger, *Has Feminism Changed Science?* (Cambridge, Mass.: Harvard University Press, 1999).

[4] bell hooks defines feminism as the struggle to end sexist oppression by opposing all forms of domination (*Feminist Theory: From Margin to Center* [Boston: South End Press, 1984]). In this definition, there is no room for "natural" forms of human domination.

[5] Sandra Harding, ed., *The "Racial" Economy of Science* (Bloomington: Indiana University Press, 1993); Cynthia Fuchs Epstein, *Deceptive Distinctions: Sex, Gender, and the Social Order* (New Haven, Conn.: Yale University Press, 1988).

[6] For a discussion of this phenomenon in terms of innovative teaching techniques such as "collaborative learning," see Maralee Mayberry, "Reproductive and Resistant Pedagogies: The Comparative Roles of Collaborative Learning and Feminist Pedagogy in Science Education," in Maralee Mayberry and Ellen Cronan Rose, eds., *Meeting the Challenge: Innovative Feminist Pedagogies in Action* (New York: Routledge, 1999).

[7] Joni Seager, *The State of Women in the World Atlas* (New York: Penguin Books, 1997), 14, 90.

[8] Center for the American Woman and Politics, Rutgers University, New Brunswick, N.J., 1994.

[9] Women have made important gains in many other areas of public policy and politics. For a review of these gains and the organizational efforts behind them, see Susan Hartmann, *From Margin to Mainstream: American Women and Politics since 1960* (Philadelphia: Temple University Press, 1989).

[10] For a discussion of the limitations of this model in relation to computers, see Paul N. Edwards, "From 'Impact' to Social Process: Computers in Society and Culture," in S. Jasanoff et al., eds., *Handbook of Science and Technology Studies* (Thousand Oaks: Sage Publications, 1995). For a discussion of the conventional model, see E. M. Rogers, *The Diffusion of Innovations,* 4th ed. (New York: The Free Press, 1995), 132–60, esp. fig. 4–1.

[11] Donna Haraway, *Modest_Witness@Second Millennium* (New York: Routledge, 1997), 95; Edwards, "From 'Impact' to Social Process."

[12] Carolina Farm Stewardship Association, *Newsletter,* March-April 1999, 5. For an examination of the problems that economic development poses for the ecosystem, see Kenneth Arrow et al., "Economic Growth, Carrying Capacity, and the Environment," *Science* 268 (1995): 520–21. For a discussion of the scientific reasons for concern, see Martha Crouch, "Debating the Responsibilities of Plant Scientists in the Decade of the Environment," *The Plant Cell* 2 (1990): 275–77, and her "How the Terminator Terminates," Edmonds Institute Occasional Paper Series, Edmonds, Wash., 1999.

[13] Haraway, *Modest_Witness@Second Millennium,* 95. The current practice of publishing new rules and regulations in the *Federal Register* and inviting comment is a limited attempt to encourage public participation in decision making.

[14] Trisha Gura, "Estrogen: Key Player in Heart Disease among Women," *Science* 269 (1995): 771–73; Sue Rosser, *Women's Health—Missing from U.S. Medicine* (Bloomington: Indiana University Press, 1994).

[15] Richard Sobol, *Bending the Law: The Story of the Dalkon Shield Bankruptcy* (Chicago: University of Chicago Press, 1991). See also Leslie Laurence and Beth Weinhouse, *Outrageous Practices: How Gender Bias Threatens Women's Health* (New Brunswick, N.J.: Rutgers University Press, 1994). For a general discussion of the ethics of research in universities, see David Shenk, "Money + Science = Ethical Problems on Campus," *The Nation,* March 22, 1999, 11–18.

[16] For a discussion of FDA guidelines for the participation of women in clinical trials, see Linda Ann Sherman, Robert Temple, and Ruth B. Merkatz, "Women in Clinical Trials: An FDA Perspective," *Science* 269 (1995): 793–94; Curtis Meinert, "The Inclusion of Women in Clinical Trials," *Science* 269 (1995): 795–96; and S. Jody Heymann, "Patients in Research: Not Just Subjects, but Partners," *Science* 269 (1995): 797–98.

[17] Jocelyn Kaiser, "Breast-Implant Ruling Sends a Message," *Science* 275 (1997): 21; James Rosenbaum, "Lessons from Litigation over Silicone Breast Implants: A Call for Activism by Scientists," *Science* 276 (1997): 1524–5.

[18] Gary Taubes, "The Breast-Screening Brawl," *Science* 275 (1997): 1056–9; Sasha Nemecek, "Hold the Hormones? The Good and the Bad about Postmenopausal Estrogen Therapy," *Scientific American,* September 1997, 38–39; Nancy Fugate Woods, "Midlife Women's Health: Conflicting Perspectives of Health Care Providers and Midlife Women and Consequences for Health," in Adele Clarke and Virginia Olesen, eds., *Revisioning Women, Health, and Healing* (New York: Routledge, 1999); Anne Fausto-Sterling, *Myths of Gender: Biological Theories about Women and Men* (New York: Basic Books, 1992).

[19] "Women: Absent Term in the AIDS Research Equation," *Science* 269 (1995): 777–80; Rosser, *Women's Health,* 37, 81; Bernadine Healy, "Women's Health, Public Welfare," *Journal of the Ameri-*

can Medical Association 266, 4 (July 24/31, 1991): 566–68; Dorothy Smith, *The Conceptual Practices of Power.* Boston: Northwestern University Press.

[20] Rosser, *Women's Health,* 90–91.

[21] Londa Schiebinger, *Has Feminism Changed Science?* (Cambridge, Mass.: Harvard University Press, 1999), 119.

[22] Fausto-Sterling, *Myths of Gender.*

[23] Virginia Morell, "Zeroing in on How Hormones Affect the Immune System," *Science* 269 (1995): 773–75.

[24] For a discussion of the debates surrounding these initiatives, see Schiebinger, *Has Feminism Changed Science?* and Healy, "Women's Health, Public Welfare."

[25] For a review of the controversies surrounding these initiatives, see A. Clarke and V. Olesen "Revising, Diffracting, Acting," in their edited volume *Revisioning Women, Health, and Healing* (New York: Routledge, 1999), 14–17.

[26] From their website at http://www.blackfamilies.com/community/groups/WomensHealth/Goals.html.

[27] Carolyn Merchant, *The Death of Nature: Women, Ecology and the Scientific Revolution* (New York: Harper and Row, 1980); Londa Schiebinger, "The History and Philosophy of Women in Science," *Signs: Journal of Women in Culture and Society* 12, 2 (1987): 305–32; Evelyn Fox Keller, *Reflections on Gender and Science* (New Haven, Conn.: Yale University Press, 1985), esp. ch. 3, "Spirit and Reason at the Birth of Modern Science," 43–65.

[28] Scott South and Glenna Spitze, "Housework in Marital and Nonmarital Households," *American Sociological Review* 59 (June 1994): 327–47; see also Joan Wallach Scott, "The Mechanization of Women's Work," *Scientific American* 247 (1982): 167–85.

[29] Judy Wajcman, *Feminism Confronts Technology* (University Park: Pennsylvania State University Press, 1991), 100.

[30] *Falling through the Net: A Survey of the "Have Nots" in Rural and Urban America* (Washington, D.C.: U.S. Department of Commerce, 1995); *Falling through the Net II: New Data on the Digital Divide* (Washington D.C.: National Telecommunications and Information Administration, 1998).

[31] M. Schrange, "Criticism: Beware the Computer Technocrats: Hardware Won't Educate Our Kids," *Educational Media and Technology Yearbook* 20 (1994):64–65; R. G. Nichols, "An Incomplete Caution: 'Beware of the Computer Technocrats,'" *Educational Media and Technology Yearbook* 20 (1994): 66–69; R. Sutton, "Equity and Computers in the Schools: A Decade of Research," *Review of Educational Research* 61, 4 (Winter 1991): 475–503.

[32] *Falling through the Net II: New Data on the Digital Divide.*

[33] For a review of this literature, see E. M. Rogers, *Diffusion of Innovations,* 4th ed. (New York: The Free Press, 1995), 429–40.

[34] Jessica Rosenberg and Gitana Garofalo, "Riot Grrrl: Revolutions from Within," *Signs: Journal of Women in Culture and Society* 23, 3 (1998): 809–13.

PREMENSTRUAL SYNDROME, WORK DISCIPLINE, AND ANGER

Emily Martin

Looming over the whole current scene in England and the United States is the enormous outpouring of interest—the publishing of magazine and newspaper articles, popular books and pamphlets, the opening of clinics, the marketing of remedies—devoted to premenstrual syndrome.

The dominant model for premenstrual syndrome (PMS) is the physiological/medical model. In this model, PMS manifests itself as a variety of physical, emotional, and behavioral "symptoms" which women "suffer." The list of such symptoms varies but is uniformly negative, and indeed worthy of the term "suffer." Judy Lever's list in her popular handbook serves as an example (Table 1).[1]

The syndrome of which this list is a manifestation is a "genuine illness,"[2] a "real physical problem"[3] whose cause is at base a physical one.[4] Although psychological factors may be involved as a symptom, or even as one cause, "the root cause of PMT [short for premenstrual tension, another term for PMS], no matter how it was originally triggered, is physical and can be treated."[5] This physical cause comes from "a malfunction in the production of hormones during the menstrual cycle, in particular the female hormone, progesterone. This upsets the normal working of the menstrual cycle and produces the unpleasant symptoms of PMT." Astonishingly, we are told that "more than three quarters of all women suffer from symptoms of PMT."[6] In other words, a clear majority of all women are afflicted with a physically abnormal hormonal cycle.

Various "treatments" are described that can compensate a woman for her lack of progesterone or her excess of estrogen or prolactin. Among the benefits of this approach are that psychological and physical states that many women experience as extremely distressing or painful can be alleviated, a problem that had no name or known cause can be named and grasped, and some of the blaming of women for their premenstrual condition by both doctors and family members can be stopped. It seems probable that this view of PMS has led to an improvement from the common dismissals "it's all in your mind," "grin and bear it," or "pull yourself together." Yet, entailed also in this view of PMS are a series of assumptions about the nature of time and of society and about the necessary roles of women and men.

. . . [In] the nineteenth century . . . menstruation began to be regarded as a pathological process. Because of ideas prevailing among doctors that a woman's reproductive organs held complete sway over her between puberty and menopause, women were warned not to divert needed energy away from the uterus and ovaries. In puberty, especially, the limited amount of energy in a woman's body was essential for the proper development of her female organs.

> Indeed physicians routinely used this energy theory to sanction attacks upon any behavior they considered unfeminine; education, factory work, religious or charitable activities, indeed virtually any interests outside the home during puberty were deplored[7] . . .

This view of women's limited energies ran very quickly up against one of the realities of nineteenth-century America: many young girls and women worked exceedingly long and arduous hours in factories, shops, and other people's homes. The "cult of invalidism" with its months and even years of inactivity and bed rest, which was

TABLE 1 A List of the Symptoms of Premenstrual Syndrome from a Popular Handbook

Complete Checklist of Symptoms		
Physical Changes		
Weight gain	Epilepsy	Spontaneous bruising
Skin disorders	Dizziness, faintness	Headache, migraine
Painful breasts	Cold sweats	Backache
Swelling	Nausea, sickness	General aches and pains
Eye diseases	Hot flashes	
Asthma	Blurring vision	
Concentration		
Sleeplessness	Lowered judgment	Lack of coordination
Forgetfulness	Difficulty concentrating	
Confusion	Accidents	
Behavior Changes		
Lowered school or work performance	Avoid social activities	Drinking too much alcohol
	Decreased efficiency	Taking too many pills
Lethargy	Food cravings	
Mood Changes		
Mood swings	Restlessness	Tension
Crying, depression	Irritability	Loss of sex drive
Anxiety	Aggression	

Source: Judy Lever and Michael G. Brush, *Pre-menstrual Tension,* © 1981 by Bantam Books; reproduced by permission.

urged on upper-class women, was manifestly not possible for the poor. This contradiction was resolved in numerous ways: by detailing the "weakness, degeneration, and disease" suffered by female clerks and operatives who "strive to emulate the males by unremitting labor"[8] while callously disregarding the very poor health conditions of those workers;[9] or by focusing on the greater toll that brain work, as opposed to manual work, was thought to take on female bodies. According to Edward Clarke's influential *Sex in Education* (1873), female operatives suffer less than schoolgirls because they "work their brain less. . . . Hence they have stronger bodies, a reproductive apparatus more normally constructed, and a catamenial function less readily disturbed by effort, than their student sisters."[10]

If men like Clarke were trying to argue that women (except working-class women) should stay home because of their bodily functions, feminists were trying to show how women could function in the world outside the home in spite of their bodily functions. Indeed, it is conceivable that the opinions of Clarke and others were in the first place a response to the threat posed by the first wave of feminism. Feminists intended to prove that the disciplined, efficient tasks required in the workplace in industrial society could be done by women when they were menstruating as well as when they were not.

In *Functional Periodicity: An Experimental Study of the Mental and Motor Abilities of Women During Menstruation* (1914), Leta Hollingworth had 24 women (who ironically held research and academic jobs) perform various tests of motor efficiency and controlled association both when they were and when they were not menstruating. These included tapping on a brass plate as many times as possible within a brief time;

holding a 2.5-mm rod as steady as possible within a 6-mm hole while trying not to let it touch the edges; naming a series of colors as quickly as possible; and naming a series of opposites as quickly as possible. Ability to learn a new skill was also tested by teaching the subjects to *type* and recording their progress while menstruating and not. The findings: "the records of all the women here studied *agree* in supporting the negative conclusion here presented. None of them shows a characteristic inefficiency in the traits here tested at menstrual periods."[11]

Similarly, in *The Question of Rest for Women During Menstruation* (1877), Mary Putnam Jacobi showed that "women do work better, and with much greater safety to health when their work is frequently intermitted; but that those intermittences should be at short intervals and lasting a short time, not at long intervals and lasting longer. Finally that they are required at all times, and have no special reference to the period of the menstrual flow."[12] Given the nature of the organization of work, men would probably also work better if they had frequent short breaks. What is being exposed in these early studies, in addition to the nature of women's capacities, is the nature of the work process they are subjected to.

It is obvious that the relationship between menstruation and women's capacity to work was a central issue in the nineteenth century. When the focus shifted from menstruation itself to include the few days before menstruation, whether women could work outside the home was still a key issue. It is generally acknowledged that the first person to name and describe the symptoms of premenstrual syndrome was Robert T. Frank in 1931.[13] Two aspects of Frank's discussion of what he called "premenstrual tension" deserve careful attention. The first is that he carried forward the idea, which flourished in the nineteenth century, that women were swayed by the tides of their ovaries. A woman's ovaries were known to produce female sex hormones, and these were the culprit behind premenstrual tension. His remedy was simple and to the point: "It was decided to tone down the ovarian activity by roentgen [x-ray] treatment directed against the ovaries."[14]

Frank reserved x-ray treatment for the most severe cases, but it was not long before the influence of female hormones on a woman was extended to include her emotional states all month long. In an extraordinary study in 1939, Benedek and Rubenstein analyzed psychoanalytic material from therapy sessions and dreams on the one hand and basal body temperature and vaginal smears on the other from nineteen patients under treatment for various neurotic disturbances. They were able to predict when the patients had ovulated and menstruated from the physiological record as well as from the psychoanalytic record. . . . But Benedek and Rubenstein went far beyond showing simple correlations between hormones and emotions. Without evidence of a causal link one way or the other, they concluded that "human [they meant 'adult female'] instinctual drives are *controlled by* gonadal hormone production" (emphasis added).[15]

Benedek and Rubenstein may have been unusually avid in their attempt to derive women's emotional states from hormones. But their study was still being quoted approvingly and elaborated on in the late 1960s. One later study (1968) concluded that "the menstrual cycle exercises gross influences on female behavior."[16] It was not until the 1970s that some researchers began to insist that women's moods had important social, cultural, and symbolic components and that even though *correlation* between biochemical substances and emotional changes can be observed, "the direction of causality is still unclear. Indeed, there is abundant evidence to suggest that biochemical changes occur in *response* to socially mediated emotional changes."[17]

The second aspect of Frank's study that deserves attention is his immediate interest in the effect of premenstrual tension on a woman's ability to work, such that in mild cases employers have to make provision for an employee's temporary care and in severe ones to allow her to rest in bed for one or two days.[18] It strikes me as exceedingly significant that Frank was writing immediately after the Depression, at a time when the gains women had made in the paid labor market because of World War I were slipping away. Pressure was placed on women from many sides to give up waged work and allow men to take the jobs.[19]

Can it be accidental that many other studies were published during the interwar years that showed the debilitating effects of menstruation on women?[20] Given this pattern of research finding women debilitated by menstruation when they pose an obstacle to full employment for men, it is hardly surprising that after the start of World War II a rash of studies found that menstruation was not a liability after all.[21] "Any activity that may be performed with impunity at other times may be performed with equal impunity during menstruation," wrote Seward in 1944, reversing her own earlier finding in 1934 that menstruation was a debility. Some of the evidence amassed for this conclusion seems astoundingly ad hoc: Seward argues that when women miss work because of menstrual complaints they are indulging in "a bit of socially acceptable malingering by taking advantage of the popular stereotype of menstrual incapacitation." Her evidence? That when a large life insurance company discontinued pay for menstrual absenteeism after a limited time allowance, menstrual absenteeism markedly declined![22] She missed the point that if people need their wages and have used up their sick leave, they will go to work, even in considerable discomfort.

After World War II, just as after World War I, women were displaced from many of the paid jobs they had taken on.[23] The pattern seems almost too obvious to have been overlooked so long, but as we know there was a spate of menstrual research after the Second World War that found, just as after the first, that women were indeed disabled by their hormones. Research done by Katherina Dalton in the 1940s was published in the *British Medical Journal* in 1953,[24] marking the beginning of her push to promote information about the seriousness of premenstrual syndrome. As we will see, one of her overriding concerns was the effect on women's performance at school and work and the cost to national economies of women's inability to work premenstrually.

Although Dalton's research fit in nicely with the postwar edging of women out of the paid work force, it was not until the mid to late 1970s that the most dramatic explosion of interest in PMS took place. This time there were no returning veterans to demand jobs for which women were suddenly "unqualified"; instead, women had made greater incursions into the paid work force for the first time without the aid of a major war.

> First single women, then wives, and then mothers of school-aged children were, in a sense, freed from social constraints against work outside the home. For each of these groups, wage labor was at one time controversial and debatable, but eventually employment became a socially acceptable—and even expected—act.[25]

Many factors were responsible for women's emergence in the paid work force: the second wave of feminism and stronger convictions about women's right to work, a lower birth rate, legislative support barring sex discrimination, increasing urbanization, and growth in educational opportunities for women.[26] It goes without saying that women's move toward center stage in the paid work force (as far away as equality still remains) is threatening to some women and men and has given rise to a variety of maneuvers designed to return women to their homes.[27] Laws has suggested that the recent burgeoning of emphasis on PMS is a "response to the second wave of feminism." I think this is a plausible suggestion, made even more convincing by the conjunction between periods of our recent history when women's participation in the labor force was seen as a threat, and, simultaneously, menstruation was seen as a liability. . . .[28]

Many PMS symptoms seem to focus on intolerance for the kind of work discipline required by late industrial societies. But what about women who find that they become clumsy? Surely this experience would be a liability in any kind of social setting. Perhaps so, and yet it is interesting that most complaints about clumsiness seem to focus on difficulty carrying out the mundane tasks of keeping house: "You may find you suddenly seem to drop things more often or bump into furniture around the house. Many women find they tend to burn themselves while cooking or cut themselves more frequently."[29] "It's almost funny. I'll be washing the dishes or putting them away and suddenly a glass will just jump out of my hands. I must break a glass every month. But that's when I know I'm entering my premenstrual phase."[30] Is there something about housework that makes it problematic if one's usual capacity for discipline relaxes?

On the one hand, for the numbers of women who work a double day (hold down a regular job in the paid work force and come home to do most of the cooking, cleaning, and child care), such juggling of diverse responsibilities can only come at the cost of supreme and unremitting effort. On the other hand, for the full-time homemaker, recent changes in the organization of housework must be taken into account. Despite the introduction of "labor-saving" machines, time required by the job has increased as a result of decline in the availability of servants, rise in the standards of household cleanliness, and elaboration of the enterprise of childrearing. . . .[31]

Perhaps the need for discipline in housework comes from a combination of the desire for efficiency and a sense of its endlessness, a sense described by Simone de Beauvoir as "like the torture of Sisyphus . . . with its endless repetition: the clean becomes soiled, the soiled is made clean, over and over, day after day. The housewife wears herself out marking time: she makes nothing, simply perpetuates the present."[32] Not only sociological studies[33] but also novels by women attest to this aspect of housework:

> First thing in the morning you started with the diapers. After you changed them, if enough had collected in the pail, you washed them. If they had ammonia which was causing diaper rash, you boiled them in a large kettle on top of the stove for half an hour. While the diapers were boiling, you fed the children, if you could stand preparing food on the same stove with urine-soaked diapers. After breakfast, you took the children for a walk along deserted streets, noting flowers, ladybugs, jet trails. Sometimes a motorcycle would go by, scaring the shit out of the children. Sometimes a dog followed you. After the walk, you went back to the house. There were many choices before nap time: making grocery lists; doing the wash; making the beds; crawling around on the floor with the children; weeding the garden; scraping last night's dinner off the pots and pans with steel wool; refinishing furniture; vacuuming; sewing buttons on; letting down hems; mending tears; hemming curtains. During naps, assuming you could get the children to sleep simultaneously (which was an art in itself), you could flip through *Family Circle* to find out what creative decorating you could do in the home, or what new meals you could spring on your husband.[34]

Here is Katharina Dalton's example of how a premenstrual woman reacts to this routine:

> Then quite suddenly you feel as if you can't cope anymore—everything seems too much trouble, the endless household chores, the everlasting planning of meals. For no apparent reason you rebel: "Why should I do everything?" you ask yourself defiantly. "I didn't have to do this before I was married. Why should I do it now?" . . . As on other mornings you get up and cook breakfast while your husband is in the bathroom. You climb wearily out of bed and trudge down the stairs, a vague feeling of resentment growing within you. The sound of cheerful whistling from upstairs only makes you feel a little more cross. Without any warning the toast starts to scorch and the sausages instead of

> happily sizzling in the pan start spitting and spluttering furiously. Aghast you rescue the toast which by this time is beyond resurrection and fit only for the trash. The sausages are charred relics of their former selves and you throw those out too. Your unsuspecting husband opens the kitchen door expecting to find his breakfast ready and waiting, only to see a smoky atmosphere and a thoroughly overwrought wife. You are so dismayed at him finding you in such chaos that you just burst helplessly into tears.[35]

Needless to say, by the terms of the medical model in which Dalton operates, the solution for this situation is to seek medical advice and obtain treatment (usually progesterone).[36] The content of the woman's remarks, the substance of what she objects to, escape notice.

A woman who drops things, cuts or burns herself or the food in this kind of environment has to adjust to an altogether different level of demand on her time and energy than—say—Beng women in the Ivory Coast. There, albeit menstrually instead of premenstrually, women specifically must not enter the forest and do the usual work of their days—farming, chopping wood, and carrying water. Instead, keeping to the village, they are free to indulge in things they usually have no time for, such as cooking a special dish made of palm nuts. This dish, highly prized for its taste, takes hours of slow tending and cooking and is normally eaten only by menstruating women and their close friends and kinswomen.[37] Whatever the differing demands on Beng as opposed to western women, Beng social convention requires a cyclic change in women's usual activities. Perhaps Beng women have fewer burned fingers.

For the most part, women quoted in the popular health literature do not treat the cyclic change they experience as legitimate enough to alter the structure of work time. However, several of the women I interviewed did have this thought. One woman expressed this as a wish, while reinterpreting what she had heard about menstrual huts (places of seclusion used by women in some societies when they are menstruating):

> [Does menstruation have any spiritual or religious significance for you?] I like the idea of menstrual huts a great deal. They intrigue me. My understanding is it's a mysterious thing in some ways. It infuriates me that we don't know more about it. Here are all these women—apparently when you get your period you go off to this hut and you hang around. [Because you're unclean?] That's what I feel is probably bull, that's the masculine interpretation of what's going on passed on generally by men to male anthropologists, whereas the women probably say, "Oh, yeah, we're unclean, we're unclean, see ya later." And then they race off to the menstrual hut and have a good time. (Meg O'Hara)

Another got right to the heart of the matter with simplicity:

> Some women have cramps so severe that their whole attitude changes; maybe they need time to themselves and maybe if people would understand that they need time off, not the whole time, maybe a couple of days. When I first come on I sleep in bed a lot. I don't feel like doing anything. Maybe if people could understand more. Women's bodies change. (Linda Matthews)

. . . These women are carrying on what amounts to a twin resistance: to science and the way it is used in our society to reduce discontent to biological malfunction and to the integrity of separate spheres which are maintained to keep women in one while ruling them out of the other.

Given that periodic changes in activity in accord with the menstrual cycle are not built into the structure of work in our society, what does happen to women's work during their periods? Much recent research has attempted to discover whether women's actual performance declines premenstrually. The overwhelming impression one gets from reading the popular literature on the subject is that performance in almost every respect does decline. According to Dalton's influential account, women's grades drop, they are more likely to commit crimes and suicide, and they "cost British industry 3% of its total wage bill, which may be compared with 3% in Italy, 5% in Sweden and 8% in America."[38] Yet other accounts make powerful criticisms of the research on which these conclusions are based: they lack adequate controls, fail to report negative findings, and fail to report overall levels of women's performance in comparison to men's.[39] Still other studies find either increased performance or no difference in performance at all.[40]

Some women we interviewed expressed unforgettably the double message that women workers receive about PMS:

> Something I hear a lot that really amazes me is that women are discriminated against because they get their period. It makes them less capable to do certain kinds of work. It makes me angry. I never faced it in terms of my own personal experience, but it's something I've heard. I grew up thinking you shouldn't draw attention to your period, it makes you seem less capable than a man. I always tried to be kind of a martyr, and then all of a sudden recently I started hearing all this scientific information that shows that women really do have a cycle that affects their mood, and they really do get into bad moods when they have their periods. I don't know whether all of a sudden it gives legitimacy to start complaining that it's okay. I think I have a hard time figuring out what that's supposed to do. Then again you can look at that as being a really negative thing, medical proof that women are less reliable. It's proven now that they're going to have bad moods once a month and not be as productive. (Shelly Levinson)

I think the way out of this bind is to focus on women's experiential statements—that they function differently during certain days, in ways that make it harder for them to tolerate the discipline required by work in our society. We could then perhaps hear these statements not as warnings of the flaws inside women that need to be fixed but as insights into flaws in society that need to be addressed.

What we see from the list of PMS symptoms in Table 1 is not so much a list of traits that would be unfortunate in any circumstance but traits that happen to be unfortunate in our particular social and economic system, with the kind of work it requires. This consideration gives rise to the question of whether the decreases reported by women in their ability to concentrate or discipline their attention are accompanied by gains in complementary areas. Does loss of ability to concentrate mean a greater ability to free-associate? Loss of muscle control, a gain in ability to relax? Decreased efficiency, increased attention to a smaller number of tasks?

Here and there in the literature on PMS one can find hints of such increased abilities. Women report:

> No real distress except melancholy which I actually enjoy. It's a quiet reflective time for me.

> My skin breaks out around both ovulation and my period. My temper is short; I am near tears, I am depressed. One fantastic thing—I have just discovered that I write poetry just before my period is due. I feel very creative at that time.[41]

Others find they "dream more than usual, and may feel sexier than at other times of the cycle."[42]

> A sculptor described her special abilities when she is premenstrual. "There is a quality to my work and to my visions which just isn't there the rest of the month. I look forward to being premenstrual for its effect on my creativity, although some of the other symptoms create strains with my family." Another woman, prone to depression, described in the journal she kept, "When I am premenstrual I can write with such clarity and depth that

> after I get my period I don't recognize that those were my thoughts or that I could have written anything so profound."[43]

> I don't know what it is, but I'll wake up one morning with an urge to bake bread. I can hardly wait to get home from work and start mixing the flour, kneading the dough, smelling the yeast. It's almost sensual and very satisfying. Maybe it's the earth-mother in me coming out. I don't know. But I do enjoy my premenstrual time.[44]

> I have heard that many women cry before their period. Well, I do too. Sometimes I'll cry at the drop of a hat, but it's a good crying. I'll be watching something tender on TV or my children will do something dear, and my eyes fill up. My heart is flooded with feelings of love for them or for my husband, for the world, for humanity, all the joy and all the suffering. Sometimes I could just cry and cry. But it strengthens me. It makes me feel a part of the earth, of the life-giving force.[45]

And from my interviews:

> I dream very differently during my period; my dreams are very, very vivid and sometimes it seems that I hear voices and conversations. My dreams are very vivid and the colors are not brighter but bolder, like blues and reds and that's also very interesting. The last three days I feel more creative. Things seem a little more colorful, it's just that feeling of exhilaration during the last few days. I feel really great. (Alice Larrick)

> I like being by myself, it gives me time to forget about what people are thinking. I like the time I don't have to worry about talking to anybody or being around anybody. It's nice to be by yourself. Time alone. (Kristin Lassiter)

Amid the losses on which most accounts of PMS focus, these women seem to be glimpsing increased capacities of other kinds. If these capacities are there, they are certainly not ones that would be given a chance to flourish or would even be an advantage in the ordinary dual workday of most women. Only the exception—a sculptor or writer—would be able to put these greater emotional and associative capacities to work in her regular environment. Perhaps it is the creative writing tasks present in most academic jobs that lead to the result researchers find puzzling: if premenstrual women cannot concentrate as well, then why are women academics' work performance and concentration better than usual during the premenstrual phase?[46] The answer may be that there are different kinds of concentration: some requiring discipline inimical to body and soul that women reject premenstrually and some allowing expression of the depth within oneself that women have greater access to premenstrually.

We can gain some insight into how women's premenstrual and menstrual capacities can be seen as powers, not liabilities, by looking at the ethnographic case of the Yurok.[47] Thomas Buckley has shown how the Yurok view of menstruation (lost in ethnographic accounts until his writing) held that

> a menstruating woman should isolate herself because this is the time when she is at the height of her powers. Thus, the time should not be wasted in mundane tasks and social distractions, nor should one's concentration be broken by concerns with the opposite sex. Rather, all of one's energies should be applied in concentrated meditation on the nature of one's life, "to find out the purpose of your life," and toward the "accumulation" of spiritual energy.[48]

Michelle Harrison, with a sense of the appropriate setting for premenstrual women, says poignantly, "Women who are premenstrual often have a need for time alone, time to themselves, and yet few women actually have that time in their lives. One woman wrote, 'When I listen to music I feel better. If I can just be by myself and listen quietly, then the irritability disappears and I actually feel good. I never do it, though, or rarely so. I feel guilty for taking that time for myself, so I just go on being angry or depressed.'"[49] What might in the right context be released as powerful creativity or deep self-knowledge becomes, in the context of women's everyday lives in our societies, maladaptive discontent.

A common premenstrual feeling women describe is anger, and the way this anger is felt by women and described by the medical profession tells a lot about the niche women are expected to occupy in society. An ad in a local paper for psychotherapeutic support groups asks: "Do you have PMS?—Depression—irritability—panic attacks—food cravings—lethargy—dizziness—headache—backache—anger. How are other women coping with this syndrome? Learn new coping mechanisms; get support from others who are managing their lives."[50] Anger is listed as a symptom in a syndrome, or illness, that afflicts only women. In fuller accounts we find that the reason anger expressed by women is problematic in our society is that anger (and allied feelings such as irritability) makes it hard for a woman to carry out her expected role of maintaining harmonious relationships within the family.

> Serious problems can arise—a woman might become excessively irritable with her children (for which she may feel guilty afterwards), she may be unable to cope with her work, or she may spend days crying for no apparent reason. Life, in other words, becomes intolerable for a short while, both for the sufferer and for those people with whom she lives . . . PMT is often referred to as a potential disrupter of family life. Women suffering from premenstrual irritability often take it out on children, sometimes violently . . . Obviously an anxious and irritable mother is not likely to promote harmony within the family.[51]

This entire account is premised on the unexamined cultural assumption that it is primarily a woman's job to see that social relationships work smoothly in the family. Her own anger, however substantial the basis for it, must not be allowed to make life hard on those around her. If she has an anger she cannot control, she is considered hormonally unbalanced and should seek medical treatment for her malfunction. If she goes on subjecting her family to such feelings, disastrous consequences—construed as a woman's *fault* in the PMS literature—may follow. For example, "Doctor Dalton tells the story of a salesman whose commissions dropped severely once a month, putting a financial strain on the family and worrying him a great deal. Doctor Dalton charted his wife's menstrual cycle and found that she suffered from severe PMT. This affected her husband, who became anxious and distracted and so less efficient at his job. The drop in his commissions coincided with her premenstrual days. Doctor Dalton treated his wife and cured the salesman!"[52]

Not only can a man's failure at work be laid at the doorstep of a woman's PMS, so also can a man's violence. Although the PMS literature acknowledges that many battered women do nothing to provoke the violence they suffer from men, it is at times prone to suggest that women may themselves bring on battering if the man has a "short fuse": "[The woman's] own violent feelings and actions while suffering from PMT could supply the spark that causes him to blow up."[53] Or consider this account, in which the woman is truly seen as a mere spark to the man's blaze:

> One night she was screaming at him, pounding his chest with her fists, when in her hysteria she grabbed the collar of his shirt and ripped so hard that the buttons flew, pinging the toaster and the microwave oven. But before Susan could understand what she had done, she was knocked against the kitchen wall. Richard had smacked her across the face with the back of his hand. It was a forceful blow that cracked two teeth and dislocated her jaw. She had also bitten her tongue and blood was flowing from her mouth . . . [Richard took her to the emergency room that night and moved out the next morning.] He was afraid he might hit her again because *she was so uncontrollable* when she was in a rage. [Emphasis added.][54]

In this incident, who was most uncontrollable when in a rage—Richard or Susan? Without condoning Susan's actions, we must see that her violence was not likely to damage her husband bodily. A woman's fists usually do not do great harm when pounding a man's chest, and in this case they evidently did not. Ripping his clothes, however unfortunate, is not on the same scale as his inflicting multiple (some of them irreversible!) bodily injuries that required her to be treated in a hospital emergency room. The point is not that she was unable to injure him because of her (presumed) smaller size and lesser strength. After all she could have kicked him in the groin or stabbed him with a knife. The point is, she chose relatively symbolic means of expressing her anger and he did not. Yet in the PMS literature *she* is the one cited as uncontrollable, and responsible for his actions. The problems of men in these accounts are caused by outside circumstances and other people (women). The problems of women are caused by their own internal failure, a biological "malfunction." What is missing in these accounts is any consideration of why, in Anglo and American societies, women might feel extreme rage at a time when their usual emotional controls are reduced.

That their rage is extreme cannot be doubted. Many women in fact describe their premenstrual selves as being "possessed." One's self-image as a woman (and behind this the cultural construction of what it is to be a woman) simply does not allow a woman to recognize herself in the angry, loud, sometimes violent "creature" she becomes once a month.

> I feel it is not me that is in possession of my body. My whole personality changes, making it very difficult for the people I live and work with. I've tried. Every month I say, "This month it's going to be different, I'm not going to let it get hold of me." But when it actually comes to it, something chemical happens to me. I can't control it, it just happens.[55]

> Something seems to snap in my head. I go from a normal state of mind to anger, when I'm really nasty. Usually I'm very even tempered, but in these times it is as if someone else, not me, is doing all this, and it is very frightening.[56]

> It is something that is wound up inside, you know, like a great spring. And as soon as anything triggers it off, I'm away. It is very frightening. Like being possessed, I suppose.[57]

> I try so hard to be a good mother. But when I feel this way, it's as if there's a monster inside me that I can't control.[58]

> I just get enraged and sometimes I would like to throw bookshelves through windows, barely feeling that I have control . . . these feelings of fury when there's nothing around that would make that necessary. Life is basically going on as before, but suddenly I'm furious about it. (Meg O'Hara)

> I was verbally abusive toward my husband, but I would really thrash out at the kids. When I had these outbursts I tended to observe myself. I felt like a third party, looking at what I was doing. There was nothing I could do about it. I was not in control of my actions. It's like somebody else is taking over.[59]

> Once a month for the last 25 years this wonderful woman (my wife) has turned into a .[60]

. . . Women say they feel "possessed," but what the society sees behind their trouble is really their own malfunctioning *bodies*. Redress for women may mean attention focused on the symptoms but not on the social environment in which the "possession" arose. The anger was not really the woman's fault, but neither was it to be taken seriously. Indeed, one of women's common complaints is that men treat their moods casually:

> Sometimes if I am in a bad mood, my husband will not take me seriously if I am close to my period. He felt if it was "that time of the month" any complaints I had were only periodic. A few weeks ago I told him that until I am fifty-five he will have taken me seriously only half the time. After that he will blame it on menopause.[61]

Or if husbands cannot ignore moods, perhaps the moods, instead of whatever concrete circumstances from which they arise, can be treated.

> The husband of a woman who came for help described their problem as follows, "My wife is fine for two weeks out of the month. She's friendly and a good wife. The house is clean. Then she ovulates and suddenly she's not happy about her life. She wants a job. Then her period comes and she is all right again." He wanted her to be medicated so she would be a "good wife" all month.[62]

Marilyn Frye, in discussing the range of territory a woman's anger can claim, suggests: "So long as a woman is operating squarely within a realm which is generally recognized as a woman's realm, labeled as such by stereotypes of women and of certain activities, her anger will quite likely be tolerated, at least not thought crazy." And she adds, in a note that applies precisely to the anger of PMS, "If the woman insists persistently enough on her anger being taken seriously, she may begin to seem mad, for she will seem to have her values all mixed up and distorted."[63]

What are the sources of women's anger, so powerful that women think of it as a kind of possessing spirit? A common characteristic of premenstrual anger is that women often feel it has no immediate identifiable cause: "It never occurred to me or my husband that my totally unreasonable behavior toward my husband and family over the years could have been caused by anything but basic viciousness in me."[64]

Women often experience the depression or anger of premenstrual syndrome as quite different from the depression or anger of other life situations. As one woman described this difference: "Being angry when I know I'm right makes me feel good, but being angry when I know it's just me makes me feel sick inside."[65]

Anger experienced in this way (as a result solely of a woman's intrinsic badness) cannot help but lead to guilt. And it seems possible that the sources of this diffuse anger could well come from women's perception, however inarticulate, of their oppression in society—of their lower wage scales, lesser opportunities for advancement into high ranks, tacit omission from the language, coercion into roles inside the family and out that demand constant nurturance and self-denial, and many other ills. Adrienne Rich asks:

> What woman, in the solitary confinement[66] of a life at home enclosed with young children, or in the struggle to mother them while providing for them single-handedly, or in the conflict of weighing her own personhood against the dogma that says she is a mother, first, last, and always—what woman has not dreamed of "going over the edge," of simply letting go, relinquishing what is termed her sanity, so that she can be taken care of for once, or can simply find a way to take care of herself? The mothers: collecting their children at school; sitting in rows at the parent-teacher meeting; placating weary infants in supermarket carriages; straggling home to make dinner, do laundry, and tend children after a day at work; fighting to get decent care and livable schoolrooms for their children; waiting for child-support checks while the landlord threatens eviction . . .—the mothers, if we could look into their fantasies—their daydreams and imaginary experiences—we would see the embodiment of rage, of tragedy, of the overcharged energy of love, of inventive desperation, we would see the machinery of institutional violence wrenching at the experience of motherhood.[67]

Rich acknowledges the "embodiment of rage" in women's fantasies and daydreams. Perhaps premenstrually many women's fantasies become reality, as they experience their own violence wrenching at all of society's institutions, not just motherhood as in Rich's discussion.

Coming out of a tradition of psychoanalysis, Shuttle and Redgrove suggest that a woman's period may be "a moment of truth which will not sustain lies." Whereas during most of the month a woman may keep quiet about things that bother her, "maybe at the paramenstruum, the truth flares into her consciousness: this is an intolerable habit, she is discriminated against as a woman, she is forced to underachieve if she wants love, this examination question set by male teachers is unintelligently phrased, I will not be a punch-ball to my loved ones, this child must learn that I am not the supernatural never-failing source of maternal sympathy."[68] In this rare analysis, some of the systematic social causes of women's second-class status, instead of the usual biological causes, are being named and identified as possible sources of suppressed anger.

If *these* kinds of causes are at the root of the unnamed anger that seems to afflict women, and if they could be named and known, maybe a cleaner, more productive anger would arise from within women, tying them together as a common oppressed group instead of sending them individually to the doctor as patients to be fixed.

> And so her anger grew. It swept through her like a fire. She was more than shaken. She thought she was consumed. But she was illuminated with her rage; she was bright with fury. And though she still trembled, one day she saw she had survived this blaze. And after a time she came to see this anger-that-was-so-long-denied as a blessing.[69]

To see anger as a blessing instead of as an illness, it may be necessary for women to feel that their rage is legitimate. To feel that their rage is legitimate, it may be necessary for women to understand their structural position in society, and this in turn may entail consciousness of themselves as members of a group that is denied full membership in society simply on the basis of gender. Many have tried to describe under what conditions groups of oppressed people will become conscious of their oppressed condition. Gramsci wrote of a dual "contradictory consciousness, . . . one which is implicit in his [humans'] activity and which in reality unites him with all his fellow-workers in the practical transformation of the world; and one, superficially explicit or verbal, which he has inherited from the past and uncritically absorbed."[70] Perhaps the rage women express premenstrually could be seen as an example of consciousness implicit in activity, which in reality unites all women, a consciousness that is combined in a contradictory way with an explicit verbal consciousness, inherited from the past and constantly reinforced in the present, which denies women's rage its truth.

It is well known that the oppression resulting from racism and colonialism engenders a diffused and steady rage in the oppressed population.[71] Audre Lorde expresses this with power: "My response to racism is anger. That anger has eaten clefts into my living only when it remained unspoken, useless to anyone. It has also served me in classrooms without light or learning, where the work and history of Black women was less than a vapor. It has served me as fire in the ice zone of uncomprehending eyes of white women who see in my experience and the experience of my people only new reasons for fear or guilt." Alongside anger from the injustice of racism is anger from the injustice of sexism: "Every woman has a well-stocked arsenal of anger potentially useful against those oppressions, personal and institutional, which brought that anger into being."[72]

Can it be accidental that women describing their premenstrual moods often speak of rebelling, resisting, or even feeling "at war"?[73] It is important not to miss the imagery of rebellion and resistance, even when the women themselves excuse their feelings by saying the rebellion is "for no apparent reason"[74] or that the war is with their own bodies! ("Each month I wage a successful battle with my body. But I'm tired of going to war.")[75]

Elizabeth Fox-Genovese writes of the factors that lead women to accept their own oppression: "Women's unequal access to political life and economic participation provided firm foundations for the ideology of gender difference. The dominant representations of gender relations stressed the naturalness and legitimacy of male authority and minimized the role of coercion. Yet coercion, and frequently its violent manifestation, regularly encouraged women to accept their subordinate status."[76] Looking at what has been written about PMS is certainly one way of seeing the "naturalness" of male authority in our society, its invisibility and unexamined, unquestioned nature. Coercion in this context need not consist in the violence of rape or beating: sometimes women's violence is believed to trigger these acts, as we have seen, but other times it is the women who become violent. In a best-selling novel, a psychopathic killer's brutal murders are triggered by her premenstruum.[77] In either case, physical coercion consists in focusing on women's bodies as the locus of the operation of power and insisting that rage and rebellion, as well as physical pain, will be cured by the administration of drugs, many of which have known tranquilizing properties.[78]

Credence for the medical tactic of treating women's bodies with drugs comes, of course, out of the finding that premenstrual moods and discomfort are regular, predictable, and in accord with a woman's menstrual cycle. Therefore, it is supposed, they must be at least partially caused by the changing hormonal levels known to be a part of the cycle. The next step, according to the logic of scientific medicine, is to try to find a drug that alleviates the unpleasant aspects of premenstrual syndrome for the millions of women that suffer them.

Yet if this were to happen, if women's monthly cycle were to be smoothed out, so to speak, we would do well to at least notice what would have been lost. Men and women alike in our society are familiar with one cycle, dictated by a complex interaction of biological and psychological factors, that happens in accord with cycles in the natural world: we all need to sleep part of every solar revolution, and we all recognize the disastrous consequences of being unable to sleep as well as the rejuvenating results of being able to do so. We also recognize and behave in accord with the socially determined cycle of the week, constructed around the demands of work-discipline in industrial capitalism.[79] It has even been found that men structure their moods more strongly in accord with the week than women.[80] And absenteeism in accord with the weekly cycle (reaching as high as 10 percent at General Motors on Mondays and Fridays)[81] is a cause of dismay in American industry but does not lead anyone to think that workers need medication for this problem.

Gloria Steinem wonders sardonically

> What would happen if suddenly, magically, men could menstruate and women could not?
>
> Clearly, menstruation would become an enviable, boast-worthy, masculine event:
>
> Men would brag about how long and how much.
>
> Young boys would talk about it as the envied beginning of manhood. Gifts, religious ceremonies, family dinners, and stag parties would mark the day.
>
> To prevent monthly work loss among the powerful, Congress would fund a National Institute of Dysmenorrhea.[82]

Perhaps we might add to her list that if men menstruated, we would all be expected to alter our activities monthly as well as daily and weekly and enter a time and space organized to maximize the special powers released around the time of menstruation while minimizing the discomforts.

PMS adds another facet to the complex round of women's consciousness. Here we find some explicit challenge to the existing structure of work and time, based on women's own experience and awareness of capacities that are stifled by the way work is organized. Here we also find a kind of inchoate rage which women, because of the power of the argument that reduces this rage to biological malfunction, often do not allow to become wrath. In the whole history of PMS there are the makings of a debate whose questions have not been recognized for what they are: Are women, as in the terms of our cultural ideology, relegated by the functions of their bodies to home and family, except when, as second best, they struggle into wartime vacancies? Or are women, drawing on the different concepts of time and human capacities they experience, not only able to function in the world of work but able to mount a challenge that will transform it?

Notes

1. Lever 1981:108. Other examples of uniformly negative symptomatology are Halbreich and Endicott 1982 and Dalton 1983.
2. Lever 1981:1
3. Ad for a drug in *Dance* magazine, Jan. 1984:55
4. Few accounts reject the description of PMS as a disease. One that does is Witt, who prefers the more neutral term "condition" (1984:11–12). It is also relevant to note that I do not experience severe manifestations of PMS, and there is a possibility for that reason that I do not give sufficient credit to the medical model of PMS. I have, however, experienced many similar manifestations during the first three months of each of my pregnancies, so I have some sense that I know what women with PMS are talking about.
5. Lever 1981:47
6. Lever 1981:2, 1. Other estimates are "up to 75%" (Southam and Gonzaga 1965:154) and 40% (Robinson, Huntington and Wallace 1977:784)
7. Smith-Rosenberg 1974:27
8. Clarke 1873:130
9. Ehrenreich and English 1973:48
10. Clarke 1873:133–34
11. Hollingworth 1914:93
12. Jacobi 1877:232
13. Frank 1931
14. Frank 1931:1054
15. Benedek and Rubenstein 1939 II:461
16. Ivey and Bardwick 1968:344
17. Paige 1971:533–34
18. Frank 1931:1053
19. Kessler-Harris 1982:219, 259, 254–55
20. Seward 1934; McCance 1937; Billings 1934; Brush 1938
21. Altmann 1941; Anderson 1941; Novak 1941; Brinton 1943; Percival 1943
22. Seward 1944:95
23. Kessler-Harris 1982:295
24. Dalton and Greene 1953
25. Weiner 1985:118
26. Kessler-Harris 1982:311–16; Weiner 1985:89–97, 112–18
27. Kessler-Harris 1982:316–18
28. Laws 1983:25. I am working on a more extensive study of the literature on menstruation and industrial work from late nineteenth century to the present, including publications in industrial hygiene as well as medicine and public health.
29. Lever 1982:20
30. Witt 1984:129
31. Vanek 1974; Scott 1980; Cowan 1983:208

32. de Beauvoir 1952:425
33. Oakley 1974:45
34. Ballantyne 1975:114
35. Dalton 1983:80
36. Dalton 1983:82
37. Gottlieb 1982:44
38. Dalton 1983:100. These figures are still being cited in major newspapers (Watkins 1986).
39. Parlee 1973:461–62
40. Golub 1976; Sommer 1973; Witt 1984:160–62
41. Both quoted in Weideger 1977:48
42. Birke and Gardner 1982:23
43. Harrison 1984:16–17
44. Witt 1984:150
45. Witt 1984:151
46. Birke and Gardner 1982:25; Bernstein 1977
47. Powers 1980 suggests that the association generally made between menstruation and negative conditions such as defilement may be a result of *a priori* western notions held by the investigator. She argues that the Oglala, Plains Indians, have no such association. This does not mean that menstruation is *never* regarded negatively, of course (see Price 1984:21–22).
48. Buckley 1982:49
49. Harrison 1984:44
50. *Baltimore City Paper* 20 April 1984:39
51. Birke and Gardner 1982:25
52. Lever 1981:61
53. Lever 1981:63
54. Lauersen and Stukane 1983:18
55. Lever 1981:25
56. Lever 1981:28
57. Lever 1981:68
58. Angier 1983:119
59. Lauersen and Stukane 1983:80
60. Letter in *PMS Connection* 1982, 1:3. Reprinted by permission of PMS Action, Inc., Irvine, CA.
61. Weideger 1977:10
62. Harrison 1984:50
63. Frye 1983:91
64. Lever 1981:61
65. Harrison 1984:36
66. On isolation of housewives, see Gilman 1903:92.
67. Rich 1976:285
68. Shuttle and Redgrove 1978:58, 59
69. Griffin 1978:185
70. Gramsci 1971:333
71. Fanon 1963; Genovese 1976:647
72. Lorde 1981:9, 8
73. Dalton 1983:80; Harrison 1984:17; Halbreich and Endicott 1982:251, 255, 256
74. Dalton 1983:80
75. *PMS Connection* 1984, 3:4
76. Fox-Genovese 1984:272–73
77. Sanders 1981
78. Witt 1984:205, 208; Herrmann and Beach 1978
79. Thompson 1967
80. Rossi and Rossi 1974:32
81. Braverman 1974:32
82. Steinem 1981:338

References

Altmann, M. 1941 "A Psychosomatic Study of the Sex Cycle in Women." *Psychosomatic Medicine* 3:199–225.
Anderson, M. 1941 "Some Health Aspects of Putting Women to Work in War Industries." *Industrial Hygiene Foundation 7th Annual Meeting:* 165–69.
Ballantyne, Sheila 1975 *Norma Jean the Termite Queen.* New York: Penguin.
Benedek, Therese and Boris B. Rubenstein 1939 "The Correlations Between Ovarian Activity and Psychodynamic Processes. I. The Ovulative Phase; II. The Menstrual Phase." *Psychosomatic Medicine* 1(2):245–70; I(4):461–85.
Bernstein, Barbara Elaine 1977 "Effect of Menstruation on Academic Women." *Archives of Sexual Behavior* 6(4):289–96.
Billings, Edward G. 1933 "The Occurrence of Cyclic Variations in Motor Activity in Relation to the Menstrual Cycle in the Human Female." *Bulletin of Johns Hopkins Hospital* 54:440–54.
Birke, Lynda and Katy Gardner 1982 *Why Suffer? Periods and Their Problems.* London: Virago.
Brinton, Hugh P. 1943 "Women in Industry," pp. 395–419 in *Manual of Industrial Hygiene and Medical Service in War Industries,* National Institutes of Health, Division of Industrial Hygiene. Philadelphia: W. B. Saunders.
Brush, A. L. 1938 "Attitudes, Emotional and Physical Symptoms Commonly Associated with Menstruation in 100 Women." *American Journal of Orthopsychiatry* 8:286–301.
Buckley, Thomas 1982 "Menstruation and the Power of Yurok Women: Methods in Cultural Reconstruction." *American Ethnologist* 9(1):47–60.
Clarke, Edward H. 1873 *Sex in Education; or a Fair Chance for the Girls.* Boston: James R. Osgood and Co.
Cowan, Ruth Schwartz 1983 *More Work for Mother: The Ironies of Household Technologies from the Open Hearth to the Microwave.* New York: Basic Books.
Dalton, Katharina 1983 *Once a Month.* Claremont, CA: Hunter House.
Dalton, Katharina and Raymond Greene 1983 "The Premenstrual Syndrome." *British Medical Journal,* May:1016–17
de Beauvoir, Simone 1952 *The Second Sex.* New York: Knopf.
Ehrenreich, Barbara and Deirdre English 1973 *Complaints and Disorders: The Sexual Politics of Sickness.* Old Westbury, New York: The Feminist Press.
Fanon, Frantz 1963 *The Wretched of the Earth.* New York: Grove Press.
Fox-Genovese, Elizabeth 1982 "Gender, Class and Power: Some Theoretical Considerations." *The History Teacher* 15(2):255–76.
Frank, Robert T. 1931 "The Hormonal Causes of Premenstrual Tension." *Archives of Neurology and Psychiatry* 26:1053–57.
Frye, Marilyn 1983 *The Politics of Reality: Essays in Feminist Theory.* Trumansburg, NY: The Crossing Press.
Genovese, Eugene D. 1974 *Roll, Jordan, Roll: The World the Slaves Made.* New York: Vintage.
Gilman, Charlotte Perkins 1903 *The Home: Its Work and Influence.* Urbana: University of Illinois Press (1972 reprint).
Golub, Sharon 1976 "The Effect of Premenstrual Anxiety and Depression on Cognitive Function." *Journal of Personality and Social Psychology* 34(1):99–104.
Gottlieb, Alma 1982 "Sex, Fertility and Menstruation among the Beng of the Ivory Coast: A Symbolic Analysis." *Africa* 52(4):34–47.
Gramsci, Antonio 1971 *Prison Notebooks.* New York: International Publishers.
Griffin, Susan 1978 *Woman and Nature: The Roaring Inside Her.* New York: Harper and Row.
Halbreich, Uriel and Jean Endicott 1982 "Classification of Premenstrual Syndromes," pp. 243–65 in *Behavior and the Menstrual Cycle,* Richard C. Friedman, ed. New York: Marcel Dekker.
Harrison, Michelle 1984 *Self-Help for Premenstrual Syndrome.* Cambridge, MA: Matrix Press.
Herrmann, W. M. and R. C. Beach 1978 "Experimental and Clinical Data Indicating the Psychotropic Properties of Progestogens," *Postgraduate Medical Journal* 54:82–87.
Hollingworth, Leta 1914 *Functional Periodicity: An Experimental Study of the Mental and Motor Abilities of Women During Menstruation.* New York: Teacher's College.

Ivey, Melville E. and Judith M. Bardwick 1968 "Patterns of Affective Fluctuation in the Menstrual Cycle." *Psychosomatic Medicine* 30(3):336–45.

Jacobi, Mary Putnam 1877 *The Question of Rest for Women During Menstruation.* New York: Putnam's Sons.

Kessler-Harris, Alice 1982 *Out to Work: A History of Wage-Earning Women in the United States.* New York: Oxford University Press.

Lauersen, Niels H. and Eileen Stukane 1983 *PMS Premenstrual Syndrome and You: Next Month Can Be Different.* New York: Simon and Schuster.

Laws, Sophie 1983 "The Sexual Politics of Pre-Menstrual Tension." *Women's Studies International Forum* 6(1):19–31

Lever, Judy with Dr. Michael G. Brush 1981 *Pre-menstrual Tension.* New York: Bantam.

Lorde, Audre 1981 "The Uses of Anger." *Women's Studies Quarterly* 9(3):7–10.

———. 1982 *Chosen Poems: Old and New.* New York: W. W. Norton.

McCance, R. A., M. C. Luff, and E. E. Widdowson 1937 "Physical and Emotional Periodicity in Women." *Journal of Hygiene* 37:571–614.

Novak, Emil 1941 "Gynecologic Problems of Adolescence." *Journal of the American Medical Association* 117:1950–53.

Oakley, Ann 1974 *The Sociology of Housework.* New York: Pantheon.

Paige, Karen E. 1971 "Effects of Oral Contraceptives on Affective Fluctuations Associated with the Menstrual Cycle." *Psychosomatic Medicine* 33(6):515–37.

Parlee, Mary 1973 "The Premenstrual Syndrome." *Psychological Bulletin* 80(6):454–65.

Percival, Eleanor 1943 "Menstrual Disturbances as They May Affect Women in Industry." *The Canadian Nurse* 39:335–37.

Powers, Marla N. 1980 "Menstruation and Reproduction: An Oglala Case." *Signs* 6:54–65.

Price, Sally 1984 *Co-wives and Calabashes.* Ann Arbor: University of Michigan Press.

Rich, Adrienne 1976 *Of Woman Born.* New York: Bantam.

Robinson, Kathleen, Kathleen M. Huntington, and M. G. Wallace 1977 "Treatment of the Premenstrual Syndrome." *British Journal of Obstetrics and Gynaecology* 84:784–88.

Rossi, Alice S. and Peter E. Rossi 1977 "Body Time and Social Time: Mood Patterns by Menstrual Cycle Phase and Day of the Week." *Social Science Research* 6:273–308.

Sanders, Lawrence 1981 *The Third Deadly Sin.* New York: Berkley Books.

Scott, Joan Wallach 1980 "The Mechanization of Women's Work." *Scientific American,* March: 167–85.

Seward, G. H. 1934 "The Female Sex Rhythm." *Psychological Bulletin* 31:153–192.

Shuttle, Penelope and Peter Redgrove 1978 *The Wise Wound: Eve's Curse and Everywoman.* New York: Richard Marek.

Smith-Rosenberg, Carroll 1974 "Puberty to Menopause: The Cycle of Femininity in Nineteenth-century America," pp. 23–37 in *Clio's Consciousness Raised,* Mary Hartman and Lois W. Banner, eds. New York: Harper and Row.

Sommer, Barbara 1973 "The Effect of Menstruation on Cognitive and Perceptual-Motor Behavior: A Review." *Psychosomatic Medicine* 35(6):515–34.

Steinem, Gloria 1981 *Outrageous Acts and Everyday Rebellions.* New York: Holt, Rinehart and Winston.

Thompson, E. P. 1967 "Time, Work-Discipline, and Industrial Capitalism." *Past and Present,* 38:56–97.

Vanek, Joan 1974 "Time Spent in Housework." *Scientific American* 231(5):116–20.

Watkins, Linda M. 1986 "Premenstrual Distress Gains Notice as a Chronic Issue in the Workplace." *Wall Street Journal,* 22 Jan.

Weideger, Paula 1977 *Menstruation and Menopause: The Physiology and Psychology, the Myth and the Reality.* New York: Delta.

Weiner, Lynn Y. 1985 *From Working Girl to Working Mother: The Female Labor Force in the United States, 1820–1980.* Chapel Hill: University of North Carolina Press.

Witt, Reni L. 1984 *PMS: What Every Woman Should Know about Premenstrual Syndrome.* New York: Stein and Day.

ENGENDERING ENVIRONMENTAL THINKING
A Feminist Analysis of the Present Crisis

Ruth Perry

UNPAID REPRODUCTIVE LABOR

Once, at a time of great stress in my life, I bought a cottage on a salt marsh south of Boston. I found the tidal rhythms infinitely soothing, a reminder that life was not structured by semesters or fiscal years. Twice every day the tides flush the channels, making silvery little waterways in what otherwise looks like a meadow. Seabirds—especially seagulls but also egrets, heron, cormorants, and ducks—swim in it, rest on it, or circle around the marsh, fishing. When an especially high tide comes in, the channels fill to overflowing; twenty-five times or so in the course of the year, particularly in the winter when the tides are deepest, the marsh floods into a little lake.

Wetlands are the most productive ecosystems in the world. They produce more organic matter than tropical rain forests. They control flooding by storing tidal overflows, thus limiting erosion and buffering uplands from the effects of storms. They clean and filter water by trapping sediment in the tangle of marsh plants, and quite literally slow down the flow of water long enough to permit plant roots to absorb this sediment even when it is toxic. A study of a Pennsylvania marsh showed "significant reductions in BOD (biochemical oxygen demand), phosphorous, and nitrogen within three to five hours in samples taken from heavily polluted waters flowing through a 512-acre marsh."[1] Ironically, given the destruction of so much natural marshland, experiments are now being conducted using man-made wetlands as tertiary treatment facilities for domestic and industrial waste. Many wetland plant species are peculiarly adapted to fix nitrogen, and marsh plants figure centrally in the recycling of carbon and methane as well. The constant tidal influx keeps these lands abundantly supplied with plankton and algae and other nutrients so that they are invaluable as spawning and breeding grounds. Thus, although wetlands comprise only 5% of the landscape, they contribute disproportionately to the sustenance of the environment—and hence to the perpetuation of the natural world and the health of its citizens.

By the mid 1980s, 58% of the wetlands in the United States had been filled in for real estate developments, agriculture, highways, used as landfills or garbage pits, or polluted by drilling for fossil fuels. Most of this appropriation of wetlands occurred between 1950 and 1980.

The work that wetlands do to maintain the environmental balance—to sweeten the water and the air, to provide suitable breeding grounds for a great variety of plant and animal species, to fix nitrogen and recycle carbon, to absorb toxicity and purify the land—this work, the work of reproducing the world, is not valued, not even noticed, and certainly not counted in any measure of national wealth. There is no way to add in the work that wetlands do given the way we now calculate the GNP (Gross National Product), a figure based on the aggregate cash transactions of the nation—but not on the health of its natural resources or even its people. Given this definition of wealth, any financial profit, however insignificant, is thought more valuable when weighed in the balance than these irreplaceable amphibious centers of life; they are traded away casually for the kind of profit that *can* be counted in the GNP. On August 9, 1991, in order to stimulate the flagging money-based economy, the United States government redrafted the official definition of a wetland so as to remove millions of acres of wetlands from federal protection, and permit their sale to businessmen in the private sector with interests in real estate, transportation, oil, timber, and finance. Short-term gains for individuals—so long as they are the kind of profits that show up on the balance sheets of the present accounting system—matter more than infinitely renewable gains in the quality of air and water and regional biodiversity. The value that wetlands create accrues to everyone and therefore is not to the advantage of anyone in particular. The service of cleaning and renewing common resources can be sold for the temporary profit of a handful of businessmen.

The analogy to housekeeping is obvious: in the culture of commodity capitalism, no one values the labor of maintenance, of subsistence, the labor that makes possible domestic life as opposed to the labor that produces commodities or commodified services. In our society the labor of maintenance—reproductive labor in the largest sense of the phrase—is unappreciated because unremunerated. What is not paid for is not valued in our culture; and the reproductive labor of women, whether as unpaid housewives or "unskilled" cleaning women or babysitters, is notoriously undervalued by our society. By reproductive labor I mean such activities as raising children, preparing food, tending the old and sick, cleaning and mending, what Adrienne Rich calls "the activity of world-protection, world preservation, world-repair—the million tiny stitches, the friction of the scrubbing brush, the scouring cloth, the iron across the shirt, the rubbing of cloth against itself to exorcise the stain, the renewal of the scorched pot, the rusted knife-blade, the invisible weaving of a frayed and threadbare family life, the cleaning up of the soil and waste left behind by men and children. . . ."[2]

Such labors that reproduce the conditions for life have always been understood and valued in subsistence cultures. They were probably not even conceived of as separable from labor that produced goods until industrialization, with the shift to a cash economy, commodification of labor, and production for a market. Prior to this, class determined who would perform these maintenance functions; perhaps power is always evidenced by who, symbolically speaking, cleans up and takes out the garbage. But the commodification of labor and alienation from subsistence that industrialization brought with it restructured the economies of everyday life in ways that were distinctly gendered as well as class based. Increasingly, tasks associated with reproduction of the conditions for life were understood to be women's work, the responsibility of women of all classes, while the work of production was man's work, performed and remunerated in the formal economy whose meaning came precisely from its being disconnected from private domestic life.

This sexual division of labor in the public and private spheres evolved first in eighteenth-century English society as a cultural marker of the middle class. While middle-class men pursued profit in the marketplace, their women were creating new spaces for living insulated from the pressures of that world, as geographically separate from the public world of finance and government as the suburbs, where a man kept his wife and family, were distant from the city where he did his business. Henry Thrale, the brewer, was thought odd because he settled his wife and children in a house next door to his brewery in the heart of industrial London rather than outside of the city, as was becoming more usual for eighteenth-century industrialists.[3] This physical separation of functions simultaneously granted the importance of women's reproductive labor in the private sphere while setting the terms for its devaluation. These newly feminized functions—tending and educating children, arranging basic subsistence for one's family in the form of clean and mended clothes, warm and comfortable shelter, nourishing cooked food, and most importantly unconditional emotional support to offset the calculations of the market—these were distinguished from the money-making business of life in spaces increasingly thought of as women's domain. Middle-class women performed these unremunerated tasks and superintended female servants who earned scarcely more than their board, as proof of their difference, their "softer" instincts, and their unsuitability for public affairs or high wages.

While these cultural redefinitions were transforming English urban society—the rise of the middle class, the development of the suburbs, the evolution of new arenas of domestic life presided over by women—rural life was also being transformed forever by the commercialization of agriculture. During the second half of the eighteenth century, lands that from time immemorial had belonged to no one in particular were seized as private property in an unprecedented sequence of Parliamentary Enclosure Acts proposed and partially financed by large landowners and representatives of the Church of England. Although there had been enclosure of common lands in England since the sixteenth century, this appropriation was on an entirely new scale. In the first sixty years of the eighteenth century, from the reign of Queen Anne through that of George II, 244 such Acts were passed, amounting to the removal of 337,876 acres from public holdings. But under George III, 3,554 Acts were passed and 5,686,400 acres were "improved"—fenced, removed from common usage, and put into production.[4] In the last half of the eighteenth century, one-quarter of England's arable land was taken out of common usage and assigned to individual property owners. This privatization of what had hitherto been common land, available to all for fodder, fuel, herbs, berries, barks, and kitchen gardens, was justified as being a more efficient use of land, a more complete exploitation of the country's natural resources, contributing to the general prosperity measured as productions for domestic and foreign markets. Landowners with capital could invest in the latest technologies (irrigation ditches, breeding stock, fertilizers) and apply these new techniques of agriculture to reclaiming "waste" lands, as they were called, for large-scale production. Thus, in the same period as the distinction deepened between unremunerated reproductive labor increasingly done by women and productive labor for wages increasingly done by men, common lands that had provided subsistences and recreation to communities for centuries were being fenced by individuals for private gain. Both women's reproductive labor and the free resources of nature were being appropriated to stoke the market economy—a pattern repeated, as we shall see, in twentieth-century examples of capital-driven development.

The immediate result of transferring these fallow lands from those to whom they had use value to those with the capital and technology to extract maximum exchange value from them, was increased production by private owners on an unprecedented scale. Manufacture as well as agriculture thrived in England as never before during this period. The newly mechanized textile industry produced Lancashire cottons and Yorkshire woolens in astonishing profusion, as Adam Smith, Patrick Colquhoun, and other economic commentators never tired of pointing out. Grain poured in from Warwickshire, Leicestershire, the Midlands, Oxfordshire, Gloucestershire, and Worcestershire—the soil made more profitable by irrigation, rotating crops, and new fertilizers. The mania for production spread to breeding livestock, and sheep and cows too began to be grown on a grander and grander scale.[5]

It has been estimated that the rents landlords extracted from their land doubled in those parts of England enclosed in this period (the Midlands, Northamptonshire, Warwickshire, Leicestershire, Lincolnshire, East Riding). Arable land went from renting at 14 shillings an acre to 28 shillings an acre and grasslands for pasture from 40 shillings to 3 pounds an acre. Even counting in the cost of fencing and the legal fees for the paperwork, large-scale agriculture was one of the best investments of the age.[6]

But there were social costs to this increased productivity. Food prices began their long upward climb, encouraged by the growth of the market and encouraging in turn the enclosure of more land for profit. Thousands of cottagers squatting on common lands were displaced and their centuries-old reciprocal, ecological relationships to forests, fens, and swamps were abruptly terminated. Successive waves of historians have argued that enclosure and industrialization ultimately raised the standard of living for all Englishmen and produced whole new categories of jobs for those displaced from their land. Progress entails disruption, so the argument goes, but in the long run, the whole nation benefits. Others argue that only a fraction profited from the enclosures: only those with education, capital or connections benefited from this re-allocation of land. Although enormous gains in productivity are undeniable, there was tremendous turnover in the landholders of enclosed areas during this period—as much as 60% in some places—and at least one third of the existing farms disappeared in the process.[7]

Recently it has also been argued that if the enclosures of the late-eighteenth century affected the entire cottager class in England, pauperizing many by reducing their access to subsistence and forcing them off the land altogether, women may have suffered especially from this movement from subsistence to waged labor. For one thing, women are always paid less than men when they enter the labor market, even when they put in the same hours doing the same work. But more importantly, the enclosures made serious inroads on women's ability to contribute to the subsistence of their households. Women had generally seen to the chores involved in keeping chickens or a cow, in maintaining kitchen gardens, or in gathering wild herbs in season, as extensions of their other forms of reproductive labor such as caring for children, cooking, preparing medicines, and the like. These labors which, because they depended on the natural world, included habits that reproduced the resource base, were made more difficult or even altogether impossible by the enclosures. Women, in particular, were thus impoverished and made vulnerable by the enclosure of common lands, because their tasks in a subsistence household economy were worth more to their families than their labor in a waged economy.[8] Without access to the commons, a woman could not earn a little extra with her butter and eggs at the local Saturday market; and without access to domestic animals and a kitchen garden, the lives of her family were impoverished of contact with the natural world. Thus, these two factors combined in eighteenth-century England to impoverish women in particular and to interrupt traditional ecological habits of life: 1) the gendering and devaluing of reproductive labor in a market economy and 2) the enclosure of common land.

As I have said, the work that wetlands do is central to reproducing the conditions for life, but we have no mechanism in our post-industrial world for assessing its value or for recognizing its contribution to our collective well-being. True cost benefit analysis of the natural resource base has made as much headway as the "wages for housework" campaign of the late 1970s—which is to say almost none. This is true despite the paradoxical fact that all people, men and women alike, have to live on the earth and share its resources.

In our own time, as in the eighteenth century, there is a dramatic correlation between increased production of commodities and the privatization of public resources. Barry Commoner noted in 1971 in *The Closing Circle: Nature, Man & Technology,* that the economy of the previous thirty years literally fed off the environment. The relationship between high profits and damage to the environment was not accidental, he argued. In the post-World War II era, what extended margins of profit were techniques of manufacture and delivery that made use of the free natural resource base. In his analysis, the most profitable new enterprises were based on innovative technologies that replaced older, less polluting manufacturing processes. He instanced the production and use of detergents rather than soap, transportation by truck instead of by train, and the manufacture of synthetic materials rather than the growth and extraction of natural plant fibers as examples of new industries whose profit margins were assured only by positing an infinite world in which to freely dispose of polluting by-products. In other words, manufacturers exercised their citizenly rights to use their country's natural resources at a rate that far exceeded what they were entitled to as individuals. The excess, which constituted their profit, could be said to be subsidized by the publicly owned resource base. After demonstrating that farmers' profits were directly correlated to their use of high nitrogen fertilizers, Commoner concluded that there is "evidence that a high rate of profit is associated with practices that are particularly stressful toward the environment and that when these practices are restricted, profits decline."[9] Use, not ecological maintenance, he tells us, is rewarded by our present economic system.

NO MAN'S LAND

The degradation of the environment in the United States, the pollution of our air and water, is the twentieth-century equivalent of the enclosure of the commons. Just as in the eighteenth century enclosing landlords appropriated for private profit what had hitherto belonged in common to those living in a given locale, the use of public-access land, water, and air for industrial processes uses up what belongs to all for the profit of few. Moreover, as in the eighteenth century, the loss of the commons has been accompanied by a distinctive feminization of poverty, a phenomenon at least in part owing to the same configuration of cultural forces that contributed to the feminization of poverty in eighteenth-century England: undervaluing women's labor in the public sector and assuming their unpaid reproductive labor in the private sphere. The degradation of natural resource bases from which women are expected to reproduce the conditions for life—clean water and air for washing and drying clothes and household articles, safe land for children to roam in, and wild plants and a patch of garden to supplement their family's diet—is seen as lamentable but unavoidable. So long as no one's livelihood is threatened—defined as profit in the commercial sector—environmental degradation is seen as a necessary evil, trivial to the extent that its immediate visible impact is on women and children.

Perhaps for this reason, because environmental degradation impinges most directly on women's work of subsistence and maintenance—given our current sexual division of labor—or because the health and safety of families is still seen to be women's responsibility, women have responded most actively to the present ecological crisis. Grassroots activists at the local level, internationally, tend to be women. (Inevitably, as these movements become bureaucratized, men often move into leadership positions.) At every stage, from discovering the problem—whether dangerous industrial by-products, contaminated ground water, hazardous waste dumps, or inadequate sewage treatment—to organizing the community and lobbying the powers that be to clean it up, it is women who act for the safety of their neighborhoods. At home for longer stretches of the day, doing domestic chores and caring for children, comparing stories with neighbors, women often are the first to notice mysterious chemical barrels in vacant lots, odd smells or stinging eyes, or the sudden coincidence of too many deformed births in an area.

This past June, in Las Playas de Tijuana, a Mexican border town, a group of women calling themselves The Association of Las Playas Housewives managed to stop the opening of Mexico's first chemical incinerator. Despite the assurances of Chemical Waste Management of Mexico, Inc. to the contrary, these women were convinced that the fumes from incinerated toxic waste would be a health hazard to everyone in the vicinity who had to breathe the air. Chemical Waste Management, a Chicago-based company, built the facility to dispose of some of the toxic waste building up from foreign manufacturers along the 2,000 mile United States-Mexico border. The Las Playas

Housewives, who pressured the government to revoke the plant's license after investigating the health and safety record of similar toxic incineration facilities, are now afraid that a North American Free Trade Agreement will reverse their temporary victory and authorize the relicensing of the plant. Ultimately, they fear that plants like this, on the Mexican side of the border, will be used to process chemical waste from United States manufacturing operations.[10]

The Las Playas Housewives, operating outside formal institutional channels, are only one example among thousands of women around the world mobilizing against local environmental disasters. Possibly as an extension of their responsibility for children, possibly because they are underpaid and undervalued by the commercial sector and hence not invested in protecting local industries or defending business interests, women are often the ones who begin the unremunerated, supererogatory labor of organizing to protect their environments. I am not claiming that it is in women's nature to protect the earth, nor even that women are particularly suited to take care of others. I am simply observing that the majority of unpaid environmental activists around the world *are* women. . . .

I have argued that the labor of reproducing the conditions for life, scorned in the past as "women's work," is crucial to the survival of the earth. I have sketched a situation in which nature's mechanisms of sustainability are not being preserved and in which business profits are tied to extraordinary consumption of natural resources. We need to reeducate our society's estimation of reproductive labor, and what is implicated in that estimation, the status of women. Some feminist theorists have framed this issue as a problem in the definition of national wealth and national security. The GNP, after all, is comprised of all the goods and services produced in the money economy but not the labor that reproduces the conditions for life.[11] The GNP does not measure economies of subsistence and needs satisfaction—such as gardening, fishing, barter, cleaning, raising children—even though these activities often underwrite and make possible the production of commodities for profit.

As the production of commodities and commodified services rises in so-called developing countries, calculated by such measures as a rising GNP, women in these countries are increasingly impoverished, as measured by health, nutrition, life span, and access to cash. Development always seems to entail lengthening the working day of women, as if the costs of industrialization are borne especially by women. One explanation for this is that capitalism erodes the material base of women's subsistence production by commodifying more and more of that material base. Bina Agarwal describes this alienation of natural resources in India from women who rely on them for their livelihood. "Because women are the main gatherers of fuel, fodder, and water," she says, "it is primarily their working day (already averaging ten to twelve hours) that is lengthened with the depletion of and reduced access to forests, waters, soils." She reports that the hardship caused by scarcity of these natural resources in Uttar Pradesh has caused a rise in young women's suicide rates in recent years.[12] Vandana Shiva's example of the women of Garhwal also shows the way women bear the ecological costs of modernization in unremunerated labor in the private sphere. Because industrial needs for wood in that region exceed the regenerative power of the forest ecosystem, women who could once gather all the fuel and fodder they needed in a few hours must now travel by truck up to two days to collect what they need.[13] The unanimous consensus about the decade 1975–1985, named, ironically, the United Nations decade for women, is that "with a few exceptions, women's relative access to economic resources, incomes and employment has worsened, their burden of work has increased, and their relative and even absolute health, nutritional and educational status has declined."[14] Overvaluing the production of commodities while undervaluing the functions that reproduce life leads inescapably to the impoverishment of women.

It has been suggested that one corrective would be to compute the GNP differently and to make the unit of measurement the household and not the enterprise.[15] This would have the salutary effect of putting women back into the equation. Arguably, a nation's wealth is comprised of the net worth of each collective household; that might be a better measure of the well-being of its citizens than its profit-making businesses. As if to illustrate the principle that women's access to public resources is through their households rather than through new business enterprises, a group of women in a village in India recently opposed a scheme to cut down a tract of oak forest in order to establish a potato-seed farm. They argued that the project would take away their only local source of fuel and fodder, thus adding five kilometers to their daily collection journey, and that the cash that would accrue to their men from the project would not necessarily benefit themselves or their children.[16]

Nor do these forces operate only in the countries of the southern hemisphere. In the United States the devaluation of the labor of social reproduction—in this case raising children—together with disproportionate power given to those interested solely in profitable enterprise (rather than in citizens' health and safety) has created a particularly ugly situation in the controversy over lead paint. Although the harmful effects of even low doses of lead paint to children are so well documented that its use was outlawed in most West European countries and Australia in the early twentieth century, it was legal in the United States until 1978, when it was banned from use in homes, on furniture, and on toys. Today, lead paint is still legally manufactured and sold in the United States for painting outdoor structures such as bridges and water towers. But the primary health hazard posed by lead paint is what remains on the walls and woodwork of most older housing in the northeastern United States insofar as lead is released into the air every time anyone opens a window or door, or brushes against a painted surface. Lead dust taken in through the nose or mouth ends up inert in the bones of most people over seven, but in children under that age it circulates in the blood until it lodges in the soft tissue of the brain where it is highly neurotoxic. It is estimated that 10–12% of the children under six in the United States "lead belt" have neurotoxic levels of lead in their blood sufficient to cause reduced I.Q., attention deficit disorder, hyperactivity, learning disability and impaired growth.[17] Notwithstanding the thorough understanding of the neurotoxicity of lead to growing children, public health departments do not, as a rule, subsidize lead paint removal. Moreover, mothers rather than landlords continue to be blamed for the damage it does to their children's health.

[It has been] suggested that what keeps this problem intractable is that male policymakers simply do not take seriously their responsibility for the safety of homes, which are considered women's domain. It is a notorious fact that the most polluted air in the United States is indoor air, the air of the home, the air in women's space, saturated with the gasses emitted from plastics and cleaning products. As far-fetched as it sounds, the sexual division of labor in our culture that makes women responsible for the health and safety of their families apparently disconnects men from responsibility for these issues. . . .

SUSTAINING KNOWLEDGE

Feminists have also observed that women's special knowledge about the environment is often ignored or passed over as old wives' tales or superstition. As the primary agricultural workers in many societies, not to mention the gatherers of fuel and water, women's traditional knowledge about sustainable resource use, accrued slowly over generations, is often overlooked by those who make policy about economic development projects. Just as the labor that women do is not valued—women's unpaid labor of love, to use Hilary Rose's phrase—so women's non-commodified knowledge about the reproductive processes of the natural world is insufficiently valued. Bina Agarwal notes that poor rural women in India have "an elaborate knowledge of the nutritional and medicinal properties of plants, roots, and trees," which can be called upon during drought or famine conditions. She also notes that hill women usually manage seed selection for their communities, having learned more about nature and agriculture "in the process of their everyday contact with and dependence on nature's resources," a function of the gendered division of labor in that society.[18] This knowledge about environmental processes must also exist among poor rural women in our own country who similarly depend on a reciprocal relationship with their local natural environment and thus have a stake in maintaining it. Yet I cannot imagine the EPA seriously entertaining a proposal to collect, codify, and put to use this lore.

Although we need to develop cleaner industrial processes, and to test the effects of chemical by-products on living organisms, much environmental thinking is not a matter of technical training so much as a matter of common sense. At a recent conference on women and the environment, two intelligent women without technical training told their stories about how they fought to end the dumping of hazardous substances in their home towns. Each demonstrated how quickly they could learn everything technical that they needed to know about the particular toxins being produced and buried in their neighborhoods, despite the deliberate mystification of some public health officials concerned to keep the public ignorant and to protect commercial interests. One described how she had slowly and painstakingly, over years, collected stories of cancer cases in her neighborhood, putting pins on a map every time she heard of a new case. She told us that these instances of cancer had clustered just where the water flowed and where the wind tended to blow. There was a simple elegance to her description that was like the best scientific observation. Such direct information about natural processes is too often passed over in preference for technically sophisticated but locally uninformed conjectures about the environmental effects of industrial processes.

Let me note in passing, too, the ecofeminist contribution to a gendered analysis of environmental issues. Both in foregrounding the metaphorical connections between the body of the earth and the bodies of women and in explaining how social justice and environmental justice are inextricably linked, ecofeminists insist on the continuities between how we treat the natural world and how we treat each other. According to an ecofeminist analysis, pollution reveals social dominance whereas sustainable production, that is, the reproduction of subsistence, is the visible sign of well-balanced interactions between humans and the natural world. Ecofeminists reject the view that the planet's processes can be understood merely mechanistically, its bio-masses reduced to "natural resources" available for exploitation by humans. Instead, they see the whole as a set of interlinked processes involving earth, air, water, and organic life. "Life on earth is an interconnected web, not a hierarchy," as Ynestra King puts it. "Human hierarchy is projected onto nature and then used to justify social domination. Therefore, ecofeminist theory seeks to show the connections between all forms of domination, including the domination of nonhuman nature, and ecofeminist practice is necessarily antihierarchical."[19]

Ecofeminists sometimes argue that women themselves have been thought of as if they were "natural resources," and thus "know" what it feels like to be viewed that way. As evidence for this way of thinking, one might begin by observing that everyone's first environment is a woman. Gerda Lerner's claim that the earliest form of slavery was the reification and appropriation by men of women's reproductive capacity is an historical argument based upon this difference.[20] Sherry Ortner's important essay "Is Female to Male as Nature is to Culture?" was an early meditation on the social meanings of this cultural analogue between attitudes towards nature and attitudes towards women.[21] Thus men's disrespectful attitudes towards women and nature could be said to reflect and reinforce one another.

In closing, let me observe that in our own day the most intractable opposition to environmental legislation comes from multinational corporations, the latest avatar of the absentee landlord enclosing publicly held resources for private profit. These multinational corporations represent a further attenuation in the journey away from subsistence, the ultimate triumph of productive values over reproductive values. Accountable neither to families, neighborhoods, municipalities, or even nations, stripped of any organic relation to place, these multinationals pose the greatest threat of all to our environment. Increasingly empowered to invalidate the environmental agendas set by our own elected legislative bodies, they represent the disembodied privilege of profit. For example, although DDT has been banned for more than twenty years in the United States following the publication of Rachel Carson's *The Silent Spring,* the General Agreement on Trade and Tariffs (GATT) could force United States citizens to import DDT-laden produce again on the grounds that our pesticide laws are a barrier to trade.[22] A law passed in Nassau County, Long Island, requiring that newspapers published there be printed on 50% recycled paper, was challenged by Canada as a "barrier to trade," spurred on by the Canadian Pulp and Paper Workers Union. Our ban on importing asbestos was recently challenged by the terms of the United States-Canada trade agreement. Although upheld in the end, our law was pronounced extreme and it was recommended that a less "trade distorting" alternative would be to require people working with asbestos to wear gloves and goggles. In the summer of 1992, George Bush refused to sign the biodiversity treaty in Rio on the grounds that it posed a danger to biotechnology industries.

Empirically and theoretically, the greatest threat to our world lies in permitting the transfer of political authority from citizen's groups to multinational corporations. Such a move will completely disempower those whose labor reproduces our social world, and definitively locate it with those who produce commodities and commodified services. The implications for women's status, women's knowledge, and the reproductive labor of subsistence and maintenance within such a system are appalling. As political authority for environmental decisions is transferred from elected officials responsive to people to appointed boards adjudicating conflicts between multinational corporations, we will witness the final disappearance of the concept of the commons and a publicly owned resource base.

Entities larger than nations, regional blocs like the EEC, are likely to be the powers negotiating future world trade agreements. How will citizens' groups be able to influence the priorities of these regional blocs? Who will speak up for the rights of neighborhoods, communities, families, individuals? How can we retain control of the environments in which we live in the face of such international pressures? We need to reestablish the fundamental claims of ordinary people to clean air, water, and safe soil as part of a basic economic bill of rights. We need to affirm the importance of small-scale invisible economies that create subsistence even when they are weighed against corporate profits. The quality of our lives and the health of our world depends on our ability to reauthorize a society that gives full value to the labor of reproducing the conditions for life.

Notes

I wish to thank all those who participated in the "En/Gendering Environmental Thinking" conference at MIT in May, 1992, without whom this paper would never have been written.

1. Jon A. Kusler, *Our National Wetland Heritage* (An Environmental Law Institute Publication), 1.
2. Adrienne Rich, "Conditions for Work: The Common World of Women," Foreward to *Working it Out,* eds. Sara Ruddick and Pamela Daniels (New York: Pantheon, 1977), xvi.

3. Mary Nash, Hester Thrale's biographer, conjectures that urban pollution may have accounted for Hester Thrale's many miscarriages. For information on the suburban estates of eighteenth-century men of fortune, see Catherine Hall and Lenore Davidoff, *Family Fortunes: Men and Women of the English Middle Class 1780–1850* (Chicago: University of Chicago Press, 1987), especially chapter 8.
4. W. Hasbach, *A History of the English Agricultural Labourer,* trans. Ruth Kenyon (London: P.S. King & Son, 1908), 57–8.
5. Harriet Ritvo, "Possessing Mother Nature: Genetic Capital in Eighteenth-Century Britain" in *Early Modern Conceptions of Property,* ed. John Brewer and Susan Staves (New York: Routledge, forthcoming).
6. Michael Turner, *Enclosures in Britain 1750–1830* (London: Macmillan, 1984), 39, 41.
7. Turner, *Enclosures,* 72–75.
8. Bridget Hill, *Women, Work, and Sexual Politics in Eighteenth-Century England* (Oxford: Basil Blackwell, 1989), especially chapter 3. After the first family wage law in 1795, the infamous Speenhamland Act, women's wages in England were sometimes fixed below subsistence which made them unable any longer even to earn enough to support themselves independently.
9. Barry Commoner, *The Closing Circle: Nature, Man & Technology* (New York: Knopf, 1971), 262.
10. "Women Blocked Incinerator," *The Boston Globe,* June 15, 1992, 33.
11. Marilyn Waring, *If Women Counted: A New Feminist Economics* (New York: HarperCollins, 1988).
12. Bina Agarwal, "The Gender and Environment Lessons from India," *Feminist Studies* 18 (Spring 1992): 138.
13. Vandana Shiva, *Staying Alive: Women, Ecology, and Development* (London: Zed Books, 1989), 8.
14. DAWN, *Development Crisis and Alternative Visions: Third World Women's Perspectives,* (Bergen: Christian Michelsen Institute, 1985), 21, quoted in Vandana Shiva, *Staying Alive, 3.*
15. At the feminist environmental conference held at MIT in May, 1992, both Joni Seager and Gita Sen suggested that computing a nation's wealth by households rather than by businesses would reorient the national accounting system to include women's work.
16. Bina Agarwal, "The Gender and Environment Debate: Lessons from India," 147. In *If Women Counted* Marilyn Waring asks: "Why do nutritional deficiencies result, when family food availability declines as subsistence (nonmonetary) farmland is taken for cash crops and men get paid an income?" (19)
17. Alliance to End Childhood Lead Poisoning, 1992, quoted in newsletter of the Citizen's Clearinghouse for Hazardous Waste, *Everybody's Backyard,* June 1992.
18. Bina Agarwal, "The Gender and Environment Debate: Lessons from India," 142. Parallel arguments about women's knowledge of sustainable processes elsewhere in the world can be found in Jodi L. Jacobson's 1992 Worldwatch Paper 110, "Gender Bias: Roadblock to Sustainable Development."
19. Ynestra King, "The Ecology of Feminism and the Feminism of Ecology" in *Healing the Wounds: the Promise of Ecofeminism,* ed. Judith Plant (Philadelphia and Santa Cruz: New Society Publishers, 1989), 19.
20. Gerda Lerner, *The Creation of Patriarchy* (New York: Oxford University Press, 1986), especially chapter 2.
21. Sherry B. Ortner, "Is Female to Male as Nature Is to Culture?" in *Women, Culture and Society,* eds. Michelle Zimbalist Rosaldo and Louise Lamphere (Stanford: Stanford University Press, 1974), 67–89.
22. Kristin Dawkins, Institute for Agriculture and Trade Policy, February 1993.

BETWEEN FATHERS AND FETUSES
The Social Construction of Male Reproduction and the Politics of Fetal Harm

Cynthia R. Daniels

In contemporary American political discourse, "crack babies" have been treated as *filius nullius*—as if they had no biological fathers. With no link between fathers and fetuses, no inheritance of harm could be attributed to the father's use of drugs. The absence of fathers in debates over drug addiction and fetal harm has had profound consequences for women, for it has dictated that women alone bear the burden and blame for the production of "crack babies."

Since at least the late 1980s, and in some cases far earlier, studies have shown a clear link between paternal exposures to drugs, alcohol, smoking, environmental and occupational toxins, and fetal health problems. Yet men have been spared the retribution aimed at women. In fact, while women are targeted as the primary source of fetal health problems, reports of male reproductive harm often place sperm at the center of discourse as the "littlest ones" victimized by reproductive toxins, somehow without involving their male makers as responsible agents.

Scientific research linking reproductive toxins to fetal health problems reflects deeply embedded assumptions about men's and women's relation to reproductive biology. Critical analysis of the nature of fetal risks thus requires not only that the biology of risk be examined but that the "collective consciousness" that shapes scientific inquiry on gender difference be assessed. As Evelyn Fox Keller states, this consciousness is constituted by "a set of beliefs given existence by language rather than by bodies" (1992, 25). Debates over fetal risk are not so much about the prevention of fetal harm as they are about the *social production of truth* about the nature of men's and women's relation to reproduction.

Challenging the science and politics of fetal harm requires deconstructing the three symbols that constitute debate over fetal health risks: the "crack baby," "pregnant addict," and "absent father." These symbols "frame" political debate about addiction and fetal health, providing the lens through which science is developed and policy is made. As Kathy Ferguson has said of this process of framing, "The questions we can ask about the world are enabled, and other questions disabled, by the frame that orders the questioning. When we are busy arguing about the questions that appear within a certain frame, the frame itself becomes invisible; we become *enframed* within it" (Ferguson 1993, 7; emphasis in original; also see Fraser 1989).

In debates over fetal harm, this process of framing takes place in many social locations: in science labs, where the priorities of research are defined; in editorial rooms, where reporters decide which news warrants coverage and what slant to take on stories; and in courts and legislatures, where decisions are made regarding the definition of and culpability for social problems. As Paula Treichler has argued, contests over meaning—over the terms of political debate—have significance not just because they help to determine the distribution of material resources but because they legitimate the disproportionate power of actors to define (or contest) social reality (1990, 123).

My purpose in this article, therefore, is not simply to question the causality of fetal harm but to make visible the frame that has constructed understandings of causality.

Science informed by gender myth is not just empirically suspect, but is politically loaded. That is, it helps to produce public health policies that target women and absolve men from culpability for fetal harm. This process is deeply racialized as well as gendered. As Mary Poovey has argued, ideological formulations of gender are "uneven" in the sense that they hold different implications for those positioned differently within the social formation (1988, 3). In similar context, the science and politics of fetal risks have held far different consequences for Anglo-American than for African-American women in the United States. So too, as fathers are drawn into the circle of fetal causality, it may well be low-income African-American men who become the target of social and political retribution.[1]

In this article, I examine the cultural characterizations of sperm and male reproduction in science, news stories, and public policy that have shielded men from culpability for fetal health problems.[2] After a brief discussion of the social construction of maternity and paternity, I analyze the symbols of the "crack baby," "pregnant addict," and "absent father" as central to public discourse on fetal harm. Finally, I explore the range of complex questions about biological gender difference generated by the politics of fetal risks and the problematic nature of the idea of individual causality in discussions of fetal harm.

Questions about the nature of fetal hazards enrich and complicate discussions of gender difference and biological reproduction. To what extent is it possible or desirable to collapse all gender distinctions in procreation as socially and historically constructed? How are the critical links between fathers and fetuses to be recognized without undermining women's exclusive claims to their bodies? While the father-fetal connection is essential to discussions of fetal risk, it may complicate women's claim to reproductive choice in other contexts.

SOCIAL CONSTRUCTIONS OF MATERNITY AND PATERNITY

. . . On one level, it is not surprising that scientists exploring the sources of fetal health problems would look first to women. The maternal-fetal relationship seems certain, clear, and direct. It is publicly visible, and it appears to be exclusive. Unlike paternity, maternity is unquestionable. By contrast, the link between fathers and fetuses is both less certain and less visible. Questions of causality for men appear more complicated because the link between fathers and fetuses must always pass through the female body.

Yet the connection between fathers and fetuses is obscured less by biology than by the social construction of procreation. Despite appearances, questions of causality are as complex for women as they are for men. The maternal-fetal body is socially and biologically permeable. Maternal and fetal health are deeply affected by a woman's access to social resources such as health care and food, by her exposure to environmental toxins, and by her relationships with her sexual partner, her family, and her community. While men's physical distance from gestation creates the illusion that men's relation to fetal health is tangential, in reality, a man's use of drugs or alcohol or his exposures to toxins long before conception can profoundly affect the health of the children he fathers. . . .

Debates over fetal harm have been constituted by the analytically distinct and antithetical categories of male virility and vulnerability. Men were assumed either to be invulnerable to harm from the toxicity of drugs, alcohol, and environmental and occupational hazards or to be rendered completely infertile by any vulnerability to risk. In particular, sperm that crossed the line from virile to vulnerable by being damaged by reproductive toxins were assumed to be incapable of fertilization. And the converse operated as well: men not rendered infertile by their toxic exposures were assumed to be immune from any other form of reproductive risk (such as genetic damage).

Social constructions of maternity, by contrast, have been firmly aligned with assumptions of women's vulnerability. The science of reproductive risks historically developed in response to women's occupational exposures, where it was assumed that the physical stress and toxic exposures of the workplace would result in the degeneration of women's reproductive systems. Protective labor law selectively exaggerated the vulnerabilities of white women to occupational hazards and virtually ignored risks to working women of color.[3] Until well into the twentieth century, science, policy, and law deeply reflected the association of maternity with vulnerability.

Feminists have successfully challenged this association in the fields of occupational and environmental health. Yet since the 1980s, assumptions of maternal vulnerability have been reconstructed around risks to the fetus mediated through the maternal body. The idea of women's "hypersusceptibility" to risk thus shifted from assumptions of women as victims to women as vectors of fetal risk (Kenney 1992; Blank 1993; Daniels 1993).

Accompanying this shift from maternal to fetal vulnerability has been the development of the metaphor of the "pregnant addict" as "antimother" in public discourse. The image of the pregnant addict has become a racialized and gendered "condensation symbol"—one that evokes a whole range of unspoken associations about women, motherhood, race, and sexuality.[4] As Wahneema Lubiano argues, "Categories like 'black woman,' 'black women,' or particular subsets of those categories, like 'welfare mother/queen,' are not simply social taxonomies, they are also recognized by the national public as stories that describe the world in particular and politically loaded ways—and that is exactly why they are constructed, reconstructed, manipulated, and contested. . . . They provide simple, uncomplicated, and often wildly (and politically damaging) inaccurate information about what is 'wrong' with some people" (1992, 330–31). Condensation symbols operate as a kind of public shorthand, suggesting related narratives that remain latent—reminders of associations that work best when not fully or explicitly articulated.

The category of the "pregnant addict" is thus saturated with social meaning. Drug-addicted women have become magnets for social anxieties produced by a whole range of social and political transformations. For those distressed by women's drift from "selfless motherhood," pregnant addicts represent women's refusal to postpone their momentary "pleasure" (addiction) for the interests of the fetus. For those concerned with racial order and welfare dependency, pregnant addicts represent female desire and reproduction out of control, with women of color producing "damaged" babies at the state's expense.[5] Contests over meaning—over the very existence, for instance, of a category of women who can be called "pregnant addicts" or of infants we can call "crack babies"—have powerful political significance for defining the nature and causes of fetal health problems.

The cultural associations of paternity with virility and maternity with vulnerability formed the context within which the symbols of the crack baby, pregnant addict, and absent father emerged at the center of debate over fetal hazards.[6]

"CRACK BABIES" AND "PREGNANT ADDICTS"

It is October 1996 and in South Carolina Cornelia Whitner is about to enter prison for an eight-year term for criminal child neglect for having a baby born with cocaine metabolites in its system. In Racine, Wisconsin, Deborah Zimmerman is the first woman in the United States charged with the attempted murder of her fetus for drinking alcohol during her pregnancy. She faces up to forty years in prison. And in Chesterfield, New

Hampshire, Rosemarie Tourigny, who is twelve weeks pregnant, is charged with endangering the welfare of a child after police find that her blood alcohol level is two times the limit for drunken driving. Lester Fairbanks, the town's acting police chief, reported that he arrested Tourigny because, "She can pickle herself all she wants, but that child doesn't have the opportunity to decide whether it's going to be retarded or not. . . . Somebody has to have responsibility for her unborn child." Tourigny, the local newspaper reports, plans to have an abortion.[7]

The prosecution of pregnant women for fetal neglect and abuse first emerged during the 1980s and continues today. Media attention began to focus on babies affected by maternal drug use with the release of a study in 1988 by Ira Chasnoff, director of the National Association for Perinatal Addiction Research and Education (NAPARE), which reported that 375,000 babies were born every year "exposed to illicit drugs in the womb" (Chasnoff 1989, 208–10). The study was fundamentally flawed in a number of ways. Chasnoff's sample was biased by the fact that thirty-four of the thirty-six hospitals surveyed were public inner-city hospitals. The study made no distinction between a single use of illegal drugs and chronic drug addiction during pregnancy, and it did not document the actual effects of drug use on newborn infants.

The limitations of Chasnoff's study were never reported. Instead, the press picked up and exaggerated the study's findings, often reporting that 375,000 babies were born every year "addicted to cocaine" (Brody 1988a, 1; 1988b, C1; Stone 1989, 3). As the distinctions between drug use and abuse collapsed, the reported numbers of crack babies exploded. By 1990, news stories reported that one out of every ten children was born "addicted to crack cocaine" or damaged by women's use of drugs (Daniels 1993). By 1993, nine influential national daily newspapers had run more than 197 stories on pregnancy and cocaine addiction alone.[8]

The mind-set created by this public discourse encouraged physicians, nurses, and social workers to attribute many serious problems experienced by infants at birth to the use of drugs or alcohol by the child's mother, particularly in low-income inner-city neighborhoods.

Symptoms associated with "crack babies" ranged from very specific conditions that could, in fact, be tied to maternal drug use (such as drug withdrawal) to low birth weight, small head circumference, irritability, respiratory problems, gastrointestinal problems, and diarrhea—conditions that could easily be caused by poor nutrition or a host of environmental factors.[9] More highly controlled studies estimated that approximately 41,000 babies were born nationally with clear symptoms of drug-related health problems (such as drug withdrawal symptoms), a far cry from the 375,000 presented by NAPARE as having been exposed to drugs in the womb (Dicker and Leighton 1990). The results of these studies were never reported by the national press, just as the press rarely reports research showing little or no association between moderate drug and alcohol use and fetal health problems (Koren and Klein 1991).[10]

The sense of social distress created by images of addicted babies wired to tubes in hospital incubators fed a profound need to blame. Public concern over crack babies contains all of the characteristics of a response to plague—fueling the impulse of privileged populations to locate, target, and contain one group as the primary source of contamination and risk (Mack 1991). As Linda Singer has observed in relation to the spread of AIDS, the epidemic "provides an occasion and rationale for multiplying points of intervention into the lives and bodies of populations" (1993, 117). The policy response to the plague narrative was to find a target population to blame, and poor inner-city women were the most obvious targets. Newspaper stories contributed to this impulse by presenting images of African-American women as virtual monsters, snorting cocaine on the way to the delivery room and abandoning horribly damaged babies in hospitals.

In some instances, drug use was characterized as a form of child abuse in utero, where cocaine "literally batters the developing child" (see Brody 1988a, 1; Stone 1989, 3).

Criminal prosecutors responded to the sense of crisis by targeting pregnant women for prosecution. By 1993 at least two hundred, and some estimate up to four hundred, women had been charged with fetal drug delivery, fetal abuse, or manslaughter (in cases where pregnancy had ended in a stillbirth). Despite the fact that almost every case challenged in the courts has resulted in the dismissal or acquittal of charges against women, prosecutors continue to bring criminal charges against women they suspect of drug or alcohol use during pregnancy. To date, almost all of these cases have been brought against African-American women.[11]

What has been the response of state and federal public health agencies to women and fetal health? Public health departments have produced warning labels on wine, beer, and liquor bottles and cans and on cigarette packages and an avalanche of public notices about pregnancy and alcohol consumption for display in restaurants and bars. Such labels stigmatize women by perpetuating assumptions that only women are vulnerable to risk and that women, therefore, are the primary source of fetal harm. Men are left entirely out of the frame as social attention focuses exclusively on the maternal-fetal nexus.

By implying women's ignorance or ill intentions, public health warnings aimed at pregnant women legitimate an atmosphere that encourages public retribution against women by focusing exclusively on individual behavior and not on the social and political causes of low birth weight, fetal birth defects, or other health problems. Retribution is invited by the fact that public health warnings aimed at men (e.g., for heart disease, high blood pressure, cigarette smoking, and steroid use) focus on behaviors that cause harm to *self*, whereas messages aimed at women focus exclusively on women's harm to *others* (the fetus).

One New Jersey public health ad displays an image of a pregnant woman holding a drink and warns, "A pregnant woman never drinks alone."[12] Yet a pregnant woman also never drinks without the effects of her home, her job,and her physical, social, and political environment. Even symptoms specific to drug or alcohol abuse, such as drug withdrawal or fetal alcohol syndrome, are complicated by simple factors such as poor nutrition. For instance, one study of pregnancy and alcohol use (that controlled for age, smoking, drug abuse, reproductive history, medical problems, socioeconomic status, and race) found that women who consumed at least three drinks a day but ate balanced diets experienced a rate of Fetal Alcohol Syndrome (FAS) of only 4.5 percent, while women who drank the same amount and were malnourished had an FAS rate of 71 percent (Bingol et al. 1987). The study showed that poor nutrition is tied directly to wealth. It also demonstrated that FAS is a measure not only of maternal alcoholism but also of economic class. There has been no press coverage of this study.

Public campaigns to "stem the tide of crack babies" are clearly racialized, primarily targeting women of color in low-income communities. Scientific research has supported the racialized nature of debate by focusing studies heavily on drugs used most commonly in poor inner cities (such as crack) and not on substances most often abused by higher-income women (such as prescription drugs). Public health warnings typically silhouette African-American or Latina women and are often produced in Spanish and directed at inner-city neighborhoods. One giant billboard of a baby tied to tubes in an incubator literally hangs over the heads of women in an African-American Los Angeles neighborhood, with the message: "He couldn't take the hit. If you're pregnant, don't take drugs" (Mitchell 1991, B1). . . .

Counteracting the symbol of the pregnant addict/antimother requires breaking the exclusive connection between pregnant women and "crack babies." The circle of causality has widened since feminist advocates began influencing media coverage of the issue and news stories began suggesting the links between fetal health and the combined effects of poverty, addiction, and exposures to workplace and environmental toxins.

But drawing fathers into the circle of causality, essential to deconstruction of the symbol of the pregnant addict, has proven more difficult. Both metaphorically and literally, fathers were absent from virtually all of the news stories on fetal health and addiction. The absence of fathers in news reports of crack babies was made easier to believe by the racial subtext of the story: African-American women are often characterized as abandoned, single mothers—women dangerously unconstrained by nuclear family relations.

The "absent father" came to represent not only men's physical distance from the out-of-wedlock child but also men's distance from fetal harm. Embedded in scientific research and newspaper and magazine stories were also assumptions about male reproduction that posed serious barriers to the father-fetal connection.

VIRILE FATHERS AND THE "ALL OR NOTHING" SPERM THEORY

Scientific literature on reproductive toxicity has traditionally dismissed the links between paternal use of drugs and alcohol (or exposure to occupational or environmental toxins) and harm to fetal health because it was assumed that damaged sperm were incapable of fertilizing eggs. Indeed, male reproductive success was defined as the ability to penetrate an egg. Because penetration was the measure of normalcy, those sperm that succeeded were assumed to be healthy. By defining male reproductive health along the principles of this "all or nothing" theory, most scientific studies until the late 1980s dismissed the possibility that defective sperm could contribute to fetal health problems. The "all or nothing" theory was based on certain culturally imbued assumptions about the reproductive process. As Emily Martin has so well documented, scientists characterized the egg as the passive recipient and the sperm as conqueror in the process of fertilization (1991). . . .

The theory of sperm competition is predicated on the idea that female infidelity is biologically founded and that only the healthiest sperm survive the competition initiated by the female: "Females mate with several males because this allows them to pit the sperm of different males against each other in their reproductive tracts. In this way, they ensure that they are fertilized by the best-quality sperm" (Mason 1991, 29; Bellis and Baker 1990). . . .[13]

The assumption that men harmed by toxic exposures would be rendered infertile deflected research away from the connections between fathers and fetal harm. As a result of the "virile sperm" theory of conception, scientific studies, until the late 1980s, focused almost exclusively on infertility as the primary outcome of hazardous exposures and the main source of reproductive problems for men. Male reproductive health was defined by "total sperm ejaculate," and healthy reproductive function was measured by "ejaculatory performance"—measures of volume, sperm concentration and number, sperm velocity and motility, sperm swimming characteristics, and sperm morphology, shape, and size (Burger et al. 1989).

Scientists who did try to pursue the father-fetal connection, such as Gladys Friedler at Boston University, who was the first to document a link in mice between paternal exposure to morphine and birth defects in their offspring in the 1970s, had difficulty funding their research or publishing their work. The significance of Friedler's work is that she found mutagenic effects from paternal exposures not only in the progeny of male mice exposed to morphine and alcohol but also in the second generation, or "grandchildren," of exposed mice. In all cases, she controlled for maternal exposures so that causality could be more clearly linked to paternal exposures.[14] Cultural constructions of male reproduction made Friedler's work simply unbelievable. . . .

THE EVIDENCE OF MALE-MEDIATED DEVELOPMENTAL TOXICOLOGY

Male reproductive exposures are now proven or strongly suspected of causing not only fertility problems but also miscarriage, low birth weight, congenital abnormalities, cancer, neurological problems, and other childhood health problems (Davis et al. 1992, 289).

Because adult males continuously produce sperm throughout their lives, the germ cells from which sperm originate are continuously dividing and developing. Sperm take approximately seventy-two days to develop to maturity and then move for another twelve days through the duct called the epididymis, where they acquire the ability to fertilize an egg (Moore 1989).[15] During this developmental process, sperm may be particularly susceptible to damage from toxins since cells that are dividing are more vulnerable to toxicity than cells that are fully developed and at rest, as are eggs in the female reproductive system.

Studies of male reproductive health and toxicity have concentrated primarily on the effects of occupational and environmental exposures of men and less on the effects of what scientists refer to as men's "lifestyle factors," such as drinking, smoking, or drug use.[16]

A number of events triggered studies of male reproduction during the 1970s and 1980s.[17] In 1977, men working at an Occidental Chemical plant in Lathrop, California, noticed a pattern of sterility among their coworkers. In the 1950s, the company had actually funded research on the carcinogenicity and reproductive effects of the pesticide produced there, DBCP (dibromochloropropane), but had quietly shelved the research after findings demonstrated associations between DBCP exposures and reproductive effects in lab animals (Robinson 1991, xiii–xv). Later studies confirmed that the men's sterility was linked to their DBCP exposure, and the chemical was banned from further use in the United States. By 1980, researchers had documented not only sterility but also increases in spontaneous abortion resulting from paternal exposure to DBCP (Kharrazi, Patashnik, and Goldsmith 1980). Seventeen studies have now evaluated the impact of pesticides and herbicides on male reproduction and paternal-fetal health (Olshan and Faustman 1993, 195).

Other studies have analyzed the effects of occupational exposures on paternal-fetal health, many of which have found significant associations between paternal exposures and fetal health problems. Paints, solvents, metals, dyes, and hydrocarbons have been associated with childhood leukemia and childhood brain tumors (Olshan and Faustman 1993, 196). Thirty-nine studies have examined the relationship between occupational exposures and spontaneous abortion. Toluene, xylene, benzene, TCE (trichloroethylene), vinyl chloride, lead, and mercury have all been associated with increased risks of spontaneous abortion (Lindbohm et at. 1991; Savitz, Sonnenfeld, and Olshan 1994).[18]

In analyses by occupation, janitors, mechanics, farmworkers, and metal-workers have been reported to have an excess of children with Down's syndrome (Olshan and Faustman 1993, 196). One study of 727 children born with anencephaly found correlations for paternal employment as painters (Colie 1993, 7). Painters and workers exposed to hydrocarbons have also been shown to have higher rates of children with childhood leukemia and brain cancer (Savitz and Chen 1990). More than thirty studies have examined the relationship between paternal occupation and childhood cancer (Holly et al. 1992; Olshan and Faustman 1993, 197). . . .

Whether addressing occupational, environmental, or "lifestyle" exposures, there are problems with many of the studies on male-mediated teratogenicity. It is difficult, for instance, to specify the nature of men's exposures to toxic substances at work or in war. It is also difficult to get a sample size large enough to provide conclusive results, especially for conditions that are typically rare in children. And, as in all epidemiological studies, it is difficult to control for confounding factors, such as the effects of multiple chemical exposures and alcohol or drug use.

While the problem of confounding variables is common to all epidemiological studies of reproductive toxicity, for cultural reasons scientists are more acutely aware of these when studying men. For instance, studies of paternal effects are routinely criticized for not controlling for maternal exposures, while studies on women virtually never control for the exposures of fathers. Studies on men's occupational and environmental exposures rarely control for men's use of drugs or alcohol. Studies that do focus on the effects of lifestyle factors on men's reproduction are criticized for not controlling for men's workplace exposures, while studies of women and drug use do not control for women's occupational exposures.

Still, even given the limitations of scientific knowledge, it is clear that men can pass on genetic defects to children. Down's syndrome and Prader-Willi syndrome have been passed to children through the paternal germ cell. The question is whether similar processes can occur when environmental exposures cause genetic mutations in sperm (Colie 1993).

The biological processes of male-mediated teratogenicity have also been examined through clinical studies on animals and studies of the effect of toxic exposures directly on sperm. All of the problems of confounding variables associated with epidemiological research can be avoided by conducting animal studies. The earliest studies of the effects of illicit drugs, for instance, were conducted on mice.

What is the evidence of paternal-fetal effects of drugs, alcohol, and cigarette smoking?

Smoking

In a study of more than fourteen thousand birth records in San Francisco, researchers found associations between paternal smoking and various birth defects, including cleft lip, cleft palate, and hydrocephalus (Savitz, Schwingle, and Keels 1991). Significant associations also have been found between paternal smoking and brain cancer in children and between paternal smoking and low birth weight.[19] In addition, cotinine, a metabolite of nicotine, has been found in seminal fluid, although researchers are unsure what effect this might have on fetal health (Davis 1991a, 123; Davis et al. 1992, 290).

Bruce Ames of the University of California, Berkeley, has suggested that the link between smoking and birth defects could be due to smokers' low levels of vitamin C. Vitamin C helps to protect sperm from the genetic damage caused by oxidants in the body, yet the vitamin is depleted in the body of cigarette smokers. Ames found that men with low levels of the vitamin experienced double the oxidation damage to the DNA in their sperm (Schmidt 1992, 92).

Alcohol Use

Paternal alcohol use has been found to cause low birth weight and an increased risk of birth defects. In animal studies, paternal exposure to ethanol produced behavioral abnormalities in offspring. Alcoholism in men is known to produce testicular atrophy. Case reports suggest an association between paternal drinking and "malformations and cognitive deficiencies" in children of alcoholic men.[20]

Cocaine and Other Illicit Drugs

A 1990 study found that cocaine increased the number of abnormal sperm and decreased sperm motility in men. In a 1991 clinical study, Ricardo Yazigi, Randall Odem, and Kenneth Polakoski found that cocaine could bind to sperm and thereby be transmitted to the egg during fertilization. Reports of cocaine "piggybacking" on sperm have led to controversy in the scientific community over whether this could contribute to birth defects (Brachen et al. 1990; Yazigi, Odem, and Polakoski 1991). In animal studies, opiates (such as morphine and methadone) administered to fathers, but not mothers, have produced birth defects and behavioral abnormalities in the first *and* second generations of the father's offspring (Friedler and Wheeling 1979; Friedler 1985). Drug addiction in men using hashish, opium, and heroin has been shown to cause structural defects in sperm (El-Gothamy and El-Samahy 1992). Despite the limitations of scientific research on male reproduction, few scientists question that biological mechanisms exist for establishing links between paternal and fetal health.

The following sections analyze the coverage of research on male-mediated fetal risks by three different kinds of print media: popular scientific magazines, magazines for general readership, and nine influential U.S. daily newspapers.[21]

MALE REPRODUCTION IN POPULAR DISCOURSE— THE GENERATION OF SPERM PERSONHOOD

As scientific research began to explore the possibility that sperm could be damaged by toxic exposures, sperm began to take on distinctive personality traits in stories in popular magazines and newspapers reporting scientific research on male reproductive hazards.[22] Despite newspapers' claims to a higher level of "objectivity" in reporting, many stories in newspapers share a language and imagery common in popular magazine articles on male reproductive toxicity. Sympathy for sperm damaged by reproductive toxicity was specifically generated by the personification of sperm.

Sperm were characterized as the "little ones" produced by men. One magazine article tells the story of "Harry" as he tries to overcome an infertility problem by improving his diet and exercising regularly: "Harry's attitude was that . . . the condition of his whole body *ought* to affect the condition of the little ones it produced" (Poppy 1989, 69). Sperm development here becomes a distinctive form of male gestation: "For seventy-four days or so, these cells lie passive in their tubules, growing quietly. Then the young sperm move along to the epididymis, a comma-shaped coil of tubing behind the testicle that would stretch for twenty feet if straightened out. For twelve days they finish maturing and gain the ability to swim" (69). In this story of gestation, the physiology of the male body is reconstructed as well: "The two testicles at the heart of a man's hopes each contain about seven hundred feet of tightly coiled seminiferous tubes" (69).[23]

Sperm also have distinctive personal traits. They have heads (sometimes more than one) and tails (sometimes misshapen). Some are "vigorous, well-aimed swimmers," while others "swim in dizzy circles and never head in the right direction" (Small 1991, 49). Sperm voyage, travel, and navigate. One scientific study reported that sperm even have a sense of smell and that "swimming sperm navigate toward a fertile egg by detecting its scent" (Angier 1992a, A19; also see Friend 1992, A1).

Publications as diverse as *Cell, Esquire,* and the *New York Times* share accounts that impart a consciousness to sperm. The "kamikaze" and "sperm competition" theories of Bellis and Baker suggest that sperm collaborate and compete as fraternity "brothers" or "enemies." One article in the *New York Times* reporting Bellis and Baker's research suggested that kamikaze sperm are "self-sacrificing" as they "commit suicide" for the good of the group (Browne 1988, C6).[24] In part, this characterization was generated directly from reports in scientific journals. For instance, in an article in *Cell*, Bennett Shapiro suggests that sperm face three existential dilemmas in reproduction—whether to swim, whether to pursue an egg, and whether to fertilize an egg, all of which shorten the "life span" of the sperm (1987). Popularized accounts of Shapiro's theory capitalized on his imagery, suggesting that human sperm were faced with the ultimate question, "Do I give up my autonomy and individuality for the chance to fertilize an egg, or do I spurn responsibility and lead an independent and happy-go-lucky—but meaningless—existence?" (*Discover* 1987, 10–11).

With sperm personified as such, toxins that could damage male reproductive health are cast not as an assault on fetal health but as an assault against man's sperm. It turns out, one story reports, that "sperm is more fragile and potentially more dangerous than previously thought" (Merewood 1991, 54). In fact, it is the fragility of sperm—the literal and metaphorical blurring of the distinction between the vulnerable and the virile—that precisely makes sperm "more dangerous."

The visual images accompanying popular magazine stories reinforce sympathy for the sperm (and men) as victims. In 1991, *Health* magazine ran a story titled "Sperm under Siege" with visuals of bottles of chemicals and alcohol pointed threateningly at a group of sperm circling around a center target (Merewood 1991). A story in *Parenting* magazine presented an image of a man and his sperm huddled under an umbrella as chemical bottles, beer cans, and martini glasses rained down on them (Black and Moore 1992). One might expect men and their sperm to be characterized as victims in cases where men were involuntarily exposed to toxins at work, but both of these stories focused on men's (presumably voluntary) use of drugs and alcohol.

Although eggs have been characterized as "aggressors," stories of reproductive toxicity do not portray eggs as the victims of toxicity. While a *New York Times* story on women and drugs describes cocaine "repeatedly battering the child in a *U.S. News and World Report* story on men and toxins describes sperm as "battered by chemicals" (Brody 1988b, C1; Schmidt 1992, 96). Of the stories in popular magazines on the effects of drugs or alcohol on male reproduction, only one contained images of men and babies, and this was of a father and healthy child with the subtitle, "The importance of the father in making healthy babies has been underappreciated" (Schmidt 1992, 96).[25] Only once the frame shifts to stories of soldiers affected by wartime exposures do images of sick children (and their mothers) begin to emerge in news coverage.

NEWSPAPER COVERAGE OF MALE REPRODUCTIVE HAZARDS

What kind of newspaper coverage has been generated by research on men and fetal health? Of the nine national daily newspapers I surveyed—those that often define the "news agenda" for local media coverage—only seventeen stories since 1985 have reported possible connections between all paternal exposures and fetal health effects (five on chemical wartime exposures in Vietnam and the Persian Gulf, five on cocaine, four on smoking, two on workplace exposures, and one article covering all causes).[26] By contrast, since 1985 these papers have run more than two hundred stories on pregnant women and cocaine addiction alone.

Since 1985, the *New York Times* has run a total of three stories and one op-ed piece on the links between paternal exposures and fetal health effects: one focused on the impact of cocaine, one on paternal smoking, and two on men's occupational exposures.[27] There has been no *New York Times* coverage of the links between paternal alcohol consumption and fetal health. By contrast, the *New York Times* alone has run at least twenty-seven stories on pregnant women and crack.[28]

Even in newspaper stories that address the connection between paternal exposures and fetal health, certain patterns of reporting emerge that function to reduce male culpability for fetal harm.

First, while men are absent from stories on maternal-fetal harm, *women are always present* in news stories on paternally mediated risks. In none of the stories are fathers solely responsible for fetal harm. In all of the stories that draw connections between paternal exposure to drugs, alcohol, or smoking and fetal harm, maternal exposure was also mentioned as a possible source of harm. In this way, male responsibility is always shared with women. One *New York Times* article modifies masculine responsibility in the following way: "If the effect is proven true, cocaine-using fathers may have to share more of the responsibility with cocaine-using mothers for birth defects in children" (1991b, C5). The same article further implicates women by suggesting that "sperm could pick up the drug in the reproductive tract of a cocaine-using woman after intercourse, opening the way for damage to the fetus by that route." A *Chicago Tribune* article reviewing a range of paternally mediated risks concludes that "women no longer have to carry the full responsibility for bearing a healthy infant" and that these "new data suggest that both may be responsible" (Merewood 1992, sec. 6, 8). Like child care and dishwashing, the man of the nineties now shares responsibility for reproductive risks with women. Particularly in discussions of drug-related risks, the presence of the pregnant woman means that the father is never cast as the primary source of harm. No article suggests or implies that "drug-clean" women may produce harmed babies as a result of their partner's drug use.

As a result of the nature of the exposures, culpability is treated somewhat differently in stories regarding men's wartime exposures. In the context of both the Vietnam War and the Persian Gulf War, stories specifically addressing male-mediated harm always include images of mothers with their ailing children.[29] The fathers/soldiers and mothers/wives thus become joint victims of military irresponsibility.

Second, *maternally mediated fetal risks are assumed to be certain and known.* Evidence of male-mediated risks are often prefaced with statements such as: "While doctors are well aware of the effects that maternal smoking, drinking and exposure to certain drugs can have on the fetus, far less is known about the father's role in producing healthy offspring" (Merewood 1992, sec. 6, 8). *U.S. News and World Report* begins its article on paternal-fetal harm, "It is common wisdom that mothers-to-be should steer clear of toxic chemicals that could cause birth defects. . . . Now similar precautions are being urged on fathers-to-be" (Schmidt 1992, 92).

Third, research on men is always *qualified and limited.* A *Chicago Tribune* story on men's role in producing healthy babies, for instance, states, "Research like this may sound convincing, but Dr. David Savitz . . . warns that it's far too early to panic. 'We have no documented evidence that certain exposures cause certain birth defects,' he says" (Merewood 1992, sec. 6, 8). An article in the *Atlanta Constitution* reports that "cocaine use in fathers is unlikely to cause the same problems in babies as cocaine use by their mothers, which include premature birth, an elevated risk of death, growth retardation and nerve and behavior problems." Still, the same article later states that "research on rodents indicates males exposed to cocaine are more likely to have offspring with nervous, hormonal or behavioral problems" (Perl 1991, F3). A *New York Times* story repeats the reservations of one researcher: "But epidemiological studies cannot prove cause and effect, said Dr. John Peters. . . . In real life, people are exposed sporadically to combinations of substances that might interact. . . . To show more dramatic associations, he said, scientists would need to study *hundreds of thousands of people over many years*" (Blakeslee 1991, A1; emphasis added). Yet there are no such studies of women. Similar reservations are common in stories regarding wartime exposures, suggesting that "infant deaths and birth abnormalities are in line with expected percentages in the general population" (Serrano 1994, A12).

Fourth, male culpability is further reduced by the fact that news articles on paternal exposures to illegal drugs are *always contextualized by reference to "involuntary" environmental and workplace exposures.* As in many of the stories in popular magazine articles, newspaper stories often refer to drug use, alcohol consumption, and smoking as "lifestyle factors" (Merewood 1992) and place these with a string of possible exposures including "pesticides and workplace chemicals" (see Blakeslee 1991; Merewood 1991). Even the newspaper stories reporting the "piggybacking" of cocaine on sperm suggest that workplace chemicals may "latch onto sperm" in the same way (Perl 1991, F3). All of this suggests the uncertainty of linking men's drug abuse to fetal harm and the difficulty of narrowing causality to illegal drug use. These are precisely the kinds of qualifications and complications absent from reporting on maternal drug use. Perhaps not surprising, while newspaper coverage of wartime exposures mentions confounding problems associated with men's multiple chemical or occupational exposures, rarely do such stories suggest that the etiology of birth defects might be traced to soldiers' drug use.

Fifth, in stories on paternally mediated harm from drugs, alcohol, or cigarette smoking, *the language and images of harmed children and "crack babies" are absent from stories on men.* A sterile scientific terminology is used to describe studies on paternal "lifestyle" exposures, with the language of "suffering crack babies" replaced by "damaged DNA," "abnormal offspring," and "genetic anomalies." One *New York Times* story linking vitamin C deficiencies (produced by male cigarette smoking) with fetal damage reported: "The study demonstrated a direct relationship between a diet low in vitamin C and increased DNA damage in sperm cells. . . . Any damage to this genetic structure may predispose a man to having children with genetic anomalies" (1992, C12). After reporting that children of fathers who smoke have been found to be at increased risk for leukemia and lymphoma, the article ends with the recommendation of a physician that men who smoke "either modify their diets to include fruits and vegetables or take a vitamin C supplement each day." While sperm "delivers," "transports," or "carries" the drug to the egg in such stories, it never "assaults" the fetus as stories on drug use and women imply. In stories on drug addiction, smoking, and alcohol consumption, when the sperm is not presented as itself a victim, sperm acts as a shield for men—deflecting or capturing the blame that might otherwise be placed on the father.

Indeed, in newspaper stories on drugs, alcohol, and smoking, the only images to accompany these stories were photographs or cartoon images of sperm. Yet of the 853 column inches dedicated to pregnancy, alcohol, and drug abuse by the *New York Times* in one two-year period, almost two hundred column inches were taken up by images of crack babies and their drug-addicted mothers (Schroedel and Peretz 1993). . . .

Clearly, reporters play an important role in framing and interpreting stories and imparting meaning to scientific research. Science reporters often pick up stories from professional journals such as the *Journal of the American Medical Association* or the *New England Journal of Medicine.* But what is the source of the slant on the story? The complex process of "framing" takes place at multiple levels. Clearly, science is skewed in terms of the kinds of questions and answers legitimated for research. The absence of research on men and fetal health, of course, precludes public knowledge of paternal-fetal risks, even in cases where the experience of men and women may suggest relations of causality, such as in the California DBCP case (see Robinson 1991).

Second, once research is initiated, embedded assumptions about gender may skew or color scientific methodology and the interpretation of findings, diminishing the importance of paternal-fetal associations. As Koren et al. have found, editors of science journals often play an important role in screening out reports that violate standards of scientific "believability" (1989). After scientific research makes it into print in professional science journals, newspaper reporters screen findings through the complex lens of social meanings they bring to the research (see Tuchman 1978, 1983, 1993). In the phrasing of a question, in what is "taken for granted," the framing of a story takes place not at the level of individual "bias" or conscious intention but through what Stuart Hall calls the "logic of social processes." As Hall argues in relation to television broadcasting, "The ideology has 'worked' in such a case because the discourse has spoken itself through him/her [the broadcaster]. Unwittingly, unconsciously, the broadcaster has served as a support for the reproduction of a dominant ideological discursive field" (1982, 88). . . .

PATERNAL EFFECTS AND "POLITICAL CORRECTNESS"

Evidence of paternal-fetal harm has generated virtual silence from public health authorities and the courts. In an editorial in *Reproductive Toxicology,* Anthony Scialli argues that the impulse to link paternal exposures with fetal effects is a result not of science but of "political correctness": "There has been no quarrel that testicular toxicants can produce fertility impairment, but paternally mediated effects on conceived pregnancies is a different matter altogether." He concedes that "several" studies on paternally mediated effects have been "nicely performed and reported," but taken as a whole they are "difficult to interpret" (1993, 189). Of those who defend the evidence of paternal-fetal links, he concludes: "The people who make these accusations appear to believe that paternally-mediated effects *must* occur in humans, for the sake of fairness. . . . It is argued that because father and mother make equal genetic contributions to the conceptus, they must have equal opportunity to transmit toxic effects. Students of developmental biology understand that there is nothing equal about male and female contributions to development. . . . There are several million unequivocal examples of children damaged by intrauterine exposure to toxicants encountered by the mother during gestation. There are no unequivocal examples for paternal exposures" (189). . . .

Even in cases where men are exposed to known reproductive hazards, scientists have been remarkably reluctant to recommend the most simple restrictions on men. Controversy still exists, for instance, over whether men who are undergoing chemotherapy should abstain from procreation during treatment. Cyclophosphamide, used during chemotherapeutic treatment, is a known female reproductive hazard, and rodent studies indicate it might cause miscarriage, birth defects, and childhood tumors in the children conceived by men during treatment. Yet at the first major medical meeting on male-mediated developmental toxins at the University of Pittsburgh in 1992, men were given "conflicting advice" about whether to postpone procreation during cancer treatment (or "bank" sperm before treatment).

In addition, in 1992 the journal *Human Reproduction* published a recommendation stating that sperm saved in the early stages of chemotherapy was safe "based on the belief that since the drugs did not kill sperm . . . the sperm were healthy" (Miller 1992, 5). Yet others argued that sperm that survive therapy may be more likely to carry genetic defects. One researcher simply recommended that men use condoms to protect their partners during treatment. But other scientists at the conference were wary of "confusing the public with the results of animal studies that may not apply directly to humans." "Speculation tends to get us into trouble," stated Jan Friedman, a clinical geneticist and specialist in birth defects (Miller 1992, 5).

Clearly, it is not the nature of the risk as much as the symbolic construction of the population targeted that has determined the public response to fetal harm.

BLAME AND ABSOLUTION: PUBLIC POLICY AND THE TARGETING OF WOMEN

When science fails to produce clear explanations for a risk to human health, the public response often results in an impulse to blame a target group in order to reestablish a sense of order and social control. But it must be remembered that who is absolved in this process is as important as who is blamed. Absolution is a privilege of those who have successfully distanced themselves from fetal risks. But this distance may be determined more by the social and political power of those who can place themselves outside the frame of causality than by true evidence of risk. . . .

The symbols used to frame understandings of addiction and fetal risk are important not only because they misdirect science, policy, and law but because, as they are currently constructed, they make it possible—and even incite the public—to target women and exculpate men for fetal harm. Anne Schneider and Helen Ingram have noted that in this process, state officials are likely to provide beneficial policy to powerful, positively constructed groups and to devise punitive punishments for those who are negatively constructed (1993). What are the specific conditions that have made the punitive targeting of women possible?

Targetability requires, first, the ability to *isolate* the target population—to draw sharp distinctions between those who are "clean" and those who are "corrupt." Research that focuses so heavily on the impact of crack cocaine on pregnancy makes it easier to distinguish between the clean and the corrupt for women.[30] By contrast, the scientific research on men focuses primarily on workplace and environmental toxins and only secondarily on smoking, alcohol consumption, and drug use. Links between fathers and fetuses therefore potentially implicate not a narrow category of men but men as a class for fetal health problems. Indeed, it seems likely that if and when men do become the targets of blame for fetal health problems, the focus may well be first on inner-city men of color who use crack cocaine.

Second, the symbolic frame used to shape science and policy makes it easier to target women as it casts them as violating dominant norms of acceptable social behavior and thus as acceptable objects of coercive state regulation. Since smoking and drinking have been culturally associated with masculinity, this hardly seems like a violation of acceptable behavior for men. Moreover, men as workers or as soldiers (in the case of Agent Orange or Gulf War exposures) are at risk as a result of fulfilling, not neglecting, their obligations as "good fathers" and citizens. Men are put at risk not by their own misbehavior but by the irresponsibility of others. The discourse of victimization thus pushes women to the center and men to the periphery as the cause of fetal harm.

CONCLUSION

The social meaning imparted to female gestation of the fetus has created the illusion that the connection between the mother and fetus is not only direct but exclusive. After the "fleeting" contribution of the father, women are assumed to be the primary sources of both fetal health and fetal harm. But this is clearly a social and political, as well as a biological, construction. Deconstructing the myths of maternity and paternity that have so far informed debates over fetal risk requires drawing men into reproduction. Yet there is an irony embedded in the politics of fetal harm. Male power in reproduction has often centered around men's claim of ownership over the fetus. In questions of fetal harm, just the opposite is true, for in this case, men's power is enhanced by their distance from the fetus. Ironically, there are similarities in the arguments made by those who defend women's right to reproductive choice and those who argue that men are more distant from fetal health problems. Both stress the significance of the fact that the fetus is a part of the pregnant woman's body. Both stress that only women mix their "body-labor" with the fetus in reproduction. From the pro-choice point of view, because gestation imposes a unique set of burdens on women, women alone must be granted the immutable right to consent to (or reject) pregnancy (McDonagh 1993).

But from the point of view of debates over fetal harm, gestation also means that there is an additional avenue for fetal harm not shared in the same way with men. It is clearly true that men's actions can have a profound effect on fetal health—both before conception and throughout pregnancy. But while the comparability of paternal and maternal sources of fetal harm is recognized, the distinction between men's and women's roles in procreation must not be collapsed. The recognition of this difference is essential both to women's right to choice and to the true protection of maternal and fetal health.

Science and media representations driven by assumptions of maternal-fetal vulnerability, on the one hand, and male virility, on the other, have led to both the negative targeting of women and the systematic neglect of men's health needs. Recognition of male vulnerability is thus essential to the science and politics of fetal harm. Yet it is important that, in the process of responding to political risks, the discussion not retreat into a position that denies the significance of gender difference and, in doing so, reinstitutes the essentialized invulnerable male body as referent for public policy and law.

Ultimately, talk about comparability of male and female risks perpetuates the misguided focus on individual causality and directs attention away from the more profound social determinants of parental and fetal health—good nutrition, good health care, and a clean and safe environment. Until the symbols of the crack baby, pregnant addict, and absent father are deconstructed in the public mind, pregnant women—and not poverty, poor health, violence, the disease of addiction, or irresponsibility on the part of men—will continue to be seen as the greatest threat to fetal health.

Notes

1. Challenging the methodological individualism of scientific research on fetal health problems, which focuses so heavily on "aberrant" individual behavior and too easily dismisses the social causes of fetal health problems, is thus equally essential to challenging the racial and gender politics of fetal harm.
2. A more detailed discussion of the rise of the concept of fetal rights and fetal protectionism can be found in Daniels 1993.
3. Baer 1978; Kessler-Harris 1982; Lehrer 1987; Daniels 1991, 1993.
4. The term *condensation symbol* is adopted from Edelman 1988, 73. For elaborations of the racialized construction of womanhood and maternity, see Lubiano 1992; and Crenshaw 1993.
5. The ideological construction of maternity/femininity and the pattern of public debates over fetal harm also reflect the history of medical discourse on women and public health risks. Particularly in relation to sexually transmitted diseases, and now in relation to women and AIDS, women are cast not as the victims of harm but as the vectors of risk for innocent children and men (Women and AIDS Book Group 1990; Corea 1992).

6. A more detailed analysis of the social and political construction of these concepts can be found in my longer treatment of this issue in Daniels 1993, where I analyze the scientific, media, policy, and legal discourses surrounding the emergence of the idea of fetal protectionism and fetal rights.
7. Information on these cases is derived from Cornelia Whitner v. State of South Carolina, On Writ of Certiorari, Appeal from Pickens County, South Carolina Supreme Court Opinion No. 24468, July 15, 1996; State of Wisconsin v. Deborah J. Zimmerman, State of Wisconsin, Circuit Court Branch 5, Racine County, File No. 96-CF-525, September 18, 1996; and Vigue 1996. For coverage of the Zimmerman case, also see O'Neill, Eskin, and Satter 1996.
8. These calculations are based on a review of the on-line ProQuest newspaper index. The nine newspapers on which my research is based are the *New York Times, Wall Street Journal, Washington Post, Christian Science Monitor, Los Angeles Times, Chicago Tribune, Boston Globe, Atlanta Constitution/Atlanta Journal,* and *USA Today.*
9. For a complete discussion of the symptoms associated with fetal cocaine exposure, see Zuckerman 1991, 26–35.
10. There are two stages to the "screening" process by which research makes it into the press. First, science journals review, accept, or reject reports of findings. Koren et al. have found a predisposition by professional scientific journals against reporting negative (or "null") associations between drug use and fetal risks (1989). Once scientific reports began to appear in journals, Koren and Klein 1991 found a similar predisposition by the press against reporting negative findings. Null associations are thus doubly burdened by the editorial processes of review in both journals and newspapers.
11. Personal interview with Lynn Paltrow, August 6, 1993, at the Center for Reproductive Law and Policy, New York City. Total numbers are now difficult to calculate since so many women are charged by local prosecutors who do not report their cases to any central, national source. For documentation of the first 167 cases, see Paltrow 1992.
12. Public health ad by the N.J. Perinatal Cooperative, 1993.
13. Multiple mating, Bellis and Baker argue, is most useful when a female is "unable to judge ejaculate quality from a male's appearance" (1990, 997).
14. Personal interview with Gladys Friedler, April 1990, Bunting Institute, Radcliffe College, Boston. For the earliest published studies of Friedler's work, see Friedler and Wheeling 1979; Friedler 1985, 1987–88.
15. This is the earliest article I have found that suggests abnormal sperm may be capable of fertilization because, as researchers postulate, speed may be more important than size or shape to the ability of a sperm to fertilize an egg.
16. For comprehensive reviews of the literature on male-mediated reproductive toxicology, see Davis et at. 1992; Colie 1993; Friedler 1993; and Olshan and Faustman 1993.
17. Some of the earliest epidemiological research studied the effects of radiation exposures on children born to men who survived the atomic bombs at Nagasaki and Hiroshima. But few associations were found between paternal exposures and childhood health problems, possibly due to the fact that so few men conceived children in the immediate aftermath of the bombing (in the six months after exposure, when effects of radiation are strongest). See Yoshimoto 1990; and Olshan and Faustman 1993, 198.
18. For useful tables summarizing these epidemiological associations and for good discussions of the strengths and limitations of these studies, see Olshan and Faustman 1993; Savitz, Sonnenfeld, and Olshan 1994; and Wright 1996.
19. Studies of paternal smoking have also shown a strong link to lower birth weight for babies, in one study 8.4 ounces below average (if a father smoked two packs a day). See Davis 1991a, 123; Savitz and Sandler 1991, 123–32; Merewood 1992, 8; Zhang and Ratcliffe 1993; and Martinez et al. 1994.
20. See Little and Sing 1987; Colie 1993, 3–9; Friedler 1993; Olshan and Faustman 1993, 197; Cicero et al. 1994.
21. Index searches were done on Uncover and ProQuest up to 1993 under all appropriate terms for male reproductive risks and fetal harm, including but not limited to various combinations of the terms *sperm, fetal risks, male reproduction, men and occupational/environmental hazards, addiction, birth defects, male fertility,* etc.

22. The personification of sperm is not a new phenomenon, but one that has been resurrected in new form in the 1990s. In the seventeenth century, scientists theorized that sperm actually contained miniature versions of man. The tiny sperm homunculus entered the uterus and attached itself to the womb, where it was simply nurtured by the woman. In fact, it was not until the nineteenth century that science confirmed the existence and importance of the female egg to the reproductive process. See Davis et al. 1992, 290.
23. Emily Martin has noted, and this is certainly confirmed by my research, that descriptions of male reproduction are clearly obsessed with measurements of tubule length (Martin 1991).
24. On the question of male self-sacrifice, one *New York Times* article reported a study that suggested that the energy required to produce sperm significantly shortened the lives of earthworms and that the same might be true of men. Worms whose sperm production was suspended lived significantly longer than worms that produced sperm throughout their life cycle (Angier 1992b, A18).
25. Few popular articles present negative images of men and the effects of toxicity, and those that do have been almost exclusively in British journals. One story in the *Economist* linking paternal drinking to fetal harm (titled "Sins of the Fathers") contained an image of a father sleeping on a couch with a baby playing on the floor next to him, the caption reading "Daddy's Boy" (*Economist* 1991, 87). Another story in the British journal *New Scientist* contained a photo of a man smoking while holding an infant on his lap, with the caption, "Smoking fathers leave a legacy of damage" (Wright 1993, 10). In the American context, the only reference I have found to paternal-fetal conflict appeared in a 1992 *Hastings Center Report.*
26. In addition to the *New York Times* articles cited previously, these stories are *Atlanta Constitution* 1990, B2; Friend 1991, A1; 1996, A1; *New York Times* 1991a, B8; Perl 1991, F3; Scott 1991, A1; *Wall Street Journal* 1991, A1; 1996, B5; *Washington Post* 1991, A8; Merewood 1992; Schmidt 1992; Serrano 1994, A1; Moehringer 1995, A3; and Nesmith 1996, A14. One *New York Times* story reported that "Vitamin C Deficiency in a Man's Diet Might Cause Problems for Offspring" but mentioned cigarette smoking as a potential cause of the problem in only one line (*New York Times* 1992, C12).
27. Blakeslee 1991, 1; Davis 1991b, A27; *New York Times* 1991a, B8; 1991b, C5.
28. Calculated from indexes in the on-line catalog ProQuest.
29. Serrano 1994; Moehringer 1995, A1; Friend 1996, A3; Nesmith 1996, A1; *Wall Street Journal* 1996, B5.
30. While all pregnant women who smoke and drink are suspect, it is simply not possible to subject these women—of all races and classes—to prosecution. This is not to say that women have not been prosecuted for alcohol addiction. Such cases are detailed in my interview with Paltrow (n. 14 above).

References

Angier, Natalie. 1992a. "Odor Receptors Discovered in Sperm Cells." *New York Times,* January 30.

———. 1992b. "In Worm, at Least, Making Sperm Is Found to Shorten a Male's Life." *New York Times,* December 3.

Atlanta Constitution. 1990. "Use of Cocaine May Reduce Male Fertility, Study Indicates." *Atlanta Constitution,* February 14.

Baer, Judith A. 1978. *The Chains of Protection: The Judicial Response to Women's Labor Legislation.* Westport, Conn.: Greenwood.

Bingol, N., et al. 1987. "The Influence of Socioeconomic Factors on the Occurrence of Fetal Alcohol Syndrome." *Advances in Alcohol and Substance Abuse* 6(4):105–18.

Black, Rosemary, and Peter Moore. 1992. "The Myth of the Macho Sperm." *Parenting* 6(7):29–31.

Blank, Robert. 1993. *Fetal Protection in the Workplace: Women's Rights, Business Interests and the Unborn.* New York: Columbia University Press.

Brachen, M. B., B. Eshenazi, K. Sachse, J. E. McSharry, et al. 1990. "Association of Cocaine Use with Sperm Concentration, Motility and Morphology." *Fertility and Sterility* 53:315–22.

Brody, Jane E. 1988a. "Widespread Abuse of Drugs by Pregnant Women Is Found." *New York Times*, August 30.

———. 1988b. "Cocaine: Litany of Fetal Risks Grows." *New York Times*, September 6.

Browne, Malcolm W. 1988. "Some Thoughts on Self Sacrifice." *New York Times*, July 5.

Burger, Edward J., Jr., Robert G. Tardiff, Anthony R. Scialli, and Harold Zenick, eds. 1989. *Sperm Measures and Reproductive Success*. New York: Liss.

Chasnoff, Ira. 1989. "Drug Use and Women: Establishing a Standard of Care." *Annals of the New York Academy of Science* 562:208–10.

Cicero, Theodore J., Bruce Nock, Lynn H. O'Connor, Bryan N. Sewing, Michael L. Adams, and E. Robert Meyer. 1994. "Acute Paternal Alcohol Exposure Impairs Fertility and Fetal Outcome." *Life Sciences* 55:33–36.

Colie, Christine F. 1993. "Male Mediated Teratogenesis." *Reproductive Toxicology* 7:3–9.

Corea, Gena. 1992. *The Invisible Epidemic*. New York: Basic.

Crenshaw, Kimberle. 1993. "Whose Story Is It, Anyway? Feminist and Antiracist Appropriations of Anita Hill." In *Race-ing Justice, En-gendering Power*, ed. Toni Morrison, 402–40. London: Chatto & Windus.

Daniels, Cynthia R. 1991. "Competing Gender Paradigms: Gender Difference, Fetal Rights and the Case of Johnson Controls." *Policy Studies Review* 10(4):51–68.

———. 1993. *At Women's Expense: State Power and the Politics of Fetal Rights*. Cambridge, Mass.: Harvard University Press.

Davis, Devra Lee. 1991a. "Paternal Smoking and Fetal Health." *Lancet* 337 (January 12): 123.

———. 1991b. "Fathers and Fetuses." *New York Times*, March 1.

Davis, Devra Lee, Gladys Friedler, Donald Mattison, and Robert Morris. 1992. "Male-Mediated Teratogenesis and Other Reproductive Effects: Biological and Epidemiologic Findings and a Plea for Clinical Research." *Reproductive Toxicology* 6:289–92.

Dicker, Marvin, and Eldin Leighton. 1990. "Trends in Diagnosed Drug Problems among Newborns: United States, 1979–1987." Paper presented at the annual meeting of the American Public Health Association, New York City, November.

Discover. 1987. "The Existential Decision of a Sperm." *Discover*, August, 10–11.

Economist. 1991. "Sins of the Fathers." *Economist*, February 23, 87.

El-Gothamy, Zenab, and May El-Samahy. 1992. "Ultrastructure Sperm Defects in Addicts." *Fertility and Sterility* 57(3):699–702.

Fraser, Nancy. 1989. *Unruly Practices: Power, Discourse, and Gender in Contemporary Social Theory*. Minneapolis: University of Minnesota Press.

Friedler, Gladys. 1985. "Effects of Limited Paternal Exposure to Xenobiotic Agents on the Development of Progeny." *Neurobehavioral Toxicology and Teratology* 7:739–43.

———. 1987–88. "Effects on Future Generations of Paternal Exposure to Alcohol and Other Drugs." *Alcohol Health and Research World*, Winter, 126–29.

———. 1993. "Developmental Toxicology: Male-Mediated Effects." In *Occupational and Environmental Reproductive Hazards*, ed. Maureen Paul, 52–59. Baltimore: Williams & Wilkins.

Friedler, Gladys, and Howard S. Wheeling. 1979. "Behavioral Effects in Offspring of Male Mice Injected with Opioids Prior to Mating." In *Protracted Effects of Perinatal Drug Dependence*, vol. 2, *Pharmacology, Biochemistry and Behavior*, S23–S28. Fayetteville, N.Y.: ANKHO International.

Friend, Tim. 1991. "Sperm May Carry Cocaine to Egg." *USA Today*, October 9.

———. 1992. "Sperm Follow Their Noses." *USA Today*, January 30.

Hall, Stuart. 1982. "The Rediscovery of 'Ideology': Return of the Repressed in Media Studies." In *Culture, Society and the Media*, ed. Michael Gurevitch, Tony Bennett, James Curran, and Janet Woollacott, 56–90. New York: Methuen.

Hastings Center Report. 1992. "Paternal-Fetal Conflict." *Hastings Center Report*, March/April, 3.

Holly, Elizabeth, Diana Aston, David Ahn, and Jennifer Kristiansen. 1992. "Ewing's Bone Sarcoma, Paternal Occupational Exposure, and Other Factors." *American Journal of Epidemiology* 135:122–29.

Kenney, Sally. 1992. *For Whose Protection? Reproductive Hazards and Exclusionary Policies in the United States and Britain*. Ann Arbor: University of Michigan Press.

Kessler-Harris, Alice. 1982. *Out to Work*. New York: Oxford University Press.

Kharrazi, M., G. Patashnik, and J. R. Goldsmith. 1980. "Reproductive Effects of Dibromochloropropane." *Israel Journal of Medical Science* 16:403–6.

Koren, Gideon, K. Graham, H. Shear, and T. Einarson. 1989. "Bias against the Null Hypothesis." *Lancet* 2(8677):1440–42.

Koren, G., and N. Klein. 1991. "Bias against Negative Studies in Newspaper Reports of Medical Research." *Journal of the American Medical Association* 266(13):1824–26.

Lehrer, Susan. 1987. *Origins of Protective Labor Legislation.* Albany, N.Y.: SUNY Press.

Lindbohm, Marja-Lusa, Kari Hemminki, Michele G. Bonhomme, Ahti Anttila, Kaarina Rantala, Pirjo Heikkila, and Michael J. Rosenberg. 1991. "Effects of Paternal Occupational Exposure on Spontaneous Abortions." *American Journal of Public Health* 81:1029–33.

Little, R. E., and C. F. Sing. 1987. "Father's Drinking and Infant Birth Weight: Report of an Association." *Teratology* 36:59–65.

Lubiano, Wahneema. 1992. "Black Ladies, Welfare Queens, and State Minstrels: Ideological War by Narrative Means." In *Race-ing Justice, En-gendering Power,* ed. Toni Morrison, 323–63. London: Chatto & Windus.

Mack, Arien, ed. 1991. *In Time of Plague.* New York: New York University Press.

Martinez, Fernando, Anne Wright, Lynn Taussig, and the Group Health Medical Associates. 1994. "The Effect of Paternal Smoking on the Birthweight of Newborns Whose Mothers Did Not Smoke." *American Journal of Public Health* 84:1489–91.

Mason, George. 1991. "Female Infidelity—May the Best Sperm Win." *New Scientist,* January, 29.

McDonagh, Eileen. 1993. "Good, Bad and Captive Samaritans: Adding in Pregnancy and Consent to the Abortion Debate." *Women and Politics* 13(3/4):31–49.

Merewood, Anne. 1991. "Sperm under Siege." *Health,* April, 53–76.

———. 1992. "Studies Reveal Men's Role in Producing Healthy Babies." *Chicago Tribune,* January 12.

Miller, Susan Katz. 1992. "Can Children Be Damaged by Fathers' Cancer Therapy?" *New Scientist* 135:5.

Mitchell, John L. 1991. "Billboard's Message Is Graphically Anti-Drug." *Los Angeles Times,* March 30.

Moore, Harry. 1989. "Sperm You Can Count On." *New Scientist,* June 10, 38–91.

Nesmith, Jeff. 1996. "Studies Link Agent Orange to Birth Defects in Children of Vietnam Vets. *Atlanta Constitution,* March 15.

New York Times. 1991a. "Study Links Cancer in Young to Father's Smoking." *New York Times,* January 24.

———. 1991b. "Cocaine-Using Fathers Linked to Birth Defects." *New York Times,* October 15.

———. 1992. "Vitamin C Deficiency in a Man's Diet Might Cause Problems for Offspring." *New York Times,* February 12.

Olshan, Andrew F., and Elaine M. Faustman. 1993. "Male-Mediated Developmental Toxicity." *Reproductive Toxicology* 7:191–202.

O'Neill, Anne Marie, Leah Eskin, and Linda Satter. 1996. "Under the Influence." *People,* September 9, 53–55.

Paltrow, Lynn. 1992. "Criminal Prosecutions against Pregnant Women: National Update and Overview." Center for Reproductive Law and Policy, New York City.

Perl, Rebecca. 1991. "Cocaine May Travel to Egg through Sperm, Study Says." *Atlanta Constitution,* October 9.

Poovey, Mary. 1988. *Uneven Developments.* Chicago: University of Chicago Press.

Poppy, John. 1989. "Upwardly Motile: A Man's Guide to Raising Healthier, Heartier, Happier Sperm." *Esquire,* June, 67–70.

Robinson, James C. 1991. *Toil and Toxics: Workplace Struggles and Political Strategies for Occupational Health.* Berkeley and Los Angeles: University of California Press.

Savitz, D., and J. Chen. 1990. "Parental Occupation and Childhood Cancer: Review of Epidemiological Studies." *Environmental Health Perspectives* 88:325–37.

Savitz, D., and D. P. Sandler. 1991. "Prenatal Exposure to Parents' Smoking and Childhood Cancer." *American Journal of Epidemiology* 133:123–32.

Savitz, D., P. J. Schwingle, and M. A. Keels. 1991. "Influence of Paternal Age, Smoking and Alcohol Consumption on Congenital Anomalies." *Teratology* 44:429–40.

Savitz, D., Nancy Sonnenfeld, and Andrew Olshan. 1994. "Review of Epidemiologic Studies of Paternal Occupational Exposure and Spontaneous Abortion." *American Journal of Industrial Medicine* 25:361–83.

Schmidt, Karen F. 1992. "The Dark Legacy of Fatherhood." *U.S. News and World Report,* December 14, 92–96.

Schneider, Anne, and Helen Ingram. 1993. "Social Construction of Target Populations: Implications for Politics and Policy." *American Political Science Review* 87(2):334–47.

Schroedel, Jean Reith, and Paul Peretz. 1993. "A Gender Analysis of Policy Formation: The Case of Fetal Abuse." Paper presented at the Western Political Science Association meeting, Pasadena, Calif., March 18–20.

Scialli, Anthony. 1993. "Paternally Mediated Effects and Political Correctness." *Reproductive Toxicology* 7:189–90.

Scott, Janny. 1991. "Study Finds Cocaine Can Bind to Sperm." *Los Angeles Times,* October 9.

Singer, Linda. 1993. *Erotic Welfare.* New York: Routledge.

Stone, Andrea. 1989. "It's 'Tip of the Iceberg' in Protecting Infants." *USA Today,* August 25.

Treichler, Paula A. 1990. "Feminism, Medicine and the Meaning of Childbirth." In *Body/Politics: Women and the Discourses of Science,* ed. Mary Jacobus, Evelyn Fox Keller, and Sally Shuttleworth, 113–38. New York: Routledge.

Tuchman, Gaye. 1978. *Making the News.* New York: Free Press.

———. 1983. "Consciousness Industries and the Production of Culture." *Journal of Communications* 33(3):330–41.

———. 1993. "Realism and Romance: The Study of Media Effects." *Journal of Communications* 43(4):36–41.

Vigue, Doreen Iudica. 1996. "Pregnant Woman Booked for Drinking." *Boston Globe,* August 15.

Wall Street Journal. 1991. "World-Wide: Fathers Who Smoke." *Wall Street Journal,* January 24.

———. 1996. "Birth Defects May Relate to Agent Orange Herbicide." *Wall Street Journal,* March 15.

Washington Post. 1991. "Fathers' Smoking May Damage Sperm." *Washington Post,* January 25.

Women and AIDS Book Group. 1990. *Women, AIDS and Activism.* Boston: South End.

Wright, Lawrence.1996. "Silent Sperm." *New Yorker,* January 15, 42–55.

Yazigi, Ricardo A., Randall R. Odem, and Kenneth L. Polakoski. 1991. "Demonstration of Specific Binding of Cocaine to Human Spermatozoa." *Journal of the American Medical Association* 266:1956–59.

Yoshimoto, Y. 1990. "Cancer Risk among Children of Atomic Bomb Survivors: A Review of RERF Epidemiologic Studies." *Journal of the American Medical Association* 264:596–600.

Zhang, Jun, and Jennifer Ratcliffe. 1993. "Paternal Smoking and Birthweight in Shanghai." *American Journal of Public Health* 83:207–10.

Zuckerman, Barry. 1991. "Drug-Exposed Infants: Understanding the Medical Risk." *Future of Children* 1 (Spring): 26–35.

FEMINIST AI PROJECTS AND CYBERFUTURES

Alison Adam

Feminist research can have a pessimistic cast. In charting and uncovering constructions of gender, it invariably displays the way in which the masculine is construed as the norm and the feminine as lesser, the other and absent. This work is no different in that respect. . . . But as both Tong (1994) and Wajcman (1991) argue, feminism is a political project and the best research is where action proceeds from description. Taking that on board for the present project involves not just using feminist approaches to criticize, but also the more difficult task of thinking through the ways in which AI research *could* be informed by feminist theory, and I make some suggestions below as to the form such research might take.

A second part of that action concerns the question of locating an appropriate feminist response to the burgeoning interest in the cultures surrounding intelligent information technologies. This includes not only AI but also the currently fashionable technologies of Virtual Reality (VR) and the Internet, both involving and related to longer established techniques from AI. Here the issue is marrying the analysis of the preceding chapters to the areas of intelligent software technology which are currently exciting considerable levels of commentary. The challenge then becomes charting a course between the Scylla of a 'nothing changes' pessimism and the Charybdis of a gushingly unrealistic 'fabulous feminist future' (Squires 1996).

FEMINIST AI PROJECTS

The fact that AI projects consciously informed by feminist concepts are thin on the ground is hardly surprising (but see e.g. Metselaar 1991). Having set up a few small projects over a period of years I have found myself questioning just what I was trying to do. I knew I was not trying to somehow 'convert' male colleagues to my way of thinking. I have never seen either my own work, or the mass of feminist literature I have consulted along the way, as proselytizing attempts to convince recalcitrant men. I can understand how feminist writers who elicit the popular response of 'that won't convince many men', are irritated by the naivety of such comments and the way they miss the point of their endeavour. But women academics working in technological departments face pressures either not to do such work at all or only to address certain aspects. These pressures can range from whispers of 'not exactly mainstream' (which because it is a whisper I mishear as 'not exactly malestream') to actually being told not to pursue such work if they want to maintain their career prospects.[1]

Almost the only kind of work which attracts a level of respectability for women working within science and technology departments, at least in the UK, involves WISE (women into science and engineering) type attempts to attract more women and girls into the subject area; for instance, I have found male peers puzzled if I do not make myself available for university-run women into science and engineering workshops. 'I thought that's what you were interested in.' This is the acceptable face of liberal feminism (Henwood 1993) where the *status quo* is left unchallenged, where women constitute the problem, for not entering computing in the numbers that they should, and where almost any attempt to boost student numbers in an underfunded and over-stretched university environment is seen as a good thing.

However those of us not prepared to wear the acceptable face of feminism return to our 'not exactly malestream' projects. Those who do projects such as these are making a statement; namely that this is research that matters, that deserves to be taken seriously and that its qualities should be judged on its own merits. And this takes more courage than many of us could reasonably be expected to muster, given the pressures I describe, and the fact that many do not have the luxury of permanent 'tenured' positions in their institutions.

If such work is not undertaken in the spirit of evangelism neither does it properly fit the notion of the successor science of the standpoint theorists (Harding 1991). This is because it is not trying to build an alternative 'successor' AI. It is, rather, and more modestly, showing ways in which AI can be informed by feminist theory and can be used for feminist projects. As Jansen (1992: 11) puts it so colourfully, it is in the spirit of 'feminist semiological guerrilla warfare . . . to transform the metaphors and models of science'. Additionally, paraphrasing Audre Lorde's (1984) metaphor it would be nice 'to demolish the master's house with the master's tools.'[2] This requires a great deal of imagination. Undeniably there are contradictions. I am reminded of the occasion when a man asked at a gender and technology workshop, 'How would a fighter plane designed by a feminist look any different?'[3] If my immediate response would be that feminists do not design fighter planes then perhaps I should acknowledge that feminists do not design AI applications either. But this will not do as it loses sight of the political project. Hoping for change means showing how change can be made no matter how modest the beginnings.

The projects I describe below are indeed quite small. Such projects do not attract research funding and must often be tackled within the confines of final year undergraduate and masters (MSc) level dissertations. This means that individual projects are short and continuity between one project and another is difficult. I also want to make it clear that my role in these projects was as originator and supervisor, and that the results and many of the ideas and novel questions which emerged belong to the individuals who tackled the projects, most notably Chloe Furnival (1993) for the law project and Maureen Scott (1996) for the linguistics project, both of which are described below.

Some interesting problems emerge. Almost all of the students who have attempted the projects are women; the one man who built some software for teaching the history of the First and Second World Wars had to remind *me* that I had originally cast the project in terms of achieving a less gender biased approach to teaching history. As the project proceeded, I had unconsciously assumed that he was not really interested in the gender aspects, and had mentally 'written them out' of his project for him—hoist by my own petard. The women who have worked on these projects are computing students, though several are conversion masters degree students who have a humanities or social science first degree, and who generally have little background in feminist theory. There is no doubt that this makes for a difficult project, for not only do I ask that they get to grips with a new subject matter, but also it is a subject matter which requires a way of thinking completely different from the technical paradigm within which they have begun to work. In addition they are often expected to apply this to the production of a software model. But it is interesting and heartening that they invariably become absorbed by the feminist literature and usually have to be persuaded not to read any more, to get on with the business of pulling the project together. Apart from anything else it allows me to relive the excitement of my own arrival at feminism.

AI AND FEMINIST LEGAL THEORY

One of the most fertile areas for research into AI applications in recent years has been the law (see e.g. Bench-Capon 1991). Part of the appeal of the law is the way that, on the surface, legal statutes appear to offer ready-made rules to put into expert systems. A 'pragmatist/purist' debate has crystallized around this issue. Purists (e.g. Leith 1986) argue that there are no clear legal rules, the meaning of a rule is made in its interpretation, and that legal rules are necessarily and incurably 'open-textured'. We cannot know, in advance, all the cases to which a rule should apply, hence its meaning is built up through its interpretation in courts of law.

A good example, which illustrates these difficulties, was reported in the British media as I was considering this question. A woman who wished to be inseminated with her dead husband's sperm had taken her case to the High Court. Before he died the couple had been trying to have a baby. They had discussed a different case where sperm had been extracted from a dying man to inseminate his wife, and agreed that they would do the same if ever in this position. Tragically the man fell ill with bacterial meningitis. His sperm was extracted by physicians as he lay dying. However a High Court ruling was made that she could not be inseminated because, crucially, her husband's signature was never obtained; it could not have been, as he was in a coma when the sperm was removed. Mary Warnock, architect of the relevant legislation, stated that the committee which drafted the Human Fertility and Embryology Bill would certainly have permitted this case, but had never foreseen that a case like this would occur and so had not allowed for it in the statute (see the *Guardian*, 18 October 1996: 1).

Pragmatists, as the name suggests, believe that it is possible to represent legal rules meaningfully, although it is hardly a trivial task. Unsurprisingly pragmatists tend to be drawn from the ranks of computer scientists who favour predicate logic and its variants for the representation of truths in the world. Either way, it can be argued that legal expert systems embody traditional views on jurisprudence, by analogy with prior arguments on traditional epistemology and expert systems.[4] Just as feminist epistemology offers a challenge to traditional epistemology, so too does feminist jurisprudence offer a significant challenge to more traditional forms of jurisprudence. The aim of the project I describe here was to build a legal expert system to advise on UK Sex Discrimination Law founded on principles from feminist jurisprudence. It was envisaged that this system could be used by individuals, many of whom would be women, who would have little knowledge of this area of the law or of past cases which might resemble their case. Was the end product informed by these principles distinguishable from an equivalent project not founded on these principles? As the scale of the project was such that the end product was never used in a practical setting, it is not possible to answer this question definitively. In any case I argue that it was the path to the product, the journey not the destination, which was important in acting as an example of an AI informed by feminism.

Although developing in parallel ways, feminist jurisprudence appears a more practically orientated discipline than much writing in feminist epistemology, in its aim to integrate legal theory with political practice. Both disciplines have moved on from exposing violations of equal rights and sexist biases to become mature philosophical disciplines in their own right. In thinking about the women's movement in relation to the law, two areas stand out. First, there is women's use of the law to promote their rights, with the achievement of often partial liberal measures ironically reinforcing women's oppression rather than undoing it. Second, there is the potentially more radical effort of feminist jurisprudence, which seeks to question the naturalness of legal power and knowledge, foundational beliefs about the law, and the way that legal reasoning transforms the imagined examples from male lives into a form of doctrine taken to be objective and normative (MacKinnon 1982; 1983; Grbich 1991).

Furnival (1993) points out that UK Sex Discrimination Law provides a good example of the use of these ideas in practice, particularly when we note that it is up to the individual to prove that her rights have been violated (Smart 1989: 144–6; Palmer 1992: 6). Linda Sanford and Mary Donovan (1993: 200) argue that many women have so little sense of themselves as persons with rights, that they experience considerable difficulty in recognizing when their rights have been violated. Other women may recognize that their rights are being transgressed in some way, but cannot bring themselves to make a complaint as this might brand them 'troublemakers'. Under the circumstances, any computer system designed to advise women on this area of the law would have to be presented as an unthreatening adviser which could show a client that she may have a case by analogy with past cases. The balance is important. It is unfair to offer users hope of legal redress for hopeless cases as the process of making and winning a case rests on an existing order, no matter how feminist the principles on which the system was built. On the other hand, offering examples of past cases which bear some resemblance to the present case leaves the question of whether or not to proceed open to the users, rather than making a decision for them. It is important not to make too grand a claim for what is, after all, a modest piece of work and this recognizes that considerably larger resources would be required to test out the hypotheses contained in this research.

FEMINIST COMPUTATIONAL LINGUISTICS

Given the growing interest in gender and language, computational models of language provide a potentially fertile ground for feminist projects. If feminist linguistic models challenge the models of traditional views of language, then how might this challenge be incorporated into the design of an AI system which analyses language? The project reported in this section sought to add a gender dimension to software tools which model conversational analysis (Scott 1996). This involved criticizing and augmenting a model of the repair of conversational misunderstandings and non-understandings (Heeman and Hirst 1995; Hirst et al. 1994; McRoy and Hirst 1995). The end product of the project was a formal (i.e. logic-based) model which could potentially be used to predict the outcomes of inter-gender miscommunications, and which forms the basis for a design of a computer system which could be built to perform the same task.

Why should anyone want to build computational models of language? There are a number of reasons why the ability to represent natural language in a computer system would be desirable. First of all, a highly useful application could be found in providing natural language interfaces to existing computers systems, e.g. spreadsheets, databases, operating systems or indeed anywhere where it is currently necessary to know a series of commands. Automatic abstracting, automatic translation, intelligent language based searches for information—all these hold promise.

Part of the process of understanding language is to understand when there has been a misunderstanding between speakers and to repair that misunderstanding in a meaningful way when it occurs. This is, once again, suggestive of Collins's (1990) and Suchman's (1987) assertions that the reason that machines do not share our form of life rests upon the 'interpretative asymmetry' which exists in the interactions between humans and machines. Human beings are good at making sense of the bits and pieces of ordinary conversations, the half sentences, the 'ums' and 'ers', and so on; so good that they can make sense of almost anything and they are not easily put off. As yet, computers do not have this ability and until they do, an asymmetry in the ability to interpret utterances will remain. Hence a computer system which had some ability to repair natural language misunderstandings would clearly be of benefit in tackling this asymmetry in interpretative powers. However, the point is whether or not it is realistic to believe that a machine that can understand natural language is possible. Clearly some, such as Searle (1987), Dreyfus (1992) and Collins (1990), do not regard it as realistic. But even if, by analogy with their arguments, a full natural language understanding system might not be a possibility, then, just as expert systems can still be useful where we provide much of the nexus of understanding and background knowledge, so too could a partial natural language-processing interface be of considerable interest.

The project was inspired by an example of the finessing away of 'social factors' which is such a pervasive feature of AI and computing in general. In putting together their model of conversational misunderstanding, Graeme Hirst and his colleagues (Hirst et al. 1994) appear to have removed the subtle nuances which made the interaction into a misunderstanding in the first place. The aspect which I examine here relates to gender. Yet there are clearly many others. Race and class are two obvious dimensions; age and size are two others. This is another situation in which embodiment is important, because, of course, the speakers are bodied individuals interacting in all sorts of physical ways connected to their linguistic utterances. For instance, the following reported misunderstanding (ibid.: 227) involves, at the least, age and gender.

> *Speaker A:* Where's CSC104 taught?
> *Speaker B:* Sidney Smith Building, room 2118, but the class is full.
> *Speaker A:* No, I teach it.

Hirst (ibid.) describes how the misunderstanding occurs. Speaker B assumes that A's plan is to take course CSC104, when in fact her plan is to teach it. However a number of salient facts within this example are not revealed by reading the written text alone. At the time of the reported misunderstanding, speaker A was a graduate student, and in her twenties, while B was a male administrator. Age seems to have had something to do with the misunderstanding: speaker A was young enough, and female enough, to be mistaken for a student.

An older speaker A might or might not have had the same problem-perhaps she would have been mistaken for a student's mother instead! It is interesting to speculate, in a society which values signs of youth in women, whether there might be some value in attempting to gain authority by appearing older. But this only serves to show how complex is the relationship between gender and age. True, A as a young man might have the same problem. But I wonder if a middle-aged male A would have fared differently. And what about the gender of B? The mantle of authority which men assume as they grow older is much harder for women to acquire. Women may be perceived as 'menopausal', which in Western society is almost always seen as pejorative rather than authoritative in middle life.[5] There are different ways of not taking a woman seriously which may vary according to her perceived stage in life. Hence I argue that the meaning of the misunderstanding is not readily available to us unless we have some means of reading between the lines in this way.

The large body of literature on gender and language which now exists provided a useful backdrop against which to locate this project. Chapter four noted that Spender's (1980) and Lakoff's (1975) work exerted considerable influence in the assertiveness industry of the 1980s. However, for this example, a much more pertinent body of work can be found in Deborah Tannen's research (1988; 1992; 1994), some of which is aimed at a more popular market. Most pertinently, *You Just Don't Understand* (Tannen 1992), demonstrates the sheer complexity of male and female linguistic interaction. Coupled with this, Pamela Fishman (1983) suggests that there are a number of interesting features about the way that men and women approach a conversation. She argues that women put in much more effort than men in initiating and maintaining a conversation. She also maintains that women are most often the agents of repair in misunderstandings in mixed (i.e. between men and women) conversations. If this is the case, then there is a good argument for a natural language understanding system which aims to repair speech understanding, to look at women's models of repair, if indeed they are the experts.

The complexities of men's and women's linguistic interactions are such that it seems impossible to uncover the layers of meaning in conversational misunderstandings in a model which is gender blind. For instance, Tannen (1992) offers a number of examples of misunderstandings which can only be made understandable in the light of the genders of the participants.

Hirst and his colleagues' research on the analysis of mis- and non-understandings includes a number of top-level action schemas which are used to describe the actions of the parties in a conversation. These include things like accept-plan(NameOfPlan) which signals the speaker's acceptance of the plan and reject-plan(NameOfPlan) which signals that the speaker is rejecting the plan which is being offered by the other speaker. These top-level schemas are decomposable into surface linguistic actions.

Combining Tannen's (1992) analyses with Hirst's research (Hirst et al. 1994), Scott (1996) suggests that there are a number of distinct patterns in the forms of female to female, male to male and mixed conversations so that a predictive model can be developed, that is, she claims that it is possible to predict the response expected to each form, following particular gender patterns. As women work harder to maintain a conversation, this suggests that a woman will avoid terminating a conversation using reject-plan as a man might do; instead she might use postpone, expand or replace to elicit another response from her conversant. With this revised format, Scott was able to produce more exact analyses of a number of conversations. Using the new model in the design of a conversation analysis tool gives a potential for misunderstandings to be predicted. Knowing the genders of the conversants, if a man responds with a form that is not expected by a woman, or *vice versa,* an analysis tool would recognize the beginnings of a misunderstanding possibly even before the participants can.

In this description, I am aware of the dangers inherent in suggesting that women's and men's linguistic interactions follow universal patterns. This is clearly not the case. Indeed the model described here is a white, middle-class, Anglo-American English one, which probably does not even fit, for example, New York Jewish speech, where interruptions are more common (Tannen 1994). It cannot be claimed that the model would suit cultures outside those for which it was designed. Yet making the cultural roots of the model explicit serves to underline the difficulties of generalizing linguistic misunderstanding.[6]

CONTRADICTIONS AND POSSIBILITIES

In reporting these two projects I am aware of unresolved contradictions. The computer systems that were designed and built were just as disembodied and unsituated, relying on the same symbolic representation structures as those I have criticized in preceding chapters. In going through this reflexive process I begin to understand the traditional plea of the computer scientist: 'we had to start somewhere'. And there seems to me no choice but to start where we did. Even if, *pace* Lorde (1984: 110), we may suspect that 'the master's tools will never dismantle the master's house', there are as yet no other tools and we cannot know unless we try. In the law project it could be argued that we have an example of a 'fighter plane designed by a feminist', in other words something which does not look substantially different from a computer system designed along more traditional lines. At the nuts and bolts level of the computer program it would be hard to point definitively at perceived differences. I have argued that it is the way the system is to be used which is different. Yet at the same time I concede that this project uses entirely conventional techniques of knowledge representation and programming, which I have criticized as being unable to capture all the important things about knowledge, especially women's knowledge. So in a real sense I am criticizing the projects in which I am involved for at least some of the same reasons that I am criticizing conventional AI projects. But I do not mean this criticism to be interpreted as an argument not to do the work at all, for either my own or other AI projects. I would follow the lead of Brooks (1991) and his colleagues, who in acknowledging the enormous problems involved in building Cog, nevertheless argue that they had to start somewhere.

Some of the same contradictions are inherent in the linguistics project. The first, more particular, concern involves the critique of the relationship between modern linguistics and predicate logic, following Nye (1992) (discussed in chapter four), given that this project follows the logic of the original research, albeit while suggesting modifications and amendments. The original could have been criticized without offering these alternatives, but I suggest that then the critique would have lost much of its force; it is important to criticize these pieces of work both from the point of view of feminism and in their own terms (i.e. 'using the master's tools').

The second concern mirrors a recent controversy arising from Suchman's (1994b) criticism of Winograd's (1994) Coordinator system. Some of Suchman's earlier writing (1987) would seem to argue against the way that, following Hirst's original logic, we saw the conversational interactions in terms of 'plans'. This is developed in her later argument which is directed against the way that speech act theory has been encapsulated in the language/action perspective described in *Understanding Computers and Cognition* (Winograd and Flores 1986), and the way that this is exemplarized in the Coordinator system. The two basic concepts in speech act theory are that language is a form of action and second, that language and action can be represented formally—they are, in principle, amenable to representation by a computer system. Under this view, Suchman (1994b: 179) argues that language is treated as instrumental, 'a technology employed by the individual to express his or her intentions to others'. The Coordinator system is one of the best known attempts to implement these ideas in a computer system. It asks speakers to make the content of a given utterance explicit by categorizing it from a range of options. The problem is that the adoption of speech act theory as a foundation for the design of computer systems brings with it an agenda of discipline and control over the actions of members of an organization.

Suchman points to the way that communication is taken to be the exchange of intent between speakers and hearers in speech act theory but she argues that the analyses of actual conversations demonstrate the interactional, contingent nature of conversation (Suchman 1994b). So a speaker's intent is always shaped by the response of the hearer. This has led commentators such as John Bowers and John Churcher (1988) to the conclusion that human discourse is so indeterminate that any computer system designed to track the course of an interaction by projecting organized sequences will inevitably, albeit unwittingly, coerce the users. The Coordinator system tries to get round this difficulty by having users categorize their utterances themselves in order to make implicit intention explicit. This allows them to set up a basic structure around the idea of 'conversation for action', entailing requests, promises, declarations (Suchman 1994b: 183–4).

> The picture of the basic conversation for action unifies and mathematizes the phenomena it represents. It works by transforming a set of colloquial expressions into a formal system of categorization that relies upon organization members' willingness to re-formulate their actions in its (now technical) vocabulary. . . . Once encapsulated and reduced to the homogeneous black circles and arrows of the diagram the 'conversation' is findable anywhere. At the same time, the specific occasions of conversation are no longer open to characterization in any other terms.
>
> (ibid.: 185)

Yet, as Suchman argues, such a process reduces the complexity of the actions being categorized to the simplicity of the category. This, then, suggests that the Coordinator is a tool to bring its users into the compliance of an established social order, so the designers of computer systems become designers of organizations.

Clearly, arguments such as these could apply equally well to the design of the modest system I have described above. We were attempting to categorize the utterances in conversations between men and women, albeit according to models developed by feminist linguists. At the same time we were making some sort of claim our model was better than the original version which failed to take account of gender and other factors. So we were claiming that our model was at least potentially better in explanatory power and predictive power, that is, it could be used to predict what sort of response would be likely in inter-gender conversations. Although currently far from this stage, if our model were ever implemented in a natural language computer system used in an organizational setting, we might well find ourselves introducing a computer system which preserved stereotypical expectations of interactions and thus preserved an existing social order and power structure. I find myself impaled on the horns of a dilemma where a weak 'I had to start somewhere' will hardly suffice to prise me off.

CYBERCULTURE

Practical AI projects informed by feminist ideals offer one view of how we can begin to think about future directions for intelligent systems. However there are other, broader, ways of thinking about the future in terms of intelligent computer technology and feminism. The alternative route is via 'cyberculture', the term used to describe the explosion of interest in cultures developing round virtual reality (VR), the Internet and including AI and A-Life, many of which speaks in a markedly futuristic voice. Few cultural commentators can fail to marvel at the extraordinary efflorescence of cyberculture—a burgeoning interest from the social sciences has quickly spawned a number of anthologies (Aronowitz, Martinsons and Menser 1996; Benedikt 1994; Dovey 1996; Ess 1996; Featherstone and Burrows 1995; Gray 1995; Shields 1996). And indeed it is marked by a number of interesting features, not least of all its relationship to feminism.

First of all, in its popular form it is a youth culture. At first sight it appears to go against the grain of a more general world-view which is sceptical about the progress of science and technology; a number of prominent scientists are aware of this malaise to the extent that they wish to set up a counter-attack (Gross and Levitt 1994). Cyberculture appeals to youth, particularly young men. Clearly it appeals to their interest in the technical gadgetry of computer technology, and in this it has been strongly influenced by the 'cyberpunk genre' of science fiction, which although offering a distinctly dystopian vision of the future, at least offers alternative heroes in the form of the macho 'console cowboys'. To 'jack in' to 'cyberspace' appears to offer a way of transcending the mere 'meat' of the body, once again signalling the male retreat from bodies and places where bodies exist.

Jacking in, *cyberspace* and *meat* are metonymic cyberpunk terms which have entered the lexicon of cyberculture, many of them from William Gibson's (1984) *Neuromancer*, the first cyberpunk novel. In *Neuromancer*, the hero, Case, logs onto, or jacks into, cyberspace through a special socket implanted in his brain. Cyberspace is a shared virtual reality, a 'consensual hallucination' where the body that one chooses to enter within cyberspace has bodily sensations and can travel in the virtual reality. Meat-free, but sinister artificial intelligences inhabit cyberspaces, having finally downloaded themselves and having left their obsolete, merely meat, bodies behind. But these images are a far cry from contemporary cyberspace and the current mundanities of logging onto a computer, and of experiencing the Internet, often rather slowly, through the interface of screen and keyboard.

A BODY-FREE EXISTENCE

The relevance of the body is demonstrated by Stone's (1994: 113) observation.

> The discourse of visionary virtual world builders is rife with images of imaginal bodies freed from the constraints that flesh imposes. Cyberspace developers foresee a time when they will be able to forget about the body. But it is important to remember that virtual community originates in, and must return to the physical. No refigured virtual body, no matter how beautiful, will slow the death of a cyberpunk with AIDS. Even in the age of the technosocial subject, life is lived through bodies.

One wonders what sort of bodies virtual reality developers will have in store for us. For instance, Thalmann and Thalmann (1994) picture a perfect, blonde, red-lipped Marilyn Monroe lookalike seemingly without irony. And writing as a prominent mainstream AI roboticist, apparently quite separately from and rather earlier than cybercultural influences, Moravec (1988) has proposed the idea of *Mind Children*. Moravec's opinions belong more to the realm of the science fiction writers than to hard-nosed engineering based roboticists, for he envisions a 'postbiological' world where:

> the human race has been swept away by the tide of cultural change, usurped by its own artificial progeny. . . . Today, our machines are still simple creations, requiring the parental care and hovering attention of any newborn, hardly worthy of the word 'intelligent.' But within the next century they will mature into entities as complex as ourselves, and eventually into something transcending everything we know—in whom we can take pride when they refer to themselves as our descendants.
>
> (ibid.: 1)

Moravec's style is heavily informed by a sociobiology untempered by his uncritical enthusiasm for all things AI. Our DNA, he suggests, will find itself out of a job when the machines take over—robots with human intelligence will be common within fifty years. Of course, futuristic pronouncements such as this are always safe bets: make them far enough ahead and you will not be around to be challenged when the time is up; closer predictions can always be revised if the deadline expires before the prediction comes true.

But I think there are two important issues at stake in projecting a body-free existence. The first concerns birth, the second escape, which is discussed in the following section. Moravec sees his robots as his progeny and this has strong parallels with the way that Brooks sees his robot baby, Cog, as a child to be brought up. Do these roboticists have real children?[7] Feminists might question *why* they feel the need to have robot children. Coming from a different direction, Easlea (1983) has noted the prevalence of sexual and birth metaphors in the development of the atomic bomb in the Manhattan project. During the testing of the bomb, the question was whether there would be a violent explosion rather than a relatively harmless radioactive fizzle. In the terminology of the Los Alamos scientists, the problem was to give birth to a 'boy' and not to a 'girl' (ibid.: 94).

> Alas, as Mary Shelley persuasively suggests in *Frankenstein,* an obsessive male desire to outdo women in creative ability can only too easily lead to tragic consequences. . . . To his credit, however, Frankenstein did try to 'give birth' to a *living* thing. The Los Alamos scientists . . . were attempting to give birth to the most potent instruments of death then conceivable, two nuclear weapons which they affectionately christened with the male names, Little Boy and Fat Man. But, like Frankenstein, the physicists found that the challenge of creating a 'monster' is one thing; the challenge of keeping control over it in a masculine world is quite another.
>
> (ibid.: 97–8)

The metaphor of 'the pregnant phallus' seems apposite in these attempts to remove creative power from the realm of the female. But even if the roboticists are not creating weapons of destruction, like all parents they may not be able to control the actions of their offspring. Jansen (1988; 1992) has pointed to the way in which several AI scientists express their dream of creating their own robots, of 'becoming father of oneself' (Jansen 1988: 6, quoting Norman Brown from Bordo 1987: 456).

Helmreich (1994) points to the way that A-Life researchers take this view one step further in their creations of 'worlds' or 'universes'. He asked a researcher how he felt in building his simulations. The reply was, 'I feel like God. In fact I am God to the universes I create' (ibid.: 5). Katherine Hayles (1994: 125, quoted in Helmreich 1994: 11) suggests that the way that A-Life scientists talk of their computers brings an image of 'a male programmer mating with a female program to create progeny whose biomorphic diversity surpasses the father's imagination'. The desires are to make the body obsolete, to play god in artificial worlds, and to download minds into robots. Such desires are predicated on the assumption that if a machine contains the contents of a person's mind then it *is* that person. The body does not matter; it can be left behind.

> Inevitably the question must be raised. Which minds? Since the capacity of the most powerful parallel processing machines (connection machines) will be finite, not everyone will be able to get out of their bodies or off the planet. Some of 'us' will be stepped on, incinerated or gassed. So, who gets downloaded into the programs?
>
> [. . .]
>
> The new evolutionary logic dictates the answer. The best minds, of course, the kinds of minds that are most readily available for modeling in the AI laboratories of MIT, Stanford and Carnegie-Mellon University: minds of upper middle-class, white, American, male, computer scientists.
>
> (Jansen 1992: 8–9)

The options then are to create an artificial world and be god, to download the mind into a robot, or to enter the realm of pure intellect in cyberspace. All these views involve both the assumption that it is possible to leave the body behind, and also a masculinist desire to transcend the body, a thread running through the whole of AI. This, of course, leads to the idea of escape.

CYBERSPACE AS ESCAPE

The idea of transcendence and escape is important in the rhetoric of cyberculture. Indeed some authors (Schroeder 1994) suggest that therein lies cyberculture's appeal; as a means of producing new forms of expression and new psychic experiences, which transcend mundane uses of technology. The fusion of technology and art with cyberspace is the medium of this transformation. This offers an alternative to drug culture, since VR and related information technologies offer a seemingly endless supply of new experiences but without the toxic risks of drugs. Ralph Schroeder (ibid.: 525) points out the tension between the technical problems which have yet to be solved and the world-view of human wish-fulfilment which has been projected onto the technology. In popular form probably the most readily available forms of cyberculture are the cyberpunk nightclub and cybercafe, which spring up in the middle of UK and US cities. In addition, a number of North American magazines, fanzines sometimes just termed 'zines, proclaim themselves the denizens of cybercultures. These include *Mondo 2000* and *bOING bOING*, neither of which are widely available in the UK. In that they uphold the traditionally macho values of cyberpunk, they are unlikely to find a mass audience amongst feminists. Balsamo (1996: 131–2) sums up their style:

> Interspersed throughout the pages of *Mondo 2000* and conference announcements, a tension of sorts emerges in the attempt to discursively negotiate a corporate commodity system while upholding oppositional notions of countercultural iconoclasm, individual genius, and artistic creativity. The result is the formation of a postmodern schizo-culture that is unselfconsciously elitist and often disingenuous in offering its hacker's version of the American dream.

CYBERCULTURE FOR FEMINISTS

I argue that the cyberpunk version of cyberculture, with its masculine attempts to transcend the 'meat', holds little obvious appeal for feminists. Feminist analysis has gained great momentum in recent years, in many areas, not least within science and technology and cyberculture, at least in its popular form, lacks a critical edge. The lack of criticism manifests itself in several different ways. First of all, popular cyberculture is in danger of becoming ensnared in the nets of technological determinism, a determinism from which both modern science and technology studies, and gender and technology research have long wrestled to be free. The arguments for and against technological determinism need not be rehearsed in detail again here but broadly speaking, for cyberculture, they offer a view which takes technological development as inevitable, as having its own inner logic, and in which society dances to technology's tune, rather than the other way round. In cyberculture, determinist views are given voice in predictive statements about what sort of technology we will have ten, twenty or fifty years hence. As I have already suggested such predictions are always subject to revision, and so the owners of the predictions need never really be called to account.

But the point I wish to make here is that such technological predictions also carry along with them a prediction of how the technology will be used. For instance, the prediction that the widespread availability of teleshopping means that we will sit at home making purchases denies the complex physical and emotional pleasures of bargain hunting, the serendipitous find, the desperate need for a cappuccino on the way, the surprise of bumping into an old friend, the journey home with the parcels and the trip back next week to exchange the clothes that did not fit.[8]

Statements about the availability of intelligent robots fifty years hence does not mean that we have to use them in any particular way, or that we must download our minds into their bodies. Some of us may not wish to lose the pleasures of the body.[8] The high priests and priestesses of cyberculture are expert in futurespeak, in blending an almost mystical way of writing with a view that the advances on which they depend may be just around the corner. Jaron Lanier, who coined the term 'virtual reality' in the late 1980s (Schroeder 1993: 965) is particularly enthusiastic about shared virtual environments. He suggests that VR has 'an infinity of possibility . . . it's just an open world where your mind is the only limitation . . . it gives us this sense of being who we are without limitation; for our imagination to become shared with other people' (Lanier 1989, quoted in Schroeder 1993: 970). This becomes a way of building a shared sense of community, which Lanier sees as increasingly lost in American cities where people live in cars and no longer meet in the street. Brenda Laurel ends her book, *Computers as Theatre,* with the prophecy, 'the future is quite literally within our grasp . . . (it will) blow a hole in all our old imaginings and expectations. Through that hole we can glimpse a world of which both cause and effect are a quantum leap in human evolution' (Laurel 1991: 197–8, quoted in Schroeder 1994: 521). There is a strong sense of a utopian desire to escape to a virtual community, to a better world which at the same time signals a dissatisfaction with the old one.

> Cyberspace and virtual reality . . . have seemed to offer some kind of technological fix for a world gone wrong, promising the restoration of a sense of community and communitarian order. It is all too easy to think of them as alternatives to the real world and its disorder.
> (Robins 1996: 24)

Given that cyberculture draws so much from the rhetoric of cyberpunk fiction there are interesting tensions. Cyberpunk's future world is dystopian; there are no communities, only dangerous, alienating urban sprawls. Yet cyberculture looks to a future utopia where communities will spring up on the Internet, somehow to replace the old communities which people feel they have lost. Kevin Robins (ibid.: 25) sees a tension between the utopian desire to re-create the world afresh, in a virtual culture which is heavily dependent on the rhetoric of technological progress on the one hand, and dissatisfaction with and rejection of the old world on the other. Part of this hope manifests itself in the promise of a digital voice for groups traditionally far removed from political and economic power (Barry 1996: 137). For instance, Jennifer Light (1995) argues that the computer-mediated communications on the Internet, as they escape centralized political and legal control, may diversify and offer alternative courses of action for women.

But if there is a determinism at work in the utopian view of the future which such utterances seem to suggest, there is also a determinism in the uncritical acclaim with which future advances in the technology are hailed. Truly intelligent robots, shared virtual realities and cyberspace rest on technological advances which have not yet happened and may never happen. These technologies rest on the bedrock of particular advances in AI; they are by no means separate. This means we need to keep a cool head when thinking about VR and cybertechnology. It seems that cyberculture has yet to come to grips with the criticisms made about the possibility of truly intelligent technologies elaborated in chapter two. Truly realistic, virtual spaces and our virtual bodies within them have to respond in all the unimagined ways which might present themselves. For instance, Jon Dovey (1996: xi–xii) describes his first encounter with a VR system, wearing a headset and glove. Inserting a smart card into a slot and negotiating obstacles was fine, but when he tried to grab a packet of cigarettes hurtling by (the system was sponsored by a tobacco company), he fell over and the program continued to run despite his prostrate form. If the arguments of Dreyfus and Collins are to be taken seriously, in other words, arguments that we cannot capture all we know in a formal language, because what we know we know by dint of having bodies and growing up in particular cultures, then cyberculture needs to address these in relation to VR and cyberspace.

THE COMFORT OF CYBORGS

If popular cyberculture offers little comfort for feminists then it may be that we should look elsewhere within the groves of cyberculture, to the writings of academic theorists and to studies of women's use of the Internet and VR, down among the MUDs and MOOs.[9]

While sociological studies of cyberculture are proliferating, one of the most potent images to emerge is that of the cyborg, or cybernetic organism. The idea of the cyborg hails from cyberpunk fiction and film but also predates it in older images of the fusion of human and machine. The cyborg is not a feminist invention, indeed in its manifestation in films such as *Terminator* and *Robocop* it is the epitomy of masculine destruction, yet it has been appropriated as a feminist icon, most famously in Haraway's 'A cyborg manifesto' (1991b). It is difficult to overestimate the influence of her essay which John Christie (1993: 172) describes as having 'attained a status as near canonical as anything gets for the left/feminist academy'.

In Haraway's hands the cyborg works as an ironic political myth initially for the 1980s but stretching into and finding its full force in the next decade; a blurring, transgression and deliberate confusion of boundaries of the self, a concern with what makes us human and how we define humanity. Her vision, coming before the upsurge of interest in VR and the naming of cyberculture, sees modern war as a cyborg orgy, coded by C^3I, command-control-communication-intelligence (Haraway 1991b: 150). In our reliance on spectacles, hearing aids, heart pacemakers, dentures, dental crowns, artificial joints, not to mention computers, faxes, modems and networks, we are all cyborgs, 'fabricated hybrids of machine and organism' (ibid.).

The cyborg is to be a creature of a post-gendered world. As the boundary between human and animal has been thoroughly breached, so too has the boundary between human and machine. The transgression of boundaries and shifting of perspective signals a lessening of the dualisms which have troubled feminist writers, and this means that we do not necessarily have to seek domination of the technology. This is a move away from earlier feminist theories towards a thoroughly postmodern feminism, which has since become a more mainstream part of feminist theory in the ten to fifteen years since Haraway's essay. Her cyborg imagery contains two fundamental messages:

> first, the production of universal, totalizing theory is a major mistake that misses most of the reality . . . and second, taking responsibility for the social relations of science and technology means refusing an anti-science metaphysics, a demonology of technology, and so means embracing the skilful task of reconstructing the boundaries of daily life. . . . It is not just that science and technology are possible means of great human satisfaction, as well as a matrix of complex dominations. Cyborg imagery can suggest a way out of the maze of dualisms in which we have explained our bodies and our tools to ourselves. This is a dream not of a common language, but of a powerful infidel heteroglossia.
>
> (ibid.: 181)

Why has Haraway's essay held such an appeal for feminists? It is partly due to the language she uses, the mixture of poetry and politics. Christie (1993: 175) notes 'its ability to move with a kind of seamless rapidity from empirically grounded political recognition of the profound and deadly military-industrial technologies to a cyborg empyrean'. It is also clear that slanting the picture, transgressing boundaries between machine, human and animal, strikes a significant chord with Actor-Network Theory research which has been emerging at around the same time in the science and technology studies arena. All this has caused an upsurge of academic interest in the programme of cyborg postmodernism, which, in terms of gender, sexuality and the body is found most notably in the work of Stone (1993; 1994; 1995), especially on boundary transgressions, and Balsamo (1996) on VR and bodies.

CYBERFEMINISM

If Haraway's 'A cyborg manifesto' has played so vital a role in spawning a feminist cyborg postmodernism, feminists may be disappointed in some of its offspring. For instance, in looking at the lure of cyberculture, Judith Squires (1996: 195) argues:

> whilst there *may* be potential for an alliance between cyborg imagery and a materialist-feminism, this potential has been largely submerged beneath a sea of technophoric cyberdrool. If we are to salvage the image of the cyborg we would do well to insist that cyberfeminism be seen as a metaphor for addressing the inter-relation between technology and the body, not as a means of using the former to transcend the latter.

It seems as if Squires is arguing that cyberfeminism, if indeed there is such a thing, is in danger of falling into the same trap with regard to the body, as cyberculture in general, which promotes a particularly masculine connotatation of the new continuity of mind and machine. As I shall discuss below, although there are some feminist approaches to cyberculture which do not suffer from the same problems, it is with the writings of Sadie Plant, self-declared cyberfeminist, that Squires takes issue. Plant has done more than possibly any other writer, at least in the UK, to bring issues of women and cybernetic futures to a more popular audience (e.g. Plant 1993). Squires describes Plant's style as one which 'shares the apoliticism of the cyberpunks but also invokes a kind of mystical utopianism of the eco-feminist earth-goddesses' (Squires 1996: 204).

In addition, Plant's writing has a universalizing tendency against which Haraway and many other feminist writers have fought a long battle, arguing that women's experiences are not all of a piece. This manifests itself in statements such as 'Women . . . have always found ways of circumventing the dominant systems of communication' (Plant 1993: 13); 'they (women) are . . . discovering new possibilities for work, play and communication of all kinds in the spaces emergent from the telecoms revolution' (Plant 1995: 28); 'Women are accessing the circuits on which they were once exchanged' (Plant 1996: 170). But who are these women? Even allowing for the fact that some of this material was written for a more popular audience, it does not seem quite enough to say that 'facts and figures are as hard to ascertain as gender itself in the virtual world' (Plant 1995: 28). At least by the time of Plant's most recent writing there have been a number of empirical studies of women's use of the Internet, and many more on women and computing in general, some of which offer facts and figures (see for example Adam et al. 1994; Adams 1996; Grundy 1996; Herring 1996; Light 1995; Shade 1994; 1996). The lack of reference to these or any studies like them makes it difficult to know who are the women about which Plant is talking. This is a pity, given the rather pleasing image that she creates of women subverting the Internet towards their own ends.

There is plenty of evidence to show that women are still much in the minority in Internet usage, even in the USA, the most wired country in the world (Pitkow and Kehoe

1996). There is a tension between some women clearly finding the Internet a potent means of communication with one another, as witnessed by the proliferation of women's news groups, and the negative effects of stories about sexual harassment. It is this tension which prompts Kira Hall (1996) to talk of two forms of cyberfeminism. First, what she terms 'liberal cyberfeminism' sees computer technology as a means towards the liberation of women. On the other hand 'radical cyberfeminism' manifests itself in the 'women only' groups on the Internet which have sprung up in response to male harassment.

Susan Herring's (1996) well-researched study of discourse on the Internet shows that computer-mediated communication does not appear to neutralize gender. As a group she found women more likely to use attenuated and supportive behaviour whilst men were more likely to favour adversarial postings. These she linked to men favouring individual freedom, while women favour harmonious interpersonal interaction. And these behaviours and values can be seen as instrumental in reproducing male dominance and female submission.

There is also the view that interactions in cyberspace can magnify and accelerate inequalities and harassment found elsewhere, which is broadly the conclusion of Carol Adams's (1996) study of cyberpornography.

> [M]ultiple examples—including overt computer-based pornography and a careful analysis of male privilege in cyberspace—powerfully confirm feminist analyses of society and pornography. Indeed, it appears that certain features of cyberspace can accelerate and expand the male dominance and exploitation of women already familiar to us "in real life" (IRL).'
>
> (ibid.: 148)

In case we imagine that all we have to do is literally to pull the plug, we should take heed of Stephanie Brail's story of the harassment she received by way of anonymous, threatening, obscene e-mail messages which she was unable to trace. These came in the wake of a 'flame war', an exchange of aggressive e-mail messages (or 'flames'), in a news group on alternative magazines, where she and others wished to talk about 'Riot Grrls', a post-feminist political group. 'At the mention of Riot Grrls, some of the men on the group started posting violently in protest . . . I . . . had no idea how much anti-female sentiment was running, seemingly unchecked, on many Usenet forums' (Brail 1996: 7). So fearful did she become, that she made sure the doors in her house were always locked and she practised self-defence. Brail adds that the real result is that she never gives out home phone numbers and addresses now and has stopped participating in Usenet news groups—'And that is the true fallout: I've censored myself out of fear' (ibid.).

If it is difficult to recognize the women in Plant's writing, it is also difficult to recognize the technology. There is a mystical, reverential tone with which she treats 'complex dynamics, self-organizing systems, nanotechnology, machine intelligence' (Plant 1995: 28).

> The connectionist machine is an indeterminate process, rather than a definite entity. . . . Parallel distributed processing defies all attempts to pin it down, and can only ever be contingently defined. It also turns the computer into a complex thinking machine which converges with the operations of the human brain.
>
> (Plant 1996: 174–5)

Unfortunately she threatens to become overwhelmed by the mystical qualities of these systems which organize themselves outside our control, and seems perilously close to Dennett's 'Woo Woo West Coast Emergence'.

Even Plant's metaphor linking women with weaving and the jacquard loom to the computer will not stand up very well when one considers that, for example, both in the cotton industry of North West England and in the silk industry centred on Macclesfield in Cheshire, the higher status and pay accruing to weavers made it, largely, although by no means completely, the domain of men rather than women. The control of jacquard hand-looms, a form of technology often linked to early computer design, was entirely in the hands of men, as the work was considered to be too skilled and too heavy for women (Collins and Stevenson 1995). It was spinning rather than weaving which was mainly the domain of working-class women.

But it is the loss of the political project, originally so important in Haraway's cyborg feminism which is most problematic in Plant's elaboration of cyberfeminism. Some of the reason for the loss is possibly because Irigaray is the only feminist writer to which Plant relates her work, and of all French feminist writing, in Irigaray is the least sense of there being any point in attacking the structures of patriarchy. More importantly, the problem may also relate to the coupling of cyberfeminism to cyberpunk, which deliberately sets itself apart from politics. Squires (1996: 208) finds this the most disquieting aspect of cyberfeminism; for although cyberpunk offers no hope of a better world, Plant is claiming that cyberfeminism offers women a better future, but with no political basis to back this up.

ALTERNATIVE FEMINIST FUTURES

In its cynicism over traditional political structures and its enthusiasm for information and communications technologies, cyberfeminism forgets that women's relationship to technology is not always positive. However there is much other research which can be used to paint a more balanced picture, which shows what use women *are* making of the new cybertechnologies and which can be used to preserve a sense of political project, even if there is no consensus as to what the politics should be.

Lyn Cherny and Elizabeth Reba Weise's *wired_women* (1996) collection paints a fascinating picture of some women's actual uses of Internet technology. As Howard Rheingold suggests on the back cover of the book, these are 'women who know their net culture from the inside', so they could well be candidates for Plant's cyberfeminists, subverting the pathways of the Internet for their own ends. It is no criticism to point out that the writers in this collection are highly educated North American women, doctoral students and computer professionals, clearly confidently enjoying and at home with their technology, with jobs and positions that not only provide the necessary technical equipment, but also permit them access and the time to use it. They are amongst the elite of technically confident women, yet amidst the cheerful humour and their easy natural usage of the new jargon there are many tales of male harassment on the news groups and bulletin boards.

Alongside the *wired_women* collection there are a number of studies, some of which are more directly focused on gender than others and which manage to eschew a 'doom and gloom' approach, yet at the same time offering more realistically positive pictures of feminist futures in computing than cyberfeminism manages to paint. Grundy's (1996) research on women working in computing in the UK, does make suggestions about 'What is to be done', though she acknowledges that a start is only now being made in moving beyond liberal feminism. Sherry Turkle's (1996) accessible and detailed psychological study of people's relationships and sense of self in relation to computers, although not allying itself explicitly to feminist theory, provides a sensitive discussion of gender and gender-swapping in on-line discussion groups. Ellen Balka (1993), Susan Herring (1993), Leslie Shade (1994) and Jennifer Light (1995) report detailed studies of women's use of computer networks. James Pitkow and Colleen Kehoe's (1996) surveys report an apparently massive increase of women's use of the world wide web, which is of considerable interest to feminist positions, although, incredibly, they manage to make no comment as to why this might be happening.[10]

The point I am making is that, in addition to the burgeoning cyberculture literature, there are increasing reports of women's use of computing, though much of the material I have cited above is North American in origin (and therefore not necessarily applicable elsewhere), and relates to networked information technologies rather than the specifically 'intelligent' technologies of VR, AI, A-Life and so on. Although it is very much feminist in tone, it does not usually engage with particular theoretical feminisms, especially not at an epistemological level.

However there is a recent attempt to combine a reading of popular cyberculture, the technology of VR and feminist theory in relation to the body, in Balsamo's *Technologies of the Gendered Body: Reading Cyborg Women* (1996). Balsamo's chief concern is what is happening to the image of the gendered material body in cosmetic surgery, body building, pregnancy surveillance and VR. She is anxious to avoid technological determinism and in seeing technologies as holding limited agency themselves, she argues against the idea that technologies will necessarily expand the control of a techno-elite (ibid.: 123). Nevertheless she wants to argue that VR technologies are involved in reproducing dominant power relations and in particular that repression of the material body in VR does not create a gender-free culture.

In questioning how VR engages socially and culturally marked bodies, she suggests its appeal lies in the illusion of control over unruly, gendered and raced bodies at a time when the body appears increasingly under threat. In this sense the new technologies reproduce traditional ideas of transcendence, 'whereby the physical body and its social meanings can be technologically neutralized' (ibid.: 128). VR seems to offer us whatever body we want. Although cyberpunk fiction portrays the body as an obsolete piece of meat, this does not change the way in which power is played out along old gendered lines. Where Haraway (1991a) sees a 'demonology of technology' from both advocates and critics of cyberculture, Balsamo wants to question how far VR technologies will promote a rationalization of everyday life or the kind of decentralization and pluralism which Haraway advocates. Balsamo sees the need to bring together both the practices of cyberpunk and feminist theory although she guards against the apparently apolitical view that new information technologies necessarily bring better ways of using them.

She argues that far from being gender-free, women find that gender follows them onto the new communication technologies. In an argument which bears out the experiences of the *wired_women* she states:

> If on the one hand new communication technologies such as VR create new contexts for knowing/talking/signing/fucking bodies, they also enable new forms of repression of the material body. Studies of the new modes of electronic communication, for example, indicate that the anonymity offered by the computer screen empowers antisocial behaviors such as 'flaming' and borderline illegal behaviors such as trespassing, E-mail snooping, and MUD-rape. And yet, for all the anonymity they offer, many computer communications reproduce stereotypically gendered patterns of conversation.
>
> (Balsamo 1996: 147)

Such communication is graphically illustrated by some of the terminology that has crept in. Brail (ibid.: 142) calmly states that:

> a 'wanna fuck' is simply an email request for a date or sex. An email asking for a date is not in and of itself harassment, but what bothers many women on the Internet and on online services is the frequency and persistence of these kinds of messages.

Similarly, the terminology for asking a woman to stop posting messages to a news group is called a 'shut up bitch'. As these are terms used by men talking to women they have a specifically gendered vector. I wonder if there is a similar term that men use in relation to men, or women use for men (or are men less likely to be silenced altogether?). If these are examples of common parlance it begins to surprise me that women want to use the Internet at all. There is now a real need to hear of women's positive experiences of computer-mediated communication to balance such a picture.

CONCLUSION

I have been trying to build a bridge between artificial intelligence and feminist theory. In particular I have tried to show how AI is inscribed with a view from mainstream epistemology, however implicit that view might be. In the process it as been necessary to uncover the ways in which women's and others' knowledge is ignored and forgotten in the building of real AI projects.

Feminist epistemology has been a useful tool in this process, partly because it allows an analytical scepticism to reside alongside a measure of realism and also because it is much more sociologically relevant than its more traditional counterparts. I have tried to show, through the medium of Cyc and Soar as paradigm projects, how symbolic AI reflects a subject who is a masculine rationalist ideal, Lloyd's (1984) 'man of reason'. Assuming that the subject need not be made explicit denies the possibility of a genuinely pluralistic discourse and is a kind of 'we' saying. This assumes that we all agree, that is if we are all reasonable people who belong to one of Foley's (1987) 'nonweird' perspectives. But the 'nonweird' perspective is the privileged, white, middle-class, male perspective, and an assumption that this does not even have to be made explicit is a way of silencing other perspectives.

In Cyc, this perspective is 'TheWorldAsTheBuildersOfCycBelieveItToBe'. In a strategy which mirrors the excessively simple 'cat sat on the mat' examples of mainstream epistemology, their authority maintains its hegemony and resists challenge by the use of a set of trivial and apparently apolitical examples with which it would seem churlish to quibble. Soar too is based on a set of experiments carried out on unrealistically bounded logico-mathematical problems carried out by a limited number of male college students in the 1960s and 1970s, with the assumption arising from this that their results can be extrapolated to apply to a wider domain of subjects and problem solving situations.

Dreyfus's (1972; 1979; 1992) critique of the way the propositional/skills distinction is handled in symbolic AI in general, and in the Cyc system in particular, remains important for a feminist analysis. Symbolic AI is good at representing the former, but not the latter. In keeping with mainstream epistemology, AI elevates propositional knowledge to a higher status than non-propositional knowledge—it assumes that skills knowledge can be reduced to propositional knowledge. Lenat and Feigenbaum (1991) assume that Cyc's assertions bottom out in 'somatic primitives'. Even so, I have argued that a simple equation of masculine ways of knowing with propositional knowledge and feminine ways of knowing with non-propositional knowledge does not do justice to the ways that gender is inscribed in the knowledge which AI systems represent. Dalmiya and Alcoff (1993) argue that we need ways of expressing gender-specific experiential knowledge, where the truth of some propositions may not be expressible in a gender-neutral language. This raises the whole question of the rational/irrational dualism and how this is maintained by the primacy of formally defined languages in a process of logocentrism.

The way that a number of aspects of knowing are not reducible to propositional knowledge, but rely instead on some notion of embodied skill, points to the role of the body in the making of knowledge. This is of particular interest in constructing a feminist critique because of the ways in which women have traditionally been assigned the role of caring for bodies, leaving men free to live the life of the mind (Lloyd 1984; Rose 1994). Additionally embodiment has become an issue for AI and is addressed through the related domain of artificial life.

I argue that feminists are unlikely to find much comfort in screen-based A-Life systems, even those that promise virtual reality implementations, as they are strongly predicated on a deterministic sociobiology. Situated robotics offers a more promising line as attempts are made to locate these robots physically in an environment and have them interact with it. However both feminist theory and Collins's (1990) research from the science and technology studies direction, suggest that there are parts of knowledge which can only be transmitted by being culturally situated. Cog, the robot baby, is physically situated but it remains to be seen whether it can be culturally situated in the appropriate sense. The embodiment that such robots possess is of a rather limited form. Their wanderings in the world, removing drinks cans, finding the centres of rooms and so on is rather aimless. To paraphrase a popular saying, we might suggest that they 'get an A-Life'. They might find more of a purpose to artificial life if they could learn to love each other, to care for and look after one another, or indeed look after us. In other words they could take on the forms of embodiment more usually associated with women's lives, i.e. the looking after and caring for bodies, young and old.

Looking at feminist visions of the future through intelligent technologies, the situation reveals some tensions. Feminist AI projects may attempt to 'dismantle the master's house with the master's tools' but they must be wary of inadvertently building on neat extensions to his house by mistake. Feminist readings of popular cyberculture are ambivalent. It seems unlikely that the promise of Haraway's (1991b) earlier rendering of cyborg imagery can be realized through current manifestations of cyberfeminism. However further research on women's use of computing technology at least offers the hope of alternative, more promising, readings.

In a sense I am telling but one more version of an old story. But by extending the bridge to other work on gender and technology, and in particular new information and communication technologies, I hope to show the possibility, at least, of bringing to empirical studies of where women find themselves in relation to these technologies a thoroughgoing, theoretically informed feminism. As the bridges are built I hope too that it will be possible to keep sight of the political project of feminism, for to show the markers of women's oppression is also to show that things can be different. By continuing to build on the practical projects just begun, and through women's refusal to give up the ground made in relation to the technology, we gain a glimpse, however small, of how things could be different.

Notes

1. In this section I allude to some of my own experiences, working in the computing department of a UK university; other reported examples have been drawn from experiences of colleagues both in my own and in other institutions, but of course anonymity must be preserved. The WiC newsletter, published several times per year, gives many stronger examples.
2. I have to thank the members of the Society of Women in Philosophy e-mail list (SWIP List) for introducing me to this term and its significance.
3. The occasion was the gender and technology session of the British Society for the History of Science/American Association for the History of Science Joint Meeting, July 1988, Manchester, UK.

4. This argument is elaborated more fully in Adam and Furnival (1995).
5. See chapter three, note 11.
6. Full project details are available in an unpublished report, Scott (1996). The latter is available on request from the author.
7. Lynne Stein, a senior roboticist in the Cog team has two real children. It is interesting to note that an article about her work stated this while no mention was made of her male colleagues' human offspring (Cog 1994).
8. This is analogous to the arguments made for having books on the Internet, rather than the 'real books' which we currently use. Apart from anything else, this denies the physical pleasures of books; not only do they look and feel nice, they often nice too.
9. See Turkle (1996: 11–14) for definitions and descriptions of these and similar terms.
10. Pitkow and Kehoe (1996) report the results of four surveys in January 1994, October 1994, April 1995 and October 1995. The surveys covered the USA and Europe, but they do not state which European countries. As a percentage, female usage of the world wide web grew from 5.1 per cent in the first survey to 29.3 per cent in the fourth. However the first survey had 1,500 respondents growing to 23,300 responses for the fourth. The authors comment: 'This represents a strong shift in the increased acceptance and use of the Web by women' (ibid.: 107). Even allowing for the marked quantitative differences in the surveys, this seems to suggest a very considerable growth in women's Internet usage in a space of only eighteen months, which surely invites an explanation.

References

Adam, Alison (1998) *Artificial Knowing: Gender and the Thinking Machine.* New York: Routledge.

———(1996) 'Constructions of gender in the history of artificial intelligence', *IEEE [Institute of Electrical and Electronics Engineers] Annals of the History of Computing* 18, 3: 47–53.

Adam, Alison and Furnival, Chloe (1995) 'Designing intersections-designing subjectivity: feminist theory and praxis in a sex discrimination legislation system', *Law, Computers and Artificial Intelligence* 4, 2: 161–74.

Adam, Alison, Emms, Judy, Green, Eileen and Owen, Jenny (eds) (1994) *IFIP Transactions A-57, Women, Work and Computerization: Breaking Old Boundaries -Building New Forms*, Amsterdam: Elsevier/North-Holland.

Adams, Carol (1996), '"This is not our fathers' pornography": sex, lies and computers', pp. 147–70 in Charles Ess (ed.) *Philosophical Perspectives on Computer- Mediated Communication*, Albany, N.Y.: State University of New York Press.

Balka, Ellen (1993) 'Women's access to online discussions about feminism', Electronic Journal of Communications/La Revue Electronique de Communication 3, 1 [to retrieve file by e-mail send the command: send balka v3n193 to comserve@vm.its.rpi.edu].

Balsamo, Anne (1996) *Technologies of the Gendered Body: Reading Cyborg Women*, Durham, N.C. and London: Duke University Press.

Barry, Ailsa (1996) 'Who gets to play? Access and the margin', pp. 136–54 in Jon Dovey (ed.) *Fractal Dreams: New Media in Social Context*, London: Lawrence & Wishart.

Bench-Capon, Trevor (ed.) (1991) *Knowledge-Based Systems and Legal Applications*, London: Academic Press.

Bordo, Susan (1987) *The Flight to Objectivity: Essays on Cartesianism and Culture*, Albany, N.Y.: State University of New York Press.

Bowers, John and Churcher, John (1988) 'Local and global structuring of computer-mediated communication', *Proceedings of the ACM Conference on Computer-Supported Cooperative Work*, Portland, Oreg.: 125–39.

Brail, Stephanie (1996) 'The price of admission: harassment and free speech in the wild, wild west', pp. 1441–57 in Lynn Cherny and Elizabeth Reba Weise (eds) *wired_women: Gender and New Realities in cyberspace*, Seattle, Wash.: Seal Press.

Brooks, Rodney A. (1991) 'Intelligence without representation', *Artificial Intelligence* 47: 139–60.

Cherny, Lynn and Weise, Elizabeth Reba (eds) (1996) *Wired-women: Gender and New Realities in Cyberspace*, Seattle, Washington: Seal Press.
Christie, John R. R. (1993), A tragedy for cyborgs', *Configurations* 1: 171–96.
Cog (1994) 'Evolutionary Cog', 'Rebel with a cause', ' A woman's work', *The Times Higher Education Supplement* 1126, June 3: 16–17.
Collins, Harry M. (1990) *Artificial Experts: Social Knowledge and Intelligent Machines*, Cambridge Mass.: MIT Press.
Collins, Lorraine and Stevenson, Moira (1995) *Macclesfield: The Silk Industry*, Chalford, Stroud: Chalford Publishing.
Dovey, Jon (ed.) (1996) *Fractal Dreams: New Media in Social Context*, London: Lawrence & Wishart.
Dreyfus, Hubert L. (1992) *What Computers Still Can't Do: A Critique of Artificial Reason*, Cambridge, Mass. And London: MIT Press.
Easlea, Brian (1983) *Fathering the Unthinkable: Masculinity, Scientists and the Nuclear Arms Race*, London: Pluto Press.
Fishman, Pamela M. (1983) 'Interaction: the work women do', pp. 89–101 in Barrie Thorne, Cheris Kramarae and Nancy Henley (eds) Language, Gender and Society, Rowley, Mass.: Newbury House.
Furnival, Chloe (1993) An investigation into the development of a prototype advice system for sex discrimination law', unpublished MSc dissertation, UMIST, Manchester.
Grbich, Judith E. (1991}'The body in legal theory', pp. 61–76 in Martha A. Fineman and Nancy S. Thomadsen (eds) *At the Boundaries of Law: Feminism and Legal Theory*, New York and London: Routledge.
Grundy, Frances (1996) *Women and Computers*, Exeter: Intellect Books.
Hall, Kira (1996) 'Cyberfeminism', pp.147–70 in Susan C. Herring (ed.) *Computer- Mediated Communication: Linguistic, Social and Cross-Cultural Perspectives*, Amsterdam and Philadelphia, Penn.: John Benjamins Publishing.
Haraway, Donna (1991a) *Simians ,Cyborgs and Women: The Reinvention of Nature*, London: Free Association Books.
———(1991b) 'A cyborg manifesto: science, technology and socialist-feminism in the late twentieth century', pp. 149–81 in Donna Haraway *Simians, Cyborgs and Women: The Reinvention of Nature*, London: Free Association Books [originally published in *Socialist Review* (1985) 80: 65–107].
Harding, Sandra (1991) *Whose Science? Whose Knowledge? Thinking from Women's Lives*, Milton Keynes: Open University Press.
Hayles, N. Katherine (1994) 'Narratives of evolution and the evolution of narratives', pp. 113–32 in John L. Casti and Anders Karlqvist (eds) *Cooperation and Conflict in General Evolutionary Processes*, Chichester: John Wiley.
Helmreich, Stefan (1994), 'Anthropology inside and outside the looking-glass worlds of artificial life', unpublished paper, Department of Anthropology, Stanford University, Stanford, Calif. [Available from author at this address or by e-mail on stefang@leland.stanford.edu]
Henwood, Flis (1993) 'Establishing gender perspectives on information technology: problems, issues and opportunities', pp. 31–49 in Eileen Green, Jenny Owen and Den Pain'(eds) *Gendered by Design? Information Technology and Office Systems*, London: Taylor & Francis.
Herring, Susan (1996) 'Posting in a different voice: gender and ethics in CMC', pp. 115–45 in Charles Ess (ed.) *Philosophical Perspectives on Computer-Mediated Communication*, Albany, N.Y.: State University of New York Press.
Hirst, Graeme, McRoy, Susan, Heeman, Peter, Edmonds, Philip and Horton, Diane (1994) 'Repairing conversational misunderstandings and non-understandings', *Speech Communication* 15: 213–29.
Jansen, Sue C. (1988) 'The ghost in the machine: artificial intelligence and gendered thought patterns', *Resources for Feminist Research* 17: 4–7.
———(1992) 'Making minds: sexual and reproductive metaphors in the discourses of the artificial intelligence movement',. paper presented at the Electronic Salon: ~! Feminism meets Infotech in connection with the 11th Annual Gender Studies Symposium, Lewis and Clark

College, March. [Author's address: Communication Studies Department, Muhlenberg College, Allentown, Pennsylvania 18104, USA.]

Lakoff, Robin (1975) *Language and Woman's Place*, New York: Harper & Row.

Lanier, Jaron (1989) 'Virtual environments and interactivity: windows to the future', *Computer Graphics*, 23, 5: 8, [panel session].

Laurel, Brenda (1991) *Computers as Theatre*, Reading, Mass.: Addison-Wesley.

Leith, Philip (1986) 'Fundamental errors in legal logic programming', *The Computer Journal* 29, 6: 545–54.

Light, Jennifer (1995) 'The digital landscape: new space for women?', *Gender, Place and Culture* 2, 2: 133–46.

Lorde, Audre (1984) *Sister Outsider*, Freedom, Calif.: The Crossing Press.

MacKinnon, Catherine (1982) 'Feminism, Marxism, method and the state: toward an agenda for theory', *Signs: Journal of Women in Culture and Society* 7: 227–56.

———(1983) 'Feminism, Marxism, method and the state: toward feminist jurisprudence', *Signs: Journal of Women in Culture and Society* 8: 635–58.

Metselaar, Carolien{1991):Gender issues in the design of knowledge-based systems', pp. 233–46 in Inger Eriksson, Barbara Kitchenham and Kea Tijdens (eds) *Women, Work and Computerization* 4, Amsterdam: Elsevier/North-Holland.

Moravec, Hans (1988) *Mind Children: The Future of Robot and Human Intelligence*, Cambridge, Mass. and London: Harvard University Press.

Nye, Andrea (1992) 'The voice of the serpent: French feminism and philosophy of language', pp. 233–49 in Ann Garry and Marilyn Pearsall (eds) *Women, Knowledge and Reality: Explorations in Feminist Philosophy*, New York and London: Routledge.

Palmer, Camilla (1992) *Discrimination at Work: The Law on Sex and Race Discrimination*, London: The Legal Action Group.

Pitkow, James E. and Kehoe, Colleen M. (1996) 'Emerging trends in the WWW user population', *Communications of the ACM* 39,6: 106–8.

Plant, Sadie (1993) 'Beyond the screens: film, cyberpunk and cyberfeminism', *Variant* 14, Summer 1993: 12–17.

———(1995) 'Babes in the net', *New Statesman and Society* January 27: 28.

———(1996) 'On the matrix: cyberfeminist simulations', pp. 170–83 in Rob Shields (ed.) *Cultures of the Internet: Virtual Spaces, Real Histories, Living Bodies*, London, Thousand Oaks, Calif. and New Delhi: Sage.

Robins, Kevin (1996) 'Cyberspace and the world we live in', pp. 1–30 in Jon Dovey (ed.) *Fractal Dreams: New Media in Social Context*, London: Lawrence & Wishart.

Sanford, Linda T. and Donovan, Mary E. (1993) *Women and Self-Esteem*, Harmondsworth: Penguin.

Schroeder, Ralph (1993) 'Virtual reality in the real world: history, applications and projections', *Futures* 25, 11: 963–73.

———(1994) 'Cyberculture, cyborg post-modernism and the sociology, of virtual reality technologies: surfing the soul in the information age', *Futures* 26,5: 519–28.

Scott, Maureen (1996) Conversation analysis model to incorporate gender differences', unpublished final year project report, Department of Computation, UMIST, Manchester.

Searle, John R. (1987) 'Minds, brains and programs', pp. 18–40 in Rainer Born (ed.), *Artificial Intelligence: The Case Against*, London and Sydney: Croom Helm (first published 1980).

Shade, Lesley Regan (ed.) 1994 'Special issue on gender and networking', *Electronic Journal of Virtual Culture*, 2, 3 [to retrieve electronically send command get ejvcv2n2 package to listserv@kentvm.kent.edu).

———(1996) 'Is there free speech on the net? Censorship in the global information infrastructure', pp. 11–32 in Rob Shields (ed.) *Cultures of the Internet: Virtual Spaces, Real Histories, Living Bodies*, London, Thousand Oaks, Calif. and New Delhi: Sage.

Smart, Carol (1989) *Feminism and the Power of Law*, London and New York: Routledge.

Spender, Dale (1980) *Man Made Language*, London: Routledge & Kegan Paul.

Squires, Judith (1996) 'Fabulous feminist futures and the lure of cyberculture', pp. 194–216 in Jon Dovey (ed.) *Fractal Dreams: New Media in Social Context*, London: Lawrence & Wishart.

Stone, Allucquère Rosanne (1993) 'Violation and virtuality: two cases of physical and psychological boundary transgression and their implications', unpublished manuscript [available in electronic form from sandy@actlab.rtf.utexas.edu].
———(1994) 'Will the real body please stand up? Boundary stories about virtual cultures', pp. 81–118 in Michael Benedikt {ed.) *Cyberspace: First Steps*, Cambridge, Mass. and London: MIT Press.
———(1995) *The War of Desire and Technology at the Close of the Mechanical Age*, Cambridge, Mass. and London: MIT Press.
Suchman, Lucy A. (1987) *Plans and Situated Actions: 'The Problem of Human Machine Interaction*, Cambridge: Cambridge University Press
———(1994b) 'Do categories have politics? The language/action perspective reconsidered', *Computer Supported Cooperative Work* (*CSCW*) 2, 3: 177–90.
Tannen, Deborah (ed.) (1988) *Linguistics in Context: Connecting Observation and Understanding*, Norwood, N.J.: Ablex.
———(1992) *You Just Don't Understand: Women and Men in Conversation*, London: Virago.
———(1994) *Gender and Discourse*, New York and Oxford: Oxford University Press.
Thalmann, Nadia M. and Thalmann, Daniel (eds) {1994) *Artificial Life and Virtual Reality*, Chichester: Wiley,
Tong, Rosemarie (1994) *Feminist Thought: A Comprehensive Introduction*, London: Routledge.
Turkle, Sherry (1996) *Life on the Screen: Identity in the Age of the Internet*, London: Weidenfeld & Nicolson.
Wajcman, Judy (1991) *Feminism Confronts Technology*, Cambridge: Polity Press.

Contributors

Alison Adam is a faculty member in the Department of Computation at the University of Manchester Institute of Technology in the United Kingdom.

Ruth Bleier was a Professor in the Department of Neurophysiology at Madison, Wisconsin, and a founding member of the Women's Studies program at UW-Madison. She died January 4, 1988. She is missed.

Mary Barbercheck is an associate professor of entomology at North Carolina State University in Raleigh.

Carol Cohn is Associate Professor of Women's Studies at Bowdoin College in Maine.

Cynthia R. Daniels is a Professor of Political Science in the Department of Political Science at Rutgers, the State University of New Jersey.

Margaret A. Eisenhart is a Professor of Education and Anthropology at University of Colorado, Boulder.

Linda Marie Fedigan is a Professor of Anthropology at the University of Alberta, Canada.

Evelynn Hammonds is an Associate Professor in the Program in Science, Technology and Society at Massachusetts Institute of Technology.

Dorothy C. Holland is Professor and Departmental Chair of Anthropology at the University of North Carolina at Chapel Hill.

Dara Horn is working toward her Ph.D. in Comparative Literature at Harvard University.

Ruth Hubbard holds the position of Professor Emerita in Biology at Harvard University.

Evelyn Fox Keller is a Professor in the Program in Science, Technology and Society at Massachusetts Institute of Technology.

Suzanne J. Kessler is a Professor of Psychology at the State University of New York–Purchase.

Cynthia Kraus is a Visiting Scholar in the Department of Rhetoric at the University of California, Berkeley, and a Ph.D. candidate in the Department of Philosophy, University of Lausanne, Switzerland.

Helen E. Longino is a Professor of Women's Studies and Philosophy of Science at the University of Minnesota.

Rachel Maines currently operates the largest museum collections management firm in North America.

Emily Martin is a Professor of Anthropology of Science at Princeton University.

Ruth Perry is a Professor of Literature at the Massachusetts Institute of Technology.

Hilary Rose is currently a Visiting Research Professor of Sociology at City University,

London, Professor Emerita of Social Policy, University of Bradford, and Professor of Physic elect, Gresham College, London.

Banu Subramaniam is currently an Assistant Research Professor at the Southwest Institute for Research on Women and the Department of Women's Studies.

Janice Law Trecker was writing from West Hartford, Connecticut, when she wrote her excerpted piece.

Judy Wajcman is a Professor of Sociology at the University of Manchester in the United Kingdom.

Christine Wennerás is an Associate Professor in the Department of Clinical Bacteriology at Göteborg University, Sweden.

Agnes Wold is currently a Professor in the Department of Clinical Immunology at Göteborg University, Sweden.

Harriet Zuckerman is Senior Vice President of the Andrew W. Mellon Foundation in New York.

Permissions

Section 1a: Education

Keller, Evelyn Fox. "The Anomaly of a Woman in Physics," in *Working It Out: Twenty-Three Writers, Scientists and Scholars Talk about Their Lives,* ed. Sara Ruddick and Pamela Daniels. New York: Pantheon, 1977, 77–91. Reprinted by permission of Pantheon Books, a division of Random House, Inc.

Sands, Aimee. "Never Meant to Survive, A Black Woman's Journey: An Interview with Evelynn Hammonds," in *The Racial Economy of Science,* ed. Sandra Harding. Bloomington, Indiana University Press, 1993, 239–48.

Eisenhart, Margaret A., and Holland, Dorothy C. "Gender Constructs and Career Commitment: The Influence of Peer Culture on Women in College," in *Gender Constructs and Social Issues,* ed. T. Whitehead and B. Reid. Chicago: University of Illinois Press, Copyright © 1992 by Board of Trustees of the University of Illinois, 142–80. Used with permission of the University of Illinois Press.

Subramaniam, Banu. "Snow Brown and the Seven Detergents: A Metanarrative on Science and the Scientific Method." Reprinted by permission of The Feminist Press at the City University of New York, from *Women's Studies Quarterly* 28, nos. 1 & 2 (spring/summer 2000): 296–304, special issue, *Building Inclusive Science: Connecting Women's Studies and Women in Science and Engineering,* edited by Sue V. Rosser. Copyright © 2000 by Banu Subramaniam.

Section 1b: Careers

Horn, Dara. "The Shoulders of Giants," *Science* 280 (1998): 1354–55. Copyright © 2000, American Association for the Advancement of Science.

Wennerás, Christine, and Wold, Agnes, "Nepotism and Sexism in Peer Review." Reprinted by permission from *Nature* vol. 387; 341–43. Copyright © 1997 Macmillan Magazines, Ltd.

Rose, Hilary. "Nine Decades, Nine Women, Ten Nobel Prizes: Gender Politics at the Apex of Science," in *Love, Power, and Knowledge: Toward a Feminist Transformation of the Sciences.* Bloomington: Indiana University Press, 1994, 136–70.

Zuckerman, Harriet. "The Careers of Men and Women Scientists: A Review of Current Research." Reprinted by permission from *The Outer Circle: Women in the Scientific Community,* ed. H. Zuckerman, J. Cole, and J. Bruer. New York: W. W. Norton, 1991, 27–56. Copyright © 2000 by the National Academy of Sciences. Courtesy of the National Academy Press, Washington, DC.

Section 2: Science, Sex, and Stereotypes

Trecker, Janice Law. "Sex, Science and Education," *American Quarterly* 26, no. 4 (1974): 352–66. © 2000 The American Studies Association. Reprinted by permission of the Johns Hopkins University Press.

Cohn, Carol. "Sex and Death in the Rational World of Defense Intellectuals," *Signs: Journal of Women in Culture and Society* 12, no. 4 (1987): 687–718. © 2000 by The University of Chicago Press.

Keller, Evelyn. "Gender and Science: An Update," in *Secrets of Life, Secrets of Death: Essays on Language, Gender and Science,* New York: Routledge, Copyright © 1992, 15–36. Reproduced by permission of Taylor & Francis/Routledge, Inc.

Section 3: Constructing Gender, Constructing Science

Hubbard, Ruth. "Science, Facts, and Feminism," *Hypatia* 3, no. 1 (1988): 5–17. Reprinted with permission from Indiana University Press.

Kessler, Suzanne. "The Medical Construction of Gender: Case Management of Intersexed Infants, *Signs: Journal of Women in Culture and Society* 16 no. 1 (1990): 3–26. Reprinted with permission from the University of Chicago Press.

Bleier, Ruth. "Sociobiology, Biological Determinism and Human Behavior," *Science and Gender: A Critique of Biology and its Theories on Women.* New York, Teachers College Press, © 1984 by Teachers College, Columbia University. All rights reserved. pp. 15–48. Reprinted by permission of the publisher.

Wajcman, Judy. "The Built Environment: Women's Place, Gendered Space," in *Feminism Confronts Technology.* University Park, Pennsylvania State University Press, 1991, 110–36. Copyright © 2000 by The Pennsylvania State University. Reproduced by permission of the publisher.

Section 4: New Science, New Knowledge

Longino, Helen E. "Can There Be a Feminist Science?" in *Feminism and Science,* ed. Nancy Tuana. Bloomington: Indiana University Press, 1989, 45–57.

Maines, Rachel. "Socially Camouflaged Technologies: The Case of the Electromechanical Vibrator," © 1989 IEEE. Reprinted, with permission, from (*IEEE Technology and Society Magazine* (June 1989): 3–23.)

Fedigan, Linda Marie. "Is Primatology a Feminist Science?" in *Women in Human Evolution,* ed. Lori D. Hager, New York: Routledge, 1997, 56–75.

Kraus, Claudia. "Naked Sex in Exile: On the Paradox of the 'Sex Question' in Feminism and Science," *NWSA Journal* vol. 12 (3).

Section 5: Reproducible Insights

Martin, Emily. "Premenstrual Syndrome, Work Discipline, and Anger," in *The Woman in the Body.* Boston, Beacon Press: Copyright © 1987, 1992 by Emily Martin. 113–38. Reprinted by permission of Beacon Press, Boston.

Perry, Ruth. "Engendering Environmental Thinking: A Feminist Analysis of the Present Crisis," *The Yale Journal of Criticism* 6 (1993): 1–17. © 2000 The Johns Hopkins University Press.

Daniels, Cynthia R. "Between Fathers and Fetuses: The Social Construction of Male Reproduction and the Politics of Fetal Harm," *Signs: Journal of Women in Culture and Society* 22, no. 3 (1997): 580–616.

Adam, Alison. "Feminist AI Projects and Cyberfutures," in *Artificial Knowing*, New York: Routledge, 1998, 156–81.

Index